MUSIC

FLEMISH TAPESTRY. SIXTEENTH CENTURY

Described in Museum of Fine Arts, Boston, *Bulletin*, xxiii, no. 140, pp. 70–72
by Miss Gertrude Townsend, Curator, Department of Textiles.

ANCIENT EUROPEAN MUSICAL INSTRUMENTS

An Organological Study of the Musical Instruments in the Leslie Lindsey Mason Collection at the Museum of Fine Arts, Boston

BY

NICHOLAS BESSARABOFF

WITH A PREFACE BY
EDWIN J. HIPKISS

AND A FOREWORD BY
CANON FRANCIS W. GALPIN

PUBLISHED FOR THE
MUSEUM OF FINE ARTS, BOSTON
by October House, Inc.
NEW YORK

Second Printing 1964

Printed in U.S.A. by The Meriden Gravure Co., Meriden, Conn.

OCTOBER HOUSE, INC.

55 WEST 13TH STREET, NEW YORK, N.Y.

DEDICATED TO

THE MAKERS OF MUSICAL INSTRUMENTS
OF ALL TIMES AND ALL COUNTRIES
WITHOUT DISTINCTION OF RACE, RELIGION, OR CLASS

PREFACE

THE AUTHOR of this volume, Mr. Nicholas Bessaraboff, an American citizen born at Voronezh, Russia, has been actively interested in music since boyhood, when he played the French horn and other wind instruments.

Despite his devotion to music, he studied mechanical engineering at the Polytechnical Institute at St. Petersburg. His life's work has been divided between mechanical engineering and the study of old musical instruments.

In 1920, at Rochester, New York, he began to study seriously the history, construction, and acoustical properties of musical instruments.

The importance of our Leslie Lindsey Mason Collection of Musical Instruments and the need of a scientific rearrangement and interpretation led the Trustees to adopt a plan proposed by Mr. Bessaraboff and to ask him to write this study.

In this country there are other important public collections of musical instruments: the Crosby Brown Collection at the Metropolitan Museum of Art, New York, and the collections in the Smithsonian Institution, Washington, D. C., at the University of Michigan, Ann Arbor, Michigan, and at the Franklin Institute, Philadelphia, Pennsylvania. Specialists in this field, however, are, with few exceptions, specialists by avocation. There are, as far as we know, no educational courses devoted to the study of old musical instruments. Important books on the subject have been published abroad, especially in Germany, and this work by Mr. Bessaraboff offers a similar serious study based on the Collection of this Museum.

There have been numerous revivals of the playing of musical instruments of the past, and there is ample evidence of a real interest in the subject. It is hoped that this work will aid many in pursuing the fascinating, although difficult, study of the technicalities of old instruments and their music.

EDWIN J. HIPKISS, *Curator,*
Department of the Decorative Arts of Europe and America

BOSTON
April, 1939

CONTENTS

The Contents serves also as a classification. The numbers before the names of instruments correspond to those of individual instruments described in the text; an (*) after a number indicates that the instrument is illustrated. For the sake of completeness, there are mentioned general divisions and instruments not represented in the Collection at the Museum of Fine Arts. The terminology given on pp. 10–13 follows the sequence of terms as they occur here.

PLATES AND ILLUSTRATIONS

Medallion on the title page is a reproduction of the rose in the sound-board of Kirkman harpsichord, No. 298 of this Collection.
Frontispiece, *Music*, is a sixteenth century Flemish tapestry at the Museum of Fine Arts, Boston, Department of Textiles.

LIST OF PLATES

LIST OF ILLUSTRATIONS

PRAETORIUS' *COLUMNAE*

Reproduced in this study and listed in the numerical order of his *Theatrum Instrumentorum*

NOTE. For better legibility the scale at the bottom of Table XIV is taken from Table VIII. Both scales are identical in size and therefore interchangeable.

ABBREVIATIONS AND SPELLINGS

O.E.I. — *Old English Instruments of Music, their History and Character.* By Canon Francis W. Galpin.
The R.M.E. Catalogue — *A Descriptive Catalogue of the Musical Instruments Exhibited at the Royal Military Exhibition, London, 1890.* Compiled by Capt. C. R. Day.

Quotations from old books in foreign languages are reproduced here *verbatim* and *literatim*, without omissions. Differences in spellings, as for instance, *lira da braccio* and *lyra da braccio*, mean that in some cases the old spelling is followed. Diacritical marks for the Oriental words are kept to a minimum and sometimes are omitted altogether. Plural forms of foreign nouns are used only when absolutely necessary, and in some instances are explicitly stated. Thus, on p. 33, the Russian word *nakra* is given both in singular and plural.

Names of instruments given in technical descriptions and printed in capital letters are preferred terms and spellings. More popular, but incorrect, terms are given second place. Thus the term *flageolet* is used in this study in its strict technical sense as defined on p. 63. The so-called "English flageolet" is named here correctly, 'vertical flute.' Alternative names (one or several) are given either in the first line of the technical description, or in the explanatory statements in the text.

The numbers in parentheses at the end of technical descriptions are Museum accession numbers. The first two figures signify the year of accession.

FOREWORD

THROUGH the kindly interest of the Trustees of the Museum of Fine Arts and the expert assistance of Mr. Nicholas Bessaraboff the great desire of my life is being realized. For the object of this collection, gathered during a period of forty years, was mainly and engrossingly educational. Neither purse nor inclination led me to pay fancy prices for mere *objets d'art*, though many beautiful, historic, and decorative examples came across my path and have been incorporated in the general scheme. To me a musical instrument is a thing of life, something that will speak to us and reveal the hidden secrets of its sound. Therefore I made every effort to secure specimens that were playable or could be rendered so. To restore the ravages of time and replace the tale of years provided for me the greatest joy in their possession. It is with supreme pleasure, then, that, before I pass on, I am assured for my lifelong treasures all the care and consideration to which, by the genius of their makers and the skill of their old-world players, they are entitled. I trust that, whereas we have somewhat failed in England in displaying the stages of evolution through which instruments have passed, the Museum of Fine Arts in Boston may use many of these objects for the practical purposes to which they have been accustomed, that is, for lectures, demonstrations, and concerts of the music of their day. In this way the collection will not only retain its primary value, but will best reflect the charming personality of the lady whose memory is enshrined in its present title and whose whole life was music.

As a native of Dorchester, our old country-town in Dorset, from which, in the days of long ago, so many crossed the water to find safe refuge in Boston and its district, which I also know, I accept with true appreciation the desire of my friend, the late Mr. William Lindsey, and of the Museum authorities to provide once more in their famous city a fine and lasting abode for these later pilgrims from the homeland. It has also been a great pleasure to assist Mr. Bessaraboff, with such aid as I can still contribute, in the furtherance of the arduous but delightful task, which he has so capably undertaken and achieved, of providing this excellent catalogue.

FRANCIS W. GALPIN

RICHMOND, SURREY

INTRODUCTION

THE Leslie Lindsey Mason Collection of Musical Instruments was originally formed by the Reverend Francis W. Galpin, Litt.D., F. L. S., Canon Emeritus of Chelmsford Cathedral and Honorary Freeman of the Worshipful Company of Musicians of England. In 1916 it was acquired by Mr. William Lindsey of Boston and presented by him to the Museum of Fine Arts, Boston, as a memorial to his daughter, Mrs. Leslie Lindsey Mason, who perished with the sinking of the *Lusitania*. The whole Collection comprises five hundred and sixty-four instruments of several nations, both European and extra-European. The European section numbers three hundred and seventeen items. In the Asiatic section is a set of Chinese instruments presented to Canon Galpin by Dr. C. A. Moule.[1] The musical instruments of the American Indians of the northwest coast of North America, collected by Canon Galpin, are another interesting group.[2] At present only the European instruments are on exhibition in the Department of Decorative Arts, Gallery D-67.

This Collection cannot compare in numbers with the more extensive collections in Washington, New York, and Ann Arbor. The Boston Collection is, however, important for students, because, although small in numbers, it has been selected to illustrate the general classification of musical instruments. There are only a few instrumental types which are not represented. One peculiarity should be noted. Chronologically it is limited to a period ending about 1850. Modern developments which can be easily traced are not represented. So, for instance, the evolution of the Boehm flute is not represented at all. The oldest instrument of this Collection is the buysine (No. 198) by Sebastian Hainlein, made in 1460. There are several instruments of great historical value: the two-keyed flute (No. 43) which belonged to J. J. Quantz, court musician and flute teacher of Frederick the Great of Prussia; the virginal (No. 295) made by Andreas Ruckers in 1610, the earliest dated instrument of this celebrated maker; the harpsichord of 1798 (No. 298) by Joseph Kirkman in playing condition and used in concerts of old music at the Museum. Some instruments are of interest for other reasons, as, for instance, the crwth (No. 291) made by a very old Welshman, and the hydraulis (No. 215), a reconstruction by Canon Galpin of a Roman instrument. These are the most outstanding instruments among several in the Collection.

Originally this study was planned as a small but adequate catalogue. As the work progressed the enthusiastic opinion of the writer concerning the value of this Collection was strengthened by a more intimate knowledge of the individual instruments, derived from detailed examination. Accordingly the study became more serious and extensive than was at first designed. This study presents several features which, for convenience, are considered point by point.

Musicology and Organology

MUSICOLOGY, in the broadest definition of the term, is the science of music and of things pertaining to music, including the study of musical instruments.[3] Thus defined, musicology necessarily becomes a comprehensive but cumbersome body of disciplines. With respect to musical instruments a more specific division seems desirable. Even with such limitation, one is confronted with several indispensable lines of approach, leading so far afield that they exceed the bounds of legitimate interest. Thus, there is an ethnological approach — perhaps one of the best, with respect to the extra-European instruments. It is significant that an important classification of musical instruments is printed in a journal devoted to ethnology.[4] Ethnological studies can be of interest to a musicologist or even to a musician from a general cultural standpoint, but only a few can attempt to study the field with its own peculiar techniques. Acoustics is indispensable for the study of musical instruments. Yet one need only examine the files of the *Journal of the Acoustical Society of America* in order to find some articles on musical instruments written in a rigorous scientific manner and requiring a knowledge of differential and integral calculus. Unless a musicologist be mathematically trained, he may legitimately consider such articles outside his field. Therefore it seems that the study of music and instruments may be divided into two mutually related, yet distinct approaches. The dividing line in this case can be clearly recognized as the difference between music proper and the objective and material means for its expression. Thus the creative, artistic, and scientific aspect of music might be entitled musicology. The scientific and engineering aspect of musical instruments might be entitled organology.[5] Both musicology in the newly restricted sense and organology have a common meeting ground, the subject matter of which would be difficult to assign definitely to either discipline. For instance, the study of some musical practices of the past is not comprehensible unless both approaches be employed: namely, the study of music and musical practices as well as of the instruments employed. The existence of such a common ground is nevertheless not an excuse for musicology to annex a matter more properly belonging to organology. To express the argument in a few words: a musicologist should be able to perform music on a given instrument; an organologist should be able to build that instrument. The existence of such exceptional individuals as Mr. Arnold Dolmetsch, who is both a musicologist and an organologist, only emphasizes the point raised. For a genius there are no limitations. Men of talent need to specialize.

Synthesis

SHORTLY before the World War and immediately thereafter there were published, mostly in German, several valuable books on musical instruments and excellent catalogues of some of the most important European collections of musical instruments.[6] The Dolmetsch school is ably represented by Mr. Gerald R. Hayes, who began to publish a series of books under the general title of *Musical Instruments and their Music, 1500–1750*; the introductory volume of the series (1928) is devoted to the treatment of instrumental music in general, and develops the idea that the music of the past should be performed on the instruments for which it was written; the second volume (1930) treats of the viols and other bowed instruments. In 1930 Dr. Otto Andersson's important book, *The Bowed-Harp*, was translated into English; it throws some light on the much confused origin of bowed instruments and describes the peculiar stopping technique of the bowed-harp. Dr. Henry George Farmer has done valuable research on Persian, Arabian, and Turkish instruments. Among his publications the articles on musical instruments in the *Encyclopaedia of Islām* should not be missed.[7] The history of the lute and the rebec is not complete without data on their Oriental prototypes. The scholarly articles of Miss Kathleen Schlesinger in the *Encyclopaedia Britannica*, eleventh edition, on various musical instruments provide excellent material for study and research; since for some incomprehensible reason they were not included in the 'humanized' fourteenth edition, they should be published in book form. Of the older publications a booklet by Major Alexander Hajdecki, *Die Italienische Lira da Braccio*, published at Mostar, Herzegovina, in 1892, failed to make its impression on American writers, yet it is one of the most important pioneer works on the history of the violin family. Wind instruments, both ancient and modern, were studied in an original manner by Professor Henri Bouasse and his experimental collaborator Dr. M. Fouché. Their approach is both scientific and practical, and contributes many fresh viewpoints on this confused subject.[8]

There exists only one book in this country by an American writer which deals with the whole field of musical instruments.[9]

There are excellent studies of special fields, published mostly in the periodicals of learned societies. Among them the works of Frances Morris and Frances Densmore treat of the subject in a manner similar to this study.[10]

The old catalogues of the Crosby Brown Collection at the Metropolitan Museum of Art in New York, now bibliographical rarities, should be really credited to the British school of musicologists.[11]

The present study is the first American work in which an attempt has been made to present a systematized and organically unified statement of the best and most vital trends of such thought both of the past and present.

It is based on a comprehensive and critical research of the works of writers of several centuries ago, among which the works of Virdung, Arnolt Schlick, Martin Agricola, Ganassi, Glareanus, Zacconi, Cerone, Michael Praetorius, Mersenne, Playford, Simpson, Mace, Rousseau, Quantz, and Altenburg should be especially mentioned. Among modern works the writings of the Reverend Canon Francis W. Galpin, M. Victor Charles Mahillon, Dr. Georg Kinsky, Dr. Curt Sachs, and Miss Kathleen Schlesinger in the general field, and of Dr. Otto Andersson, Mr. Arnold Dolmetsch, Major Alexander Hajdecki, and Mr. Gerald R. Hayes in specialized fields, have had the greatest influence upon the thought of the writer.

In a certain sense this work should be regarded as a primer introducing a more comprehensive study of the best contributions in the field.

The Classification of Musical Instruments

THE general classification in this study is based on the classification published in 1910 by Canon Galpin in his well known book *Old English Instruments of Music*. It was found necessary to modify the 1910 classification in several places and bring its terminology up to date. The writer is glad to record the fact that Canon Galpin himself concurred in this, since his new classification[12] is even more radically modified. A detailed comparison of the three classifications, those of Canon Galpin of 1910 and 1937, and the one used in this study, would prove instructive.

Standard Acoustical Terminology

THE standard pertaining to this work is the *American Tentative Standard Acoustical Terminology* sponsored by the Acoustical Society of America, a scientific body of people interested in the science of acoustics as related to all fields where sound presents a problem.[13]

The standard itself has been developed under an elaborate procedure of the American Standards Association.[14]

The standard acoustical terminology is long overdue, as any one who has to deal with works on musical instruments knows only too well. Definitions of the majority of acoustical terms in this study are adopted verbatim. Unfortunately some of the most important terms such as 'the harmonic series,' 'the natural scale,' as well as the standard term for overblown tones and 'harmonics' of string instruments are not defined in the *Tentative Standard Acoustical Terminology*. A detailed discussion of supplementary definitions is incorporated in the text and notes.

Terminology

A PROPER terminology has been developed in French and German, but in English there is a deplorable lack of the most necessary terms. Parts of the French terminology have penetrated into English because of M. Mahillon's great catalogue of the Brussels Collection, which has been in existence for about fifty years. The works of Dr. Curt Sachs in German are, comparatively, too recent to have made an imprint on other languages. His indispensable books are not yet translated into English. Adding to existing terminology is an ungrateful task, exposing the innovator to criticism. The easiest way would be to translate properly or adopt a term from a foreign language. This could not be done in all cases, and certain modifications and additions have been found necessary.

Description of Instruments

AN improved terminology has permitted a more precise technical and typological description of instruments. Structural characteristics are described as if intended for those who might make copies of the instruments.

Dimensioning

This is one of the least satisfactory features in catalogues of musical instruments. No intelligent conclusions can be made nor comparative studies carried on without adequate general dimensions. The writer has been handicapped in his studies of viol sizes by the dearth of certain essential dimensions. In this study a more adequate dimensioning is attempted. It is realized that in the catalogues of larger collections such a detailed dimensioning may be found impossible. There should be an agreement as to general principles and as to the minimum number of dimensions required to describe an instrument most adequately.

General Plan

On the formal side the basis of this study is the general classification given in the Contents. Each important section has a general introduction giving the history, typology, acoustical properties, general constructional details, and tunings of the instrument of a given group. The notes under individual instruments continue some of these features with respect to that particular instrument, but in more specific detail. Explanatory and technical matters, as well as references, are given in notes placed at the end of the book. Technical matters are discussed in the Appendices.

On the subjective, inner side, the unifying thread in this work is man, who according to a philosopher is 'the measure of all things'; man with all his wisdom and foibles, achievements and failures, dignity and snobbishness, gayety and sadness. All these traits are reflected in musical instruments and their usage. Musical instruments to this writer are living entities possessing their own personalities and reflecting the collective personality of the men who have had anything to do with them. Many instruments such as the 'Jingling Johnny' (No. 6), the kettledrums, the flute, the trumpet, the horn, the Scotch bagpipe, the organ, the Irish harp, the lute, the viola da gamba, the violin, the harpsichord, the piano, and many others are to this writer not mere conglomerations of materials and means of musical expression. They are rather poems and epics reflecting the religious, social, economic, and even political relations of racial and social groups of men. Beyond musical instruments is the vast canvas of humanity. Back of the Jingling Johnny are fierce fighting men, the janizaries. The kettledrums were at one time a badge of rank and prized possessions, won on the battlefield at the price of life. The flute inspired many men in battle and delighted others in their hours of leisure. The trumpet was played at one time by a haughty caste of professional trumpeters and denied to ordinary mortals; only kings and nobles were privileged to maintain trumpeters. The horn is symbolical of the chase. The organ is a symbol of religious worship and ecclesiastical power, and as such often an object of intense hatred. The Scotch bagpipe is, indeed, an epic instrument of a noble and proud race. The Irish harp has been an inspirer of a sensitive and much abused people. A price was placed on the heads of Irish harpers by Queen Elizabeth. The lute has been sung in poetry and always evokes a haunting sense of something exotic and exquisite. The noble viol was beloved by the most cultured and sensitive musicians of its time. The violin, a haughty and tyrannical Cinderella and a one-time symbol of the revolution of the masses, is now the acknowledged queen of instruments. Finally, there is the 'lordly harpsichord' and the poetic yet exhibitionistic piano. What a fascinating, living, vital flood of emotions, aspirations, sufferings, and triumphs!

The writer is painfully aware of imperfections in the form of his expression. One needs the genius of a Walt Whitman to do justice to the subject. One can only hope that the unifying idea and feeling, the unifying thread of thought, appearing explicitly only occasionally yet invisibly always present, will be intuitively grasped by the reader; that it will inspire and stimulate his or her imagination, and fire a desire to learn to play some of the 'ancient' instruments. Some of the latter deserve the serious attention of amateurs. Recorders are already attracting the attention of many. Appreciation of the harpsichord is increasing. The viola da gamba family is being revived among several small groups abroad and in this country. Viols with their inherent qualities should be cultivated among amateurs and school children, because, if furnished with frets, they are the easiest bowed instruments to learn to play. Musically, the viols are second in importance only to the lute, and in some respects they are fully equal, if not superior, to the violin. A vast literature of wonderful music exists. The return of the viol to the universal popularity it once enjoyed would enrich our cultural life.

To Fret or not to Fret?

UNFORTUNATELY, there exists a great deal of misapprehension with respect to the fretting of the viol. The question is, should the viol be played with or without frets? Historically, viol playing was developed by musicians who were primarily lute players and transferred much of their technique to the viol. The tuning intervals between the strings on the lute (similar, with one exception, to its modern counterpart, the guitar) and on the viol are the same. Both the lute and the viol had their parts written, at a certain early period, in tablature notation. The viol, when used for song accompaniment, was very often played *pizzicato*, that is, as a plucked and not as a bowed instrument. If an historical analogy were to be followed, then, to restore the viol and its playing technique, guitar players and not violin or violoncello players would be the most logical performers. It is unfortunate that violinists should be among those who became interested in the restoration of the art of viol playing. The viol family has only one thing in common with the violin family: both families are bowed instruments. Specific differences are so numerous that it is ridiculous to think of them in the same terms. Let us enumerate only the most important differences. The real viol is fretted and the violin is not. The viol has six strings tuned in fourths and the violin four strings tuned in fifths. The bow and the bowing technique of both types are different. A reader may ask, 'Why is this question of fretting so important'? The answer is: because it involves the most important thing which justifies a separate existence of any instrumental type — *tone color*.

Fretted viols have a resonant yet very pleasant tone, quite distinct from the tone color of members of the violin family. Technical reasons for this phenomenon are discussed in the text. Therefore the question 'to fret or not to fret' is not rhetorical, but for many reasons very important.

At present there are two schools of viol enthusiasts. One of them, headed by Mr. Arnold Dolmetsch, unqualifiedly and for good reasons stands for the fretting of viols. Another school, comprising not less sincere and enthusiastic people, exclusively professional violin and violoncello players, insists that the viol should be played unfretted. So one is treated sometimes to the spectacle of violoncello players who give competent and even brilliant performances on a six-stringed instrument which to all outer appearances is a bass *viola da gamba*. If, however, one should close one's eyes, one would notice a subtle difference in tone from that of the violoncello, yet not sufficiently distinct to justify the optical illusion. Upon detailed examination of this phenomenon one discovers an unfretted *viola da gamba*. An organologist worthy of his calling should not be deceived by appearances. The objective musicological, organological, and iconographic evidence, without any important exception, tells us that the real *viola da gamba* must be fretted. The last eminent virtuoso player on the instrument, Karl Friedrich Abel (1725–87), played it fretted. Therefore, when an organologist is confronted with unfretted viols, he has to make his stand known. In this study only the fretted *viola da gamba* is regarded as a real instrument having the right to this name. The unfretted *viola da gamba* (?) is the invention of the late nineteenth century and early twentieth. With respect to the unfretted viol only two positions are possible. The first one is that the practice of playing the viol unfretted is a misconception and should be discontinued. If an objection should be raised to such an 'intolerant and dogmatic' attitude, then, in consideration of the sincere and devoted champions of the unfretted viol, the following solution is suggested: the practice should be regarded as a legitimate one, the existence of a new family of bowed instruments should be recognized by organologists, and a new name for it should be adopted.

The fretting of viols, in addition to the esthetic problem of restoring the lost tonal color of exquisite beauty, has a very practical side. One can learn to play the viol acceptably, assuming an elementary knowledge of musical notation and a moderate skill in reading music, approximately in one year. There exists a large quantity of excellent music for viol 'consorts' for two, three, four, five, or six voices which is not difficult technically for amateurs of moderate abilities. This music is interesting because much of it is written by outstanding masters and requires good musicianship, a term not synonymous with technical dexterity. The fretted viola da gamba family of instruments would provide an ideal means of musical expression for people who love music written for the bowed instruments but who cannot afford either the time or energy necessary to learn, even passably, the violin or violoncello. Not every music lover can spend four to six years' time in learning to play even the simplest quartets for the violin family. There are literally hundreds of moderately gifted music lovers who could become proficient in playing fretted viols to a half-dozen who could do the same with the violin in the same length of time. The unfretted viol is more difficult to play even than the violin, so it is out of the question for the amateur. The writer hopes that he has stated the case forcefully enough to compel an intelligent discussion of this problem in the musical press and among music teachers and school supervisors. Fretted viol playing should be taught to American school children. It is more than likely that a love for playing these noble instruments will stay for the rest of their lives, since the fretted viol does not put such a severe strain on one's time and patience as does the violin. Besides, no one is prevented from taking up the study of the violin if one has the energy, persistence, and ability. Viol playing would be an excellent preparation for that; the art of music would gain a new impetus. Since the viol is simpler in construction, the instrument could be made even more cheaply than the violin if made in quantities. If sufficient demand should arise, music would undoubtedly be published for viol consorts.

The author considers it necessary to state that two books, *Musical Wind Instruments* (London, 1939) by Dr. Adam von Ahn Carse, and *The History of Musical Instruments* (New York, 1940) by Dr. Curt Sachs, came to his attention after the MS of the present book was completed and officially submitted to the Museum authorities in August, 1939. In both cases there are some ideas and conclusions similar to those expressed in this book, yet they were reached by the author independently of the books in question.

Acknowledgments

The author is glad to make acknowledgments to the following:

Francis W. Galpin, Litt. D., F. L. S., Canon Emeritus of Chelmsford Cathedral in England, the author of *Old English Instruments of Music, A Textbook of European Musical Instruments, The Music of the Sumerians*, and many other works, for reading part of the manuscript and writing a Foreword; Miss Lotta Van Buren, New York, a specialist on old musical instruments, and Madame Matton-Painparé, Geneva, Switzerland, for data on viols; Mrs. J. Foster White, for sharing her findings on the history of the harp; Dr. Curt Sachs, noted scholar and author of many works on musical instruments, for enlightening comments on some obscure problems of organology; Mr. John A. Gould, a violin-maker, Boston, Mass., for many revealing conversations about the mysteries of the violin-making art; Dr. Frederick A. Saunders, Professor of Physics, Harvard University, for data on the acoustics of the violin; Dr. Frederick M. Watkins, Cornell University, for information on the sizes of viols in the Modena Museo Civico, gathered by him on a trip to Italy; Mr. Richard G. Appel, Assistant-in-Charge, Music Department, Boston Public Library; Mr. Robert H. Haynes, Assistant Librarian, Harvard College Library, Harvard University; Mr. Carleton Sprague Smith, Chief, Music Division, New York Public Library, for many courtesies in facilitating research; Mr. Leslie J. Rogers, Librarian, Boston Symphony Orchestra, for permission to measure and test the Wagner tubas; Mr. Edward Babson Gammons and Mr. Ellery L. Wilson, for lending several valuable books on musical instruments; Mr. Claude Jean Chiasson, Cambridge, Mass., for reading the parts of the manuscript pertaining to keyboard instruments; Mr. David Hoyt Kimball, Buffalo, New York, for reading portions of the manuscript and for many valuable suggestions; Mr. Patrick Brown, the Irish bagpipe maker, and Mr. Daniel J. Murphy, the Irish bagpipe player, both of Dorchester, Mass., for their courtesy in demonstrating the construction and playing technique of the Uilleann pipes.

To the Trustees of the Museum of Fine Arts, Boston, especially to the President, Mr. Edward Jackson Holmes and the Director, Dr. George Harold Edgell, grateful acknowledgment is made for authorizing the undertaking of this long research and the publishing of its results.

To Mr. Edwin James Hipkiss, Curator of the Decorative Arts of Europe and America, Museum of Fine Arts, Boston, further acknowledgment is due for having initiated the work and for his unfailing support during its progress.

To Mr. Ashton Sanborn, Secretary of the Museum of Fine Arts, Boston, and Editor of the Museum's publications, the author is indebted for reading through and editing the whole of the rather bulky manuscript; more important, for moral support and kindly, yet discriminating, appraisal of this work.

To Mrs. Yves Henry Buhler, Assistant, Department of Decorative Arts, Museum of Fine Arts, Boston, the author owes a debt of personal gratitude.

To Miss Elizabeth Pratt, Secretary, Department of Decorative Arts, the author is indebted for the typing of over two thousand pages of the text and corrections of the manuscript of this book, and also for correcting and revising the English. Her extraordinary patience and unfailing courtesy contributed greatly to the successful completion of an arduous task in preparing this book for print.

To Miss Caroline Bullard, Keeper of the Tolman Collection in the Library of the Museum, the author owes many thanks for compiling the Indices and doing this formidable piece of work exceptionally well.

To the American Standards Association, 29 West Thirty-Ninth Street, New York, especial acknowledgment is due for their generous permission to quote extensively and to reprint several tables from the American Tentative Standard Acoustical Terminology — Z24.1–1936. The author has the highest opinion of this standard and regards it as an outstanding contribution to the science of acoustics.

Finally to the members of the Harvard University Press the author gives his thanks for their careful attention to the technical details involved in the actual production of this book.

NICHOLAS BESSARABOFF

WORCESTER, MASSACHUSETTS
November, 1940

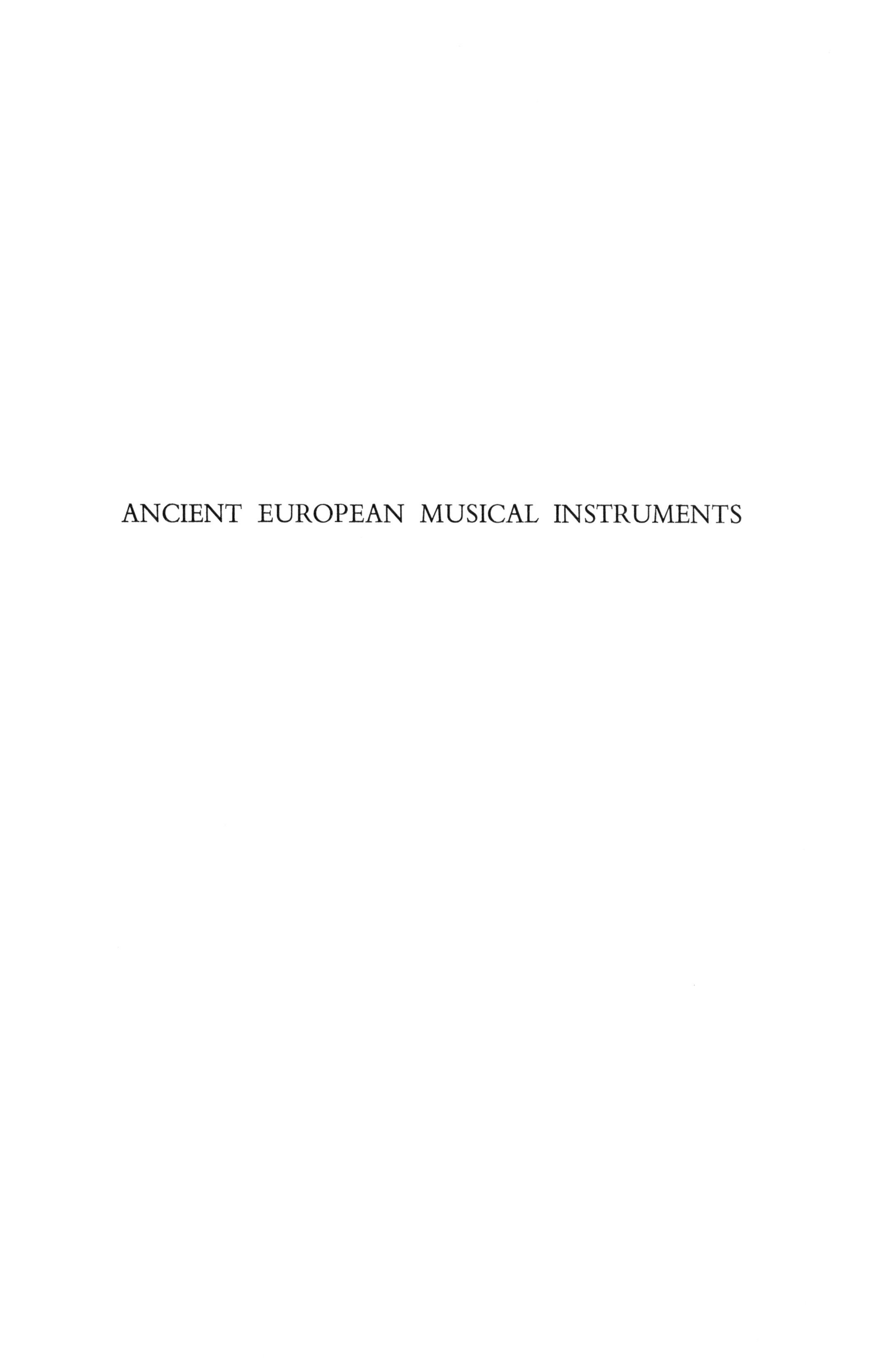

ANCIENT EUROPEAN MUSICAL INSTRUMENTS

ANCIENT EUROPEAN MUSICAL INSTRUMENTS

MUSIC is an expression of the spiritual and emotional powers of man through forms created by the architectonics of intellect. It does not exist in pages of musical notation, nor even in musical instruments. Music comes to life for brief moments during performance and then, like a veiled queen, is perceived no more. The existence of music is on a different plane from that of the other works of man, for the dimension of time is an indispensable element.

The whole complex of music is a four-dimensional space-time entity with two components or aspects. The higher-dimensional subjective aspect of this whole complex of music is a four-dimensional time component revealing itself in the three-dimensional objective sphere of perception as rhythm, melody, and interweaving contrapuntal melodic lines, in a flowing time sequence of patterns. The higher-dimensional objective aspect of the whole complex of music is a four-dimensional space component, a Platonic archetypal idea, a Kantian entity, manifesting itself in the three-dimensional objective sphere of perception as various musical instruments. These two aspects are inseparable. Music cannot manifest itself without some objective means, be that a musical instrument or the voice of a singer. True, composers of music perceive it in their creative imagination, but even thus it is the psychic and physical aspects of the composer's being that respond to the creative urge coming from within. So here is a polarity of urge and response, and that which responds becomes, as it were, an objective matrix with respect to the inner urge. The essence of music dwells in ethereal regions, beyond our limited rationalistic comprehension. 'Music of the spheres' is not entirely a metaphor.

Kant defined things-in-themselves as entities existing independently of our perceptions of space and time. When he was writing, non-Euclidean geometries and higher dimensional spaces were not conceived by the scientists of his day. Now, when concepts of space and time are completely changed and extended, a more precise definition can be given to Kantian ideas. A thing-in-itself is an entity existing independently of our perception of three-dimensional space and time; it exists in the higher-dimensional space-time manifold. Can we imagine such an entity? Very easily, if the clumsy division of time into past, present, and future be eliminated. When the imagination is freed from this limitation, then the musical instrument as a thing-in-itself will include in one unity all instruments built in the past, all instruments existing at the present time, and all instruments yet to be built. Does such an entity exist? Yes, metaphysically; on its own plane of being this existence is just as real as existence in the physical world of any material instrument. Not only that. This entity is a reality, a living force. This entity, this force influences the lives, thoughts, emotions, and imagination of its votaries; it demands devotion, inspires visions, and by its existence and manifestations teaches those in affinity with it unforgettable lessons.

How else can one account for the love, the patient hours of toil, the expenditure of material means so freely given to the study of the technique of the playing of musical instruments, the inspiration which masters of the luthier's art find in their work, the organologist's interest in the design and history of musical instruments, and the passion for collecting which takes possession of certain individuals? Not by economic motives, nor by some psychic derangement can such things be explained. Undoubtedly in some cases these things admix themselves with reasons and motives less personal.

What has all this philosophizing to do with the collection of musical instruments? A collection systematically formed and arranged is the nearest approach to the image of that oneness which is the related-manyness, that thing-in-itself, that metaphysical MUSICAL INSTRUMENT which like a many-faceted diamond reveals itself in many aspects, each of which is the individual instrument. When many musical instruments are gathered together in one place, when their different peculiarities are studied, then a more complete idea can be conceived of the Platonic idea, the Kantian thing-in-itself, that unites them all. One may not realize this consciously, only intuitively, when one comes in contact with such a collection, but the fascination is there. Those few who have had the opportunity and privilege of the actual collecting of musical instruments know the force of attraction which they exercise. This feeling is experienced by collectors of any significant objects, but musical instruments bring one into communion with some of the chosen spirits of mankind, with the history and customs of many peoples of various countries and races; they challenge one's interest and mental powers with the many riddles of their construction, and of the principles upon which that construction is based, and the almost infinite variety in application of these principles. If life is a school and if one is given a choice of subjects of study, among the most significant and fascinating subjects are musical instruments.

ACOUSTICAL TERMINOLOGY

THIS terminology is based on the *American Tentative Standard Acoustical Terminology* — Z24.1 –1936. The numbers given in the parentheses at the end of each definition correspond to those of the American Tentative Standard. When they are given without qualifications, the definitions are quoted verbatim.

General Definitions

1. *Sound.* Sound is the sensation produced through the ear by an alternative displacement of air particles set in motion by some causative means. (Based on 1.1, a and b.)

2. *Tone.* A tone is a sound giving a definite sensation of pitch and loudness which constitute its quantitative characteristics; also a subjective sense of an individual 'tone color' or timbre which is its qualitative characteristic. (Partly based on 6.1.)

3. *Note.* A note is a conventional sign used to indicate the pitch, or duration, or both, of a tone. (6.9.)

4. *Pitch.* Pitch is that subjective quality of a sound which determines its position in a musical scale. Pitch may be measured as the frequency of that pure tone having a specified sound pressure, or specified loudness level, which seems, to the average normal ear, to occupy the same position in a musical scale. The unit is the cycle per second. (3.1.)

5. *Unpitched sound.* An unpitched sound is any sound to which no definite pitch can be assigned. (1.41.)

6. *Noise.* Noise is any undesired sound. (1.42.)

7. *Cycle* (~). One complete set of the recurrent values of a periodic quantity comprises a cycle. (1.4.)

8. *Period* (T). The time required for one cycle of a periodic quantity is the period. The unit is the second. (1.5.)

9. *Frequency* (f). The number of cycles occurring per unit of time, or which would occur per unit of time if all subsequent cycles were identical with the cycle under consideration, is the frequency. The frequency is the reciprocal of the period. The unit is the cycle per second. *Note*: It is recommended that the following terms be discontinued: double vibrations (*dv*), periods per second (*pps*), and Hertz, all these being equivalent to cycles per second; and vibrations per second (*vs*), which has usually been used as the equivalent of half cycles per second. (1.6.)

10. *American standard pitch.* The standard pitch for America is based on the frequency 440 cycles per second for tone A_{49} on the pianoforte keyboard. (6.16.)

11. *Loudness.* The loudness is that subjective quality of a sound which determines the magnitude of the auditory sensation produced by that sound. (3.14.)

12. *Interval.* The interval between two tones is a measure of their difference in pitch and is usually numerically represented by the ratio of their frequencies. (6.8.)

13. *Scale.* A scale is a series of tones ascending or descending in frequency by definite intervals, suitable for musical purposes. (6.13.)

14. *Octave.* An octave is the interval between any two tones the frequency ratio of which is 2:1. (Based on 1.7 and 6.10.)

15. *Equally tempered half tone.* An equally tempered half tone is the interval between any two tones the frequency ratio of which is the twelfth root of two. (Based on 6.11.)

16. *Cent.* A cent is the interval between any two tones the frequency ratio of which is the twelve hundredth root of two. *Note*: 1 octave = 12 equally tempered half tones = 1200 cents; or a cent is one hundredth part of an equally tempered half tone. (Based on 6.12.)

17. *Just scale* (*untempered scale*). A just scale is a musical scale employing only intervals found in the harmonic series. (6.14.) See Table II.

18. *Equally tempered scale.* The equally tempered scale is a division of the octave into twelve equal intervals, called equally tempered half tones. (6.15 partly quoted.) See Table III.

EQUIVALENTS OF MUSICAL STAFF NOTATION

THERE are several equivalents of musical staff notation. The oldest and most widely used system designates the tones by letters and diacritical marks. The practical advantage it has over the newer numerical systems is the greater ease in memorizing the symbols of tones and in assigning the tones to a given octave. For this reason it is used in this study.

The lowest tone, *CCC*, is that of the 32-foot organ pipe having 16.351 cycles per second at 440 pitch. The chromatic tones are identified thus: *F*-sharp, *b'*-flat. The tuning tone of the orchestra (diapason) is *a'*. Since in this study there are many references to different standards of musical pitch, the number of cycles is specified in each particular case: *a'* = 440, *a'* = 502.6, etc. The system used in this study is referred to sometimes as the 'Helmholtz system.' This is a misnomer, since the letter system with diacritical marks differing only in form, but otherwise identical, was used in the *De Organographia* of Praetorius, published in 1619. Helmholtz himself stated that 'die Deutschen Musiker bezeichnen die Töne der höheren Octaven durch Strichelung . . .' ('the German musicians designate the tones of the higher octaves by means of accents . . .'); cf. *Die Lehre von den Tonempfindungen*, second ed., 1865, p. 28. Sometimes the octaves beginning with the alto octave are referred to as 'once-accented,' 'twice-accented,' etc.

The International System. Officially adopted by the International Music Congress in Paris on June 16, 1900, as the International System. In this system each tone of the chromatic scale is identified by its name and number; the lowest tone is *CCC* to which is assigned the number 1; the rest of the tones are identified in the numerical succession (cf. Mahillon, *Catalogue . . . de Bruxelles*, V, 1922, p. 78). The system was originated by M. Victor Mahillon and embodied in *Le matériel sonore des orchestres* (Brussels, several editions; first published in 1866). This booklet, widely used abroad, is indispensable when unambiguous identification of tones, a precise and quick reference to the absolute position of tones of the orchestral and band instruments, their compass, and the written notes of transposing instruments are required. For easy visualization the keyboard is represented at the bottom of each table. The number system of tones was found impracticable as a notation, however useful it proved to be in other respects. The principal difficulty is that no simple mnemonic rule for memorizing the numbers of tones is possible and constant reference to the table is required.

The American Standard System. See Table IV, p. 9. This system is a combination of letter and number systems. Each tone is identified by a capital letter, by an accidental, if a chromatic tone, and by a subscript number. Example: middle C is designated as C_{40}; the second partial tone of the B-flat trumpet as $B_{\flat 38}$. In principle this system is similar to that of Mahillon, except that it starts with the lowest tone of the pianoforte as its tone No. 1, and its octaves are counted from A to A. The proposed system has several defects. It introduces a new series of numbers differing by 9 from those of the International System and is as difficult to memorize as the latter. There is no provision for extending its notation below the tone A_1. Yet the lowest tone of the contrabass sarrusophone (AAA-flat) is one semitone lower than A_1; the pedal tone of the E-flat sub-bass tuba (EEE-flat) is six semitones lower; the 32-foot stop

TABLE I

EQUIVALENTS OF MUSICAL STAFF NOTATION AND NAMES OF OCTAVES

Octave Ordinal No.	Organ Pipe Length	Names of Octaves		Musical Notation and Letter Equivalents
1st	32-foot	Subcontrabass	Subcontra	*CCC* *BBB* 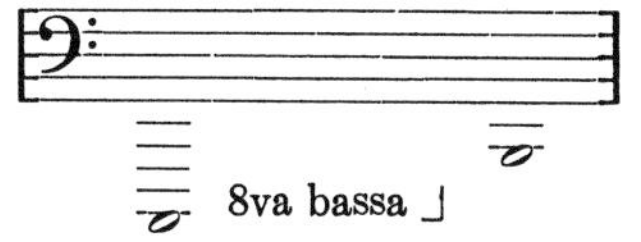 (8va bassa)
2nd	16-foot	Contrabass	Contra	*CC* *BB* 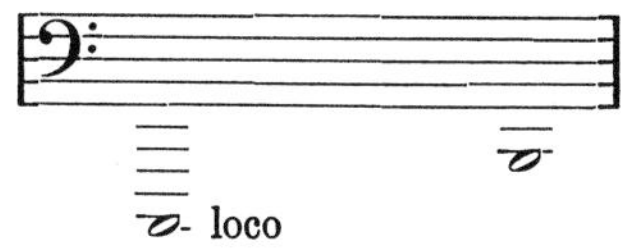 (loco)
3rd	8-foot	Bass	Great	 *C* *B*
4th	4-foot	Tenor	Small	 *c* *b*
5th	2-foot	Alto	One-line	 *c'* *a'* *b'*
6th	1-foot	Treble	Two-line	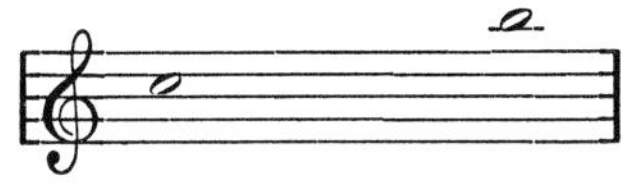 *c''* *b''*
7th	6-inch	In Alt (Rare)	Three-line	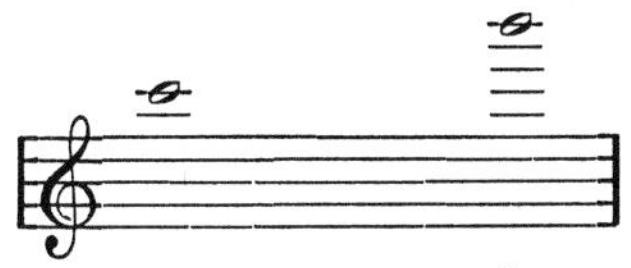 c^3 b^3
8th	3-inch		Four-line	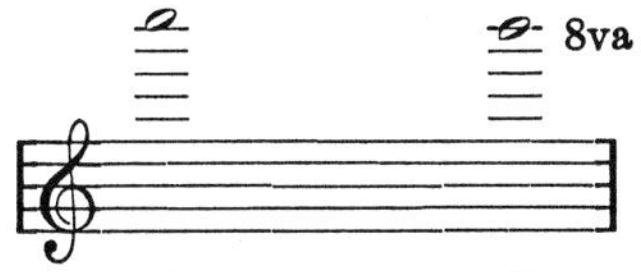 c^4 b^4 (8va)

of the organ (by no means a rare stop) descends chromatically nine semitones lower. The most serious objection is that it goes contrary to the standardized practice of dividing the octave from C to C. Upon this division is erected a complex system of solfege and trans-

TABLE II

A JUST SCALE (See 17, p. 5)

Interval	Frequency Ratio from Starting Point	Cents from Starting Point
Unison	1 : 1	0
Semitone	16 : 15	111.731
Minor Tone	10 : 9	182.404
Major Tone	9 : 8	203.910
Minor Third	6 : 5	315.641
Major Third	5 : 4	386.314
Fourth	4 : 3	498.045
Augmented Fourth	45 : 32	590.224
Diminished Fifth	64 : 45	609.777
Fifth	3 : 2	701.955
Minor Sixth	8 : 5	813.687
Major Sixth	5 : 3	844.359
Harmonic Minor Seventh	7 : 4	968.826
Grave Minor Seventh	16 : 9	996.091
Minor Seventh	9 : 5	1017.597
Major Seventh	15 : 8	1088.269
Octave	2 : 1	1200.000

TABLE III

EQUALLY TEMPERED SCALE (See 18, p. 5)

Name and Number of Tone from C_{40} in Ascending Order	Name of Interval from C_{40} as Starting Point	Frequency (cycles per second) at Standard Pitch $A_{49} = 440$ Cycles per Second	Cents from Starting Point	Frequency Ratio from Starting Point
C_{40}	Unison	261.626	0	1:1
$C\sharp_{41}$ $D\flat_{41}$	Half Tone	277.183	100	1.059463:1
D_{42}	Whole Tone	293.665	200	1.122462:1
$D\sharp_{43}$ $E\flat_{43}$	Minor Third	311.127	300	1.189207:1
E_{44}	Major Third	329.628	400	1.259921:1
F_{45}	Fourth	349.228	500	1.334840:1
$F\sharp_{46}$ $G\flat_{46}$	Augmented Fourth Diminished Fifth	369.994	600	1.414214:1
G_{47}	Fifth	391.995	700	1.498307:1
$G\sharp_{48}$ $A\flat_{48}$	Minor Sixth	415.305	800	1.587401:1
A_{49}	Major Sixth	440.000	900	1.681793:1
$A\sharp_{50}$ $B\flat_{50}$	Minor Seventh	466.164	1000	1.781797:1
B_{51}	Seventh	493.883	1100	1.887749:1
C_{52}	Octave	523.251	1200	2:1

positions, i.e., the whole pedagogics of musical training. Since M. Mahillon's booklet is so convenient for reference purposes, the rules for translation of the numbers of one system into another may be given. To translate the American number into the Mahillon number,

TABLE IV

FREQUENCIES OF THE TONES OF THE EQUALLY TEMPERED SCALE

(As used in music, named and numbered according to their positions on the pianoforte keyboard and calculated to the American Standard Pitch)

(See 10, p. 5)

Name on Pianoforte Keyboard	1st Octave No. Cycles per Second		2d Octave No. Cycles per Second		3d Octave No. Cycles per Second		4th Octave No. Cycles per Second		Name on Pianoforte Keyboard
A	1	27.500	13	55.000	25	110.000	37	220.000	A
A♯ B♭	2	29.135	14	58.270	26	116.541	38	233.082	A♯ B♭
B	3	30.868	15	61.735	27	123.471	39	246.942	B
C	4	32.703	16	65.406	28	130.813	40	261.626	C
C♯ D♭	5	34.648	17	69.296	29	138.591	41	277.183	C♯ D♭
D	6	36.708	18	73.416	30	146.832	42	293.665	D
D♯ E♭	7	38.891	19	77.782	31	155.563	43	311.127	D♯ E♭
E	8	41.203	20	82.407	32	164.814	44	329.628	E
F	9	43.654	21	87.307	33	174.614	45	349.228	F
F♯ G♭	10	46.249	22	92.499	34	184.997	46	369.994	F♯ G♭
G	11	48.999	23	97.999	35	195.998	47	391.995	G
G♯ A♭	12	51.913	24	103.826	36	207.652	48	415.305	G♯ A♭

Name on Pianoforte Keyboard	5th Octave No. Cycles per Second		6th Octave No. Cycles per Second		7th Octave No. Cycles per Second		8th Octave No. Cycles per Second		Name on Pianoforte Keyboard
A	49	440.000	61	880.000	73	1,760.000	85	3,520.000	A
A♯ B♭	50	466.164	62	932.328	74	1,864.655	86	3,729.310	A♯ B♭
B	51	493.883	63	987.767	75	1,975.533	87	3,951.066	B
C	52	523.251	64	1,046.502	76	2,093.005	88	4,186.009	C
C♯ D♭	53	554.365	65	1,108.731	77	2,217.461	..	....	C♯ D♭
D	54	587.330	66	1,174.659	78	2,349.318	..	....	D
D♯ E♭	55	622.254	67	1,244.508	79	2,489.016	..	....	D♯ E♭
E	56	659.255	68	1,318.510	80	2,637.021	..	....	E
F	57	698.456	69	1,396.913	81	2,793.826	..	....	F
F♯ G♭	58	739.989	70	1,479.978	82	2,959.955	..	....	F♯ G♭
G	59	783.991	71	1,567.982	83	3,135.964	..	....	G
G♯ A♭	60	830.609	72	1,661.219	84	3,322.438	..	....	G♯ A♭

add 9 to the American number. Thus, the lowest tone of the pianoforte will be designated in Mahillon's system as A_{10}. To translate the Mahillon number into the American number, subtract 9 from the Mahillon number, if the latter is 10 or more; this stipulation is necessary since there are no American equivalents of the Mahillon number below 10. The table of tones produced on the clavichord No. 299 and notated according to the American Standard System is given on p. 335.

Further information on details of other systems, with rather trenchant comments on the existing confusion, may be found in *The Oxford Companion to Music* by Dr. Percy A. Scholes, s.v. 'Pitch, 7,' p. 734. It should be added that, for some reason, Dr. Scholes omitted any reference to the International System; the new American Standard was published too late for inclusion in his valuable work.

CLASSIFICATION OF MUSICAL INSTRUMENTS

THE great number of factors involved renders the scientific classification of musical instruments a complicated and difficult task. An organologist, one who studies the science of musical instruments, must take into account not only the instruments used in his own time and among his own people, but also instruments used in the past which, for various reasons, have become obsolete. He must also classify properly the instruments of peoples in countries outside of Europe.

The next problem in order of difficulty is the great number of types of sound production as applied to musical instruments. Some methods of sound production are simple. The striking of a sonorous substance or a membrane, the blowing against the sharp edge of a tube, or the plucking of a string, are immediately and easily comprehensible. Sometimes, however, an organologist has to deal with an instrument like the Hindu *nyastaranga*, which is played with a cup-shaped orifice pressed against the neck, close to the larynx. A sound is produced by the sympathetic vibration of the membrane affixed inside the tube, when the performer hums a melody. This example is, of course, an extreme case; nevertheless, a classification must be so devised that even such a weird method of sound production finds its place.

The classification adopted for this study by the Museum of Fine Arts, Boston, is based on that of Canon Francis W. Galpin,[15] with certain additions and modifications. Some of the terms follow the terminology proposed by Dr. Erich M. von Hornbostel and Dr. Curt Sachs.[16]

For the convenience of the reader the classification in this study is combined with the Table of Contents, pp. ix–xv, so that the various divisions and subdivisions and the individual instruments illustrating them may be more easily found.

TERMINOLOGY

THE definition of terms follows the order of their occurrence in the classification given in the Table of Contents, pp. ix–xv. The acoustical terms, such as 'pedal,' 'partial tone,' etc., are defined on pages 42 and 43.

Idiophonic Instruments. A class of musical instruments in which a sonorous substance composing them, upon being suitably vibrated by a player, produces sound by itself without an intermediate vibrator.

Instruments Controlled Directly. A division of musical instruments which a player holds in his hands, and upon which he controls the production of tones directly by operating finger-holes, keys, valves, or pistons; by manipulating a slide; by using a plectrum, a bow, a drum-stick, etc. The direct control of an instrument does not necessarily imply the direct control of a vibrator. (See 'Reeds controlled indirectly' below.)

Rhythmic Instruments. The idiophonic and membranophonic instruments of indefinite pitch, noise-makers, used for the production of rhythmic, unpitched sounds.

Tonal Instruments. The idiophonic and membranophonic instruments producing musical tones of definite pitch.

Instruments Controlled by a Keyboard. A division including polyphonic instruments which permit the playing of chords and have a keyboard mechanism attached to them.

Instruments Controlled by Automatic Motion. A division including all the instruments which have some source of energy and motion (a spring motor, an air motor, or an electric motor) attached to them in such a way that the control exercised by a 'player' is confined to starting and stopping. The latter function on some of the instruments of this type is performed automatically.

To this division belongs an instrument vibrated by the uncontrolled motion of the surrounding air, the aeolian harp. The proper adjective applicable in this case is autonomous motion, i.e., the independent motion of air obeying its own laws.

Membranophonic Instruments. A class of instruments, the principal sound-producing medium of which is a membrane. Membranes can be set in vibration by striking, by friction, by plucking, or by induction of sympathetic vibrations by humming. To this class also belong phonographs, the membrane of which is set in motion by a needle mechanism actuated by grooves in the discs or cylinders.

Aerophonic or Wind Instruments. A class of musical instruments in which the principal sound-producing medium is the air column confined in the tubes. This column of air is set in vibration by various methods, such as (1) blowing a stream of air through a *flue* (a narrow wind-way); (2) setting a *reed* in vibration; (3) blowing air through the *lips* stretched across the rim of a mouth-piece. In this case the lips serve as vibrating 'reeds.'

In accordance with these fundamental methods of generating the primary vibrations, the aerophonic instruments are divided into three principal sections: (A) *Flue-blown*, (B) *Reed-vibrated*, (C) *Lip-vibrated*.[17] Aerophonic instruments also include the division (35) in which the vibrators of the instruments act upon the air unconfined in tubes.

Flue-blown Instruments. A section of aerophonic instruments with the air column confined in tubes (as in flutes) or in receptacles (as in ocarinas) and set in vibration by a stream of air directed by a flue against the sharp edge of a hole or of the tube itself (as in panpipes). The term *flue* is borrowed from the organ-builder's term for the narrow wind-way directing and shaping the air stream in the *flue pipes* (as contrasted with *reed pipes*). In playing such an instrument as the transverse flute, the player's lips form a flexible 'flue,' so that the underlying principle remains essentially the same.

Reed-vibrated Instruments. A section of aerophonic instruments with the air column confined in tubes (as in clarinets, oboes, etc.) or organ pipes (reed pipes), and set in vibration by reeds actuated by a stream of air forced past them. The fundamental reed types are (1) beating reeds (single and double), (2) free reeds, and, (3) ribbon reeds.

Reeds Controlled Indirectly. The reed vibrators on reed-vibrated instruments of this type are inserted in the air-reservoir (as in bagpipes), or covered by a capsule (as on cromornes, page 81) and, therefore, are not touched by the lips of the player. The tone is produced by blowing into a bag or a capsule and developing a certain amount of air pressure around the reeds. The compressed air surrounding the reed sets it in vibration by passing through the small aperture which, alternately, is closed and opened by the vibrating reed. This intermittent entry of an air stream through the aperture causes vibration of the air column in the tube, thus producing a musical tone. No particular skill is required in producing sounds on such instruments. Anyone with sufficiently strong lungs can produce a tone; but a player has no control of quality of tone, and only a limited control of its dynamics.

Polyphonic Reed Instruments. The group of instruments with indirectly controlled reeds, with an air reservoir, and two or more sounding pipes. Bagpipes with a chanter and one or more drones belong to this group.

Reeds Controlled Directly. The reed-vibrators on reed-vibrated instruments of this type are held by the player in his mouth and controlled by lip muscles. The player exercises complete control over the tone as to its quality (tone color or timbre) and its quantity (the dynamic control, piano or forte). The embouchure on instruments with directly controlled reeds, such as clarinets, oboes, bassons, is developed only after considerable practice and requires care for its maintenance. The embouchure is the adjustment of lip muscles necessary for production of correct tones on the wind instruments such as those with directly controlled reeds or lip-vibrated instruments (horns and trumpets). In the course of practice and playing the lip muscles are developed. Among players this is known as 'developing a lip.'

Lip-vibrated Instruments. A section of aerophonic instruments, the vibrator of which is the lips of the player stretched across the rim of the mouthpiece. The air passing through the lips, which serve as the vibrating 'reeds,' sets the air column in vibration. The usual names for this section of instruments are 'brass wind' and 'cup-mouthpiece' instruments. Both of these terms are incorrect. The saxophone is made of brass, but it is played with a single beating reed, and, therefore, should be classified as a reed-vibrated instrument and not a brass wind. In other words, designation by material is meaningless. 'Cup-mouthpiece' is not sufficiently inclusive, because the French horns, Wagner tubas, cornophones (Besson), and cornons (Červeny) are played with funnel-shaped mouthpieces.

Two-octave Instruments. A group of lip-vibrated instruments having a tube which permits playing partial tones of the natural scale not higher than a fourth. Some of the instruments belonging to this group produce only its pedal tone; others only the pedal and its octave, etc.

Three-octave Instruments. A group of lip-vibrated instruments having a tube of such proportions that it permits playing partial tones of the natural scale within the range of the pedal and the eighth partial tone. Exceptional players may reach tones above the latter, but the practical upper limit for band and orchestra work should be regarded as the eighth partial tone.

Instruments with Pedal Tone. A sub-group of lip-vibrated instruments having a tube of such proportions that it permits the playing of the pedal tone with assurance and good tonal quality. *Ganzinstrument* in the German terminology: the 'whole-tube' instruments.

Instruments without Pedal Tone. A sub-group of lip-vibrated instruments having a tube of such proportions that playing of the pedal tone is either impossible or, if possible, then the uncertainty of producing and of tonal quality makes it unsuitable for musical purposes. The first tone of these instruments is the second partial tone. *Halbinstrument* in the German terminology: the 'half-tube' instruments.

Four-octave Instruments. A group of lip-vibrated instruments having a tube of such proportions that it permits playing the natural scale within the range of the pedal and the sixteenth partial tone. Some players develop the ability to play still higher partial tones, but this ability is rather exceptional. The practicable upper limit for average players is the sixteenth partial tone.

Free Air Instruments. The aerophonic instruments, vibration of which acts directly upon the air surrounding them without any intermediate tube or pipe. Such instruments are sirens, electro-dynamic loud speakers, bull roarers, etc.

Chordophonic Instruments. Stringed instruments. The sound-producing medium of chordophonic instruments is a string set in vibration, either by plucking, striking, bowing, or by an air stream.

Electrophonic Instruments. Our Collection has no representatives of this class. These instruments are being invented in ever increasing numbers. Only a prophet may predict whether their appearance presages a radical change in the method of sound production and the eventual disappearance of musical instruments of the usual type, or just an addition of a new type to our instruments. At present electrophonic instruments are in the first stage of development; some of them are rather inferior in tone color and expressiveness. The fundamental principle involved in this class of instruments is the utilization of oscillating systems of high frequency employing vacuum tubes as generators of the oscillation. By suitable means these high frequency oscillations are brought down to the number of vibrations within the range of audibility. A detailed classification of electrophonic instruments can be found in F. W. Galpin, *A Textbook of European Musical Instruments*, p. 36.

CLASS I

IDIOPHONIC INSTRUMENTS OR IDIOPHONES

CLASS I: IDIOPHONIC INSTRUMENTS OR IDIOPHONES

MODERN scientific classification of musical instruments no longer retains the term 'percussion' in designating certain types of sound producers. The increasing knowledge of instruments of primitive races and of peoples outside of Europe revealed so many varieties of types and forms of sound producers which would ordinarily be classed as percussion instruments, that it has been found necessary to subdivide them into two new classes: *idiophonic instruments* or *idiophones*, and *membranophonic instruments* or *membranophones*.[18]

In the class of idiophonic instruments are included those instruments in which the sonorous substance composing them is the primary vibrating medium. For instance, a xylophone bar, consisting of a piece of wood, issues a sound upon being struck. Or a church bell, struck by the clapper, vibrates and produces sound. Idiophones are, therefore, distinguished from those instruments of which the primary vibrating medium is extraneous to the substance of the body of the instrument, like a string or a membrane.

The sonorous substance of idiophones can be set in vibration by: (1) *percussion*, or striking it with another solid substance (bell, triangle, cymbals); (2) *plucking* (music box comb, Jew's harp); (3) *friction* (Franklin's glass harmonica); (4) *blowing* (*piano chanteur*, *Ku tang*). But, irrespective of the method of exciting vibrations, it is the substance of which the instrument is made that produces sound.

Further classification of idiophones is based on the type of sound produced. In music there are two types of sound in use: (1) *unpitched sounds*, and (2) *musical tones*. The distinction between the two is based on the control of quantitative and qualitative characteristics. A musical tone is a sound controlled as to its pitch or the number of cycles per unit of time, its intensity (piano or forte), and its tone quality or tone color (timbre). An unpitched sound is a sound possessing neither definite pitch nor any particular tone color. Its only characteristic common with a musical tone is the intensity, which can be controlled within a certain range.

Therefore, idiophonic instruments are divided into producers of noise of indefinite pitch, serving for the accentuation of rhythmic patterns, and producers of tone of definite pitch; that is, into *rhythmic* and *tonal* instruments.

DIVISION I: CONTROLLED DIRECTLY

SECTION A: RHYTHMIC (UNPITCHED SOUND)

1. SISTRUM — Southern Italy type. Reproduction

Bronze body and handle. Copper rods. The instrument consists of a loop of elongated horseshoe shape with handle; four rods passing through the loop and bent at ends to prevent them from slipping out. The handle represents the base upon which sits a figure of the god Bes surmounted by a double-faced winged figure. Within the loop is a cat. Upon the top, a jackal. Length, 21.5 cm. Width, 4 cm. Length of rods, 11 cm. (17.2040)

The sistrum can hardly be regarded as a musical instrument. It is rather a sound-producing ritual implement which was used in the worship of Isis and in magical religious rites. Its purpose was to dispel evil spirits. In some districts of Abyssinia it is still so used by the priests under the name of *tsanatsel*. In the worship of Isis, the sistrum was carried in the priest's left hand, the right one holding the *ankh*, the symbol of life; the priestesses held the sistrum in the right hand. It was used in the most solemn religious services, and was frequently carried by women of the most exalted rank.[19]

2. CASTANETS — Spain

Boxwood. Two hollowed-out discs with grips. Diameter, 5 cm. Length, 7.5 cm. (17.2029)

3. CASTANETS — England

Ebony. Three pieces. Flat centerpiece with integral handle, to which are attached two castanets of a type similar to No. 2. Diameter, 4.5 cm. Length, 27.5 cm. (17.2030)

Castanets, their simplicity notwithstanding, are among the most difficult instruments to play properly. Used by Spaniards in their original form, like No. 2, i.e., in two separate pieces, they require an extraordinary skill in manipulation. The difficulty in playing them consists not only in the complex rhythmic patterns, but also in producing the proper tonal quality. Experienced players take good care of their castanets and protect them from the influence of atmospheric conditions, otherwise they refuse to 'sing.' Only those who learn to play castanets in childhood can play them well. Instruments like No. 3, with the handle, are made as a concession to the lack of inborn skill of ordinary players.

4. TRIANGLE — England

Steel. Circular steel bar bent into the shape of an equilateral triangle with two ends slightly curved outward. Steel bar striker with loop on one end. Length of side, 16.5 cm. (17.2048)
Plate VII

5. CYMBALS — England

Bronze discs with a spherical segment depression in the center. A leather loop on each end for holding. Diameter, 17 cm. Height, 4 cm. (17.2028)
Plate VII

6. JINGLING JOHNNY — Belgium, early 19th century

Turkish Crescent, Chinese Pavilion. Fig. 1, p. 19. A brass pole with wooden handle and sliding sleeve. Surmounted by a small crescent, below which is a small sphere and four bells. Further below there are (1) a round, pavilion-shaped perforated piece with twelve bells on the lower rim; (2) a large crescent with six bells; (3) a sphere with five-pointed star inside the crescent; and (4) a perforated paraboloidal skirt with twelve jingles on the lower rim. Inside the skirt there is a brass ferrule with a helical spring fixed to the pole; the sliding sleeve has a short spring attached to its top. The instrument is carried at the head of a band and assists in keeping the marching rhythm. The lower end of the pole is inserted into a leather pocket attached to a shoulder belt to facilitate the holding. The sliding sleeve is moved up and down, striking against the spring and causing the jingles and bells to jingle; hence the affectionate name bestowed upon it by the British 'Tommies.' Length, 178 cm. Diameter, 30 cm. (17.2043)

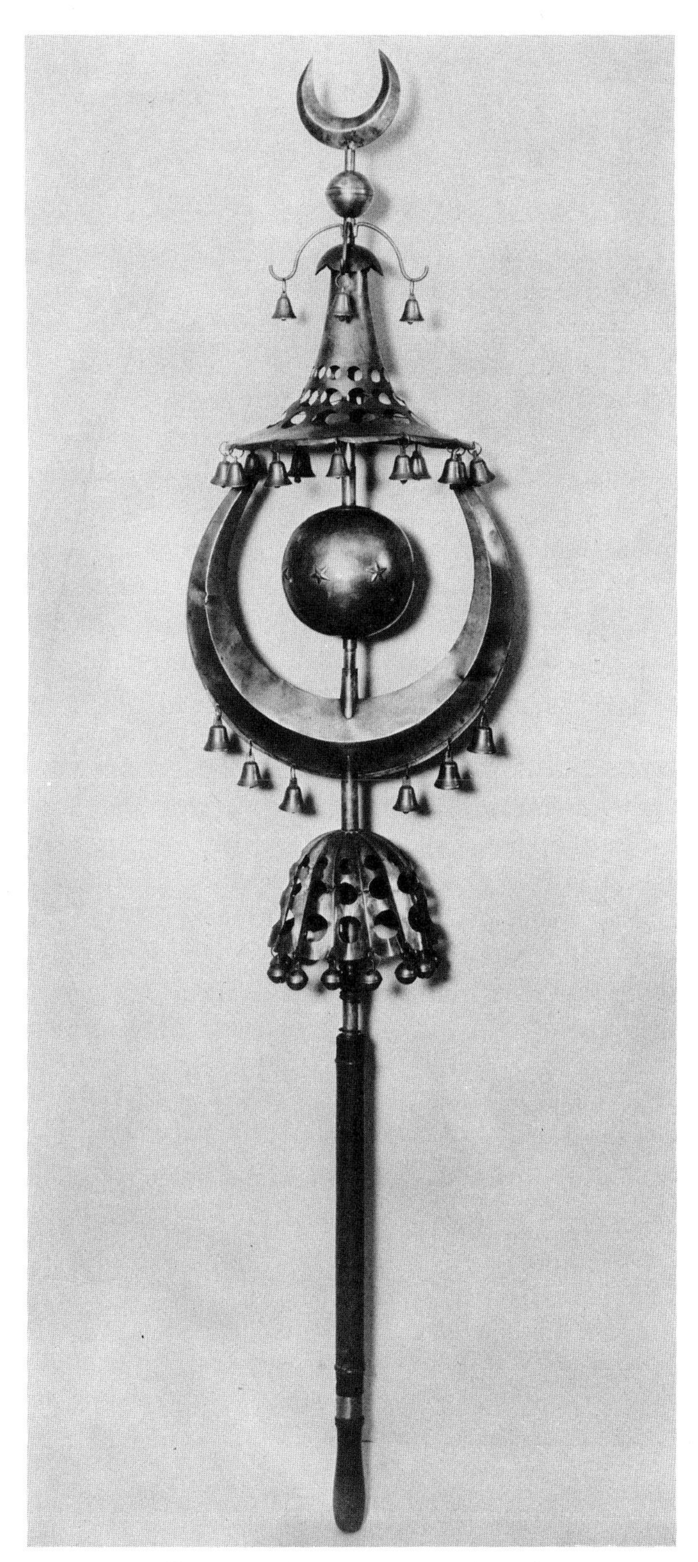

Fig. 1. JINGLING JOHNNY (No. 6)

The 'Jingling Johnny' of this Collection is a comparatively modest specimen without horsetails. There are in existence magnificent instruments with a gala array of stars, crescents, bells, jingles, horsetails, etc., the whole surmounted by imperial eagles. This type of instrument was developed in a spirit of play, under the influence of forces which revolutionized European military music and affected indirectly its orchestral music. For this reason a short historical excursion should prove enlightening.

After the conquest of Constantinople by the Turks, Europe was subject to their constant military pressure, which lasted almost to the end of the seventeenth century. Among the Turkish troops the terrible janizaries acquired a notable reputation for relentlessness, cruelty, and invincibility. *Janizaries* (corrupted from the Turkish *Yenicheri*, new troops) were the regular infantry created by the Ottoman Turks in the fourteenth century, which became their principal force and made possible the vast conquests of that and the following centuries. Organized in 1326 during the reign of Sultan Orkhan, the janizaries were conscripted among the Christian subjects of the Sultans in their boyhood, converted to Mohammedanism, and brought up under fanatical tutorship and the strictest discipline. Originally they were not permitted to marry or learn any trade; and until the development of European standing armies during the wars of the Emperor Charles V, they possessed a decisive superiority in war.

But gradually corrupting influences undermined the strength of this marvellous fighting machine. From the time of the assassination of Sultan Othman II (1622), the janizaries degenerated gradually into the tools of irresponsible adventurers and foreign intriguers. The former servants of the Sultans became their masters, demanded money at the accession of their sovereigns, influenced appointments of important dignitaries, exacted tribute from the populace. Their revolts and insubordination finally became such a burden that in 1826 the whole organization, at that time numbering over 100,000 men, was forcibly suppressed,[20] many thousands being massacred.

The janizaries had a very interesting organization and from the beginning possessed military bands.[21] They developed martial music of the most effective kind, well adapted to the business of war, both for marching and for the battlefield. During the battle the musicians were stationed by the standards of commanders[22] and played incessantly, thus encouraging the fighting spirit of their men and instilling horror into their enemies. We should remember that in those times hand-to-hand fighting was the rule, while firearms were clumsy and not very effective.

With the material available at present, it is difficult to restore the instrumentation of janizary bands.[23] Undoubtedly it varied; but toward the end of their existence, the staff band of the *Agha* (commander-in-chief) of the janizaries was constituted as follows:

There were six groups of musicians.[24]

1. Nine musicians playing the *zurna* (a kind of oboe), including their chief, who had the title of *Mehter-bachi*, the bandmaster; he also played a *zurna*.

2. Nine musicians playing the *chaghana*. This was the instrument which can be regarded as the ancestor of the Jingling Johnny, but it had no horsetails. More of this later. This

particular group was somewhat exceptional, since it consisted of the pages of the *Vezier* and was under the leadership of the *Bach-chaush*, an important officer of the janizaries, who presented petitions to the *Agha* and corresponded to a commissioned officer in charge of the band.

3. Nine musicians playing the Turkish bass drums. Their chief was the assistant band-master.

4. Nine musicians playing the cymbals. They either stood back of, or followed, when on march, the players of the preceding group.

5. Nine musicians playing *naqqāra*,[25] small kettledrums. Players of this group were seated at state functions.

6. Nine musicians playing the Turkish trumpet (*buru*).

The whole band consisted, therefore, of fifty-four players.

How did this unusual combination sound? There is a testimony of contemporary Europeans. Marsigli writes[26] "Les différens sons de tous ces Instrumens seroient durs à l'oreille, s'ils n'étoient corrigés par celui de la Grand Caisse; mais, quand ils sont tout réunis, le concert en est assés agréable."

Then we have the opinion of Schubart, who expresses it very definitely: "The character of this (Turkish) music is so warlike, that even cowardly souls throw out their chests. When one had the good fortune of listening to the performance of the janizaries themselves, whose music-choirs are usually between eighty and one hundred persons strong, then he must laugh indulgently over the clumsy aping, which among us mostly disfigures the Turkish music." Of its rhythmic qualities he speaks thus: "It loves the straightforward two-four time. . . . Meanwhile, no other kind of music requires such firm, definite and overpowering, predominating beat. Each beat is delineated so strongly, with such new manly accent, that it is wellnigh impossible to get out of step."[27]

Marsigli gives us also very interesting pictures and descriptions of mounted Turkish bands. The rank of commanders in Turkey was designated by the number of horsetail standards (*tugh*) borne before them. Thus, the *sandjak-bey* had one standard; the *beyler-bey*, two; the *vezier*, three; the *grand-vezier*, five; the sultan, in time of war, had seven or nine standards borne before him.[28]

It should be distinctly understood that these standards were the symbols of authority, dignity, and rank, and were not band instruments.[29] Figure 2, reproduced from Djevad Bey's book, gives an idea of their appearance.

The mounted band of a pasha of the three horsetail standards rank constituted a part of a very imposing cortege. We reproduce here that part of it which immediately preceded the band, as well as the band itself. The men and players were disposed as follows. (See Fig. 3.) References to the instruments are taken from Marsigli's book.

N. The honor guard of the horsetail standards (*tugh*).
P. Three horsetail standard bearers.
Q. The Pasha's color-bearer.
R. Seven *zurna* players.

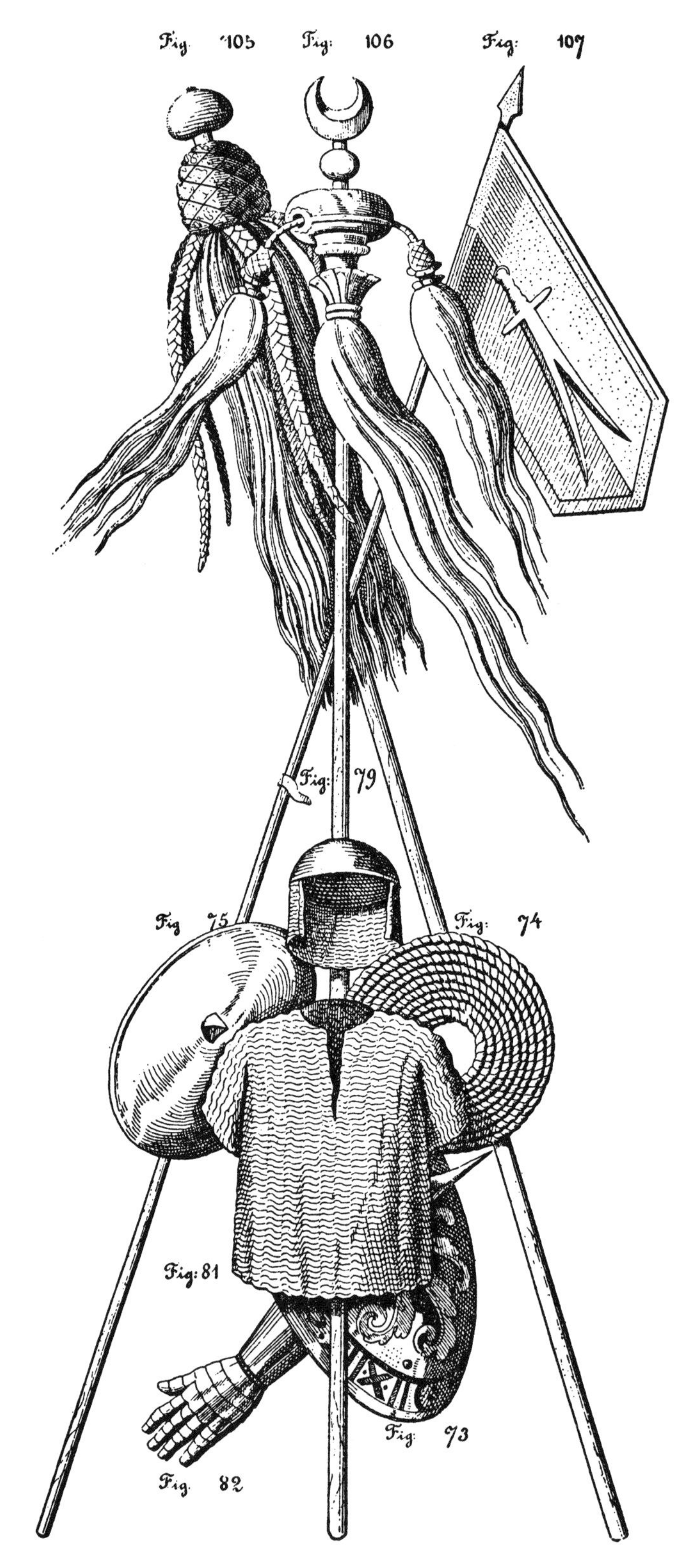

Fig. 2. THE TURKISH STANDARDS

Fig. 3. A MOUNTED TURKISH BAND

S. Seven bass drum players. (Drums on the left side of horses.)
T. Two kettledrum players with drums (*sardar-naqqāra*) placed across the saddle.
V. Five trumpeters.
X. Two cymbal players,

or twenty-three players in the band proper. This picture helps us to understand how Europeans, in their failure to appreciate the fine points of Oriental etiquette, later hung the horsetails on a musical instrument, where they are entirely out of place.

According to Kappey,[30] early in the eighteenth century Augustus II, Elector of Saxony and King of Poland, was presented by the Sultan with a complete janizary band. The novelty, picturesque appearance, and prestige of the janizaries, the manly and martial character of their music, all combined to create a profound impression on the populace, and very rapidly the vogue for 'Turkish music' spread.

Frederick the Great, King of Prussia, secured the services of real janizary musicians for several of his regiments.[31] Russia and later Austria followed his example. So, by the beginning of the nineteenth century, all European armies had their bands with 'Turkish music' as their principal element.

Affected by the spirit of the times, composers began writing 'Turkish marches.' Those of Beethoven and of Mozart (*Rondo à la Turque*) were especially popular. Gluck introduced 'Turkish music' to the opera in Vienna.[32]

Europeans, after a while, began to develop 'janizary bands.' Some of these developments were constructive and enriched the art of music. They consisted mostly of the addition of new instruments. This process resulted finally in our modern military and symphonic bands. Some of the customs were rather bizarre. One of them was the introduction of colored drum-majors and their assistants. They were dressed in the most fantastic 'Oriental' costumes, and developed a special style of playing, juggling the drumsticks, clowning, and contorting themselves for the amusement of the spectators. The remnants of this custom in our prosaic days are the 'fancy steps' and the baton jugglery of the drum-majors of marching bands. Some of the instruments underwent a remarkable change. The 'Jingling Johnny' of the Turks had rather a modest appearance.[33] The horsetail standard, for some reason, caught the fancy of the Europeans. It should be remembered that in some European armies the bands were maintained by the officers of the regiments, and there were no uniform regulations as to their instrumentation or dress. So different regiments competed in dressing their bands and in acquiring bigger and more elaborate Jingling Johnnies. As has already been mentioned, imposing hybrids of horsetail standards and 'chinoiserie' were developed, reaching absurd limits.

The 'Turkish music,' although it appeared only as a temporary fad, nevertheless left some ineradicable traces on European music. It brought the robust, manly, emotional element of martial music into the stuffy and nervous atmosphere of Europe. The wind bands still retain this invigorating influence. The Turkish bass drum and cymbals are now indispensable members of the 'Battery' of our symphonic and operatic orchestras. In skilful hands the percussion instruments, appealing to the most elementary and deeply hidden subconscious forces within ourselves, are capable of strong dramatic effects.

SECTION B: TONAL (DEFINITE PITCH)

7. BELL — Italy

Bronze. The handle is a sculptured ibis, the sacred bird of the Egyptians. Reproduction of a bell found in Pompeii. Diameter, 5.5 cm. Height, 15 cm. (17.2034)

8. CHARIOT BELL — Italy. Reproduction. First century type

Bronze. Square at bottom, tongue in the form of a ring, fastened by a piece of wire passing through a hole in the top. Loop at the top. Diameter, 2.5 cm. Height, 4.5 cm. (17.2037)

9. PEDLAR'S BELL

Red, unglazed clay. The tongue is a lump of clay tied by a piece of string through a hole in the top. Diameter, 7.5 cm. Length, 10 cm. (17.2035)

10. MULE BELL — Athens, Greece, 19th century

Wrought iron, with remnants of copper plating inside. Upper part egg-shaped, lower part elongated into an ellipsoidal opening of smaller size. Square loop on the long iron tongue. Made of one piece of sheet iron, hammered into shape, overlapped and welded on the sides. Length, 17 cm. Width, 10 cm. Height, 13.5 cm. (17.2038)

11. CURFEW BELL or HAND BELL — England, 14th century

Of wrought iron. Rectangular cross-section with rounded corners; a little smaller at the top. Large, square loop-shaped handle with a wide integral handgrip, grooved in the upper side; the handle continued within the loop through the holes in the upper wall, forming a long loop with the stem of the tongue attached to it. Welded, spherical clapper, diameter 6 cm. at the lower end of the tongue, the stem projecting 3.5 cm. beyond it. Made of one piece of hammered sheet iron about 2 mm. thick, bent and shaped by hammering, overlapped, riveted, and welded. It was formerly bronzed. Height, total, 32.5 cm. Height, body, 25 cm. Length, bottom, 18 cm. Width, bottom, 12.5 cm. (17.2039)

This is a very rare bell bound at Chalfont St. Giles, the home of Milton and associated with William Penn. It is similar to the Celtic bells of St. Patrick and others.

12. JEW'S HARP or JEW'S TRUMP — England, 19th century

Steel. Consists of a slender tongue of flattened steel wire fixed by one end to the base of an onion-shaped loop. The free end of the tongue passing between the two branches of the frame is bent at a 90° angle and has a small loop. The instrument is inserted in the mouth and the branches of the frame are held firmly between the teeth. The loop at the bent end of the tongue is plucked and set in vibration. The mouth cavity serves as a resonator. The instrument produces several partial tones of the natural scale, starting with the fourth. For this purpose, the player shapes his mouth as if intending to pronounce different vowels, which isolates and reinforces certain harmonics. Length, 7 cm. Diameter, 4.25 cm. (17.2044)

The Jew's harp is a representative of the plucked idiophonic instruments. It is of Asiatic origin and in different forms finds wide distribution in Asia, Malaysia, and Melanesia.

13. XYLOPHONE or WOODEN HARMONICA — Switzerland, 19th century

With two hammers. Fifteen strips of wood of graduated lengths strung on cords and tied to a wooden frame. Diatonic compass from *c'* to c^3. Length, 47 cm. Width, large end, 26.5 cm.; small end, 13 cm. (17.2041 a & b)

14. NAIL VIOLIN — Germany, 19th century

Of wood, with iron nails and iron wire guard. Flat, semi-circular sound-box with two C-shaped sound-holes on the top and an oval one on the bottom. Thirty-three iron nails are arranged around the curved side; the tops are protected by a wire guard. The naturals are straight, the sharps have their tops bent inward. Inside the sound-box is an inverted bridge with three feet glued to the sound-board. Light yellow varnish. Played with a bow (missing). Length, 36 cm. Width, 17.5 cm. Height of body, 4.25 cm. Total height, 13 cm. (17.2046)

The discovery of the principle of the nail violin was made by accident in 1744. The Bavarian musician, Johann Wilde, had touched a nail on the wall of his workroom with a bow and heard a strong sound. After several experiments with nails driven in the door he had found that nails of different sizes gave tones of varying pitches when stroked with a bow. An instrument with a sound-box was constructed in which the newly discovered principle of sound production was properly applied. Johann Wilde was a violinist and a viole d'amour player in the Imperial Theatre Orchestra in St. Petersburg, Russia, from 1741 to 1764.

15. GLASS HARMONICA — Europe, early 19th century

Portable instrument in a wooden cabinet with two folding legs, roll top cover, two heavy brass handles. Steel shaft running in two bearings; fly-wheel, mounted on the left side shaft extension, with a lead rim and counter-balance; small crank, mounted on the right side shaft extension, operated by a folding foot-pedal; connection between crank and pedal consisting of a rope passing through a hollow right leg. Thirty-two hemispherical glass cups of varying diameters mounted on the steel shaft between the bearings (only twenty-six actually remaining); a water-trough underneath the glasses. Length, 69 cm. Width, 33 cm. Height, 82.5 cm. Glasses, diameter, max., 18 cm.; min., 8.5 cm. (17.2047)

The glass harmonica is played in the following manner. A water-trough is filled with water deep enough to wet the rim of the smallest glass; the shaft is rotated continuously by the foot-pedal. The moistened rotating rims of the glass cups are pressed by fingertips; by varying pressure of fingertips on the rims, control of dynamic expression becomes possible within a certain limited range. The sounds produced on the glass harmonica are delicate and pleasant. But the method of sound production has a harmful effect on the player's nervous system.

This particular type of glass harmonica, the most convenient for player from a mechanical standpoint, was invented by Benjamin Franklin in 1762. The principle involved was not new at the time. Franklin first heard a performance on musical glasses in London in 1757. Two performers in that city, E. H. Delaval and an Irishman, Richard Puckeridge (Pockrich), attracted his attention by their skilful performances on the musical glasses. Struck by the beauty of the sounds elicited by them from a set of ordinary beer glasses filled to different heights with water and rubbed on their rims by the fingertips, Franklin experimented for some time and evolved a successful type of glass harmonica. It became very popular in England and on the Continent. Among performers who gave concerts on the glass harmonica can be mentioned Marianne Davies, to whom Benjamin Franklin presented his own instrument; the blind player, Marianna Kirchgesser; and the Bohemian pianist, Johann Ludwig Dussek. The compass of our own instrument is from *g* to e^3; diatonically from *g* to *c′*, chromatically from *c′* to e^3.

DIVISION II: INSTRUMENTS CONTROLLED BY A KEYBOARD

16. METAL HARMONICA or KEYBOARD GLOCKENSPIEL Italy, 18th century

Rectangular walnut box with a hinged cover. Twenty-five bronze bars underslung from a cross-bar. The keys lift bronze balls attached to the brass ribbon springs and strike them against the sounding bars. Compass of two octaves from *d″* to d^4, the naturals of boxwood, the sharps of ebony. Length, 58.5 cm. Width, 36.5 cm. Height, 12.5 cm. (17.2042)

Canon Galpin suggested that "this is probably the type of instrument intended by Mozart to be used in the opera *Die Zauberflöte* (1791, Vienna) under the title *Strumento d'acciaio*. This is an early small example, but the required solo can and has been played on it."

DIVISION III: INSTRUMENTS CONTROLLED BY AUTOMATIC MOTION

17. MUSICAL BOX Switzerland, 19th century

Small wooden box with hinged cover. A spring motor operates the cylinder with small steel pins; these pins pluck the tongues of a steel comb. Plays two tunes, "The Bay of Biscay" and "The Banks of Allan Water." Length, 11.75 cm. Width, 8.25 cm. Height, 6.25 cm. (17.2045)

CLASS II

MEMBRANOPHONIC INSTRUMENTS OR MEMBRANOPHONES

CLASS II: MEMBRANOPHONIC INSTRUMENTS OR MEMBRANOPHONES

THE vibrator of membranophonic instruments is, as the name implies, a membrane stretched over a receptacle which may serve either as a resonator (as in drums), or merely as a frame (as in tambourines). Methods of setting a membrane in vibration are as follows: (a) striking, (b) friction, (c) blowing, (d) plucking.

The first method, striking, is used almost exclusively on European instruments. The membranes are struck either with drumsticks or different parts of the hand: fingers, knuckles, and parts of the palm. Other methods are rather exceptional, though, for special effect, friction is used in playing the tambourine, the thumb being rubbed close to the rim. However, this is done principally for producing a tremolo effect on jingles attached to the tambourine, the membrane participating but little in the total sound effect.

Blowing conjoined with speaking, singing, or humming sets the membranes of such instruments as the *kazoo* (No. 24) or the *zazah* (No. 25) in vibration by producing a sympathetic vibration in the membrane by the impact of air particles. Direct blowing will not produce any sounds on these instruments.

It is on the instruments of primitive peoples and of those outside of Europe that the application of principles other than striking for producing sound on membranophonic instruments should be studied.

Membranophones are divided similarly to idiophones into *rhythmic* and *tonal* instruments. In Europe all drums belong to the first section; the only exception are the kettledrums, which are tuned to a definite tonal pitch. In Asia there are many types of tuned drums.

DIVISION I: CONTROLLED DIRECTLY

SECTION A: RHYTHMIC

18. TABOR — DRUM AND STICK — England, 19th century

A shallow wooden barrel with shellacked sides; two gaily painted wooden hoops laced with rope, with leather tags for tightening the two skin heads. Lower head has a snare. Diameter, 27.5 cm. Height, 11.5 cm. (17.2026 a & b)

The tabor is of very ancient origin. In 1823 a specimen of the two-headed drum was found in Egypt at Thebes.[34] The tabor is played with a pipe (*chûrula*, No. 69). The drum is suspended by a loop on the left arm, drumstick is held by the right hand; the pipe is played by the left hand. In England the pipe and tabor were used by the masses of people from the fifteenth to the eighteenth century for the Morris dance. Recently, they have been revived for folk-dancing.

19. SIDE DRUM — Flanders, 18th century

Brass barrel, two skin heads held by wooden loops laced with cord braces and tightened with leather tags. Two snares below. Diameter, 45.5 cm. Height, 44 cm. (17.2020)

This is a battle-scarred specimen with a short mark on the barrel. A typical infantry drum of the type used in Europe at least as far back as the sixteenth century. Praetorius[35] gives a picture of a pair of *Soldaten Trummeln* in his *Theatrum Instrumentorum.*

20. BASS DRUM — England, ca. 1810

Wooden barrel, overlapped and riveted with three rows of flat-headed brass rivets. Painted white scroll, decorations, no inscriptions. Two painted wooden hoops held with cord braces and tightened with leather tags. One hoop braced with sheet iron patches (riveted on). Two drumsticks. Diameter, 65 cm. Height, 73.5 cm. (17.2021 a & c)

21. BASS DRUM — England, ca. 1815

Wooden barrel built up with two shells of equal height. Two wooden hoops, braced and tightened with cord and tags. On the barrel is painted a large red square with the inscription: 'DARTMOUTH INDEPENDENT HARMONY BAND.' Below are white and blue ensigns with the flagstaffs crossed and a small scroll inscribed "Unity is strength." Diameter, 72 cm. Height, 80 cm. (17.2022)

The bass drums Nos. 20 and 21 have proportions differing materially from those of modern ones, which are shallow and of larger diameter.

The bass drum came to Europe with the janizary bands (see Note under No. 6). Marsigli, and after him Djevad Bey,[36] both give pictures of Turkish bass drums of the same proportions as those in our Collection.

SECTION B: TONAL

22. PAIR OF KETTLEDRUMS — England, 19th century

The bodies of both drums are made of brass hemispherical shells covered with vellum drum heads. The smaller drum has five tuning screws; the larger one, six. Pair of drumsticks with whalebone handles; the wooden heads are covered with a thin layer of sponge. Small kettledrum: diameter, 61 cm.; height, 37 cm. Large kettledrum: diameter, 67.5 cm.; height, 38 cm. (17.2019 a & b)

Kettledrums, like trumpets, were aristocrats among instruments. Possession of them was the prerogative of royalty and nobility. Used at court functions, in the church, on important state occasions, a token of distinction permitted only to the life guards and mounted regiments which had won them on the battlefield, the kettledrums always held a high position, until social changes brought them down to the orchestra platform and the theatre pit. It is only when borne across the saddle at the front of a mounted regiment, embellished with richly embroidered drum-banners and played on by a gorgeously uniformed drummer, that they preserve something of their former glory. For the kettledrums came from the Orient, where they already had an heroic past and were clothed with legends and traditions. Some of these traditions were adopted by the Europeans.

It is almost certain that the first instruments came into possession of Occidental peoples by capture in battle. Borne with the colors, they were defended in the Orient to the last man. For this reason their possession by a regiment was a badge of hard-won distinction. The reverse was also true, and the loss of the kettledrums has caused the disbanding of a unit which had so disgraced itself.

There were three points of contact which brought the kettledrums into Europe. On the eastern shores of the Mediterranean they came into the possession of the Crusaders; in the Southwest they penetrated through the contact of the Spaniards with the Moors; and they came to Western Europe through Russia, Poland, and Hungary. But, before attempting any historical investigation, it is worth mentioning that there were, and still are, several distinct types of kettledrums, differing more in size than in shape. Dr. Curt Sachs in the *Real-Lexikon*[37] discriminates between two types of kettledrums in Europe. This is true of Western Europe, but if Eastern Europe (the old Russia of the pre-Peter-the-Great period) were included, then there are more than two types.

For percussion instruments of the drum type, the generic word in Arabian is *naqqāra*; specifically, the word means the kettledrum.[38] Hence come the antiquated words: English — *nakers*; French — *nacaire*; Spanish — *nacara*; Russian — *nakra* (plural: *nakri*).

In Western Europe the earliest traceable date in the history of kettledrums is 1303, when the term *naccherone* was used.[39] In 1304 Janino le Nakerer is mentioned in the list of minstrels[40] of King Edward I. In 1309 Joinville, the chronicler of King Louis the Saint, writes of the Saracens: "La noise que il menoient de leur nacaires et de leurs cors sarrazinnoiz, estoit espoventable à escouter."[41] In 1347 we have the testimony of Froissart that nakers were among the instruments used at the triumphal entry of Edward III into Calais.[42]

Chaucer mentions nakers in *The Knight's Tale*:

> Pypes, trompes, nakers, clariounes,
> That in the bataille blowen blody sounes.[43]

Very important historical testimony concerning the relative size of kettledrums is given by Père Benoit, who writes of the embassy sent by Ladislaus V, King of Hungary, to Charles VII, King of France, in 1457 to ask for the hand of his daughter, Magdalen. He writes about 'tabourins' which were like large kettles.[44] Dr. Sachs, commenting upon this, remarks that in the middle of the fifteenth century the large-sized kettledrums were already known in Hungary, but not in Western Europe.

In this connection it is interesting that Henry VIII tried to procure from Vienna kettledrums which could be carried across the saddle, "after the Hungarian manner."[45] This is additional testimony that the Hungarian drums differed from those in use in Western Europe and England.

Pictorial evidence at our disposal gives us an opportunity to judge the relative sizes of small kettledrums.[46] But their actual size can be judged more closely by a pair of Turkish kettledrums in the Vienna collection of musical instruments.[47] Their date is sixteenth to seventeenth century and the diameter is 20 cm. Marsigli's engraving, Fig. 3, page 23, indicates the size of kettledrums as approximately that of those in the Vienna collection.

Thus far we have been dealing with two sizes: (1) The small kettledrums of about 20 cm.

in diameter, *nakers* or *sardar-naqqāra*.[48] (2) The large-sized 'Hungarian' or Hussar kettledrums. Their exact size is not known.

In Russian sources[49] we have references to the following types: (1) *Bubni* (*nakri*) *malie* (the small kettledrums, *nakers*). (2) *Bubni velikie* or *nabati* (kettledrums of very large size). (3) *Tulumbaz*. (4) *Litavri*.

The Russian word *buben* (pl. *bubni*) has two meanings: (a) a tambourine, and (b) a kettledrum. The latter with respect to military instruments is a more ancient meaning.[50] The early Russian reference in the *Troitzkaia Letopis*, [51] under the year of 1216, says: "There were in Prince Iuri's (troops) 13 standards, and of trumpets and *bubni* sixty; and they say about (Prince) Iaroslav (that he had) 17 standards, and of trumpets and *bubni* forty."

Perhaps the first reference to *nakers* in the Russian language is the statement in the *Nikonova Letopis* under 1453: "The Turks, after proclaiming their prayer, began playing *surni* and beating *vargani* and *nakri*."[52]

A very curious testimony about two types of kettledrums, as used in the Orient in the second half of the fifteenth century (1466–72) is given in the *Travels of Athanasius Nikitin*, a Russian merchant, who was in Persia and in India in those years. He tells us: ". . . went the sultan to *Teferich*, and with him twenty great viziers, also three hundred elephants covered by steel armor . . . also one hundred camels with *nagaras*,[53] and three hundred trumpeters." And further: "At *Melik-tuchar* . . . every night his court is guarded by one hundred men in armour, and twenty trumpeters, and ten *nagaras*, also ten *bubni velikie* [that] are beaten by two men."[54]

In 1589, in *Opisnaia Kniga* (the record book) of Tsar Boris Godunov, there are mentioned "seven nakri great and small."[55] These references help in establishing the development of Russian terminology. In the eleventh century the kettledrums were called *briazalo*;[56] in the thirteenth and fourteenth centuries, they were named *bubni*; and in the fifteenth century they were known as *nakri*.[57]

The *velikie bubni* were also called *nabati* (singular, *nabat*). This word is the Russianized Arabian word *naubat*. The *naubat*, also called *mahanagara*, is a kettledrum of very large size.[58] Dr. Giles Fletcher, who was in Russia at the end of the sixteenth century, tells us that "They [the Russians] have drummes besides of a huge bignesse, which they carry with them upon a boarde layde on foure horses, that are sparred together with chaines, every drumme having eight strikers or drummers, besides trumpets and shawmes, which they sounde after a wilde manner, much different from ours."[59] *Nabati* were used for assembly calls for troops: "the grand duke ordered *nabati* beaten for men to assemble," we read in *Sophiisky Vremennik* in the year 1553.[60]

Further, during the same year, the grand duke "ordered to beat *nabati*, and many *nakri* and play *surni*."[61] They were also used for giving an alarm when the Tatars were approaching. In this the Russians were following the custom of the Tatars themselves, from whom they borrowed the large kettledrums. One curious fact should be mentioned. At a later date and into the beginning of the twentieth century, within the writer's time, fire alarms in Russia were given by a special middle-sized alarm bell (*nabatniy kolokol*). Such bells were used for this purpose only. But instead of the usual 'ring the bell,' the words used in connection with this alarm bell were 'beat the *nabat*,' a reminder of the days when the *nabat*, a large kettledrum, was used for this purpose.

In the East the *naubat* or *kūs*[62] was included in the orchestras which were stationed in the *naubat-khana*, or the 'salute-building.'[63] In the palaces of some Oriental potentates the *naubat-khana* was constructed on a lavish scale, with quarters for the musicians on duty and a gallery for the performers.[64] Upon the entrance and exit of potentates and nobles, the salute was sounded by the orchestra.

Finally, in the Russian record books of property belonging to the tsars, there are numerous references to another type of kettledrum, not mentioned in any European sources, namely, the *tulumbaz*.[65] The Russians used this word in designating a type of kettledrum, Fig. 4, page 36.

A single *tulumbaz*, not a pair as usual with kettledrums of ordinary size, was used, mostly for hawking,[66] and was struck, not with a stick but with a *voshaga*, a wooden ball affixed by a thick leather strap to the handle.

The drums themselves were made of iron, copper, silver, and of the steel used for armor.[67] They were richly adorned, as is shown by the following references in the list of Tsar Michail Theodorovich (Romanov) of 1640. (1) "*Tulumbaz* of gold-plated copper, the edges garnished with black velvet, (the shell) covered with violet morocco leather; the drum banner is of silk embroidered with gold and morocco inlay. Sent as a gift to the Tsar by the Kizilbash Shah Abbas in the year of 1627." (2) "Two iron *tulumbaza*, inlaid with gold, the edges covered with striped silk tape, holding cords of green silk, the saddle pillow of rose velvet. Presented to the Tsar by the Georgian Tsarevitch in the year of 1634."

It should be remembered that when a *tulumbaz* was carried by mounted men, there was a pillow attached on the right side of the saddle for protecting the drum shell from banging.

In the list of 1687 we find a "silver *tulumbaz*, smooth; upon it six gold-plated silver medallions, covered with precious red garnets and lapis lazuli; body covered with green velvet affixed with silver nails. The weight of it is four pounds with half-a-pound. . . ."

The beaters, *voshagi*, were made to match the drums. The list of 1687 mentions "six *voshagi*, that beat upon *tulumbazi*, embroidered with gold and silver, the handles covered with violet velvet. . . ."[68]

Finally, the *litavri*[69] were the usual type of cavalry kettledrums made of copper or silver, with richly embroidered drum banners of expensive materials with gold braids, silken cords and tassels. There are no definite references as to the time of their introduction, but they appear in the sixteenth century.

This excursion into history shows that there is available interesting material throwing light upon the customs and traditions in connection with kettledrums. These customs and traditions are the richest and most colorful in the Orient; they are almost intact in Russia of the pre-Peter-the-Great period, when Oriental influences were strongest there. As the lack of references to *tulumbaz* and *nabat* types in Western literature shows, the farther West we go, the more we find that these instruments and the customs associated with them

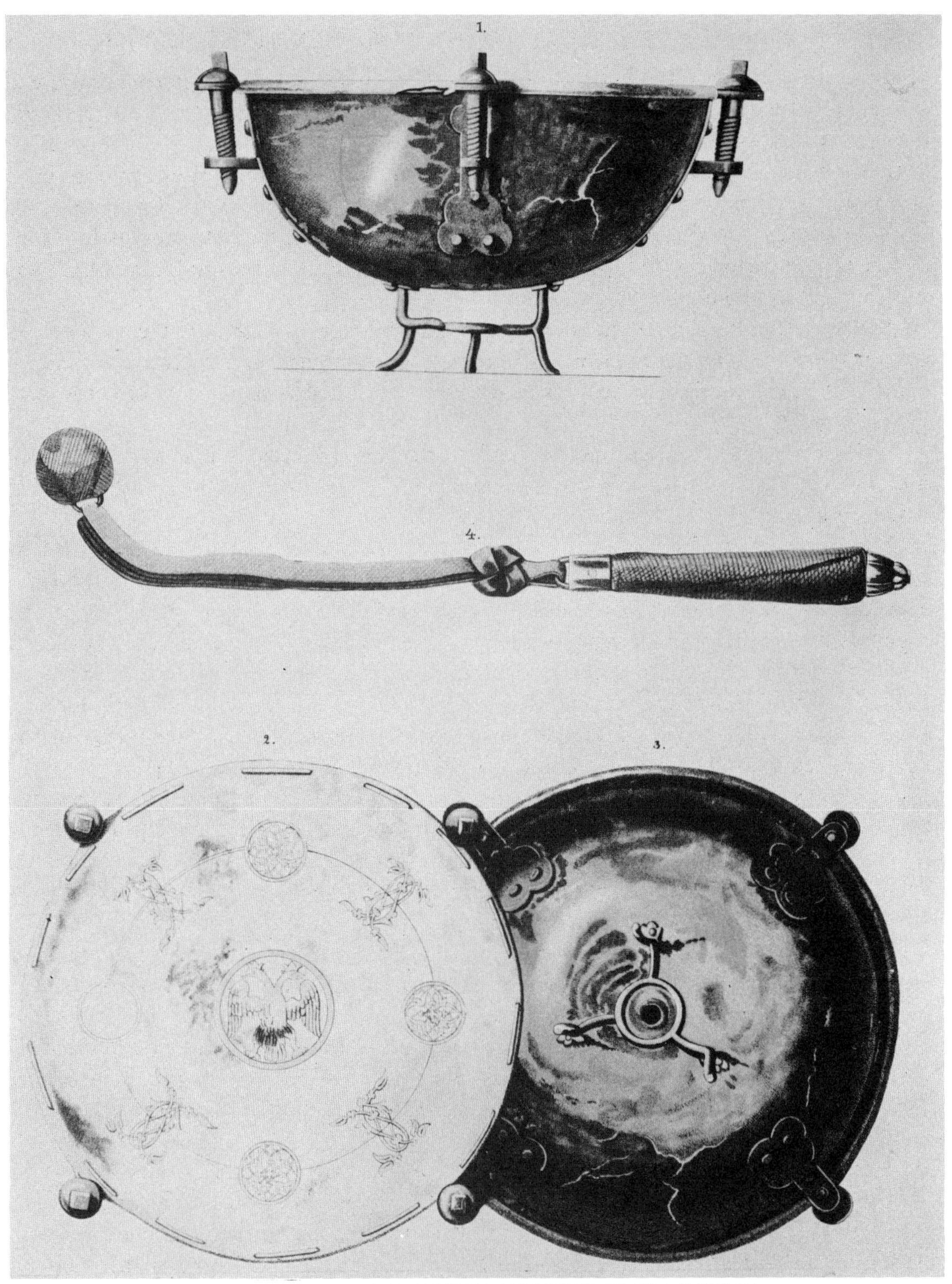

FIG. 4. THE *TULUMBAZ* IN THE MOSCOW ARMS MUSEUM

(*Oruzheinaia Palata in the Kremlin*)

1. Side view. 2. Top view. 3. Bottom view. 4. *Voshaga*, for beating the *tulumbaz* (enlarged).

tend to disappear. A richly adorned *tulumbaz* was a proper present to send to Russian tsars by rulers of neighboring countries. It seems that there is no counterpart of such a custom in Western Europe, or at least the facts wait upon discovery.

23. ONION FLUTE — 17th-century type. Reproduction

Conical tube of stained wood with bell and detachable spherical cap. Turned with heavy mouldings. At the smaller end there is a hollow conical plug covered with onion skin (hence the name) or some other membrane. Played by humming into the hole, in the tube near the cap. Called also 'Eunuch's flute.'[70] Diameter, 10.5 cm. Length, 54 cm. (17.2031)
Plate I

24. KAZOO — U. S. A.(?)

Tube of boxwood with four imitation finger-holes. A perforated tin band placed over the hole covered with a membrane. The upper part serves as a mouthpiece. Played by humming into the mouthpiece. Diameter, 2.5 cm. Length, 14 cm. (17.2032)
Plate I

25. ZAZAH or VOICE FLUTE — England, 19th century

A cylindrical tube of stained boxwood with a membrane covered by a perforated cap. A sound tube near the membrane. The tube has three finger-holes, which are used to produce a kind of tremolo when two of them are stopped and the third is trilled by shaking the finger on it. The finger-holes have no effect on intonation. Diameter, 2.7 cm. Length, 17 cm. (17.2033)
Plate I

CLASS III

AEROPHONIC INSTRUMENTS OR AEROPHONES

CLASS III: AEROPHONIC OR WIND INSTRUMENTS

THE modern scientific term designating wind instruments is derived from two Greek words ἀήρ (ἀερο in its combining form), air, and φωνή, voice, sound, tone; hence the term 'aerophonic' instruments or aerophones.[71] This class should be divided into two subclasses: 'free-air' aerophones and 'vibrating air-column' aerophones. A representative of the first type is the siren, which produces sounds without any long tubes and acts on the surrounding air almost immediately; another example is the bull-roarer.[72] Since this type has but few representatives it is incorporated in the general classification only as Division IV, *Free Air Instruments*.

The more numerous and important type of aerophone is that which includes those instruments having as a vibrating element a certain volume of air partly separated from the surrounding atmosphere by a tube or a receptacle. The typical representative of the first type is the flute, of the second type, the ocarina. The type having a tube as a separator shapes the separated volume of air into an air column the length of which varies in accordance with the pitch of the instrument: higher pitched instruments have shorter tubes, lower pitched ones have longer tubes.[73]

The following terminology is based in part on the American Tentative Standard Acoustical Terminology Z24.1–1936, supplemented by definitions of such terms as the 'harmonic series,' 'overblowing,' the 'pedal tone,' etc., which are necessary in the subsequent discussion. As heretofore, the numbers in the parentheses at the end of each definition correspond to those of the American Tentative Standard; when they are given without qualifications, the definitions are quoted verbatim.

Frequencies

1. *Periodic wave or quantity.* A periodic wave or quantity is an oscillating quantity the values of which recur for equal increments of the causative variable factor.[74] (Based on 1.3.)

2. *Frequency (f).* The number of cycles occurring per unit of time (1.6, partly quoted; for complete quotation see p. 5, 9).

3. *Fundamental frequency.*[75] A fundamental frequency is the lowest component frequency of a periodic wave or quantity (1.8 partly quoted).

4. *Basic frequency.* The basic frequency of any wave is that frequency which is considered to be the most important. In a driven system it would, in general, be the driving frequency, while in most periodic waves it would correspond to the fundamental frequency. (1.10.)

5. *Harmonic.* A harmonic is a component of a periodic wave or quantity having a frequency which is an integral multiple of the fundamental frequency. For example, a com-

ponent the frequency of which is twice the fundamental frequency is called the second harmonic. (1.9.)

6. *Subharmonic.* A subharmonic is a component of a complex wave having a frequency which is an integral submultiple of the basic frequency.

The term subharmonic is generally applied in the case of a driven system the vibration of which has frequency components of lower frequency than the driving frequency. (Based on 1.13.)

7. *Harmonic series of frequencies.*[76] The harmonic series of frequencies is a set of frequencies each member of which is a harmonic. Between the harmonics there exists the following interval relationship:

a. The numbers under the notes serve both as the ordinal numbers identifying the place of constituent members in the series and as the abstract numbers used as either multipliers or divisors in calculating the frequency of harmonics. *b.* The frequency of the first (lowest) member of the series is the fundamental frequency of the whole series. *c.* The frequency of the *n*th member of the series is the product of the fundamental frequency and the abstract number corresponding to the *n*th ordinal number. Thus, the tenth harmonic has a frequency ten times that of the fundamental frequency. *d.* The note example above illustrates the interval relationship between the members of the series only, and is not limited to any particular set of frequencies connected with some standard pitch. This relationship is invariant for any value of the fundamental frequency of the series. With the change of that value, the whole series of harmonics change their frequencies so as to keep the same relative intervals and remain the integral multiples of the changed fundamental frequency. *e.* The harmonic series has two aspects: a simultaneous aspect when the fundamental frequency and its harmonics are regarded as the component members of a compound tone and constitute a *chord*; and a seriatim aspect when its interval relationship is regarded as the basis of the harmonic and the natural scales of tones (see the definitions 7 and 10 below); in other words, when this relationship is a *scale*. The abbreviation, 'the harmonic series,' can be used.

Tones

1. *Simple tone.* A simple tone is one which consists of a single frequency. (6.3.)

2. *Compound tone.* A compound tone is one which consists of more than a single frequency. (6.4.) *Note*: The component frequencies of a compound tone may or may not bear an integral relation to its basic frequency.[77]

3. *Partial.* A partial is a component of a compound tone. Its frequency may be either higher or lower than that of the basic frequency and may or may not bear an integral relation to the basic frequency. (1.11.)

4. *Harmonic*. A harmonic is a partial the frequency of which is an integral multiple of the fundamental frequency. (Based on 6.7.)

5. *Overtone*. An overtone is a partial having a frequency higher than that of the basic frequency. (1.12.) *Note*: Overtones are identified by the same ordinal numbers as the members of the harmonic series of frequencies.[78]

6. *Harmonic tone*. A harmonic tone is a compound tone the partials of which are harmonics.[79]

7. *Harmonic scale of tones*.[80] The harmonic scale of tones is an idealized scale, consisting of harmonic tones the fundamental frequencies of which have the same interval relationship as the harmonic series of frequencies. *Note*: The harmonic scale of tones is represented by the same notes as the harmonic series of frequencies, each note in this case symbolizing a compound tone; the lowest pitched tone of this scale is called the fundamental tone and is assigned the ordinal number 1; the rest of the harmonic tones are identified by the same ordinal numbers as the members of the harmonic series of frequencies. The abbreviation, 'the harmonic scale,' can be used.

8. *Fundamental tone*. The fundamental tone of the harmonic scale of tones is one having the lowest fundamental frequency.[81]

9. *Partial tone*. A partial tone is a compound tone produced on musical instruments by such means as vibrating strings stopped lightly at the nodal points or by tubes overblown in a certain manner.[82]

10. *Natural scale of tones*.[83] A natural scale of tones is an actual scale of partial tones produced by some musical instrument. *Note*: Natural scales of various types of musical instruments vary in the number and sequence of partial tones and serve as the basis of their classification. The simplified term 'the natural scale' can be used.

11. *Overblowing*. Overblowing is the intensifying of the velocity and pressure components of the vibrating column of air in an aerophonic (wind) instrument in such a way that it sounds a partial tone.

12. *Pedal tone*. A pedal tone is a compound tone produced by an aerophonic instrument without overblowing. *Note*: The pedal tone produced by the tube of fixed acoustical length is the lowest pitched tone of its natural scale; it corresponds to the fundamental tone of the harmonic scale of tones. The pedal tone can be referred to as 'the pedal.'[84]

13. *Tone color*. The tone color of a tone is a qualitative characteristic which distinguishes the tones produced by a voice or some musical instrument from those of another voice or musical instrument.[85] *Note*: Tone color is also referred to as the 'timbre.'

14. *Formant*. A formant is a group of harmonics the intensity of which remains constant when the tones of a musical instrument change within a certain range of the scale. The formant affects and in a considerable degree determines the tone color of tones produced by an instrument. The change of tone color in various registers of the same instrument (as, for example, on the clarinet) is due to some change of the formant.[86]

The correspondencies between some important acoustical terms used in this study are summarized in the following tabular form.[87]

Compound Tone	Helmholtz's Scale	Natural Scale (Overblown tones)
Harmonic Series of Frequencies	Harmonic Scale of Tones	Natural Scale of Tones
Fundamental Frequency	Fundamental Tone	Pedal Tone
Partial	......	Partial Tone
Harmonic	Harmonic Tone	......

Tonality and Tonal Position of Aerophonic Instruments

AN aerophonic instrument is usually identified by the voice it plays in its own family, by the family name, and by its tonality. For example: the tenor trombone in B-flat. It should be understood that the acoustical tonality of an instrument is not necessarily its musical tonality. Thus, although the tenor trombone is pitched in B-flat, it is treated in musical notation as a non-transposing instrument in C. In the case of reed instruments the musical tonality and the lowest tone produced by a given instrument, and therefore the scale playable on it, are not related directly. Thus the tonality of the clarinet is determined by the pitch of the third partial tone overblown from the nominal low F. The general rule for the determination of the acoustical tonality of aerophonic instruments (except clarinets) can be formulated very simply: the acoustical tonality of an aerophonic instrument is identical with the pitch of the pedal tone or that of the second partial tone of its natural scale.[88]

In some instances the musical tonality of an instrument coincides with its acoustical tonality, but sometimes this is not the case. Thus the nominal tonality of the old flutes was one tone above their musical tonality; so the soprano flute pitched in C had *d'* as its lowest tone and because of that tone was known as the flute in D. Since the compass of the flute was gradually extended down to *b* such a designation by the lowest tone lost its meaning. Irrespective of the acoustical tonality of the instrument, its musical tonality remained unchanged. Likewise the variations of the lower compass extension on reed instruments make the designation of tonality by their lower tone impracticable. Thus, the lowest tone of the bassoon is either BB-flat or AA, depending upon whether it has an ordinary bell joint or an extension joint. Yet musically both instruments are treated as non-transposing instruments in C. Further particulars can be found in Note 91.

The tonal position of an aerophonic instrument is the place it holds in its own family: soprano, alto, tenor, etc. It is determined, theoretically, by the absolute pitch of its natural scale. If the limits of various voices could be agreed upon and some tone such as the pedal or the second partial tone were chosen as a characteristic tone, then it would be possible to determine the tonal position of an instrument without ambiguity. The voice designation then would become also the pitch designation of a given instrument. This ideal condition is not present in actual practice. Thus the alto flute is referred to as the tenor or even as the bass (!) flute. The althorn is called the tenorhorn in England, etc. In addition, owing to the differences in the acoustical properties of various types of instruments and variations of their downward compass extension, the absolute pitch of the natural scale is not always practicable for the determination of the tonal position. For instance, in order to place the clarinet in a correct tonal position, its characteristic tone (the third partial tone overblown from the nominal F, as already stated) has to be transposed one octave lower. The notation of transposing instruments presents another difficulty. Thus the acoustical tonalities of the tenor trombone, the bass tuba, and the contrabass tuba are respectively, B-flat, F or E-flat, and C or BB-flat. Yet all these instruments have their parts written in the bass clef and are therefore treated musically as non-transposing instruments. How is their tonal position to be determined: by their acoustical scale or by their musical scale? Therefore, in order to settle in which voice a given instrument plays in its own family, four factors have to be decided upon: (1) the nomenclature of voices, (2) a definite selection of a certain tone as the characteristic tone for a given type of instrument, depending upon its acoustical properties, (3) the proper musical notation of the characteristic tone, and (4) the absolute limits on the general scale of tones defining the voices, or what amounts to the same thing, the tonal position of an aerophonic instrument.

The necessity for factor (3) should be explained. Fipple flute parts are notated in some cases at their true pitch (for instance, the alto and tenor recorders). If the tonal position were to be determined from their notation, the instruments would be placed too high.[89] So their lowest tone has to be transposed one octave lower to place the alto and tenor recorders in a proper tonal position with respect to the rest of the family.

In the next section are given the note limits for various voices. Owing to the difference of acoustical properties and musical notation of the characteristic tone, no general rule for the determination of the tonal position can be given. Each instrumental type has to be treated individually. In this study the following rules are adhered to for establishing the tonal position of aerophonic instruments.[90]

1. *The transverse flutes and ordinary vertical flutes.* The nominal pedal tone at its true tonality,[91] notated at the actual pitch.
2. *The recorders.* The pedal tone notated one octave lower.[92]
3. *The flageolets.* The nominal pedal G notated a fourth higher.[93]
4. *The pipes.* The second partial tone notated one octave lower.[94]
5. *The clarinets.* The third partial tone overblown from the nominal low F, notated one octave lower.[95]
6. *The shawms, oboes, English horns, bassoons.* The nominal pedal C notated at the actual pitch.
7. *The lip-vibrated aerophones* ('brass wind'). The second partial tone notated at the actual pitch.

Designation of the Tonal Position of Aerophonic Instruments[96]

THE rules just formulated for the characteristic tones and their notation[97] permit the designation of the tonal position of aerophonic instruments without ambiguity as to the pitch position. It is possible now to assign the limits of tones for each individual voice. Below the staff are given the equivalents in three systems: (1) the old letter system used in this study; (2) the Mahillon International System; and (3) the American Tentative Standard System.

	SUB-CONTRABASS		SUB-BASS		CONTRABASS		BASS		BARITONE-TENOR	
	8va	loco								
1	AAA♭	DD♭	DD	GG	AA♭	D♭	D	G	A♭	d♭
2	9	14	15	20	21	26	27	32	33	38
3	?	D♭5	D6	G11	A♭12	D♭17	D18	G23	A♭24	D♭29

	ALTO		SOPRANO		SOPRANINO		OCTAVE		OCTAVINO	
1	d	g	a♭	d′♭	d′	g′	a′♭	d″♭	d″	g″
2	39	44	45	50	51	56	57	62	63	68
3	D30	G35	A♭36	D♭41	D42	G47	A♭48	D♭53	D54	G59

The procedure for finding the proper designation of a tonal position of an instrument, assuming that its family, acoustical properties, and musical notation conventions are known, is the following.

1. Determine the absolute pitch of the characteristic tone given in the rules on p. 45.

2. Write down this tone in its proper notation in case the absolute pitch of the characteristic tone is not used in this determination.

3. Find the proper place of the characteristic tone in its proper notation in note example. The voice name is then determined unambiguously.

Example a. The recorder sounds *f′* with all finger-holes stopped. The parts are notated at its true pitch. Transposing *f′* one octave lower, the note will be *f*. This is between *d* and *g*, or the instrument is the alto recorder in F.

Example b. The recorder sounds *f* with all finger-holes stopped. The parts are notated one octave lower; the lowest tone is therefore normally written as *F*, and no transposition is necessary. The note falls between *D* and *G*; the instrument is the bass recorder.

Classification of Aerophones

The aerophones are classified in this study under four main divisions listed in the general classification on pages ix–xiii. The most important is Division I, the directly controlled aerophones. They are subdivided into three main sections in accordance with the fundamental method of sound production, namely: (A) Flue-blown, (B) Reed-vibrated, and (C) Lip-vibrated aerophones.

DIVISION I: INSTRUMENTS CONTROLLED DIRECTLY

SECTION A: FLUE-BLOWN

THE fundamental method of tone production on instruments of this section is the blowing of a stream of air shaped and directed by a flue[98] against the sharp edge made in a tube or a receptacle. The 'flue' may be the lips of a player as in the flutes, or a passage made in the mouthpiece as in the recorders. Hence the division of flue-blown aerophones into two subsections: (a) aerophones in which the air stream is directed by the lips, and (b) mouthpiece-blown aerophones.

SUB-SECTION a: AIR STREAM DIRECTED BY THE LIPS

Group 1: Vertically Blown

THE instruments in the Collection belonging to this group are the panpipes and the vertical flutes, *auloi*. The panpipes consist of several small pipes of different lengths with the bottom end closed and the top end open. They are held in a vertical position against the lower lip, so that a stream of air can be blown across the open end, and will strike the inner edge of the tube. This motion of the air stream against the edge produces fluctuating eddies, which cause the vibration of the air column inside the tube.[99]

The vertical flutes (*auloi*), Nos. 29 and 30, both came from Greece, but their prototype is, it seems, the Arabian *nay*. Both ends of the tube of the *aulos* are open. The production of sound on these simple instruments is extremely difficult and requires a special knack.

26. PANPIPES — Southern Europe

Syrinx. Reed. Nineteen pieces of reed closed at the bottom, placed side by side; held together by four narrow strips of reed tied with string. Compass: c″–f^4; diatonic scale. Length, 23 cm. Height, longest pipe, 17 cm.; shortest pipe, 3 cm. (17.1842)
Plate I

27. PANPIPES — Spain, 19th century

Flauta de Pan. Iron, tinplated. Nine tubes. Wire loop for a cord. Compass: e^3–f^4; diatonic scale. Length, 7 cm. Height, 7 cm.; 3 cm. (17.1844)
Plate I

28. PANPIPES — Southern France

Boxwood. Trapezoidal flat piece of boxwood with an ear having a small hole by which it is hung. Eleven tubes bored into the piece. Unvarnished. Compass: c^3–f^4; diatonic scale. Used by itinerant Basque dealers. Length, 7.5 cm. Height, 10.5 cm. (17.1843)
Plate I

29. VERTICAL FLUTE Greece, 19th century

Aulos. Cylindrical brass tube with six finger-holes in the front and one thumb-hole in the rear; chamfered upper edge. Length, 25.5 cm. Diameter (outside), 14 mm. Bore, 12.5 mm. (17.1829)
Plate I

30. VERTICAL FLUTE Greece, 19th century

Aulos. Cylindrical reed tube with six finger-holes in the front and one thumb-hole in the rear; the joint membrane, located about 8 mm. from the lowest finger-hole, is pierced through; chamfered upper edge. The outside surface is almost completely covered with an engraving of the battle of Navarino (1827). Length, 31.5 cm. Diameter (outside), 18 mm. Bore (approx.), 11 mm. (17.1828)
Plate I

Group 2: Transversely Blown

THE transversely blown aerophones, among which is the orchestral flute, embody a principle of sound production which is artistically important, since it gives to the player the possibility of controlling the quality of tone and a continuous dynamic control from piano to forte within comparatively wide limits.

The basic instrument of this group is the keyless flute, Fig. 5. This represents the instrument in its most primitive form.

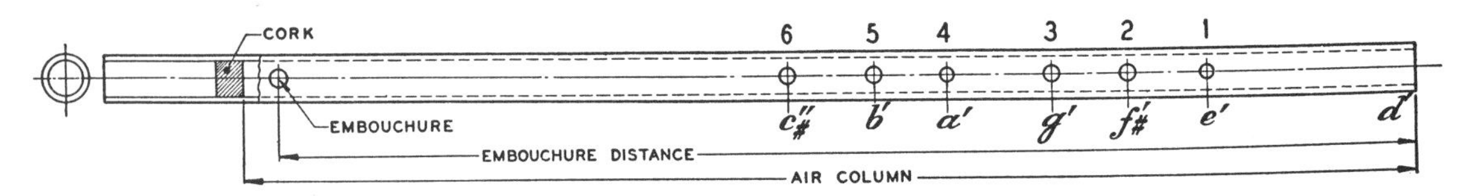

FIG. 5. A PRIMITIVE FLUTE

A cylindrical tube with a bore of 19 mm. in diameter is plugged at one end with a cork and is open on the opposite end. Close to the cork is located the mouthpiece or 'embouchure,' which may have various shapes: circular, elliptical, rectangular with rounded corners, etc.; it is undercut so that the orifice on the outside surface of the tube is smaller than one on the inside surface. There are six finger-holes on the tube, which permit a shortening or lengthening of the acoustical length of the tube and therefore a variation of the pitch of tones produced by it. The sound is generated by the fluctuating eddies caused by the stream of air striking the sharp edge of the embouchure and setting the air column in vibration. The shape, size, and location of the embouchure has important influence upon the quality of tone of the flute; the 'embouchure distance' is the distance between the centre of the embouchure and the plane of the open end of the tube; this dimension is given for each instrument in the technical description.[100]

The fundamental scale of ancient flutes was that of D-major. The playing range was from d′ to a³, but the third octave was rather difficult to produce in tune. The tones of the second octave were overblown tones, with the same fingerings as those of the first octave, except for certain tones (c″ and d″) which required the c″-sharp hole (numbered 6 on Fig. 5) as the vent-hole. Since the fundamental scale of the ancient flute was, as stated, the D-major, such tones as f′ and c″ required the 'cross-fingering' or 'forking,' which was also used for the playing of chromatic tones.[101] The cross-fingered tones required from a player greater care in production; altogether the ancient flutes demanded better musicianship from the performers.[102] In the hands of a fine musician the ancient flute is a charming instrument.

The designation of tonalities of the flute requires an explanation. The old system was to name a flute for the lowest actual tone it produced; thus the soprano instrument of the flute family was called the flute in D. Its true tonality was, of course, that in C, since the lowest tone sounded in unison with d′ on the keyboard instrument, and, therefore, the soprano flute was a non-transposing instrument.[103] The practice persisted when the compass of the flute was extended to c′. The same system was applied to other instruments of the flute family; the true tonality was always one tone lower than the nominal tonality. The practice was discontinued only in comparatively recent times. In this study the tonality of the flute is given at its true pitch. The flute in F means that its nominal tone c′ (whether actually on the instrument or not) sounds f′ or f, depending upon whether the flute is higher or lower than the standard instrument.

The bore of the flute was originally cylindrical. About 1680 the bore was changed to an inverted conoidal one. The actual form of the bore of the conoidal flute calls for a comment. Fig. 6 represents a section of a typical one-keyed flute.

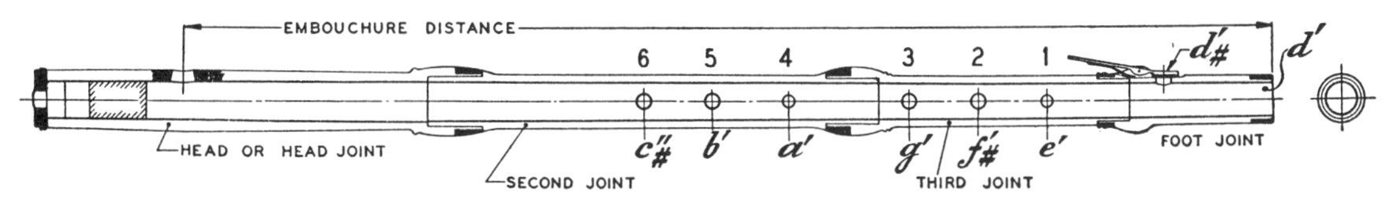

FIG. 6. SECTION OF THE ONE-KEYED FLUTE
The finger-holes are shown in the plane of projection

The head-joint had, nominally, a cylindrical bore. Since the cylindrical reamer would drag on wood and it would be difficult to make a clean bore, the actual reamers for the head-joint were given a small clearance angle, that is, they were made with a slight taper. Therefore, the actual bore of the head-joint was conoidal, however little it departed from the true cylindrical form. Some makers were not very particular as to how the small diameter of the head-joint was fitted; on some flutes the narrow end was at the embouchure, on others the wide end; on some instruments, it seems, the same reamer was used both on the head-joint and on the second body-joint, since measurements show that on some flutes the taper of both joints is identical.[104]

The transverse flute, an instrument of respectable antiquity, came to Europe from the Orient at some period not yet definitely determined. There are reasons to believe that the transverse flute was known to the Greeks and Romans.[105] The earliest Italo-Byzantine images on caskets of the ninth or tenth century are preserved in Florence, Italy.[106] One of the most interesting objective proofs both of its Oriental origin and of the early period of its appearance in Europe is the fresco on the stairway wall of the Cathedral of St. Sophia in Kiev, Russia. This dates from the eleventh century and is reproduced in Fig. 7.

The musician in the upper left-hand corner holds a transverse flute, but to his left, which is contrary to the method usually adopted.[107] There are many references to the flute in Western European literature,[108] but the most important representation of it is in Sebastian Virdung's *Musica getutscht und auszgezogen*, published in 1511 in Basel; it is called a *Zwerchpfeiff*. Martin Agricola gives the complete family, consisting of the descant (*d'*), the alto and tenor (*g*), and the bass (*d* or *c*); he calls it the *Querchpfeiff* or *Schweitzerpfeiff*, the last name alluding to its use by the Swiss troops as a military instrument.[109]

Praetorius gives a description, pictures, and the tone compass of the transverse flute and similar instruments of his time, including among them the *Schweitzerpfeiff* or *Feldtpfeiff* (table ix, fig. 4, reproduced here on p. 67); he tells us that the latter had a somewhat different fingering from that of the transverse flute and was used with drums. The ordinary flutes were the *Cant* (the lowest tone is *a'*), the *Tenor-Alt* (d'; he remarks on p. 22 of *De Organographia* that these flutes were used as a descant similarly to the recorder of the same pitch), and the *Bass* (*g*). The embouchure distances of Praetorius' flutes are of interest: they are 33.7 cm. for the *Cant*, 53 cm. for the *Tenor-Alt*, and 77.5 cm. for the *Bass*.[110]

The first key (the closed *d'*-sharp key) was added to the flute about 1660; this is surprising because the recorders and shawms of Virdung's, and other wind instruments of Praetorius' time had keys. The conoidal bore was introduced about 1680. Further history of the flute is uneventful. The *c'* and *c'*-sharp keys were added about 1722; the *e'*-flat key is discussed on p. 56 under No. 43. The *f'*, *g'*-sharp, and *b'*-flat keys were added in the second half of the eighteenth century. The high c'' and d'' keys appeared at the turn of the eighteenth century.[111]

The history of the Boehm flute is a separate story in itself. This Collection has no Boehm flute.

Keyless Flutes

31. TRANSVERSE FLUTE. Flanders type, ca. 1600. Reproduction

Schweizerpfeife. Cylindrical bore. Cylindrical tube of pearwood. Circular embouchure and six finger-holes. Cork inserted close to the embouchure. Length, 68.5 cm. Diameter (outside), 23 mm. Bore, 17 mm. Embouchure, diameter, 8 mm. Embouchure distance (to centre), 57.5 cm. (17.1745)
Plate II

For more instruments of this type, see the Royal Military Exhibition *Catalogue*, plate i.

32. FIFE England, late 19th century

In B-flat (French pitch, a' = 435). Cylindrical bore. Boxwood, stained dark brown; in two parts, with brass tips. The head and the body turned with slight taper on outside. Elliptical embouchure and six finger-holes. Stamped 'C' under the embouchure. Length, 35.5 cm. Diameter, max., 22 mm. Bore, 10.5 mm. Embouchure, 9 x 10 mm. Embouchure distance, 30 cm. (17.1863)
Plate II

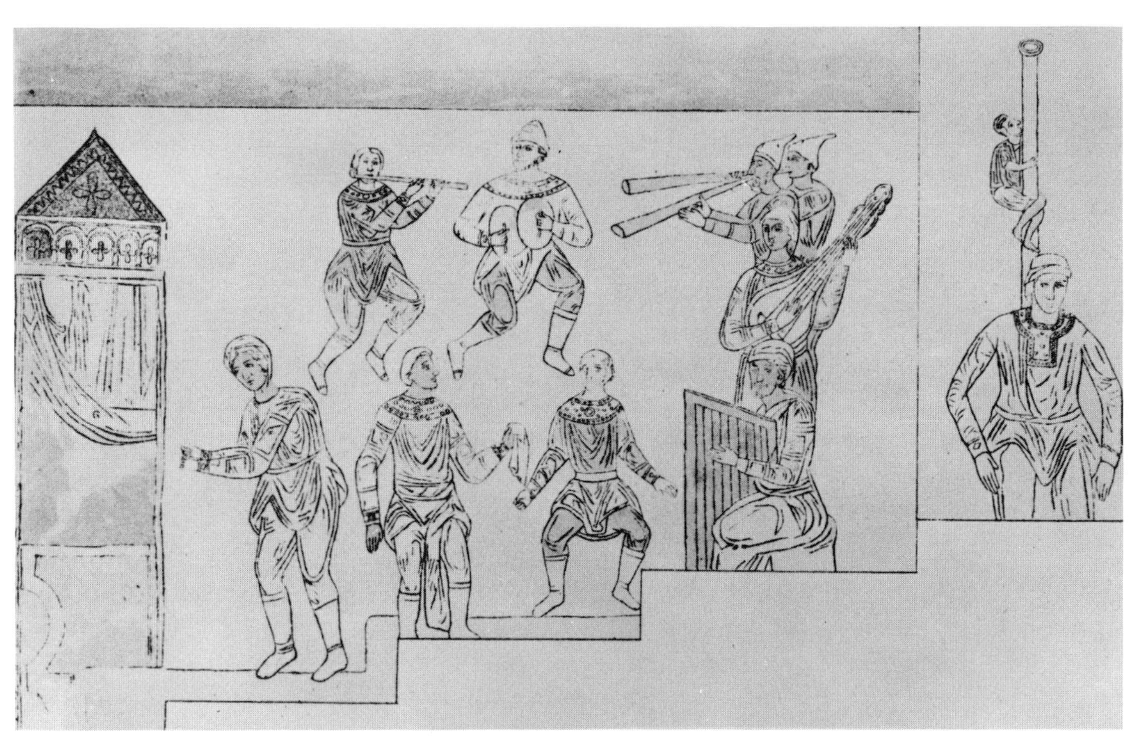

FIG. 7. A FRESCO IN THE CATHEDRAL OF ST. SOPHIA, KIEV, RUSSIA
Eleventh century, representing 'Skomorohi'

33. FIFE London, England, ca. 1800

In B-flat. Cylindrical bore. Boxwood, varnished a light yellow-brown. Brass tips. Tapered toward ends, the largest diameter being at the embouchure. Circular embouchure and six finger-holes. Stamped 'C' and maker's name in the scroll: 'V. Metzler, London.' Length, 38 cm. Diameter, max., 22 mm. Bore, 11.2 mm. Embouchure, diameter, 9 mm. Embouchure distance, 31 cm. (17.1860)
Plate II

34. WALKING-STICK FLUTE England, late 19th century

In B-flat. Conoidal bore. Maple, stained dark brown. Made in three parts in the form of a walking stick with an ellipsoidal head; brass tips. Elliptical embouchure, six finger-holes, and two vent-holes. Length, 90 cm. Diameter, head, 3.5 cm.; at embouchure, 22 mm.; at vent-holes, 20 mm. Embouchure, 9 x 10 mm. Embouchure distance (from centre of vent-holes), 31.5 cm. The size of the bore could not be measured. (17.1864)
Plate II

35. CONCERT FLUTE London, England, the second half of the 19th century

In C (a′ = 435). Conoidal bore; lowest tone is d′; chromatic experimental flute. Mahogany, varnished light brown; ivory tips. The tube is made in three parts: the head, long body joint, and the very short foot joint with a finger-hole for the right little finger. An adjustable cork with a threaded stem and ivory depth indicator; moved by means of the threaded head-cap. Elliptical embouchure and ten finger-holes; the hole nearest to the embouchure and covered by the left thumb is made in two circular segments, with a dividing bridge slightly inclined to accommodate the thumb. On the centre-line of the fourth hole (counting from the foot-joint), and at an angle of 90° to it, is a threaded hole stopped by a plug with a circular nut, which is prevented from rotating by an ivory eyelet with a small square-headed ivory set-screw. Length, 61 cm. Diameter, max., 3.5 cm.; min., 21 mm. Bore, head, cylindrical, 19 mm.; body, conoidal, max., 19.5 mm.; min., 11 mm.; length, 39.8 cm. Embouchure, 10 x 13 mm. Embouchure distance, 51.7 mm. (17.1866)
Plate II

This extremely interesting instrument was made for the late Dr. Burghley, of Camden Town, the first to suggest (in 1845) the idea of the well known Briccialdi B-flat key.[112] The instrument is practicable and gives the complete chromatic scale from *d′* to *c″*-sharp without cross-fingering. The significance of the plugged hole is unknown. The double hole is intended to produce *c″* and *c″*-sharp; when the half-hole nearest the embouchure is covered, the tone is *c″*-sharp; when the second half (farthest away) is covered, the tone is *c″*. The finger-holes are rather large; the six regular holes are 10 mm. in diameter; the right and left little finger-holes are 8 mm.; the right thumb-hole is also 10 mm.; left thumb- (double) hole is 10 x 4 mm. All finger-holes are rather closely spaced and conveniently located for the fingers.[113]

One-Keyed Flutes

KEYLESS flutes were in general use down to 1660–70. About this time Lulli introduced the flute into the orchestra. Approximately at the same time some unknown inventor added the D-sharp key to the flute and the body of the instrument was made in several joints: the head joint, the body joint, and the foot (or tail) joint. The body joint was later further subdivided, and the upper part was made in several interchangeable lengths, so that the pitch of the instrument could be adjusted.[114] The joint proper was made as a pin-and-socket joint.[115] The air-tightness was secured by wrapping the 'pin' part of the joint with a waxed linen thread or 'lapping.' To prevent the sockets from cracking, ornamental rings of brass, horn, or ivory, called 'tips,' were fitted on them.

The tuning slide appeared in the middle of the eighteenth century. J. J. Quantz claimed it as his own invention.[116] The cork or stopper required an adjustment, since its position with respect to the embouchure affected the pitch of tones produced by overblowing.[117] To facilitate this adjustment, the cork was furnished with a threaded stem of ivory, and the head-cap had a female thread engaging the thread on the ivory stem of the cork. See the design on No. 43. Sometimes the stem was extended through the hole in the head-cap and served as an indicator of the position of the cork, but this device was not very practicable. The flutes Nos. 35, 45, 46, 48, 49 have this device.

The transverse flute family consisted of several members, the number of which varied at different periods. The flutes of Martin Agricola (1528) and of Praetorius (1619) have already been mentioned. In the middle of the eighteenth century, in addition to the standard flute in C, there were the small *Quartflöte* in F (the lowest tone *g'*), the *flûte d'amour* in A (the lowest tone *b*), the large *Quartflöte* in G (the lowest tone *a*), and the 'bass' flute in F (the lowest tone *g*). By the end of the eighteenth century, the flute family received an addition in its upper register, when the octave flute in C with a conoidal bore made its appearance. The lowest tone of this piccolo flute was *d''*, one octave above the old standard flute.[118]

The modern flute family consists of the following instruments:

I. *Octavino Flutes*:	1. Piccolo in E-flat.
II. *Octave Flutes*:	2. Piccolo in D-flat (Bands).
	3. Piccolo in C (Orchestras).
	4. Piccolo in B-flat.
	5. Piccolo in A-flat.
III. *Sopranino Flutes*:	6. Terzflute in E-flat.
IV. *Soprano Flutes*:	7. Flute in D-flat (Bands).
	8. Flute in C (Orchestras).
	9. Flute in B-flat.
	10. Flute in A.
V. *Alto Flutes*:	11. Alto Flute in G.
	12. Alto Flute in F.
	13. Alto Flute in E-flat.
VI. *Tenor Flutes*:[119]	14. Bass Flute in D-flat.
	15. Bass Flute in C.

36. FLUTE London, England, early 19th century

In F. *Quartflöte*. Lowest tone is *g'*. Conoidal bore. Boxwood, varnished light yellow; ivory tips. Four joints. Elliptical embouchure, six open finger-holes, square key of brass (D-sharp). Stamped with the three plumes of the Prince of Wales and 'late Goulding & D'Almaine, So(ho) Square, London.' Length, 44.5 cm. Diameter, max., 26 mm. Bore, max., 14.5 mm.; min., 12 mm.; length of conoidal part, 29.5 cm. Embouchure, 9 x 11 mm. Embouchure distance, 39.2 cm. (17.1862)
Plate II

37. FLUTE Germany (?), early 19th century

In E-flat. *Terzflöte*. The lowest tone *f'*. Conoidal bore. Maple, varnished light yellow-brown; horn tips. Four joints. Elliptical embouchure, six open finger-holes, square key of brass (D-sharp). Length, 52 cm. Diameter, max., 26 mm. Bore, max., 14 mm.; min., 11 mm.; length of conoidal part, 35 cm. Embouchure, 8.5 x 10 mm. Embouchure distance, 46 cm. (17.1861)
Plate II

38. CONCERT FLUTE Paris, France, ca. 1670(?), by Chevalier

In C. Conoidal bore. Boxwood, varnished light yellow-brown; ivory mounted. Made in four parts: head cap, head with very broad ivory ring, body with finger-holes, and a short foot-joint. Circular embouchure with ivory bushing, six finger-holes, square brass key (D-sharp). Stamped 'Chevalier' over the dolphin trade-mark. Length, 69.2 cm. Diameter, max., 3.7 cm. Bore, max., 18 mm.; min., 15 mm.; length of conoidal part, 40 cm. Embouchure, diameter, 9 mm. Embouchure distance, 56.5 cm. (17.1846)
Plate II

This excellently made instrument is identical in shape with the flute represented in the etching by Bernard Picart in the hands of one of the most famous of French flutists, Jacques Hotteterre-le-Romain[120] (d. 1760–61).

39. CONCERT FLUTE Germany, 18th century

In C. Conoidal bore. Boxwood, varnished light yellow-brown; horn tips, scalloped ivory ring at the foot-joint orifice. Made in four parts: the head, second and third body joints (which correspond to the single body joint of the Chevalier's Flute, No. 38), and foot-joint. Elliptical embouchure, six finger-holes, square key of silver (D-sharp). Length, 61.5 cm. Diameter, max., 3.1 cm. Bore, max., 17.5 mm.; min., 13 mm.; length of conoidal part, 41.3 cm. Embouchure, 9 x 11 mm. Embouchure distance, 53.5 cm. (17.1854)
Plate II

40. CONCERT FLUTE Rome, Italy, ca. 1724

In C, high chamber pitch. Conoidal bore. Ivory, with incised lines and circles in red and black. Made in four parts, like the previous instrument, but each joint is made up of several pieces; the lower head-joint and foot-joint have screw-thread connection. Elliptical embouchure, six finger-holes, square key of silver (D-sharp). Length, 57.5 cm. Diameter, max., 3.3 cm. Bore, max., 20 mm.; min., 14.5 mm.; length of conoidal part, 39.5 cm. Embouchure, 9 x 10 mm. Embouchure distance, 51.8 cm. (17.1847)
Plate II

This instrument is described in the Royal Military Exhibition *Catalogue* on p. 30, no. 51. The tonality of this flute is determined there as that in *e'*-flat (i.e., in d'-flat, since the R. M. E. *Catalogue* listed its flutes according to the old system). R. S. Rockstro probably referred to this flute in paragraph 429, p. 229 of his treatise.

41. CONCERT FLUTE Paris, France, ca. 1756, by Thomas Lot

In C. 'Tertia minore' pitch (a' = 400). Boxwood, varnished light yellow-brown. Ivory tips and cap. Made in four parts, like No. 39. Elliptical embouchure, six finger-holes, square D-sharp key of silver. Two body-joints are stamped 'T★Lot,' above a lion rampant. Length, 64.5 cm. Diameter, max., 3.3 cm. Bore, max., 19.2 mm.; min., 16 mm.; length of conoidal part, 44.4 cm. Embouchure, 8.5 x 9.5 mm. Embouchure distance, 57.2 cm. (17.1850)
Plate II

Described in the Royal Military Exhibition *Catalogue* on p. 31 under no. 53. The low pitch of this flute is very close to the 'tertia minore' pitch of Praetorius (a' = 396.4) as determined by Mr. A. J. Hipkins (see p. 359 of this study). The sizes of the head bore are: the cork end, 19.2 mm., the end adjoining the second body-joint, 18 mm. The difference in the bore sizes at the junction plane of the head-joint and the body-joint is 1.2 mm., so the bore abruptly expands by this amount. This peculiarity, commented on in the R. M. E. *Catalogue*, can be explained simply by the fact that the maker intended to match the head-joint and the body-joint, since both have the same diameter (19.2 mm.), but either erroneously drilled the embouchure close to the wide end, or finish-reamed the bore of the head-joint from the wrong end. The fact that the bore of the head-joints on the ancient flute is tapered was referred to before; practically all the flutes of this Collection have conoidal bores in the head-joints, the taper varying from one which is scarcely perceptible to one which is rather large, as on this instrument. The usual method is to match the bores of the head- and the body-joints; a smaller diameter of bore of the head-joint is located at the cork end. This practice has been consistently carried out with the rest of the flutes in the Collection (except the metal-lined heads) and corresponds to the best modern practice: on the Boehm flute the bore of the head-joint decreases gradually toward the cork end; the shape of the bore is quasi-paraboloidal.[121] The date, ca. 1756, was estimated by its former owner, Mr. Carli Zoeller.[122]

42. CONCERT FLUTE Germany, 18th century

In C. Conoidal bore. Ebony, ivory tips and screw-cork. Made in four parts like No. 39. Elliptical embouchure, six finger-holes, square D-sharp key (silver). Body-joints and foot-joint stamped 'I. Hoffman,' with trade-marks above and below the name. Length, 61.8 cm. Diameter, max., 3.3 cm. Bore, max., 17 mm.; min., 13 mm.; length of conoidal part, 41.6 cm. Embouchure, 8 x 9 mm. Embouchure distance, 54.6 cm. (17.1853)
Plate II

Referred to in the Royal Military Exhibition *Catalogue* on p. 32, under no. 58.

Two-Keyed Flute

43. CONCERT FLUTE Rome, Italy, before 1725

In C. Conoidal bore. Boxwood, varnished light yellow-brown, ivory tips and screw-cork. Made in four parts like No. 39. Elliptical embouchure, six finger-holes; closed square key (D-sharp) and open square key (C-sharp), both keys of silver. Body-joints stamped 'I. Biglioni in Roma'; the second joint stamped '4.' Length, 63.5 cm. Diameter, max., 3.2 cm. Bore, max., 18 mm.; min., 10.5 mm.; length of conoidal part, 44.3 cm. Embouchure, 8.5 x 10 mm. Embouchure distance, 57 cm. (17.1852)
Plate II

This important historic instrument belonged to Johann Joachim Quantz (1697–1773), the distinguished flute-player who was the teacher and the court composer of Frederick the Great of Prussia. It is described in the Royal Military Exhibition *Catalogue* on p. 30, under no. 50. The detailed description with many dimensions is in Rockstro's *Treatise*, pp. 229 ff., paragraphs 430 to 433 inclusive. Mr. Rockstro's sizes are correct, except the head bore, which he gives as cylindrical in shape and .74 of an inch in diameter (18.8 mm.; pp. 231 ff.). The true shape of the head bore consists of two truncated cones with a common small diameter. Counting from the cap end of the head, the end diameter is 18.8 mm.; the small diameter, 18 mm.; the diameter at the body-joint, 18.5 mm.; the common small diameter is located 3.1 cm. from the cap end and 2.2 cm. from the centre of the embouchure, the latter being 5.3 cm. from the cap end.

This instrument is interesting also because it has an extra key (c′-sharp), but unfortunately this is not Quantz's famous *e*′-flat key which he introduced in 1726 while he was staying in Paris. Although well accepted in Germany, this latter innovation was coldly received abroad. One may wonder, indeed, why this enharmonic key was introduced at all when there were several tones on the ancient flute which required correction. The subsequent history of flute development proceeded on more practical lines.

J. J. Quantz's life can be found both in R. S. Rockstro's *Treatise* and in Mr. H. Macaulay Fitzgibbon's *The Story of the Flute*.

Multiple-Keyed Flutes

44. CONCERT FLUTE England, ca. 1800

In C. Conoidal bore. Boxwood, varnished light yellow-brown, ivory tips; the cap is lost. Made in four parts like No. 39. Elliptical embouchure, six finger-holes, one of which (the F-sharp hole) is enlarged. Four square brass keys: D-sharp, F-natural, G-sharp, and B-flat. Length, 59.5 cm. Diameter, max., 3.3 cm. Bore, max., 17.5 mm.; min., 12 mm.; length of conoidal part, 39.5 cm. Embouchure, 9.5 x 11 mm. Embouchure distance, 52.8 cm. (17.1849)
Plate II

The fundamental scale of the ancient flute was, as stated, that of D-major; the finger-holes opening consecutively gave this scale without cross-fingering. The C-major scale, which became the basic scale of secular music, lacked the lowest tone (*c*′), and the tones *f*′ and *c*″ had to be cross-fingered. Such essential chromatic tones as *g*′-sharp and *b*′-flat also had to be cross-fingered. Therefore the logical steps in the evolution of the key mechanism were the addition to the flute of such keys as would, first, permit the elimination of cross-fingerings, and, secondly, extend the compass of the flute. The new additional keys on the flute were those for *f*′-natural, *g*′-sharp, and *b*′-flat. Neither the names of the inventors nor the exact date of this innovation are known positively. This flute represents therefore the next step in evolution.

The addition of keys to the mechanism of wind instruments is not regarded by all as a desirable development. There are people who think that the old, mechanically primitive instruments required better musicianship from the performer and demanded better ear training. Their contention is that if it were possible to play a wind instrument so much out of tune, it was also possible to play it in tune, provided one had a good sense of pitch. Modern acoustical research supports this contention.[123] Any competent instrumentalist knows from his struggles to play in tune that the wind instrument, especially the 'brass wind,' is not rigidly fixed in pitch, and that it is possible to play out of tune even on the clarinet, as amateur clarinetists demonstrate so convincingly. The whole tendency in the evolution of musical instruments is to replace the skill of a performer by the greater perfection of the complicated mechanism.[124] This enables even mediocre musicians to perform acceptably. Of course, much is gained by correctness of tone production and technical dexterity, but for some people the loss of certain intimate qualities and the personal touch far outweigh the advantages gained. Each gain in one direction means the loss of some quality in the other. This is a general philosophical question: is there such a thing as 'progress'?

45. CONCERT FLUTE London, England, ca. 1810

In C. Conoidal bore. Boxwood, varnished light yellow-brown, ivory tips and screw-cork. Made in five parts: the head, of two parts with a tuning slide, the bore, entirely lined with tin-plated brass tubing, two body-joints, and a foot-joint. Circular embouchure. Six finger-holes. Six silver keys with round heads and metallic pads, riveted with round-headed silver rivets so that the pads can be rotated. The keys are mounted between the brass plate linings of the knobs; the bores of the keyholes have metal bushings. The keys are disposed as follows: open C-natural and C-sharp articulated keys, closed D-sharp key on the foot-joint; F-natural key on the lower right-hand body-joint; G-sharp and B-flat keys on the second body-joint. All joints are stamped 'Astor & Horwood' over the head of unicorn trade-mark. The head-joint is stamped under the embouchure 'Astor & Horwood, 79 Cornhill, London. Patent.' Length, 64.5 cm. Diameter, max., 3.5 cm. Bore, max., 18 mm.; min., 9.5 mm.; length of conoidal part, 43.8 cm. Embouchure, diameter, 9 mm. Embouchure distance, 56 cm. (17.1851)
Plate II

Described in the Royal Military Exhibition *Catalogue* on p. 39 under no. 85. This flute is very similar to No. 44, but has two semi-tones added to its compass at the lower end of the scale, thus illustrating the second direction of the flute's evolution mentioned in connection with No. 44. The c′-natural and c′-sharp keys are open because the basic instrument still remains the flute with D-major scale. The open keys on the Boehm flute are constructed on an entirely different principle.[125]

46. CONCERT FLUTE London, England, ca. 1810, by William Henry Potter

In C. Conoidal bore. Ivory, silver mounted; ivory screw-cork. Made in five parts with a tuning slide and metal-lined head like No. 45. Elliptical embouchure (slightly irregular: the curvature of the playing side is somewhat greater), six finger-holes. Eight silver keys: open C-natural and C-sharp articulated keys, closed D-sharp key on the foot-joint; two F-natural keys, a regular one and a long F-natural shake key (with long lever actuated by the left little finger) on the lower (right-hand) body-joint; G-sharp, B-flat and a long C-natural shake key (actuated by the right thumb) on the second body-joint. All joints are stamped 'Potter, London, Patent.' Length, 65 cm. Diameter, max., 3.1 cm. Bore, max., 19 mm.; min., 10.5 mm.; length of conoidal part, 45.4 cm. Embouchure, diameter, 9 x 10 mm. Embouchure distance, 57.6 cm. (17.1848)
Plate II

Described in the Royal Military Exhibition *Catalogue* on p. 32 under no. 59 and represented on plate i, fig. H. This instrument is an example of the ultimate development of the standard multiple-keyed flute. The eight keys were the practical minimum necessary for mitigating the deficiencies of the basic D-major scale of the ancient flute. Although many attempts to increase the number of keys were made, none of them gained universal acceptance. The next step in the development of the flute was not an evolutionary but a revolutionary one, which changed the bore back to the cylindrical, the disposition and size of the tone-holes, the shape and position of the embouchure, the shape of the head-joint (quasi-parabolic), and reformed the fingering. This much-resisted change was made in 1847 by Theobald Boehm.

Low-Pitched Flutes

47. FLÛTE D'AMOUR Germany, ca. 1700

Alto flute in A. The lowest tone is *C*. Conoidal bore. Boxwood, stained yellow brown; ordinary cap, signed in ink 'KRAFFT.' Made in four parts like No. 39. Elliptical embouchure, six finger-holes, square D-sharp key of brass, stamped 'I. W. Oberlender' in a scroll and the letter 'O' beneath, on all four joints. Length, 73 cm. Diameter, max., 3.7 cm. Bore, max., 19 mm.; min., 15 mm.; length of conoidal part, 48.2 cm. Embouchure, 9 x 10 mm. Embouchure distance, 67.3 cm. (17.1855)
Plate II

Described in the Royal Military Exhibition *Catalogue* on p. 31 under no. 54 and also in Rockstro's *Treatise* on pp. 285 f. Another historical instrument. It belonged, it is said, to the celebrated violoncellist Krafft, a member of Haydn's orchestra. The a′ and e′ holes are bored at an angle, so that the distance between the orifices on the inside wall of the tube is increased without undue spread of the fingers. It is difficult to say why flutes in A were called 'flûtes d'amour,' since there was no *Liebesfuss* on them to change the tone color as on the oboe d'amore; Dr. Curt Sachs suggested that the reason should be sought in the identity of tonality with the oboe d'amore, which is also in A.[126]

48. ALTO FLUTE[127] London, England, ca. 1800, by William Henry Potter

In A. Conoidal bore. Ebony, ivory tips and screw-cork. Made in four parts like No. 39. Elliptical embouchure, six finger-holes. Four closed round silver keys with soft metal pads; the bores

of the key-holes have silver bushings. The keys are the same as on No. 44. The head is stamped 'WILLm HENy POTTER, Johnson's Court, Fleet Street, London.' Length, 77.3 cm. Diameter, max., 3.6 cm. Bore, max., 18 mm.; min., 13 mm.; length of conoidal part, 51.3 cm. Embouchure, 9 x 10 mm. Embouchure distance, 67.6 cm. (17.1856)
Plate II

Referred to in the Royal Military Exhibition *Catalogue* on p. 33 under no. 63. The flute is by William Henry Potter, and not by Richard Potter, as stated there on p. 33. The suggestion there that it was a B-flat flute of its time is interesting.

49. FLAUTO DI VOCE London, England, 1811

Alto flute in G. Conoidal bore. Boxwood, varnished yellow-brown; ivory tips. Made in four parts. The head is made of a block of oval cross-section, in which are bored two parallel holes with a very slight taper in each. The bores are connected by a passage. The opening is covered by an elliptical ivory cover with cork stopper. The regular screw-cork is inserted into that part of the hole which has the embouchure. The second body-joint has a large circular hole (15 mm. diameter) which is covered by a thin skin membrane. This hole is located 32 mm. above the C-sharp hole, measuring from the centres of the holes. Elliptical embouchure, six finger-holes bored obliquely. Two finger-holes are stopped by keys, the E-hole and the C-sharp hole; these keys are open. In addition there are four closed standard keys: D-sharp, F-natural, G-sharp, and B-flat. The keys are of silver-plated brass mounted in knobs; the pads are of leather held by brass discs with small screws. The head- and the foot-joint are stamped with the Royal Arms and 'Wigley & McGregor, Patentees, 161 Strand, London.' On the head is stamped the number '7' below the maker's name (the factory number of the flute?), and on the oval ivory head-cover is engraved the name of the original owner of the instrument: 'Benj.n Rotch Jun.r, Castle Hall, June 1811.' Length, 67 cm. Diameter, max., 3.5 cm. Head, width, 5.9 cm.; thickness, average, 4.5 cm. Bore, max., 21 mm.; min., 16 mm.; length of conoidal part, 47.2 cm. Embouchure, 9.5 x 11 mm. Embouchure distance, actual, 57.8 cm.; measured on centre line (approx.), 75 cm. (17.1857)
Plate II

Described in the Royal Military Exhibition *Catalogue* on p. 35 under no. 68. The patent was granted in 1810 to Malcolm McGregor, a musical instrument maker of London.[128] The large hole covered by a thin skin membrane added the tone color referred to as 'reedy.'

50. BASS FLUTE London, England, 1811–16

In C, an octave lower than the concert flute. The lowest tone is *d*. Conoidal bore. Boxwood, stained dark yellow-brown; ivory tips, ordinary boxwood cap. Made in six parts. The head is made in three parts: the embouchure joint, the U-shaped connecting brass tube, and the head-joint proper, the whole forming a 'U' with unequal arms. The body proper consists of two joints. There is also the foot-joint. Elliptical embouchure, six finger-holes bored straight. The E, G, A, and C-sharp holes are stopped with long brass keys; these keys are normally open. The bores of the holes stopped with keys are lined with brass bushings. In addition there are four standard closed brass keys, as on No. 49. The joints are stamped with the Royal Arms, 'Wigley & McGregor Patentees, 161, Strand, London' and the figure '5.' Length, 87 cm. Diameter, max., 4 cm. Bore, max., 24 mm.; min., 17 mm.; length of conoidal part, 70.5 cm. Embouchure, 14 x 15 mm. Embouchure distance, actual, 65.5 cm.; measured on centre line (approx.), 100 cm. (17.1858)
Plate II

The real bass instrument of the flute family should have its pedal tone located between *G* and *D*. Since the nominal pedal tone of this flute is only *c* (actually not on the instrument), its correct designation should be the tenor flute. The bass flute is described and pictured by Martin Agricola. In the 1528 edition of his *Musica Instrumentalis Deudsch*[129] the actual lowest tone is given as *D* (an octave too low?) and therefore its tonality is in C. In the 1545 edition the lowest tone is given as C and therefore its tonality should be in B-flat. Praetorius' bass flute is in F. If I have read correctly Mersenne's obscure references to the bass flute, then the French bass flutes of his time (1637) were also in B-flat.[130] The so-called bass flute of later periods was either the tenor or the alto flute.

51. ALTO FLUTE London, England, ca. 1810

In F, low pitch. Conoidal bore. Boxwood, stained grey-brown; ivory screw-cork. Made in four parts like No. 39. Elliptical embouchure bored in the ivory plug inserted in the head. Six regular finger-holes. Five closed hemispherical cup keys of brass: D-sharp, F-natural. G-sharp, B-flat, and a long C-natural shake key. Closed octave key stopping small (1 mm. diameter) vent-hole located 22.8 cm. below the embouchure. The head is stamped 'G Flute.' The second body-joint is stamped below the crown '*WILLm BAINBRIDGE*, fecit, 34 Windmill St., Finsbury Sq.e, London.' Large, rather clumsy instrument. Length, 90.5 cm. Diameter, max., 5 cm.; min., 18 mm.; length of conoidal part, 60 cm. Embouchure, 10.5 x 11 mm. Embouchure distance, 81 cm. (17.1859)
Plate II

This very large instrument is marked 'G Flute.' The A-hole sounds approximately *c*-sharp at 440 cycles per second; the tonality stamped on the instrument leads to the conclusion that it was the low pitched (a' = 420 cycles per second) alto flute in F.

SUB-SECTION b: MOUTHPIECE BLOWN (FLUE-BLOWN)

'FLUE-BLOWN' aerophones take their name from the 'flue,' which is the windway in the foot of a flue-pipe of the organ. They are also called 'fipple-flutes' or 'whistle-flutes.' Fig. 8, representing a section of the recorder, shows more clearly the reason for these terms.

The bore of instruments of this type is stopped at the top with a plug called the 'fipple.' Between the fipple and the body of the flute a wedge-shaped passage or windway is cut out. This is called the 'flue,' the wide end of which is at the mouthpiece and the narrow end at the bottom of the fipple. Below the fipple an opening, the 'mouth,' is cut out, having a sharp edge, the 'lip.' In playing, the mouthpiece is taken between the lips and the instrument itself is held in front of a player in an inclined position, like the oboe or the clarinet. The air blown into the slit comes out of the narrow end of the flue in the form of a thin ribbon. The striking of this air stream against the lip produces fluctuating eddies and sets the air column in vibration. The essential dimension is the 'lip distance,' which is the distance between the lip edge and the open end of the tube. This distance, as on the organ pipes, is the effective dimension influencing the pitch of the fipple-flute.[131]

Some fipple-flutes have their mouthpieces covered by a cap which forms an air chamber over it. The shape and size of this chamber is immaterial, since it does not affect the acoustic properties of the fipple-flutes. Sometimes a piece of sponge is put inside the cap to absorb the moisture of the breath. The air is blown into the air-chamber in various ways: (1) through a slit in the upper edge of the cap, as on the basset recorder No. 58; (2) through a small mouthpiece inserted in the cap, as on the *flûte-à-bec* No. 54, the flageolet No. 67, and the multiple flutes Nos. 75, 76, and 77; (3) through a crook, as on the bass recorder No. 59. The large instruments require a cap to permit the attachment of the crook and thus facilitate

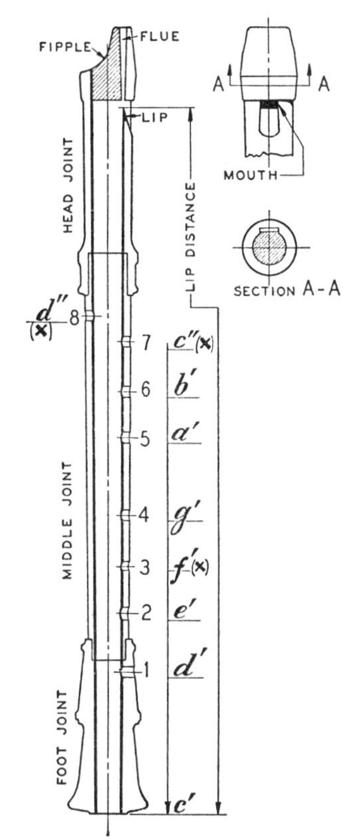

Fig. 8. SECTION OF THE RECORDER
'X' — Cross-fingering

handling. On the small instruments, such as the flageolet No. 67, the cap is made extra long. This is for structural reasons also, since a longer instrument is more convenient to hold and to finger than a very short one.

Flue-blown aerophones have an indirect control of tone production. On the transverse flute, the player has to spend considerable time in gaining control of the tone as to both its quality and its dynamic expression. He has to train his lip muscles to behave in a certain way, to practise constantly to keep the lips in condition, and to take good care not to disturb or injure his 'embouchure.'[132] On the fipple-flute anyone can produce a tone merely by blowing into the instrument. No lip training is necessary. Yet it should not be thought that tone production on the fipple-flute requires no technique. The simplest technique is on those instruments with cap-covered fipple mouthpieces. Control over quality of tone is very limited; the vibrato is possible; the dynamic control, within certain limits, is under the player's will. The tone is uniform, since there is greater air resistance and the air-chamber acts as an equalizer. The breath control is easier, since the recorder, for instance, is too easy to blow and requires more expert breath control. The tone of the cap-covered fipple-flute is very pleasant, although somewhat impersonal. The overblown tones are produced mostly by increased air pressure. Tonguing is less effective. On the fipple-flute with an uncovered mouthpiece not only the dynamic, but also the tone color control is possible within certain limits. The same instrument in the hands of two players does not sound exactly the same.[133] The overblowing requires a certain amount of skill, since not only the increase of pressure but the placing of breath in the mouth cavity enter as factors in producing overblown tones.

Classification of Fipple-Flutes by Families

A FAMILY of instruments in organology is a specific division of instruments of the same type into a set, the individuals of which differ from each other only by their pitch and size. Other characteristics of instruments, especially the acoustic and tonal properties, remain the same. Thus, it is not correct to regard the oboe, the English horn, and the bassoon as belonging to the same family merely because their tubes are conical and all are double reed instruments. There is the oboe family, the incomplete English horn family, and the complete bassoon family; the tone color of each of these families is quite individual, and the instruments of the same tonality and pitch, but of different families, are not alike in timbre. This important question of classification of musical instruments into families is discussed more fully later.

There are four basic families of fipple-flutes in use in Europe: the vertical flutes, recorders, flageolets, and pipes. These families differ not only in their fingering but also in the acoustical properties of their tubes, in the number and disposition of the finger-holes, and in the overblowing technique and the number of overblown partial tones used in their scales.

The Vertical Flute Family

THE basic vertical flute, Fig. 9, has an inverted conoidal bore, that is, one which is wider at the mouthpiece and narrower at the open end. The vertical flute is made to overblow an octave by increase of the air pressure and velocity and by direction of the breath about 45° against the palate.[134] The number of finger-holes is six and all of them are placed at the front. The nominal basic scale is that in D-major. The compass extension is several tones over two octaves; the upper extension depending mostly upon the skill of the player. Thus in many respects the vertical flute is similar to the keyless transverse flute.

The Recorder Family

THE recorder, Fig. 8, page 61, has an inverted conoidal bore. It overblows an octave.[135] There are seven finger-holes in the front and a thumb-hole in the rear. The nominal basic scale, that of C-major, is produced with the tones f′, c″, and d″ cross-fingered.[136] In practical fingering the tones beginning with e″ and up are produced by overblowing with the thumb-hole 'pinched,' that is, the tones are produced by placing the thumbnail so that the hole 8 is half-covered and serves as a vent-hole.[137] The normal compass extension of the recorder is two octaves and one tone; several additional tones are possible, but they are too shrill. The tone of the recorder is very pleasant, soft, and sympathetic.

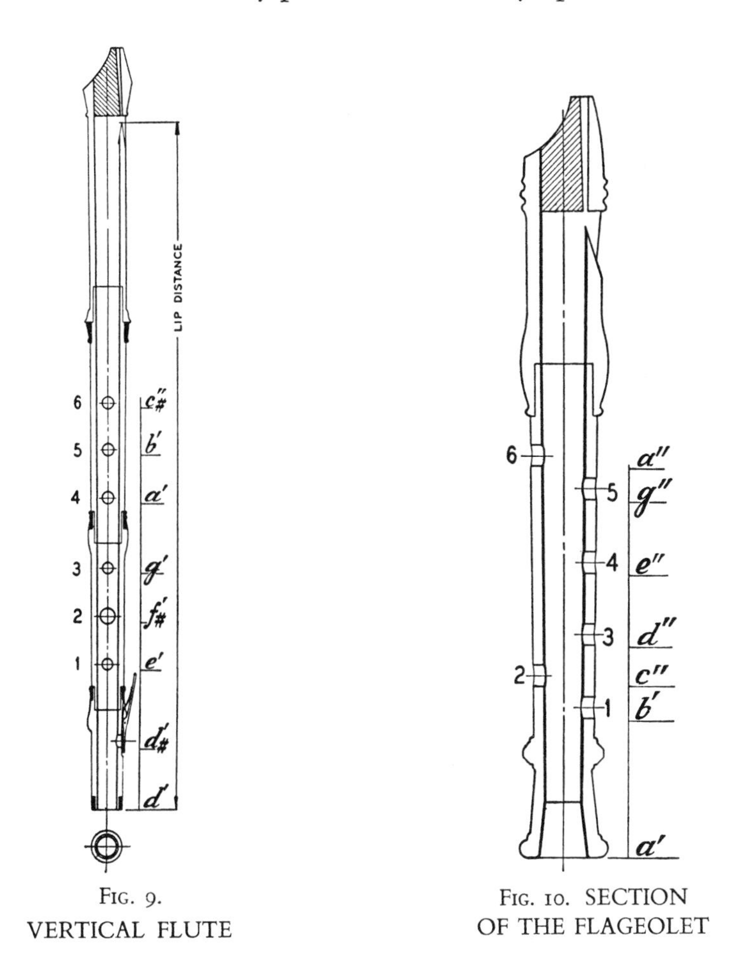

FIG. 9.
VERTICAL FLUTE

FIG. 10. SECTION
OF THE FLAGEOLET

The Flageolet Family[138]

THE flageolet has an inverted conoidal bore with very slight taper and a short conoidal flare at the open end of the tube. The flageolet overblows an octave. There are four finger-holes in the front and two thumb-holes in the rear. The nominal basic scale is that of G-major. The lowest tone is produced with all the finger- and thumb-holes stopped and the lower end opening of the tube partly covered by a finger of the right hand.[139] The f″ is cross-fingered. Beginning with b″ the tones are produced by overblowing with the left-hand thumb-hole 6 pinched, as in the recorder family. The normal compass extension of the keyless flageolet is one octave and a sixth (from g′ to e^3).

The Pipe Family

THE pipe has an inverted conoidal bore with a very slight taper; it is regarded as having, nominally, a cylindrical bore. The finger-holes, only three in number, are located at the lower end, two in the front and a thumb-hole in the rear. The fingered scale of the pipe differs from other fipple-flutes in the greater use of the overblown partial tones. It is similar in this respect to the brass wind instruments with ascending valves. The pedal tone of the

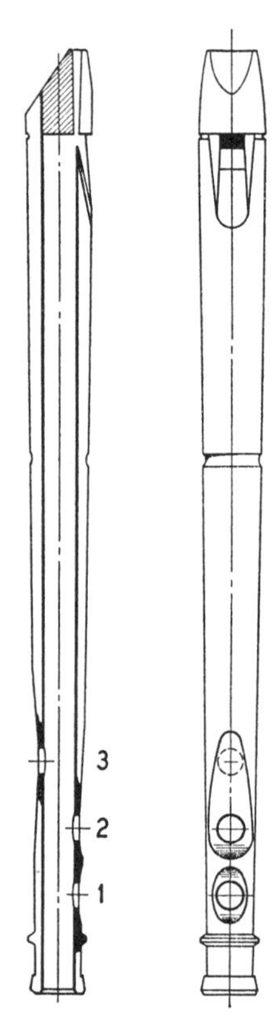

FIG. 11. SECTION AND FRONT VIEW OF THE PIPE

pipe and three fingered-tones based on it are playable only pianissimo and are not used in regular playing.[140] The playing scale is based on the second, third, fourth, and the fifth partial tones of the pipe overblown with all finger-holes stopped. In the acoustical property of its tube, the pipe is similar to the lip-vibrated aerophone ('brass-wind') without the pedal tone.[141]

Vertical Flutes

52. VERTICAL FLUTE London, England, 19th century

In C. Lowest tone d′. Cylindrical bore. Made of drawn brass tubing. Six finger-holes; the fipple is made of lead. Stamped trade-mark with the monogram 'I&H' and the words 'London made' are

soldered on the tubing. The letter 'D' is stamped above the trade-mark. Length, 57 cm. Diameter, outside, 19.5 mm. Bore, 18 mm. Lip distance, 54.2 cm. (17.1838)
Plate I

53. VERTICAL FLUTE London, England, early 19th century

In C. Lowest tone *d'*. Conoidal bore. Boxwood, varnished light yellow; ivory tips. Made in four parts. Six finger-holes, the F-sharp hole enlarged; square silver key (D-sharp). Stamped 'G. French, London.' Length, 55.5 cm. Diameter, max., 3.9 cm. Bore, max., 17 mm.; min., 14 mm.; length of conoidal part, 38 cm. Lip distance, 50.5 cm. (17.1839)
Plate I

In addition to the maker's stamp, 'Boston' and a partially obliterated word are also stamped on the head.

54. FLÛTE-À-BEC London, England, ca. 1810

A vertical flute in A-flat. Lowest tone is a'. Conoidal bore. Boxwood, varnished yellow-brown; ivory mouthpiece and conoidal finger-guides. Made in three parts: a cap with mouthpiece, head joint with a fipple, flue, and lip, and body-joint. Seven finger-holes in the front, thumb-hole in the rear. Four round brass keys: D-sharp, F-natural, G-sharp, and B-flat. Stamped 'T. Prowse, Hanway Street, London,' and 'New Patent.' Length, 47.5 cm. Diameter, max., 3.6 cm. Bore, max., 15 mm.; min., 12 mm.; length of conoidal part, 27 cm. Lip distance, 33.3 cm. (17.1840)
Plate I

Described in the Royal Military Exhibition *Catalogue* on p. 17, under no. 29. Although the disposition of holes is that of the recorder, the resemblance is only superficial. The basic scale of this instrument is in D-major, and therefore it is a vertical flute. The lowest hole is for the nominal c'-sharp. The F-sharp hole (the third from the bottom) is enlarged.[142] The thumb-hole is used for overblowing. The lowest tone (nominally c'-sharp) sounds a' at 440 cycles per second; the tone c' (not actually on the instrument) would sound a'-flat; hence the tonality of this flute.

55. VERTICAL PICCOLO FLUTE England, early 19th century

Piccolo Flageolet. In C. The lowest tone is c^3-sharp. Conoidal bore. Rosewood, stained dark mahogany-brown; ivory tips and mouthpiece. Made in three parts similarly to No. 54, with an inner mouthpiece. Seven finger-holes in front; the eighth, a thumb-hole, is stopped by a small cup-shaped silver key. The F-sharp hole (third from the bottom) is enlarged, the seventh hole is reduced in diameter by the ivory plug. Small silver pins between the holes serve as finger-guides. The instrument was used for teaching birds to sing. Length, 23 cm. Diameter, max., 2.5 cm. Bore, max., 8.5 mm.; min., 5.5 mm.; length of conoidal part, 12.8 cm. Lip distance, 13.9 cm. (17.1813)
Plate I

This tiny instrument could be appropriately called a 'piccolino,' since it stands an octave higher than the orchestral piccolo flute. Its fundamental scale is that of D-major and the compass covers one octave and a sixth. The small key serves a double purpose: it is the octave key and also sharpens all tones of the lower octave a semitone without cross-fingering. Bainbridge patented a key in 1807 which produced a similar effect.[143] The instrument is described in the Royal Military Exhibition *Catalogue* on p. 16 under no. 26.

The Recorder Family

THE recorder, the *flûte douce* of the French,[144] the *Blockflöte* of the Germans, the *flauto* of the Italians, is historically one of the most important wind instruments. The recorder family is becoming once more a living entity, welcomed back by many serious enthusiasts. The acoustic properties of recorders have already been described (p. 62f.); their history will now be discussed.

The first complete description of the recorder family with pictures, diagrams of the right- and left-handed methods of playing, and fingering charts, was given in the *Musica getutscht* (1511) by Sebastian Virdung.[145] The recorder family, it can be safely conjectured, developed in the second half of the fifteenth century, or possibly earlier. Virdung's recorder family consisted of the descant recorder in G (*g′*); the tenor recorder in C (*c′*); and the bass recorder in F (*f?*).

The bass recorder of Virdung had a key for the lowest hole, the lever of which had two touch-pieces so that either the right- or left-handed player could be accommodated. The key mechanism was enclosed in a protective perforated guard sleeve called the fontanelle.[146]

Martin Agricola does not add anything essential to our knowledge, since in many parts his book was a versified transcription of Virdung's *Musica getutscht*; many illustrations were borrowed from Virdung. Nor does Luscinius give much help.

Zacconi in *Prattica di Musica*[147] gives the compass of his *flauti* (recorders) as canto, *g* to *f″*; tenore, *c* to *a′*; basso, *F* to *b*.

The notation of parts for the canto and the tenore is an octave too low.[148] The terminology of Zacconi is the same as that of Virdung and Agricola and differs from that of Praetorius. Praetorius, of course, supplies excellent information about the status of the recorder family, which is represented on table ix of *Theatrum Instrumentorum* (reproduced here as Fig. 12, on the opposite page). The recorder family of 1619 is tabulated below.

The Recorder Family of Praetorius (1619)

No.	Name	Tonality and Pitch		Lip Distance (cm.)
		Basic*	Alternative	
1	Klein Flöttlin	A(a″)	G(g″)	17.8
2	Cant	D(d″)	E(e″)	23.8
3	Cant	C(c″)	....	26.2
4	Alt	A(a′)	G(g′)	37
5	Tenor	D(d′)	C(c′)	55
6	Basset	G(g)	F(f)	88
7	Bass	C	B-flat	131
8	Gross-Bass	G	F	182

* The basic tonality of recorders is given by Praetorius on page 34 of *De Organographia*. The tonality is referred to that of the cornett which is in A (the lowest tone is *a*); hence the tonality and pitch of the *Klein Flöttlin*, which is two octaves higher than the cornett.[149] Both the basic and alternative tonalities were given by Praetorius in *Tabella Universalis*, p. 21 of *De Organographia*.

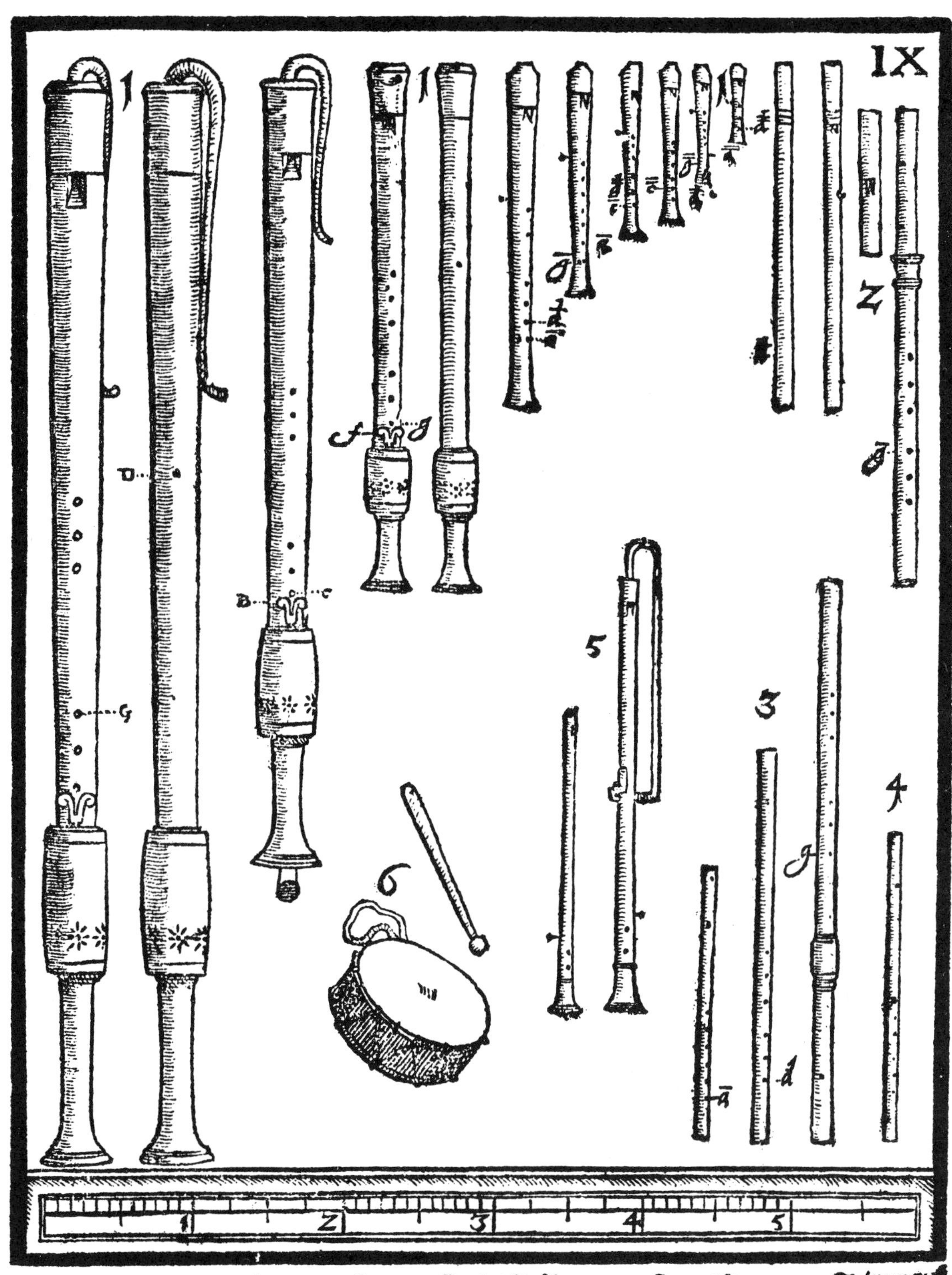

1. Blockflöiten/ ganz Stimwerck. 2. Dolzflöit d g. 3. Querflöiten/ ganz Stimwerck
4. Schweizer Pfeiff. 5. Stamentien-Baß vnd Discant. 6. Klein Päuckin:
zu den Stamentien Pfeifflin zugebrauchen.

FIG. 12. PRAETORIUS, TABLE IX

1. Fipple-flutes, the whole family. 2. Vertical Flute, d'–g(?). 3. Transverse Flutes, the whole family. 4. Fife. 5. Bass Pipe and Treble Pipe. 6. Small Drum: used with a small Pipe.

There is one small instrument which is either overlooked or not quite correctly classified. It is the *Klein Flötlin mit vier Löchern* of Agricola[150] and the *gar Kleine Plockflötlein* of Praetorius. It is the small fipple-flute with three finger-holes in the front and a thumb-hole in the rear. Agricola's fingering table shows that it overblows the octave, the thumb-hole being partly covered for the overblown octave; so in this respect it is similar to the recorder family. Both Agricola and Praetorius treat it as a separate instrument, since the lowest tone was played with the open end hole partly covered by a finger; in this respect it was similar to the flageolet family.[151]

A tabulated history of the recorder family can be found in Dr. Curt Sachs' *Handbuch.*[152] The best and most exhaustive treatise on recorders is the book by Mr. Christopher Welch, *Six Lectures on the Recorder and other Flutes.*[153]

Canon Galpin kindly supplied the following information about the reproduction of the recorders Nos. 56, 57, 58, and 59.

As a large number of old specimens passed through my hands when I was helping Mrs. Crosby Brown to form her collection, I was able to take measurements of bore, etc., of some of the less common wind instruments. I also was in correspondence with the authorities of continental museums (which I knew personally) and found them willing to send me details of others. Having drawn out all to scale, I got one or other of the English wind-instrument-making firms to make the body of the instrument with the correct bore. Then I fitted the instrument up with the necessary finger-holes and brass keys, as shown in the work of Praetorius and Mersenne. From this you can see that they are not *facsimiles* of any particular specimen, but playable reproductions of the old types. I required them for practical use and many of them have been played at lectures in London and elsewhere, even the Great Bass Shawm (No. 132), which the late Sir Frederick Bridge of Westminster Abbey delighted in.

Specifically, Canon Galpin stated that Nos. 56 and 57 were made in London and finished by him; No. 58 is the "reproduction of a sixteenth century instrument in my present collection"; and No. 59 is a reproduction of the type found at Verona, Brussels, Berlin, Vienna. A letter from Canon Galpin, January 21, 1936.

56. TREBLE RECORDER — Reproduction

In G. Lowest tone g′. Conoidal bore, with slightly flaring bell. The tube is made of one piece of pearwood stained dark brown. Eight holes in front, the lowest one on the left stopped with wax; thumb-hole in the rear. Length, 45 cm. Diameter, at lip, 2.7 cm.; bell (outside), 3.5 cm. Bore, max., 21 mm.; min., 17 mm.; bell, 25 mm.; length of conoidal part, 32 cm. Lip distance, 39.5 cm. (17.1805)
Plate I

57. TENOR–ALTO RECORDER — Reproduction

In D. Lowest tone d′. Conoidal bore with a slightly flaring bell. The tube is made of pearwood, stained light brown. The holes as on No. 56. Length, 64 cm. Diameter, at lip, 3.5 cm.; bell (outside), 4.3 cm. Bore, max., 25 mm.; min., 19 mm.; bell, 32 mm.; length of conoidal part, 48 cm. Lip distance, 57 cm. (17.1806)
Plate I

The 'Tenor-Alto' is a name derived from Praetorius. In his *Tabella Universalis*, p. 21 of *De Organographia*, Praetorius gives several recorder consorts in which the same instruments played different voices depending upon the combination in which they participated. For convenience in comparing those consorts they are tabulated below:

Consort No.	Names and numbers of Recorders from Table on p. 66					
	3 Cant	4(56) Alt	5(57) Tenor	6(58) Basset	7(59) Bass	8 Gross-Bass
1...........	Descant	Tenor-Alt	Bass	....	....	....
2...........	....	Descant	Tenor-Alt	Bass	....	....
3...........	....	....	Descant	Tenor-Alt	Bass	....
4...........	....	....	....	Descant	Tenor-Alt	Bass

This table follows Praetorius, but the numbers of the instruments are reversed. The numbers in the parentheses are those of the recorder in this Collection corresponding to those of Praetorius. Only consorts 2 and 3 could be formed from the recorders in our Collection.

58. BASSET RECORDER — Reproduction

In G. The lowest tone is *g*. Made of walnut stained dark reddish-brown. Conoidal bore without flare at the lower end. The tube is made of one piece. The fipple is covered with a cap having a slit which serves as an air conductor. A perforated fontanelle. The cap and the fontanelle are mounted with brass rings. Six finger-holes in front; the lowest (first) hole is stopped with an articulated key having a double finger-touch lever; the key mechanism is enclosed within the fontanelle; thumb-hole in the rear. Length, 92 cm. Diameter, at fontanelle, 6.5 cm. Bore, max., 34 mm.; min., 28 mm.; length of conoidal part, 82.2 cm. Lip distance, 82.2 cm. (17.1807)
Plate I

59. BASS RECORDER — Reproduction

In C. The lowest tone is *c*. Made of walnut, stained dark reddish-brown. The tube is made in two parts, the body and the foot-joint; the cap serves as a receptacle for the S-shaped crook. The perforated fontanelle is on the foot-joint. The cap and fontanelle are mounted with brass rings. Six finger-holes in the front: the lowest (first) hole is stopped with an articulated key having a double finger-touch lever; the key mechanism is enclosed within the fontanelle; an S-shaped crook of brass; thumb-hole in the rear. Length (to the top of the cap), 133.5 cm. Diameter at fontanelle, 9 cm. Bore, max., 45 mm.; min., 36 mm.; length of conoidal part, 128.8 cm. Lip distance, 128.8 cm. (17.1808)
Plate I

60. TREBLE RECORDER — England, late 18th century

In A. The lowest tone is *a'*. Conoidal bore. Walnut, stained dark mahogany reddish-brown. Made in three parts: the head, the body, and the foot-joint. Seven finger-holes in front, thumb-hole in the rear. Length, 37.5 cm. Diameter, max., 3.5 cm. Bore, max., 13 mm.; min., 8 mm.; length of conoidal part, 25 cm. Lip distance, 33.5 cm. (17.1738)
Plate I

61. TREBLE RECORDER Germany (?), 18th century

Flûte douce. In G. The lowest tone is g'. Conoidal bore. Beautifully turned and carved ivory. Made in three principal parts, as is No. 60, but each part is made of several pieces skilfully joined by screw threads. The mouthpiece is in the form of a fish's head; the head is beautifully carved with a foliated design; the foot-joint is finely carved, with a scalloped rim. Seven finger-holes in front, thumb-hole in the rear. Length, 43.5 cm. Diameter, max., 4.2 cm. Bore, max., 16 mm.; min., 10 mm.; length of conoidal part, 28 cm. Lip distance, 37.3 cm. (17.1809)
Plate I

Described in the Royal Military Exhibition *Catalogue* on p. 7 under no. 2.

62. TENOR RECORDER England, ca. 1800

In D. The lowest tone is d'. Conoidal bore. Pearwood, varnished blackish-brown. Made in three parts. Seven finger-holes in front, thumb-hole in the rear. On the bottom is scratched 'Neave, Maker.' Length, 61.5 cm. Diameter, max., 5 cm. Bore, max., 21 mm.; min., 14 mm.; length of conoidal part, 41.7 cm. Lip distance, 53.5 cm. (17.1804)
Plate I

Flageolets

63. FLAGEOLET France, 19th century

In A; low chamber pitch (a'= 420). Small tapered conoidal bore with a slight flare at the bottom. Ebony, with ivory tips and mouthpiece. Made in two parts. Four finger-holes in front, two thumb-holes in the rear. Stamped 'Tibouvile, Frère.' Length, 19.8 cm. Diameter, max., 2.3 cm. Bore, max., 9 mm.; min., 7.5 mm.; length of conoidal part, 12.3 cm. End bore, bottom diameter, 9 mm.; flare length, 2 cm. Lip distance, 16 cm. (17.1819)
Plate I

The tonality of flageolets given in the technical descriptions is acoustical and not musical tonality. See Note 93 for particulars.

64. FLAGEOLET France, 19th century

In G; low chamber pitch (a' = 420). Small tapered conoidal bore with a slight flare at the bottom. Boxwood, wax finish; made in two parts. Four finger-holes in front, two thumb-holes in the rear. Length, 20.6 cm. Diameter, max., 2.5 cm. Bore, max., 12 mm.; min., 9.5 mm.; length of conoidal part, 12.1 cm. End bore, bottom diameter, 13 mm.; flare length, 15 mm. Lip distance, 17.1 cm. (17.1817)
Plate I

The basic instrument of the flageolet family.

65. FLAGEOLET England, 19th century

One key. In G; low chamber pitch (a' = 420). Small tapered conoidal bore with a slight flare at the bottom. Boxwood, painted dark reddish-brown. Made in two parts. Four finger-holes in front, two thumb-holes in the rear. D-sharp square brass key mounted on knobs. Length, 22.3 cm. Diameter, max., 3.2 cm. Bore, max., 11 mm.; min., 8.5 mm.; length of conoidal part, 12.6 cm. End bore, bottom diameter, 13 mm.; flare length, 1 cm. Lip distance, 16.8 cm. (17.1841)
Plate I

66. FLAGEOLET Paris, France, second half of 19th century

One key. In D; low chamber pitch (a′ = 420). Small tapered conoidal bore, slightly chamfered at the bottom. Rosewood, stained dark reddish-brown. Ivory tips and mouthpiece. Made in two parts. Four finger-holes in front, two thumb-holes in the rear. D-sharp key of silver, round and mounted on knobs. Stamped 'Thibouville, Père (?) & Fils, à Paris.' Length, 26.5 cm. Diameter, max., 3 cm. Bore, max., 11 mm.; min., 10 mm.; length of conoidal part, 16.5 cm. Lip distance, 22.4 cm. (17.1818)
Plate I

67. FLAGEOLET Paris, France, late 19th century

In G; low chamber pitch (a′ = 420). Seven German-silver keys. Small taper conoidal bore with a slight flare at the bottom. Ebony, German-silver tips, ivory mouthpiece. Made in four parts: the mouthpiece pipe, the air chamber joint, the lip joint, and the body joint containing the finger-holes. Four finger-holes in front, two thumb-holes in the rear. The keys are D-sharp, F-sharp, G-sharp, B-flat, C-natural, high E-flat, and two shake keys with long levers for a semi-tone and one tone shakes for all the tones, including the cross-fingerings. Stamped 'Gautrot Aine, A Paris, Brevete' with a lyre over it. Length, 39.3 cm. Diameter, max., 12 mm.; min., 10 mm.; length of conoidal part, 12 cm. End bore, bottom diameter, 13 mm.; flare length, 1.5 cm. Lip distance, 16.8 cm. (17.1820)
Plate I

This is the modern keyed flageolet. The newest instruments use the Boehm system of keys and their tonality is either in D-flat or in C.

Pipes

68. PICCO PIPE London, England, late 19th century

Picco's Tibia.[154] Very slightly tapered conoidal bore with rounded flare at the bottom. Boxwood, wax finish. Two finger-holes in front, one thumb-hole in the rear. Stamped 'London' and 'D' and 'O' at the thumb-hole, 'A' and '1' at the top front finger-hole, and 'G' and '2' at the lower finger-hole. Length, 9.5 cm. Diameter, max., 2.2 cm. Bore, max., 11.5 mm.; min., 10.75 mm.; length of conoidal part, 5.6 cm. End bore, flare diameter, 16 mm.; flare length, 4 mm. Lip distance, 6 cm. (17.1810)
Plate I

Described in the Royal Military Exhibition *Catalogue* on p. 13, under no. 20. This pipe with all its finger-holes stopped and the end opening completely closed gives a nominal tone c'' which sounds g^3. The actual sounds produced by the gradual opening of the end hole are from g^3 to c^4 continuously; that is, the chromatic tones from g^3 to c^4 are possible. From c^4 to f^4 inclusive the diatonic scale is fingered; g^4 is played either with all finger-holes open or as the third partial tone of the tube. The pedal tone and three tones based on it can be fingered; but they are almost beyond the limit of audibility, and the slightest increase of air pressure makes the pipe speak the second partial tone. Canon Galpin in his *Old English Instruments of Music* called this instrument 'Picco Pipe, or Little Recorder.'[155] Technically the name of recorder cannot be applied to this little instrument; it is a real pipe in the sense of this word as defined on p. 64 under the Pipe Family.

69. CHÛRULA — France, late 19th century

Basque pipe. In D-flat. The lowest tone is *d''*-flat. Very slightly tapered conoidal bore. Boxwood, unvarnished. Two large finger-holes in front, thumb-hole in the rear. The tube is cut out at the finger-holes to provide a better grip. The lip is faced with a thin piece of tin. Length, 31.8 cm. Diameter, max., 2.4 cm. Bore, max., 10.25 mm.; min., 9.5 mm.; length of conoidal part, 28.5 cm. Lip distance, 28.5 cm. Finger-holes, diameter, 8 mm. (17.1814)
Plate I

The *chûrula* is played with the string drum, the *tambourin à cordes*, or the *toontoona*,[156] described in this section under No. 72. The player holds the pipe in his left hand, stopping the two holes in the front with his index and middle fingers, supporting the pipe on the under side with his ring finger, and stopping the hole in the rear with his thumb. The overblowing is done by smart tonguing and by directing the breath at different angles against the palate. The earliest fingering table of the instrument can be found in Mersenne's *Harmonie universelle*, book v, p. 231.

70. TABOR PIPE — England, late 19th century

In B-flat. The lowest tone is *b'*-flat. Very slightly tapered conoidal bore. Boxwood, unvarnished. Two large finger-holes in front, thumb-hole in the rear. Length, 37 cm. Diameter, max., 2.6 cm. Bore, max., 11 mm.; min., 10 mm.; length of conoidal part, 33.2 cm. Lip distance, 33.2 cm. (17.1811)
Plate I

The 'pipe and tabor' are inseparable in practical usage. For a description of the tabor see No. 18 on p. 31. The pipe and tabor are represented in *Cantigas de Santa Maria*,[157] and were known as *Flautilla y Tamboril*. The combination is popular in France (Provençal), England, the Netherlands, and Spain. Shakespeare requires the pipe and tabor in *The Tempest*.[158] At the present time they are used in Morris dances.

71. BASS TABOR PIPE — Reproduction

Bass Schwegel, *Stamentienbass*. In C. The lowest tone is *d''* (the second partial tone of the natural scale; the pedal tone is not available). Slightly tapered conoidal bore. Pearwood, unvarnished. Made in two parts: the body and the cap. Two holes in front and thumb-hole in the rear. The bell has slightly flaring bore at the end. A brass crook with a horn mouthpiece. Length, without crook, 64 cm. Diameter, max., 2.9 cm. Bore, max., 14 mm.; min., 12 mm.; length of conoidal part, 55.7 cm. End bore, diameter, 21 mm.; flare length, 7.5 cm. Lip distance, 55.7 cm. (17.1812)
Plate I

This instrument is built on the pattern of the instrument represented on table ix, fig. 5, of Praetorius, *Theatrum Instrumentorum*, reproduced here on p. 67. Praetorius' instrument had a lip distance of 63.5 cm.; this should be compared with the lip distance of 67.2 cm. derived from the drawing of the *Stamentien-Pfeiff* no. 1022 of the Brussels Collection.[159] In Praetorius' time the family of tabor pipes had three members: the descant, with its lowest tone *d''* (actual), the tenor (*g'*), and the bass (*c'*).

72. TAMBOURIN À CORDES France, second half of 19th century

String drum. Irregular oblong sound-box hollowed out of a solid block of maple forming the body of the instrument; light walnut sound-board. Six gut strings, fixed to the projecting block at the bottom, pass over the saddle-block (nailed to the sound-board), over the upper bridge with U-shaped wire staples, over the top saddle-block to the six boxwood tuning pegs inserted in the top and protected by two horn-shaped guards. The sound-board is decorated with two hexafoils and conventionalized plant pattern and perforated by many small holes; the decorations are made lighter in color than the rest of the sound-board. Stained light greenish-brown and varnished. Linen covered stick attached by a gut string. Length, 91 cm. Width, 17 cm. Ribs, height, 7 cm. Vibrating length of strings, 68 cm. (17.1781 a & b)
Plate I

This instrument is also known as the *tambourin du Béarn*, *tamburina*, and *tountouna*.[160] In playing it is held on the left side in a vertical position with the left elbow pressing it against the body. The sound is produced by a linen-covered stick held in the right hand. Since this drum is always played with the *chûrula* (No. 69), the strings are tuned alternately to the tonic and the dominant (the second and the third partial tones) of that pipe. Assuming the tonality of the pipe in C, the tuning of the string drum would be:

Multiple Flutes

73. DVOJNICE Croatia, 19th century

Double vertical flute. Made out of a solid block of holly-oak. Two slightly divergent cylindrical bores. The tubes, separated about half-way down by a hole cut through the stock, have a thin connecting rib left at the bottom. Three finger-holes in the left-hand pipe and four finger-holes in the right-hand pipe. Rough burnt-in decorations; the connecting rib has a circular hole. The top end has a wide mouthpiece and two fipples. Length, 31.3 cm. Width, top, 3.5 cm.; bottom, 5 cm. Thickness, 1.7 cm. Bore, diameter, 13 mm. Lip distance, 27.6 cm. (17.1826)
Plate I

Double flutes were known in pre-Christian times in ancient Greece and those countries under Greek cultural influence. This instrument is indigenous among the Southern Slavs. The melody is played on the right-hand pipe, which has four finger-holes; the second voice plays mostly in thirds; in certain combinations the third (differential) tone is heard. Additional information can be found in the catalogue of the Brussels Collection.[161] Acoustically, the *dvojnice* No. 73 gives pedal tones and second and third partial tones, as does the pipe.

74. DOUBLE VERTICAL FLUTE London, England, early 19th century

Double flageolet. In C and in E. Elliptical solid block of wood with broad mouthpiece and two parallel conoidal bores; maple, varnished dark yellow-brown. Seven double finger-holes in front, double thumb-hole in the rear. Stamped with the three plumes of the Prince of Wales, 'F. Lehner,' and the monogram 'F.L.' Length, 31.5 cm. Width, top, 3.7 cm.; bottom, 3.2 cm. Thickness, average, 2.3 cm. Bore, max., 13 mm.; min., 8 mm. Lip distance, left-hand, 28 cm.; right-hand, 25.3 cm. (17.1821)
Plate I

75. DOUBLE VERTICAL FLUTE — London, England, ca. 1830

Double flageolet. In A-flat and in G-flat. Conoidal bore. Boxwood, stained black; ivory tips and mouthpiece. Made in four principal parts; the cap, which serves as an air-chamber for both tubes; the lip-stock with a double bore; two tubes of unequal length. The lip-stock has two lips cut in it; each lip can be silenced by a cut-off shutter operated by a key. The shorter tube has for its lowest tone a′-flat; six finger-holes, of which the first one from the top is partially plugged; four silver keys nominally called C-sharp (open), D-sharp, F-natural, and high D-natural (the last three closed). The longer tube has g′-flat for its lowest tone; four finger-holes; five keys, nominally called low B and C keys, F, high B, and C, of which two low keys are open and operated by long articulated levers. Stamped 'Simpson, 266 Regent Street, Oxford Street, London, Patent.' Length, 53.5 cm. Diameter, max., 6.6 cm. Short tube: bore, max., 16 mm.; min., 10.5 mm.; length of conoidal part, 26.2 cm.; lip distance, 33.6 cm. Long tube: bore, max., 16 mm.; min., 10 mm.; length of conoidal part, 32.2 cm.; lip distance, 39.3 cm. (17.1822)
Plate I

This instrument is described in the Royal Military Exhibition *Catalogue* on p. 20, under no. 37. The actual tones produced by the tubes, with all keys and finger-holes closed, at 440 cycles per second, are as given in the technical description.

The term 'double vertical flute' is given preference instead of the traditional name 'flageolet' because the acoustical properties of the tubes and the disposition of the finger-holes are those of the vertical flute and not of the flageolet. There is no reason why a confusing terminology should be perpetuated. The cut-off shutter which controls access of air into the flues of the pipes is also called the 'wind-cutter.'

76. DOUBLE VERTICAL FLUTE — London, England, ca. 1830

Double flageolet. In A-flat. The lowest tone is a′-flat. Conoidal bores. Boxwood, varnished light yellow; ivory tips and mouthpiece. Constructed similarly to No. 75, but both tubes are of equal length. The left-hand tube (corresponds to the shorter tube of No. 75) has six finger-holes and the same keys, the latter of brass. The right-hand tube has four finger-holes and a vent-hole opposite the C-sharp key. There are four brass keys on the right-hand tube: low C-sharp, F, B, and high C. Stamped 'Simpson, 260 Regent Street, Oxford Street, London, Patent.' Length, 47.5 cm. Diameter, max., 6.5 cm. Bore, max. (both tubes), 15 mm.; min., 10 mm.; length of conoidal part, 26.5 cm. Lip distance, 33.5 cm. (17.1823)
Plate I

77. TRIPLE VERTICAL FLUTE — London, England, 1830

'Trio flageolet.' In A-flat and in G-flat. Conoidal bores. Boxwood, stained light yellow; ivory tips and mouthpiece; silver keys. The fundamental instrument is constructed similarly to No. 75. The third tube is attached to the air-chamber cap by a short nipple, the same mouthpiece serving all three tubes. The lip-stock has two lips with wind-cutters and also two keys for the shorter tube stamped 'New C Key,' 'New D Key' (nominal high C and D keys). The shorter tube (left-hand) has six finger-holes and the following keys: low C-sharp, D-sharp, F-natural, high D (the duplicate of one on the lip-stock), and high E. The lower end bore of the longer tube is covered by a cap with a vent hole. It has four finger-holes and five keys: low B-natural (open), D, F-natural, high B-natural, and high C, the last four keys being closed. The third side-tube is made in three parts: a lip-stock with an auxiliary air-chamber, fipple, and wind-cutter; a receptacle tube plugged

with cork at the bottom; a long decorative extension tail-piece screwed into the ivory tip of the receptacle tube at the lower end. There is only one open finger-hole on the receptacle tube marked 'F-natural'; four silver keys, a', b', c'', d''. The instrument is stamped 'Bainbridge, Inventor, 35 Holborn Hill, London, New Patent.' The keys have a silversmith's mark of 1830 and the initials 'WB' in a rectangle (not identifiable). Length, 57.2 cm. Width, 11.5 cm. Thickness, 6.5 cm. Short (left-hand) tube, bore, max., 14 mm.; min., 11 mm.; length of conoidal part, 26.8 cm.; lip distance, 33.4 cm. Long (right-hand) tube, bore, max., 15 mm.; min., 11 mm.; length of conoidal part, 27.5 mm.; lip distance (to centre of vent hole), 38 cm. Side-tube, bore, max., 27 mm.; min., 22 mm.; effective length of receptacle, 18 cm. (17.1824)
Plate I

An unusual and very rare instrument. Very few triple vertical flutes were made. Their inventor was W. Bainbridge, a specialist in multiple flutes. The third tube works on the same acoustical principle as the ocarina. It is a receptacle and not a tube; the keys work in the reverse order: those for the higher tones are located further away from the lip. A similar instrument is described in the Royal Military Exhibition *Catalogue* on p. 21, under no. 41.

Whistles

78. BIRD-WHISTLE — Switzerland

In the shape of a bird. Made of pine with eyes, wings, and feathers burnt into the wood; marked 'Interlaken.' One finger-hole. Length, 15 cm. Diameter, 3.6 cm. (17.1831)
Plate I

79. BOATSWAIN'S PIPE — England, 19th century

Boatswain's whistle. German silver. Consists of a small spherical receptacle with a circular opening at the top, thin curved pipe, reinforcing plate, and rib; a copper ring to attach it to a cord. The pitch is indefinite, as it depends upon the strength of the blower. Length, 11.3 cm. Diameter of the ball, 19 mm. (17.1830)
Plate I

A small shrill whistle used by the boatswain and his mates to call ('pipe') sailors to their various duties; used also as a salute for ranking officers and important visitors on a ship. Good piping is an art.

80. MILITARY WHISTLE — London, England, 19th century

German-silver tube with mouthpiece, lip, and three finger-holes with raised circular sockets; circular cap with knurled rim and a cord ring. The lowest tone is b'-flat (all finger-holes stopped). Stamped 'Rudall Rose Carte & Co., 20 Charing Cross, London.' Length, 12 cm. Diameter, 19 mm. (17.1833)
Plate I

81. DOUBLE WHISTLE — England, 18th century

Made of ivory with two parallel tubes. Length, 4.8 cm. Width, 2.3 cm. Thickness, 1 cm. (17.1834)
Plate I

82. OCARINA — Budrio, Italy, after 1860, by G. Donati

Sopranino in G. The lowest tone is g″. Brown earthenware, painted black, with traces of gilt ornament. Brass mouthpiece. Tuning cork with wooden button. Eight finger-holes in front, two thumb-holes in the rear. Two gilt labels (not legible, but similar to those of No. 83). Length, 14.2 cm. Diameter, max., 4.5 cm. (17.1835)
Plate I

83. OCARINA — Budrio, Italy, after 1860

Bass in G. The lowest tone is g. Brown earthenware, painted black. Seven finger-holes in front, one thumb-hole in the rear. Two gilt labels. One with maker's name 'G. Donati, Budrio, Bologna.' Length, 37 cm. Diameter, max., 11 cm. (17.1836)
Plate I

84. OCARINA — England, 1912

Sopranino in E-flat. The lowest tone is e″-flat. In the shape of a fish; of pottery, gilded. Eight holes in front, one thumb-hole in the rear. Registration mark of Staffordshire. Length, 17.5 cm. Width, 6 cm. Thickness, 4.4 cm. (17.1837)
Plate I

85. PITCH PIPE — England, ca. 1860

Rectangular pipe with mouthpiece, fipple, and lip; long slider with graduated lead scale inlaid in the groove. Pipe body of mahogany, slider of pine. Intended for a′ = 452′. Pipe: length, 36 cm.; width, 3.2 cm.; thickness, 3.7 cm.; lip distance, 31.5 cm. Slider, length, 35.5 cm. (17.1816)
Plate I

86. FOOL'S FLUTE — Reproduction

Jester's flute. Unvarnished maple. Made in three parts: the head has mouthpiece, a hollow spherical chamber with two perforated conical nozzles (one is lost), and a body with dummy bore and finger-holes. Length, 40.5 cm. Diameter, max., 6.2 cm. (17.1865)
Plate I

This simulacrum of a musical instrument was used in the eighteenth century in France for playing practical jokes. The hollow ball was filled with flour; the unwary but eager spectator who would ask to 'play' it, would have his face covered with the flour forced through the nozzles by his breath.

SECTION B: REED-VIBRATED AEROPHONES

Reed-vibrated aerophones have the vibrations of the air-column generated by the 'reed,' made of reed, cane, or a thin lamina of bone, metal, or some other elastic material. The reeds of European musical instruments are divided into three principal groups: single beating reeds, double beating reeds, and free reeds. Reed-vibrated aerophones, depending upon the type of reed used, are divided respectively into single-reed, double-reed, and free-reed aerophones. Further subdivision is made according to the mode of control exercised by the player over the reed. There are reed-vibrated aerophones with the reed covered by a cap, so that the reed is controlled indirectly. On others the player takes the reed in his mouth and exercises a complete tonal and dynamic control. This essential difference in the mode of reed control is recognized in the general classification by the introduction of two sub-sections: (a) *Reeds controlled indirectly*, and (b) *Reeds controlled directly*. Finally, the acoustical properties of reed-vibrated aerophones differ according to the shape of the bore of their tubes. Those with cylindrical tubes act as stopped pipes and the first overblown tone of their natural scale is a twelfth, or they 'overblow a twelfth'; those with conical tubes act as open pipes and 'overblow an octave.'[162]

Single-reed aerophones. Single-reed aerophones consist essentially of a tube and a single-reed 'mouthpiece.' A 'mouthpiece' is a technical term not necessarily implying that it is actually taken by the player in the mouth: on aerophones with indirectly controlled covered reeds, the reed cannot be taken into the mouth, since it is completely enclosed in the cap. Therefore, in the specific technical sense, a 'mouthpiece' is the generator of vibrations. In this particular instance the single reed is the vibration generating agent. The simplest type of the single reed is the straw-reed, Fig. 13. It is made of a portion of a reed with one end closed[163] and the integral tongue sliced off its side. The first cut is taken at an angle of 45° and the reed is cut to the depth of about one quarter of its diameter; then the knife is flattened and the rest of the cut is made more or less parallel to the centre line of the reed. Straw reeds are used on hornpipes, pibgorns, and bagpipe drones.

The clarinet mouthpiece, Fig. 14, is more elaborate. It consists of (1) the mouthpiece proper, (2) a separate single reed, and, (3) a ligature affixing the reed to the mouthpiece.

The clarinet mouthpiece is so shaped that the bore is cut into a curving chamber with an opening on the side. The important surface, on the side to which the reed is fixed, is the 'facing.' From AB to CD the facing is flat. This portion is sometimes referred to as the 'table.' From the line CD up to the tip the facing is curved. This curved portion is called the 'lay.' The contact of the reed with the facing ceases at the line CD where the table ends and the lay begins; between the lay and the inner flat surface of the reed there is, therefore, a clearance permitting the reed to flex toward the lay. The elastic resistance of the reed bent toward the lay provides the return force reacting against the pressure of the stream of air impinging upon it in playing. The size of clearance is measured by the width of the 'tip opening.' The shape of the curve of the lay, the size of the tip opening, and the length of the lay have an important influence upon the tone. The longer lay facilitates emission and improves the quality of the lower register, but the upper register becomes somewhat thin; the shorter lay makes the lower tones less rich, but improves the quality of the upper register. Selection of the proper shape and length of the lay, the size of the tip opening, etc., is made to suit the instrument and the individual player. With so many variable factors involved, it is a delicate operation.

The clarinet (saxophone) reed is made from the *Arundo donax*, a reed plant which grows wild on the shores of the Mediterranean. The inner surface of the reed is perfectly flat. The upper part of the outer surface is bevelled off to a very thin edge, slightly curved at the top to conform with the curve of the tip of the mouthpiece. In action the single reed beats (vibrates) against the facing and interrupts what otherwise would be a continuous stream of air. These interruptions create intermittent impulses setting the air column inside the tube in vibration. The number of beats is proportional to the pitch of the tone produced; control of the quality of tone, dynamics, and pitch is exercised by a delicate lip action which governs the stiffness of the reed; for overblowing, the air pressure is increased and the vibrating length of the reed is decreased by the lip adjustment. On the clarinet dynamic control of tone is

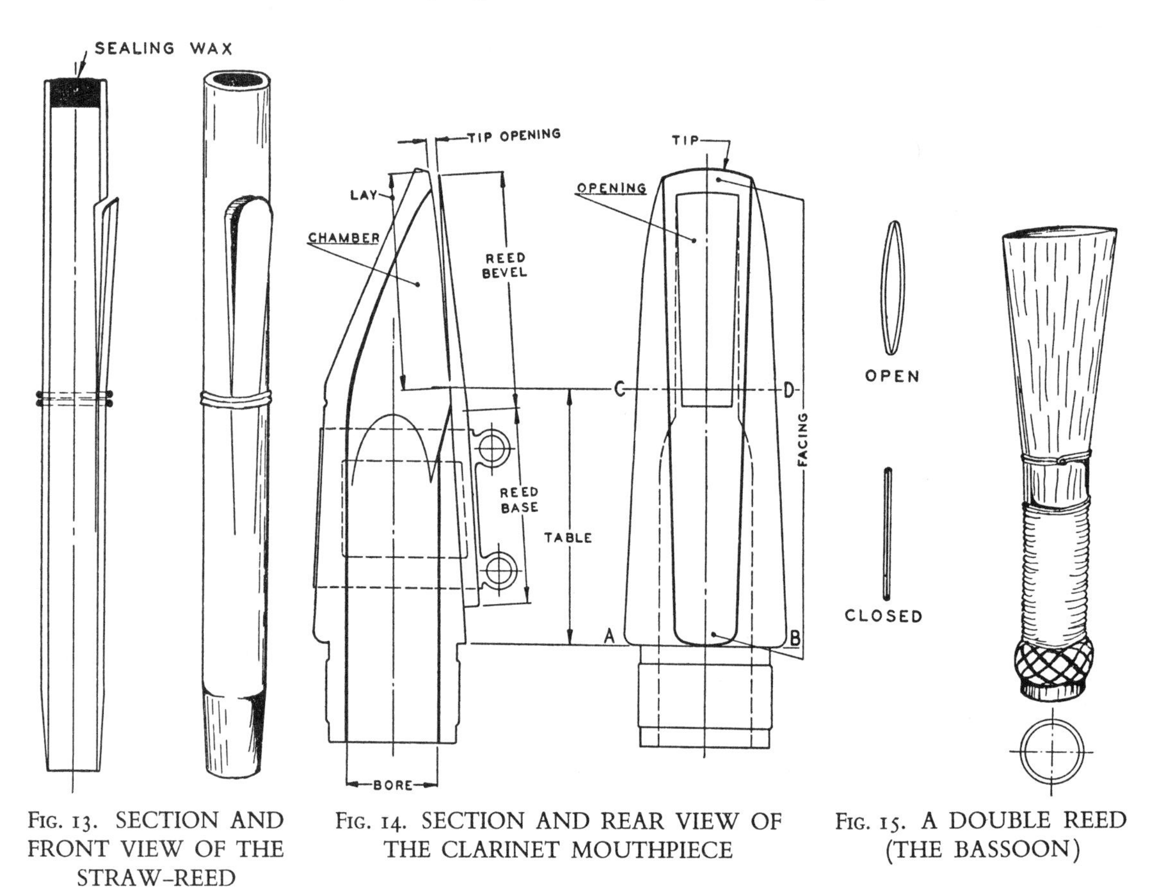

Fig. 13. SECTION AND FRONT VIEW OF THE STRAW-REED

Fig. 14. SECTION AND REAR VIEW OF THE CLARINET MOUTHPIECE

Fig. 15. A DOUBLE REED (THE BASSOON)

possible from the gentlest pianissimo almost beyond the limit of audibility, up to a limit which the reed can stand and still produce a tone of acceptable quality.

Double-reed aerophones. Double-reed aerophones consist essentially of a tube and a double reed. The double reeds are made of two blades of reed or two laminae of some elastic material, and are so shaped that they form at the top a narrow ( ) -shaped slit; at the lower end the reeds are formed into a circular-shaped tube which is connected to the main tube of the instrument.[164] The action of the double reed is also of the beating type, but both laminae beat against one another so that the slit alternately closes up and opens; this alternate action interrupts the continuous stream of air. These interruptions create, as with the single reed, intermittent impulses setting the air-column inside the tube in vibration. The directly controlled double reeds, such as those used on orchestral instruments, permit complete control of tone and expression. The French school of oboe and bassoon playing developed its technique to the limit of its possibilities. Oboists and bassoonists trained in that school are considered the finest. Double-reed instruments, especially of the smaller size like the oboe, are very difficult to play, since very little air can pass through the narrow slit between the reeds. The oboe player's problem in breath control is to change the stale air in the lungs quickly enough. The pressure of air necessary for playing double-reed instruments is considerable and fatigues the player. Yet the tone color of the orchestral double-reed instruments is so individual and interesting that they are indispensable members of the ensemble.

Free reeds. This type of reed is not of importance in the art of music. It is used almost exclusively on popular instruments: mouth harmonicas and accordeons; harmoniums, and many unusual types such as the melophone, No. 223. The free reed consists essentially of a thin rectangular tongue of metal affixed to a slotted frame. The size of the opening in the frame is slightly larger than the size of the tongue, so that it can vibrate without any constraint except for the elastic resistance of its own body. The free reed can be actuated by the positive air pressure and also by the vacuum created by suction. Mouth harmonicas have reeds of both types.

SUB-SECTION A: REEDS CONTROLLED INDIRECTLY

Aerophones with indirectly controlled reeds ('covered reeds') are important from an historical standpoint. Many instruments of this type have been used in Europe in the past. At present the bagpipes are still in use.

The reeds on such instruments are enclosed either in a rigid cap forming an air-chamber of a fixed volume, or in a bag providing a distensible air-chamber. Anyone can produce tones by inflating the air-chamber and raising the air pressure until the reed begins to 'speak.' Expressive playing and tone control are not possible. Dynamic control is possible only to a limited extent.

Group 1: Single Beating Reed Aerophones

Sub-group i: With Cylindrical Tube

87. SINGLE HORNPIPE — Greece, 19th century

Reed tube with five equally spaced finger-holes and a bell made of the tip of a cow's horn, in which a hole is cut for the insertion of the tube. The top of the tube has a round washer, which is inserted in a gourd forming the air-chamber (the gourd is lost). Single beating straw reed. Length (including reed), 25.5 cm. Tube, inside diameter (approx.), 7 mm.; length, 14 cm. (17.1887)
Plate I

88. DOUBLE HORNPIPE — Greece (?)

Instrument similar to No. 87, but with two parallel tubes, two horn bells, two reeds. The tubes are inserted in a circular piece of wood which is fitted into the air-chamber (lost). Length (including reeds), 25 cm. Tubes, inside diameter (approx.), 8 mm.; length, 12.5 cm. (17.1888)
Plate I

This instrument came from England with a tag identifying it as a Greek double hornpipe. It is possible that it is really a part of the *souqqarah* (*Zuqqara*), an Arabian bagpipe. Cf. V. C. Mahillon, *Catalogue . . . de Bruxelles*, i, p. 412; also C. Sachs, *Real-Lexikon*, p. 434 a.

89. PIBGORN Wales, 19th century

Cylindrical tube of walnut with six equally-spaced finger-holes in the front, a thumb-hole in the rear. The air-chamber is at the top. The bell has two lips of unequal length with serrated edges, both made of horn. Small single beating straw reed. Length, 44 cm. Tube, outside diameter, 17 mm.; bore (approx.), 8 mm.; length, 20.5 cm. (17.1884)
Plate I

The rigid air-chamber on this instrument has no mouthpiece; the large circular opening at the top is pressed around the lips and the thin edge forms an effective air-seal. The tone is very pleasant. Additional information can be found in *Six Lectures on the Recorder and other Flutes*,[165] by C. Welch.

90. STOCK AND HORN Scotland, 19th century

Double bore. Ebony tube flattened in the front and partly flattened in the rear, embellished white bone tip and five inlaid bars and two diamond-shaped inlays; seven double finger-holes in the front, two thumb-holes in the rear. Cow-horn bell and wooden cap with mouthpiece. Two single beating straw reeds covered by the cap. Length, 57 cm. Tube, outside diameter, max., 2 cm.; diameter of bores, 3.5 mm.; length, 27.7 cm. Bell, diameter, 6 cm. (17.1885)
Plate I

Cf. C. Welch's *Six Lectures on the Recorder and other Flutes*, p. 17, note.

Sub-group ii: With Conoidal Tube

91. SIGNAL HORN Argentina, 19th century

Made of cow's horn, with the tip faced off to provide a clearance in the form of a cavity similar to a clarinet mouthpiece. The reed is of very thin bone, tied by a silk thread. The mouthpiece cap is lost. Length, 31 cm. Diameter, max., 7.2 cm. (18.2257)
Plate III

Group 2: Double Beating Reed Aerophones

Sub-group i: With Cylindrical Tube

DOUBLE beating reed instruments with a cylindrical bore in their tubes and with covered or uncovered reeds are not used in modern orchestras. The acoustical properties of cylindrical tubes with double reeds are similar to those with single reeds. The tubes act as stopped pipes and the first overblown tone of their natural scale is a twelfth, the same as that of the clarinet family. For some reason this type was not very successful. This was not due to a lack of diligence. There were several families of instruments, such as the cromornes, the racketts ('the sausage bassoons'), the sourdines.[166] The most probable reasons for lack of success were the mechanical difficulties with the narrow bores of some of the instruments, i.e., the racketts and sourdines, and the complexity of the key mechanism required to span such a long interval as a twelfth. These instruments disappeared before the clarinet was developed, so the knowledge gained in the construction of the instruments of the clarinet family was not available to their makers.[167] No attempts, to the writer's knowledge, have been made to develop cylindrical tube instruments with the double reed, applying to them a modern mechanism.

The Cromorne Family. Cromornes were in general use in Europe from the fourteenth to the seventeenth century.[168] They are represented in works of art, the most conspicuous example being, perhaps, the series of woodcuts by Hans Burgkmair. They are represented in Virdung's *Musica getutscht*, in Martin Agricola, and in Praetorius' *Theatrum Instrumentorum*, table xiii (reproduced here on p. 82, fig. 16). The bore of the cromorne is cylindrical, of large diameter, with a short conical flare at the open end. The double reed of the bagpipe type (with a long shank) is covered with a cap; at the top of the cap (on a smaller-sized instrument) is a mouthpiece with a narrow slit for the air; on larger-sized instruments the mouthpiece is inserted in the side of the cap as seen in Praetorius' table xiii. The cromorne family in the early seventeenth century consisted of five members:

1. Small descant — *c′ — d″*
2. Descant — *g — a′*
3. Tenor-alto — *c — d′*
4. Chorist bass — *C — g*
5. Great bass cromorne — (a) *BB♭ — c*; (b) *AA — d*

Cromornes No. 4 and No. 5 had compass extension keys.

The cromorne family is represented in this Collection by two instruments, Nos. 92 and 93.

92. TREBLE CROMORNE — Italy, early 17th century

Soprano in A. J-shaped tube of maple, covered with black leather. Reed cap (not original) with mouthpiece. Brass staple (or crook) for holding the double reed. Bore is cylindrical except at the end, where it flares slightly. Eight finger-holes (one of which is stopped with wax) and one vent-hole in the front, a thumb-hole in the rear. Length, 52 cm. Diameter of tube, outside, 2.2 cm. Bore, 7.5 mm. Length of air column (with reed), 60 cm. Flare, diameter at the end, 1.5 cm. (17.1891)
Plate III

93. ALTO CROMORNE — 17th century type. Reproduction

In D. J-shaped tube of maple. Reed cap with mouthpiece. Brass staple for reed. Brass tips. Bore and holes as on No. 92. Length, 62 cm. Diameter of tube, outside, 1.8 cm. Bore, approximate diameter, 6 mm. Length of air column (with reed), 75 cm. Flare, diameter at the end, 1.5 cm. (17.1892)
Plate III

Sub-group ii: With Conoidal Tube

THE double reed in conjunction with a conoidal tube proved itself a more vital type than the preceding one. The conoidal tubes overblow the octave; the covered reeds permit the overblowing[169] if the pressure is sufficiently high and a vent-hole is provided on the tube

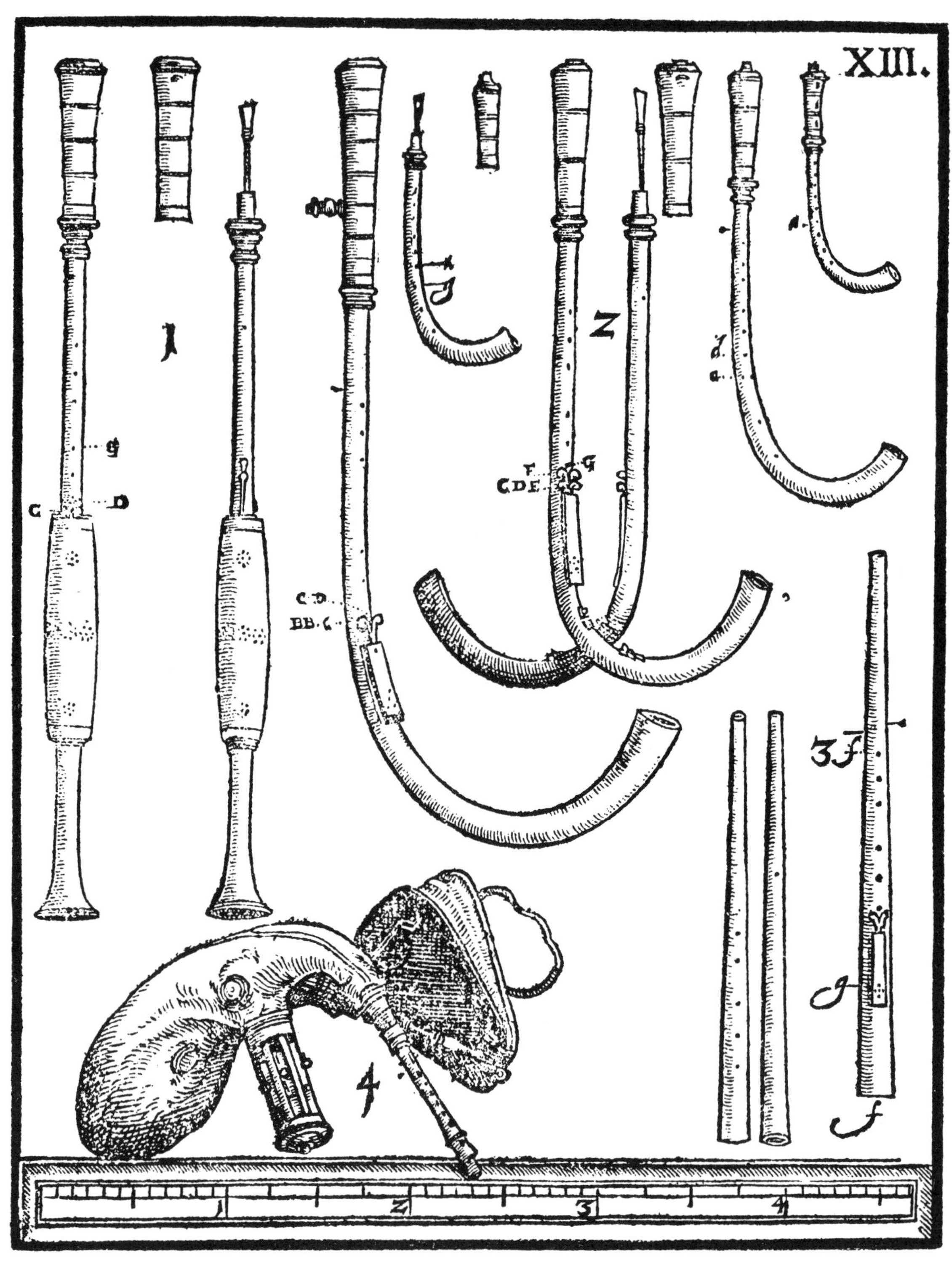

1. Baſſett: Nicolo. 2. Krumbhörner. 3. Cornetti muti: ſtille Zincken.
4. Sackpfeiff mit dem Blaßbalg.

Fig. 16. PRAETORIUS, TABLE XIII

1. Basset: *Nicolo*. 2. Cromornes. 3. Mute Cornetts: silent Zinks. 4. Bagpipe with bellows. (The bourdon cylinder is of the same type as one on the musette No. 102.)

for this purpose; the only limitation is the upward compass extension, which is less than on the instruments with uncovered reed and depends entirely upon the number of the finger-holes. Thus on the oboes with covered reeds and seven finger-holes the overblown tones add only a sixth; on the eight-hole chanter of the Uilleann bagpipe, a seventh is added by overblowing.

94. PRACTICE CHANTER — Ireland, 18th century. Repaired ca. 1881

Made of ivory, with engraved silver mounting. Conoidal bore. The tube and the reed cap are of composite construction. Seven finger-holes in the front, a thumb-hold in the rear, two vent-holes on both sides. The silver band just above the bell is marked with 'J.C.' (Jas. Crichton?) in a rectangle and the London silversmiths' mark of 1881–82. Length, total, 45.5 cm. Diameter, max., 3.5 cm. Bore, min., 4.5 mm.; max., approx., 13 mm.; length of conoidal part, 32 cm. Length of air column (with reed), 40 cm. (17.1915)
Plate IV

95. HAUTBOIS DE POITOU — France, late 18th century

In D. Boxwood, wax finish, with ivory tips. The reed cap is not original. The tube is made in three parts: the upper and middle body joints and the bell. The instrument is finely moulded. Six finger-holes in the front, two of which (the third and the fourth) are double; a thumb-hole in the rear. Three square brass keys mounted on knobs: C, D-sharp, and long C-sharp key actuated by the little finger of the left hand. Two vent-holes on the bell. Length, total, 58.7 cm. Diameter, max. (bell), 5.7 cm. Bore, min., 5 mm.; max., 15.5 mm.; length of conoidal part, 41.4 cm. Length of air column (with reed), 53 cm. (17.1917)
Plate IV

Mersenne in the *Harmonie universelle*[170] gives a whole family of these oboes with the covered reed. The family consisted of the descant ('dessus') in D(*d'*), the tenor ('taille') in in G(*g*), bass ('Basse de Haut-bois de Poictou') in F(?); the last instrument is represented on p. 306 of the *Harmonie universelle*, bent in two like a bassoon, with the open key operated, it seems, by the thumb, thus extending the compass down to E(?).

96. HAUTBOIS DE POITOU — France, 19th century

In G. Keyless. Maple, stained light brown. The tube is made in two parts: the body joint and the bell; the reed cap with mouthpiece. Six finger-holes in front and one hole that is not stopped by a finger; a thumb-hole in the rear; two vent-holes on the bell. Length, total, 39.5 cm. Diameter, max. (bell), 5.2 cm. Bore, min., 5.5 mm.; max., 10 mm.; length of conoidal part, 25 cm. Length of air column (with reed), 35.2 cm. (17.1916)
Plate IV

97. FOGHORN — Shetland Islands

Conical tube of sheet steel with hemispherical bell and mouthcap covering a double reed of brass. Painted red. Length, 45 cm. Diameter, bell, 14 cm. (17.1929)

Group 3: Polyphonic Reed Instruments

This group of directly controlled aerophones with covered reeds enclosed in a distensible air-chamber is limited to bagpipes. Bagpipes are divided into two specific sub-groups: (i) the bagpipe inflated by a player's lung-power, and (ii) the bagpipe inflated by bellows operated by a player's arm. Further subdivisions are based on specific details such as (1) the kind if pipes (drone, chanter, regulator), (2) the number of each kind of pipes, (3) the type of drones (the pipes or the cylinder with slides as on the musette, No. 102), (4) the kind of reeds (single or double), (5) the type of bore (cylindrical or conoidal), (6) the type of pipe (open or closed), (7) the number of finger-holes and keys (if any), (8) the scale and peculiarities of playing technique.

The history of the bagpipe is one of the most controversial subjects in musicology and is rivalled in this respect only by that of the Irish harp. It is accordingly suggested that this subject be studied in standard works.[171]

Sub-group i: Bagpipes Inflated through a Blow-Pipe

The simplest bagpipe of this sub-group consists essentially of three principal elements: (1) a blow-pipe, (2) a bag, and (3) sounding pipes. The simplest instrument, actually, is the *Platerspiel*, which consists of a blow-pipe, a bag made out of a bladder, and a sounding pipe or chanter with finger-holes. Sometimes this instrument is identified with the cromorne.[172]

The typical bagpipe has as the possible minimum two sounding pipes of different kinds, the drone and the chanter. The blow-pipe is taken in the player's mouth and serves to conduct the air into the bag. At its inner end is attached a leather flap valve which prevents the air from passing back. This allows the player to take a breath, and also permits him to increase the pressure of the air in the bag by squeezing the latter with the arm, thus exercising a certain amount of dynamic control over the reeds. The bag is made of specially treated leather, pliable and water proof. To the bag are attached several 'stocks' — short cylindrical pieces of wood drilled through and counterbored so as to provide sockets for the insertion of the pipes from the outside and to protect the reeds inside the bag.

The drones are furnished with single beating reeds ('straw reeds'); each drone issues one continuous tone only. The chanter plays the melody.

In playing, the bag is taken under the arm (usually the left one) and inflated through the blow-pipe. The drones, depending upon their number and size, are variously disposed. The chanter is held in the front of the player in a slightly inclined vertical position. The finger-holes are not covered by the finger-tips, as is usual on other wind instruments, but are stopped by the fingers, which are kept in the most conveniently natural way with respect to the finger-holes.

The music of the bagpipes, especially that of the Scotch Highland bagpipe, affects the emotions strongly. It is passionately loved by many and disliked just as intensely by others. The perpetual pedal of the drones induces a philosophical calm in lovers of the bagpipe and completely unnerves the haters. Paradoxically, the chanters in this dialectical entity, so prosaically called the bagpipe, supply the excitement of change. Perhaps this strident antithetic juxtaposition of such contrasting elements may provide a clue to the violent emotional reactions to bagpipe music.

98. BINIOU — Brittany, 19th century

Breton bagpipe. Chanter and one drone. Leather bag covered with black velvet. Three stocks. The blow-pipe of ebony is tipped with ivory and inlaid with tin ornamentation. The drone of ebony is in three parts with flaring bell, tipped with brass rings and also inlaid with tin; cylindrical bore. The chanter of ebony; conoidal bore; seven finger-holes in the front, the lowest located to the left for the left little finger; two vent-holes on the sides. Length (bag and drone), 72 cm. Drone, bore, 7 mm.; length (without reed), 41 cm. Chanter, bore, min., 4 mm.; max., 15 mm.; length of conoidal part, 14 cm. (17.1934)

This instrument is a typical bagpipe of the simplest construction. For further details, see Dr. C. Sachs' *Real-Lexikon*, p. 47 a, s.v. 'Biniou.'

99. CORNEMUSE — France, ca. 1750

Chanter and one drone, both with cylindrical bore. Leather bag covered with brocaded silk, gilt braid, and fringe. Two stocks of ivory. Ivory blow-pipe with a leather flap which serves as a stop-valve for air. The ivory cap serves as an air-chamber for the chanter and has an auxiliary cap for the drone connected with it; both inserted in one stock. A chanter with bell, both of ivory, seven holes in the front (the lowest one consists of two small holes for half-stopping), a thumb-hole in the rear. The drone has a small decorative bell. The chanter cap is stamped 'P.G'; the bag is marked 'Gaillard.' Length (bag and chanter), 70 cm. Drone, bore, 4 mm.; length (without reed), 19 cm. Chanter, bore, 4 mm.; length (including reed), 28 cm. (17.1935)

A less typical instrument, with the drone in a subordinate position.

100. GREAT HIGHLAND BAGPIPE — Scotland, early 19th century

Piob Mor. Chanter and three drones. Black leather bag. Five stocks. The blow-pipe is of ebony with an ivory mouthpiece. The drones are of ebony, ivory tips, furnished with single reeds; the bells of the drones have a pear-shaped inside profile somewhat similar to that of the English horn; the bore is cylindrical, in two steps: the bell joints have increased bores (12.5 mm.). The chanter is of ebony with an ivory disc at the end; conoidal bore, double reed; seven finger-holes in the front, a thumb-hole in the rear, two vent-holes on the sides. Length (bag and long drone), 102 cm. Short drones, bore, 9 mm.; length (without reed), 35.5 cm. Long drone, bore, 10 mm.; length (without reed), 64 cm. Chanter, bore, min., 4 mm.; max., 20 mm.; length (without reed), 36.5 cm. (17.1931)

The great Highland bagpipe is more than merely a musical instrument: it is an embodied legendary epic. The *Piob Mor*, the great pipe, is the musical instrument of war, the inspirer of men in battle. In peace it is a great story-teller, condescending at times to play for amusement, but only to prove its versatility. To appreciate to a certain extent what the Highland bagpipe means to a Scotsman one must read with sympathy such a book as Sir Alexander Duncan Fraser's *Some Reminiscences and the Bagpipe*. One can then understand that to some people certain musical instruments are much more than a skilfully fashioned colligation of various materials.

The most interesting and typical part of the Highland bagpipe is the chanter and its scale. Dr. Alexander J. Ellis found that the scale of a correctly constructed Scotch chanter is identical with that of the Arabian and Persian, the *zalzal*.[173] It starts on g′ and goes up to a″, but not by the intervals of our tempered scale; in round numbers of cents the following comparative tabulation may be found useful:

H. S.*	g′		a′		b′		c″		d″		e″		f″		g″		a″
Cents		200		200		150		150		200		150		150		200	
E. T.*	g′		a′		b′		c″		d″		e″		f″		g″		a″
Cents		200		200		100		200		200		100		200		200	

*H. S. = the Highland scale. E. T. = the equal tempered scale. The intervals between *b′* and *d″*, and *e″* and *g″*, both of which are equal to 300 cents, are divided on the Scotch Highland chanter into two equal intervals of 150 cents. Therefore, the tone *c″* of the chanter is one quarter of a tone flatter than *c″*-sharp of the equal tempered scale; the same is true of the intervals between *e″* and *g″* with respect to the chanter's *f″*. For the real values of intervals, see the references given in Note 173.

The drones are tuned an octave apart in the key of A-major: the large drone to *A* and the small drones to *a* in tune with the *a′* of the chanter. The tunes are written in the keys of G (one sharp), D (two sharps), and A (three sharps). Modulations are possible without introducing a complicated mechanism.

101. ZAMPOGNA — Italy, early 19th century

Calabrian bagpipe. Two plain drones and two drones with finger-holes inserted in one large stock. The blow-pipe is attached to the second stock. The bores of all the pipes are conical. Two plain drones, short and long, made of walnut in two parts. Right-hand drone (short) of walnut made in two parts: the body-joint has five finger-holes in the front and two vent-holes on the sides and the bell has an additional vent-hole, the bell opening being narrower, as on the English horn; the body and the bell are held together by a rough screw thread. Left-hand drone (long) is also made in two principal parts, but the body-joint is made of three tubes permanently fastened together by broad iron rings; three finger-holes in the front, one key the mechanism of which is covered by a fontanelle with perforations; the bell has four vent-holes, a constricted bell opening as on the left-hand drone; the body and the bell are joined by a screw thread. Length (bag and long left-hand drone), 235 cm. Short drone, bore, 5(12) mm.; length (without reed), 28.5 cm. Long drone, bore, 7(18) mm.; length, 59 cm. Left-hand drone, length, total, 75 cm.; bore, min., 7 mm.; max., 15 mm.; length of conoidal part, 58.5 cm. Right-hand drone, length, total, 127 cm.; bore, min., 7 mm.; max., 18 mm.; length of conoidal part, 96 cm. (17.1937)

The *zampogna* is a bagpipe which has no chanter. All four pipes are drone pipes, two of which are plain and two have finger-holes. The size of the fingered pipes is such (58.5 and 96 centimeters) that they cannot be considered chanters. The *zampogna* serves as an accompaniment instrument for the *piffero*, a small keyless oboe, played by another player.[174]

Sub-group ii: Bagpipes Inflated by Bellows

The principal difficulty in playing the lung-inflated bagpipe is not so much the amount of air required, but rather the considerable pressure necessary for proper operation of the reeds. Only people with strong lungs can bring the air pressure in the bagpipe to the proper level; the physical exertion is very fatiguing. Bellows were attached to the bag for an obvious reason. After the bag is inflated and the pressure brought to a desired point, which is done very quickly with properly constructed bellows, the physical labor involved in maintaining the air supply at the necessary pressure is surprisingly small. The air pressure can be increased for overblowing very easily by accelerating the pumping of the air and by squeezing the bag with the arm.

102. MUSETTE — France, ca. 1750

Two chanters and six drones. Leather bag covered with blue velvet and silver braid. Three stocks; one of which has attached to it the bourdon cylinder, and extends 12.5 cm. into the bag, forming a protective cap for the drone reeds. The bag is inflated by bellows. Two chanters are attached to one stock; the smaller chanter is fixed on the larger. The bourdon consists of a rosewood cylinder in which are drilled sixteen cylindrical bores connected into six independent systems forming the tubes of the drones. The pitch of the drones is regulated by seven sliders of ivory (*layettes*) fitted into swallowtail grooves, the bottoms of which are covered with leather. The ivory sliders have steel shoes that are pressed against the leather bottom of the grooves by steel springs, thus insuring an airtight fit. The drones are fitted with double reeds. The large chanter (*le grand chalumeau*) has an open cylindrical bore with a flaring bell, seven finger-holes in the front, one of which (the lowest) is double as on No. 99 for half-stopping, and a thumb-hole in the rear; two vent-holes on the bell; no keys. The small chanter (*le petit chalumeau*) consists of a small closed tube with six silver keys; it is attached so that it is parallel to the large chanter. Both chanters are made of ebony and both are fitted with double reeds. The stocks, the bourdon, and the chanters are tipped with ivory; the whole instrument is of excellent workmanship. Bellows. Length (bag and chanter), 72 cm. Bourdon, length of cylinder, 17.6 cm.; length of longest drone (approx.), 95 cm.; length of the shortest drone, 12 cm.; bore, longest drone, 5 mm.; shortest drone, 3 mm. Large chanter, bore, 4 mm.; length (without reed), 29 cm. Small chanter, bore, 3 mm.; depth of bore, 5.5 cm. (17.1936 a & b)

The French *musette* attracts attention by its "rustic Watteau-like grace."[175] The instruments are of exquisite workmanship, the bags and bellows covered with costly fabrics, the keys of solid gold or silver, the color schemes finely chosen. The *musette* owes all this to the unusual attention paid to it at certain periods of its history, when it became the instrument of fashion of French court ladies in the seventeenth and eighteenth centuries. The bellows-inflated bag could be workeu very easily even by ladies, and the clumsy drones were replaced by a small and compact cylinder. The whole appearance and design of the *musette* show that it was intended for people of refinement and breeding.[176]

As already mentioned in the technical description, the drone cylinder had sixteen bores interconnected into six systems of tubes of various lengths; the tubes had double reeds; therefore, except that the tubes had no finger-holes, the drone cylinder is built on the same

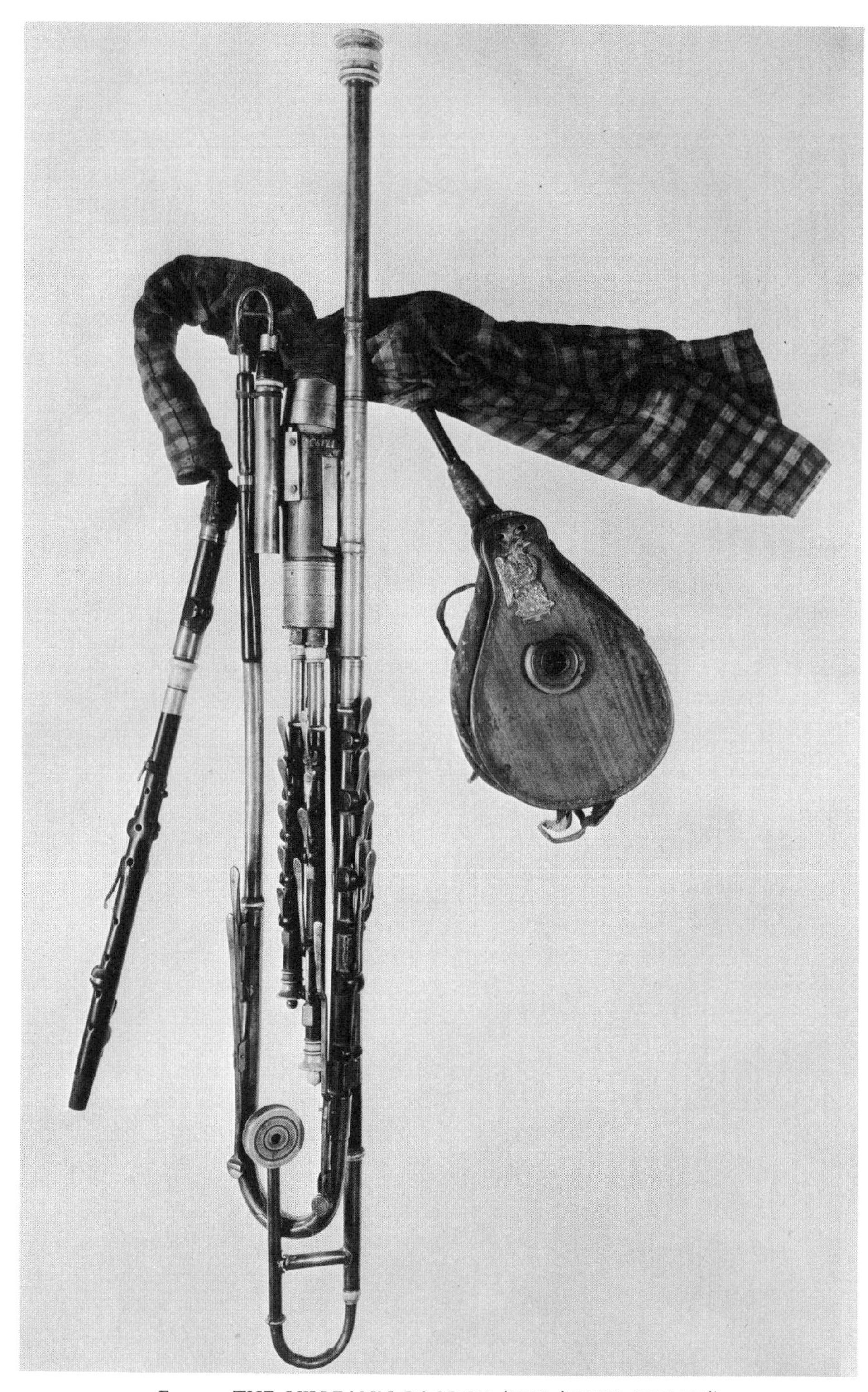

Fig. 17. THE UILLEANN BAGPIPE (THE 'IRISH ORGAN')

principle as the rackett or the 'sausage bassoon.' The pitch of each drone was regulated by sliders; on this *musette*, No. 102, two of the drones have two sliders and can be tuned in two tonalities. The tuning of the drones of this instrument is as follows:

Drones 4 and 6 could be tuned either in C or D. The large chanter has a compass from *f'* to *a''*; the small chanter extends the compass up to d^3. The *musette* is undoubtedly related to the Irish Uilleann bagpipe and appeared in the early seventeenth century. The small chanter was added about 1650 by M. Hotteterre.[177] The tone of the *musette* is pleasant; the construction of the drones and chanters is such that the usual sharpness of tone of the bagpipe is subdued and refined.

103. UILLEANN BAGPIPE — Ireland, early 19th century

Uilleann pipes. Union pipes. Irish bagpipe. Fig. 17, p. 88. Chanter, two drones, three regulators. Leather bag covered with plaid cotton. Three stocks. The bag is inflated by bellows embellished with a brass eagle marked with a figure '8.' Large stock, to which are attached drones and regulators, with a shut-off valve for drones. Short drone of ebony made in three parts with an elongated horn tip. Long drone of ebony in three parts: the reed-joint is folded twice, trumpet-wise; the middle joint almost completely enclosed in the brass tube, and the bell-joint of brass ending with a circular box of ivory with a vent-hole. Both drones are furnished with single beating reeds. Chanter of ebony, ivory tips; seven finger-holes in the front, one thumb-hole in the rear; seven square brass keys mounted on knobs. First treble regulator of ebony with ivory tips and closed end-cap into which is inserted the 'tuner,' a brass wire with an ivory ball; to this wire is fastened, inside the tube, a long piece of rush with the pulpy part uncovered; four brass keys (square) mounted on knobs. The lowest key has a long touch piece. Second treble regulator constructed similarly to the first one; five brass keys. Differential bass regulator of complicated construction; it is attached to the stock in two places and connected by passages with the air supply at both ends. The reed is fastened to a long separator, which is inserted in the tube in such a way as to divide the air column into two parts (see Fig. 19, B, p. 92). The differential regulator (Fig. 19, A) is essentially a U-shaped tube consisting of the following parts: a brass tube attached to the stock by a tapered slide-plate joint and containing a separator, in which is inserted a reed covered by a long brass tube cap with a large moulded ivory stopper; the body is of ebony with four brass keys; a U-shaped crook with three brass keys; a long tube with conoidal bore tapering toward the upper end. A small brass crook ('B') connects this tube to a cylindrical brass receptacle ('A') attached to the stock by a tapered slide-plate joint. Length (bag and regulator), approx., 110 cm. Drones, short, bore, 4.5 mm.; length, 27 cm.; long, bore, 7 mm.; length, 70.5 cm. Chanter, bore, min., 6 mm.; max., 12 mm.; length of conoidal part, 44.5 cm. Regulators, first treble, bore, min., 6 mm.; max., 11 mm.; length of conoidal part, 45.5 cm.; second treble, bore, min., 6 mm.; max., 10 mm.; length of conoidal part, 33 cm.; double-bass, bore, min. (at reed), 6 mm.; max., 14 mm.; length of conoid, 76.5 cm.; cylindrical part, bore, 19 mm.; length, 46 cm. (17.1930)
Fig. 17; Fig. 18; Fig. 19

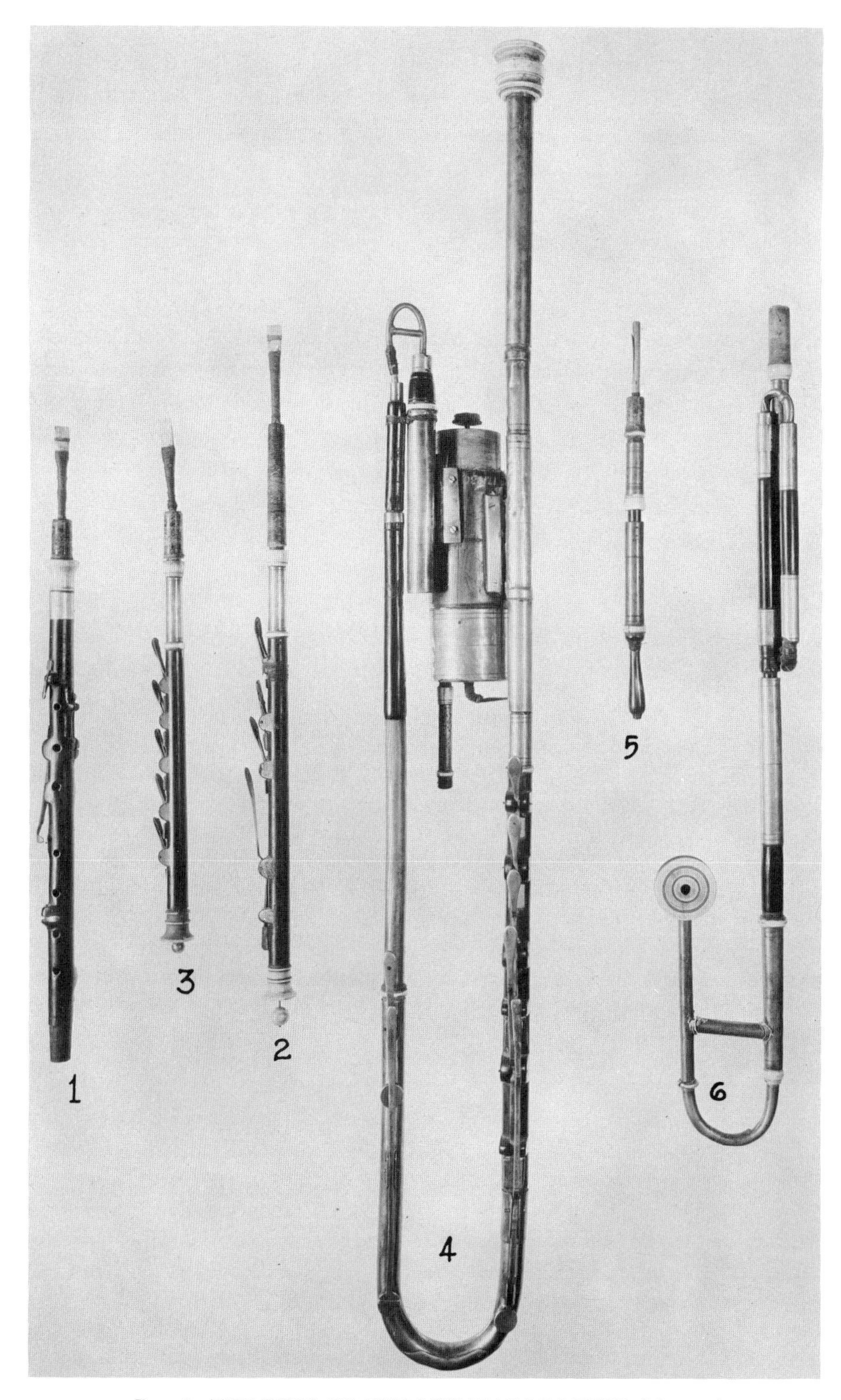

FIG. 18. THE PIPES OF THE UILLEANN BAGPIPE (NO. 103)
1. Chanter. 2. First treble regulator. 3. Second treble regulator.
4. Differential bass regulator. 5. Short drone. 6. Long drone.

The Uilleann ('elbow') bagpipe made its appearance about 1588 and therefore preceded the *musette*.[178] Its improved form dates from the beginning of the eighteenth century. The Irish bagpipe has three types of pipes: (1) the chromatic keyed chanter with conoidal bore and the double reed; (2) the cylindrical bore drones with straw reeds; and (3) the keyed regulators with stopped conoidal bore pipes and double reeds. Regulators are found only on the Irish Uilleann pipe. The full set of pipes is furnished, in addition to the chanter, with three drones and three regulators; sometimes a fourth (D-bass) regulator is added; the number of pipes is not standardized. The basic scale of the chanter is that of D-major and extends from *d'* to d^3-sharp; the second octave beginning with *e''* is overblown and high tones are produced with the thumb-hole 'pinched' as on the recorder.[179] The chanter playing technique of the Uilleann pipe differs from any other bagpipe in this particular; that the end opening of the chanter rests on the right knee and the pipe is played with the end opening 'stopped' for all the tones except lowest *d'*; for playing this tone the chanter is lifted off the knee. Since this operation is repeated many times during playing, the old pipers tied a piece of kid leather to their knee. Modern chanters have a special valve affixed to the lower end. The valve is kept open by a spring when the chanter is lifted off the knee and is easily closed when the chanter rests on it. The drones have no peculiarities, except, perhaps, their shape, and the fact that they can be silenced by the shut-off valve on the stock. The most distinctive feature of the Uilleann pipe is the regulators. No description of these interesting pipes exists in printed literature and there is a misapprehension of their true nature.[180] The essential technical point about the regulators is that they are stopped and filled with compressed air. To prevent them from speaking they are closed at the bottom and have no open keys. The regulators speak only when the keys are opened. The long pieces of rush tied to the wire passing through the end cap are intended for a fine adjustment of the pitch of the regulators. The pulling out lowers the pitch and pushing in raises the pitch; the rush also softens the tone.[181] The instrument of this Collection has a differential regulator of a somewhat unusual construction. It is represented in Fig. 18 (4) and Fig. 19. It has seven keys, combining in one tube the third and fourth regulators, which are made separate on some pipes.

Fig. 19 (B), representing a section of the separator, shows that the air enters into the circular clearance between the outer brass tube and the separator and surrounds the reed. On the other side the air enters first into a cylindrical receptacle A, goes through the small, narrow bore crook B, and fills the rest of the tube. Since the whole tube is air-tight, the air-pressure equalizes itself on both sides of the reed. When one of the keys is lifted, the air pressure in the tube under the reed is lowered; the small bore of the crook B creates a resistance and prevents the quick escape of the air from the bag. The lowering of pressure under the reed creates a flow of air through the reed and causes the reed to speak.[182] The closing of the key restores the equilibrium once more. On the short regulators no such elaborate arrangement is necessary, since the leakage of air through the reed is sufficient to restore immediately the equilibrium in their tubes. In a long, low-pitched tube this seepage of air would not be sufficiently quick and the reed would speak sluggishly.

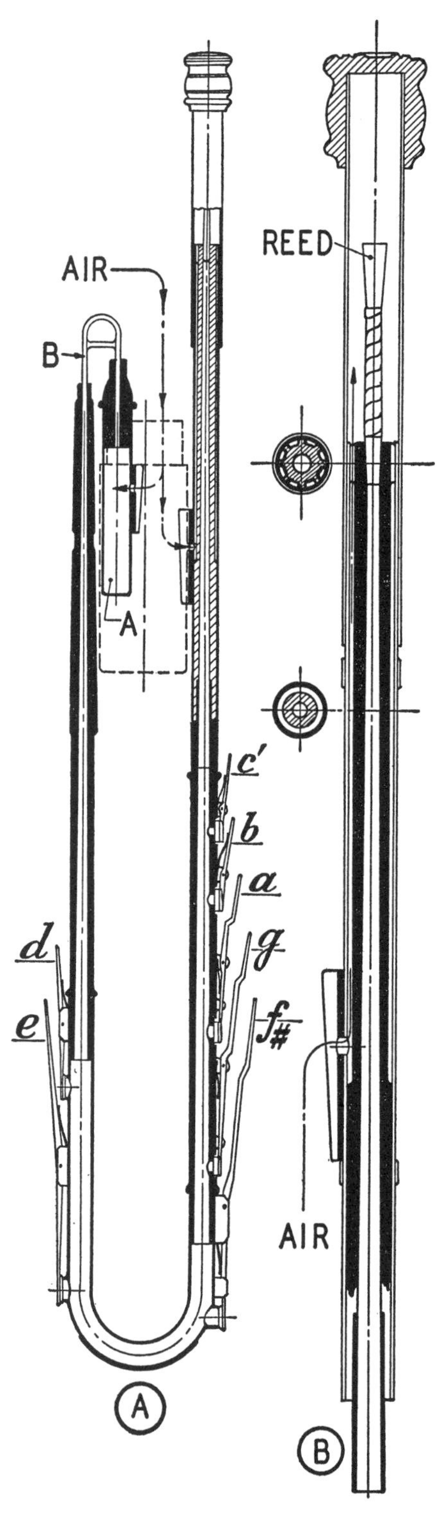

FIG. 19. SECTION OF THE DIFFERENTIAL BASS REGULATOR

A, Section with keys in the plane of projection.

B, Enlarged section of the separator with the reed.

The keys on the regulators give the following tones:

The short drone is tuned to *a'* of the chanter; the long drone is tuned to *A*, two octaves lower. The instrument is played with the player seated, the bag under his left arm, the bellows strapped to the body, and their movable part tied to the right arm near the elbow; hence the name *uilleann* or 'elbow' pipe. The drones and regulators are held across the right leg in an inclined position. The regulators are played in two ways. The old way was to press the keys with the wrist of the right arm. The key levers were made long and closely spaced to permit this, but at the best it was very difficult. The new method is to limit the melody to such tones only as can be stopped with the left hand alone. The right hand is taken off the chanter and the regulator keys are pressed by the fingers. This is a practical compromise; even then the Uilleann pipe is not easy to play.

104. LOWLAND BAGPIPE — Scotland, 19th century

Chanter and three drones. Leather bag covered with green woollen cloth, fringe on edges. Three stocks, silver tips. Drones of different lengths, conoidal bores of very small taper; silver and ivory tips. Chanter with cylindrical bore; seven finger-holes in the front, a thumb-hole in the rear. Bellows. Length (bag and chanter), 74 cm. Drones, short, bore, 4(3) mm.; length, min., 17.3 cm.; medium, bore, 4(3) mm.; length, min., 24 cm.; long, bore, 5(3) mm.; length, min., 34.3 cm. Chanter, bore, 3.5 mm.; length, 19.5 cm. All lengths of pipes are given without reeds. (17.1932 a & b)
Plate IV

The Lowland bagpipe is a smaller Highland pipe inflated by bellows. It is used mostly for dancing. As the name indicates, it is the instrument of the Scottish Lowlands. The drones are held either across the right arm or the right thigh, depending on whether the player stands or sits while playing. The scale of the chanter is the same as that of the Highland bagpipe. The sound of the Lowland bagpipe is less strident.

105. NORTHUMBRIAN BAGPIPE — England, 19th century

Chanter and four drones. Leather bag covered with dark blue velvet. Three stocks, silver tips. Drones of ivory richly embellished with silver tips and long joint tubes of silver; inverted conoidal bores with very small taper and stopped at the ends; single reeds. Chanter of ebony, cylindrical bore, stopped at the lower end; seven finger-holes in the front, a thumb-hole in the rear; seven silver keys mounted on knobs. The chanter is stamped 'C. (?) REID.' Length (bag and chanter), 84.6 cm. Drones, average bore, 3.5 mm.; effective lengths (with reeds), 1, 20 cm.; 2, 24 cm.; 3, 31 cm.; 4, 37 cm. Chanter, bore, 4 mm.; effective length (with reed), 29 cm. (17.1933 a & b)

The Northumbrian bagpipe is called also the 'Border pipe,' because Northumberland is a Border county. The chanter and the drones are stopped at the lower end, and their pitch is regulated by small adjustable stoppers drawn in and out by small silver balls attached to the stems of the stoppers. The 'effective length' means the actual length of the air column, not doubled.

Group 4: Free Reed

106. MOUTH HARMONICA Germany, early 20th century, by F. A. Boehm

Free reed mouth organ. Wedge-shaped oblong block of wood, containing set of free reeds giving 32 chromatic tones. Protected on both sides by segment-shaped metal shields; metal bell at larger end. Trade mark 'Trombona.' Length, 15 cm. Diameter, bell, 5.7 cm. (17.1741)

The only representative of the directly controlled free reed instruments in this Collection.

SUB-SECTION a: REEDS CONTROLLED DIRECTLY

Group 1: Single Beating Reed

Sub-group i: With Cylindrical Tube

The Clarinet Family

THE clarinet family has an important place in modern music. The soprano and bass clarinet are indispensable members of an orchestra. In modern military and 'symphonic' bands clarinets hold the same relative position as the strings in the orchestra. The tonal qualities of clarinets of different sizes, while preserving the family resemblance, possess strongly marked individual characteristics. The high-pitched clarinets are shrill and spicy; the middle register instruments are lyrical and elegiac; the low-pitched instruments are mysterious in pianissimo and dramatic in forte.

Certain idiosyncrasies of the clarinet will become more comprehensible after their construction and acoustical properties have been examined. The clarinet mouthpiece is described on p. 77 and p. 78, Fig. 14. The bore of the clarinet is nominally regarded as cylindrical; this is correct with respect to the middle part only.

Fig. 20 shows the exact shape of the bore of a clarinet (No. 114). From A to B the bore of the clarinet is an inverted conoid; from B to C it is cylindrical; from C to D it is an expanding conoid; from D to the bell opening it is a continuous curve.

The tube of the clarinet is usually made in four separate parts: 1, the barrel; 2, the top joint, or left-hand joint[183]; 3, the lower joint, or right-hand joint; 4, the bell. The old instruments were not standardized as to the number of joints. The number of finger-holes in the front is seven and there is a thumb-hole in the rear. The lowest finger-hole (producing the tone *g* when open) was stopped by the little finger of the right hand and had to be bored much higher than its proper position. To compensate for this, it was bored slanting downward toward the bell, made rather smaller and longer than usual. To make this possible the body had that bulbous enlargement in the lower part which is so marked a characteristic of the old type clarinet. On the newer clarinets, Iwan Mueller's open low F-key eliminated the necessity for this makeshift, and the G-hole was located in its proper place and made of proper size, while the number of the finger-holes in the front was reduced to six.

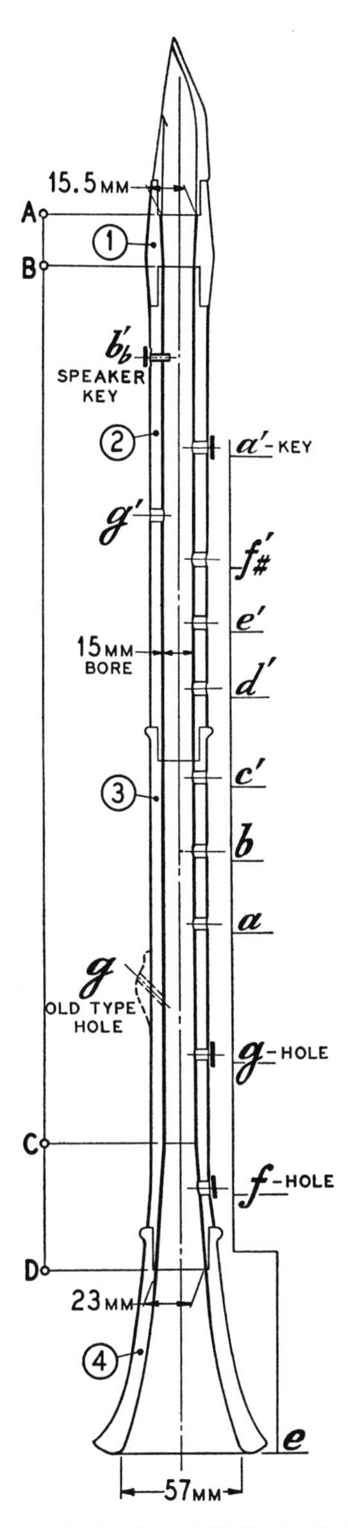

FIG. 20. SECTION OF THE CLARINET

The tube of the clarinet acts as a stopped pipe, that is, it sounds approximately one octave lower than the open pipe, or the conoidal tube (the oboe, saxophone) of the same length. The natural scale of the clarinet falls into the odd or 1, 3, 5, 7, series; the first overblown tone is a twelfth. This wide interval presents many problems both for the maker and the player of the clarinet: a greater number of keys complicates the mechanism; the odd partial tones complicate the fingering, since the similar tones of the next octave do not repeat the fingering of the lower octave.[184] The tone of the clarinet is not uniform in its coloring. There are several registers, each with a peculiar tone color. This difference is partly due to the peculiarities of the fingering. From the nominal *e* to *f'* the tones are reedy and dark in coloring; this register is called the *chalumeau* register.[185] From *g'* to *b'*-flat the rear thumb-hole has to be opened; these few tones form the intermediate or *throat* register and are the weakest and most uninteresting tones on the clarinet. The tones from *b'* up comprise the *clarino* or the *clarion* register[186] and sound bright and crystalline. Sometimes the clarino register is limited by c^3 and the tones beginning with the d^3 and upward form the fourth or high register.[187]

Overblowing on the clarinet is facilitated by the 'speaker' or the 'twelfth' key covering a small hole. Its history is treated in connection with various instruments representing the successive stages of clarinet evolution.

Before the modern key mechanism was developed, clarinets had to be built in many tonalities. Therefore the clarinet family had many members. Some of them are of historical interest only. The clarinets in actual use at present vary from time to time, but the general tendency is to increase the number of voices, especially in the lower register.

The modern clarinet family, reduced to a practical size,[188] consists of the following instruments:

Octave	1. Clarinet in A-flat	(*c'*)
Sopranino	2. Clarinet in G	(*b*)
	3. Clarinet in F	(*a*)
	4. Clarinet in E-flat	(*g*)
	5. Clarinet in D	(*f*-sharp)
Soprano	6. Clarinet in C	(*e*)
	7. Clarinet in B-flat	(*d*)
	8. Clarinet in A	(*c*-sharp)
Alto	9. *Clarinette d'amour* in G	(*B*)
	10. Basset horn in F	(*F*)
	11. Alto clarinet in E-flat	(G)
Baritone	12. Bass clarinet in B-flat	(*D*-flat)[189]
	13. Bass clarinet in A	(*C*)
Bass	14. Contrabasset horn in F	(*AA*)
	15. Contrabass clarinet in E-flat	(GG)
Contrabass	16. Contrabass clarinet in B-flat	(*DD*)[190]

107. CHALUMEAU Reconstruction, 18th-century type

Primitive form used in Europe. Walnut, stained brown. Cylindrical bore without bell. Eight finger-holes in the front, one of which is stopped with wax; a thumb-hole in the rear. Single reed attached to the mouthpiece by a thread. Length, 25 cm. Diameter, max., 2.9 cm. Bore, 13 mm. (17.1870)
Plate I

This is a reconstruction of the primitive instrument from which the clarinet is supposed to have been developed. No actual primitive chalumeau may be found in the European collections and the term itself is one of the mysteries of organology. In the past it designated a conoidal tube instrument with double reed, or a cylindrical tube instrument, either with double or single reed. In the eighteenth century the 'chalumeau' meant specifically an instrument with cylindrical bore and single reed. It is so described and pictured in the *Encyclopédie* of Diderot and d'Alembert (1767, s.v. 'Lutherie'). The reconstruction of our instrument follows the description of the *Encyclopédie*. The chalumeau produced a nominal scale from *f* to *g'*, the actual pitch depending upon the size of the tube; overblown tones were not used. The name of the low register of the clarinet came from this instrument.[191]

M. Mahillon describes a small clarinet (*Catalogue . . . de Bruxelles*, ii, p. 204, no. 906) the original of which is in the Bavarian National Museum in Munich; our instrument is similar in many respects to the Bavarian instrument, except that the latter has two keys.

108. CLARINET Reproduction, late 17th-century type

In C. Two keys. The earliest form with a *b'*-natural key. Tube of maple, stained brown. Cylindrical bore without bell. Made in three parts: long mouthpiece, body, and bell-joint. Seven finger-holes in the front, of which the lowest is double for half-stopping; a thumb-hole in the rear; two square brass keys for *a'* and *b'*. The reed is tied by a string. Length, 49.4 cm. Diameter, max., 4 cm. Bore, 13 mm. (17.1871)
Plate I

The early history of the clarinet is uncertain. Its invention is usually credited to Johann Christoph Denner (1655–1707), a famous wood-wind instrument maker of Nuremberg, Germany, about 1690. Yet this alleged fact is not so well established as some writers assert. The original of this instrument is in the Bavarian National Museum in Munich. It represents the first step in the evolution of the two-keyed clarinet. The holes stopped by two closed keys are located above the finger-holes, are of equal diameter and of normal size; both are placed directly opposite one another. The scale made by successive opening of the finger-holes and the keys is:

Several important points should be noticed: (1) the tone *f* is the 'bell' tone produced with all finger-holes closed; (2) the tone *f*-sharp is produced with one of the two small twin holes open;[192] (3) the tone *g* is produced with both small twin holes open; (4) the tone *a′* is produced with either one of the two keys open, since the holes covered by the keys are of the same diameter and, as just stated, are located opposite one another; (5) the tone *b′* is produced with both keys open.

Additional information is given in the *Catalogue . . . de Bruxelles* under no. 911, where M. Mahillon states that it overblows a twelfth.[193] It is possible to play overblown tones when either one of the two keys is open very slightly, but the front key is not so convenient to operate as the thumb key; the process is rather uncertain and difficult. A similar instrument is also represented in the Royal Military Exhibition *Catalogue* on plate iv, fig. b, and described in 'Errata.' The scale given in the R. M. E. *Catalogue* is not correct. The tone *b′*-flat is given as being produced by the second key. This cannot be done with any degree of certainty, since a full opening of the key produces the tone *a′* (see point (4) above) and a partial opening causes the instrument to overblow.

109. CLARINET — Reproduction, early 18th-century type

In C. Two keys. J. C. Denner type with a *b′*-flat speaker key. Walnut, oil finish. Made in three parts: mouthpiece with 'bulb,' body, and a bell-joint with a flaring bell. Seven finger-holes in the front, the lowest being on the bell-joint, and a thumb-hole in the rear; two square brass keys for a′ and b′-flat. The reed is tied by a string. Length, 59 cm. Diameter, max. (bell), 6.8 cm. Bore, 14 mm. Length of cylindrical part, 48 cm. (17.1872)
Plate I

The difficulty in overblowing a clarinet of primitive type (No. 108) led to the second stage in the two-keyed clarinet's evolution. The rear key-hole was made considerably smaller and located nearer to the mouthpiece. The scale of the clarinet with this improvement remained the same as that of No. 108, with these important exceptions: (1) when both the front key (No. 1 on the scale in the previous note) and the thumb-key were open, the tone produced was *b′*-flat and not *b′*-natural; (2) the thumb-key also served as the 'speaker' or the 'twelfth' key for overblowing of the tones beginning with *c″*, with satisfactory results; (3) the tone *b′*-natural could be produced only by cross-fingering. The exact time of this improvement, ascribed to Johann Denner, the son of J. C. Denner, is not known; possibly it was made before 1720. Several two-keyed clarinets of this type are in existence, belonging to the same early period and made by other makers.[194] The original of instrument No. 109 of this Collection is described in the *Catalogue . . . de Bruxelles* under no. 912.

The third and final step in the evolution of the fundamental clarinet was made about 1720(?) and is usually credited to Johann Denner. It consisted in lengthening the tube and adding a third, the open low E-key. This addition eliminated cross-fingering for the *b′*-natural tone; it could be overblown now from the low *e* with the same fingering as this last tone, except that the speaker-key would be open as on any overblown tone. A three-keyed clarinet is described in the *Catalogue . . . de Bruxelles* under no. 913.

Since there is some slight confusion as to the successive stages of the evolution of the clarinet, the following summary may be found useful.

1. *Prototype*. A primitive folk instrument, the *chalumeau*. Compass from *f* to *g′*; no overblown tones. No. 107.

2. *First Step*. Two keys are added, located above the finger-holes. The key-holes are of equal diameter, normal size, and are drilled opposite one another. Compass from *f* to c^3; the tones from *c″* and above are overblown by partly opening *either* of the two keys. The tone *b′*-flat is cross-fingered. No. 108.

3. *Second Step*. The thumb-key hole is made of small diameter and shifted closer to the mouthpiece, becoming (a) the speaker-key hole and (b) the tone hole for producing the tone *b′*-flat; the tone *b′*-natural now has to be cross-fingered. Compass from *f* to c^3. No. 109.

4. *Third Step*. The tube is lengthened and the low E-key is added; the tone *b′*-natural is overblown from the low *e*. Compass from *e* to c^3. The evolution of the fundamental clarinet was completed and further evolution consisted in improving the key mechanism. The only essential departure was made in Mozart's time, when basset horns and a few soprano clarinets were built with a compass extension down to nominal low C. Basset horns still retain this feature; but soprano clarinets with low C remained merely an experiment.

110. CLARINET — London, England, ca. 1800

In E-flat. Six keys. Boxwood, stained light yellow-brown. Ivory tips. Made in six parts: mouthpiece, barrel, three body-joints, and bell. Seven finger-holes in the front, a thumb-hole in the rear. Three square brass keys on the lower body-joint: e (open), f-sharp, and g-sharp; the two lowest keys have long levers operated by the left little finger. Three keys on the upper body-joint: a′, the a′-shake, and the speaker-key. Stamped 'Goulding & Company' on the body-joints and 'Goulding, 45 Pall Mall, London' on the bell. Length, 49 cm. Diameter, max. (bell), 6.3 cm. Bore, 12 mm. Length of cylindrical part, 41.5 cm. (17.1873)
Plate I

Further development of the clarinet consisted in the addition of more keys. The first chromatic keys, *f*-sharp and *g*-sharp, were added between 1760 and 1770 by Berthold Fritz of Brunswick, bringing the total number of keys to five. The sixth key, *c′*-sharp, was added by Xavier Lefebvre (Lefevre) in 1790. Although clarinet No. 110 has six keys, it is really a five-keyed instrument, since the *a′* shake-key is a duplicate. Described in the Royal Military Exhibition *Catalogue* on p. 114, under no. 232.

111. CLARINET — London, England, early 19th century

In C. Eight keys. Boxwood, stained light yellow-brown and spotted. Ivory tips. Made in five parts: mouthpiece, barrel, two body-joints, and bell. Seven finger-holes in the front, a thumb-hole in the rear. Four round brass keys mounted on knobs on the lower body-joint: e, f-sharp, g-sharp, and b-natural correction key. Four brass keys on the upper body joint: e′-flat, a′, the a′-shake, and the speaker key. Stamped with the imperial crown over laurel leaves and 'D'Almaine & Co., late Goulding & D'Almaine, Soho Square, London.' Length, 57.7 cm. Diameter, max. (bell), 7.5 cm. Bore, 13 mm. Length of cylindrical part, 46.5 cm. (17.1876)
Plate I

Described in the R. M. E. *Catalogue* on p. 114, under no. 234.

112. CLARINET Brunswick, Germany, late 18th century

In B-flat. Six keys. Boxwood, stained light yellow-brown. Made in five parts: mouthpiece, barrel, upper body-joint, a short lower body-joint, and a long bell-joint with a little finger-hole and three keys mounted on it. Seven finger-holes in the front, a thumb-hole in the rear. The square keys of brass are mounted on knobs and are similar to those of No. 110. Stamped 'H. C. Tolcke, Bronsvig.' Length, 67 cm. Diameter, max. (bell), 6.9 cm. Bore, 14 mm. Length of cylindrical part, 56 cm. (17.1875)
Plate I

Described in the R. M. E. *Catalogue* on p. 113, under no. 231.

113. CLARINET London, England, late 18th century

In A. Five keys. Boxwood, stained light yellow-brown. Ivory tips. Made in six parts similarly to No. 110. Seven finger-holes in the front, a thumb-hole in the rear. The three square lower keys of brass are e, f-sharp, and g-sharp; two upper keys, a′, and the speaker key; all keys are mounted on knobs. Stamped 'A. Bland & Weller, No. 28 Oxford Street.' Length, 68.5 cm. Diameter, max. (bell), 6.9 cm. Bore, 14 mm. Length of cylindrical part, 58 cm. (17.1874)
Plate I

Described in the R. M. E. *Catalogue* on p. 113, under no. 228.

317. CLARINET Paris, France, before 1794

In B-flat and A. Five keys. Ebony; ivory tips. Made in six parts: mouthpiece, barrel, three body-joints, and bell. The lower body-joint and bell are common to both instruments, but the other parts are in duplicate. Seven finger-holes in the front, thumb-hole in the rear. The three square lower keys are e, f-sharp, and g-sharp; two upper keys, a′ and the speaker key; all keys are mounted on knobs. Stamped 'Amlingue à Paris.' Length, B-flat, 67.5 cm.; A, 71 cm. Diameter, max. (bell), 6.8 cm. Bore, 14 mm. (38.1750)

Authenticated instruments are very rare finds. This fine clarinet set belonged to Captain Bryant P. Tilden. It came into the Museum's possession intact, in a fine case, and with the following letter:

My Clarionett

was bo't for me by my music master D'Anglebert, a German professor at Bordeaux in 1794. It was made, years previous, by Amlingue of Paris. I paid twenty silver crowns (6 livres ca.) on account of its superior excellence. My music lessons were on every day — during one hour: about 18 mo. at three francs per lesson.

It has now travelled with me six times, to various parts of Europe and Asia Minor. Twice to Brazils. [A check mark is inserted here.] Four times to China, — besides many trips shorter distances, Java, Manilla, etc. etc. etc. making over 200,000 miles.

Near St. Helena. Ship Globe from Canton for Philadelphia.
April 8th 1832

Bryant P. Tilden.

Below is added the check mark and the following postscript:

3 times more. Batavia Manila and Canton. Sept. 1837.

The original of the letter is now preserved in the Museum.
Gift of Mrs. Henry B. Chapin.

114. CLARINET London, England, ca. 1870

In B-flat. Thirteen keys. Rosewood, key and trimmings of German silver. Made in five parts, like the modern standard instruments. Bore of the modern type. Six finger-holes in the front, a thumb-hole in the rear. Standard keys, no rings. The keys are e (open), f (open), f-sharp, g-sharp, b-flat, b, c′-sharp, e′-flat, f′, g′-sharp, a′, the a′-shake, and the speaker key. All keys are mounted on pillars. The barrel is stamped 'Riviere & Hawkes, 28 Leicester Sq-re, London.' Length, 67 cm. Diameter, max. (bell), 8.4 cm. Bore, 15 cm. (17.1877)
Plate I

This instrument represents a developed type of the thirteen-key clarinet. In the early nineteenth century (ca. 1812) the famous clarinetist, Iwan Mueller, designed a thirteen-key clarinet and improved it acoustically. As stated already, the G-hole on the old clarinets was bored obliquely in the bulbous enlargement of the lower body joint; see p. 95, Fig. 20. On the Mueller clarinet a special open key with a long lever was provided for the tone *f*, permitting acoustically correct location of the G-hole. The thirteen-key clarinet became a standard instrument, just as did the eight-keyed flute. Further evolution of the clarinet is not represented in this Collection, since the modern instrument has been developed along different lines by the adaption of a mechanism somewhat similar to that of the Boehm flute.

115. ALTO CLARINET London, England, early 19th century

In F. Thirteen keys. Boxwood, stained dark brown. Ivory tips. Made in six parts: ivory mouthpiece, bent brass crook, three body-joints, and bell. Six finger-holes in the front; a thumb-hole in the rear. Ten of the original brass keys (square, mounted on knobs), supplemented later by three more mounted on saddles; the keys are the same as on No. 114. Stamped 'Key, London,' over the head of a unicorn and 'Charing Cross' below. Length, 86.5 cm. Diameter, max., 9.2 cm. Bore, 14.5 mm. (17.1878)
Plate I

The alto clarinet was built in F and E-flat, the lowest nominal tone E sounding *A* and G respectively. It possesses a beautiful, rich, and sonorous tone; it is used in wind bands. The alto clarinet should not be confused with the basset horn described in the next section, from which it differs not only in compass (the basset horn descends to nominal C), but also in tone; the alto clarinet sounds more open and vigorous. For this reason the basset horn parts should not be played on the alto clarinet.

The Basset Horn

THE word 'basset' was the old German name applied to a string double bass of reduced size. The 'basset horn' has the same tonal position as the alto clarinet. It differs from the alto clarinet in having a narrower bore and a softer, more sympathetic tone.[195] Another important difference between these two types of instruments is that the alto clarinet descends to the nominal tone E; the basset horn has a longer tube and the so-called 'basset keys' which extend the compass down to the nominal C.[196] On basset horn No. 116 only the C-key is added; on No. 117 the additional keys are D and C; finally, on No. 118, the downward extension is completely chromatic. The shape of the basset horn varied considerably; it was, perhaps, one of the least standardized instruments. The tubes were bent at an angle varying from sixty to ninety degrees;[197] sometimes the barrel, as on No. 116, was also bent backward to accommodate the player. At the lower end the tube was shortened by affixing a special box with three parallel interconnected bores, somewhat along the lines of the 'sausage bassoon' (No. 125). The bell was made of brass and diverged considerably more than on the smaller-sized clarinets.

The basset horn appears to have been invented about 1770 by Mayrhofer of Passau.[198] It was one of the most beloved wind instruments of the late eighteenth and the early nineteenth centuries. Mozart, who liked the clarinet, was especially fond of the basset horn, and wrote many important parts for this instrument. Among them the basset horn *obligato* to the aria "Non più di Flori" in the opera *Clemenza di Tito* is, perhaps, the best known. In his *Requiem* the basset horn replaces the clarinet. Beethoven wrote for it in the *Prometheus* overture. The list could be extended to greater length.[199]

116. BASSET HORN — Dresden, Germany, 1791

In F. Seven keys. Incomplete diatonic extension to *c*. Boxwood, stained light yellow-brown, horn tips, brass bell. Made in seven parts: mouthpiece, barrel-joint bent backward, right-hand (upper) body-joint, 120° elbow-joint, left-hand (lower) body-joint, the stock of irregular triangular shape with three parallel bores joined by passages and covered with corks forming a continuous tube, and a bell. Six finger-holes in the front; thumb-hole in the rear. The keys are *c* (open key, long lever operated by right thumb), *e* (open, long lever, left little finger), *f*-sharp (closed, right thumb), *f* (open), *g*-sharp (closed), *a'*, the speaker key; all keys are mounted on knobs. Stamped on the stock 'Grundmann, Dresden, 1791,2,' under two crossed swords. Length, 90 cm. Diameter, max. (bell), 15 cm. Bore, 14.5 mm. Length of air column (approx.), 110 cm. (17.1881)
Plate III

117. BASSET HORN — Vienna, Austria, early 19th century

In F. Fourteen keys. Complete diatonic extension to *c*. Boxwood, stained dark brown, ivory tips, brass bell. Made in eight parts: ivory mouthpiece, barrel, left-hand (upper) body-joint, ivory 120° elbow, a short right-hand (lower) joint, a short key-joint holding six key levers, stock with extended tube and three parallel bores joined as on No. 116, and a flattened brass bell. Six finger-holes in the front, one of which (the third from the top) is bored double for half-stopping; a thumb-hole in the rear. The keys are *c* (open key, long lever operated by right thumb), *d* (open, long lever, right thumb), *e* (open, long lever, left little finger), *f* (open), *f*-sharp (long lever, left little finger), *g*-sharp (closed), *b*-flat, *b*, *c'*-sharp, on the ivory elbow, *e'*-flat, *f'*, *a'* (two duplicate keys), the speaker-key. The low *c*, *d*, and *e* keys are enclosed in brass cages. The keys beginning with *b*-flat and upwards are mounted on brass saddles. Stamped on the stock 'Griesbacher, K. K. Hof Instr. Macher in Wien, 2,' under the imperial crown. Length, 91 cm. Bell, major axis, 12.7 cm. Bore, 15 mm. Length of air column (approx.), 110 cm. (17.1882)
Plate III

118. BASSET HORN — Dresden, Germany, early 19th century

In E-flat. Sixteen keys. Chromatic extension to *c*. Boxwood, stained dark brown, brass bell. Made in seven parts: mouthpiece, barrel (ivory tips), left-hand (upper) body-joint, 120° elbow,

right-hand (lower) body-joint, an irregularly shaped stock with three parallel bores, and a flattened brass bell. Six finger-holes in the front; a thumb-hole in the rear. The keys are *c* (open), *c*-sharp (open), *d* (closed), *e*-flat (open); the levers of the *c*, *c*-sharp, and *e*-flat keys are interlocked, so that by pressing on the low *c* lever all these open keys can be closed simultaneously; the rest of the keys are similar to those on No. 117. Stamped on the stock 'H. Grenser & Wiesner, Dresden,' under a king's crown. Length, 98 cm. Bell, major axis, 16 cm. Bore, 15 mm. Length of air column (approx.), 118.5 cm. (17.1883)
Plate III

Described in the R. M. E. *Catalogue* on p. 128, under no. 273.

119. BASS CLARINET Chiaravalle, near Pavia, Italy, ca. 1815, by Nicola Papalini

In C. Five keys. Pearwood, stained dark brown; horn tips. Made in five parts: mouthpiece, crook, barrel, body, bell. The crook and the body are carved out of two separate slabs to make possible the forming of the bore of serpentine shape; the halves are glued together and fastened by iron pins. Nine finger-holes in the front, of which the second and the eighth are double; the first and the fifth finger-holes are stopped by the middle joints of the left-hand and right-hand respectively; two thumb-holes in the rear; a vent-hole on the bell. The keys are *c* (open key), *d* (closed key), *f*, *a'*, and the speaker key. The *d* key is located in the rear and operated by the right thumb. All keys are of brass and are mounted on knobs. Length, 68 cm. Diameter, bell, 10 cm. Bore, 20 mm. (17.1879)
Plate III

The unorthodox form of this clarinet is a clever experiment in the reduction of the length of the model and in bringing together the finger-holes, of which there are eleven. Two of the finger-holes, as already mentioned in the technical description, were covered by the middle joints of the fingers, so that the total number of fingers required for stopping the finger-holes was nine. The holes and the keys are rather conveniently located.

120. BASS CLARINET England, late 19th century

In B-flat. Theatre model with a bassoon-like butt-joint and upturned bell. Twenty keys. Boxwood, stained bark brown. Made in five parts: mouthpiece, nickel-silver mouth-pipe, left-hand (upper) body-joint, butt-joint with two bores of unequal length, and a bell of German silver turned upward and outward in the front of the instrument. Four finger-holes in the front; a thumb-hole in the rear. The third and fourth finger-holes are stopped by open keys. The others are modern in type with circular pads, forged levers, mounted on pillars; some are mounted on hinge tubes. The keys are *C*, *C*-sharp, *D*, *E*-flat (all of which are mounted in the rear of the butt and operated by the right thumb), *E*, *F*, *F*-sharp, *G*-sharp, *B*-flat, *B* (in duplicate), *c*, *c*-sharp, *e*-flat, *f* (in duplicate), *g*-sharp, *a*, the *a* shake-key, a speaker-key. Length, 84.5 cm. Diameter, bell, 12 cm. Bore, 21 mm. Length of air column (approx.), 155 cm. (17.1880)
Plate III

Described in the R. M. E. *Catalogue* on p. 126, under no. 267. This instrument was intended for the opera theatre orchestras; the bell of this model is farther away from the floor of the orchestra pit and closer to the audience than the usual type.[200]

Invention of the bass clarinet is credited to G. Lot, who built a 'basse-tube' in 1772. Among those who contributed to its development should be mentioned Heinrich Grenser

(1793) of Dresden, G. Streitwolf (1833) of Göttingen, and Adolphe Sax (1836), then of Brussels. Grenser's bass clarinet in bassoon form is now in the Grossherzogliches Museum in Darmstadt and is described in the R. M. E. *Catalogue.*[201] Streitwolf's instrument is in E-flat, an octave lower than the alto clarinet, and is now in the Berlin Museum. One of the A. Sax instruments is in the same place.[202]

Sub-group ii: With Conoidal Tube

The use of the single reed with a conoidal tube has already been encountered on the primitive signal horn No. 91 with the covered reed. This type can be regarded as a representative of similar instruments much older than those now used in Europe and America. The interest attached to this combination is due to the disputed claims made for Adolphe Sax — who never made them himself — that he was the first to use it on the saxophone. In this Collection there is an interesting instrument, the *alto fagotto*, No. 121, originally invented under the name 'Caledonica' (see the next page), which has a conoidal bore and is played with the single reed mouthpiece. There is no reason to believe that Sax knew of instruments of this type. His fertility in invention is so well known that it requires no exaggeration.

The bass clarinet of Desfontenelles of Lisieux, built in 1807, was regarded by Constant Pierre as the model which Sax followed in the building of the saxophone.[203] The superficial resemblance is striking, but the acoustic property of the tube should be the decisive argument. Conoidal tubes with reed mouthpieces (either single or double reed) behave like open organ pipes as to their pitch and overblow an octave. Mr. Jaap Kool, who played on the Desfontenelles instrument, found that it overblows a twelfth, and, therefore, is a clarinet and not a saxophone.[204] This settles the problem presented by the Desfontenelles clarinet. The original patent drawing of the saxophone family [205] shows that only a few members of it had a 'tobacco-pipe' bell; the smallest and the largest members are shown there with straight bells. Evidently Sax had not attached any particular significance to the form usually associated with the saxophone.

Therefore, if any claims should be made as to the priority of applying the single reed mouthpiece to a conoidal tube, they should be granted to the inventor of the 'Caledonica.'

121. ALTO FAGOTTO London, England, ca. 1830

In C. Conoidal bore. Bassoon-shaped instrument with a mouthpiece of clarinet type. Eight keys. Boxwood, stained dark brown, tipped with brass ferrules. Made in six parts: mouthpiece, brass crook, wing-joint, butt, long joint, a short bell with a slightly contracted orifice. The brass keys are cup-shaped; some are mounted on knobs and some on saddles. The keys are *d* (open), *e*-flat, *f* (open), *f*-sharp, *g*-sharp, *c'*-sharp, a cross-fingering correction key, and a speaker-key. Stamped 'Wood & Ivy, late Geo. Wood, New Compton S(treet), 50, Soho, London.' Length, 54 cm. Diameter, bell, 6.4 cm. Bore, min., 3 mm.; max., 26 mm.; length of conoidal part, 101 cm. Length of air column (approx.), 107 cm. (17.1890)
Plate III

The *alto fagotto* was the name given by an English maker to the improved instrument invented by the Scottish bandmaster William Meikle ca. 1820, and called by the inventor the 'Caledonica.' The R. M. E. *Catalogue* on p. 77 describes our instrument under no. 158 and an earlier instrument of the same type under no. 157. Both instruments are called 'Dulcian, in *c*.' Mr. A. J. Hipkins in *Musical Instruments*, plate xli, also called a similar instrument the 'dolciano' and "upon the high authority of Mr. Harry Lazarus, clarinet-player" stated that it was called 'tenoroon.' This confusion of nomenclature was settled by Mr. F. G. Rendall, who stated in an article, "The Saxophone before Sax,"[206] that the correct English name of this instrument is the 'alto fagotto.' The stamped inscription of the 'dolcian' no. 157 in the R. M. E. *Catalogue* states clearly 'Invented by William Meikle.' The original Meikle's instrument, the 'Caledonica,' is now at the University of Edinburgh.[207] Our instrument is built on the bassoon pattern, the bore, shape, and key mechanism being very similar to the bassoons of that period. The tone is very pleasant; it has a singing quality, but is not very strong. The tonal position of this instrument is tenor, since its pedal tone is *c*.

122. SAXOPHONE Paris, France, ca. 1850

Alto in E-flat. Conoidal bore tube of brass with downward bent mouth-pipe and upturned bell; detachable mouthpiece. Eighteen tone-holes of various diameters covered by keys with chamois pads. Two independent octave keys. Engraved on the bell 'Adolphe Sax & Cie. à Paris,' and the factory number '5828.' Length, 58 cm. Diameter, bell, 14.3 cm. Bore, min., 12.5 mm.; max., 60 mm.; length of conoidal part, 82 cm. Length of air column (approx.), 105 cm. (17.1889)
Plate III

The saxophone was first built by Adolphe Sax in 1841. The whole family was patented in 1846. Georges Kastner as early as 1848 mentioned the following instruments: the sopranino in F or in E-flat, the soprano in C or in B-flat, the alto in E-flat, the alto-tenor in B-flat, the tenor-baritone (properly the bass) in E-flat, the bass (the contrabass) in C or B-flat, the contrabass (the sub-bass) in F or in E-flat.[208] This proves that A. Sax had in mind a complete orchestral series of saxophones (in C and in F) and the band series (in B-flat and E-flat). The saxophone of this Collection built in Sax's factory is one of the earlier instruments, as can be judged by the factory number.[209] The saxophone is a much abused and derided instrument, rather unjustly so. In the hands of a player with good musical taste and a solid musical training the saxophone becomes an expressive instrument with a fine and individual tone. One needs only to refer to the cantabile in Bizet's Suite, *L'Arlesienne* which is written for the E-flat saxophone. When played on the clarinet it loses that haunting wistfulness so clearly intended by the composer, which only the saxophone can impart to this fine melody. For more complete references to saxophone parts in modern music, Mr. Cecil Forsyth's *Orchestration* should be consulted.[210]

The tube of the saxophone has a wide conoidal bore. The mouthpiece is similar to that of the clarinet, but differs in some specific details. The saxophone overblows an octave. The basic scale of the saxophone is almost identical with that of the old one-keyed flute: the tones *d'*, *e'*, *g'*, *a'*, *b'*, *c''*-sharp are fingered in the same way on both instruments; the old flute fingering for the tone f'-sharp is used on the saxophone (and also on the Boehm flute) for the tone f'-natural. The saxophone of this Collection has the old style independent octave key: the lower octave key was used for overblowing the tones from d'' to g''-sharp; the upper octave key, located on the mouthpipe, was used for the tones from a'' upward; the left-hand thumb had to be shifted as the tones changed their range. On the modern instrument the octave keys are interconnected, and only one thumb-lever operating both keys is needed.

Antoine Joseph (Adolphe) Sax (1814–94) was born in Dinant, Belgium. His father, Charles Joseph Sax, was a prominent musical instrument maker in Brussels. This Collection has two instruments made by Sax's father; the key bugle No. 174 and the *cor omnitonique* No. 194. Adolphe Sax had a many-sided genius. Early in life he manifested great musical abilities and a predilection for making musical instruments. He found in his father a sympathetic tutor. Later Sax studied clarinet playing in the Brussels Conservatoire under M. Bender. This training helped him later when he returned once more to instrument making. Before Sax removed to Paris, he perfected the bass clarinet and invented the double bass clarinet.

In 1842 Sax emigrated to France and opened a small shop in the Rue St. George in Paris. Very soon he attracted attention by his unusual abilities and the business began to grow. The middle of the nineteenth century was a very propitious time for an inventive genius. New types and models of instruments, especially in the brass group, were appearing in great numbers. This prolific inventiveness of many people had no coördination; instruments varied in tonalities and shapes; very few of them were practicable. Sax brought order into chaos; he can be regarded as the outstanding influence in the development of the modern wind band. In rapid succession he developed the saxophone family (before 1846) and the saxhorn and saxotromba families (1845). These families were built in the same standard tonalities, those in B-flat and E-flat; the individual members constituted homogeneous tonal groups. The valve mechanisms were simplified and made more practicable; the tubings were standardized in the bore; and the shape and tone of the instruments were so improved that rivals had to abandon their models and copy those of Sax. This involved him in bitter and expensive court suits with the infringers and created many enemies.

In 1845 Adolphe Sax presented a memorandum to the French War Ministry in which he made definite recommendations for the reorganization of the French Army Bands. A special Committee was appointed to investigate the merits of Sax's proposal. Michele Enrico Carafa (1787–1872), the director of the Paris Conservatoire de Musique, made a counter-proposal.[211] On April 22, 1845, in the Champs de Mars, one of the significant events of music took place: a contest between two bands. One, the old style band of forty-five musicians, consisting mostly of professors and advanced pupils of the Conservatoire, was led by M. Carafa. Another, of only thirty-eight musicians (owing to intrigue, several hired by Sax failed to appear), was led by Sax. This contest was very interestingly described by M. Oscar Comettant in his biography of Adolphe Sax.[212] Although handicapped by the incomplete band, Sax won a decisive triumph. Thus more enemies were added. The decision of the

Committee was in favor of Sax, whose recommendations were followed. Since the saxhorn family made a foundation for military bands, Sax had practically a monopoly for some time in supplying the French Army Bands with brass instruments.

The rest of Sax's life consisted of a series of triumphs over his adversaries in patent struggles, intrigues against him, more improvements in instruments.[213] Sax had many influential friends both in the government and in musical circles and unprecedented opportunities for becoming rich. Nevertheless his artistic and essentially unbusinesslike temperament eventually robbed him of his business and of a considerable fortune which he had at one time. His precious collection of old musical instruments was sold. On February 6, 1894, Adolphe Sax died in Paris, penniless and almost forgotten.

Group 2: Double Beating Reed

Sub-group i: With Cylindrical Tube

THE plan of coupling a directly controlled double reed with a cylindrical tube had not shown much vitality.

As already stated (p. 81) the difficulty of spanning such a large interval as a twelfth, since cylindrical tubes overblow a twelfth, undoubtedly had much to do with the failure of the instruments of this type to survive.[214] Another reason, also mentioned, was that on some instruments of this type the bores were of very small diameter. The moisture of the breath would swell the wood and make them smaller, or close up the passage completely.[215] This was especially true of the 'sausage bassoons' (No. 125). Several families of instruments existed in which the cylindrical tubes were vibrated by uncovered double reeds. Among them can be mentioned: 1. The Racketts ('sausage bassoons'). 2. The Sourdines.[216] 3. The Tartoelds.[217]

The courtaud (No. 124) of Mersenne existed, it seems, only as an individual instrument. The 'Kortholt' of Praetorius had a covered reed.[218]

123. AULOS — Reconstruction

Reed pipe allegedly similar to that used by the ancient Greeks. Cylindrical wooden tube with five finger-holes in the front and a thumb-hole in the rear. Length, including reed, 36.5 cm. Diameter, 1.7 cm. Bore, 7 mm. (17.1895)
Plate III

The history of the *aulos* is too long and complicated to be even touched upon in a short note. There is an excellent article by Miss Kathleen Schlesinger in the *Encyclopaedia Britannica*.[219] Among the sources mentioned there the article by Professor Albert A. Howard, "The Αὐλός or Tibia," is especially valuable.[220]

124. COURTAUD — Reconstruction, after Mersenne

Cylindrical body of maple, stained dark brown. Two flaring caps bound with brass ferrules. Brass staple for the double reed. The U-shaped air column is formed by two long bores joined at the bottom by a cross-bore, the extra holes plugged by wooden plugs. Six finger-holes in the

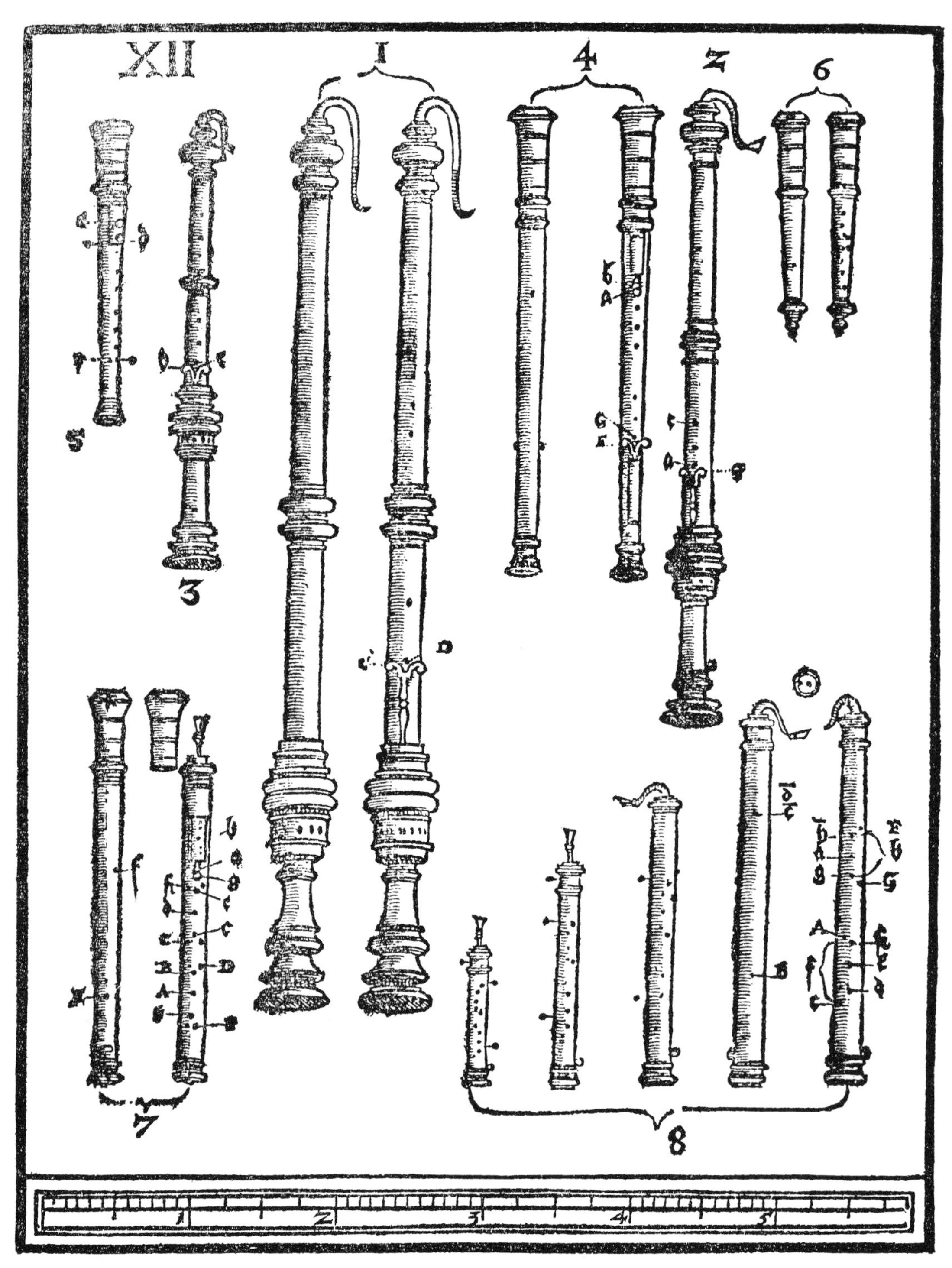

1. Baß vom Baſſanelli. 2. Tenor vnd Alt Baſſanelli. 3. Diſcant Baſſanelli. 4. Baſs vom Schryari. 5. Tenor, Alt Schryari. 6. Cant Schryari. 7. Kortholt. oder Kurtzpfeiff: 8. Ein gantz Stimwerck von Sordunen.

FIG. 21. PRAETORIUS, TABLE XII

1. Bass Bassanello. 2. Tenor-Alto Bassanello. 3. Treble Bassanello. 4. Bass Schryari. 5. Tenor-Alto Schryari. 6. Treble Schryari. 7. Curtal or *Kurzpfeiff*. 8. A complete family of Sourdines. (For Bass Sourdine, see p. 127, Fig. 24, representing Praetorius, table x.)

front, very small in diameter (2 mm.); six large holes (5 mm. bore) bored in the funnel-shaped protruding plugs (three of them dummies) and the rear tube; two thumb-holes and a vent-hole in the rear. Length, body, 61 cm. Diameter, body, 3.8 cm. Bore, 5 mm. Length of air column (including reed), 116 cm. (17.1893)
Plate III

No actual instruments, to the writer's knowledge, have reached our times. This instrument was reconstructed by Canon Galpin from the description and drawings found in Mersenne's *Harmonie universelle*.[221] The funnel-shaped protruding plugs were called *tetines* by Mersenne. Their function was to enable the player to use his finger-joints in addition to his finger-tips and thus control a larger number of the finger-holes without resorting to the key mechanism. This principle was applied later by Papalini to his peculiarly shaped bass-clarinet No. 119.

125. RACKETT — Reproduction of an early 17th-century type

Sausage bassoon. Short cylindrical body of maple, stained dark brown. Two caps, short mouth-pipe; brass staple for reed and a pirouette. The air column is formed by seven parallel bores, the central one serving as the initial duct; all the bores are connected so as to form one continuous air passage. Ten finger-holes; additional eight holes in a diamond formation. Length, including reed, 23 cm. Body, diameter, 5 cm.; length (without caps), 11.2 cm. Bore, 6 mm. Length of air column (including reed), 83 cm. (17.1894)
Plate III

This freakish instrument, despite its shortness, has a very deep tone. The cylindrical pipe acts as a stopped pipe and sounds an octave lower than an open pipe of the same length. The tonality of this instrument (unfortunately not in a playable condition) can be estimated as that of the bass in F, equivalent to the bassoon in F of the size approximately equal to No. 147. Praetorius described the entire family of the sausage bassoons, consisting of 1. Cant, *G* to *d'*. 2. Tenor-Alto, *C* to *g*. 3. Bass, *FF* to *c*. 4. Great Bass, *DD* to *A* or, *CC* to *G*.

The last instrument descended to the 16-foot C, much to Praetorius' surprise, since its body was only 11 Brunswick inches long (26.2 cm.), as stated by him in *De Organographia.* The tone of the sausage bassoon was rather quiet, and Praetorius stated that even in a consort it sounded *keine sonderliche gratiam* ("without any special distinction"). It was only when the racketts were played by a good musician with a *viola da gamba*, or in conjunction with some other string or wind instrument and accompanied by a harpsichord, that they sounded well, particularly in the bass.[222] Such instruments as the racketts, sourdines, cromornes, and courtaud, all of them having a cylindrical bore, were not overblown in Praetorius' time.[223] A schematic drawing of the sausage bassoon's tube and the peculiar disposition of the finger-holes can be found in the fourth volume of the *Catalogue . . . de Bruxelles* on p. 183, where the 'diamond' formation is clearly represented.

Sub-group ii: With Conoidal Tube

THE double reed has an affinity with the conoidal tube. The most vital and artistic 'wood-wind' instruments of the modern orchestra belong to this sub-group. The oboe, *oboe d'amore*, English horn, bassoon, contrabassoon, and the newer heckelphone, all possess undeniable individuality of tone color. These instruments, with the exception of the contrabassoon, are on a high artistic plane and have considerable power of expression and technical agility. Fine nuances of phrasing are possible, especially if players are trained in the French school of double reed playing.[224]

There exist several families of conoidal tube aerophones with the directly controlled double reed. The family classification in dictionaries and books on instrumentation (the 'oboe family') is not suitable for scientific purposes, because it deals only with contemporary instruments. In organology a more precise and scientific division is necessary, because an organologist is concerned with a large number of specifically dissimilar instruments, some little used and many obsolete. The table on page 111 provides the basis for subsequent discussion.

This table shows that for each tonal position there are several instruments, sometimes in the same tonality, possessing different specific characteristics. The present terminology is not definite. For instance, the English horn is referred to as the 'alto oboe.' This is meaningless, since there is the alto oboe proper, and the same term may with equal right be applied to the alto shawm, the discant fagott, the *oboe da caccia*, and the alto sarrusophone. Even less appropriate is the use of the term 'oboe family.' Unless properly qualified in each case, it may mean one of these three things: (1) All the conoidal bore double reed instruments. (2) The heterogeneous 'oboe family' of dictionaries and instrumentation books. (3) The oboe family proper. At one time there existed a whole family of real oboes, comprising soprano (C), mezzo-soprano (A), alto (F), baritone (C), and bass (F). All these instruments are true oboes, similar in bore, bell construction, and tone color to the soprano oboe. Only the soprano member of the true oboe family has survived. Such instruments as the *oboe d'amore* (A), English horn (F), and the *hautbois baryton* (C) are now called, respectively, mezzo-soprano, alto, and baritone oboe. They preëmpt the names of the obsolete members of the oboe family, although they possess neither structural nor tonal similarity to the real oboes. Thus by default a questionable terminology established itself. No other science would tolerate for a moment such loose terminology and classificational blunders as are found in writings on musical instruments. So, perhaps, it would not be amiss to define more precisely the term, 'a family of musical instruments.'

In this study the general classification is brought down to generic aggregates only. The whole ladder of classification consists of the following steps: 1. Class. 2. Division. 3. Section. 4. Sub-section. 5. Group. 6. Sub-group.

In accordance with considerations of necessity and sufficiency, some classes descend only to the third step of the ladder (Classes I and II; see General Classification, p. ix). In some cases the fifth step is necessary (Class III, Division I, Section A, p. x). At present the sixth step, a sub-group, is the last step. In each of these cases the last respective step of the ladder is a generic group.[225]

A further subdivision below the generic group must be, of necessity, into specific groups. These specific groups are called families. A family of musical instruments is defined as an

DOUBLE REED AEROPHONES WITH CONOIDAL BORE

(Directly controlled reeds)

Tonal Position	Name of Instrument	Tonality
Sopranino	1. Oboe (Military)	E-flat
	2. Piccolo Heckelphone	F
	3. Terz-Heckelphone	E-flat
	4. Sarrusophone	E-flat
Soprano	1. Discant Shawm (No. 129)	C
	2. Oboe (Band)	D-flat
	3. Oboe (No. 134)	C
	4. Oboe (Band)	B-flat
	5. Sarrusophone	B-flat
Mezzo-Soprano	1. *Oboe basso* (No. 138)	A
	2. *Oboe d'amore*	A
	3. Discant Fagott (*Exilent*)	A
Alto	1. Small Alto Shawm	G
	2. Large Alto Shawm	F
	3. Discant Fagott	G
	4. Alto Oboe (Nos. 139 and 140)	F
	5. *Oboe da caccia* (No. 142)	F
	6. English Horn (No. 144)	F
	7. Sarrusophone	E-flat
Baritone (Tenor)	1. Tenor Shawm (No. 131)	C
	2. Baritone Oboe (No. 141)	C
	3. *Hautbois baryton*	C
	4. Heckelphone	C
	5. *Fagottino* (No. 146)	C
	6. Tenor Sarrusophone	C
Bass	1. Basset Shawm	G
	2. Bass Oboe	F
	3. Single Curtal (No. 145)	G
	4. Tenoroon (No. 147)	F
	5. Baritone Sarrusophone	E-flat
Contrabass	1. Bass Shawm (*Bombardo*) (No. 132)	C
	2. Bassoon (No. 148)	C
	3. Bass Sarrusophone	B-flat
Sub-bass	1. Great Bass Shawm (*Bombardone*)	GG
	2. *Quart Fagott*	GG
	3. *Quint Fagott*	FF
	4. Contrabass Sarrusophone	EE-flat
Sub-contrabass	1. Double Bassoon (No. 152)	CC
	2. Subcontrabass Sarrusophone	BBB-flat

Note: Numbers in parentheses refer to instruments in this Collection.

aggregate of instruments which have similar acoustical properties and essential structural characteristics, and differ only in their size and the tonal position. By similarity of acoustical properties is meant principally the similarity of the partial tones of the natural scale and the affinity of tone color. By essential structural characteristics is meant the features affecting the tone color of instruments. For instance, the geometrical similarity of the bore is essential; in the case of the conoidal bore instruments, the taper of the conoid should be the same, as far as practicable; in the cylindro-conoidal tubes the relative lengths of the cylindrical and conoidal parts should be the same. In the case of the wood-wind instruments the shape of the bell, as on the *oboe d'amore*, English horn, and the 'hautbois baryton,' affecting as it does the tone color, is of importance. The form of the tube is not essential; it can be bent upon itself several times without disturbing acoustical properties.[226] The similarity of the key or valve mechanism is a desirable but not a mandatory factor in grouping instruments into families.[227]

The double reed instruments with conoidal tube and directly controlled reed have the same acoustical characteristic in common: they overblow an octave and the partial tones of their natural scale enter into a 1, 2, 3, 4, . . . series.[228] Here the similarity stops. Classified by their specific attributes, the conoidal double reed instruments may be divided into the following families: 1. The primitive instruments. 2. The shawm family. 3. The oboe family.[229] 4. The *oboe d'amore* family (incomplete). 5. The bassoon family. 6. The sarrusophone family. 7. The heckelphone family (incomplete).

The reasons for this division are given as the study unfolds.

In books on instrumentation, modern double reed instruments are brought together into one group. As already stated, this is not correct scientifically, and can be justified only for practical reasons.[230] The tabulation below enumerates the double reed instruments called for in modern scores; it also shows the heterogeneous character of such grouping. The words in parentheses refer to the family.

The Orchestral Double Reeds

Sopranino	Piccolo heckelphone	(Heckelphone)
	Terz heckelphone	(Heckelphone)
Soprano	Oboe	(Oboe)
Mezzo-soprano	*Oboe d'amore*	(*Oboe d'amore*)
Alto	English horn	(*Oboe d'amore*)
Baritone	Heckelphone	(Heckelphone)
Contrabass	Bassoon	(Bassoon)
Sub-contrabass	Double bassoon	(Bassoon)

The Primitive Instruments

126. WHITHORN — Oxfordshire, England, 19th century

Rustic reed pipe. Conical tube formed of willow bark twisted when green and fastened together with white thorn prickers. A double reed of soft willow bark. Length, 37.5 cm. (17.1897)

Used in England by villagers in Oxfordshire during the Whit Monday hunt.

127. PASTORAL PIPE France, 19th century

Musette. In F. Conoidal bore. Rosewood; stained dark brown, ivory tips. Made in two parts: body and bell-joint. Seven finger-holes in the front; a thumb-hole in the rear; two vent-holes. Length, 36.5 cm. Diameter, bell, 5.8 cm. Bore, min., 5.5 mm.; max., 14 mm.; length of conoidal part, 32 cm. (17.1914)
Plate IV

128. MUSETTE BRETONNE Brittany, France, 19th century

In A. Ebony, ivory tips and ivory bell rim. Finely moulded conical tube with a widely flaring bell. Made in two parts. Seven finger-holes in the front. Length, 34.5 cm. Diameter, bell, 9 cm. Bore, min., 4.5 cm.; max., 16 mm.; length of conoidal part, 28.5 cm. (17.1898)
Plate IV

The Shawm Family

THE immediate predecessor of the mediaeval double reed instrument in Western Europe was the Arabian *zamr*. Typical instruments of the shawm family made their appearance as early as the fourteenth century.[231] The nomenclature of shawms is rather complex. The word 'shawm' was spelled formerly as 'shalm,' 'shalmie,' and was akin to the German *Schalmei* and the Old French *chalemel*. These words came from Mediaeval Latin *calamellus*, a diminutive of the Latin *calamus*, a reed, a cane, hence a pipe. The alternative names in English were 'bumbarde,' 'pommer'; *Bombarde, hault-bois, gros-bois* in French; *bombardo* in Italian; *Bombardt, Bomhart, Pommer* in German. A typical instrument of the shawm family had seven finger-holes in the front, the lowest being duplicated as on the recorder for right- and left-hand players. On the larger instruments the lowest hole was covered by a key with a double touch-piece. The key mechanism was covered by a fontanelle as on the recorder. The reed was affixed to the staple or 'crook,' a conoidal brass tubing, straight or bent, according to the size of the instrument. A peculiar part not found on modern orchestral instruments was the 'pirouette,' a turned piece of wood partly surrounding the reed and permitting the player to take in his mouth only a certain length of the reed. The larger shawms, it seems, had no pirouettes.[232] The pirouette is still used on Oriental double reed instruments.

The earliest image and description of the shawm is found in Virdung's *Musica getutscht*. The smaller instrument was called the *Schalmey*. The larger instrument with the key and fontanelle was called the *Bombardt*. Martin Agricola does not add much to our knowledge. Praetorius, as always, gives complete information. According to him the name 'bombart' with all its different variations was derived from 'bombio,' to bumble, to buzz, to make a loud explosive noise. The shawm family of his time is given in tabulated form on p. 114.

The discant shawm No. 2, according to Praetorius (*Tabella Universalis*, in *De Organographia*, p. 22, x), has as its two lowest tones *d'* and *e'*; No. 3 the same as *c'* and *d'*. The small alto shawm No. 4 the same as *g* and *a*; the great alto shawm No. 5 (referred to on p. 13 of *De Organographia*) the same as *f* and *g*. Both alto shawms Nos. 3 and 4 had their lowest tones (*g* and *f* respectively) controlled by the key. Since the instruments Nos. 2 and 3 had no keys, it is possible that Praetorius gave them their two lowest tones for the sake of uniformity. The tenor-pommer No. 6 had four keys: *C, B, A, G.* The bass-pommer No. 7 also had four keys: *F, E, D, C.* The great bass-pommer No. 8, represented on Table VI, fig. 3 and reproduced in this study on p. 354, had four keys: *BB*-flat, *AA, GG, FF.* Among the shawm family Praetorius includes also the *nicolo*, a basset-pommer referred to in *De Organographia* on pages 22 and 36; it is represented on table XIII, fig. 1, reproduced in this

THE SHAWM FAMILY

(Praetorius, 1619)

No.	Table XI	Nomenclature: Praetorius	Nomenclature: Italian (1619)	Compass
1	Fig. 5	Gar kleine Discant Schalmey		$b' - b^3$
2	Fig. 4	Discant Schalmey	Piffaro	$d' - b''$
3		Discant Schalmey		$c' - g''$ (a'')
4	Fig. 3	Klein Alt-Pommer	Bombardo Piccolo	$g - d''$
5		Gross Alt-Pommer		$f - c''$
6	Fig. 2	Basset- or Tenor-Pommer		$G - g'$
7	Fig. 1	Bass-Pommer	Bombardo	$C - b$ (c')
8	Fig. 3 (Table VI)	Gross Bass-Pommer	Bombardone	$FF - e$ (f)

study on p. 82. The *nicolo* of Praetorius has two keys and the reed is covered with a cap. For this reason the *nicolo* should not be regarded as a member of the shawm family, but as an instrument properly belonging to Sub-section a, reed instruments with indirectly controlled reed.

The tonal qualities of the shawm were described by Mersenne as follows:

> Quant à leur [shawms] Musique elle est propre pour les grandes assamblées, comme pour les Balets (encore que l'on se serve maintenant des Violons en leur place), pour les Nopces, pour les Festes des village, & pour les autres resiouyssances publiques, à raison du grand bruit qu'ils font, & de la grand Harmonie qu'ils rendent, car ils ont le son le plus fort & le plus violent de tous les instrumens, si l'on excepte la Trompette.[233]

Mersenne gives a *Pavanne* in six parts for a consort of shawms; one of the parts (*Seconde Taille ou Basse Taille*) is written for the *sacquebute* or slide trombone. The other parts are written for the following shawms: Premier dessus, *d'–d''*; Second dessus, *d'–c''*; Haute-contre, *g–f'*; Première Taille, *G–d'*; Basse, *GG–c.*

The shawm family is important historically, since it appears that several members of the orchestral family have developed from it. Oboes are improved discant shawms. English horns are modified alto shawms. Bassoons, contrary to the usual statements, have not developed from the bass shawms, but have evolved parallel to them. These questions will be discussed more completely in the sections on the respective instruments.

129. TREBLE SHAWM — Reconstruction, 17th-century type

In C. Conoidal bore. Walnut, stained dark brown. Made in four parts: short wooden staple, long body-joint, bell, and a fontanelle. Six finger-holes in the front; one large (8 mm.) hole under

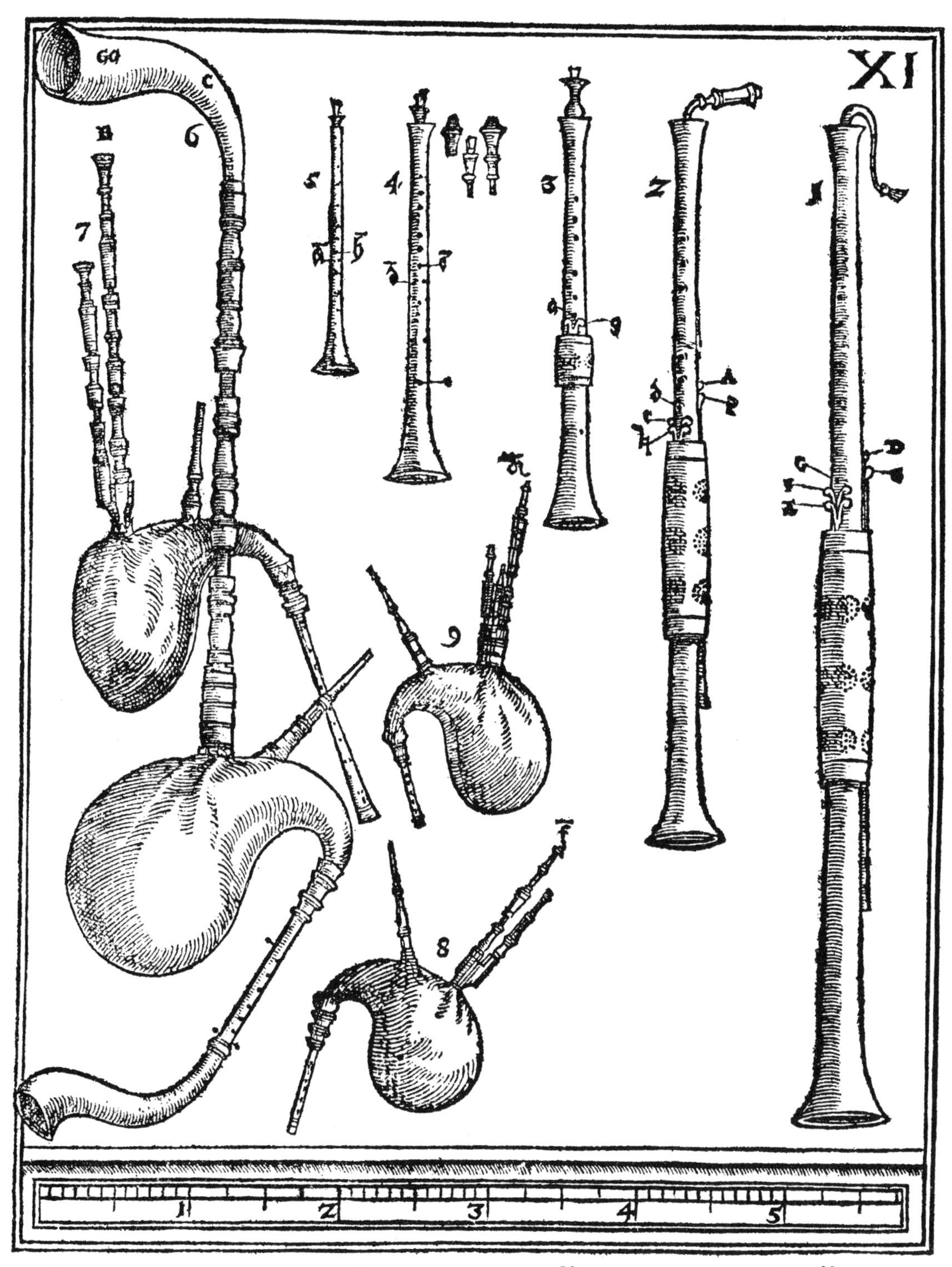

1. Bas-Pommer 2. Baſſet oder Tenor-Pommer. 3. Alt Pommer.
4. Diſcant Schalmey. 5. Klein Schalmey. 6. Groſſer Bock.
7. Schaper Pfeiff. 8. Hümmelchen. 9. Dudey.

Fig. 22. PRAETORIUS, TABLE XI

1. Bass Shawm (Pommer). 2. Basset or Tenor Shawm (Pommer). 3. Alto Shawm (Pommer). 4. Treble Shawm. 5. Small Shawm. 6. Great Bock (large bagpipe). 7. *Schäferpfeife* (middle-sized bagpipe). 8. *Hümmelchen* (small-sized bagpipe). 9. *Dudey* (smallest-sized bagpipe with three drones).

the fontanelle, not accessible for fingering and not stopped by any key; two vent-holes on the bell-joint. Length, without reed, 63.8 cm. Diameter, bell, 7.3 cm. Bore, min., 3 mm.; max., 18 mm.; length of conoidal part, 51 cm. (17.1901)
Plate III

The construction of this instrument is a puzzle. The fontanelle covers up a large hole, which serves therefore as a vent-hole and determines the lowest tone of the instrument (*d'*, sounding a semitone higher). Dr. Georg Kinsky suggested that the fontanelle on the treble shawm is merely a formal decorative feature.[234] Several instruments such as no. 957 (Brussels), no. 67 (Berlin), no. 1303 (former Heyer Collection now in Leipzig), show that it was not an accidental practice. The distance from the pirouette to the centre of the hole under the fontanelle is 43.3 cm. on our instrument. Since the instrument sounds *d'* when all six finger-holes are closed (the fingering for the tone d'), its tonality is that of C, as in the case of the old flutes.

130. ALTO SHAWM — Reconstruction, 17th-century type

In F. Conoidal bore. Boxwood, stained dark brown; the fontanelle is of pine. Made in four parts: pirouette, long body-joint, bell-joint, and the fontanelle. Six finger-holes on the body-joint; one key, stopping the hole located on the bell-joint, the mechanism of which is protected by the fontanelle and a lever with two touch-pieces projecting outside. Two vent-holes on the bell-joint. Length, without reed, 91.5 cm. Diameter, bell, 10.3 cm. Bore, min., 3 mm.; max., 27 mm.; length of conoidal part, 82 cm. (17.1902)
Plate III

The instrument is represented on Plate III with the fontanelle removed and the key mechanism exposed. There is an excellent drawing and description of a similar mechanism in Mr. Christopher Welch's *Six Lectures on the Recorder and other Flutes.*[235] The fontanelle is a protective cover over the key mechanism. It is a barrel-shaped thin-walled shell of wood with brass rings at both ends; there are many small holes, drilled in ornamental patterns, to let the sound out. This fascinating word 'fontanelle' can, of course, be found in Praetorius, and was discovered there by Dr. Georg Kinsky. [236]

131. TENOR SHAWM — Reconstruction, 17th-century type

In C. Conoidal bore. Walnut, stained dark brown. Made in six parts: pirouette, staple, long body-joint, fontanelle-joint, bell-joint, and the fontanelle. The finger-holes and the key mechanism are like that on No. 130. Length, without staple, 109 cm. Diameter, bell, 12.9 cm. Bore, min. (without staple), 6 mm.; max., 24 mm.; length of conoidal part (with staple), 118 cm. Length of the air column, including reed, 131 cm. (17.1903)
Plate III

132. BASS SHAWM — Reconstruction, 17th-century type

In C. Conoidal bore. Walnut, stained dark brown. Made in five parts: crook, long body-joint, fontanelle-joint, bell-joint, and the fontanelle. Six finger-holes in the front. Four keys, two located in the front and operated by the little finger and two in the rear. The key mechanism is protected by a very long fontanelle (46.5 cm.) and the lowest key is enclosed in a brass guard located at the

rear. Length, without crook, 184.5 cm. Diameter, bell, 16.3 cm. Bore, min. (without crook), 7 mm.; max., 40 mm.; length of conoidal part (with crook), 203 cm. Length of air column, including reed, 218.5 cm. (17.1904)
Plate III

This is the instrument which the late Sir Frederick Bridge, organist of Westminster Abbey, liked so well. (See p. 68; the letter from Canon Galpin.) The tone of this bass shawm, when played with the bassoon reed, is soft and velvety, quite unlike that of the bassoon in quality. The most interesting feature of this instrument is the key mechanism. There are four keys, two in the front and two in the rear. The rear keys are operated by the thumb. The lowest key giving *C* has a very long lever which is covered by the fontanelle for most of its length; the rest is enclosed in a brass guard which Mersenne called *la poche* (*Harmonie universelle*, liv. v, p. 297). Both pairs of keys have their key levers so disposed that, by pressing the levers located outside, two key-holes are covered simultaneously. This interlocking feature anticipated in principle later interlocking arrangements on the key mechanisms of the 'wood-wind' instruments of the eighteenth and nineteenth centuries. There is only one instrument of the shawm family which is larger, namely, the gigantic bass shawm represented by Praetorius in table vi, fig. 3, the body length of which is 10 feet, 5 inches (Brunswick), or 297 cm. The only actual instrument which has reached our time is now preserved in the Collection of Old Musical Instruments in Berlin;[237] it measures 271.5 cm. A copy of it is in the *Catalogue . . . de Bruxelles* (no. 987); the total length, including the crook and the reed, is given there as 323 cm.

The Oboe Family

THE modern oboe is an ultra-refined, almost effeminate descendant and the sole survivor of what at one time promised to be a complete family of oboes. Originally a military instrument [238] with a coarse piercing tone, the oboe gradually became more civilized and finally developed into one of the most expressive and sensitive instruments of the modern virtuoso symphony orchestra.[239] The French should be given the credit for this transformation.

The oboe family, using the word 'oboe' in a narrowly specific sense, consists of the following instruments:

Sopranino	1. Oboe in E-flat	(Military)
Soprano	2. Oboe in D-flat	(Military)
	3. Oboe in C	(Orchestra)
	4. Oboe in B-flat	(Military)
Mezzo-soprano	5. 'Oboe basso' in A [240]	
Alto	6. Alto oboe in F	
Baritone	7. Baritone oboe in C	
Bass	8. Bass oboe in F	

All these instruments are true oboes. Organologically the oboe is a double reed aerophone having a medium tapered conoidal bore and moderately flaring bell. The latter is of two types. The old type bell, Fig. 23, 1 (p. 119), has a slightly contracted opening intended to subdue to a certain extent the coarse tone of the old oboe. The modern oboe bell, Fig. 23, 3, is plain, without the undercut. It should be noted that 'modern' is a relative term, since the alto oboe No. 139, made in the eighteenth century, has the bell without the undercut. The shawms also had plain bells. Among the instruments comprising the oboe family the following require comment.

The 'oboe basso' (No. 5), or 'grand hautbois' of the French, is not to be confused with the *oboe d'amore*. Although similar in pitch, they differ in construction of the bell, the 'oboe basso' having an ordinary oboe bell of the old type, and the *oboe d'amore* a pear-shaped bell; for details, see under No. 138, p. 121. The alto oboe in F differs likewise from the English horn. The baritone oboe is constructed on the soprano oboe lines. The heckelphone, which sometimes is called a 'baritone oboe,' can be so called only with the understanding that in this instance the term 'oboe' is used in a generic sense, really meaning a double reed instrument with a conoidal bore.[241] The existence of such instruments as the alto oboes No. 139 and No. 140 and the baritone oboe No. 141 shows that there is a necessity of being careful, at least in work on organology, in the grouping of instruments; otherwise there will be an unfortunate confusion.[242]

The ancestor of the modern soprano oboe in C was the discant shawm. The oboe differed from the latter instrument in bore and key mechanism. The coarse and loud tone of the early oboes, already mentioned, was due to a much wider and coarser reed (see under Nos. 135 and 136). At first the oboe had two keys, the open *c'* key, and the closed *d'*-sharp key; these were introduced at the end of the seventeenth century.[243] Gerhard Hoffmann is usually credited with the addition of two keys, g'-sharp and a'-sharp. Dr. Curt Sachs, however, challenged Hoffmann's influence on the evolution of the oboe.[244] The octave key appeared shortly after the middle of the eighteenth century. At the end of the eighteenth century a Parisian oboe-maker, Christophe Delusse, changed the bore and improved the key mechanism. Early in the nineteenth century, the oboe method of Sellner, published in Vienna in 1825, shows nine keys: *c'*, *c'*-sharp, *d'*-sharp, *f'*, *f'*-sharp, *g'*-sharp, *a'*-sharp, and *c''*-natural, and, of course, an octave key facilitating the overblowing of tones of the second octave. Brod, Triébert, and Buffet should be mentioned among those who contributed to the evolution of the oboe. Frédéric Triébert (d. 1878) deserves special mention, since his work contributed to the development of the modern oboe key mechanism. The modern oboe is not represented in our Collection.

The oboe made its first appearance in the Paris Salle du Jeu de Paume de la Bouteille on March 19, 1671, in Robert Cambert's *Pomone*.[245] It was a very primitive instrument having only two keys. The technical descriptions of the oboes in this Collection show that the third and fourth finger-holes were not of the normal large size, but each was replaced by two small holes located side by side; the tube had flat spots provided for the finger-tips to facilitate the stopping and half-stopping of these double holes. On such oboes the scale was played as follows. With the instrument completely stopped, the oboe would give its lowest tone *c′*; the opening of the *c′*-key gave the tone *d′*, since this key is normally open and is located over the *d′*-hole. The first (the lowest) finger-hole, when uncovered, sounded *e′*; the second hole gave *f′*-natural. The third finger-hole, being a double hole, was stopped in two ways: to produce *f′*-sharp one small hole only was uncovered; when both small holes were open the tone produced was *g′*. Likewise, the fourth hole with one small hole open would give *g′*-sharp, and both small holes open would sound *a′*. The fifth hole gave *b′* and the

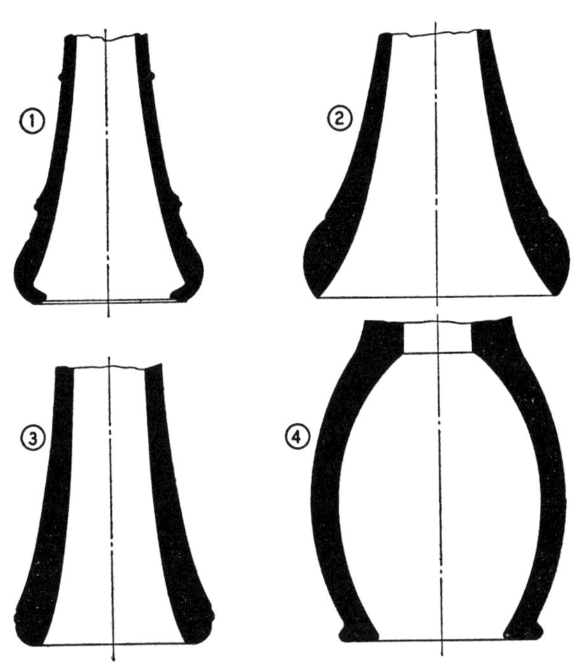

FIG. 23. BELLS OF DOUBLE REED INSTRUMENTS
1. Oboe bell, old type. 2. Oboe da caccia bell. 3. Oboe bell, modern. 4. Pear-shaped bell (*Liebesfuss*) used on the *oboe d'amore*, English horn, and the 'hautbois baryton.'

topmost hole gave a very difficult and uncertain *c″*-sharp. The tone *c″*-natural had to be cross-fingered. There was no octave hole in the rear to facilitate the playing of overblown tones. Yet the old oboe players, by stopping and increasing the air pressure, managed to reach as high as d^3. The modern oboe has an elaborate key mechanism with two 'octave' keys.

133. OBOE — Germany, 18th century

The lowest tone is *c′*. Pearwood, stained dark reddish-brown. Made in three parts: two body-joints and a bell. Six finger-holes in the front, of which the third and the fourth are double. Three square brass keys, c-key (open) and *d′*-sharp key (doubled), mounted on knobs. Two vent-holes on the bell-joint. The bell opening is slightly narrowed. Stamped 'I. W. Koenigsperger.' Length,

without reed, 57 cm. Diameter, bell, 5.8 cm. Bore, min., 7 mm.; max., 20 mm.; length of conoidal part, 47.5 cm. (17.1908)
Plate IV

134. OBOE France, 18th century

The lowest tone is *c'*. Ivory. Finely made instrument, constructed similarly to No. 133. The keys are made of silver-plated brass. Length (without reed), 58.4 cm. Diameter, bell, 5.8 cm. Bore, min., 5.5 mm.; max., 21 mm.; length of conoidal part, 48 cm. (17.1905)
Plate IV

135. OBOE London, England, 18th century

The lowest tone is *c'*. Boxwood, stained light yellow. Constructed like No. 133, except for the key mechanism. The keys are *c'*, *c'*-sharp with a long lever operated by the left little finger (evidently a later addition), and *d'*-sharp; made of silver, mounted on knobs. Stamped 'W. MILHOUSE, London.' Length (without reed), 56.8 cm. Diameter, bell, 5.7 cm. Bore, min., 5 mm.; max., 22 mm.; length of conoidal part, 47 cm. (17.1909)
Plate IV

Described in the Royal Military Exhibition *Catalogue* on p. 88, under no. 186. An old reed, of the early nineteenth century, was attached to this oboe at the time of the Royal Military Exhibition, London, 1890; it measured 9.5 mm. across the top. The modern oboe reed measures about 8 mm.

136. OBOE Venice, Italy, 1815

The lowest tone is *c'*. Ebony, with ivory tips and key. Made in three parts like No. 133. Six finger-holes in the front, of which the third one is double. Stamped 'FORNARI,' 'A VENEZIA,' '1815,' under starfish emblem. Extra joint. Length (with the upper joint, no. 1), 56.5 cm. Diameter, bell, 5.8 cm. Bore, min., 6 mm.; max., 22 mm.; length of conoidal part, 47.5 cm. Length of interchangeable joints: no. 1, 23.8 cm.; no. 2, 23.1 cm. (17.1906)
Plate IV

Described in the R. M. E. *Catalogue* on p. 87, under no. 185. The additional top joint is for change of pitch. The old reed attached to this oboe measured 11 mm. in width, or about 3 mm. more than the modern oboe reed.

137. OBOE London, England, late 18th century

The lowest tone is c'. Two keys. Pearwood, stained dark brown. Ivory tips. Constructed like No. 136, except that the keys are made of silver, and the c' key is slightly ornamented. Stamped 'KUSDER, LONDON.' Length, 58.8 cm. Diameter, bell, 6.6 cm. Bore, min., 5 mm.; max., 19 mm.; length of conoidal part, 57.5 cm. (17.1907)
Plate IV

Described in the R. M. E. *Catalogue* on p. 86, under no. 178.

138. GRAND HAUTBOIS France, 18th century

Oboe basso. Mezzo-soprano oboe in A. The lowest tone is *a*. Two keys. Boxwood, stained light brownish-yellow. Made in four parts: short brass staple, left-hand body-joint, right-hand

body-joint with a broad ivory ring around the socket, a bell with a moderate flare and narrowed opening, similar to that of the standard oboes of the eighteenth century. Six finger-holes in the front, of which the third and the fourth are double; two silver keys, c and c-sharp, mounted on knobs; two vent-holes on the bell. Stamped 'BIZEY' under a fleur-de-lis. Length (without staple), 61.7 cm. Diameter, bell, 5 cm. Bore, min., 5 mm.; max., 21 mm.; length of conoidal part, 52 cm. Length of air column (including reed), 70 cm. (17.1910)
Plate IV

Described in the R. M. E. *Catalogue* on p. 92, under no. 202, where it is called *Oboe d'amore*. Although this instrument is pitched in A, the same tonality as the *oboe d'amore*, nevertheless its constructional features show that it is an oboe. The typological feature distinguishing it from the *oboe d'amore* is the bell. The latter is described in the R. M. E. *Catalogue* as "pear-shaped and contracted at the mouth, where it measures only 1-3/8 inches [35 mm.] in diameter." The size is correct; the bell, as Plate IV shows, is just an ordinary oboe bell of the old type, with the typical oboe undercut; the bells of the soprano oboes (Nos. 133 to 137 inclusive) and the bell of the alto oboe No. 139 in this Collection are contracted. See Fig. 23, 1. This is a regular feature of the old oboes.[246] Therefore it is difficult to understand why the bell of this instrument was described as 'pear-shaped,' when this term is usually reserved for the type represented on Fig. 23, 4. The tone of this instrument is more akin to that of the old-fashioned oboe than to the *oboe d'amore*; the latter is more akin to the tone of the English horn. The instrument is really a 'grand hautbois' or an 'oboe basso.'[247]

139. ALTO OBOE — Newark, England, 18th century

Tenor Oboe. In F. The lowest tone is *f*. Short model. Boxwood, stained dark brown. Made in three parts: a short brass staple, bent slightly backward, left-hand (upper) body-joint, right-hand body-joint and bell made in one piece; the bell has a very slight flare outside and practically continues the conoidal bore. The opening is not narrowed. The left-hand joint is tipped with ivory, the right-hand with brass. Six finger-holes in the front; two square brass keys, *c'* and *d'*-sharp, mounted on knobs; no vent-holes on the bell. Stamped 'MILHOUSE, NEWARK.' Length, (without staple), 72.5 cm. Diameter, bell, 4.9 cm. Bore, min., 7.5 mm.; max., 23 mm.; length of conoidal part, 63.5 cm. Length of air column (including reed), 84.7 cm. (17.1911)
Plate IV

The absence of vent-holes is a somewhat unusual feature of this instrument. The distance from the bell to the end of the staple (measured along a straight line) is 80.5 cm. Described in the R. M. E. *Catalogue* on p. 92, under no. 203.

140. ALTO OBOE — England, early 18th century

Tenor Oboe. In F. The lowest tone is f. Long model. Boxwood, stained dark brown. Made in three parts: left-hand body-joint, right-hand body-joint (with the keys), and the bell-joint; the bell has a normal flare and a narrowed opening. Six finger-holes in the front, two square brass keys, *c'* and *d'*-sharp, mounted on knobs. Stamped 'CALEB GEDNEY.' Length (without reed), 84.8 cm. Diameter, bell, 7.3 cm. Bore, min., 5.5 mm.; max., 25.4 mm.; length of conoidal part, 74.5 cm. Length of air column (including reed), 90 cm. (17.1912)
Plate IV

Designed along the orthodox lines of the soprano oboe. Has two vent-holes on the bell. Described in the R. M. E. *Catalogue* on p. 92, under no. 204.

141. BARITONE OBOE England, ca. 1760

Basset Oboe. In C. The lowest tone is *c*. Four keys. Maple, stained black-brown. Made in four parts: a brass crook, left-hand body-joint, right-hand body-joint (with three keys), a bell with moderate flare and plain opening. Six finger-holes in the front; three brass keys, *c*, *c*-sharp, *d*-sharp, the levers of the c and c-sharp keys being interlocked so that the c-key is automatically closed when the c-sharp key is pressed down; the fourth key is the speaker-key; two vent-holes on the bell. All keys are mounted on brass saddles. Length (without crook), 100.5 cm. Diameter, bell, 5.7 cm. Bore, min., 9 mm.; max., 24 mm.; length of conoidal part, 94 cm. Length of air column (including reed), 122 cm. (17.1913)
Plate IV

Described in the R. M. E. *Catalogue* on p. 93, under no. 206. This instrument is the real oboe. The 'Basset-Oboe' or 'Basse de musette' of the former Heyer Collection, no. 1352 (*Kleiner Katalog*, p. 157), has a bore of wide taper, and therefore is not an oboe in the specific sense. M. Mahillon describes two instruments of the same size as no. 1352; another, no. 972, pitched in A, has the same taper of the bore.[248] M. Mahillon infers quite correctly that these two instruments are members of a family the name of which is not known.

Oboe d'amore Family

THE insertion in our classification of the *oboe d'amore* family of double reed instruments is suggested here for two reasons. (1) There exists three instruments, the *oboe d'amore*, the English horn, and the baritone oboe (d'amore), all three with pear-shaped bells and similar tone color. (2) There exist several types of double reed instruments of the same pitch as these instruments (see Table, p. 111) which differ specifically from them in construction and tone color. Since a family of musical instruments should include only members with the same specific characteristics, the suggested division only adheres to the well established rules of classification followed in other fields.[249]

At present there are only two active representatives of this incomplete family: (1) the mezzo-soprano *oboe d'amore* in A, and (2) the English horn in F. Both instruments have the pear-shaped bell (*Liebesfuss*, Fig. 23, 4), the inside of which is not a smooth transition from the conoidal bore, but an abrupt expansion into an ovoidal form with a contracted bell opening. Both have the same peculiar nasal timbre, setting them apart from the oboes proper.

The history of the *oboe d'amore* family is highly uncertain. The *oboe d'amore* in A or in G was introduced, probably, in the early eighteenth century.[250] The English horn has two traditional forms, straight and curved, which strongly suggest its probable origin. Both these forms were developing side by side. The ancestor of the straight tube English horn is the alto shawm in F (see Table on p. 114, No. 5). An improved bore, pear-shaped bell (*Liebesfuss*), and improved key mechanism added to the straight tube of the alto shawm would be the logical steps in this development. Several instruments of this type exist.[251]

Evolution of the curved form English horn is represented in this Collection by three instruments: the *oboe da caccia*, No. 142; the curved English horn, No. 143; and the angular English horn, No. 144. The *oboe da caccia* developed, probably, from some primitive instrument originally used, as the name implies, by huntsmen. It has a wide flaring bell (represented in section, Fig. 23, 2, p. 119). The tone is robust and rough.[252] The next step is represented by No. 143, which is a rebuilt *oboe da caccia*; the pear-shaped bell is added to subdue the tonal roughness.

Difficulty in making the curved bore led to the technological simplification shown by No. 144. The tube was made in two straight parts turned on a lathe; a short angular connecting joint presented less difficulties in making than a long curved bore. Improvements in the key mechanism made the angular form unnecessary.

The name, English horn, is of unknown origin. An attempt to derive it from *cor anglé* (an 'angled horn'), was made by Canon Galpin.[253] Later, according to this theory, it was corrupted into 'cor anglais' or the 'English horn.'

There are also some lower pitched members of the *oboe d'amore* family. Triébert constructed the 'hautbois baryton' about 1825 for the famous oboe-player Vogt. His son Frédéric made several similar instruments. M. Loree made one for the Paris Exposition of 1899, an octave lower than the soprano oboe.[254] The German firm Wilhelm Heckel built baritone oboes for a time, as did also the French firm Evette and Schaeffer in Paris. These instruments have a *Liebesfuss* and therefore belong to the *oboe d'amore* family.[255]

The *oboe d'amore* and the *oboe da caccia* were used by J. S. Bach. After Bach's death the *oboe d'amore*, a lovely instrument with a sympathetic and ingratiating tone, disappeared from use; it was revived by M. Mahillon in 1874, with all modern improvements of the key mechanism. Since then modern composers, notably Richard Strauss, have used the *oboe d'amore* in their compositions. The English horn is firmly intrenched in the orchestra.

142. OBOE DA CACCIA — Italy, late 18th century

Alto in F. The lowest tone is *f*. Curved form. Two keys. Walnut, covered with leather. Made in two parts, a curved brass staple and a tube with a bell. The bulb, into which the staple is inserted, and the bell were both turned on a lathe. The central curved part of the tube, octagonal in shape for three-quarters of its length, has a curved bore carved out of two slabs of wood. The slabs were glued together and the whole instrument was then covered with leather. Six finger-holes in the front, of which the third and the fourth are double; two brass keys, *c* and *c*-sharp, mounted on knobs; two vent-holes on the bell. The bell has a large flare, with a plain opening. (See Fig. 23, 2, on p. 119.) Length (without staple), 72 cm. Diameter, bell, 10 cm. Bore, min., 8 mm.; max., 24 mm.; length of conoidal part, 73 cm. Length of air column (measured on straight line, with reed), 97 cm. (17.1918)
Plate IV

J. S. Bach used the *oboe da caccia* effectively in his scores. Yet one technical point should be noted. Evidently the English horn, under its different names, was not known to him. These two instruments, the *oboe da caccia* and the English horn, differ in bore. The *oboe da caccia* has a wider bore with a slightly greater taper than the English horn. The bells of the two instruments are entirely different. Their tone color differs considerably, the *oboe da caccia* sounding more rough and virile. Therefore in performing the scores of J. S. Bach the replacement of the *oboe da caccia* by the English horn, especially when the latter is played with all the refinements of French technique, is not correct. As in many other cases, it is primarily the problem of a correct recovery of the ancient tone color.[256] Whether such recovery would be acceptable to modern ears accustomed to the refined and feminine tones of our double reed instruments is a question of personal taste.

143. ENGLISH HORN — Italy; original part of the instrument late 18th century; repaired by Fornari ca. 1820

Cor Anglais. In F. The lowest tone is *f*. Curved form. Six keys. This instrument was originally an *oboe da caccia* similar to No. 142; in its present form it has obviously been remade. Made in three parts: two curved, leather-covered body-joints of pearwood tipped with horn and ivory ferrules, and a pear-shaped bell with a *Liebesfuss*, also tipped with ivory. Six finger-holes in the front, of which the third is double. The key mechanism was made in three stages: (1) the original keys, *c* and *d*-sharp, are flat brass keys mounted on knobs; (2) the *c*-sharp, *g*-sharp, and *b*-flat keys are mounted on brass saddles, and were added probably by Fornari, whose name is stamped on the bell; (3) the speaker key is located at the front and is connected by a bent link to the thumb-lever at the back, both the speaker key and the thumb-lever being mounted on pillars; since the R. M. E. *Catalogue* description[257] does not mention this key, it was, evidently, added after 1891. The bell is stamped 'FORNARI, A VENEZIA' in an oval composed of stars. Length (without staple), 72 cm. Diameter, max. (bell), 6.8 cm. Bore, min., 5 mm.; max., 20 mm.; length of conoidal part, 75 cm. Length of air column (with reed), 85 cm. (17.1920)
Plate IV

144. ENGLISH HORN — Vienna, Austria, ca. 1835

Cor Anglais. In F. The lowest tone is *e*. Ten keys. The tube is bent in the middle at an angle of 120 degrees. Boxwood, stained dark red-brown, ivory tips. Made in six parts: a brass staple slightly bent back, a moulded 'bulb' with an ivory tip, left-hand body-joint, an ivory 120° elbow, right-hand body-joint, and a pear-shaped bell with the *Liebesfuss*. The brass cup-shaped keys are: *b* (open), *c′* (open), *c′*-sharp, *d′*-sharp, *f′*, *f′*-sharp (in conjunction with hole), *g′*-sharp, *b′*-flat, *c″*, and the speaker key. All the keys are mounted on knobs. The *b* and *c′*-sharp key have long levers operated by the left little finger; the b′-flat key also has an extended lever operated by the right thumb. Finely made instrument stamped 'Kuss, Wien,' under an imperial eagle. Length (without staple), 77 cm. Diameter, max. (bell), 6.7 cm. Bore, min., 5 mm.; max., 19 mm.; length of conoidal part, 68 cm. Length of air column (with reed), 87 cm. (17.1919)
Plate IV

The Bassoon Family

THE origin of the bassoon has not been determined with any degree of certainty. The phagotus of Afranio is not an ancestor of the bassoon.[258] The more plausible theory of its descent from the bass shawm does not stand searching criticism, as Dr. Curt Sachs has shown in his *Real-Lexikon*.[259] Even the usual explanation that the Italian name, *fagotto*, is a reference to its fancied resemblance to a bundle of sticks (fagots) is anachronistic, since the early instruments were made from a solid block of wood and not separated into joints as were the later instruments.[260] The known history of the bassoon can be divided into three periods. (1) The earlier stage when the bassoon was made in one piece, this period ending in the second half of the eighteenth century. (2) The middle period, when the bassoon acquired its present form, but still remained a rather primitive instrument, ending in the first quarter of the nineteenth century. (3) The modern period, when the bassoon emerged both artistically and mechanically into its present position as one of the most important and colorful instruments of the modern orchestra. The evolution of the bassoon in the last period divided itself into two main streams, French and German. The French school of bassoon-making continued along the original lines of development; the key mechanism has organically evolved into its present relative perfection.

The proportions of the French bassoon are so chosen that they emphasize its feminine, lyrical, and elegiac aspect. The French bassoons possess a pleasant singing quality of tone. The German bassoons are built with a different bore and key mechanism. The masculine and dramatic aspect of the bassoon is brought into prominence by the German school of bassoon-making.[261] A choice between the two is difficult, because, since neither type of bassoon possesses all the desirable qualities of an ideal instrument, any preference becomes a matter of personal taste. With this necessary discrimination in mind, it is possible to say, in general, that the bassoon has a peculiar ability to express the most contradictory moods, varying from the solemn to the ridiculous, from the gay and happy to the pathetic and lugubrious. Only the bassoon can so well express droll and clownish moods, or become impertinent, even impudent. In the hands of a good player the bassoon discourses the language of emotions with dramatic, lyrical, elegiac eloquence, or becomes humorous and impish. To call the bassoon 'the clown of the orchestra' is to insult this noble instrument; it can be clownish if called for, but this is only one aspect of the many it is capable of expressing. Added to this is an extraordinary technical agility and unusually wide range, from *BB*-flat to *e''*-flat, or even *e''* or f''.

The earliest instruments, which as we know from Praetorius were called 'Dolcianen' or 'Fagotten,' were built along the lines of the curtal (No. 145). Two conoidal bores were bored in a solid block of wood of elliptic cross-section. At the bottom of the bores there was provided a passage by the cutting out of a portion of the dividing wall between the two bores and the plugging of the bottom hole with a cork cover. Zacconi (1592) mentions only two types of instruments of the bassoon family: *Fagotti Chorista*, C to b (?), and *Dolciane*, c to d' (g'); the second type corresponds to Praetorius' *Alt-Fagott* (table x, no. 6), but descends one tone lower. The bassoon family of Praetorius is presented below in tabulated form.

The instruments Nos. 2 and 6 are mentioned in *Tabella Universalis*, p. 23, of *De Organographia*.

All the bassoons of Praetorius were made from a single block of wood. The smaller sizes had no keys. The larger sizes, beginning with the single curtal (No. 4 of the table above), had two keys, E and F. It is usually stated that the first two keys on the bassoon were D and F; this is true only of some instruments. As will be shown under No. 145 there were two types of two-keyed bassoon. The lowest tone of the early bassoon should be also noted. It was nominal C. In this connection the scale and tonal position of the bassoon should be discussed.

The structure of the bassoon differs radically from other instruments. The flute, clarinet, oboe, and saxophone have their finger-holes and keys so disposed that the higher part of their register is controlled by the left hand and the lower part is controlled by the right hand. Any additional tones lower than the basic tone of the scale, such as *b*-natural and *b*-flat on

THE BASSOON FAMILY

(Praetorius, 1619)

No.	Table X	Tonal Position	Name	Compass
1................	Fig. 7	Soprano	*Discant Fagott* 'Exilent zum Chorist Fagott'	*a – c''*
2................		Alto	*Discant Fagott*	*g – c''*
3................	Fig. 6	Alto	*Alt Fagott*	*d* – ?
4................	Fig. 5	Bass	*Fagott Piccolo* Single Curtal 'Basset or Tenor to the Chorist Fagott'	*G – g'*
5................	Fig. 3	Contrabass	*Fagott* Double Curtal *Chorist Fagott*	*C – g'*
6................		Sub-bass	*Quart Fagott* *Fagott grando*	*GG – a*
7................	Fig. 2	Sub-bass	*Quint Fagott* *Doppel-Fagott*	*FF – g*

the oboe or the extra tones on the basset-horn, are regarded as extension tones and are controlled by additional keys operated by the right hand.

The bassoon has a tube doubled up upon itself and both thumbs are used to stop the finger-holes in the lower range of the instrument. On the bassoon the left hand controls the production of both the highest and the lowest tones; this is true of both old and modern instruments. Therefore, the bassoon fingering is based on a principle differing from other instruments, and comparisons between the bassoon and, say, the oboe, are hardly relevant. The fingering of Praetorius' *Chorist-Fagott*, table x, fig. 3, for example, would proceed as follows. It is assumed that the ascending diatonic scale is being fingered. The lowest tone *C* is produced by stopping all finger-, thumb-, and key-holes. One important detail: the right-hand thumb has to do double duty by holding the *E*-key down and stopping simultaneously the *E*-hole.[262] The tone *D* is produced by opening the *D*-hole, the one nearest to the bell and stopped by the left-hand thumb. The tone *E* sounds when the *E*-hole is uncovered by shifting the right-hand thumb downward over the *E*-key touch-piece. The tone *F* was made by lifting the right-hand thumb from the *E*-key, the flap of which heretofore covered the

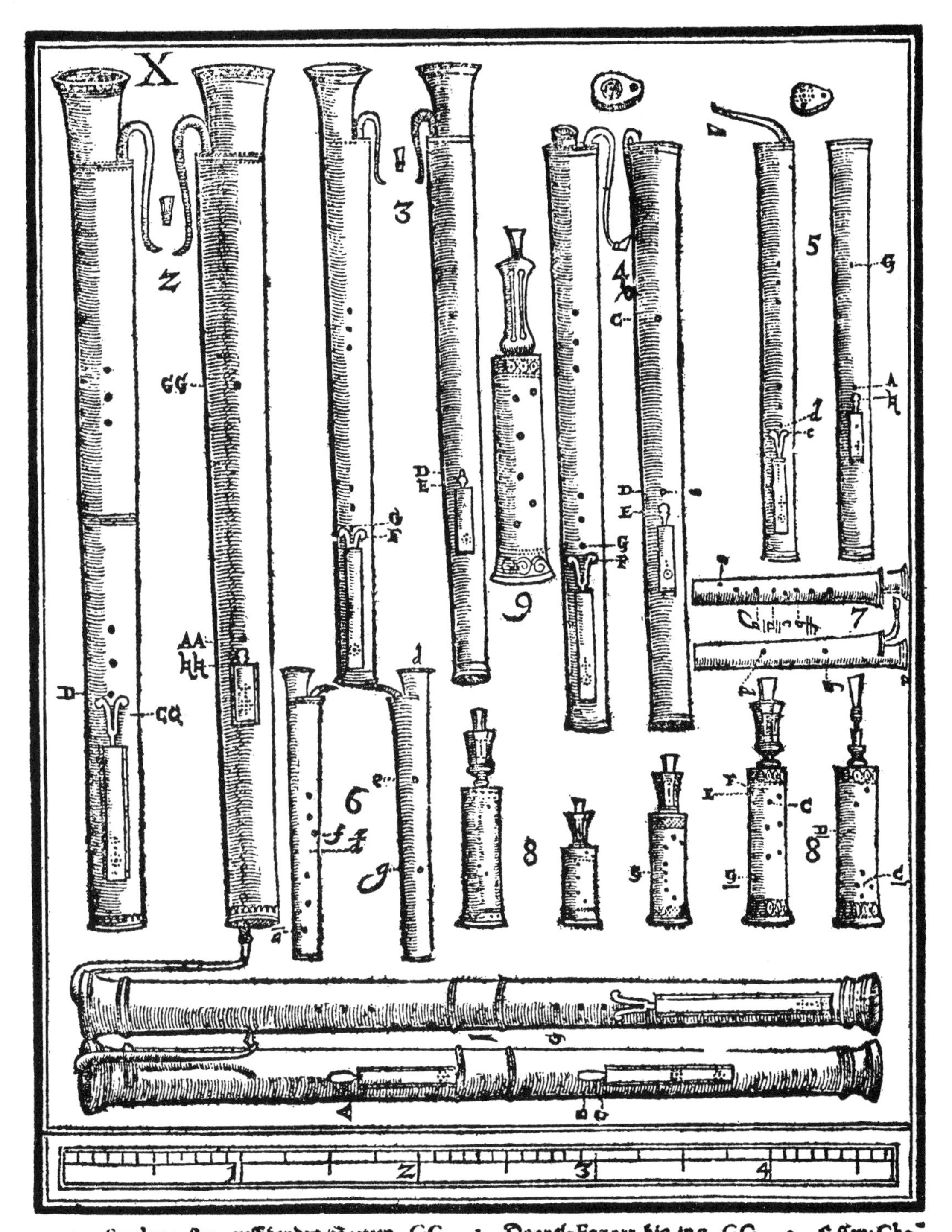

1. Sorduen-Bas auff beyden Seitten. GG. 2. Doppel-Fagott bis ins GG. 3. Offen-Chorist-Fagott C. 4. Gedact Chorist-Fagott. C. 5. Singel Korthol. Basset oder Tenor zum Chorist-Fagott, G. 6. Alt. d. 7. Discant oder Exilent zum Chor-Fagott. a. 8. Stimmwerck Racketten. 9. Groß-Rackett/ so tieff als der gar Grosse Baß-Bombard, CC, Uff 16. Fuß-Thon.

NB Bnden 1. 2. 3. 4. 5. stehen die Buchstaben des Clavis beym Loch/ do es zugemacht wird. Im 6. 7. & 8. 9. aber stehen die Buchstaben des Clavis, do das Loch offen bleibt.

FIG. 24. PRAETORIUS, TABLE X

1. Bass Sourdine, both sides, GG. 2. Double Bassoon, descending to GG. 3. Open Chorist-Bassoon, C. 4. Covered Chorist-Bassoon, C. 5. Single Curtal. Basset or Tenor for Chorist-Bassoon, G. 6. Alto [-Bassoon], *d*. 7. Discant or Exilent [-Bassoon] for Chorist-Bassoon, *a*. 8. Family of Racketts. 9. Great Rackett, as deep as Great Bass-Bombard, CC, with 16-foot tone.

N.B. On the instruments 1, 2, 3, 4, and 5, letters of the tones are shown at the finger-holes which are to be stopped. But on 6, 7, 8, and 9, letters of the tones are shown at the finger-holes which remain open.

F-hole. The tone G sounds when the *F*-key is released. The rest of the scale is produced by the successive uncovering of the finger-holes located in the front of the instrument. With all holes and keys open the Chorist-Fagott sounds *f*.

The fundamental scale on the Chorist-Fagott is the C-major scale, which should be regarded as the basic scale of the bassoon.[263] The tonal position of the members of the bassoon family can be determined by the lowest tone of their basic scale. The instruments with the extension tones are treated in the usual way.[264] The orchestral bassoon is regarded as a non-transposing instrument. This is a sound tradition and convenient musical practice based on the old scale of the early Chorist-Fagott.

The overblowing technique of the bassoon is somewhat peculiar. The basic scale of the instrument played without overblowing extends from *C* (*BB*-flat or *AA*) to *f*, or, counting from *C*, one octave and a fourth. The lowest octave of the bassoon can be overblown as that of any other wood-wind instrument, but in practice the lowest tones from *BB*-flat to *F* inclusive are not overblown, since they would duplicate the tones from *B*-flat to *f*, which are already on the instrument and can be played without overblowing. Therefore the first overblown tone of the bassoon is *g*, which is overblown from G as the basic tone.

The tones from *g* to *f′* are overblown an octave; the tone *g′* is overblown as the fourth partial tone from G (that is as a double octave). The tone *a′* is overblown from *d* as a twelfth; from *b′* up the fingerings become complex and depend upon the system of key mechanism. On the old bassoon the upper limit of the compass was *g′*. In this connection it should be noted that Praetorius gave the overblown tones up to *d′*; the tones *e′*, *f′*, and *g′* are printed in solid black in *Tabella Universalis* (p. 23 of *De Organographia*, under no. 3). The old bassoon overblew easily up to *d′* inclusive; above that, owing to the proximity of the upper holes to the reed and the shortness of the remaining effective length of the tube, the tones were less certain. The refinements of the bore, the auxiliary means for easier overblowing of the higher tones, and the extension of the bassoon compass upward, were the work of the nineteenth century.

The further evolution of the bassoon will be briefly indicated. In Mersenne's time (1636) the bassoon still had two keys. At the time when the *Pomone* of Cambert was produced (1671) the compass was extended to the low *BB*-flat and the key to produce this tone added. In 1687 Daniel Speer in *Unterricht der musicalischen Kunst* gave the fingering of the 'Bass Fagott,' which had two keys disposed similarly to those of the bassoon of Praetorius' time.[265] Mattheson in *Das Neu-eröffnete Orchester* (1713) gave the normal compass of the bassoon from *C* to *f′* or *g′*, thus confirming Praetorius.[266] He also stated that some instruments descended to *BB*-flat or even *AA*. The fourth key, G-sharp, was added some time in the first quarter of the eighteenth century; in the Brussels Collection there is a bassoon (no. 997) made by G. de Bruijn in 1730 which has a closed key producing the tone G-sharp.[267] The fifth key was the low E-flat key.

In 1807, a most valuable series, the *Instrumental Assistant*, was published at Exeter, New Hampshire. The second volume has as a sub-title *with Instructions for the French Horn and Bassoon*. It was compiled by Samuel Holyoke, A.M., "from late European publications."[268]

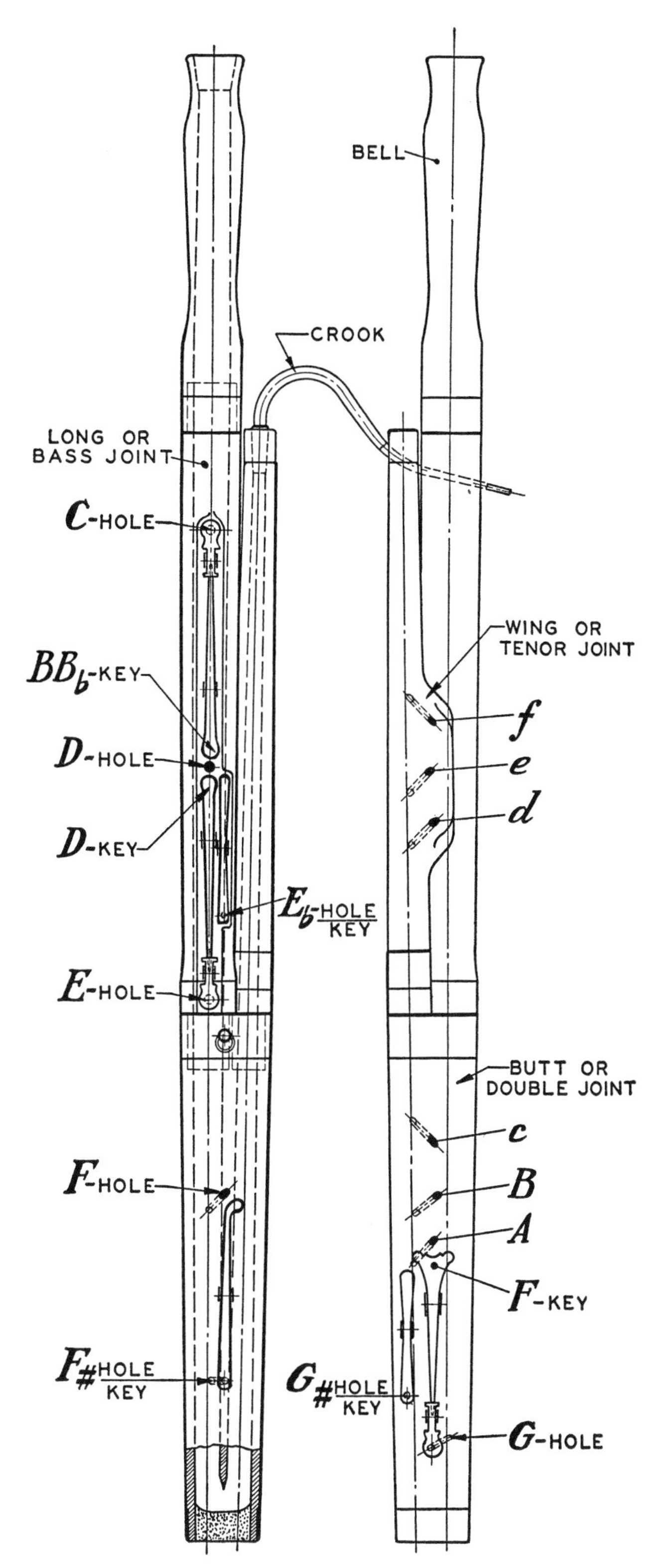

FIG. 25. FRONT AND REAR VIEWS OF THE SIX-KEYED BASSOON

The bassoon described by him had 14 holes and 6 keys. Since this book is a great rarity and one of the few published in any country about that time, a few quotations will be of interest. On page vi Samuel Holyoke states: "The Bassoon is imperfect, and requires the assistance of a good musical ear to blow it in tolerable tune." On page vii he gives a detailed description of the bassoon at the turn of the century (1800) which is so excellent that it will be quoted verbatim. The bassoon represented on Fig. 25 to illustrate Holyoke's description is No. 148 of this Collection, drawn to scale; the only addition is the F-sharp key, which is not on Milhouse's instrument. It should be noted that Holyoke counts the tone-holes from the highest downward; therefore the finger-holes of the tones from *f* to *A* are "the first 6 holes . . . stopped with the fingers." Position of the hands is standard: the left hand is above the right hand. The keys G-sharp, F-sharp, and E-flat are closed keys; the rest are open keys.

The Bassoon has 14 holes, as represented by 14 lines in the Scales [the fingering chart], 8 of which are stopped with the thumbs, and fingers, and 6 with the keys. The first 6 holes are stopped with the fingers. The 7th, with F, or great lower key. The 8th, with A-flat or G-sharp key, which is the small key at the bottom.

The 9th, with the F-sharp key, or the key governed with the right thumb. The 10th, is the right hand thumbhole. The 11th, with the long key above the right hand thumb hole, which is governed with the left hand thumb. The 12th, with the small key above the right hand thumb hole which is the E-flat or D-sharp key.

The 13th is the left hand thumb hole.

The 14th, with the upper long, or double B-flat key, which is the lowest note on the Bassoon; to make which you must stop at once with your left thumb, two keys and one hole, as may be seen by the scales.

Some remarks on fingering the ascending scale on the bassoon may be found of interest. The lowest tone, *BB*-flat, is produced with all finger-holes and open keys stopped; as explained by Holyoke, the left-hand thumb has a triple duty to perform. To produce the tone *C*, the BB-flat key is released and the left-hand thumb remains on the D-hole and the D-key. The tone *D* is produced by sliding the left-hand thumb down the D-key lever, still holding it down, and opening the D-hole. The other fingerings present no exceptions, but the operation of some keys is rather interesting. In fingering the ascending chromatic scale on the bassoons of the old type (or their modern lineal descendants) the key E-flat is opened before the D-key is released. This rather unusual order is explained by the fact that the E-flat key is a closed key and the D-key is an open one; therefore, in order to produce E-flat the D-key must be kept closed, otherwise the bassoon would sound *E*; by pressing the E-flat key, its hole will speak E-flat; to produce *E* both levers, E-flat and D, must be simultaneously released; the E-flat will cover up its hole and the D-lever will raise its key-flap and the bassoon will speak *E*. Likewise in playing the descending scale the F-lever must be pressed simultaneously with the F-sharp lever, if the tone F-sharp is desired; the closing of the F-sharp key produces the tone *F*, if the F-lever is kept closed. If the keys are counted on the bassoon in the descending order, the F-key is encountered first; it is located in the front of the instrument. The F-sharp key, located in the rear, follows (not precedes!) the F-key. Again the explanation of this seeming incongruity is the fact that the F-key is an open key and covers the G-hole; the F-sharp key is a closed key and produces its tone only when it is open and the F-key closed.

Among the bassoon-makers who contributed to the development of the bassoon the names of J. F. Simiot (first quarter of the nineteenth century) of Lyons, France, and F. G. Adler (d. 1854) of Paris should be mentioned. Simiot added in 1808 the keys for *B*-natural and *C*-sharp, and in 1823 the keys for *F*-sharp, *c*-sharp, and *f*-sharp. Adler made many improvements in the key mechanism; in 1827 he constructed the 15-key bassoon; in 1839 he extended the compass up to *e''*-flat. The Stradivari of the bassoon was Jean Nicolas Savary *jeune* of Paris, whose bassoons had a singing quality of tone. The present-day French bassoons are built after Savary's model.[269]

The modern German bassoon is a development along lines departing from the old tradition. Carl Almenräder, a bassoon-player and later a court musician of the Duke of Nassau in Biebrich and Wiesbaden, in 1820 designed a bassoon with many improvements. In 1831 he took into partnership Johann Adam Heckel, an instrument-maker. From this partnership has grown the firm of Wilhelm Heckel, outstanding among wood-wind instrument builders. The somewhat meagre details of the evolution of the Almenräder-Heckel bassoon can be found in a booklet, *Der Fagott.*[270]

145. SINGLE CURTAL — Reproduction, early 17th-century type

Bass in G. The lowest tone is G. Two keys. Boxwood, stained a blackish-brown. Made in three parts: a brass crook with a circular brass shoe, the body of oval cross-section with a double bore, and a short bell; bound with brass ferrules. Six finger-holes in the front; two thumb-holes in the rear. Two open brass keys: one in the front, F (actually gives *c*) with two touch pieces, another one in the rear, D (actually gives A); both keys have their mechanisms protected by perforated brass boxes. Length, 65.8 cm. Width (major axis), 6.2 cm. Bore, min. (crook orifice), 4 mm.; max., 27 mm.; length of conoidal part, 134.5 cm. Length of air column (with reed), 142.5 cm. (17.1921) Plate III

The original instrument, of which this one is a simplified copy, is preserved in the Germanic Museum in Nuremberg. The *Catalogue . . . de Bruxelles* has a facsimile copy (no. 991) described and pictured on pp. 264 and 265 of the second volume. The dispositon of the rear open key differs from that of Praetorius in that it covers the *E*-hole when the key lever is pressed down and therefore produces the tone *D*. Praetorius' instruments had the rear key cover the F-hole and the key when pressed down gave the tone *E*. This is an essential constructional difference, since it affected the fingering technique of the two-keyed bassoon. Thus Daniel Speer's fingering, already mentioned, refers to this type of bassoon with the D-key and not to Praetorius' type. A conclusion which can be drawn from this is that Praetorius' bassoons with the E-key were instruments of an earlier type.

The name 'curtal' with its various spellings comes from the old French word *courtault*, meaning 'short.' There were two kinds of curtals: a higher pitched 'single curtal' in G and a larger instrument in C, the familiar Chorist-Fagott, which was called a 'double curtal.' The meaning of the adjectives 'single' and 'double' has been explained by Canon Galpin in his *Old English Instruments of Music.*[271]

146. BASSOON Germany, early 18th century

Fagottino. Baritone in C. The lowest tone is B-flat. Three keys. Boxwood, stained light yellowish-brown; brass tips. Made in five parts: brass crook, wing (or tenor) joint, butt, long joint, and a bell. The bore is conoidal up to the bell; the bore of the bell is an inverted conoid narrowing toward the orifice. Six finger-holes in the front; two thumb-holes in the rear. Three square brass keys (open): B-flat, d, and f; mounted on knobs. The bell and the body-joint are richly moulded. Stamped: 'I. C. Denner' in a scroll and the letter 'D' underneath. Length, 63.5 cm. Width, butt, 4.2 cm. Bore, min. (crook orifice), 3.5 mm.; max. (end of the long joint), 21 mm.; length of conoidal part, 105.5 cm. Bell, orifice diameter, 19 mm. Length of air column (with reed), 124.5 cm. (17.1922)
Plate IV

This instrument is similar in construction to nos. 427 and 998 of the Brussels Collection.[272] It is a richly profiled and finely made instrument, probably by I. C. Denner's sons. Played with the bassoon reed, it gives rich, reedy tones in the register where the deeper pitched orchestral instrument sounds more like a violoncello. For this reason, if for no other, the instrument should be revived, as it produces a tone color absent from the present double reed orchestral family.[273] In its tonal position this fagottino is equivalent to the baritone oboe. The inverted conoidal bore of the bass joint, a feature also present on bassoons Nos. 147, 148, and 149, and to a lesser extent on No. 150, was intended to soften the lower tones.

147. BASSOON Ireland, middle of the 18th century

Tenoroon. Bass in F. The lowest tone is *E*-flat. Four keys. Boxwood, stained blackish-brown; brass tips. Made in five parts like No. 146. The bore is also similar to that of No. 146. Six finger-holes in the front; two thumb-holes in the rear. Four brass keys mounted on saddles: *B*-flat, *d*, *f*, and *g*-sharp. Stamped 'Blockley' under the emblem of an Irish harp. Length, 83 cm. Width, butt, 6.2 cm. Bore, min. (crook orifice), 2 mm.; max. (end of long joint), 24 mm.; length of conoidal part, 156 cm. Bell, orifice diameter, 21 mm. Length of air column (with reed), 167.7 cm. (17.1923)
Plate IV

Higher-pitched bassoons were built down to the middle of the nineteenth century. The French firm of Buffet-Crampon still builds on order bassoons in D, E-flat, F, and even in G, an innovation introduced by them at the Universal Exposition in Paris, 1889.[274] The alternative name, 'tenoroon,' was applied to alto fagotto (No. 121; this is not correct: see p. 105). Described in the R. M. E. *Catalogue* on p. 76, under no. 152, where it is suggested that it was probably made by Stanesby.

148. BASSOON Newark, England, late 18th century

Contrabass in C. The lowest tone is BB-flat. Five keys. Maple, stained dark brown; brass tips. Made in five parts like No. 146. The bore is like that on No. 146. Six finger-holes in the front; two thumb-holes in the rear. Five brass keys: *BB*-flat, *D*, *E*-flat in the rear; *F* and *G*-sharp in the front; the *F*-key has a double touch piece; all the keys are mounted on saddles. The maker's name is only partly legible: 'M . . . OUSE, N . . . RK'; stands for 'MILHOUSE, NEWARK.' Length, 122.8 cm. Width, butt, 7.5 cm. Bore, min. (crook orifice), 4 mm.; max. (end of the long

joint), 30 mm.; length of conoidal part, 217 cm. Bell, orifice diameter, 27 mm. Length of air column (with reed), 248 cm. (17.1925)
Plate IV

This bassoon was made by the same Milhouse of Newark who made the oboe No. 139 of this Collection.

149. BASSOON France, late 18th century

Contrabass in C. The lowest tone is BB-flat. Nine keys. Boxwood, stained light yellow; brass tips. Made in five parts like No. 146. The bore is like that on No. 146. Six finger-holes in the front; two thumb-holes in the rear. The instrument has been considerably changed: the long joint shortened and the key mechanism altered. The original instrument had but five keys: *BB*-flat, *D*, *E*-flat (now removed and the hole and the saddle socket plugged with wood), *F*, and *G*-sharp. Subsequently, *F*-sharp, *B*-correction key, *c*-sharp, *f*-sharp, and *a'* keys were added. The original keys are mounted on saddles; the new keys are 'home made' and mounted on wire loops. Length, 114 cm. Width, butt, 6.7 cm. Bore, min. (crook orifice), 4 mm.; max. (end of long joint), 32 mm.; length of conoidal part, 212 cm. Bell, orifice diameter, 30 mm. Length of air column (with reed), 237 cm. (17.1924)
Plate IV

Unfortunately, this fine bassoon was mercilessly cut down to make it of higher pitch than it originally was. The additional keys are amateur work, not in keeping with the original five keys. The workmanship shows that it is, probably, of French origin.

150. BASSOON England, late 19th century

Contrabass in C. The lowest tone is BB-flat. Seventeen keys. Rosewood, stained dark brown; German silver keys and tips. Made in five parts like No. 146. Conoidal bore, except the bell-joint which becomes very slightly narrower toward the orifice (about 75 per cent of its length), then gradually flares out. Six finger-holes in the front; one thumb-hole in the rear. The key mechanism is of a modern type mounted on pillars. *BB*-flat, *C*, and *D* keys are interlocked. The *B*-natural key is located on the long joint and is not interlocked with the C-key. The vent-hole key on the crook is interlocked with the three highest keys. No maker's name; all the joints are stamped: '20x–I.' Length, 127.2 cm. Width, butt, 6.5 cm. Bore, min. (crook orifice), 4 mm.; max. (end of long joint), 34 mm.; length of conoidal part, 209.5 cm. Bell, minimum diameter, 32.5 mm. Length of air column (with reed), 243.5 cm. (17.1926)
Plate IV

A modern bassoon; probably the experimental model of an English maker.

151. BASSOON Paris, France, ca. 1860

Contrabass in C. The lowest tone is *BB*-flat. Twenty-nine keys. Rosewood, stained dark brown. German silver keys and trimmings. Made in six parts: crook, two left-hand joints, a U-shaped connecting tube (German silver), two right-hand joints; the whole body of the instrument forming a U-shaped tube with unequal arms. The bore is conoidal throughout, with a slightly flaring bell. There is no wing joint or butt. No finger-holes. All holes, twenty-nine in number, are covered with cup-shaped keys operated by a very ingenious, but exceedingly complicated, mechanism based on that of the Boehm flute. Stamped 'A. MARZOLI, A PARIS, BREVETÉ,' the monogram 'ABM,' and the number '92' on the bell. Length, 132.7 cm. Width, 8.5 cm. Bore, min. (crook

orifice), 4 mm.; max., 44 mm.; length of conoidal part, 251.5 cm. Length of air column (with reed), 261.5 cm. (17.1927)
Plate IV

Described in the R. M. E. *Catalogue* on p. 79 under no. 166. This instrument originally belonged to the band of one of the battalions of the 60th Rifles of England. The first instrument of this type was developed by Triébert, and exhibited in 1862 at the London Exposition, where it received the Prize Medal. It is similar to no. 3119 of the Brussels Collection (cf. the *Catalogue . . . de Bruxelles*, v, pp. 92 f.). This bassoon is one of the several attempts to improve an admittedly defective instrument. Its key mechanism is constructed on the Boehm's flute principle, the features being ingenuity and extreme complexity. Since there are no finger-holes, all stopping is done by keys. The mechanism of this type was found impracticable. In addition, the radical modification of the tube and elimination of oblique finger-holes so affected the tone color that it sounds more like a sarrusophone. All serious departures from the time-honored model of the bassoon were penalized by alteration of the tone color so that it no longer sounded like a bassoon. The bassoon of today remains an imperfect instrument and requires excellent musicianship, but, if the lessons of history are read aright, it can be improved only in detail, not in substance.

152. DOUBLE-BASSOON — Vienna, Austria, ca. 1835

Contrabassoon. Contrafagotto. Subcontrabass in C. The lowest tone is BBB-flat (high pitch). Nine keys. Maple, stained dark brown; brass extension tube and bell; brass tips. Made in eight parts: crook, crook extension pipe (both of brass), wing-joint, intermediate joint, butt, long joint (all these are of wood), brass extension tube, and a bell. The bore is conoidal up to the end of the wooden long joint; the brass extension tube is cylindrical. Six finger-holes in the front, two thumb-holes in the rear. Nine cup-shaped brass keys mounted on pillars. The keys have the standard arrangement, except for the old style *c*-sharp key, which is mounted in the rear above the F-hole and is operated by the right-hand thumb. Stamped on the butt 'Stehle, formals Kuss, Wien'; on the brass ferrule binding the butt is engraved: 'Kaiser. K. Hof-Capellen Instrument.' Length, 263 cm. Width, butt, 10 cm. Bore, conoidal, min. (crook orifice), 6.5 mm.; max. (wooden long joint), 50 mm.; length, 365 cm.; cylindrical, brass tube, inside diameter, 48.5 mm.; length, 94 cm. Bell, diameter, 18.5 cm., length of effective part, 32 cm. Length of air column (with reed), 495 cm. (17.1928)

The R. M. E. *Catalogue* on p. 81, under no. 170, lists a contrabassoon, built by Stehle, which belonged to the Vienna Imperial Capella; it has eight keys, descending only to CC, and its length is given as six feet six inches (198.3 cm.). Our instrument has nine keys (*BB*-flat, *D*, *E*-flat, *F*, *F*-sharp, *G*-sharp, *B*-correction key, *c*-sharp key on the wing joint, and the old style *c*-sharp key, which is located on the butt-joint, and, as already stated, is operated by the right-hand thumb.[275] The hole for this key is drilled into the wing-joint side of the double bore in the butt, and is located inside the bore above the C-hole. In conjunction with the *c*-sharp key on the wing-joint this tone is produced with greater ease and in better tune. The lowest tone on our instrument is close to *BBB*-natural at a′-440 cycles per second; this means that the instrument sounds *BBB*-flat, high pitch. It seems, therefore, that the brass tube of the bell-joint was lengthened and one extra key added to extend the compass of the instrument one tone lower. The original instrument was built between 1835 and 1845.

SECTION C: LIP-VIBRATED AEROPHONES

THE third great section of aerophones comprises those instruments in which the lips of a player serve as the vibrator. The simplest lip-vibrated aerophones consist of a tube open at both ends and a mouthpiece. The mouthpiece on some instruments, made out of animal horn or wood, is sometimes cut in the tube itself; the more usual method is to make the mouthpiece separate. Lip-vibrated aerophones are known as 'trumpets' (in the generic sense), 'cup-mouthpiece instruments,' 'brass wind,' or simply 'brass.' None of these names is sufficiently inclusive; some are misleading.

The classification of lip-vibrated aerophones is a complex and somewhat uncertain task. The only correct basis is a natural scale of simple tubes of fixed length. The geometrical shape of the bore of the tube is of secondary importance, since the basic acoustical properties are similar both in the conoidal and cylindrical tube instruments.[276] The uncertainty exists with respect to both the lower and higher registers of the natural scale, as will be seen presently.

It is possible to state without qualification that the true playing technique of lip-vibrated aerophones is based exclusively on overblowing. This principle is not affected by the existence of lateral hole instruments, such as cornetts and serpents, on which the scale is produced in a manner similar to the transverse flute and recorders. Such technique is not true brass technique. The intermediate type of instrument, the keyed bugle, having large lateral key covered holes and no finger-holes, was using the overblowing technique almost to the same extent as the valved instruments. As soon as the valve mechanism on the 'brass wind' reached a relative state of perfection, the lateral hole instruments went out of use. Therefore, the normal method for producing tones on the lip-vibrated aerophones is by overblowing. Detailed description of the technique of brass instruments is given on pp. 169–173.

In general it is possible to state that theoretically all lip-vibrated aerophones produce the complete natural scale, or a 1, 2, 3, 4, 5, . . . series of partial tones; theoretically, this series of tones should extend upward indefinitely. In practice limitations exist to the upward compass; generic classification is based on this upward limit. There also exists the ability or inability of lip-vibrated aerophones to produce the pedal tone; specific classification is based on the presence or absence of the pedal tone.

Specific Classification of Lip-Vibrated Aerophones

THE logic of classification requires that generic division should be established first. Historically, specific division was noticed first and generic division was for the most part implied, but never explicitly formulated. As a matter of fact, several writers have mistaken specific division for generic and have reached erroneous conclusions with respect to the inauguration of the 'new era' in the construction of brass-wind instruments at the time of the introduction of the valve mechanism.[277] Therefore our present task is to prove that the presence or absence of the pedal tone is a *specific* and not a generic characteristic.

The problem is, perhaps, as old as the lip-vibrated instruments themselves. It was explicitly stated for the first time (1636) when Mersenne noticed that not all trumpeters knew of the existence or could produce the tone one octave below that usually considered to be the first tone on the trumpet. His comment is very illuminating.

> Il faut aussi remarquer que le ton, que l'on appelle ordinairement le premier, ou le plus bas de la Trompette, n'est pas celui dont on use ordinairement, & que j'ay nommé UT, car elle descend encore d'une Octave entière, quoy que plusieurs Trompettes ne le croyent pas, parce qu'ils ne le peuvent fair, ou qu'ils ne l'ont jamais essayé.[278]

The enumeration of the partial tones of the trumpet by Mersenne on page 249, livre v of *Harmonie universelle*, as well as the note example on the banner of the trumpet pictured on page 267 of the same work, leave no doubt that Mersenne referred to the pedal tone. The old-time German trumpeters had a special term for it, *Flattergrob*; no better description of the pedal tone of the trumpet can be given, because it is a rough, fluttering tone.

Therefore, in Mersenne's time it was a well known fact that some players were unable to produce the pedal tone on the trumpet. This lack of ability of some players to produce the pedals on the brass instruments complicates the entire problem of their correct classification. The same problem had to be faced in 1854 when Dr. Carl Schafhäutl wrote an article on musical instruments, with reference to those exhibited in Munich at that time.[279] He noticed, quite correctly, that the proportions of the tube had a decisive influence upon the ability of the instrument to produce the pedal tone. The wide bore tubes produced the pedals easily, with a sonorous, rich quality of tone; the narrow bore tubes either completely refused to 'speak' or behaved capriciously, depending upon whether a player had or had not a lip for producing pedal tones. Dr. Schafhäutl divided brass-wind instruments into two groups: (1) 'Ganzinstrument,' or whole-tube instrument group, the bore proportions of which permitted the utilization of the entire length of the tube, so that the pedal tone had the same pitch as an open organ pipe with a length equal to the tube of the brass instrument; and (2) 'Halbinstrument,' or the half-tube instrument group, which, although theoretically capable of producing the pedal, in practice, by producing the second partial tone as the lowest tone, utilized, as it were, only one half the length of the actual tube. Thus the French horn in C should be capable of producing a 16-foot *CC*, since its tubing is about this length (515 cm., exactly); whereas the lowest tone it can produce is only 8-foot *C*. In the actual grouping of instruments Dr. Schafhäutl did not adhere strictly to acoustical principles. He depended also on the current local musical usage, which was not to employ pedal tones on the flügelhorn. In that early period of brass instrument-making, when the new designs of the valved instruments were appearing quite frequently, such a lack of strict discrimination was excusable, and in no sense invalidated Dr. Schafhäutl's indispensable grouping. With the greater knowledge of the qualitative properties of lip-vibrated aerophones at our disposal a more precise statement is possible. To the writer's knowledge this problem of the pedal tone with respect to standard brass instruments has never been consistently investigated.

Anticipating somewhat, the principal families of lip-vibrated aerophones are as follows: 1. The Bugle-Tuba-Flügelhorn-Saxhorn Family.[280] 2. The Horn Family. 3. The Trombone Family. 4. The Trumpet Family.

It will be noted that the first family has a somewhat complex name. All these names are equivalent and designate only one type of instrument, the bugles. Theoretically, the bore of the bugle should be a conoid with a wide taper; in practice, certain lengths of cylindrical tubing are introduced in various places on the bore; the extent and proportion of the relative lengths of the conoidal and cylindrical tubing, as well as the size of the taper, varied with different manufacturers and in some cases constituted a proprietary model. Patent litigation in the past has developed many questionable practices, one of which was the unnecessary multiplication of names not only of individual instruments, but also of essentially identical family groups. The bewildering nomenclature of brass instruments of the nineteenth century is one of the results of this struggle. Now as to the pedal tone.

1. *The instruments of the bugle (tuba-flügelhorn-saxhorn) family are without exception whole-tube instruments with pedal tone.* The only qualification is with respect to the BB-flat bugle or the contrabass tuba, on which the pedal tone and several valved tones (on the four-valved instruments) in the lowest register are not sufficiently sonorous. There is some confusion about the pedal tone of the bugles (saxhorns). For instance, the high-pitched saxhorns are regarded as half-tube instruments and the low-pitched saxhorns (tubas) as whole-tube instruments. It happens that the whole family of bugles (saxhorns) has the pedal tone and therefore such division is incorrect acoustically. It is true that musically the upper saxhorns are treated as if they had no pedal tone, mostly because they are built with three valves only. This was not always so. Plate xx in G. Kastner's *Manuel général de musique militaire*, represents the whole family of saxhorns with *four* piston valves, ranging from the sopranino in *E*-flat to the bass in *E*-flat; the fourth valve ('Quartventil') would be a senseless addition if the pedal tone were not available; it is added only when the interval between nominal C and F-sharp is to be filled on the valved brass instrument, provided that C (the pedal) is easily available. The question might be asked: 'why are the four-valved sopranino, soprano, and alto bugles (flügelhorns) not being built today?' The answer is that only a few instruments of this type were built; the parts in the bands are written for the generally used three-valve instruments;[281] the tones of the soprano bugle in the lower valved octave would duplicate the better sounding tones of the baritone bugle of the same pitch. In other words, in some cases the problem is not whether the pedal tone is available or not, but what to do with it when it is available. This is again a musical and not an acoustical problem.[282]

2. *The instruments of the horn family belong to two specific groups: the lower horns from B-flat basso to the F-horn inclusive are half-tube instruments without pedal tone; the upper horns beginning with the G-horn are whole-tube instruments with pedal tone.* This statement goes contrary to the generally accepted notion that all the horns are half-tube instruments. Any horn player who plays the double horn or a B-flat single horn[283] will laugh at such a notion and then will proceed to disprove it by producing *BB*-flat (in unison with the lowest tone of the bassoon), then blandly valve the following tones: *AA* (the 2nd valve), *AA*-flat (the 1st valve), *GG* (the 3rd valve), in acceptably good tune; *GG*-flat (2 and 3), *FF* (1 and 3), and finally *EE* (1, 2, and 3), these last three tones being rather difficult to produce. Moreover in the United States there is a five-valve single French horn in B-flat.[284] The

existence of this model, actually used by some professional horn players, disposes of any unqualified statements that horns are half-tube instruments having no pedal tone.

The horn family is an example of important acoustical characteristic change within the family.

3. *The trombone in the higher positions is a whole-tube instrument with pedal tone; in the lower positions it is a half-tube instrument without pedal tone.*

The statement is shocking. Here is an instrument which changes its acoustical characteristic according to the location of the slide. The facts are well known. The tenor-trombone has the following playable pedal tones: *BB*-flat, *AA*, *AA*-flat, in the first, second, and third positions respectively; some good trombonists can play *GG* of the fourth position without much trouble, but below that the pedals refuse to 'speak.' Therefore, what is the tenor-trombone; a whole- or half-tube instrument? The correct answer is that it is both. So here we are confronted with a case where one and the same instrument changes its specific acoustical characteristic.

4. *Instruments of the trumpet family should be divided into two groups similarly to those of the horn family: the lower trumpets from the B-flat (basso) to the E inclusive are half-tube instruments without pedal tone; the higher trumpets from F to A-flat*[285] *are whole-tube instruments with pedal tone.*

Only the true trumpets are considered here and not modern instruments pitched in B-flat and higher. Mersenne's statement and Berlioz' remarks about the trumpet should be studied.[286]

Therefore, to summarize, it is possible to say that the bugle family has the pedal tone on all its members; the horn and the trumpet families change the characteristic within the family; the trombone family changes the characteristic with the instruments themselves.

Conclusions: (1) The presence or absence of the pedal tone is a specific and not a generic characteristic. (2) It is practically useful for determination of the playable ranges of instruments and in cases when the desirability of the fourth valve on the instrument is considered. (3) The change of this characteristic, whether within the family or within the individual instrument, does not split either a family or an instrument into separate generic groups. In the case of horns and trumpets it is not necessary; in the case of trombones it is not possible. (4) A generic acoustical classification of lip-vibrated aerophones should exist.

To prevent any misunderstanding, it should be taken into consideration that the whole argument is based, in addition to the well known facts, on the following assumptions:

1. The instruments considered are average good instruments furnished with proper mouthpieces.[287]

2. An average competent performer is taken as a norm.

3. Only simple, fixed lengths of tubings and their acoustical properties are considered, specifically: the natural instruments with interchangeable crooks (horns and trumpets) are regarded as individual instruments for each crook; the slide instruments are regarded as compound instruments, each standard position being regarded as an elementary acoustical unit;[288] the valved instruments are studied as simple tubes with the valves in the 'off' posi-

tion, thus the valve horn in F is regarded as a natural horn crooked in F; the inclusion of the valve crook on the valved instrument is regarded as the change of crook on the natural horn.

These assumptions are also valid for the following discussion.

Generic Classification of Lip-Vibrated Aerophones

THE problem of pedal tone and its availability concerns the lowest register of lip-vibrated aerophones. This, as we have seen, is an old problem which is brought out here in sharper relief than heretofore. It has been shown that the presence or absence of the pedal tone can serve only as a basis for the specific grouping of lip-vibrated aerophones, since it changes not only within a family, but even on individual instruments (trombone). The generic classification of lip-vibrated aerophones is based on their upper register. The question of what is the upper limit of partial tones on brass instruments is even more uncertain, at least in the mind of some writers upon the subject. Much depends upon the ability of a player and current practice. In old scores trumpet and horn parts are written as high as the twentieth partial tone and in some individual instances even higher. Again, in Germany a special practice of producing higher partial tones was cultivated, the so-called 'Clarinblasen'; but such a technique is an accomplishment of exceptional individuals which cannot be taken as a norm. There are certain well established facts which may be taken as a guide for the generic classification of lip-vibrated aerophones.

There are three clearly recognizable groups of lip-vibrated aerophones: 1. Two-octave instruments. 2. Three-octave instruments. 3. Four-octave instruments.

These terms are based on the following ranges of partial tones of the natural scale produced by various types of lip-vibrated aerophones:

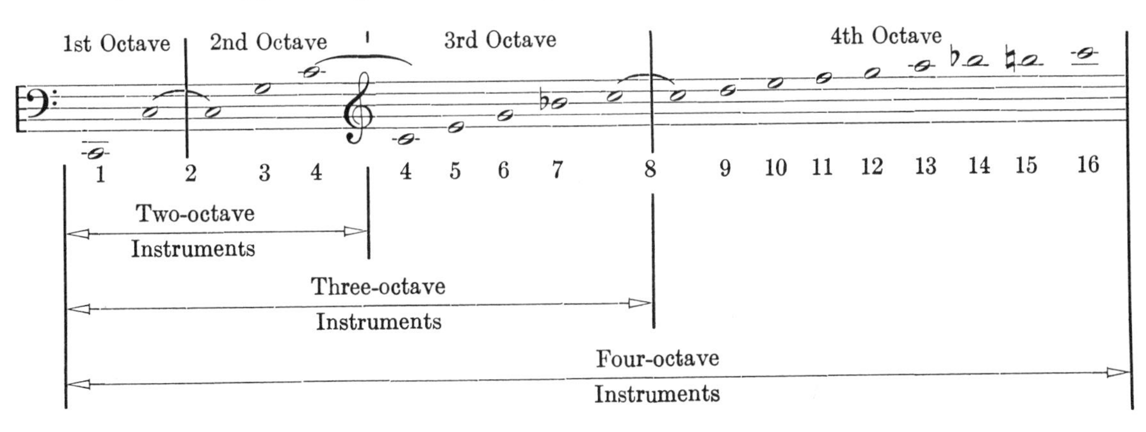

The first group, *two-octave instruments*, is so called because their partial tones range from the pedal tone to the fourth partial tone inclusive. Some primitive instruments made of animal horns, tusks, or tree bark and having short, large bores produce only the pedal tone; some produce the pedal and the second partial tone, etc., not exceeding the fourth partial tone; anything above that produced by some exceptional player should be regarded as a primitive 'Clarinblasen.'[289] The tone color of such an instrument is either dull or rough and brutal; owing to the small number of overtones it is uninteresting. Since the pedal tone is always producible on instruments of this group there are no sub-groups.

The second group, *three-octave instruments*, has a range of partial tones from the pedal tone to the eighth partial tone inclusive. Some exceptional players can produce partial tones above the eighth by means of the 'Clarinblasen' technique, but practical experience shows that it is wiser to stay within this limit.[290] The slide trombones belong to this group, as well as the modern valve instruments invented in the nineteenth century: bugles (tubas, flügelhorns, saxhorns of all sizes), cornets, valve trombones, modern high trumpets (in B-flat, C, D, E-flat, and F), saxotrombas, and saxtubas. The tone color of these instruments is more suitable for military bands; some instruments like the euphonium (the baritone bugle) have a fine tone not devoid of a certain degree of nobility. Nevertheless they are inferior to the next group, which may be regarded as the aristocracy of the brass wind instruments.

The third group, *four-octave instruments*, reaches normally as high as the sixteenth partial tone. Exceptionally gifted players may exceed this limit by the 'Clarinblasen' technique. Horns and real trumpets belong to this group. The tone color is rich and noble, abounding in overtones.[291] It is interesting to note that both natural trumpets and horns were developed by our ancestors because they needed instruments with a greater number of partial tones than those supplied by the short hunting horn and bugle. This could be done only by lengthening the tubing. Horns have retained their place in the modern orchestra because they cannot be replaced. The old time trumpet, a magnificent, manly, noble instrument gave way to an upstart, the high B-flat (or C) trumpet, which, while superior in agility and easier to play, is inferior in tone color to its predecessor.

A 'New Era' in the Construction of Brass Wind Instruments

'Brass wind' instruments possess an unusual power in stirring certain elementary emotions of the human heart. Their value on the battlefield has been recognized throughout the ages. In the nineteenth century the growth of militarism encouraged the development of military bands. The invention of a valve mechanism solved the old problem of providing the brass with a chromatic scale. Instrument makers were faced with a choice of two groups of instruments to which they could apply valves: the old four-octave group, consisting of two families of natural horns and trumpets of various tonalities, or the very primitive three-octave instruments, such as the bugle and the post-horn. A group of keyed chromatic instruments already existed: the keyed bugle; the alto, tenor, and bass ophicleide, descendants of the older cornett family of the Middle Ages. The imperfections of keyed instruments were too glaring: a complicated key mechanism and poor tonal quality, especially in the upper register. There was a need for simple, reliable instruments which could be quickly mastered by enlisted or conscripted and for the most part illiterate soldiers. Horns and trumpets were not only difficult to play, but were also incapable of being developed into complete families, both in the high and the low tonal position.[292] Their principal value consisted in the ability to produce a diatonic scale in the upper part of their register without any valves. Their lower register was somewhat uncertain, because of the narrow bore of their tubing and their small mouthpieces. Owing to the large number of partial tones, the valve mechanism seemed almost superfluous.[293] Previous experience gained with keyed bugles and ophicleides taught instrument makers that the three-octave instruments were better suited for this development. The earliest valve instruments were in the soprano register: the valved bugle and the valved post-horn.[294] Deeper pitched instruments with valves were experimented with; the alto-cors, tenor-cors, and the early bass tubas had rather narrow bores. Especially in France the valved post-horn developed into an incipient family of cornet-à-pistons. Following the bad example of horns and trumpets, valved instruments were built with crooks and in many unnecessary tonalities. The early valve mechanisms were crude affairs, and the tubes of the instruments were bent into irrational, impracticable shapes, with sharp bends, and were badly proportioned. The real reform was instituted by Adolphe Sax. Realizing that the three-octave instruments were the only type suitable for military music, he first selected the best type to be developed into a complete family, the bugle. He established two standard tonalities, B-flat and E-flat, for the whole family. The bore of the bugles was modified somewhat by being made with a smaller taper. This improved the tonal quality of his instruments without changing either the generic or specific acoustical characteristics of the true bugle. His newly named instruments, the saxhorns, were a practical compromise between the wide-tapered bugles and narrow-tapered ophicleides. The saxhorns were built in two parallel families with three and four valves.[295] Sax also developed another family of instruments intended primarily for cavalry, the saxotrombas, the tubes of which were proportioned between those of the saxhorn and the trombone.[296] Finally, for Halévy's opera *Le Juif errant* Sax built special instruments which had an unusually powerful tone.[297] So the great reform, begun by others but finally developed to a practical stage by Adolphe Sax, consisted in the elevation of the lowly bugle, a three-octave instrument, to a position of predominance in the brass world. This completed the earlier trend, when keyed instruments and early valved post-horns[298] had begun to encroach upon the position formerly held by the trumpet and horn. Three-octave instruments, with their wide intervals between partial tones, were useless in military band music unless made chromatic by some means. With a relatively perfect valve mechanism which could span the wide intervals between the partial tones, three-octave instruments became a practical possibility, and a 'new era' in the construction of the brass wind was inaugurated.

What happened to the four-octave instruments? The horn, after a long and bitter resistance on the part of the old hornists, finally became a three-valved instrument. Being indispensable, horns remained firmly established in the orchestra and retained their position in the better bands. The trumpet was subjected to ignominy. The old time trumpet is, perhaps, one of the most difficult brass instruments, sharing with the horn the difficulty of playing its closely packed partial tones and being more fatiguing to blow. The valve mechanism could not convert it into a melodic instrument, since its tonal position was too low[299] and the old difficulties were not eliminated. Bands needed a flexible valved soprano instrument. This need was at first supplied by the cornopean, which was essentially a valved post-horn, and then by its more advanced descendant, the cornet-à-pistons. Trumpeters began to abandon their aristocratic instrument, which, through the rise of democratic ideals in Europe, had inevitably lost caste. This trend was resisted and ridiculed, but the practical requirements of the band relegated the trumpet to the secondary voice. Finally a high pitched soprano instrument appeared, a soprano valve trombone played with a trumpet mouthpiece and built in the traditional trumpet shape. With trader's shrewdness it was called the B-flat trumpet. Gradually it displaced the real trumpet in the orchestra, a thing which should never have occurred. Eventually it not only replaced the low-pitched trumpet, but at one time threatened to eliminate even the cornet-à-pistons from the band.

What did this new era mean acoustically and artistically? Acoustically it meant that the natural scale of brass wind instruments was raised an octave. This brought the wider intervals between partial tones to the same tonal position as that of the old horn and trumpet. A comparison of the old C trumpet and its modern substitute should make this clear.[300]

No. 1 represents the essential partial tones of the old time trumpet in C, an instrument with a length of tube slightly over 8 feet, at its true pitch. No. 2 represents the corresponding partial tones of the modern trumpet in C with a length of tube slightly over 4 feet. In this particular case the old low trumpet with its ponderous, solemn, and magnificent tone was replaced by a more certain, agile, brilliant, shrill, and more playable instrument, that blends with the trombone, but is tonally inferior.[301] Certainty in hitting the right tones is a desirable thing, but this is a quantitative and not a qualitative requirement.

In general, the more practicable but tonally inferior three-octave instrument has become predominant in band music and invaded the orchestra. The bass (saxhorn) tuba in F, the tenor (saxhorn) tuba in B-flat, the high soprano and sopranino 'trumpets,' and the bass trumpet, all became as acceptable in the orchestra as the regular members. Thus the noisiness of the orchestra has increased, while the quality of the orchestral tone has not improved.[302]

The four-octave instruments possess superior tone, but have a serious limitation. The tones of the fourth octave are produced successfully on long, narrow-bore tubes with small mouthpieces. This structural characteristic affects the acoustical properties of the tubes both in the low and high tonal positions. If the length of the tube of a given bore exceeds a certain limit, the instrument loses its pedal tone. Thus the horn in G (tube length 348 cm.) has the pedal tone, but the horn in F (391 cm.) has no pedal tone. If the tube is shorter than a certain length, the instrument becomes limited as to the number of partial tones producible in the high register and the quality of tone changes. Thus in the horn family the shortest tube which still retains the horn tone is that of the B-flat horn *alto*. In the trumpet family it is that of the G-trumpet. The instruments pitched above these are no longer true horns or trumpets; this point will be discussed at length later. Therefore horns are limited, practically, to the bass and tenor voices, and trumpets to tenor and alto voices. The story of Wagner tubas and bass trumpet will show this more clearly.

Richard Wagner began composing at a time when the valved brass instruments provided a new means of musical expression. One of the aspects of the vast change in music was the radical alteration of the dynamic level of the orchestra. The number of instruments increased, especially in the wind section. Both reed and brass wind instruments were considerably improved, and new wind instruments were added. The string section was increased for obvious reasons. All this raised the sonority of the orchestra to an unprecedented degree. It is difficult for us to realize the impact of the new instrumentation of Berlioz, and especially Wagner, upon their contemporaries. Only a detailed study of sonorities of each instrument and of the total effect of all instruments used in the orchestras of the pre-Berlioz-Wagner era can give an adequate basis for the understanding of this aspect of the widespread and often venomous opposition to the 'music of the future.' The opposition to the new technique of orchestration was both general and specific. Thus in the middle of the nineteenth century there was staged a battle between old-time hornists, who preferred the natural hand horn, and adherents of the newly developed valve horn. Perhaps it would not be amiss to consider the background of this battle, since the story is interesting and typical.

The old-time hornists were acutely aware of the loss of certain qualities brought about by the introduction of the valve horn. It is usually explained that the natural tones of the hand horn had a better quality than the allegedly bad tones produced by the valves. The real explanation is slightly different. The so-called 'hand-stopping' technique requires that the horn be played more muffled, as will be presently explained. When the crooks were used for the change of tonality of the horn, hand-stopping caused no particular difficulties. After the valves were added to the horn, the old hornists attempted to treat them as crooks, i.e., to press a valve down and play the valve horn as if it were a natural horn; it should be remembered that the majority of horn parts at that time were written for natural horns. They soon found that the valves (especially the old type of imperfect design and workmanship) were less suitable than crooks for playing the horn hand-stopped. Some tones were not so good as those produced with crooks. This was a misunderstanding of the true purpose of the valves, which was to eliminate the hand-stopping altogether. Yet there were more valid objections against the valve horn which cannot be dismissed as a misconception.

The old type natural narrow-bore horns had a soft and refined tone even when played completely open. The funnel-shaped mouthpiece depicted on p. 149 had much to do with this softness of tone. The invention of the hand-stopping technique permitted the diatonic scale to be played on a valveless horn in the most used third octave; some chromatic notes were also possible. The right hand had to be inserted in the bell so that it could be conveniently located for playing 'open,' partially stopped ('single-stopped'), and completely stopped ('double-stopped'). To minimize the disparity between the open and stopped tones and equalize the sonority of the whole scale, the hand hornists muffled the horn considerably more than is now done. This greater muffling, coupled with the naturally soft tone of the narrow-bore horn, produced a tone of quiet, veiled, and mysterious quality admired by the discriminating musicians of that time. Contrary to the usual opinion, the natural horn played with this technique, provided its tone was not forced, produced a more uniform scale than one would expect. Addition of the valves to the horn permitted the chromatic scale to be performed with uniform quality of tone and equalized sonority over the whole compass and at different dynamic levels. Those horn players who liked valve horns realized that excessive muffling and subdued sonority were no longer necessary and played more 'open' and more loudly. This increase of sonority was followed also by the development of the technical resources of the horn due to addition of the valves. Horn music changed so much that some hornists thought the character of the instrument was being spoiled. The real objections, therefore, concerned loss of the intimate qualities of the hand horn, change of tone quality, increasing loudness, and change of the type of music written for the horn.

Johannes Brahms, having played the hand horn when a boy in Hamburg, admired it tremendously. His famous *Horn Trio* in E-flat major (Op. 40) was originally intended for natural hand horn (*Waldhorn*) and not valve horn (*Ventilhorn*). In a letter to Richard Heuberger he wrote, "If the performer is not obliged by the stopped notes to play softly, the piano and the violin are not obliged to adapt themselves to him and the tone is rough from the beginning."

It should be taken into consideration that the piano of Brahms' period was not so loud as the modern instrument. Even then the pianist and violinist had to subdue themselves so as not to overpower the hornist. This gives an idea of the softness of the hand horn tone and suggests a proper dynamic level for performing Brahms' *Horn Trio*.[303]

The type of music composed by Berlioz and Wagner needed horns of a new kind. Suitable instruments which received a widespread acceptance, at least in this country, in Germany, and in Russia, were built only when the German makers introduced, in 1903, the modern wide-bore horn. That Wagner was not entirely satisfied with the sonority of the narrow-bore horn of his time, even when played less muffled, may be judged by the fact that he invented the famous Wagner tubas, more broad in tone than the contemporary horns. In retrospect one may venture an opinion that Wagner had in mind a sonority of the modern wide-bore horn. This can be inferred from the fact that the Wagner tubas, the tenor in B-flat and bass in F, are large-bore analogues of the French horns in B-flat *alto* and in F. For some reason (perhaps to prevent the horn players from holding the hand in the bell) the military elliptical flügelhorn model was selected for the Wagner tubas. In accordance with Wagner's ideas, these tubas were to be played by the French horn players of the second quartet, who could use their mouthpieces interchangeably. There is a great deal of misinformation about these unusual instruments, so the following data about their sizes, tonal and acoustical properties may be of interest.

Both sets of Wagner tubas owned by the Boston Symphony Orchestra are furnished with four valves. The first three valves on all instruments are the usual 1, ½, and 1½ tone valves. The fourth valve on the Uhlmann set is the 'Quartventil,' lowering the pitch a fourth (2½ tones). The fourth valve on the Kruspe set lowers the pitch a major third (2 tones); this arrangement simplifies the fingering according to the system used by the German cavalry trumpeters.[304]

DIMENSIONS OF THE WAGNER TUBAS

(Boston Symphony Orchestra)

Instrument and Maker	Bore			Length of Air-column[2]	Bell Dia.	Length of tube up to the Valves
	Min.	Near Valves	Max.[1]			
Tenor in B-flat (L. Uhlmann)	0.9	1.2	12.5	277	19.5	43.5
Tenor in B-flat (E. Kruspe)	0.9	1.1	10	277	20	45
Bass in F (L. Uhlmann)	0.9	1.3	12.5	372	19.5	44
Bass in F (E. Kruspe)	0.9	1.3	11	373	21	44
French Horn in F (Wide bore)[3]	0.8	1.2	9.5	380	30.5	220

Sizes are given in centimeters.

1 This size is measured according to the method given on p. 166; it is the size 'd' on the diagram.
2 Without the mouthpiece.
3 Dimensions added for comparison. On the horn in F the valves are located five times as far from the mouthpiece as on the Wagner bass tuba in F.

The Wagner tenor tuba and bass tuba differ both in tonal and acoustical properties. The tenor tuba has a sonorous and easily playable pedal tone; using the valves, it is possible to descend as low as *FF*. In the upper register the tenor tuba plays with ease up to the eighth partial tone inclusive; the tenth partial tone is already difficult, and the twelfth partial tone is the highest playable. The tone color is akin to the tenor horn of the cornet family. Therefore the tenor tuba in B-flat is a whole-tube instrument more properly belonging to the three-octave sub-group. The bass tuba has no pedal tone; using the valves, it is possible to descend only to *BB*-flat. This point has been checked by the writer personally; paradoxically, the higher-pitched B-flat Wagner tenor tuba descends lower than the Wagner bass tuba in F; this is true also of the B-flat and F horns. In the upper register the bass tuba plays as easily as the French horn in F up to the sixteenth partial tone inclusive. The tone color is almost that of the wide-bore French horn played with an open bell, but more hollow and 'other-worldish' (C. Forsyth). Therefore the Wagner bass tuba in F is a four-octave half-tube instrument.

The Wagner tubas bring out strongly the following point. Widening of the horn bore in the tenor tonal position to a greater extent than it is done on the modern wide-bore horn in B-flat *alto*, leads to a change of generic acoustical characteristic. The Wagner tuba in B-flat is, practically, a three-octave instrument which can be forced and played fortissimo. Widening of the horn bore in the bass tonal position, if done discreetly, leaves the basic acoustic characteristic unchanged; although the Wagner bass tuba in F has a bore of larger taper than the modern wide-bore horn in F, it still remains a four-octave half-tube instrument. Thus the Wagner tuba in F is a true horn, with a peculiar timbre, but a horn, nevertheless. Its tone cannot be forced beyond a certain limit; and in the low register it is not so broad as one would expect of a bass instrument. The conclusion is inescapable that a true bass horn, having a broad and sonorous tone approaching that of the bass tuba of the saxhorn family, is not possible. A moderate widening of the bore does not seem to produce the desired result, as long as the mouthpiece remains as small as the horn mouthpiece with which the Wagner tubas are customarily played. If the bore of the bass instrument were widened sufficiently and a larger mouthpiece attached, the tone in the low register would become more solid, but it is certain that the tube would acquire the characteristics of a narrow-bored cornet. This conclusion is based on a similar experience with the Wagner bass trumpet. Wagner wanted a trumpet pitched an octave lower and more broad in tone than the trumpet in C used in his time. It should be remembered that the trumpet in C of Wagner's period of activity was an 8-foot instrument, yet played at the same pitch as the modern high-pitched trumpet in C. As originally planned by Wagner, the bass trumpet was to play an octave below the classical trumpet. This would mean a tube length of about 16 feet, or substantially the same length as the tube of the horn in C *basso*. The cylindrical tube of this length having a narrow trumpet bore is not feasible. The practical solution was to increase the bore and raise the natural scale one octave. This operation converted an intended four-octave instrument (trumpet) into a three-octave instrument (trombone). So the actual bass trumpet of Wagner is really a valve trombone in C built in a trumpet form.

In general, the four-octave instruments with either a conoidal tube (horns) or a cylindrical tube (trumpets) are not suitable for development into the real bass and contrabass instruments. To retain their ability to produce partial tones of the fourth octave of the natural scale, such instruments must, of necessity, have narrow bores and small mouthpieces. If the bores are widened and the mouthpieces enlarged, the resulting instruments are cornets and trombones, and not horns and trumpets. In other words, bass horns and bass trumpets, retaining the tonal and acoustical characteristics of their respective families, yet possessing the broad and powerful tone of true bass instruments, are not feasible. Likewise there can be no true soprano trumpets nor soprano and alto horns.[305]

If the high-pitched horns in the soprano or alto positions were constructed, their partial tones above the eighth would be found very difficult and only the partial tones below that considered practicable; this would mean that the soprano and alto 'horns' are really three-octave instruments.[306]

Summary. 1. The generic and specific acoustical characteristics of the tubes of lip-vibrated aerophones depend primarily on length and proportions of tubing.[307]

2. The generic classification of lip-vibrated aerophones is based on the upper compass extension. There are at least three distinctly recognizable groups, which differ not only in the number of practically producible partial tones, but also in their tonal quality and their adaptability of development into complete families.

3. The first group, *two-octave instruments*, is composed mostly of primitive conoidal bore

instruments, producing the pedal tone and a limited number of partial tones not exceeding the fourth partial tone. The tonal qualities are poor and the instruments of this group are not adaptable for artistic uses. No sub-group.

4. The second group, *three-octave instruments*, is composed both of cylindrical and conoidal bore instruments normally producing partial tones up to the eighth inclusive. This group has two sub-groups: the whole-tube instruments with the pedal tone and the half-tube instruments without pedal tone. The tonal qualities of the instruments of the second group are superior to those of the first group and inferior to those of the third group. There is a recognizable difference in tonal qualities between the instruments belonging to different sub-groups, as, for instance, between the flügelhorn and the cornet-à-pistons, both of which nominally have a conoidal bore.

The instruments of the second group with the pedal tone are eminently adaptable for development into complete families; less adaptable for the same purpose if they have no pedal tone.[308] Only the most indispensable valved instruments of this group are admitted as regular members of the orchestra. Primarily they are wind band instruments.

5. The third group, *four-octave instruments*, is composed of both cylindrical and conoidal bore instruments, normally producing partial tones up to the sixteenth inclusive. This group has two sub-groups: the majority of instruments belong to the half-tube sub-group having no pedal tone; the higher pitched instruments belong to the whole-tube sub-group with the pedal tone. The tonal qualities of the instruments of this group are superior to those of any other brass instruments. The horns are indispensable members of the orchestra and blend well with all groups, strings, 'wood-wind,' and 'brass.' The trumpets, unfortunately, owing to many causes, have not been retained in the orchestra. Instruments of this group have a serious limitation, in that no complete families of four-octave instruments are practically possible, since both high-pitched and low-pitched instruments change their generic acoustical characteristic to that of the second group. Example: the high B-flat trumpet in the high tonal position and the bass trumpet in the low tonal position are three-octave instruments.

Construction of Lip-Vibrated Aerophones

As has been already stated, lip-vibrated aerophones consist essentially of a tube and a mouthpiece. Nominally the geometrical shapes of the tubes are cylindrical and conoidal.[309] There are no strictly cylindrical tube instruments used in European instrumental music; the actual 'cylindrical' tube instrument has a conoidal section with a flaring bell affixed to the cylindrical portion of the tubing. The old hunting horn of fixed pitch (like No. 191 of this Collection by Raoux) has a conoidal tube for its entire length. The natural hand horn with tuning slide and 'crooks' has a cylindrical portion affixed to the conoidal tubing. The modern valved instruments have a cylindrical portion inserted where it is required by practical consideration. Therefore, strictly speaking, there are no purely cylindrical or conoidal tubes in actual practice: with a few exceptions, brass instruments have cylindro-conoidal bores. The relative length of the cylindrical and conoidal portions determines the sub-section to which the instruments are assigned. Thus the trumpet and trombone having two-thirds of their length cylindrical and only one third quasi-conoidal are regarded as cylindrical tube instruments.[310]

Mouthpieces. The mouthpiece of a lip-vibrated aerophone is one of the most important and the least scientifically investigated parts. Mouthpiece-making is still an art and not a science. Therefore, one is forced of necessity to speak in general qualitative and not quantitative terms. The mouthpieces are divided into three general types in accordance with their shapes: (1) the cup-shaped type, (2) the funnel-shaped type, and (3) the elongated cup type, combining both previous types.

A typical cup-shaped mouthpiece, that of the trumpet, is represented on Fig. 26. 'A' is the old type and 'B' is a modern type. The principal parts of the cup-shaped mouthpiece are the cup and the backbore. The old type trumpet mouthpiece had a semi-spherical cup.[311] The backbore was a conoid. The orifice (3) where the cup and backbore communicated, called the 'groin' or 'throat,' had a very slightly rounded edge. Important elements of the cup-shaped mouthpiece are the following: the rim, the surface set on the lips of the performer; the cup diameter (1); the rim width (2); the throat diameter (3); the cup depth (4); the throat edge (5); the backbore length (6); the backbore base diameter (7). The length of mouthpiece under the cup is known as the shank; at the lower end the shank has a taper fitted into the bore of the instrument.

A modern trumpet mouthpiece differs from its ancient prototype in two important particulars. The throat edge has a larger radius and the backbore is not conoidal; its true shape differs with each mouthpiece-maker, and in some cases the generator is not a straight line but a curve of complex form. The cup depth, the throat diameter, the throat edge radius, and the shape of the backbore, all these are important elements affecting the quality of tone, correctness of pitch of the partial tones, and ease of producing the upper partial tones of the normal range, as well as the 'Clarinblasen' extension of the normal range of partial tones.[312] The tone quality imparted to cylindrical bore instruments (meaning for the most part trumpets, since the trombone mouthpiece differs from the true trumpet type by the shape and depth of the cup and length of the backbore) by the cup-shaped mouthpiece is rich in overtones, especially in the discordant seventh partial, majestic and incisive; somewhat hysterical if forced; when properly played, manly and martial in forte, and solemn and serious in piano.[313]

A typical funnel-shaped mouthpiece is the old type French horn mouthpiece, Fig. 27. It was usually made out of a thin sheet of brass brazed at the joint and with its edge rolled under to form a rim. There was no cup or backbore, the form of the curve approaching that of the exponential horn. Used in conjunction with the true conoidal tubes of the old hunting horn, and later with the cylindro-conoidal tubes of the natural horn, the funnel-shaped mouthpiece imparts a smooth, dreamy, mysterious quality to the tone. This type of mouthpiece is somewhat sluggish for tonguing, but for long tenuto tones that give one a feeling of contact with infinity itself there is no better type.

The elongated cup mouthpiece varies from the comparatively shallow cup of the high-pitched bugle to the funnel-shaped cup of a modern French horn mouthpiece. In this case art, the imagination of the maker, and the personal idiosyncrasies of the player have full sway, so it would be useless to attempt to find any 'typical' example. There is only one feature in common: the 'edge' radius (Fig. 26, 'A,' 5) on this type is very large, so that transition from the cup to the backbore is very gradual. The quality of tone imparted to the cylindrical and conoidal tubes is mellow without being sluggish; tonguing is possible with excellent results.

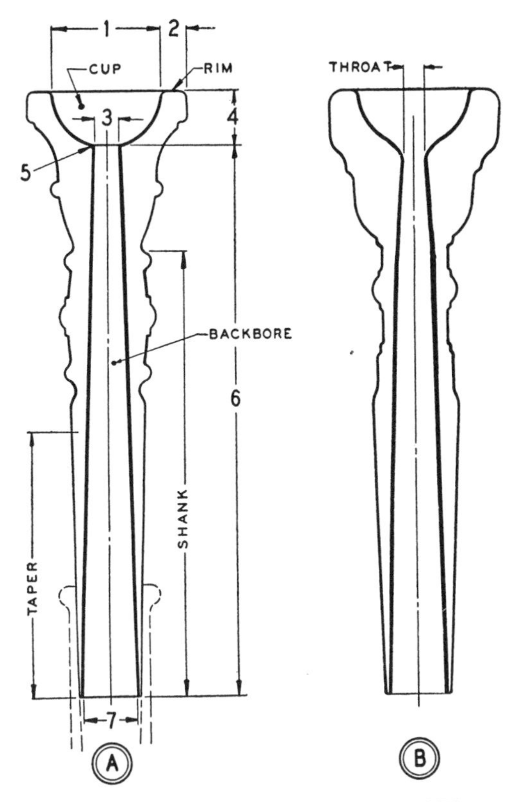

FIG. 26. TRUMPET MOUTHPIECES
A, old type, with a sharp throat edge (5), the conoidal backbore having a rectilinear generator. B, modern type, with a rounded throat edge, the backbore having a curvilinear generator.

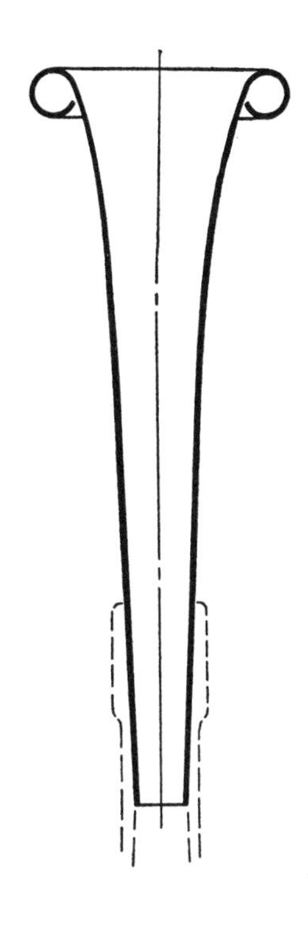

FIG. 27. THE FRENCH HORN MOUTHPIECE, OLD TYPE

Families of Lip-Vibrated Aerophones

THE classification of lip-vibrated aerophones, if made at all, has to be based both on the structure of the tubes and on their acoustical properties. [314]

A superficial examination of a lip-vibrated aerophone, combined with a measurement of proportions of its tube, permits its assignment to a certain sub-section: it is a 'cylindrical' or a 'conoidal' instrument. Without actual experience with instruments of similar type, one is not in a position to say to which group or sub-group an instrument belongs. To do this the instrument must be actually played. An example will elucidate the point. The cornet-à-pistons and the flügelhorn (soprano saxhorn) are both conoidal bore instruments.[315] The cornet-à-pistons has a moderately tapered bore; the flügelhorn has a wide-tapered bore; but between the two 'typical' conoidal bores there are innumerable intermediate ones. The early cornet-à-pistons had a narrow taper and the following properties: the pedal tone, if playable at all, was execrably out of tune; the valved tones below the written middle c′ were badly out of tune; some players were peculiarly fitted to extract a vulgar nasal tone and could do no better. True, in the hands of a good player the old narrow-tapered cornet-à-pistons sounded very well. The flügelhorn is precisely the reverse: the pedal tone sounds well; the valved tones below middle c′ are fine,[316] the tone is mellow and pleasant, if less flexible; no player could make it sound badly. The cornet-à-pistons makers made improvements by changing the taper of the bore, so that sometimes it is very difficult to decide whether one has in his hands a cornet-à-pistons or a narrow-tapered flügelhorn with a cornet mouthpiece.[317] This example shows some of the difficulties encountered with the conoidal bore brass instruments. Another example. It would seem that the trombone is a fairly well standardized instrument; at least it seems that there are not many elements to be modified. Yet at one time in this country the old wide-bore, large bell model was gradually reduced to a 'brilliant' sounding instrument — a caricature of a trombone, with a narrow bore and small bell, which among discriminating musicians was known as a 'pea-shooter.' A noble, magnificent instrument was reduced to a vulgar simulacrum. Both this and the previous example show another difficult aspect: what constitutes a cornet or a trombone or a trumpet? In other words, is there such a thing as a standard type of any brass instrument? The answer, of course, is no. In addition, an organologist's task is not made any easier by the many intermediate types of instruments introduced mostly in the hectic period between 1840 and 1900. For instance, there are saxotrombas of Adolphe Sax and the 'army trombones' of Červeny. Are they different instruments or essentially of the same type? Neither of these families belongs to the old traditional families.[318] Again, is there much difference between the Wagner tuba, Besson's cornophone, and Červeny's cornon? All of these instruments have conoidal bore tubes and are played with mouthpieces of the French horn type. Can a cornophone or the cornon of the same tonal position as the Wagner tuba be used interchangeably with the latter instrument?

Family Classification of Lip-Vibrated Aerophones

THE old lateral hole instruments, such as the cornett (including the serpent), the keyed bugle, and the ophicleide are somewhat outside the normal line of evolution of 'brass' instruments. The true brass instrument produces its tones, as already stated, by overblowing; the slide, the crooks, and the valve crooks only change the total length of the tubing. All tones produced by such instruments as the slide trombone, the natural horn with crooks, and a valved instrument, are the partial tones of a certain fixed (if only for a moment, as on instruments with slides and valves) length of tubing. No 'cross-fingering' is possible on true brass instruments. The lateral hole instruments follow the technique of the 'wood-wind' instruments and use cross-fingering for producing some chromatic tones. This constitutes a generic difference between the lateral hole lip-vibrated aerophones and the true 'brass.' Therefore the following discussion is with respect to the latter type only.

The scientifically correct method for classification of brass wind instruments is the consideration of the structural and acoustical properties of simple, fixed length tubes. There are two important reasons for this procedure. The first one is that the early instruments had tubes of fixed lengths. Later, when the slide mechanism was added to the cylindrical instruments (trombones, and, still later, the slide trumpets) and the crooks to the horns and trumpets, this change involved no change in acoustical principle. The second reason is that the only difference between an instrument with a slide and one with a crook is that on the slide instrument the length of tubing is changed conveniently and quickly and on the crooked instrument laboriously and slowly; this is a quantitative, mechanical factor and does not affect the basic acoustical principle. When the valve mechanism was invented, a rapid and convenient change of 'crooks' eliminated this mechanical superiority of the slide over the crook: the valved instruments are even more agile than the slide instruments. It matters not whether a brass instrument is a simple tube, or one furnished with a slide, crook, or a valve mechanism: at the moment of production of any partial tone the length of tubing remains fixed. This is obvious in the case of the simple tubes and those furnished with interchangeable crooks; on a slide instrument the slide has to be momentarily stopped and on a valve instrument the valve has to be held down, if only for a moment. Therefore, in classifying brass instruments the first operation is the assignment to a proper sub-section: a cylindrical or a conoidal instrument; the second operation is to determine to which group and sub-group the instrument belongs acoustically. This is done on the slide instruments by examining each standard position as if it were a separate instrument; on the crook instruments by trying each crook; and on the valve instrument by treating the addition of each valve and combination of valves as a separate instrument.[319]

The families of brass wind instruments, classified according to their structural and acoustical characteristics, are given in the following table.

FAMILIES OF LIP-VIBRATED AEROPHONES

Basic	Intermediate	Derivative
Horns	......	......
......	Horn-Tubas	......
......	Cornets (Post-Horns)	......
Bugles	......	......
......	Saxotrombas	......
Slide Trombones	......	Valve Trombones
Trumpets	......	......

The tonal position of a lip-vibrated aerophone is determined by the actual pitch of the second partial tone as stated on p. 45. Valved instruments have their tonal position determined in the same way as natural instruments; that is, the pitch of the second partial tone of the shortest length of their tubes, with the valves 'off,' is taken into consideration.

Technical Description of the Families of Lip-Vibrated Aerophones [320]

Cornets. Conoidal bore instruments with narrow taper tubes and bell of medium size; three-octave instruments without pedal tone;[321] elongated cup mouthpiece with a medium shallow cup. Instruments belonging to the family are post-horns, cornopeans, cornet-à-pistons. The cornet family consists of the following members:

Octave	1. Cornet in C
	2. Cornet in B-flat
	3. Cornet in A-flat
Sopranino	4. Cornet in E-flat
Soprano	5. Cornet in C
	6. Cornet in B-flat [322]
Alto	7. Althorn in F [323]
	8. Althorn in E-flat
	9. Althorn in D
Tenor	10. Tenorhorn in B-flat [324]
	11. Tenorhorn in A

Horn-Tubas.[325] Conoidal bore instruments with medium taper tubes and bells of various sizes; a funnel-shaped French horn type mouthpiece. Instruments belonging to the family: Wagner tubas ('Waldhorntuben,' 'Ringtuben'), the prim-horn and the cornons of Červeny, the cornophones of Fontaine-Besson. The Wagner tubas are built only as the tenor in B-flat and the bass in F. Červeny's cornons are built as the alto in E-flat, the tenor in B-flat, the bass in E-flat, the contrabass in BB-flat. The cornon was invented in 1846 and the whole set was developed in 1872 by Vaclav F. Červeny. The cornophones were developed by Fontaine-Besson of Paris in 1880 under the name of cornons, and patented in 1890 under the name of cornophones.[326] The cornophones range from the soprano in B-flat to the bass in F or in E-flat.[327]

Bugles. Conoidal bore instruments with wide taper tubes and bells of various sizes; three-octave instruments with pedal tone; an elongated cup mouthpiece with depths of cups varying from medium to medium-deep. The numerous family of the wind instruments, used mostly in the wind bands; they are furnished with three, four, five, and, in some cases, with six valves.[328] As stated already, instruments of the bugle family are known under many names (p. 136). The bugle-tuba-flügelhorn-saxhorn family consists of members each of which could be called, in a generic sense, with equal justification a bugle, tuba, flügelhorn, or saxhorn.[329] The most commonly used names are given in the following list.

Sopranino	1. Flügelhorn in F [330]
	2. Flügelhorn in E-flat
Soprano	3. Flügelhorn in C
	4. Flügelhorn in B-flat [331]
Alto	5. Althorn in E-flat [332]

Baritone	6. Baritone in B-flat
	7. Euphonium in B-flat [333]
	8. Bass in B-flat [334]
Bass	9. Bass Tuba in F [335]
	10. Bass Tuba in E-flat
Contrabass	11. Contrabass Tuba in BB-flat [336]
Sub-bass	12. Sub-bass Tuba in EE-flat [337]
Sub-contrabass	13. Sub-contrabass Tuba in CC.
	14. Sub-contrabass Tuba in BBB-flat [338]

Horns. Conoidal bore instruments with narrow taper tube and large flaring bell; four-octave instruments; [339] a funnel-shaped or elongated cup mouthpiece with a deep cup. Instruments belonging to the family: the hunting horns (fixed pitch), the hand horns (natural French horns with pitch varied by crooks or inventions), and valved French horns. The horns form an incomplete family, which begins with the baritone and extends down to the contrabass. There are no soprano nor alto members in the horn family.[340] The acoustical sub-group changes within the family.[341] The following list shows the tonal position, the tonality, and the acoustic sub-group characteristic of the horn.

Baritone	1. Horn in B-flat *alto*	Whole-tube
	2. Horn in A	Whole-tube
	3. Horn in A-flat	Whole-tube
Bass	4. Horn in G	Whole-tube
	5. Horn in F	Half-tube
	6. Horn in E	Half-tube
	7. Horn in E-flat	Half-tube
	8. Horn in D	Half-tube
Contrabass	9. Horn in C	Half-tube
	10. Horn in B	Half-tube
	11. Horn in B-flat *basso*	Half-tube

One may occasionally find in old scores tonalities in F-sharp and in C-sharp (low), but they are somewhat unusual. The list of crooks given here is a representative one. Berlioz lists also a crook in C-alto, but this is a very unusual crook. The double French horn (valve) in B-flat and F is a tenorbass instrument somewhat similar to the tenorbass trombone.

Slide Trombones. Cylindro-conoidal bore instruments with two-thirds of their tube length cylindrical, one-third conoidal, with a bell of medium size; three-octave instruments; a cup-shaped mouthpiece with deep cup and short backbore. The slide trombones have the pedal tone in the three highest positions and no pedal tones in the lower positions. The slide trombone family consists of the following members:

Soprano	1. Soprano Trombone in B-flat [342]
Alto	2. Alto Trombone in F
	3. Alto Trombone in E-flat

Tenor	4. Tenor Trombone in C [343]
	5. Tenor Trombone in B-flat
	6. Tenorbass Trombone in B-flat [344]
Bass	7. Bass Trombone in G ('Terzposaune')
	8. Bass Trombone in F ('Quartposaune')
	9. Bass Trombone in E-flat ('Quintposaune')
Contrabass	10. Contrabass Trombone in BB-flat

Valve Trombones. Cylindro-conoidal bore instruments with two-thirds of the tube length cylindrical, one-third conoidal, with a bell of medium size; three-octave instruments with pedal tone. The valve trombone family is divided into two sub-families: (1) the 'trumpets,' played with a trumpet type mouthpiece, its members in the octave, sopranino, soprano, and alto tonal positions; (2) the 'trombones,' played with a trombone type mouthpiece, its members in the soprano, alto, tenor, and bass tonal positions. The nomenclature is not consistent either as to type or the tonal position; this applies especially to the valve trombones proper, some of which are made in trumpet form and miscalled 'trumpets.' In general, the 'trumpets' are built with three valves on the trumpet model. The 'trombones' are built with three or four valves on the trombone or the trumpet model.[345] Individual members of the valve trombone sub-families are enumerated below.

The Valve Trombone Sub-family 1: 'Trumpets'

Octave	1. Piccolo Trumpet in B-flat
Sopranino	2. Trumpet in F [346]
	3. Trumpet in E-flat
	4. Trumpet in D
Soprano	5. Trumpet in C
	6. Trumpet in B-flat (or in A)
Alto	7. Tromba contralta in F [347]
	8. Tromba contralta in E-flat

The Valve Trombone Sub-family 2: 'Trombones'

Soprano	1. Soprano Valve Trombone in C (or B-flat; Cornet mouthpiece; Jazz)
Alto	2. Alto Valve Trombone in F
	3. Alto Valve Trombone in E-flat
	4. Bass Trumpet in E-flat (Military Band)
Tenor	5. Bass Trumpet in C (R. Wagner; Orchestra)
	6. Tenor Valve Trombone in C
	7. Bass Trumpet in B-flat (Military Band)
	8. Tenor Valve Trombone in B-flat (Three valves)
Baritone	9. Tenor Valve Trombone in B-flat (Four valves)
Bass	10. Bass Valve Trombone in G (English)
	11. Bass Valve Trombone in F
	12. Bass Valve Trombone in E-flat

Saxotrombas.[348] Cylindro-conoidal bore instruments with a longer and wider tapered conoidal part and larger cylindrical bore than the trombones; medium sized bell. Three-octave instruments with pedal tone; a cup-shaped mouthpiece with deep cup and short backbore. Instruments belonging to this group: the saxotromba family of Adolphe Sax, ranging from the sopranino saxotromba in E-flat to the contrabass in BB-flat; the 'army trombone' family of Červeny, ranging from the alto in F (also in E-flat) to the sub-contra-bass (more correctly, the sub-bass) in FF.

Trumpets. Cylindro-conoidal bore instruments with two-thirds of the tube length cylindrical, one-third conoidal, with a bell of medium size; four-octave instruments;[349] cup-shaped mouthpiece either with a shallow hemispherical or medium depth cup and long backbore. The real or classical trumpets form an incomplete family which has only the alto and the tenor voice. There are no real four-octave trumpets in the soprano or the sopranino tonal positions nor a real bass trumpet in the lower position. The instruments pitched above the alto and below the tenor trumpets change their generic acoustical characteristic to that of the trombone family, i.e., become three-octave instruments and change their tone color. The following list shows the tonal position, the tonality, and the acoustical sub-group characteristics of the natural trumpets.

Alto	1. Trumpet in G	Whole-tube
	2. Trumpet in F	Whole-tube
	3. Trumpet in E[350]	Half-tube
	4. Trumpet in E-flat	Half-tube
	5. Trumpet in D	Half-tube
Tenor	6. Trumpet in D-flat[351]	Half-tube
	7. Trumpet in C	Half-tube
	8. Trumpet in B-flat	Half-tube
	9. Trumpet in A	Half-tube

The instruments enumerated above are valveless natural trumpets. There were valve trumpets built with two or three valves, having tubes of exactly the same proportion as the natural instruments; well built low-pitched valve trumpets have the same fine tonal qualities as their classical prototypes.

SUB-SECTION a: CONOIDAL TUBE

Group 1: Two-Octave Instruments

Primitive Types

THE EARLIEST primitive types of lip-vibrated aerophones with conoidal tube were made from the horns or tusks of animals. Since animal horns are hollow, no boring operation was required; the solid tips of the horns or tusks were cut off to provide an opening.[352] This opening served as a primitive 'mouthpiece.' Later, the tip was only partially cut off and some of the solid portion left. A small hole was bored through this solid portion, and the cup carved directly in the horn, forming a 'mouthpiece.'

The most common materials for such instruments were the horns of domesticated cattle. The horns of game animals, especially those of antelopes, were also used. Elephant tusks were made into finely carved instruments — the oliphants; only kings and great nobles could afford such instruments, some of which were veritable works of art.

153. SHOFAR Poland, 19th century

Ram's horn trumpet (bugle). Made of a ram's horn, straightened out and flattened; a scalloped opening edge. Engraved zigzags in three wavy, parallel lines. The integral mouthpiece of oval conoidal shape is carved out of the cut-off tip of the horn. Length, 33.5 cm. Width, 6.7 cm. Embouchure, 9 x 11 mm. Bore, initial, 5 mm. Opening, length, 6.3 cm.; width, 2.2 cm. (17.1961) Plate V

The *shofar* (*šofar*) is, perhaps, one of the most ancient instrumental types which have survived until our time. It was a ritualistic and military instrument of the ancient Hebrews and more than likely was borrowed by them from the Egyptians.[353] The R. M. E. *Catalogue* should be consulted for details of its use, and examples of typical *shofar* calls played in the Jewish Synagogues on New Year's Day and the Day of Atonement. The *shofar* is reputed to be a very difficult instrument to blow. This is not correct. Its mouthpiece is shaped in a rational manner, the cup being oval and not circular in shape; the long axis of this oval rim is pressed into the thin part of the lips and very little effort is required to produce a tone. It is assumed, of course, that a person like a horn or trumpet player, with a practiced lip used to a small mouthpiece, does the blowing. The pedal tone can be played, but it is hardly audible. The tones actually used are the second, third, and sometimes the fourth partial tones. The *shofar* sounds pleasantly if blown in the proper manner; if sheer force is used in blowing, the tone is rough.

154. BACCHIC HORN Graeco-Roman. Found in the Fayum. First century

Red earthenware bugle with low reliefs representing a young Bacchus, Silenus, and bunches of grapes. Circular embouchure, oval bell opening; conoidal bore, very rough inside. Length, 19.3 cm. Width, 6 cm. Embouchure, 17 mm. Bell orifice, length, 4 cm.; width, 3 cm. (17.1964)

155. OLIPHANT Bavaria, Germany, late 17th century

Ivory hunting horn. Irregular bore with a wooden pierced plug located 25 cm. from the bell opening. Made of an elephant's tusk, richly carved with hunting scenes and the conversion of St. Eustace.[354] Hemispherical cup mouthpiece of ivory with small orifice and conoidal backbore. Length (centre line; with mouthpiece), 99 cm. Width, major axis of bell opening, 8 cm. Bore, initial diameter, 10 mm.; plug hole, 14 mm. (17.1962)

The instrument is listed in the R. M. E. *Catalogue* on p. 143 under no. 288. The actual tones are:

The writer was unable to get the tones given in the R. M. E. *Catalogue*. The middle section of the instrument is a nineteenth-century restoration.

156. WATCHMAN'S HORN England, 18th century

Made of a twisted ox-horn; a brass bell and a brass band in the upper end; tipped at the small end with a brass ferrule. The hemispherical cup mouthpiece is of horn. Length, 85 cm. Diameter, bell, 17 cm. Bore, initial, 15 mm. (17.1966)
Plate V

157. FORESTER'S HORN England, 19th century

Made of ox-horn without mounts. No mouthpiece; the embouchure is formed by the sawing off of the horn tip. Length, 40 cm. Diameter, min., 2.2 cm.; max., 8 cm. (17.1965)
Plate V

158. FORESTER'S HORN Germany (?), 19th century

Made of a cow's horn; German silver bell, two hoops with eyelets for a chord, a mouthpipe of German silver with a fixed cup-shaped mouthpiece of ivory. Raised stamping of a leaping deer on one side. Length, 36 cm. Diameter, bell, 10.5 cm. Bore, mouthpiece, initial, 4 mm. Length of air column (approx.), 44 cm. (17.1979)
Plate V

Tubes with Lateral Holes

THE primitive two-octave lip-vibrated aerophones produced only the pedal tone and a few overblown partial tones, which in the lower range have wide intervals: the octave, the fifth, the fourth. The short tube lip-vibrated instruments were therefore almost useless for musical purposes. Long continued efforts were made to provide more tones for such instruments, so that at least a semblance of a scale could be played on them. The earliest solution of this problem was to provide lateral holes in the same manner as on the flutes and primitive double-reed instruments. Then the complete diatonic scale could be played and the cross-fingering would add a few chromatic tones. On instruments with a very short length of tube only one octave could be produced; on the longer and narrow bored instruments over two octaves. With the exception of the slide trombone, the lateral-hole instruments were the only lip-vibrated instruments which supplied a continuous scale. They were used for many centuries. Keys which were invented for the low-pitched recorder and shawm were later applied to the lateral-hole lip-vibrated instruments. This process culminated eventually in the keyed bugle and ophicleide of the early nineteenth century, which had no finger-holes, while the lateral holes were stopped with large-sized keys. The possibility of cross-fingering on the lateral-hole lip-vibrated aerophones divides them sharply from the true lip-vibrated aerophones, such as bugles, horns, and trumpets, which have no lateral holes and produce their tones by overblowing exclusively.

159. BUKKEHORN Northern Europe, 19th century

Made of a goat's horn. Mounted with a brass band near the bell. Four equally spaced finger-holes. Irregular oval shaped integral mouthpiece carved in the small end and similar to that of the *shofar*. Irregular initial bore of circular shape with two slots filed diametrically opposite one another. Length, 26.5 cm. Width, major axis of bell opening, 5.8 cm. Embouchure, 9 x 19 mm. (17.1963)
Plate V

Played with the embouchure set on the thin part of the lips and well attacked, the bukkehorn produces surprisingly sharp and snappy tones:

The tones *c''* and *f''* (in parentheses) are similar to those of the Scotch bagpipe, that is, they are equally far apart from the *b'* and *d''*, *e''*, and (non-existent) *g''*. Roughly estimated, the intervals (in cents) are:

b'		*c''*		*d''*		*e''*		*f''*
	150		150		200		150	

The Cornett Family

THE cornett (French *cornet à bouquin*; Italian *cornetto*; German *Zink*) is a lip-vibrated aerophone with lateral holes; it has a narrow-tapered conoidal bore and a cup-shaped mouthpiece. The mouthpiece was usually detachable on all but one type, the *cornetto muto*, or a mute cornett which had an integral mouthpiece bored in the pipe itself. The old writers had a curious way of classifying the cornetts by shapes and colors. With the exception of the mute cornett and the *cornetto diritto*, which had a straight body turned on a lathe, cornetts were usually curved in shape. Since the curved bore cannot be reamed out on a lathe, the cornett was made from two pieces of wood, in each of which a half-bore was carved out. Two pieces were joined so that the half-bores matched; the outside was shaped to conform to the bore and the whole securely fastened together with black leather. The mute cornett was left either unvarnished or varnished. Hence the two designations of colors. Zacconi refers to the cornetts as the *Cornetti bianchi e negri* the white and black cornetts. The 'white' cornetts were, undoubtedly, the mute cornetts, and the 'black' ones were the leather-covered curved cornetts. Praetorius confirms this nomenclature by referring to 'Cornu, Cornetto, Cornet' as a black curved Zink ('ein schwartzer krummer Zinck'); whereas 'Cornamuti' were referred to as a yellow and straight Zink ('ein gelber und gerader Zink'); undoubtedly Praetorius had in mind a newly varnished, straight, mute cornett with its bright yellow color.

Zacconi gave the compass of the white and black cornett as from *a* to *a''*. A larger size, *corno torto* or *cornone*, had a compass of *c* to *g'*. Praetorius for some reason fails to mention cornetts in his enumeration of instruments on page 13 of *De Organographia*, where he names all the wind instruments of his time. In *Tabella Universalis* he gives the following ranges of the cornett:

Klein Zink	*e'* to e^3
Zink	(*g*) *a* to *a''* (g^3)
Corno torto, Cornon, Gross Zink	(*c*) *d* to *d''*

In chapter ix Praetorius divides the cornetts into *Recti* and *Curvi*. The straight cornetts were subdivided into (1) *Cornetto diritto*, a straight cornett with a separate mouthpiece, and (2) *Cornetto muto*, with an integral mouthpiece and soft sound. *Cornetti curvi* were the ordinary black curved cornetts, which had a standard range of two octaves from *a* to *a''*; but some could, as Praetorius remarks, get the 'falset' tones *g* and even *f* below and as high as g^3 above. The tones lower than *a* were not fingered but lipped; this fact was recently confirmed by M. Henri Bouasse.[355] The largest instrument of the cornett family in the time of Praetorius was the great Cornett, *Corno* or *Cornetto torto*, also called *Cornon*, an S-shaped instrument, which gave only 11 tones and no *falset* tones; yet on some instruments the regular 15 tones could be played. The tone of the great cornett, according to Praetorius, was 'gar unlieblich und hornhafftig' ('quite unlovely and bullocky'). The smallest cornett mentioned by Praetorius was a very small *Cornettino*, a fifth higher than the ordinary cornett and "not unlovely to hear." From the fact that Praetorius mentions no serpent, which, as Mersenne correctly stated, is the bass instrument of the cornett family, we may conclude that the serpent was unknown in Germany at the time of Praetorius (1619).

Mersenne is quite enthusiastic about the tone of the cornett which he compared to "a ray of sunshine which appears through the gloom of darkness ('dans les tenebres') when it is heard among the voices in cathedral churches or chapels." [356] Mersenne also makes a statement about some players who could hold the tone for eighty, and one player, 'le sieùr Sourin d'Auignon,' for a hundred measures without taking a breath.[357] This seems quite incredible, since some writers said that the cornett is very fatiguing for the lips and lungs.[358] Paradoxically both statements are correct. The cornett, played very softly with no pressure on the lips, can be sounded for a long time without difficulty; but when blown forte and with the pressure method of blowing it is exceedingly difficult and fatiguing.

Historically the cornett is among the oldest wind instruments in Europe. Its origin should be sought in Eastern Europe and Asia Minor. In England, at least, it has been known since the late tenth or early eleventh century.[359] In Germany the cornett persisted into the nineteenth century; Wilhelm Schneider in *Historisch-technische Beschreibung der musicalischen Instrumente* (Leipzig, 1834) mentioned that, although the cornett was obsolete in his time, it was used with the trombone "not so long ago." [360] In Russia the *rozhok*, a cornett with four or, more often, with five finger-holes in the front and a thumb-hole in the rear was heard as late as 1923, when a small ensemble of *Vladimirski rozhechniki* played at the All-Union Agricultural Exposition. In the seventies of the past century N. V. Kondratiev, a peasant in the village Mihnevo, organized an orchestra of twelve members which became known not only in Russia but even abroad. In ensemble playing two sizes of the *rozhok* were used: the *maliy rozhok*, or the *vizgunok* (the 'squealer') and the *bol'shoy rozhok* or the bass, an octave below the former. The music, composed by the players themselves, was an original folk polyphony quite different from that of Western Europe.[361]

160. STRAIGHT CORNETT Norfolk, England, probably 17th century

Cornettino recto. In C. Made of an antelope's horn with an integral conoidal mouthpiece bored in the solid part of the tip of the horn. Six finger-holes in the front with countersunk edges provide convenient cup-shaped orifices for the finger tips and insure adequate stopping. No trimmings nor embellishments of any kind. Length, 45.4 cm. Diameter, bell opening (average), 4.7 cm. Embouchure, diameter, 15 mm.; depth, 19 mm. (17.1953)
Plate IV

This instrument is described in the R. M. E. *Catalogue* on p. 156, under no. 316. It was found in a Norfolk village, where it was known as the 'Harvest Horn' and had existed for generations. The instrument gives a D-major scale, the actual lowest tone sounding as *d'*-sharp at a'-440 cycles per second; in other words it stands one semi-tone sharper than our standard pitch. It overblows an octave and a twelfth with all finger-holes stopped; the e'-hole overblows only an octave; the *f'*-sharp hole is increased in size. The tone produced, when attacked forte, is very clear, somewhat deficient in the higher partial tones, yet pleasant. The tones which can be produced with an acceptable tonal quality and intonation range from *d'* to *a''*.

161. TREBLE CORNETT — Reproduction, 17th-century type

Cornetto diritto. In A. The lowest tone is a (a'-420 cycles per second). Made of maple, stained reddish-brown; tipped with brass. Cup-shaped mouthpiece of horn. Six finger-holes in the front; a thumb-hole in the rear. Length (with mouthpiece), 66.5 cm. Diameter, bell, 3.4 cm. Bore, min., 7 mm.; max., 25 mm.; ratio, max.: min., 3.6:1; length of conoidal part, 63 cm. (17.1951)
Plate IV

162. CORNETT — Reproduction, 17th-century type

Cornetto curvo. In A. The lowest tone is *a*. Made from two slabs of wood, the curved conoidal bore carved in halves which have been fastened together and covered by black leather. The outside of the tube is of irregular, octagonal cross-section. Six finger-holes in the front; a thumb-hole in the rear. The mouthpiece is lost. Length (without mouthpiece), 58 cm. Width, bell, 3.2 cm. Bore, min., 7 mm.; max., 24 mm.; ratio, 3.43:1; length of conoidal part, 55.5 cm. (17.1949)
Plate IV

Described in the R. M. E. *Catalogue* on p. 157, under no. 318, and represented there on plate vi, figure e.

163. MUTE CORNETT — Reproduction, 17th-century type

Cornetto muto. In F. The lowest tone is *f*. Made of pearwood. Straight conoidal bore; integral cup-shaped mouthpiece. Eight finger-holes in the front, one of the lowest stopped with wax; a thumb-hole in the rear. Length, 69.2 cm. Diameter, bell, 4.5 cm. Bore, min., 6 mm.; max., 29 mm.; ratio, 4.85:1; length of conoidal part, 68 cm. Embouchure, diameter, 15 mm. (17.1952)
Plate IV

Described in the R. M. E. *Catalogue* on p. 159, under no. 326, and represented there on plate vi, figure f (not on 'plate vii, fig. b,' as on p. 159; the reference on p. 256 of the R. M. E. *Catalogue* is correct).

164. GREAT CORNETT — Reproduction, 17th-century type

Corno torto. Cornone. In C. The lowest tone is *c*. Made from two slabs of wood, like No. 162, and covered with black leather. The tube is bent twice in the form of the letter S. Ivory tip at the small end. Six finger-holes in the front, and seventh hole stopped by a square brass key with a double touch-piece; a thumb-hole in the rear. The mouthpiece is lost. Length (without mouthpiece), 91 cm. Diameter, bell, 6.5 cm. Bore, min., 8 mm.; max., 50 mm.; ratio, 6.25:1; length of conoidal part, 94.5 cm. Length of air column, 97.2 cm. (17.1950)
Plate IV

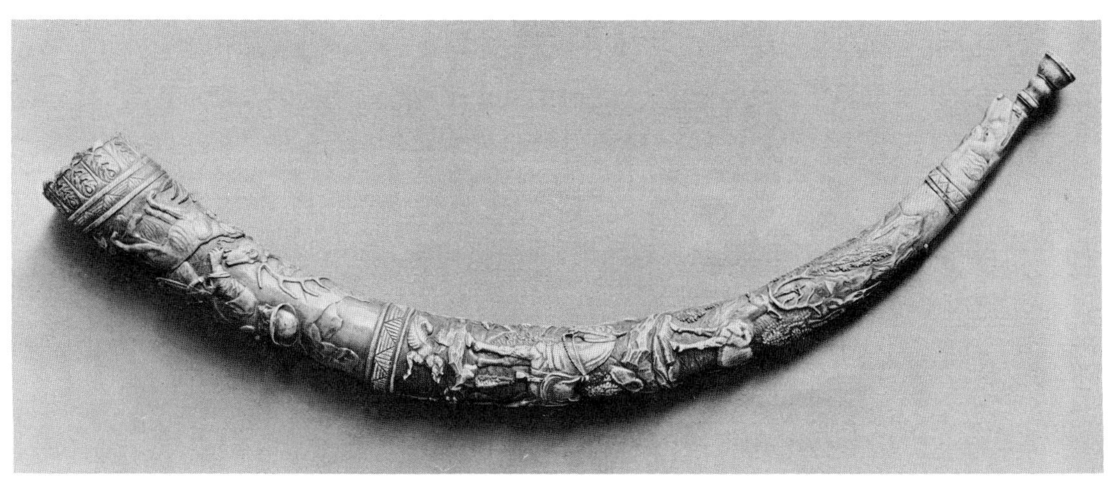

Fig. 28. OLIPHANT (No. 155)

Fig. 29. SERPENT (No. 165)

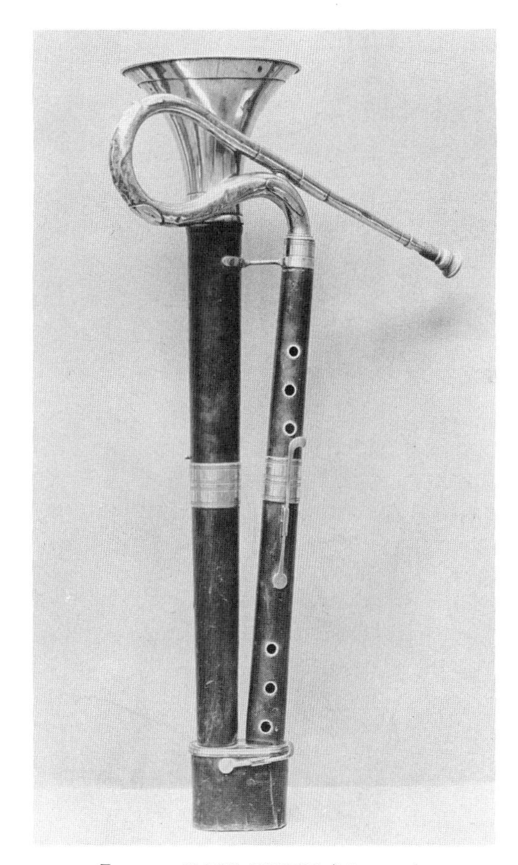

Fig. 30. BASS HORN (No. 167)

165. SERPENT Belgium, early 18th century

In C. The lowest tone is *C*. Made of pearwood in the shape of a serpent, the tube making three U-shaped bends and almost a complete circle at the end with the bell turned upward; all the bends and the bell are in one plane; carved out in halves, fastened together and covered with black leather. Wide brass ferrule at the small end; brass mouthpipe, ivory mouthpiece. Six finger-holes in the front. 'BAUDOUIN' stamped inside the bell. Length, 85 cm. Width, 43 cm. Bore, min., 1.4 cm.; max., 10 cm.; ratio, 7.14:1; length of conoidal part, 190 cm. Length of air column (with mouthpiece), 226 cm. (17.1954)
Plate IV

For several reasons the serpent is an unusual instrument. First, for its grotesque shape, which attracts immediate attention. Then, the fact that it is an ancestor of our modern bass tuba. Finally, its remarkable and hardly credible acoustical properties. The first serious study of the acoustical properties of the serpent by scientists of standing was done by Dr. Bouasse and M. Fouché. The reader is referred to *Instruments à vent*, i, pp. 376 ff., paragraphs 193, 194. The writer can only confirm the conclusions of these scientists. On the serpent it is possible to play in the lowest register the series of tones given there on p. 378, which, "among other series," comprise the scale of D-major and the tones of the first or church Dorian mode; these tones can be produced by the lips with fingerings, which normally are supposed to give an entirely different series of tones, with a perfectly correct intonation.[362] The lowest tone of the serpent of this Collection is given as *C*. As a matter of fact, this is perfectly arbitrary, since it is possible to produce around this tone a continuous glide within a very wide interval, at least a fifth, ranging from AA to E. The basic conclusion of Messrs. Bouasse and Fouché with respect to lip-vibrated aerophones is supported in the most convincing way by the serpent. This conclusion is as follows. A lip-vibrated aerophone has well-defined true partial tones, for which the tube reacts on the lips in a more stable manner and imposes frequencies and tone color in the best way; that is, these tones are the most adaptable for production by the lips in an easy and natural way. But below those true partial tones it is possible to produce tones, almost as good tonally, within an interval which in the low register may exceed a fifth; that is, the lips begin to force the emission of tones and modify the frequency. It should be realized that these 'off pitch' tones are not the most natural tones; yet with their help it is possible to correct true partial tones when they are musically faulty.[363] It is possible on the long tube instruments, such as the horn, to raise the pitch of the true partial tone slightly, but not much: the lips either slip into the next higher partial tone, or, if one plays in the lower register, simply 'break.' As one descends the scale, this upper interval between the breaking point and the true tone increases slightly, but still remains quite narrow. The interval *below* the true partial increases very rapidly and near the second partial tone becomes quite wide. For instance, on the F-horn, after a little practice, it is possible to glide continuously from *F* down to *C* and produce the latter tone in tune and hold it securely without the lips breaking for a certain length of time; it is possible also to play the tones separately within the same interval and to produce, among other possible tones, a chromatic scale from *C* to *F* by the lip action alone. True, this is by no means easy; but the whole point is that it is possible. Therefore, the contention of Professor Bouasse that the lip-vibrated aerophones are instruments of variable pitch having no rigidly fixed partial tones is merely a statement of scientifically demonstrable fact.[364] More on this subject on p. 187.

The invention of the serpent is credited to Canon Edme Guillaume of Auxerre about 1590. Dr. Curt Sachs states that there exist some serpents of Italian make of an earlier date, and grants to Canon Guillaume only the honor of introducing the serpent into France.[365] The serpent was used in churches for supporting the choir singers in Plain Song and chorals. Later it became a member of the military band and was even used in the orchestra.

166. BASS HORN — Belgium, ca. 1800

Basson russe. In C. The lowest tone is *C.* Made of bird's-eye maple in the shape of a bassoon; stained light yellow. The instrument consists of a long brass mouthpipe, wing joint, butt, long (bass) joint, and a brass bell; all wood parts are tipped with wide brass bands. Six finger-holes in the front. Four round brass keys mounted on saddles which give the following tones: *C*-sharp, *E*-flat, *F*-sharp, and *B.* The B-key can also be used as an octave key. The E-hole is bored into both large bores of the butt. Length, 106.5 cm. Width, butt, 9.3 cm. Bore, min., 1.2 cm.; max. (end of long joint), 5 cm.; ratio, 4.15:1; length of conoidal part, 221 cm. Length of air column (with mouthpiece), 256 cm. (17.1957)
Plate V

The Russians can be accused of many sins, but the invention of the *basson russe* is not among them. According to Gerber, an Italian musician Regibo residing in Lille, France, improved the form of the serpent by giving it a more practicable form of a bassoon-shaped tube; the date of this improvement is 1780.

167. BASS HORN — England, ca. 1800

In C. The lowest tone is *C.* A tube and a short butt made of pearwood. Consists of the following parts: a long brass crook; a finger-hole tube, upon which are located six finger-holes bushed with ivory and two round brass keys on saddles; a very short butt with a brass key, a long bass joint, and a brass bell with an oval orifice. Brass tips and a brace join both tubes at the top. The keys give the following tones: *C*-sharp, *F*-sharp, and B; the key-holes are also bushed with ivory. Length, 89 cm. Width (at the top), 16 cm. Bore, min., 1.4 cm.; max., 5.8 cm.; ratio, 4.14:1; length of conoidal part, 231.5 cm. Length of air column (with mouthpiece), 250 cm. (17.1955)
Plate V

This instrument is a modified form of the serpent, somewhat similar to the *basson russe,* but with a short butt joint and only one key.

168. BASS HORN — England, ca. 1800

In C. The lowest tone is *C.* Made entirely of brass. Consists of a long crook, two conical tubes brazed into a short butt-stock, and the bell; the tubes are at a slightly divergent angle and are joined by a tubular brace at the top. Six finger-holes with raised sockets on the small tube. Four round keys mounted on a saddle, the key-holes also having raised sockets. The keys give the same tone as

No. 166. Length, 89 cm. Width (at the top), 17 cm. Bore, min., 1.4 cm.; max., 6.5 cm.; ratio, 4.65:1; length of conoidal part, 228.5 cm. Length of air column (with mouthpiece), 253.5 cm. (17.1956)
Plate V

This brass model of the bass horn is credited to A. Frichot, a French refugee who lived in London about 1800. It seems that this particular model became known as the 'English bass horn' or the 'serpent anglais.' The bass horn held its place in the military band until the thirties of the nineteenth century, when it was gradually replaced by the ophicleide.

The Lateral-Hole Instruments with Keys

THE lateral-hole instruments dealt with so far were originally tubes with finger-holes and later with auxiliary keys which supplemented the finger-holes; essentially they still remained finger-hole instruments on which the fingers were used for the direct stopping of holes. We will now describe a series of instruments which have lateral holes and do not differ in principle from the former group; the difference is in mechanical construction and the greater use of partial tones. The finger-holes on instruments of this group are eliminated and the keys cover up all lateral holes; the fingers manipulate the key levers only and do not stop any holes directly. This practice permitted larger lateral holes and introduced a new variation in tone producing technique. As stated already, the older type of lateral-hole instrument permitted cross-fingering; the latter is effective on the lip-vibrated instrument with small finger-holes and is not so effective on the instrument with large lateral openings. The old type technique used partial tones very sparingly; on the cornett only the second partial tone was used. The keys were applied to the natural instruments, such as the horn, the trumpet, and the bugle, which were played with many overblown partial tones. This experience did not fail to influence the fingering technique after keys were applied. Therefore, the keyed instrument should be regarded as an intermediate step to the fully developed overblowing technique of the valve instrument. Specifically, this is the way the key bugle was played. The instrument considered is No. 171. The numbers under the notes are the ordinal numbers of the partial tones.

The first key is an open key in its normal position. When all the keys, including the first key, are closed, the key bugle No. 171 sounds:

With the first key open it sounds:

In other words, the bugle behaves so far as a three-octave whole-tube instrument with pedal tone.

With the second key open it sounds:

With the third key open it sounds:

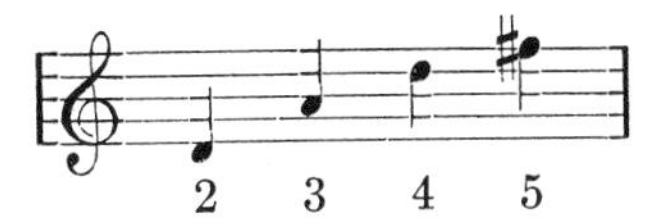

With the fourth key open it sounds:

The fifth and sixth keys give:

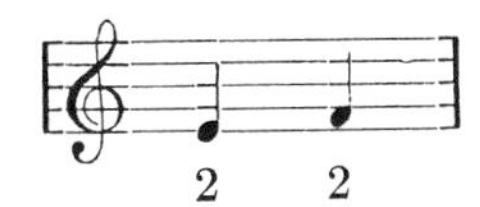

The instrument gives a complete chromatic scale from *b* to c^3. An interesting phenomenon takes place as the tube is shortened. Beginning as a regular three-octave instrument with pedal tone, the key bugle retains this specific characteristic: it remains an instrument with pedal tones.[366] The upper partial tones gradually shrink in number, and with the opening of the fourth key the shortened tube displays the properties of a two-octave instrument: the number of partial tones shrinks to two and their tonal quality becomes poor. As a result of such a change in the acoustical characteristic (in a given instance it is the generic characteristic that changes) the key bugle has a very uneven scale as to tone color produced and is difficult to keep in tune. A good musician can play a key bugle in tune, but he cannot improve the tonal qualities of the tube when it is shortened by the keys being placed close to the mouthpiece. Therefore, the principal defect of the key bugle was the uneven tone color of the scale, which produced the impression that the instrument was out of tune.[367] This defect could not be remedied. Since it is present on all lateral-hole lip-vibrated aerophones, it is not surprising that they were abandoned when the valve mechanism was invented.

The history of keyed instruments is not very complicated. The first attempt was made about 1760 by Koelbel, a horn player in the Russian Imperial Orchestra in St. Petersburg, who constructed the 'amorschall,' an improved horn with a modified bell and several keys. Although Koelbel's experiment was a failure, it inspired the application of the keys to other instruments. Anton Weidinger of Vienna applied keys to the trumpet in 1800. The first inventor who really applied keys in a systematic manner, so as to fill the large intervals between the second, third, and fourth partial tones, was Joseph Halliday, bandmaster of the Cavan militia, who invented the key bugle in 1810. This principle was extended later to the lower-pitched instruments, on which the octave interval between the pedal and second partial tone was filled by keys. Halary (Jean Hilaire Asté) invented in 1817 an improved bass horn which he called the ophicleide, a keyed serpent. He also developed the clavi-tube, a modified keyed bugle in several tonalities, and the alto instrument, the quinti-clave or quinti-tube in F and in E-flat, which later developed into the alto ophicleide. The ophicleide was built as the bass (more properly the 'baritone' by its tonal position) in C and in B-flat, and as the contrabass (properly, the 'bass') in F and in E-flat.

Note on Measuring Conoidal Bore Instruments with Bells

TABULATION of sizes given below the technical description of the key bugle No. 169 is typical for 'brass' instruments. Certain items require explanation. The tubes of cylindrical

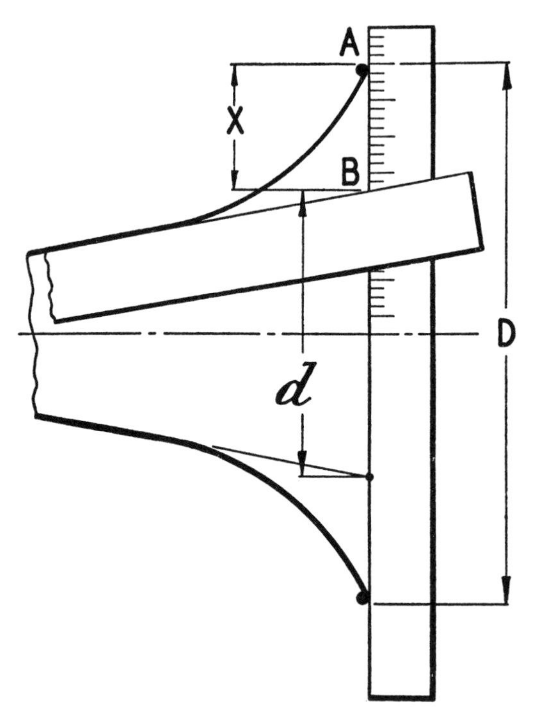

FIG. 31. METHOD OF MEASURING THE MAXIMUM DIAMETER OF CONOID

and conoidal lip-vibrated aerophones end with a truncated cone expanding into a flaring bell. Theoretically the termination of the tube should be a truncated cone without any bell. Some old type instruments of the bugle family had no bells. Thus in the middle of the nineteenth century the Prussian 'cornets' were bugles without bells. The 'Swedish cornet' still perpetuates this model. Old tubas and helicons (cf. C. Pierre, *La facture instrumentale*, Paris, 1890, p. 242) had a slightly turned rim instead of a bell. This straight termination of the tube made no noticeable difference in tonal quality, but the stubby appearance displeased the eye. Gradually the bells were made larger and larger until, as in the case of tubas, they became a decorative feature. Since there is no uniformity in size or form of bells, no consistent measurement of the conoidal part of the bore is possible until the bell is eliminated from consideration. The method of measuring the maximum diameter of conoid used in this study is represented on the diagram.

A straight-edge is laid inside the bell securely against the straight generator line of the conoid. The distance x = AB is measured by a scale put across the rim of the bell. Two times 'x' subtracted from the diameter *D* of the bell gives the maximum theoretical diameter *d* in the plane of the bell rim. In the tabulations of sizes *d* is given as: Bore, conoidal, maximum. Specifically: (1) the horns are regarded as conoidal bore instruments; the cylindrical parts of the bore, in some cases, are disregarded; (2) the trumpets and trombones have the lengths of cylindrical and conoidal parts of the bore given in each instance; (3) the cornets and bugles of this Collection are cylindro-conoidal instruments and not conoidal-cylindro-conoidal as are the modern instruments. The ratio between the maximum theoretical diameter *d* and the minimum diameter of the conoidal bore portion serves as a rough approximation for measuring the taper of the conoid. A large ratio, as in the case of horns, means a narrow taper, and vice versa. To eliminate confusion the minimum diameter of the conoid is also given.

169. KEY BUGLE — Paris, France, ca. 1825

Soprano in B-flat. Brass. Cylindro-conoidal bore. Two round keys (closed) mounted on saddles; key-holes have raised sockets. Shallow cup mouthpiece inserted into the tuning tube held in place by a wing nut. The keys give *c'* and *d'*. The fundamental tone, with both keys closed, comes out easily and in tune. Stamped on the rim of the bell: 'COURTOIS NEVEU AINE A PARIS.' Length (crooked in B-flat), 56 cm. Diameter, bell, 14.8 cm. Bore, cylindrical, diameter, 13 mm.; length, 21.5 cm.; conoidal, min., 13 mm.; max., 7.8 cm.; ratio, max.: min., 6:1; length, 107.5 cm. Length of air column (with mouthpiece), 134 cm. (17.1971)
Plate V

170. KEY BUGLE — Lierre, Belgium, ca. 1830

Sopranino in E-flat. Brass. Five round keys mounted on pillars; key-holes have raised sockets. Deep conical cup mouthpiece inserted into the tuning tube, held in place by a wing-nut. Cylindro-conoidal bore. The keys give the following nominal tones: *b*, *c'*-sharp, *d'*, *e'*-flat, *e'*, and *f'*, sounding a minor third higher; the lowest key is open, the rest are closed. Engraved on the bell: 'G. Van Engelen, ainé à Lierre.' Length (crooked in E-flat), 41 cm. Diameter, bell, 13.5 cm. Bore, cylindrical, diameter, 10.5 mm.; length, 17.5 cm.; conoidal, min., 10.5 mm.; max., 7.5 cm.; ratio, 7.15:1; length, 84 cm. Length of air column (with mouthpiece), 105.5 cm. (17.1974)
Plate V

171. KEY BUGLE — England, ca. 1830

Soprano in C. Copper; brass keys and trimmings. Cylindro-conoidal bore. Six cup-shaped keys mounted on saddles; key-holes have brass sockets; the saddle of the third key is made in the form of an inverted U and has two brass strips, the whole serving as a finger-rest for holding the

instrument. The first key (open) has a knurled head screw for the adjustment of the key clearance. The keys give the following actual tones: *b*, *c'*-sharp, *d'*, *e'*-flat, *e'*, and *f'*. Length, 45 cm. Diameter, bell, 16 cm. Bore, cylindrical, diameter, 13 mm.; length, 11 cm.; conoidal, min., 13 mm.; max., 8.8 cm.; ratio, 6.75:1; length, 105.5 cm. Length of air column (with mouthpiece), 122.5 cm. (17.1972)
Plate V

172. KEY BUGLE England, ca. 1830

'Pocket' model. Soprano in B-flat. Copper, with brass keys and trimmings. Cylindro-conoidal bore. Six flat round keys mounted on saddles; key-holes have brass sockets; a finger-rest above the first key. The tube has a very slight flare at the bell end instead of the usual bell with a wide rim. Deep conical cup mouthpiece with a silvered rim. The keys give the same nominal tones as on No. 171. Length, 27 cm. Diameter, bell opening, 8 cm. Bore, cylindrical, diameter, 11 mm.; length, 15 cm.; conoidal, min., 11 mm.; max., 6.6 cm.; ratio, 6:1; length, 117.5 cm. Length of air column (with mouthpiece), 138.5 cm. (17.1976)
Plate V

173. KEY BUGLE England, ca. 1835

Soprano in C with B-flat crook. German silver keys and trimmings. Cylindro-conoidal bore. Six cup-shaped keys mounted on saddles. Deep conical cup mouthpiece of brass with a very narrow rim. Clearance adjusting screw on the first key. The keys give the same actual (when crooked in C) tones as those on No. 171. Engraved on the bell: 'Royal Kent Bugle, Patent.' Length (crooked in B-flat), 54 cm. Diameter, bell opening, 15.2 cm. Bore, cylindrical, diameter, 12 mm.; length (with crook), 19 cm.; conoidal, min., 12 mm.; max., 9.6 cm.; ratio, 8:1; length, 121.5 cm. Length of air column (with mouthpiece), 143 cm. (17.1975)
Plate V

The Royal Kent Bugle was the name of the key bugle introduced into the English army under the patronage of the Duke of Kent, father of Queen Victoria.

174. KEY BUGLE Brussels, Belgium, 1841

Soprano in B-flat. Brass with German silver keys and trimmings. Cylindro-conoidal bore. Seven cup-shaped keys mounted on pillars (flaps of the keys have very small curvature; levers extend to the centre of the flaps). Deep conical cup mouthpiece (brass) inserted into the tuning tube. The keys give the following nominal tones: *b*, *c'*-sharp, *d'*, *e'*-flat (double for improving intonation), *e'*, and *f'*. Engraved on the bell: 'C. Sax, à Bruxelles, No. 5991.' Stamped on the rim: 'B, 1841.' Length, 50.5 cm. Diameter, bell, 17 cm. Bore, cylindrical, diameter, 11.5 mm.; length, 18.5 cm.; conoidal, min., 11.5 mm.; max., 8.6 cm.; ratio, 7.5:1; length, 119.5 cm. Length of air column (with mouthpiece), 141.5 cm. (17.1973)
Plate V

175. OPHICLEIDE Brussels, Belgium, ca. 1840

Alto in E-flat. Brass. Conoidal bore throughout, except for a short length (7.5 cm.) where the crook is inserted into the main tubing. Nine slightly cup-shaped keys mounted on pillars. Made in two principal parts: the crook and the main tube; the crook is adjustable for tuning and position. Cup-shaped mouthpiece. The keys give the following nominal tones: *B*, *c*-sharp, *d*, *e*-flat, *e*, *f*, *g*, *a*, and *b*-flat. The third and the fifth key (counting from the bell) are located at the

back and are operated by the left-hand and right-hand thumbs respectively. Engraved on the bell: 'C. Devaster, A. Bruxelles.' Length, 90.5 cm. Diameter, bell, 20.5 cm. Bore, min., 12 mm.; max., 11.5 cm.; ratio, 9.6:1; length, 210.5 cm. Length of air column (with mouthpiece), 215 cm. (17.1958)
Plate V

176. OPHICLEIDE — Paris, France, ca. 1845

Baritone in B-flat. Brass. Conoidal-cylindro-conoidal bore. Nine flat keys mounted on pillars; the first key (open) has a knurled head screw for clearance adjustment. Made in two principal parts: a crook thrice bent upon itself and held in place by a wing-nut, and the main tube; the crook is adjustable axially for tuning and for position. Cup-shaped mouthpiece. The keys give the same nominal tones as on No. 175. The third and the fifth keys have the same location and are operated as those on No. 175. Two hand-rests on the main tube for support of the instrument. Engraved on the bell: 'Guichard Breveté A Paris,' under the imperial crown and flags. Number '219' stamped on several parts. Length, 114 cm. Diameter, bell, 21 cm. Bore, min., 12.5 mm.; max., 14 cm.; ratio, 11.2:1; length, 279 cm. Length of air column (with mouthpiece), 282.5 cm. (17.1959)
Plate V

The Slide and the Valves

THERE are two types of mechanism for making the lip-vibrated aerophones completely chromatic: the slide and the valve. Acoustically both types are similar and only certain mechanical differences in construction affect the playing technique; this question will be discussed later on. Both the slide and the valves have this basic characteristic in common: a lip-vibrated aerophone, furnished either with a slide or valves, produces natural scales of tones consisting of overblown partial tones only; no 'cross-fingering' is possible. The plural 'natural scales' is used deliberately. Both slide and valve instruments produce many natural scales. There is, however, this difference. An instrument furnished with a slide can produce an infinite number of natural scales, since the slide moves continuously between certain limits and continuously changes the length of the main tubing between these limits. An instrument furnished with valves can produce only the limited number of scales necessary to make the instrument chromatic; the valve mechanism changes the length of the main tubing discontinuously, by a certain definite unit or 'quantum' (an equal tempered semitone, theoretically) or its multiple. The slide permits the playing in perfect tune in any desired temperament (just, meantone, or equal), the accuracy of pitch of the tones being limited only by the skill of the player and the accuracy of his ear.

The valve mechanism has an inherent defect which affects the accuracy of the pitch of tones produced by its means, and the player is forced to correct the pitch of the tones by 'lipping' on the ordinary valve instrument; primarily the valve mechanism is calculated for the equal temperament only.

The essential constructional difference between the slide and the valve mechanism is the following. The whole-tube valve instruments can be made completely chromatic from the pedal tones [368] upward by means of the valve mechanism. Without auxiliary valves the slide instruments cannot be made completely chromatic. Thus, on the tenor slide trombone there is an interval between the pedal tone of the first position (*BB*-flat) and the lowest tone of the seventh position (*E*) which cannot be filled in.[369] It is only on the combination slide and valve instruments (as tenor-bass trombones with the auxiliary 'Quartventil') that this interval can be filled. Less important is the impossibility of true legato playing on slide instruments. The slide has to be shifted from position to position without any intervening portamento; the sound emission has to be stopped for a certain length of time, however short. The player uses this time interval for shifting the slide and adjusting the lips to produce a partial tone in the new position. Skilful players do this with great rapidity; but if the interval between the tones requires a shift over several positions (say from the first to the sixth) there is a perceptible interruption in the continuity of sound. On valve instruments, because of the swifter action of the mechanism and the possibility of changing the valves without discontinuing the blowing, legato playing is more successful.

Acoustically the action of the slide or valve (or valves) is as follows. The pitch of a natural scale on the lip-vibrated aerophone depends upon the length of the tube, other conditions remaining the same. The shortening of the tube will raise the pitch of the natural scale; the lengthening of the tube will lower the pitch of the natural scale. In practice it has been found that the most important interval to be bridged is the fifth between the second and the third partial tones. There are seven standard positions on the slide instruments and seven valve combinations on the valve instruments.[370] The minimum number of valves to achieve this result is three on the three-octave half-tube instruments without pedal tone; if a loss of a few tones is to be tolerated, the minimum number of valves on the four-octave half-tube instruments would be two. Historically, the first valve instruments had only two valves.[371]

The action of a slide is almost self-evident. When the slide is shifted 'home' as far as it can go, the total length of tubing is the shortest possible; this position is called the first position of the slide. The natural scale of tones produced by a slide instrument in its first position is the highest possible; its true pitch depends upon the tonal position of the instrument. For the sake of simplicity let us take a tenor trombone in C.[372] Then the normal natural scale produced by this instrument in the first position is:

Some players extend the upper limit of their register to the twelfth partial tone.[373]

For the second position the slide is shifted out sufficiently far [374] to produce the following natural scale:

In the third position the natural scale sounds:

In the fourth position:

The pedal tone is designated by a crotchet, because some trombone players are unable to produce the pedal tone in the fourth position and those below the fourth.

In the fifth position:

In the sixth position:

In the seventh position:

When these natural scales are superimposed, a complete chromatic scale from G-flat to *c''* becomes possible on the C slide trombone; above that capable trombonists extend the scale chromatically up to *g''*. Two important facts should be noted in connection with the slide instruments. The first one is that a diatonic scale is not possible by merely extending the slide successively. Here is what the trombonist has to do to play a diatonic scale from *c* to *c'*.

Position	1	6	4	3	1	4	2	1
Partial Tone	2	3	3	3	3	4	4	4

In other words, in order to play such a simple scale as that of C-major (on the tenor trombone it would be the B-flat major scale) the trombonist has to shift the slide into five different positions (1, 2, 3, 4, and 6) of which the first position is taken three times, the fourth position twice, and each of the rest once; the total number of changes is eight and no adjacent tones are played in the same position. The sequence of partial tones comes out a little better since there is a certain uniformity. The largest shift is between the two adjacent tones *c* and *d*; to play *d* the slide has to be shifted from the first position to the sixth. No wonder that the slide trombone is difficult to play and that a true legato is impossible.

Another important fact is that some tones can be produced in more than one position. This fact was known to Mersenne.[375] Thus g′ (sounds f′ on the B-flat tenor trombone) can be played as the sixth partial tone in the first position, as the seventh in the fourth position, or the eighth in the sixth position.[376]

The valve mechanism is essentially similar to the slide in its action. The main tube is lengthened through the inclusion of additional lengths of tubing by means of the valves. On three-valved instruments the first valve adds two semitones, the second valve adds one semitone, and the third valve adds three semitones. This order (2, 1, 3) of adding semitones was chosen primarily because it gave the simplest fingering on four-octave instruments (trumpets and horns) in the most used third octave.[377]

By combining the valves, it is possible to produce the necessary number of additional natural scales so that the chromatic scale can be played from the nominal *f*-sharp to *c″*. In other words, the main tube with valves 'off' corresponds to the first position of the slide trombone. The six additional combinations possible with three valves correspond to the six extended positions of the slide on the trombone. Just as on the trombone it is not possible to span the interval between the lowest tone of the seventh position (the nominal *G*-flat or *F*-sharp, sounding *E* on the *B*-flat tenor trombone) and the pedal tone of the first position (the nominal *C*; *BB*-flat on the tenor trombone), so it is not possible with three valves to fill the same interval between the pedal tone and the nominal *F*-sharp. On slide instruments this defect, as has been already stated, cannot be remedied by means of the slide alone. On valve instruments the fourth valve is added; this valve adds five semitones or a fourth.[378] Obviously, the fourth valve is needed only on the whole-tube instruments with the pedal tone.

A Defect of the Valve Mechanism

THE slide on the slide trombone is shifted for each semitone not by equal amounts, but by gradually changing increments. If the slide is extended into the seventh position, then it is shifted into successive higher positions by the same relative amounts as the spacing of frets on fretted instruments; that is, the lengths of the shifts decrease with each successive higher position. Starting with the first position, the process is reversed, and the trombonist pulls the slide out more each time as he descends into each successive position. In other words, a trombonist has the same freedom in controlling the pitch of tones as a violinist. This is the inherent advantage of the slide. On valve instruments the length of the valve crooks has to be figured with respect to the length of the main tube. Just as long as single valves are used, their natural scales remain in a correct pitch relationship to the natural scale produced by the main tube. The trouble starts when two or more valves are pressed down simultaneously;

then their combined lengths are too short and give a natural scale of tones which is too sharp.[379] This defect can be remedied by a player with his lips, owing to the fact that below the true partial tones it is possible, within certain limits, to play flatter. But this process is not very convenient.[380] Therefore many inventors attempted to remedy this inherent defect of the valve mechanism by so-called compensating mechanisms which would add supplementary lengths of tubing when the valves are used in various combinations. On some systems additional valves are used; on others, by a clever combination of the tubes and valve passages, the compensatory process is effected without the necessity of complicating the fingering. Finally, A. Sax invented the independent tube system, in which the instrument was constructed with seven tubes, corresponding to the seven standard positions of the slide, and six valves, corresponding to the six valve combinations; each tube was, except for a short length from the mouthpiece to the valves, entirely independent of the others, and each had its own bell. The mouthpiece acted on the longest tube directly; the rest of the tubes were switched on by means of their own valves; no two tubes could be combined. In playing on this instrument the sounds were emitted by different bells similarly to the organ pipes. The system was a success musically, since in purity of tone it was equal to the slide instruments, except that it was not as flexible in the pitch adjustment; but the instruments were too heavy and not very convenient to play.[381]

Group 2: Three-Octave Instruments

Sub-group i: With Pedal Tone

THREE-OCTAVE instruments differ from the preceding group of two-octave instruments by having two sub-groups. Wide-tapered conoidal bore instruments produce the pedal tone with good tonal quality, fine sonority, and in good tune; this sub-group consists mainly of the bugle family and its various modifications. Narrow-tapered conoidal bore instruments either refuse to produce the pedal tone or produce it out of tune and with bad tonal quality, so that it becomes useless for musical purposes. A real explanation of this property of tubes has been given by Professor Bouasse.[382]

177. BUGLE — Berlin, Prussia, early 19th century

Signalhorn. Soprano in C (in 'Kammerton' pitch; the second partial sounds d′ at a′ = 440). German army type. Brass. Conoidal bore, funnel-shaped mouthpiece with very large bore. Half-moon shape. The bell and mouthpipe are braced by a brass rod. Two rings and an ear for leather straps. The bell is lacquered green inside. Stamped on the bell: 'Griessling & Schott, A Berlin.' Length, 52.5 cm. Width, 43 cm. Bore, min., 12 mm.; max., 11.6 cm.; ratio, 9.7:1; length, 106 cm. Length of air column (with mouthpiece), 110 cm. (17.1969)
Plate V

178. BUGLE — England, ca. 1810

Alto in G. The second partial sounds g. Copper, lacquered black. Cylindro-conoidal bore; deep conical cup mouthpiece. The tube is wound twice upon itself. Engraved on the bell: 'Kelly & Co. Pall Mall, London.' Length, 39 cm. Diameter, bell, 15.5 cm. Bore, cylindrical, diameter, 12.5 mm.;

length, 61.5 cm.; conoidal, min., 12.5 mm.; max., 8 cm.; length, 100 cm. Length of air column (with mouthpiece), 167 cm. (17.1970)
Plate V

179. LUR — Reproduction of the instrument, ca. 1000 B.C.

Bronze. Conoidal bore. Made in two principal parts, each part consisting of three joints fastened by ferrules. Cup-shaped mouthpiece. The bell end is embellished by a disc with eight hemispherical indentations; five pendants on rings near the mouthpiece. Length, 119 cm. Diameter, disc, 25 cm. Bore, min., 9 mm.; max., 64 mm.; length, 211 cm. Length of air column (with mouthpiece), 214.5. (17.1968)

The original of this instrument was found in an excavation of remnants of the Bronze Age in peat beds in Denmark and is now preserved in the Royal Museum of Antiquities of the North in Copenhagen. A similar instrument is listed in the *Catalogue . . . de Bruxelles*, ii (1909), p. 377, under no. 1156. The approximate tonality of this *lur* is E-flat and its length of tubing is close to that of the althorn in E-flat (208 cm.). M. Mahillon, *op. cit.*, p. 379, gives the number of partial tones as eight. On this point see Dr. Curt Sachs's *Real-Lexikon*, s.v. 'Lur.'

180. BUCCINA — Reproduction. 1st century B.C. type

Conoidal bore. Brass. The tube is bent into a G-shape in the same plane. Cup-shaped mouthpiece; moderately flaring bell. The instrument is braced with a turned wooden rod. Length, 132 cm. Diameter, bell, 13 cm. Bore, min., 10 mm.; max., 25 mm.; length of conoidal part, 270 cm. Length of air column (with mouthpiece), 323.5 cm. (17.1967)

The buccina or *tuba curva* was the signal instrument of the Roman infantry. The original of this instrument was found in an excavation in Pompeii and is now preserved in the National Museum in Naples, Italy. For further details, see the *Catalogue . . . de Bruxelles*, i (1893), p. 459, no. 464, and ii (1909), p. 30, for a picture. Our instrument is shorter and its approximate tonality is that of a horn in A-flat.

181. ALPHORN — Switzerland, 19th century

Alpenhorn. Conoidal bore. Trumpet-shaped wooden horn. Consists of a pine tube carved from two blocks of wood, fitted together and bound with long, narrow strips of birch bark. Wooden cup-shaped mouthpiece. Length, 98 cm. Diameter, bell, 11 cm. Bore, min., 15 mm.; max., 7 cm.; length of conoidal part, 256.5 cm. Length of air column (with mouthpiece), 260.5 cm. (17.1998)
Plate V

Sub-group ii: Without Pedal Tone

The Cornet (Post-Horn) Family

THE cornet (post-horn) family of instruments is the descendant of the French type of valveless post-horn, which originally had a short conoidal tube with a narrow tapered bore. The mouthpiece is of the elongated cup type, the cup length between that of the trumpet and the bugle, with a short shank. Owing to the combination of its tube and mouthpiece, the French post-horn began its natural scale from the second partial tone; its timbre was not particularly distinguished, a characteristic which it bequeathed to its descendants, the cornopean and the early type of the cornet-à-pistons. As the keyed post-horn No. 183 shows, the keys were applied to the post-horn. With the invention of valves the post-horn was converted into the cornopean with two and later with three piston valves. The soprano instrument was built in many tonalities.[383] Later, higher pitched instruments were added, such as the sopranino cornet in E-flat, the octave cornets in A-flat, and in high B-flat and C.

The lower pitched members of the family never descended below the tonal position of tenor instruments. An extension of the cornet family to the lower tonal position is not feasible, since the bore would be too narrow for the pitch of tones expected of bass and contrabass instruments. The althorn in E-flat and the tenorhorn in B-flat are still built in Italy with a real cornet bore. These narrow-bore instruments have a fine tone and possess the agility which is characteristic of the whole family. The althorn (the alto cornet) sounds better than the alto bugle. The latter instrument has a wider bore and is, perhaps, one of the worst sounding brass instruments. The modern soprano cornets-à-pistons have a wider taper and possess a broader tone; their pedal tone is playable.

182. POST-HORN — England, 19th century

Octave in B-flat. Conoidal bore. Copper, with brass mouthpiece. The tube is bent twice upon itself, trumpet-like, but the bends are brought closely together and soldered. Length, 28 cm. Diameter, bell, 7.5 cm. Bore, min., 7.5 mm.; max., 4.1 cm.; length of conoidal part, 66.5 cm. Length of air column (with mouthpiece), 68.5 cm. (17.1981)
Plate V

183. POST-HORN — Germany, ca. 1830

Alto in G (high pitch). Five keys. Conoidal bore. Brass. Circular wound tube (three times) with a cup-shaped mouthpiece. Five round keys mounted on saddles; the key levers are bent to conform with the shape of the instrument, except one which is mounted on a flat cross-brace. The keys give the following nominal tones: *c'*-sharp, *d'*, *e'*-flat, *e'*, and *f'*. Stamped 'A.K' with a six-petalled flower between the letters. Length, 33.8 cm. Diameter, bell, 12 cm. Bore, min., 9 mm.; max., 6 cm.; ratio, 6.65:1; length of conoidal part, 155 cm. Length of air column (with mouthpiece), 161.5 cm. (17.1983)
Plate VI

184. CORNOPEAN — Brussels, Belgium, ca. 1830

Soprano in C. Two piston valves. Cylindro-conoidal bore. Brass. The tube is made in two parts. The first part (counting from the mouthpiece) includes a tuning slide and ends in a valve tube; the second begins with a valve tube and ends in a bell; both parts are connected by a short cylindrical tube to form a continuous air column. The piston valves are inserted directly into the valve tubes, and have their travel limited by the screws passing through slots in the pistons. Cup-shaped mouthpiece. Engraved on the bell: 'C. Sax. Bruxelles. No. 6325.' Length, 29 cm. Diameter, bell, 13.2 cm. Bore, cylindrical, diameter, 9 mm.; length, 53 cm.; conoidal, min., 9 mm.; max., 5.2 cm.; ratio, 5.78:1; length, 83 cm. Length of air column (with mouthpiece), 134.5 cm. (17.1985)
Plate VI

The cornopean is the earliest form of cornet-à-pistons. The first instruments were built with only two pistons. These pistons had a peculiar construction, since they served as a continuation of the main tube and were set into the main tube much closer to the bell than the later types of cornets. The pistons were hollow and deflected the air-stream at right angles. This sharp change of direction in the main stream of air affected unfavorably the tone of the instrument, and gave the valve mechanism a bad reputation, which it had difficulties in outliving. The only good mechanical feature was the long bearing of the piston tubes, reintroduced later in the modern pistons. The German name for this type of valve is the *Schubventil*.[384]

185. CORNOPEAN — England, ca. 1840

Soprano in C, crooked in A. Cylindro-conoidal bore. Three piston valves. Copper, with German silver trimmings. The tube is made in two parts. The first part, as on No. 184, includes a tuning slide, but it is attached to a U-shaped tube into which are inserted two pistons; the second part begins with a piston tube and ends in a bell; a short cylindrical tube joins the U-shaped tube and the second part. Formerly, in addition to piston valves, there was a shake-key, the socket of which is now plugged. Engraved on the bell is a wreath, within which is inscribed 'Made by William Grayson, 5 Cooper Street, Westminster.' The crook is marked 'A-flat.' Length (with crook), 30.5 cm. Diameter, bell, 12.4 cm. Bore, cylindrical, diameter, 12 mm.; length, 80 cm.; conoidal, min., 12 mm.; max., 6 cm.; ratio, 5:1; length, 50 cm. Length of air column (crooked in C), 134 cm. (17.1989)
Plate VI

186. CORNET — London, England, ca. 1845

Patent Lever Cornet. Sopranino in E-flat. Cylindro-conoidal bore. Three disc valves. Brass. The tube is made in seven separate parts, three of which are located on the rotary discs of the valves. The shake-key has a double lever so that it can be operated either by the little finger or the thumb of the right hand. Card-holder for music soldered to the bell. Stamped name-plate attached to the bell, reading: 'By Her Majesties Royal Letters Patent. J. Shaw Inventor. Koehler Sole Maker. 35, Henrietta St.t, Covent Garden, London.' The number '189' is engraved on the name-plate. Length, 35.5 cm. Diameter, bell, 12.6 cm. Bore, cylindrical, diameter, 11 mm.; length, 61.5 cm.; conoidal, min., 11 mm.; max., 5.5 cm.; ratio, 5:1; length, 50 cm. Length of air column (with mouthpiece), 115 cm. (17.1986)
Plate VI

The R. M. E. *Catalogue* on p. 205 under no. 405 describes John Shaw's 'Patent Lever' valves, which were patented by him in 1838. The description there is correct, except for one detail mentioned later. The 'disc valves,' as they were called by the inventor, consisted of two brass discs each, one stationary and the other rotary. The stationary disc was affixed to the main tubing of the instrument in such wise that its plane was perpendicular to the axis of the main tube. It also had an additional tube (valve-crook) attached to it. This stationary disc had four holes (not two as in the R. M. E. *Catalogue*, p. 205). Another interesting detail: there was a slot (circular) in the stationary disc with holes at the ends; into these holes were inserted wax-impregnated wooden plugs, which served as the limit stops (on the modern rotary valve instruments the limit stops are made of cork and are attached outside the valve cage); the purpose of employing wood for these plugs was to reduce noise. The rotating disc had also four holes, connected in pairs by two short lengths of tubing. One of these tubes served as a continuation of the main tube, when the valve was in its normal or 'off' position, and as a connecting passage-way for the valve crook when the valve was shifted into its 'on' position. The second short tube on the rotary disc was inactive in the normal position, but in the 'on' position provided another wind-way, so that two portions of the main tube and two branches of the valve-crook could be connected into one continuous wind-way. The contacting surfaces of both discs had to be very carefully fitted in order to secure an air-tight yet easily working joint. The rotary disc was centered on the pin, affixed to the stationary disc, and held in place axially by a threaded ring with an extending rim; tightness of fit and wear take-up could be controlled by this ring. On the same centering pin was placed a small cylindrical cage with a spiral spring inside. On the outside of this cage was a lug to attach the lever which operated the valve; also a bent extension finger, which passed through a hole in the rotating disc and extended through sufficiently far to fit in the above-mentioned circular slot in the stationary disc. This protruding extension served as a stop. This rather complicated design of the stop was made to permit the winding of the spiral spring, for which at least three complete turns of the disc were necessary. The disc valves were discarded because of difficulties in keeping them air-tight.

187. CORNET — Vienna, Austria, ca. 1870

Sopranino in E-flat. Cylindro-conoidal bore. Three rotary valves. Brass, with German silver trimmings. Tuning slide in the main tube. Deep conical-shaped mouthpiece. Engraved on the bell rim reinforcing ring: 'Leopold Uhlmann, K. K. Priv. Instrumenten Fabrik. Wien.' Length, 42.5 cm. Diameter, bell, 12 cm. Bore, cylindrical, diameter, 10.5 mm.; length, 47 cm.; conoidal, min., 10.5 mm.; max., 6.4 cm.; ratio, 6.1:1; length, 64 cm. Length of air column (with mouthpiece), 117 cm. (17.1987)
Plate VI

This instrument illustrates another important variety of the valve mechanism, the so-called 'rotary valve.' The device consists of a short cylinder mounted in a cage and provided with two journals or bearing pins. The upper pin is inserted into the bushing permanently fixed to the top of the cage; the lower pin goes into that of the removable cover, which is centered in the cage and held in place by the threaded cap. The upper pin has an extension with a squared end on which is affixed a crank operated by a link rod, which is connected to the finger lever. The finger levers are mounted on the common axis and have spiral springs concealed in circular cages. The cylinders have two passages milled in them; in the 'off' position one of these passages serves as a continuation of the main tubing, while the other remains inoperative. In the 'on' position, both passages connect the 'valve crook' with the main tube and increase the length of the latter. When properly made and adjusted, the rotary valves work easily and positively. These valves are used mainly in Central Europe and Soviet Russia. In the United States the French horns are furnished with rotary valves having a flexible string connection between the finger lever and the valve crank. The majority of instruments in this country are made with piston valves.[385]

188. CORNET — Austria (Bohemia), ca. 1875

Soprano in B-flat (high pitch). Cylindro-conoidal bore. Circular shaped, 'Prince Pless Horn' type. Three double piston valves, Viennese action. Brass, with German silver trimmings. Piston levers arranged for left-hand playing as on a French horn. Music holder (detachable) of German silver. No maker's name; finely made instrument. Length, 32 cm. Diameter, bell, 12.2 cm. Bore, cylindrical, diameter, 8.5 mm.; length, 41.5 cm.; conoidal, min., 8.5 cm.; max., 6 cm.; ratio, 7.05:1; length, 84.5. Length of air column (with mouthpiece), 132 cm. (17.1988 a & b)
Plate VI

An unusual form of the cornet, shaped like a post-horn. Another unusual feature is the valve mechanism of the old Viennese action type. This mechanism was popular at certain periods, since it is very simple in construction and positive in action. Essentially it consisted of a heavy piece of brass with a long bore, which served as a part of the main tube, and six short cross-bores, to which were fixed the three pairs of tubes of the valve crooks. There were three pairs of short pistons which worked inside the valve crook tubes. In principle they were similar to those of the old cornopean pistons, except that they were working in pairs for each crook and were inserted in the crook tubes and not in the main tubing.[386] The instrument has the pedal tone of a narrow-bore bugle and should be classified as such. It is included among the half-tube instruments for musical and not acoustical reasons.[387]

189. BALLAD HORN — London, England, late 19th century

Tenor in C, with B-flat crook. Conoidal bore. Circular-shaped. Three piston valves of Perinet type. The valve mechanism is arranged for right-hand playing. Interchangeable tuning slide. Drain key on the main tube. The valve-crook slides have lines etched on them to show the extended position while playing with the B-flat crook. Mouthpiece with a cone-shaped cup. Engraved on the bell: 'W. Hillyard, Maker, 61 & 62 High St., Bloomsbury, London,' and the factory serial number '2269.' Length, 57 cm. Diameter, bell, 18.5 cm. Bore, min., 10 mm.; max., 8.3 cm.; ratio, 8.3 : 1; length (approx.), 200 cm. Length of air column (with mouthpiece), 236 cm. (17.2005 a & b)
Plate VII

This instrument is included in the Collection to illustrate the modern Perinet type piston valve. The principal difference from the early *Schubventil* is that the modern piston is not a part of the main tube as is the former type, but has only a short air passage when it is in the 'off' position and therefore does not change the direction of the main stream of air. The instrument itself is a medium-bore bugle made in a quasi-French-horn shape. It gives a good pedal tone, and is included among half-tube instruments for the same reason as the preceding one.

Group 3: Four-Octave Instruments

[*Sub-group i: With Pedal Tone*]

Sub-group ii: Without Pedal Tone

THE term 'horn' includes many types of instruments, varying from the short animal horn to the modern orchestral instrument. Here we are concerned only with a specific type:

a four-octave instrument with a narrow conoidal bore, circular-wound, and with a large flaring bell and funnel-shaped mouthpiece. The circular form of the tube with the large flaring bell was known as far back as the late fourteenth century.[388] The exact date or inventor of the real horn is unknown. The only statement that can be made with any degree of certainty is that in Cavalli's opera *Le Nozze de Tito e Pelei* of 1639 the horn parts show the tone *e*, which could be produced only by a horn in C-basso.[389] The early hunting horn was wound with a circle of large diameter, like our No. 191, so that a huntsman could carry it slung around his body. When the horn finally became a regular member of the orchestra, the diameter across the coils was decreased, so that the instrument could be conveniently held. The traditional way of holding the horn with the right hand in the bell was firmly established after Anton Joseph Hampel discovered about 1750 that the diatonic scale could be played on the natural horn by partly stopping the bell with the right hand.[390] The half-stopped tones sounded more muffled than the 'open' tones, but it should be remembered that the open tones of the old natural horn sounded less bright than those of our modern orchestral horn. There were two important reasons for this. The tubes of the old horn were of smaller bore, and the mouthpiece was of the true funnel-shaped type, as represented on page 149. So the old horn had a gentle and veiled sound which differed less from the hand-stopped tones than is usually thought. The excessive muffling which some modern players consider necessary is a vain attempt to retain the old horn tone quality on the modern instrument. When muffled too much a powerful modern horn sounds sour and choked.[391]

Reinhard Keiser first introduced the horn into the orchestra as a regular member in 1705, in his opera *Octavia*.[392]

The change in tonality on the horn was made by means of 'crooks,' supplementary lengths of tubing inserted between the main tubing and the mouthpiece. The crook changed only the tonality of the horn, otherwise the instrument remained essentially the same, capable of producing only the natural scale of tones. The mechanical part of 'crooking' the horns had several features worth touching upon. The natural orchestral horn consisted of three parts: (1) the permanent body of the instrument, which in length was slightly shorter than the length of tubing necessary to give the B-flat *alto*; (2) interchangeable crooks, which ranged from the B-flat *alto* crook to the B-flat *basso* crook; (3) the mouthpiece. The B-flat *alto* crook was very short, sometimes only sufficient to make a short transition from the small diameter of the mouthpiece end to the much larger diameter of the body tube where the crook was inserted. The result was that the horn crooked in B-flat *alto* sounded somewhat harsh and raucous.[393] With the gradual increase in the length of the crook, the horn sounded increasingly better. The optimum tonality was always considered to be that in F.[394] Below E-flat the horn began to sound stuffy. The reason was that, theoretically, the crooks should have been constructed with a conoidal bore. In practice only the initial part of the crook had a conoidal bore, the rest being cylindrical.[395] This introduction of cylindrical tubing, which on the low-pitched crook was of considerable length, spoiled the tone of the horn crooked below E-flat.[396]

It was difficult for a player to change crooks. Aside from the laboriousness of changing, the standard of lip tension varied with each crook.[397] An adjustment of the lips to the new crook could not be made without several breaks for a few bars at least; the whole process was, undoubtedly, unpleasant both for players and listeners. Opera goers in the Imperial Opera in St. Petersburg resigned themselves to this fact, consoling themselves with saying *Valtorny vsegda vrut*, meaning, 'the horns always play false.' [398] The history of the evolution of the horn mechanism will be given in the notes under individual instruments.

190. HUNTING HORN — Nuremberg, Germany, the first half of the 18th century

Bass in G. The lowest actual tone is GG. Cylindro-conoidal bore. Brass. The tube is wound two and a half times in a circle. The rim of the bell is reinforced by a wide band, upon which is engraved: 'MACHT. FRIEDRICH EHE IN NUR.NB.' Diametrically opposite is engraved a six-pointed star and the letters 'F.E.' The rest of the rim band is decorated with several stamped fleurs-de-lis. Mouthpiece (not original) has shallow conical cup. Length, 68 cm. Diameter, bell, 22.3 cm.; across the coils, 41 cm. Bore, cylindrical, diameter, 7 mm.; length, 17 cm.; conoidal, min., 7 mm.; max., 10.8 cm.; ratio, 15.4:1; length, 328 cm. Length of air column (with mouthpiece), 350 cm. (17.1999)
Plate VI

A fine-toned instrument. The mouthpiece is of the cup-shaped type, more akin to that of the trumpet. Experiments with a French horn mouthpiece show that this horn gives the pedal tone *GG* without much effort and therefore belongs to the whole-tube sub-group; it is listed in this sub-group for convenience only. Below the second partial tone (*G*) it is possible to descend as low as *D* with a continuous glide, or play any intermediate tones staccato.[399] It blows easily up to the sixteenth partial tone inclusive. The difference in the quality of tone between the open and stopped tones is not so considerable as on modern instruments.

191. HUNTING HORN — Paris, France, ca. 1700

Cor de Chasse. Bass in D. Conoidal bore. Brass. The tube is wound two and a half times in a circle. The rim of the bell is reinforced by a wide band, upon which is stamped: 'FAIT A PARIS PAR RAOUX SEULE ORDINAIRE, DU ROI PALGE (*sic*!) DU LOUVRE.' Funnel-shaped mouthpiece. Length, 81 cm. Diameter, bell, 27.5 cm.; across the coils, 54 cm. Bore, min., 6.5 mm.; max., 12.5 cm.; ratio, 19.3:1; length, 448 cm. Length of air column (with mouthpiece), 452 cm. (17.2000)
Plate VII

An exceptionally fine-toned instrument, built by a member of the famous Raoux family, who made fine horns for generations. The tube is conoidal throughout with very narrow taper. This horn gives no pedal tone; it is possible to descend as low as *AA* below the second partial tone (*D*). In the upper register it gives the partial tones up to the twentieth inclusive; the seventeenth and nineteenth partial tones (*d''*-sharp and *e''*-sharp, the actual pitch) are rather difficult; the twentieth partial tone is easy to blow, but comes out only piano. One of the features of this instrument is an exceptionally easy response: the tones speak very easily and require very little air for blowing; very long tenuto is possible without much effort. Oberon's magic horn call in Baron Karl Maria von Weber's *Oberon* overture (1826) should be heard on this instrument to appreciate that composer's intention. Played on modern instruments (especially on the B-flat horn) it sounds too prosaic and out of touch with the infinite.

192. FRENCH HORN — England, late 18th century

Hand Horn. Crooked in E. Conoidal bore. Brass. The uncrooked horn has a conoidal bore except for short lengths of cylindrical tubing for tuning slide. Crook of the conoidal bore throughout. Funnel-shaped mouthpiece with silver rim. Length, 53 cm. Diameter, bell, 28 cm.; across the coils, 27 cm. Bore, crook, min., 8 mm.; max., 11 mm.; length (effective), 186.5 cm.; horn, min., 11 mm.; max., 10.5 cm.; length (without crook), 246 cm.; ratio, max. horn: min. crook, 13.2:1. Length of air column (with mouthpiece), 436 cm. (17.2001)
Plate VI

Except for the unusual shape of the crook, this is a typical orchestral hand horn furnished with a tuning slide. An attempt was made to make the instrument with a conoidal bore throughout, since, except for short lengths of cylindrical tubing for the tuning slide, which has different diameters for each branch, the bore is strictly conoidal. Unfortunately, the horn is so badly battered in a few places that the tonal qualities could not be determined.

193. FRENCH HORN — Germany, late 18th century

Inventionshorn. Crooked in A. Cylindro-conoidal bore. Brass, with German silver trimmings. Invention is marked 'F' (evidently belonged to another instrument with longer tubing). Bell rim, reinforced with a band of German silver engraved with flowers and inscribed 'C. Lobeit.' Length, 62 cm. Diameter, bell, 29 cm.; across the coils, 32 cm. Bore, min., 8 mm.; max., 12.0 cm.; ratio, 15 : 1. Length of air column (with mouthpiece), 318 cm. (17.2002)
Plate VI

'Invention' is the name of a crook of special design. As will be more fully explained on the next page under No. 195, the changing of ordinary crooks was not always convenient for a player, since on some instruments compound crooking changed the distance between the body of the horn and the mouthpiece. Anton Hampel is credited with introducing a combination of a crook with a tuning slide called 'invention,' which not only eliminated the variation in distance, but also made a more secure arrangement which would stay in place. The ordinary crook had a tendency to loosen up and had to be tightened in place by several rotary motions in order to wedge the tapered part of the crook more tightly in the main tube of the horn. Since ordinary crooks were many in number and had to be interchangeable, on some the taper did not fit well, and the player had to be constantly on guard, otherwise sour notes and breaks would plague him. The 'invention' solved many inconveniences of the old system, but had one drawback: the inventions could not be compounded and cost more than the ordinary crook. In the R. M. E. *Catalogue* on pp. 148 f., under no. 310, is described a very fine German-built French horn with 13 'inventions'; the comments by Mr. T. S. Mann quoted there are worth reading. The table of crook lengths given there on p. 149 is correct; the exact length of the uncrooked horn should be 246 centimetres for *a′* of 435 cycles per second.[400]

194. COR OMNITONIQUE — Brussels, Belgium, 1833

The playing compass is from B-flat alto to B-flat basso. Cylindro-conoidal bore. Brass. The instrument has a conoidal bore tube of 97 cm. (measuring the tube without the mouthpiece), then a straight cylindrical tube, upon which are affixed eight oval-shaped cylindrical bore branches, arranged in such a way as to add progressively increasing length of tubing. This addition or subtraction of lengths is controlled by a sliding piston with a knob and index finger; in the body of the piston, the upper part of which is made of a solid brass rod, are five (should be eight) holes drilled through; the lower half of the piston is made of a long brass tubing open at the lower end; in the upper end, adjoining the solid portion, this piston has one hole which serves as an outlet for the air. The piston is prevented from rotating by a knob which fits into a long slit in a continuation of the tube in which the piston slides. On one side of this slot are engraved position lines and tonalities of 'crooks': 'si, la, sol, fa, mi, mi bemol, re, ut, si.' The piston now on the instrument permits the use of tonalities from B-flat alto to E-flat only. Engraved on the bell: 'C. Sax, à Bruxelles, 1833.' The inside of the bell is lacquered dark cherry-red with trophies and flowers in gold. Drain valve on the tube. Length, 65 cm. Diameter, bell, 29.5 cm.; across the coils, 35 cm. Bore, min., 8 mm.; max., 13 cm.; ratio, 16.3:1; length (B-flat alto), 276.5 cm. Length of air column (B-flat alto with mouthpiece), 281.5 cm. (17.2004)
Plate VI

A clever but not entirely practical attempt to eliminate the crook-change nuisance. The instrument is somewhat heavy and awkward to hold. This invention, by the father of the famous Adolphe Sax, was introduced shortly before valves were applied to the horn.

195. FRENCH HORN — London, England, ca. 1843

Crooked in C. Conoidal-cylindro-conoidal bore. Brass. Two disc valves, identical in design with those of No. 186. The first valve is a semi-tone valve, the second is a whole-tone valve. Two circular coiled crooks: the smaller one (in which the mouthpiece is inserted) has a conoidal bore and air-column length of 107.5 cm., and the larger intermediate one has a cylindrical bore and an air-column length of 176.5 cm. The stamped name-plate on the bell is identical with that on No. 186, except the engraved serial number, which is '86' on this instrument. Stamped on the bell rim: 'KOHLER, HENRIETTA ST., COVENT GARDEN, LONDON.' The initials of the former owner, 'W. Y. C.' are engraved on the bell in large capital letters. Funnel-shaped mouthpiece with silvered rim. Length, 62 cm. Diameter, bell, 29.5 cm.; across the coils, 33 cm. Bore, smaller crook, min., 8.5 mm.; max., 11 mm.; intermediate crook, 11 mm.; horn, max., 12.5 cm. Length of air column (horn proper), 240 cm.; ratio, max. horn bore: min. crook bore, 14.7:1. Length of air column (with mouthpiece), 528 cm. (17.2003)
Plate VII

This fine instrument is interesting because it illustrates several historical features of the horn-playing art. It shows the compound crook, of which the first part is a small conoidal bore crook which could be inserted in the instrument by itself and would pitch the horn in G. The small G-crook can be seen clearly in the picture, the mouthpiece inserted. This G-crook is inserted in an intermediate crook of large diameter, almost equal to that of the horn body proper. The mouthpiece could not be inserted in this crook without a supplementary piece, which would then convert it into an E-crook. When combined, the small and the large crooks pitch the horn in C-basso. This compounding of crooks was done to reduce the cost of the instrument, since low-pitched crooks were very long. The maximum length of the main tube of the horn had to be made so that the horn could be crooked B-flat alto. This meant that the length of the main tube was only about 250 centimetres; the B-flat basso crook was 330 centimetres long, or longer than the main tube by about 80 centimetres! The total length of tubing necessary to outfit a good horn without compound crooks would be 22.78 metres (74 feet, 9 inches), a rather astounding figure.[401] It is not surprising that compound crooking was resorted to in order to decrease the cost. Another feature of interest is two valves so arranged that the first valve lowered the horn a semitone and the second valve a whole tone, a variant of the more common arrangement. Crooks and valves did not mix very well, since the valves were good only for one particular tonality; for any other the valve slides had to be shifted out for the lower tonality and pushed in for the higher tonality. This adjustment could be made for three tonalities only: one for which the horn had valve slides especially made (usually in F), and two others a semitone and a whole tone lower. For other tonalities, either the valve horn with crooks had to be treated as a hand horn, or the part had to be transposed by the player. For a long time some composers did not understand this. Horn parts were written which could not be played in the tonality prescribed without transposition, except for a rare case when the hornist had an instrument which could be adjusted for the tonality prescribed.[402] In actual practice no hornist used crooks with a valve horn in the orchestra. Since many parts had to be transposed in any case, the hornists played everything on the valve horn in F. With the introduction of the double horn in F and B-flat (alto), the first and third horn parts were played almost entirely on the B-flat horn; finally the single B-flat horn came into existence.[403] This change can hardly be welcomed, since only exceptional horn players can make it sound like a horn: the B-flat horn has a 'sandy' tone, not the smooth, flowing tone of the F-horn. Composers are mostly responsible for this. Horn parts are so written that this versatile instrument is not only taxed to capacity but is required to play parts which are alien to its spirit. There are some conductors who should share the responsibility also.[404] After all, the horn is not a trumpet nor a trombone. No instrument can be asked to sing poetically at one moment and to discourse in stentorian tones the next. Horn players were forced to use an instrument with a large bore and short tube, the highest pitched horn which still remains a four-octave instrument, the horn in B-flat. It can discourse dramatically, but alas for poetry!

SUB-SECTION b: CYLINDRICAL TUBE

Group 1: Two-Octave Instruments

Primitive Types

THERE are very few primitive European instruments which have a short cylindrical tube of large bore giving only a few partial tones. Two examples, Nos. 196 and 197, can be called musical instruments only in consideration of the intent of their makers, since their tone is hardly musical. In the early Middle Ages there existed a straight metallic trumba without a bell, illustrated in Irish manuscripts,[405] which could be assigned to this group. Otherwise cylindrical bore instruments evolved early into the three-octave group.

196. GLASS TRUMPET — Florence, Italy

Made of greenish-white glass. Cylindro-conoidal bore with flaring bell. Gives only a fundamental tone of indifferent quality. The approximate tonality is B-flat. Length, 72 cm. (17.1978)

197. CELLULOID TRUMPET — France

Made of ivory-colored celluloid. Integral cup-mouthpiece. Gives the fundamental tone and the second partial tone (out of tune). The tonality is, approximately, G-sharp. Owing to the large initial bore (10 mm.) the tone is very bad. Length, 55 cm. (17.1980)

Group 2: Three-Octave Instruments

Sub-group i: With Pedal Tone

The Trombone Family

THE trombone, if played in good taste, is a serious, powerful, and solemn instrument. It can express some of the deepest religious emotions, dramatize a situation, or discourse epically like a bard. The fact that it is put nowadays to certain ignoble uses does not affect in the least its true stature. The trombone is fine as a solo instrument, but it is more temperamentally fitted for group work with members of its own family or with instruments in tonal affinity with its spirit. Although asked sometimes to display the agility of a youth, the trombone prefers a more dignified mode of expression. The trombone is like a man who has reached an age of discretion and concentrated power: its utterances have weight, and it cannot engage in five-o'clock-tea talk. The trombone is primarily a masculine instrument and should not be made to sound like a frivolous dandy.

The trombone of our discourse is, indeed, the slide trombone, the simplest yet almost ideal 'brass' instrument. Who invented the slide and where and when is not known. A slide was applied to the folded buysine sometime before or during the fourteenth century. If the slide is a European invention, then the most probable places for its origin would be either the Netherlands or South Germany. For the preliminary stages of the evolution of the sackbut, the predecessor of the trombone, consult an excellent article by Miss Kathleen Schlesinger in the eleventh edition of the *Encyclopaedia Britannica* and Canon Galpin's *The Sackbut, Its Evolution and History*, also Dr. Curt Sachs's *Handbuch*.[406]

The first definite information about the trombone family is found in Praetorius. It has a strangely modern sense. Praetorius describes four kinds of slide trombones.

1. The *Alt-* or *Discant-Posaun: Trombino, Trombetta picciola*, on which not only the alto but also treble parts could be played "gar wol und natürlich." Praetorius states that, owing to the small size of its tube, it does not sound so well in the ensemble as when the same high tones, through "guten Anzatz und Übung" (good embouchure and practice), are played

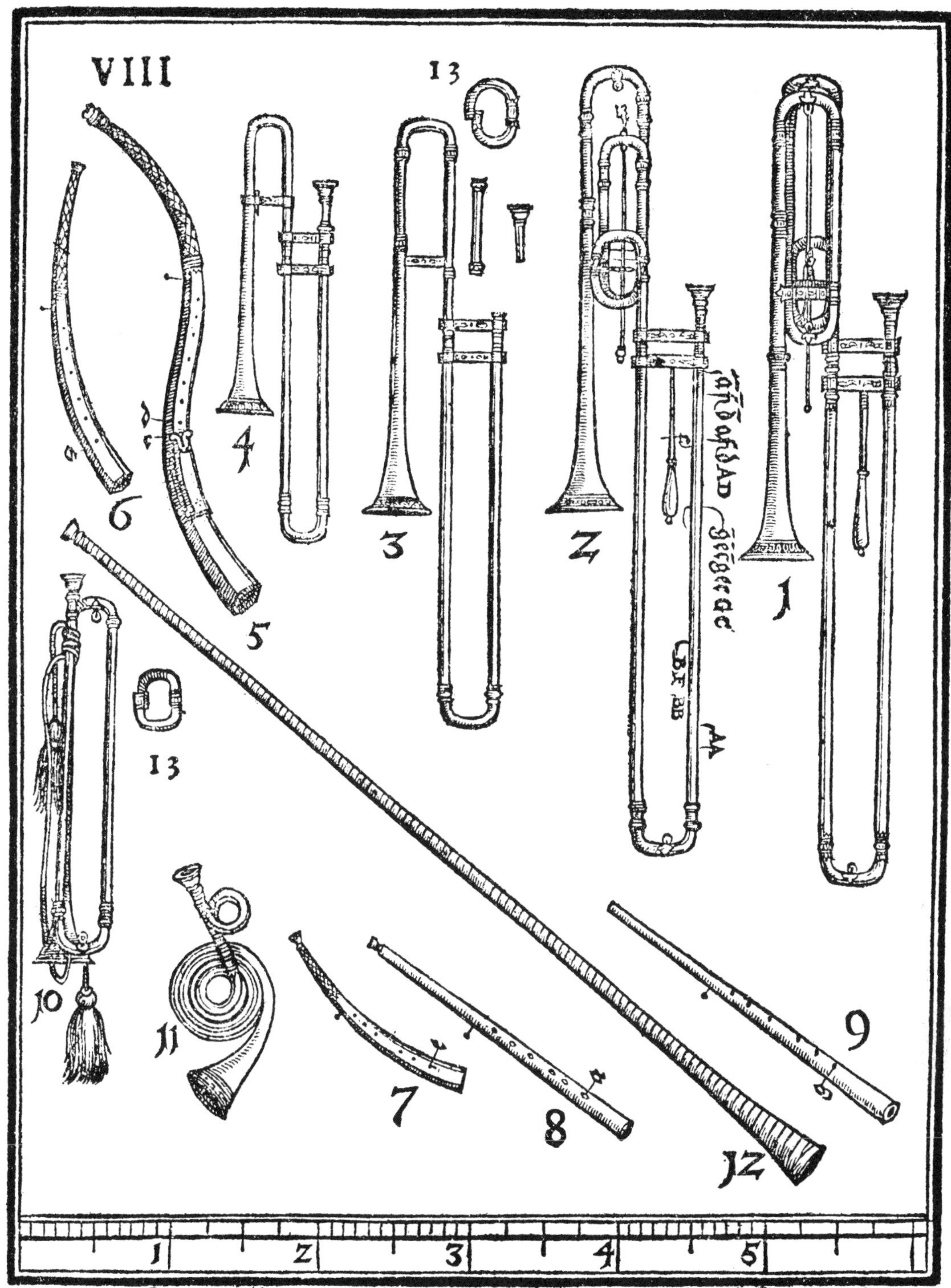

1. 2. Quart-Posaunen. 3. Rechte gemeine Posaun. 4. Alt-Posaun. 5. Corno/ Groß Tenor-Cornet. 6. Recht ChorZinck. 7. Klein DiscantZinck / so ein Quint höher. 8. GeraderZinck mit eim Mundstück. 9. StillZinck. 10. Trommet. 11. Jäger Trommet. 12. Hölzern Trommet. 13. Krumbbügel auff ein ganz Thon.

FIG. 32. PRAETORIUS, TABLE VIII

1, 2. Quart-Trombones. 3. Ordinary Trombone. 4. Alto Trombone. 5. Cornon, Great Tenor Cornett. 6. Ordinary Choir Cornett. 7. Small Treble Cornett, a fifth higher. 8. Straight Cornett with a mouthpiece. 9. Mute Cornett. 10. Trumpet. 11. Hunting Trumpet. 12. Wooden Trumpet (Alphorn). 13. Crook, transposing one tone lower.

on the tenor trombone. Modern practice is in agreement with Praetorius, although tenor trombonists know that the alto trombone parts of the classical and of some romantic composers are very difficult, owing to their extreme height. The compass of the Alt-Posaun is given by Praetorius from *B* to *d''* (e''); its tonality was therefore in F.[407]

2. The *Gemeine rechte Posaun: Tuba minor, Trombetta,* or *Trombone piccolo,* is the tenor trombone. The ordinary compass is given by Praetorius from *E* to *g'* (a'). Praetorius mentions two exceptional players. One of them, the renowned master Phileno of Munich, could play *D* (in the seventh position, 'Falset-Stimme'?) and ascended up to *c''*, *d''*, *e''* without any particular difficulty. Another player in Dresden, Erhardus Borussus, reached as high as the cornett, or *g''*, and as low as *AA*; Borussus did it with excellent technique, equivalent to that of the *viola bastarda* (the lyra viol, No. 273). The question is what Praetorius meant by his reference to *AA*; if he meant the pedal tone of the second position, then Borussus' feat was nothing astounding, since any trombone player can do this without trouble.[408] But if Praetorius meant that Borussus could descend from *E* to *AA* by pulling the slide to the seventh position and then descending to *AA* with the lips alone, then he had an exceptional lip, indeed, and, incidentally, anticipated Drs. Bouasse and Fouché by some 310 years.[409] This would mean that by the 'Falset-Stimme' technique Borussus could play *D*, *CC*, and *AA*, which Praetorius put in the *Tabella Universalis*, p. 20, in the 'Gemeine oder rechte Posaun' column. The tonality of Praetorius' tenor trombone is B-flat.[410]

3. The *Quart-Posaun: Tuba major, Trombone grando, Trombone majore,* which stands either a fourth or a fifth (the *Quint-Posaun*) lower than the tenor trombone and one octave lower than the alto trombone. Praetorius gives the lower compass as *AA*, *GG*, and *FF*; again since the lowest tone of the *Quint-Posaun* in the lowest position [411] is *AA*, the tones *GG* and *FF* can be played only as the 'Falset-Stimme.' The uppermost limit is given as *g'*. The tonality of the Quart-Posaun was in F and of the Quint-Posaun in E-flat.

4. The *Octav-Posaun: Tuba maxima, Trombone doppio, la Trombone all' Ottava basso.* Praetorius mentions that there were two kinds: one with tube twice as long as that of the tenor trombone without the crooks ("ohne Bügel"), represented on table vi, fig. 2, of *Theatrum Instrumentorum* (p. 354 of this study); another with tubes of larger bore, with crooks and, therefore, not as long as the former.[412] The lower compass extension as given by Praetorius finally settles the problem of the 'Falset-Stimme.' Praetorius states: ". . . sie ihren Thon ein *Octav* tiefer bringen und natürlich das *EE*; im *falset* aber auch, doch mit gutem Anzatz, das *DD* und *CC* erreichen kan." Or, ". . . it [the *Octav-Posaun*] brings its tone an octave deeper and [gives] naturally *EE*; but in the 'falset' it can reach with good embouchure *DD* and *CC*." No argument is possible. The *Octav-Posaun* of Praetorius was pitched in BB-flat, as are some of the modern contrabass trombones; the lowest tone in the lowest position on this instrument which is produced naturally is *EE*; in the 'falset,' i.e., by the lips alone ("mit gutem Anzatz" means that also), *DD* and *CC* are produced. These tones are not the pedal tones of any slide position; therefore they cannot be produced by any other means than 'lipping.' Perhaps we could learn a few things about brass instrument playing from the old timers.[413]

Investigations of Drs. Bouasse and Fouché support Praetorius. In *Instruments à vent* it is explained that several more tones can be produced, especially in the lower register, as stated already in our notes on the hunting horn. We quote:

"L'erreur que les instruments à embouchure de cor sont *à sons fixes*, est tellement enracinée qu'il faut insister: *au-dessous de chaque partiel vrai, l'artiste donne ce qu'il veut dans un intervalle enorme.*" [414] (The error that cup-mouthpiece instruments have fixed sound is so deeply rooted that it must be insisted: below each true partial tone *the artist gives what he wants* within an enormous interval.) It seems that Praetorius and Dr. Bouasse are in complete agreement. For once practice (1619) and theory (1929) have come together.

In the time of Praetorius (1619) the trombone had crooks (*Krumm-Bogen, Krumm-Bügel, Cromette*) and short extension pieces (*Polette*) inserted between the mouthpiece and the inner slide socket where the mouthpiece is ordinarily fixed. Both kinds of pitch changing devices are represented on table viii, fig. 3 and fig. 13; the *Polette* is the short straight piece shown separately between the tenor trombone (fig. 3) and its mouthpiece. The passage in Praetorius in which these terms can be found, as well as a somewhat indirect description of transpositions possible on slide trombones, is given in translation.

This *Instrumentum Musicum* (*Posaun*, the trombone) is especially superior to other wind instruments; in all *Consorts* and other instrumental combinations it can be used and in all tonalities (*Tonen*, the modes), and can be used somewhat higher or lower not alone by the putting on or taking off of crooks (*Krumm-Bügel, Cromette*) and other changeable pieces (called *Polette*), but also with the mouth and wind alone, without changing the crooks (*Krumm-Bogen*), by means of embouchure (*Ansatz*) and mouthpiece, by a practised and experienced artist according to his volition, by tones and semitones, it can be played and used: which on any other instruments, the fingerholes of which must be regulated by the fingers, is impossible.[415]

Praetorius is redundant in his statements. Evidently he desired to impress on his readers that not the crook changes, but the playing technique alone permitted the trombonists of his time to accommodate themselves to the many variations of pitch; this could be done by displacing the slide from its accustomed 'standard' places where the pitch differences were less than a semitone. In cases where there was some definite interval, like a semitone or a whole tone, some trombonists transposed without the help of the *cromettes* and *polettes*. Some, less skillful, used crooks. Yet it should be remembered that in our times some slide trombones have two tuning slides, one for the low and another for the high pitch.

Canon Galpin in his valuable monograph on the Sackbut brought out another very important point.[416] He has in his possession an old trombone mouthpiece shaped like the old type French horn mouthpiece. When attached to the trombone this type of mouthpiece subdues its sonority, but brings out other qualities of tone which cannot be achieved by the ordinary type: the tone becomes richer and comes out without effort. Canon Galpin suggested the revival of the old time sackbut technique of playing, "to aim at the full, round, quiet rolling tone which can only be equalled by the open Diapason of the Organ."

198. BUYSINE Germany, 1460

Herald's trumpet. Alto in D. Cylindro-conoidal bore. Brass. The tube is made in five parts with the joints reinforced by engraved brass bands. Finely engraved bulb located 30 cm. from the bell. The rim of the bell is reinforced by a wide band with a scalloped top. A loop in the lower half for a banner. Engraved on the bell rim band: 'MACHT SEBASTIAN HAINLEIN⋆M⋆CDLX.' Between the name and surname is a dove in a shield. Brass mouthpiece (not original). Length, the trumpet only, 101.7 cm. Diameter, bell, 8.7 cm. Bore, top joint, diameter, 11 mm.; length, 17.2 cm.; second joint, diameter, 11.5 mm.; length, 13.8 cm.; third joint,* diameter (average), 12.5 mm.; length, 22.4 cm.; fourth and fifth joints, diameter, min., 12.5 mm.; max., 6.5 cm.; length, 48.2 cm. Length of air column (with mouthpiece), 106.5 cm. (17.1990)
Plate VII

* The third joint is very slightly tapered toward the bell; the fourth joint is definitely conoidal; the fifth joint has a slightly flaring bell.

Sebastian Hainlein's buysine has the distinction of being the oldest dated instrument of this Collection. Its shape is practically identical with that of the *añafil* represented in the *Cantigas de Santa Maria*.[417] The solitary ring is for affixing a banner which is suspended on a string. Owing to the irregularity of the bore, the natural scale is not strictly in tune, especially the third and the sixth partial tones. Actual tones are: *D*, *d'*, *a'*-flat (instead of *a'*), *d''*, *f''*-sharp, *a''*-flat (not strictly in octave with the previous one), and d^3. The tone is clear and loud.

199. DISCANT TROMBONE Germany, 1781

Soprano in B-flat. Brass. Cylindro-conoidal bore. Made in three parts: inner slide branch, slide, and the bell branch. The mouthpiece has a deep conical cup and the inner edge of the rim is slightly undercut. The bell rim is reinforced by a brass band stamped: 'IOHANN IOSEPH SCHMIED MACHTS IN PFAFFENDORFF, 1781.' Length, 51.5 cm. Diameter, bell, 10.3 cm. Bore, cylindrical, diameter, 10.5 mm.; length (1st position), 101.5 cm.; conoidal, min., 11 mm.; max., 5 cm.; length, 28 cm. Length of air column (with mouthpiece), 134.5 cm. (17.2006)
Plate VI

The soprano instrument of the trombone family, that is, one pitched an octave higher than the tenor trombone, never became an accepted member of this august group. The lateral-hole cornett, the only soprano lip-vibrated aerophone before the invention of valves, was not a good substitute for the true 'brass' instrument, so the soprano trombone was built at intermittent intervals. The principal difficulties in playing it are the shortness of the shifts of the slide and the difficulty in stopping it in the right places. The lip correction of pitch becomes more and more difficult as the length of the tube decreases; besides, cylindrical tube instruments have less tolerance for such correction. The tone of the instrument when played with the trombone type of mouthpiece is very indifferent. No one, it seems, ever tried to use a trumpet mouthpiece. If such an experiment should be tried, then the soprano slide trombone would become the acoustical equivalent of the modern B-flat soprano 'trumpet.' The reverse of this proposition is true also. The soprano trombone furnished with valves and played with a trumpet mouthpiece remains, essentially, the soprano trombone with valves. It happens that a trumpet mouthpiece makes the soprano trombone sound brilliantly. The valve mechanism, although by no means perfection, nevertheless is mechanically more convenient than a short slide. Therefore, since the length of the tube and the bore of some soprano slide trombones are equivalent to those of the B-flat valve trumpet, and since their acoustical characteristics are the same (both are three-octave, whole-tube instruments with pedal tone), then it follows that *the B-flat trumpet is really a soprano valve trombone.* The clinching argument is that when the soprano slide trombone is played with a trumpet mouthpiece its tone really does not differ from that of the valve 'trumpet.' [418]

A very interesting conclusion follows. The modern soprano valve trumpet in B-flat (or in C) replaced the old time trumpet for these reasons: (1) it can play trumpet parts in almost all old scores (the high trumpet parts in Bach's scores excepted), although not with the same quality of tone, and (2) its timbre blends perfectly with trombones. The last fact is quite comprehensible. The modern high-pitched trumpet is a valve trombone and supplies the formerly missing soprano voice in the trombone choir.

Another and still more interesting conclusion is inescapable. Among the many brass instruments used in the modern symphony orchestras and 'symphonic' bands, one of the noblest and most eloquent voices, the real trumpet, is missing.

200. ALTO TROMBONE England, late 19th century

Alto in F. Brass. Cylindro-conoidal bore. Made in four parts: inner slide branch, slide, bell branch, and a tuning slide in the bell branch. The mouthpiece has a deep conical cup. German silver stockings on the ends of the innder slides. Length, 72 cm. Diameter, bell, 13.2 cm. Bore, cylindrical, diameter, 12.5 mm.; length (1st position), 121 cm.; conoidal, min., 12 mm.; max., 6.2 cm.; length, 58 cm. Length of air column (with mouthpiece), 185 cm. (17.2007)
Plate VI

The alto trombone can be found in many of the old classical scores and in some nineteenth-century scores. Its parts are written in the alto clef and their high tessitura causes many a fine trombonist to shake his head. That the modern trombone player, like his confrère in Praetorius' time, is equal to the task is beside the point. The alto trombone has a small but distinctive voice of its own, and if the instrument were to be experimented with as much as the modern tenor trombone, no doubt fine alto trombones could be built. Its disappearance from the orchestra was mainly due to the fact that when valves were applied to the trumpet, there were two trumpets, in F and in E-flat, which could substitute for it. In some orchestras the alto trombone parts were played on these trumpets. After both the alto trombone and the low-pitched valve trumpets disappeared from the orchestra, the first tenor trombone player was required to play the alto trombone parts. The composers wrote higher and higher for brass instruments, a tendency deplored by Widor.[419] This had one unpleasant consequence: trombonists began to ask for instruments which would produce the tones of the upper register with greater ease. This meant a smaller bore and smaller bell, a development which eventually resulted in the 'pea-shooter,' a miserably sounding effeminate caricature. Fortunately, the tendency now is to return to the old type of trombone, which can produce fine, broad tones and 'juicy' pedals.

201. TENOR TROMBONE England, late 19th century

Tenor in C. Brass. Cylindro-conoidal bore. Made in four parts as is No. 200. The mouthpiece has a semi-ellipsoidal cup. Length, 94.5 cm. Diameter, bell, 16.3 cm. Bore, cylindrical, diameter, 12 mm.; length (1st position), 191 cm.; conoidal, min., 13 mm.; max., 7 cm.; length, 59 cm. Length of air column (with mouthpiece), 255 cm. (17.2008)
Plate VI

202. TENOR TROMBONE Belgium, ca. 1850

Tenor in B-flat (high pitch). Brass 'bell over shoulder' model. Double bore type. Made in four parts, as is No. 200, except that the bell branch has two bends and the bell is turned upward. The mouthpiece has a semi-ellipsoidal cup. The bell rim is engraved with a coat of arms, and the maker's name: 'F. van Engelen te Lier.' Length, 128 cm. Diameter, bell, 17 cm. Bore, cylindrical, upper slide, 11 mm.; length, 73.5 cm.; lower slide, 12 mm.; length, 134 cm.; conoidal, min., 12 mm.; max., 7 cm.; length, 61.5 cm. Length of air column (with mouthpiece), 276 cm. (17.2011)

The 'bell over shoulder' model of brass instrument was introduced by an American inventor, Dodsworth, in 1838, and later became very popular for a time with marching bands, especially during the Civil War. There exists a whole family of saxhorns (bugles) with the long bell branches.[420] The purpose of this design was to throw the sound backward so that the marchers would get the benefit of the music. The 'bell over shoulder' instruments with valves sounded better, it was asserted, because the tubes had fewer bends. The drawback of the design was the difficulty of carrying and the danger of damaging the long bell branches. Yet inherently Dodsworth's model had its fine points, which accounted for its vogue not only in this country but abroad.

203. BUCCIN Lyons, France, ca. 1850

Tenor trombone in B-flat (high pitch). Brass. Dual bore type. No tuning slide. The instrument is constructed like an ordinary slide trombone, but the bell branch is conoidal for a greater length and bent in a semi-circle. Instead of a regular bell there is a head of a dragon with wide-open jaws; the jaws, the forked tongue, and the mouth cavity were originally painted bright red; the head was a bright olive-green, much gilded. Silverplated cup mouthpiece. German silver stockings on the inner slides. Stamped on the bell joint: 'TABARD A LYON.' Length, 110 cm. Head, length, 31 cm.; width, 12 cm. Bore, cylindrical, upper slide, 10.5 mm.; length, 71 cm.; lower slide, 11 mm.; length, 85 cm.; conoidal, min., 12 mm.; max., 6 cm.; length, 105 cm. Length of air column (with mouthpiece), 270 cm. (17.2012)

An instrument of bizarre design, belonging to a period when bands were very decorative affairs with many unusually shaped instruments and handsomely uniformed bandsmen. This type of instrument with its shaking red tongue frightened children; see the account of it in *Military Music*, by J. A. Kappey.

204. BASS TROMBONE England, late 19th century

Bass in G (high pitch). Brass. Cylindro-conoidal bore. Made in three parts: inner slide, branch slide, and a bell branch. The lower slide has an extension over which the bell branch is moved axially for tuning; the bell lock keeps the bell branch in place. The slide is furnished with a swivel

extension handle ('crutch') to enable the player to reach the lower positions. Fine sonorous instrument; pedals rather fuzzy. Length, 137 cm. Diameter, bell, 17.5 cm. Bore, cylindrical, diameter, 12 mm.; length (1st position), 183 cm.; conoidal, min., 14 mm.; max., 8.7 cm.; length, 129.5 cm. Length of air column (with mouthpiece), 318 cm. (17.2009)
Plate VI

The most interesting part of this trombone is the extension handle for shifting the slide in the lower positions. This is a very old device, found already on a trombone by Pierre Colbert, built in Reims in 1593 and now in the Rijksmuseum in Amsterdam, Holland.[421] Another fine instrument, the *Octave-posaune* built in 1612 by Isaac Ehe of Nuremberg, Germany, and now in the Germanisches Museum, also has a swivel handle.[422] Praetorius' *Octave-Posaun*, table vi, fig. 2, in the *Theatrum Instrumentorum*, already mentioned, is somewhat of the same shape as the latter instrument, the principal difference being in the construction of the bell branch. The bass trombone in G is known in Germany as the *Terzposaune*, because it is a third lower than the standard B-flat instrument. Its tone is not so fine as that of the *Quartposaune* in F. The modern instrument used in the orchestra is a practical compromise forced on players by the wide range of the bass trombone parts. Essentially it is the large bore tenorbass trombone with the *Quartventil* conveniently located for operation by the left-hand thumb. Although this type of instrument is easier to manipulate than the bass trombone with the swivel handle, the latter type is better in tone, since its proportions can be better chosen than those of the compromise type with the valve. In any case the bass trombone is very fatiguing for the player.

205. TENOR TROMBONE — London, England, late 19th century

Tenor in B-flat (high pitch). Combination slide and valve model. Brass. Cylindro-conoidal bore. Made essentially in two parts: (1) the body of the instrument, including the piston valve, valve crook, and inner slides; (2) the outer slide. German silver stockings on the ends of the inner slides. The mouthpiece has a deep conical cup. 'F. Besson, Breveté, 198 Euston Road, London,' is stamped on the bell. Length, 55 cm. Diameter, bell, 11.8 cm. Bore, cylindrical, diameter, 11 mm.; length, 189.5 cm.; conoidal, min., 12 mm.; max., 6.2 cm.; length, 75 cm. Length of air column (valve off, slide in first position), 268.5 cm. Length of valve crook, 55.5 cm. (17.2010)
Plate VI

This instrument is one of the many attempts to improve the trombone. With the valve in the 'off' position, the slide gives the four standard positions of the ordinary slide trombone. With the slide brought back into the first position, the pressing down of the valve gives the fifth position. Then the slide extends the compass down to the seventh position. The instrument is compact, but not especially convenient to play. Addition of the valve is not necessary on the tenor trombone. The standard instrument is convenient even for players with small reach. The slide trombone is the simplest functional form adequately meeting the severe requirements of modern orchestration. This is the reason why any complication, unless absolutely necessary as in the case of the bass trombone, proves impracticable.

The Trumpets

THE real trumpet is the haughty aristocrat of musical instruments. In Western Europe only emperors, kings, great nobles, and prominent municipalities enjoyed the privilege of having trumpets. Trumpeters were of 'knightly kind' and their calling was considered not a trade but a free and knightly art.[423] Many were the subterfuges for enjoying the forbidden fruit, such as a tube coiled in the form of the hunting horn. But it was of no avail! The true character of the instrument would betray itself. No one who has heard the real trumpet played will ever forget it. After all, the raison d'être of any musical instrument is the quality of its tone. The real trumpet has a rich, broad, and majestic tone; it stands to the modern B-flat trumpet in the same relation as the French horn to the melophone. This qualitative difference is due to the longer tube and more extended natural scale. The classical trumpet, as already stated, is a four-octave instrument playable between the second and the twenty-first partial tones inclusive. The modern B-flat trumpet is a three-octave instrument with the natural scale playable between the first and the eighth partial tones, although exceptional players can go as high as the twelfth. By its acoustical characteristics the modern trumpet should be more correctly classified as a soprano valve trombone.[424]

The generic property of the real trumpet (a four-octave instrument) accounts for its inherent defects and qualities. Its principal defects are the greater exertion required for execution, and the tendency to break. On the positive side is the magnificent, noble, masculine tone in the low and middle register (the so-called 'principale' register), which cannot be reproduced with the same tonal quality on the modern trumpet. In the high register, through special lip-technique, called the *Clarinblasen* (clarino-playing), very high partial tones in the sopranino register can be produced.[425] It is not feasible to produce high trumpet tones by forcing them; this will only render the lips useless in a short time. When a properly proportioned instrument with the mouthpiece fitted for the individual player is used, and, most important, if the player has an inborn ability for producing high tones,[426] then only does clarino-playing become possible. It requires exceptional breath-control, fully equal to that of virtuoso chamber music singers, since, contrary to some opinions, clarino-playing can be done very softly.[427] Properly produced, the high tones of the real trumpet possess a rich, crystal-pure, sweet, and almost unearthly quality which can be compared only with the harmonics of a fine Stradivari violin, except that the clarino tones are more interesting and touch emotions more deeply. This brings us to the problem of the high trumpet parts in the scores of Bach and Handel.

The high trumpet parts, it is usually stated, fell into disrepute because they were so loud and ear-piercing; with the invention of the clarinet a boon was granted to the listener. This might have been the case with some trumpeters who forced their tone and had no real aptitude for the clarino-playing. Disregarding certain social and political changes which made the trumpet lose its caste, it is possible to adduce the real reason for this decline. Clarino-playing requires concentration and practice on the instrument of one and the same tonality; the lips have to be kept in condition through constant exercise. With the introduction of crooks for changing tonality of the trumpet, trumpeters had to find an average practical condition so that they could play on the low B-flat crook with equal facility as on the high G-crook. They had to adopt a mouthpiece proportioned for such work; this meant that the trumpeters had to limit the upper register to the twelfth partial tone (the nominal g″), venturing beyond that only under duress. Crooks were disastrous to the art of trumpet playing.

When, after long neglect, the high trumpet parts of Bach and Handel were brought to the attention of musicians, the first reaction was that of incredulity: the parts are unplayable. At present there are three solutions to the problem. The first one is to play the high trumpet parts on high pitched wood-wind instruments, such as the sopranino E-flat clarinet and the piccolo heckelphone. This practice can be regarded only as a protest against the second solution, which is just as unsatisfactory. The second solution was suggested by music instrument makers who built high-pitched sopranino trumpets in D and in F. If there are serious objections to the replacement of real trumpets by the B-flat trumpet, these objections apply *a fortiori* to the still higher pitched 'trumpets.' Arguments are summarized below:

1. There can be no valid objections to B-flat, C, D, E-flat, F, or even higher 'trumpets' as such, provided that their true acoustical nature is clearly recognized: that they are soprano and sopranino valve trombones, three-octave instruments, with very valuable and original characteristics of their own and irreplaceable in their own field. From this should follow their correct musical usage and music should be written suitable to their genius. Certain effects are possible only on instruments of this type. Those parts conceived and written by modern composers for the B-flat and C trumpets, *in terms of these instruments*, should be played on these instruments only.

2. It should be recognized that those parts in the scores of classical, romantic, and even of some modern composers, conceived and written for real trumpets, should be played on these instruments.[428] B-flat trumpets do not substitute for the old instruments in quality of tone, dynamics, attack, etc., however much they may improve the dynamic balance, blend better with the trombones, or solve some of the practical difficulties, such as easier playing, greater freedom from breaks, etc. The old trumpet parts are transcribed for the B-flat trumpet and all well known objections against the practice of transcription apply almost without qualification in this case. The entire question is the general problem of quality as against quantity.

3. The quality of tone of the sopranino trumpets in high D and F is not the real clarino tone of the long, low-pitched, four-octave instruments. The short tubes lack overtones and the proper timbre; their sounds are shrill, owing to the paradox that the high partial tones on high-pitched brass instruments are very difficult.[429] The eighth partial tone on the sopranino trumpet in F is almost impossible, so the high-pitched brass instruments begin to approach in their tonal qualities the two-octave instruments, which, as stated already, are not distinguished for beauty of tone. At best, the old high trumpet parts are transcribed for modern sopranino valve trombones. Dr. Richard Strauss' selection of the piccolo-heckelphone becomes understandable in the light of this argument.[430] Briefly, this is a problem of proper tone color, dynamics, and general artistic effect.

4. The general conclusion is that the use of high sopranino trumpets for the Bach and Handel high trumpet parts is historically, acoustically, and artistically an incorrect solution.

What is the correct solution?

It seems that a correct solution is the return to old type classical trumpets with their long tubes and magnificent tone color, and the cultivation of clarino-playing technique. In Bach's and Handel's time this historical technique was still practised. At the end of the nineteenth century it was successfully recovered by Julius Kosleck and Walter Morrow. In our country the practical difficulties are mostly economic. Few players have a natural aptitude for clarino-playing. One has to concentrate on that register and develop special lip-technique, and is not fitted to play ordinary trumpet parts. Since performances of old works having those difficult trumpet parts are infrequent, a player could not support himself by specializing in the clarino-playing technique. Yet among the works requiring this specialized skill are some of the greatest of Bach and Handel, to mention only the *B-minor Mass*, the *Christmas Oratorio*, and the *Messiah*. Many valuable works are not performed at all, or, if performed with substitutes, lose much of their brilliance, because of the difficult technical problems presented by high trumpet parts. If some of our prominent conductors would trouble themselves to investigate this question and to accept no substitutes for the classical trumpet, the way could be found to provide support for several capable players who would be willing to specialize in clarino technique. Perhaps a jazz player may some day prove that this technique can also become popular and clear the way for its return in symphonic repertoire. Not all things accomplished by ourselves are necessarily progressive. Some old skills now lost were distinctly worth while. Their restoration is desirable for the enrichment of our life.

206. LITUUS — Reproduction of the ancient Roman Empire type

Reproduction of a Roman cavalry trumpet. Cylindro-conoidal bore. Copper, with brass mouthpiece. The approximate tonality is G. The conoidal part of the tube is curved up, forming a rimless bell. Length (with mouthpiece), 163 cm. (17.1991)

This instrument is almost identical with the reproduction no. 621 of the Brussels Collection described in the second volume of M. Mahillon's *Catalogue* on p. 29 and pictured on p. 30. The original of both instruments is preserved in the Vatican Museum in Rome and was found in the tomb of a warrior excavated in 1827 in Cervetere, Italy, formerly Caere of the Etruscans.

207. TRUMPET — Prague, Bohemia, early 18th century

Alto in E-flat. Brass. Cylindro-conoidal bore. Two bends. Wide ribbed bands at the top and around all joints of the tubing; decorative boss in the bell branch. The mouthpiece has a conical cup. The bell rim is reinforced by a brass band, engraved and stamped: 'IOSEF WOLF, PRAHA, PRAG.' Length, 68 cm. Diameter, bell, 12.7 cm. Bore, cylindrical, diameter, 9.5 mm.; length, 122.5 cm.; conoidal, min., 10 mm.; max., 5.3 cm.; ratio, max.: min., 5.3:1; length, 72 cm. Length of air column (with mouthpiece), 202 cm. (17.1992)
Plate VI

The traditional shape of the old trumpet is illustrated by this instrument. Praetorius gives the traditional tonality of the German trumpets as D, saying that they could be crooked also in C and therefore play in the Chortone pitch. In the *Tabella Universalis* (p. 20) he gives the pedal tone as *CC*, designating it in black as a 'Falset-Stimme'; the normal high tone is given as g'', that is, the normal highest tone of an average trumpeter. The 'Falset-Stimme' in altissimo is given as f^3. This extremely high tone (the twenty-first partial tone of the trumpet in C) can mean only one thing, namely, that the clarino-playing technique was practised by some trumpeters in Praetorius' time. High trumpet parts of Bach and Handel were, therefore, only a continuation of the traditional technique of trumpeters of old.

The ancient trumpeters specialized in certain registers of their instruments in a manner similar to the horn players of today.[431] The registers were divided, approximately (information on this point differs) as follows:

Part	*Partial Tones*
Clarino I	8 and upward
Clarino II	6 to 16 inclusive
Principale I	4 to 10 inclusive
Principale II (*Toccato*, Tucket)	3 to 8 inclusive
Basso	2 to 4 inclusive

Sometimes the Toccato and the Basso parts, especially in the absence of the kettledrums, were reduced to the tonic and dominant, and, except for the rhythmic variety, were monotonous for players; at the best they moved within very limited compass; yet, one may imagine, the whole ensemble sounded effective.

208. STOPF-TROMPETE Augsburg, Germany, early 19th century

Trompette à demi-lune. Soprano in A-flat. Brass. Cylindro-conoidal bore. The tube is bent in a moon-crescent form. The mouthpiece has a deep conical cup (taken from an old-fashioned bugle). Engraved on the bell rim band: 'JOH. GEORG LINTNER IN AUGSBURG,' and a small tree. Length, 50.5 cm. Diameter, bell, 11 cm. Bore, cylindrical, diameter, 10 mm.; length, 111 cm.; conoidal, max., 10.5 cm.; length, 45 cm. Length of air column (with assumed trumpet mouthpiece), 163 cm. (17.1994)
Plate VI

After Hampel's discovery of the hand-stopping technique on the horn, which consisted in various degrees of muffling the tube by a hand inserted in the bell, the same technique was experimented with, less successfully, on the trumpet.[432] To permit the player to reach the bell, the tube of the trumpet was bent in a semi-crescent form. As already stated, on the old hand horn the difference between the open and stopped tones was not so prominent; but on the trumpet this difference was so sharp that the experiment proved a failure, despite a temporary vogue.

209. CAVALRY TRUMPET London, England, ca. 1855

Alto in E-flat (high pitch). Brass. Cylindro-conoidal bore. The tube is wound twice upon itself (four bends). The tube is reinforced at the top and at the joints with long (10.5 cm.) sleeves

with chased floral ornament and twisted grooves; elaborately moulded and embellished boss on the bell branch. Regular cup-shaped, trumpet mouthpiece with rolled-in silver rim. Elaborately embossed bell rim band with flowers, musical instruments, and trophies with maker's name: 'Kohler, London, 35 Henrietta St. Cov't Garden.' The mouthpiece is stamped 'Kohler and Son, London.' Length, 41.5 cm. Diameter, bell, 12.4 cm. Bore, cylindrical, diameter, 10.25 mm.; length, 123.5 cm.; conoidal, min., 10.25 mm.; max., 6 cm.; ratio, max.: min., 5.85:1; length, 72 cm. Length of air column (with mouthpiece), 202 cm. (17.1993)
Plate VI

Here is a trumpet that is a trumpet! The mouthpiece has a large throat diameter and is especially adapted for playing from the second partial tone up to the twelfth; above that the tones are rather hard to get out. Within the compass indicated this cavalry trumpet is almost ideal as to the breadth of tone and fine quality. Not an instrument for sissies.

210. SLIDE TRUMPET — England, ca. 1810, by Astor

Crooked in E-flat. Silver. Cylindro-conoidal bore. Made in three parts: crook, instrument proper, and the slide. The tube has two bends. The slide is operated by a long hollow rod sliding over another one of smaller diameter, inside of which are concealed two gut strings attached to two brass drums with spiral springs inside. The spring drums (only one is now actually on this instrument) are enclosed in special circular cases; the drums revolve on bronze axles. Triple boss on the bell branch is elaborately chased. The tube is elaborately reinforced; all ferrules, sleeves, braces, and the spring drum cases are profusely engraved with floral designs. The monogram 'I.A' in a circle is engraved on the bell. Length, 68 cm. Diameter, bell, 11.3 cm. Bore, cylindrical, diameter, 11 mm.; length, 163.5 cm.; conoidal, min., 11 mm.; max., 5.5 cm.; ratio, 5:1; length, 40 cm. Length of air column (slide in 1st position), 210 cm. (17.1996)
Plate VI and Fig. 33

The various experiments aiming at a chromatic scale on brass instruments included the slide trumpet also. The slide on this trumpet has two positions, corresponding to the semitone and whole-tone valves on the early valve trumpet.[433]

211. KEY TRUMPET — Minerbio, Italy, 1843

Alto in G. Five keys. Brass. Cylindro-conoidal bore. The tube has four bends; tuning slide. The keys are mounted on pillars and give the following tones: g-sharp, a, b-flat, b, and c′; the fourth and fifth keys combined give c′-sharp. Silver-plated conical cup-mouthpiece. The bell rim is stamped 'Leonardo Massarenti e Fratelli in Minerbio, 1843.' Length, 41 cm. Diameter, bell, 12 cm. Bore, cylindrical, diameter, 11 mm.; length, 97.5 cm.; conoidal, max., 5.8 cm.; length, 64.5 cm. Length of air column (with mouthpiece), 168 cm. (17.1995)
Plate VI

Keys were applied to the trumpet by Weidinger (see p. 165). The instrument is similar to no. 1247 of the Brussels Collection; cf. its *Catalogue*, ii, p. 419.

212. VALVE TRUMPET — Brussels, Belgium, ca. 1840

Alto in F. Three double valves of the Viennese type. Brass. Cylindro-conoidal bore. Tuning slide. The valve mechanism consists of three long levers pivoted on one end and connected under the finger touch-pieces with valves by means of articulated rods; the valve levers are returned into

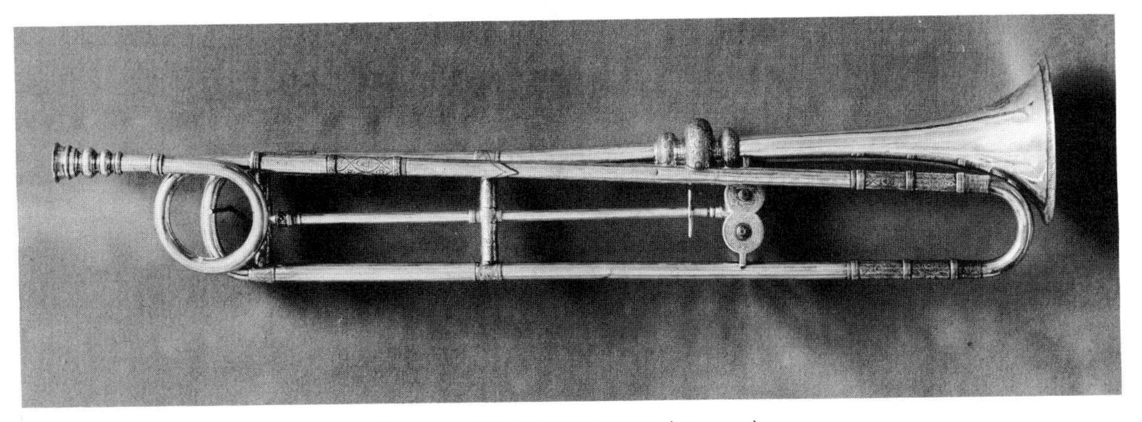

FIG. 33. SLIDE TRUMPET (No. 210)
By Astor. English, c. 1810

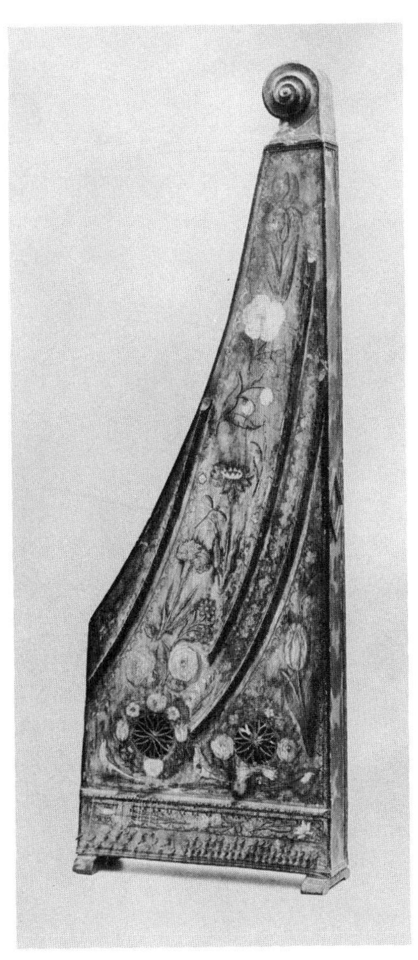

FIG. 34. SPITZHARFE (No. 226)

FIG. 35. CLARSECH (No. 233)

the initial position by flat springs with rollers; the key pivots and spring roller guides are soldered to a long strip of brass. The valve tubes are reinforced on both sides by rectangular sheets of brass. Cornet-à-pistons mouthpiece. Engraved on the bell rim band is 'C. Mahillon, Bruxelles.' Length, 40.5 cm. Diameter, bell, 12.7 cm. Bore, cylindrical, diameter, 10.5 mm.; length, 123.5 cm.; conoidal, max., 5 cm.; length, 57 cm. Length of air column (approx.), 184 cm. (17.1997)
Plate VI

The tonality of the three-valve trumpet was standardized in F, like that of the French horn, and so remained down to the end of the nineteenth century, when the alto trumpet was displaced by the soprano valve trombone in B-flat (the 'trumpet' in B-flat).

213. POST-HORN — Germany, 19th century

Alto in E-flat. Circular-wound trumpet with an althorn type mouthpiece. Brass. Cylindro-conoidal bore; the tube is coiled four times. Stamped on the bell: '531'; on the bell rim band: 'G. Eschenbach, Berlin.' Length, 32 cm. Diameter, bell, 11.5 cm.; across the coils, 17.5 cm. Bore, cylindrical, diameter, 11.5 mm.; length, 149.5 cm.; conoidal, max., 6 cm.; length, 51.5 cm. Length of air column (with mouthpiece), 207 cm. (17.1982)
Plate VI

The inclusion of the post-horn in the trumpet section requires an explanation. There is a difference between the French and the German post-horns. The French post-horn is a conoidal bore three-octave instrument with pleasant but inconsequential tone; as already stated, it is an ancestor of the cornet-à-pistons. The German post-horn is a cylindrical bore four-octave instrument. Experiments in the Museum have shown that if played with a trumpet mouthpiece, the instrument No. 213 (also No. 214) produces an excellent trumpet tone, and its natural scale is that of the E-flat alto trumpet. The regulation mouthpiece supplied with the German post-horn is a small althorn mouthpiece, not suitable for the acoustical characteristics of the tube. It spoils the tone and limits the upper register.

Praetorius mentioned that some trumpets were wound in the shape of the 'Posthorn,' but were not equal in tone to the standard instrument. Evidently he refers to the 'Jäger Trommet,' table viii, 11 (reproduced here on p. 185), which is wound as a post-horn with many coils. It is difficult to say whether the inferiority of tone of the 'Posthorn — Jäger Trommet' mentioned by Praetorius is due to the proportions of its tube or to the mouthpiece. Gottfried Reiche, the famous 'Stadtpfeifer,' a contemporary and friend of J. S. Bach, used a circular-wound trumpet similar to that of Praetorius' 'Jäger Trommet.' Additional information on circular-wound trumpets can be found in C. S. Terry's *Bach's Orchestra.*[434]

214. POST-HORN — Germany, second half of the 19th century

Alto in E-flat. Circular-wound trumpet with a cornet type mouthpiece. Two piston valves, 'Berliner Pumpen' type (short; large diameter). Brass, with German silver trimmings. Cylindro-conoidal bore. Large cornet type mouthpiece. Engraved on the bell rim band (of genuine silver): 'Ehren-Posthorn für den Postillon Heinrich Bredemeier.' The band is also engraved with the Prussian eagle and conventional floral patterns. Length, 38.5 cm. Diameter, bell, 11.3 cm.; across the coils, 20.5 cm. Bore, cylindrical, diameter, 11 mm.; length, 154 cm.; conoidal, max., 5.9 cm.; length, 47 cm. Length of air column (with trumpet mouthpiece), 208 cm. (17.1984)
Plate VI

The 'Berliner Pumpen' or 'Bombenventile' were short piston valves of large diameter invented in 1835 (?) by C. W. Moritz in Berlin.[435] This system permitted large air passages, but the bearing surface of the piston was too short and wore down rapidly. The Perinet piston, with its long body of small diameter, has proven itself superior mechanically.

DIVISION II: INSTRUMENTS CONTROLLED BY A KEYBOARD

SECTION A: FLUE AND REED PIPES

THE instruments belonging to this section are the organs. The construction and history of the organ is such a vast subject that even the most elementary discussion cannot be attempted here. Standard works on the subject should be consulted.[436]

In connection with the organ there exists an obscure and difficult problem, namely the pitches of the organ in the early sixteenth century. Since the church music of that time had a direct influence on instrumental music, certain problems, such as the tuning of the viol, can be solved only if the organ playing practices of that period are understood. The technical details can be found in Appendices B and D. Only a brief summary will be given here.

At present the basic tonality of our musical system is stabilized and set as that in C. The pitch, at least in this country, is standardized at 440 cycles per second for the tone *a'* (A_{49}). Instruments having a tonality differing from that of C are comparatively few in number. The musical notation of parts of some of them (bassoons, trombones, tubas) is written so that transposition is not necessary. Keyboard instruments, such as modern harpsichords, organs, and pianos, are set in the tonality of our musical system, that is in C. This happy and convenient condition is a recent development. Therefore, it comes as a shock to learn that in the early sixteenth century at least two musical systems existed with different pitches, and that organs were tuned as far as a fourth apart. In other words, the old timers built organs in different tonalities, just as today there are clarinets in A and in D. It seems almost incredible that such a ponderous instrument as the organ should be treated so lightly. Yet well established facts support the contention that two musical systems with distinct and widely divergent tonalities existed side by side. The real situation was, of course, much more complex. In Appendix D the principal tonalities and pitches of several historically important musical systems are given. The whole problem can be considerably simplified when attention is directed to the extremely low and extremely high pitches, as in the early sixteenth century there were definite reasons for having both the low- and the high-pitched organ. The musicians of that time found a simple and ingenious method of dealing with such a condition by establishing a certain average pitch level. This was done by selecting the tonalities of organ parts, the tuning of viols, and the pitch of wind instruments in such a way as to bring them to the best average tessitura of the human voice. Below are summarized the most important points.

1. The musical system of the church was based on the hexachord. The lowest tone of the system was *Gamma*, G.

2. In the early sixteenth century the first church mode, the Dorian, had its final tone

either D or G. The tone D was that of the theorists; the tone G was used by some practical men, and the practice, it seems, antedated the sixteenth century.

3. The keyboards of the pedal organs and the manuals had F as their lowest tone.

4. In order to utilize the keyboards more completely when the choral accompaniment was played with the pedal organ, and also because many church songs end *in gravibus* (that is, on a low tone), some organists preferred to play the Dorian mode on G.

5. If the Dorian mode were played in that tonality (G) on a medium-pitched organ (say *a'*-440), the tessitura for voices would be too high. In order to bring the tessitura of voices to a convenient pitch level, low-pitched organs were constructed.

6. If the Dorian mode were preferably played in D, for the same reason (to place the tessitura correctly) high-pitched organs were constructed.

7. The low-pitched organ was pitched so that its tonality, with respect to the pitch of our system, was in A. The high-pitched organ was pitched so that its tonality was, respectively, in D. The interval between the low- and the high-pitched organ was a fourth.

8. The organ parts were written to accommodate the organist so that he was not obliged to transpose. For the low-pitched organ in A the Dorian mode was written transposed *per quartam superiorem*, or a fourth *higher* with respect to D; for the high-pitched organ in D the Dorian mode remained in its theoretical tonality.

9. The parts for the low- and the high-pitched organ, therefore, differed in their notation; in their practical musical effect they were *in unison*.[437]

10. In some organ tablature books both systems of notation were given on the same page.[438] The probable reason was that the organist in his professional capacity was required to play both on the low- and the high-pitched organ, depending on the system used in various localities.

215. HYDRAULIS

A first-century type. Reconstruction

Hydraulus. The water organ. The instrument consists essentially of five principal parts: (1) an octagonal water-tank, (2) a wind-chest with an inverted funnel attached to it, (3) three sets of flue pipes, each set consisting of nineteen pipes, (4) a balanced action keyboard of nineteen keys, and (5) two air-pumps operated by long handles. Three cylindrical taps serve as stops governing the admission of air into the cross-channels of each set of pipes. A stand. Height, total, 201 cm. Breadth, 70.5 cm. Width, 49 cm. Pipes, inside diameter, 22 mm. Air pump cylinders, diameter, 18 cm.; stroke, 12 cm. (17.1942)

This is Canon Galpin's reconstruction of a hydraulis of the ancients from the baked uncolored clay statuette found about 1885 on the site of ruined Carthage. The model is made to a scale of one half of the assumed dimensions of the actual instrument. The model is described and illustrated by Canon Galpin in several publications.[439] The scale of this instrument consists of the following tones:

G, A, B♭, B, c, d, e♭, e, f, f♯, g,
g♯, a, b♭, b, c', c'♯, d', e'

The front row of pipes (the 'front' is the side opposite the keyboard) are 'stopped pipes.' The other two rows or 'ranks,' the octave and super-octave, are open pipes fitted with tuning rings. For the historic background of the hydraulis, based on Hebrew, Syriac, and Arabic sources, *The Organ of the Ancients, from Eastern Sources* (1931), by Dr. Henry George Farmer, should be consulted. The book has a foreword by Canon Galpin. An extensive bibliography is appended.

216. PORTATIVE ORGAN England, ca. 1800

Compass from A to f″. Trapezium-shaped oak case. Imitation half-pipes painted blue and gold. Recessed keyboard with a hinged cover, forming a music rack when open. Keys: twenty naturals and thirteen sharps. Two ranks of open flute, lead pipes (modern). Two stops. The organ is blown by a small handle on the left-hand side attached to a bellows concealed in the base. Length, 63.5 cm. Width, 36 cm. Height, 72 cm. (17.1938)

The portative organs were small organs slung from the neck and easily carried by one person in procession; the bellows were blown by one hand and the keyboard was played with the other.

217. POSITIVE ORGAN Germany, ca. 1600

Compass from c to c^4; the lowest octave is the short octave. Rectangular wooden case with a bellows at the top; twenty-one tin pipes in front with carved scrollwork; the rest of the pipes are inside the case; two side doors and a removable rear door. The feeder bellows are pumped by a leather strap on the left side; three stop handles on the right side (the fourth one is lost). The keys are of pear wood, twenty-seven naturals, eighteen sharps. Originally this organ had four ranks of pipes; only two are actually in place: the *montre* stop (tin pipes) and the four-foot stopped flute (oak pipes). The bellows are connected with the wind-chest in the base by a square oak pipe. Two wide bars passing through the iron loops in the front and the back are for carrying this organ in processions. A stand. Length, 85 cm. Width, 50 cm. Height, 109 cm. (19.1939)

The positive organ was a larger organ than the portative and usually had to be placed in position for playing. The smaller sizes of positive organs, like this one, were carried in procession by two men, the organist playing it when the procession stopped. The larger sizes were kept in churches and were shifted from place to place as the occasion required.

218. CABINET ORGAN London, England, 1792

Compass from c to f^3. Rectangular mahogany case; a folding keyboard covered by a hinged cover. The front part of the cover on the top of the case is hinged and can be operated by a foot pedal on the left side serving as a swell. Three stops on the right side. Three ranks of pipes: (1) the eight-foot *Diapason* (stopped rectangular oak pipes); (2) the *Principal* (open flute, lead pipes); (3) *the Fifteenth* (open flute, lead pipes). The keys, thirty-two ivory naturals and twenty-one ebony sharps (the lowest C-sharp was omitted by the builder). The bellows are located in the base below the wind-chest. The pumping foot-pedal, loaded with a lead weight, is on the right side. Two folding brass candle holders. Maker's name: 'Avery Londini Fecit, 1792.' Length, 102.5 cm. Width, 56 cm. Height, 119 cm. (17.1941)

219. CHAMBER ORGAN England, 18th century

Compass from c to e^4. Mahogany panelled case on stand; the keyboard is recessed and has a removable cover; the top of the case is hinged and operated as a swell by the pedal on the left side. Three drawstops, one on the left, two on the right side. Three ranks of pipes: (1) *four-foot Diapason* (stopped rectangular oak pipes); (2) *the Flute* (open rectangular oak pipes); (3) *the Fifteenth* (open flute, lead pipes). The keys, seventeen ivory naturals and twelve ebony sharps. The bellows are located in the base and pumped by the pedal on the right side; the bellows have two parallel link guides. A wind-chest for the two lower pitched ranks of pipes and a small separate one for the highest pitched rank. No maker's name. Length, 72.5 cm. Width, 35 cm. Height, 108 cm. (17.1940)

SECTION B: FREE REEDS

220. ACCORDION — London, England, ca. 1860

Rectangular wooden case decorated with wooden scrolls. Five-fold pasteboard bellows. Twenty-three touches arranged in two rows with mother-of-pearl linings; round pearl keys. The basses are arranged on both sides: the right-hand basses (2) have long levers and are operated by the finger-joints; the left-hand basses are arranged for operation by the thumb and the ring and middle fingers. Stamped 'Keith, Prowse & Co., 48 (?) Cheapside, London.' Length, 39 cm. Width, 12.5 cm. Thickness (bellows compressed), 15 cm. (17.1946)

221. CONCERTINA — England, 19th century

Hexagonal rosewood case with ornamentally perforated covers. Green leather bellows (four-fold). Two thumb-straps for holding. Twenty-four touches on either side. The reeds for each tone are doubled and are located on either side of the reed diaphragms, so that a continuous tone for a note is provided for either motion of the bellows. The brass name plate reads 'Cramer and Co.'s Artist's Concertina'; also 'Selected by Richard Blaygrove.' Diameter of the circumscribed circle, 18 cm. Width (bellows compressed), 13 cm. (17.1945)

222. ROCKING MELODIAN — Concord, New Hampshire, U. S. A., ca. 1835

Lap Organ. Teeter. Compass from F to a″. Rectangular wooden case with double bellows. The bellows are divided diagonally by a thick wooden diaphragm into two chambers. The lower (left-hand) chamber serves as the primary bellows (feeder) and the upper (right-hand) chamber as a combined wind-chest and pressure increaser. The lower chamber has a double flat steel spring; the upper chamber has a single flat steel spring. Two strip valves in the lower chamber, one strip valve in the upper chamber. The reed-frame serves as a cover for the upper chamber and the reed carrier. The reeds are protected by two removable covers with slides for the contrasting forte and piano effects; the slides are moved by a sliding lever. The touches are round ivory buttons disposed in two rows: the one nearest the player has twenty-four touches and corresponds to the naturals on the piano; the second row, with a black circle on the top of each touch, has seventeen touches corresponding to the sharps. Between the touches there is a printed paper strip with the letters of the tones. Stamped 'C. Austin, Concord, N. H.' Length, 47.5 cm. Width, 26 cm. Height (with springs in normal position), 24 cm. (17.1948)

On a similar instrument built by Abraham Prescott, also of Concord, N. H., has been found a label in which the instrument was referred to as a 'Melodian.' The label is so original that it is worth quoting in full. It is shown on the opposite page.

The compass of our instrument ranges from *F* to *a″*, or three octaves and a third. One misconception should be corrected. The majority of instruments the writer has seen have had the upper part of their bellows in a shut position, giving a wedge-shaped appearance to the instrument. An examination of the inside construction shows that the upper spring is single and usually broken off. Therefore, the normal appearance of the instrument was that of a parallelepipedal case with a diagonally divided bellows. The lower double spring in all cases remained intact.

ABRAHAM PRESCOTT

Manufacturer of

PREMIUM BASS & DOUBLE BASS VIOLS

Seraphines and Melodians

and dealer in

Musical Instruments, Umbrellas, Parasols, &c.

Instruments and Umbrellas repaired at short notice, and

WARRANTED

OPPOSITE THE COLUMBIAN HOTEL, CONCORD, N.H.

Care should be taken in blowing the Melodian to give a steady pressure, as a sudden motion may injure the tone of instrument.

The name of 'lap organ' was given to this instrument because it was held across the lap. The left side was pushed down by the forearm, the spring returning the bellows to a normal position. The dynamic nuances were controlled by the right forearm, the spring on the diaphragm providing an elastic resistance to the compression of the wind-chest bellows. The contrasting forte and piano effects were made by shifting the shutter slides. The melodian, called more commonly the melodeon, was very popular at one time and served as a small portable organ in congregational singing in small communities. It was also popular in the home and on the farm. Similar instruments can be found in the Stearns Collection of Musical Instruments, Ann Arbor, Michigan.[440] Also in the New York and Brussels Collections.[441]

223. MELOPHONE — Paris, France, after 1842

Compass from *B* to e^4, with the additional tones *G*, *G*-sharp, *A*, and *A*-sharp for octaves. A guitar-shaped case of bird's-eye maple, containing a double bellows operated by a handle affixed to two plunger rods. On the top of this case is a cover of the same shape, but smaller, with ribs of bird's-eye maple and belly of spruce with two F-holes as on a violin. The cover protects the valve mechanism, consisting of eighty-three valves with operating levers, springs, and control wires located on the top of the air chamber; the latter is split in two parts held by six hinged screws with wing-nuts, thus permitting easy access to the reeds and air valves. There is a short neck with a small decorative scroll affixed to the air chamber. On the front surface of the neck are eighty-four semicircular touches of German silver, spaced by a perforated plate into seven longitudinal rows, each containing twelve touches. An octave coupling lever is at the back of the neck. Stamped on the plate: 'Par Brevet d'Invention. Pellerin Breveté. 29 Quai Bourbon Paris.' Branded on the top of the air chamber is 'C. A. Pellerin.' Length (without handle), total, 77 cm.; body, 54 cm. Width, the lower bouts, 31.5 cm. Height, total, 19 cm.; ribs, bellows chamber, 12 cm.; ribs, cover, 7 cm. (17.1947)

The melophone was invented in 1837 by Leclerc, a Parisian watchmaker. In 1842 Pellerin bought a license and started the manufacturing of melophones. The melophone is held on the right thigh, stopped by the left hand, and the air is pumped in by the right handle. The handle was called a 'bow' (*archet*) in France. The reason for this name was that the air chamber was small and the sound lasted only as long as the handle was moved; sound was produced by moving the handle in either direction. One of the peculiarities of melophone 'bowing' technique was the possibility of a tremolo effect, which could be produced with the same rapidity as on any bowed instrument. Therefore, the term 'bow' applied to the handle was quite appropriate. Although the melophone was superseded by the harmonium, the latter instrument could not produce a tremolo. The sound of the melophone is similar to that of the accordion, but somewhat stronger, and in certain parts of the register reminds one of a trumpet. The keyboard has two peculiarities. One is that the seven longitudinal rows are spaced a fifth apart, as on a violin, so that the fingering is somewhat similar to that of the violin. Another one is that the touches are duplicated, beginning with the eighth transverse row. The octave coupler is operated by the left-hand thumb. The tones below B enumerated in the technical description sound only when the octave coupler is engaged. The operating mechanism is ingenious, but very complicated and delicate.

DIVISION III: INSTRUMENTS CONTROLLED BY AUTOMATIC MOTION

224. BARREL ORGAN — France, 19th century

Serinette. Compass from c^3 to e^4. Roughly made rectangular box of ash. Ten small organ pipes operated through a tracker mechanism by a large pin barrel with a spur gear. Small bellows inside the case. The inside mechanism is operated by a crank handle fixed to a combination worm and crank shaft. The worm engages the spur gear on the barrel and the crank operates the bellows. The barrel is mounted on a movable bracket which has on the right-hand side a projecting shift pin with eight notches. One of the notches is engaged by a latch, permitting the selection of one of the eight airs set on the barrel. The airs are listed on the label pasted inside on the cover. Length, 27 cm. Width, 22 cm. Height, 15.5 cm. (17.1943)

The French name of this miniature mechanical organ is derived from the name of the finch (*serin*). It was used for teaching finches and other birds to sing popular airs.

316. BOOK HARMONIUM — France, 19th century

Bible Harmonium. Compass from c to f^4. Small free reed organ in a book-shaped oaken case. The keys: twenty-five ivory naturals and seventeen ebony sharps. Two bellows. Length, 59 cm. Width, 30 cm. Height, 13.5 cm. (21.13)

The book-shaped organ was invented in France in the seventeenth century. When the case was folded it gave the appearance of a book in a strong binding, especially when viewed from a distance. The original instruments were real little organs with single beating reed pipes as on the regals. Our instrument is built along the traditional lines, except that the sound is produced by the free reeds; therefore it is a harmonium and not an organ.

CLASS IV

CHORDOPHONIC INSTRUMENTS OR CHORDOPHONES

CLASS IV: CHORDOPHONIC INSTRUMENTS OR CHORDOPHONES

DIVISION I: INSTRUMENTS CONTROLLED DIRECTLY

CHORDOPHONIC instruments or chordophones are the instruments which have a string or a set of strings as a primary vibrator. The word 'chordophone' is derived from two Greek words, χορδή, string (specifically, gut-string), and φωνή, sound; therefore chordophone means a 'string-sounder.' In ordinary usage this class of instruments is called 'string instruments,' 'stringed instruments,' or simply 'strings.'[442]

Strings on chordophones are held by some suitable means under tension and are set in vibration by one of the following methods: 1. Plucking. 2. Striking. 3. Bowing. 4. A stream of air.

The instruments with air-vibrated strings are exceptional. Therefore, discussion will be confined to the plucked, struck, and bowed chordophones.

Position of Parts

To make the description of chordophones more definite, the following rules in identifying the position of various parts of the instruments are adopted.[443]

The *upper end* or *head* of an instrument is that end where the tuning device (pegs, machines, etc.) is located.

The *lower end* is the opposite end.

The *front* or *belly* is that side on which the strings are fastened.[444]

The *back* is the reverse side.

The *right side* is that which in the case of the violoncello is on the player's right-hand side.

The *left side* is the opposite side.

In determining the right or left side, a confusion might arise unless some definite viewpoint were adopted as the standard one. It cannot be the playing position, as will be seen from a few examples. Regarded from the player's viewpoint, the right side of a violin in the playing position is that side where the highest string (E-string) is located. Such an identification of the sides of a violin will be the reverse of that for a violoncello.

Another example is that of the guitar. In the playing position it is so held that the lower end is on the player's right side; the sides of the guitar are in an up-and-down position. It is clear that the playing position viewpoint, in the case of the violin, gives the names of the sides in the opposite sense from that of the violoncello, an instrument of the same family and similar in shape and design; and in the case of the guitar it does not permit identifying the sides at all.

Dr. Sachs suggested an anthropomorphic viewpoint. After identifying the upper end and the front of the instrument, one should imagine himself enclosed in it so that the front side of the man would coincide with the front of the instrument. Then the sides will be identified uniquely and no confusion will be possible, whatever the playing position. Thus, the lute (see page 234, Fig. 39) is played with the right side up; its melody string (chanterelle) is on the left side and in the lowest position; the lute's left side rests on the player's knee, etc.

Types of Strings

THERE are three types of strings used on chordophones:

1. *Open strings*, or strings of constant length. They are intended to produce one tone only. Examples: Plucked: Psaltery (No. 227); Harp (No. 233). Struck: Dulcimer (No. 263). Bowed: Crwth (No. 291, two bourdons only).

2. *Stopped strings*, or strings of variable length. Their vibrating length can be temporarily changed by various methods of stopping. Examples: Plucked: Zither (No. 232); Lute (No. 242). Bowed: Bass-Viol (No. 275); Violoncello (No. 287).

3. *Sympathetic strings.* These are the auxiliary strings which add tone coloring to the tones produced by the main playing strings by resounding sympathetically with them. Examples: Viole d'amour (No. 281); Tromba Marina (No. 291; has fifty sympathetic strings; not typical of the ordinary tromba marina).

Resonant Bodies or Sound-Boxes

A STRING stretched between holders on a rigid, non-resonant base would produce a dull and subdued tone. The overtones might be present, but they would be inaudible and the more subtle tone colorings not perceptible. Therefore, additional means should be provided for amplifying the fundamental frequency and intensifying the overtones. This is accomplished by constructing a secondary vibrator, a sound-box which vibrates in resonance with the strings mounted on it. The art of making musical instruments consists in devising the sound-boxes of a proper shape and size to produce sonorous and colorful tones.

1. *Bi-partitioned type of sound-box.* A sound-box of this type consists of two principal parts: (a) the *body*, and (b) the *sound-board* or *belly*. The body is usually shaped like a half-pear. Examples: Plucked: Lute (No. 242); Mandoline (No. 248). Bowed: Rebec (No. 266).

2. *Tri-partitioned type of sound-box.* A sound-box consisting of three parts: (a) the *belly*, (b) the *sides* or *ribs*, and (c) the *back*. Examples: Plucked: Guitar (No. 256). Struck: Dulcimer (No. 263). Bowed: Violoncello (No. 287).

String Fasteners and Intermediate Supports

THE strings on chordophones are so affixed that it is possible to put them under tension to secure a desired pitch and to change that tension for tuning. Usually one end of a string is fixed permanently and not disturbed except to change it; the other end is attached to a tuning pin or peg in such a way as to permit a variation of tension.[445]

The fixed ends of the strings are held by devices of two types:

1. *Sound-board fastening*. This type consists of a cross-bar affixed to the sound-board or belly; strings are fastened to this cross-bar by a knot, loop, or pins. The cross-bar serves the double purpose of a holding device and a vibration transmitter. Examples: Guitar (No. 256); strings are held by loops. Machête (No. 254); strings are held by pins.

2. *Lower end fastening*. The strings are held at the lower end of the body by different means: (a) by pins fastened in the lower end, as the Mandoline (No. 248); (b) by pins attached to the tail-piece, which is held by (i) a hook-bar fastened to the underside, as the Lyra-Viol (No. 273); (ii) a loop affixed to the end-pin as the Sultana (No. 280).

The tuning ends of the strings are fastened to tuning pegs in two different ways.

1. The *frontal*[446] type. The strings are placed so that their tuning ends are affixed to the pegs at the front of the instrument.

2. The *occipital* type. The strings are placed so that their tuning ends are brought to the back of the head of an instrument (hence the term *occipital*) by being threaded through the holes drilled just above the nut for the stopped strings, and on the sides of the peg-box for the open strings. The string ends are fastened to the protruding ends of the tuning pegs at the back.[447]

The disposition of the tuning pegs falls into two types.

1. The *sagittal* type. The axis of the pegs is normal (perpendicular) to the front plane of the instrument, i.e., it goes from the front to the back. This type has two sub-types:

(i) *Anterior pegs*, which are inserted so that their heads are at the front. Examples: Tanbourica (No. 240); the frontal type of string tuning end fastening. Crwth (No. 291); the occipital type of string tuning end fastening; the open strings are threaded through from the front in the same manner as the stopped strings. Hurdy-Gurdy (No. 305); the occipital type of string tuning end fastening; the open strings (*bourdons*) are threaded through the cheeks of the peg-box.

(ii) *Posterior pegs*, which are inserted so that their heads are at the back. Examples: Husla (No. 269); the pegs are made in the shape of arrows. Guitar (No. 256).

2. The *lateral* type. The axis of the pegs is normal to the sides, i.e., it goes from the right to the left. The peg holes are bored in the sides or cheeks of the peg-boxes. Examples: Theorbo (No. 243). Lyra-Viol (No. 273). Baryton (No. 283).

Intermediate supports of the strings are inserted between the fixed and the tuning ends. These are the *nut* and the *bridge*. Their functions are double: structural and acoustical.

The *nut* is a notched piece of hard wood or ivory, usually placed at the top of the finger-board and just below the tuning pegs. Structurally, a nut (a) holds the strings at a definite distance from the finger-board, (b) keeps the strings placed in its notches a definite distance apart, and (c) adds a frictional resistance, helping the pegs in holding the strings. This is especially true of lutes, where the arc of contact of the strings with the nut is about 90 degrees.

Acoustically, a nut provides a definite cut-off point on a string separating the vibrating length from that which is musically ineffective. This enhances the clarity and sonority of tone, as may be judged by the difference in sonority of violin strings played open and stopped. This difference is so considerable that, with the exception of the tone *g* of the lowest string, the open tones are not used in violin playing.[448]

The *bridge* is a wedge-shaped, notched piece of hard wood, with a broad base and a narrow top. The shapes of bridges are many. Structurally, a bridge (a) supports the strings at a required distance from the sound-board, (b) keeps the strings a definite distance apart and prevents them from slipping under the pressure of the finger or the bow. Acoustically, a bridge (a) provides a definite cut-off point on a string separating the vibrating length from the musically ineffective one; in this function it is similar to the nut; and (b) serves as a vibration-transmitting element.

Sound-Post and Bass-Bar

On bowed instruments, vibrations of the strings are transmitted by the bridge to the sound-board or belly. The vibrations of the latter are transmitted to the back by the sound-post. The *sound-post* is a round stick of fine, even-grained spruce fitted between the belly and the back just snugly enough not to fall out when the instrument is unstrung, but not imposing any strain on the body. It has to be placed at a certain point, usually found by an experienced person by a method of trial and error, because the quality of the tone and sonority of an instrument depends upon its right location. The French call it *l'âme*, the soul. The function of the sound-post is not so much to transmit the vibrations between the belly and the back, as to synchronize the vibrations of both and render them uniform.

The *bass-bar* is a long piece of fine, even-grained pine, located under that foot of the bridge where the lowest string is placed. It is glued to the inside surface of the belly, and slightly inclined with respect to the centre line of the instrument. Functions of the bass-bar in influencing the tone are as follows: (a) it modifies the tone produced by the belly; the stiffer the bass-bar, the higher the tone of the belly;[449] (b) it transmits the vibrations from the foot of the bridge placed over it and distributes them over the belly, preventing at the same time any partial or segmental vibrations in its neighborhood;[450] (c) it helps to stiffen the belly structurally; but this is not its primary function, because the arched form of the belly provides sufficient resistance to strain.

SECTION A: PLUCKED

Plucked instruments are, perhaps, among the most ancient and widely distributed musical instruments used by man. The Egyptians had the harp at a very remote period. Recent discoveries in the land of the Sumerians show that the harp existed there as long ago as it did in Egypt. Chronologically the plucked instruments can be dated as far back into the past as 5000 years.[451]

Plucking of the strings is done either by the fingers or by a plectrum, the simplest form of which is a goose quill. The plectrum is also called a pick.

Plucked chordophones are divided into two sub-sections: (a) those without a neck, and (b) those with a neck.

SUB-SECTION a: PLUCKED CHORDOPHONES WITHOUT A NECK

THE distinguishing structural characteristic of the instruments of this sub-section is the absence of any extended member which would be used for stopping strings, such as a neck on a lute or a guitar. Instruments belonging to this sub-section can be divided into two groups: (1) instruments with strings parallel to the sound-board, or the lyre-psaltery-zither type; and (2) instruments having strings perpendicular to the sound-board, or the harp type. External members, such as yokes on lyres and harmonic curves with front pillars on harps, have many forms and serve as supports for the strings and auxiliary devices only. Their purpose is functional and not organic.[452]

Lyre Type

225. ROTTA — Reproduction, Germany, 5th–7th centuries.

Shallow box of oak with two extended arms, made of one piece of oak, hollowed at the lower half; thin oaken sound-board. Separate yoke joined with arms and held by oaken pins. Two narrow slits at the junction of the sound-board and arms for affixing the supporting cord which was attached to the arm of the player. Six gut strings, lower-end fastening type, attached to the boss projecting from the body; frontal type fastening of tuning ends; iron tuning pins inserted into the yoke, anterior type. Movable bridge. The original is in the Staatliches Museum für Völkerkunde, Berlin. Length, 78.5 cm. Width, upper, 21 cm.; lower, 17.25 cm. Thickness, 2.75 cm. Vibrating length of strings (aver.), 65 cm. (17.1767)
Plate VIII

The original of this instrument was found in the Würtemberg Black Forest at Oberflacht, buried in an Allemanic grave and excavated in 1846. The exact period of its use is not known, but is approximately estimated as between the fifth and the seventh century of our era.

Psalteries

PSALTERY, from the Greek *ψαλτήριον*, is derived from *ψάλλειν*, meaning to pull and let go, to pluck. But this does not mean that the instrument comes to us from classical antiquity. It is found in the Islamic civilization of the Orient, where the prototype of our psalteries is known as *qānūn*. The probable date of its appearance in Europe is in the eleventh century.[453]

The psaltery is played by plucking the strings, either by the fingers or with a plectrum. In this it differs from the dulcimer (No. 263, page 247), the strings of which are struck. The psaltery can be regarded as the ancestor of the spinet, virginal, and harpsichord.

226. SPITZHARFE — Germany, ca. 1670

The Double Psaltery. A vertical, shallow sound-box placed on two feet, with strings on both sides. Ornamented with painted Cupids, birds, and flowers. A portrait of a lady on the front. The left-hand side sound-board has one rosette sound-hole and thirty-six strings passing over a single bridge. The right-hand sound-board has two rosettes and seventy-three strings divided into two groups; a group of fifty-one strings fixed at the upper end to a curved bar and passing over a curved bridge close by, then over a straight bridge at the bottom; a group of twenty-two strings fixed to another curved bar and passing over the straight bridge at the bottom. (See Fig. 34, p. 197.) A scroll top. Height, 116 cm. Width (bottom), 39 cm. Thickness, 7.5 cm. (17.1773)

227. PSALTERY England, 1789

Shepherd's Harp. A trapeze-shaped oak case; the top board pierced with the initials HS and the date 1789. Eight strings, identified by numerals painted in white under each string on the sound-board; strings are fastened to two bars by small iron pins on the left and to the tuning pins on the right. Both bars have inserted thin strips of brass, serving as bridge. Length, narrow end, 32 cm.; wide end, 83.5 cm. Width, 27.5 cm. Height of body, 9 cm. Vibrating length of strings, shortest, 29 cm.; longest, 69.5 cm. (17.1776)
Plate VIII

Canon Galpin kindly supplied the following note: "I made special inquiry about this instrument (which came from an old farmhouse in Essex) as to the way in which it was played by the aged owner of long ago. The strings were *plucked,* not struck; hence its interest."

228. PSALTERY Germany, 19th century

A trapeze-shaped pine sound-box with bevelled edges and an ornamented sound-hole. Two bridge bars and a tuning pin bar on the top. Twenty-two doubled steel strings, both ends of which are fixed to the tuning pins; the looped ends of the strings are affixed to hooks fastened on the side of the body. Length, narrow end, 19.5 cm.; wide end, 62 cm. Width, 34 cm. Height of body, 3.5 cm. Vibrating length of strings, shortest, 12.75 cm.; longest, 47 cm. (17.1774)
Plate VIII

229. KANTELE Finland, 19th century

Psaltery. A trapezoidal sound-box made of a solid block of birch wood, with the resonating cavity covered by a thin pine sound-board. Two sound-holes: a round one and a cross-shaped one. The metal strings, twelve in number, are fixed to an iron cross-bar inserted in the holes bored in the raised horns of the scroll. They pass over a low wooden bridge located near the round sound-hole, then over a long iron bar close to the end tuning pegs. The posterior pegs inserted in the projecting ridge of the body. Length, 69.5 cm. Width, maximum, 22 cm. Height of body, 7.25 cm. Vibrating length of strings. shortest, 14.75 cm.; longest, 44.5 cm. (17.1771)
Plate VIII

The *Kantele* is the national instrument of Finland. Its praise is sung in the Finnish national epic, *Kalevala.* The legendary hero, Wainamoinen, is the reputed inventor of the five-stringed *kantele.* The ancient Russian *gusli* were built along similar lines.[454]

Zithers

THE ancestor of the zither is an old German folk instrument, the *Scheitholt* (No. 230, described below). It is not known exactly when the zither originated, but in the eighteenth century the instruments with an increased number of strings and larger and more resonant bodies began to evolve into the modern zithers. The sound-box has a curved extension either on one side (as in instrument No. 231), the *Salzburg* type, or on both sides, the

Mittenwald type. Instruments of the zither type have a set of open accompaniment strings and a fretted finger-board, over which are stretched the stopped melody strings. The stopping is done by the left hand. The melody is played with the thumb of the right hand, on which is affixed a special ring-shaped plectrum. The accompaniment strings are played with the three fingers. The little finger is not used. Modern zithers have five stopped strings. The number of open strings varies with the size from 24 to 37.

230. SCHEITHOLT — Germany, 18th–19th century

A narrow sound-box with two heart-shaped sound-holes. Peg-box with scroll at the top; five lateral pegs. Metal strings with the lower end frontal fastening. Two stopped melody strings passing over fourteen metal frets set in the sound-board. Three open strings. The ends of the pins are protected at the lower end by an ornamental guard. Played in a horizontal position with the peg-box at the player's left. Length, 64.5 cm. Width, 8 cm. Thickness of body, 2.75 cm. Vibrating length of strings, 48.25 cm. (17.1778)
Plate VIII

The *Scheitholt* had a wide distribution in Northern Germany, the mountainous districts of Bavaria and Austria, France (Vosges), and the Scandinavian countries. It still existed in the eighteenth century and even into the nineteenth century.[455] Instruments of this type are known as *langleik* (Norway), *hummel* (Sweden), *humle* (Denmark), *houmel, noordische balk* (Flanders), *epinette des Vosges* (France).

Canon Galpin added: "It is interesting to remember that the early scheitholts were played like the Hawaiian guitar, the strings being pressed down on the finger-board by a small rod held in the left hand."

This remark is based on Praetorius' statement in *De Organographia*, ii, p. 57, where he states: "Es wird aber uber alle diese Säitten unten am Stäige mit dem rechten Daumen allezeit uberher geschrumpet: und *mit eim kleinen glatten Stöcklin in der lincken Hand* uff der förder-sten Säitten hin und wieder gezogen, dadurch die Melodey des Gesanges uber die Bünde, so von Messingen Droth [Messing-Draht] eingeschlagen sind, zuwege gebracht wird." (Italics are mine.)

231. ZITHER — Germany, 18th century

Salzburg type. A shallow sound-box with a straight right-hand side and a semi-circular extension on the left-hand side. Pierced sound-hole. Gradually tapering head. Lower end frontal string fastening, anterior pegs of iron wire with loop formed heads. Two paired stopped strings pass over seventeen wire frets inserted in an ebony finger-board. Nine open strings. Length, 58 cm. Width, max., 21.5 cm.; narrow part, 12 cm. Height of body, 4 cm. Vibrating length of strings, open, 43 cm.; stopped, 41.5 cm. (17.1777)
Plate VIII

232. ZITHER — France, 19th century

Psalterion rectangulaire. A rectangular deep box with slanting, moulded ends on four ivory feet; bottom and sides of maple, sound-board of pine. Light yellow-brown varnish. The sound-board has two sunk rosetted sound-holes. An ebony finger-board with twenty-four ivory frets. Lower end frontal fastening of strings; buttons at the lower end, square-headed steel tuning pins. Four stopped strings passing over metal strips serving as the saddle and a nut. Thirteen open strings pass over two ebony bridges with thin metal strips on the top. The edges of the sound-board and of the sound-holes are inlaid in black and white. Length, 73.5 cm. Width, 22.5 cm. Ribs, height, 7.75 cm. Height, total, 10.5 cm. Vibrating length of strings, open, 52.75 cm.; stopped, 66 cm. (17.1775) Plate VIII

Harps

THE word harp is of Northern origin. In the Old Norse it was *harpa*, from *harpan*, to pluck. In Anglo-Saxon it was *hearpe*.[456]

The most ancient harp now known is the bow-harp (*Bogenharfe* in Dr. Curt Sachs' terminology), derived apparently from the hunting bow. It is shown in Egyptian tomb reliefs of Old Kingdom date (Pyramid Age, ca. 3500 B.C.). Two illustrations of the instrument, with five and seven strings respectively, have been found on a Sumerian diorite vase (ca. 3200 B.C.) at Bismya in Babylonia. It is also portrayed in the pictographic script of the Indus Valley civilization (early third millennium B.C.). The history of this interesting harp, its various forms, development, and distribution are described by Canon Galpin, in *The Music of the Sumerians . . . the Babylonians and Assyrians* (Cambridge, England, 1937). The harp found at Ur (ca. 2700 B.C.) had already been elaborated upon both artistically and musically.[457] This type of harp found a wide distribution in Asia and Africa.

The second type of harp is the angle-harp (*Winkelharfe*). Essentially it consists of a sound-box and a post inserted in the lower part perpendicularly to the plane of the sound-board. Excellent illustrations can be found in plate vi of Canon Galpin's book just mentioned, where several examples of this type are given. Its probable place of origin is the Near East in the third century B.C. It spread as far east as China and Japan.[458]

The harps of this Collection all belong to the third fundamental type, the frame-harp (*Rahmenharfe*) of triangular form. The harps of this type consist essentially of three members: (1) a *body* or *sound-box* serving as a resonator for the strings, (2) a curved neck, called the *harmonic curve*, on which are affixed the tuning pins holding the strings, and on more highly-developed types containing also the mechanism which changes the pitch of the strings, and (3) a *front pillar* (either curved or straight), functioning as a brace for any resisting strain set up by the stretched strings.

The origin of the triangular harp is uncertain. The old idea that harps with a front pillar are exclusively European instruments is no longer tenable, since, as Dr. Curt Sachs pointed out,[459] there are some Asiatic harps with a front pillar.

There are some scholars who venture to express an opinion that the triangular frame-harp came from the North. Among the adherents of this theory is Canon Francis W. Galpin. In Canon Galpin's words:

The origin of the Northern Harp is traceable to the Bow-shaped Harp. This instrument is known to have existed not only in Mesopotamia and India but also in Central Asia. It is still in use among the Ugrian Finns of Western Siberia and also among the tribes of the Caucasus region. These peoples frequently inserted a stick or wooden rod between the two ends of the bow-shaped instrument:

this enables them to obtain greater tension of strings (cf. W. Heinitz, *Instrumentenkunde*, pl. ii, and Curt Sachs, *Handbuch der Musikinstrumentenkunde*, 1930, fig. 96). In its simpler form it also appeared in the Baltic Provinces. The last harper who did not use a front rod or pillar died in Estonia over a century ago (cf. C. Engel, *Music of the Most Ancient Nations*, p. 34). The influence of the Finns was widely diffused over the greater part of Northern and Eastern Europe and was strongly exerted on the Nordic peoples. Of this harp the Cythara Anglica (the harp of the barbarian Nordic Angles) is typical — the bent front-pillar (constructionally wrong, but conspicuously present) preserves the shape of the older stick, which was bent owing to the tension of the strings. This is shown in a specimen of an Ugrian Ostyak harp in the British Museum, London, and is frequently depicted (with more or less curvature) in British MSS of the tenth and eleventh centuries. Though actual illustrations in Norway may be few or late, the crosses on the *east* coast of Scotland, exposed to Nordic influence, show this triangular instrument from the ninth to the eleventh centuries. On the other hand, it is not until the thirteenth or fourteenth centuries that we find it on the *west* coast of Scotland, as at Iona, the form having appeared in Ireland in the eleventh or twelfth centuries, as at Ardmore Cathedral (the earliest known).

The straight-pillared Harp, so common in Southern Europe, claims a different source, being connected with the Trigons of Greece and Asia Minor. (Letter from Canon Galpin of May 10, 1937.)

The origin of the Irish harp is of importance, since the oldest known specimen of these instruments is Irish. Legends and traditions ascribe the origin of the harp to Ireland. But here one has to be careful in using the term 'harp.' Very often it is applied to any open-stringed instrument which is not obviously a lyre. In a rather heated exchange of opinion on the origin of the clarsech (Irish harp) between Canon Galpin and Dr. W. H. Grattan-Flood[460] this point was not clearly established. The whole question hinges on the typological characteristics of the instruments represented on the Irish crosses, whether they were triangular frame-harps or cruits. The objective evidence points to the conclusion that there were two types of plucked string instruments played in Ireland. The earlier type was the cruit, a plucked chordophone with its strings parallel to the sound-board. The later type was the true harp, that is, an instrument with its strings perpendicular to the sound-board. It seems that Canon Galpin has proved his assertion that the 'harp' on the much discussed Ullard cross, ninth century, in County Kilkenny, Ireland, is really the quadrangular cruit.[461]

But the proof of this point does not necessarily support the theory of the Northern origin of the clarsech. The possibility that the Oriental bow-harp was brought into Ireland by Celtic tribes is not excluded. The moist climate of Ireland made the use of metallic strings more practicable. Their greater tension required more rigid structure and the addition of the front pillar would be a logical step. In other words, the clarsech might have been evolved in Ireland independently of Northern influence.[462]

Examination of historical material[463] shows that a high level of musical culture existed in ancient Ireland. There were schools of minstrels with masters and a long period of apprenticeship. The harpers were highly esteemed in Ireland and were supported by the people with other learned men, such as historians, physicians, poets, etc. Irish harpers were famous not only in their native land, but also on the Continent.

The oldest existing harp of the triangular type is the famous O'Brian's harp or *clarsech*, now in Trinity College, Dublin.[464] An instrument of this Collection, No. 233, the Bunworth Harp, represents the Irish harp at the close of its existence. The evolution of more highly developed chromatic instruments on the Continent caused the disappearance of the Irish harp. One other point should be mentioned. The tonal qualities of the wire-strung Irish and Highland harps seem to be superior to those of the gut-strung instruments. Praetorius in his *Organographia* speaks of the "lovely resonance" (*lieblichen Resonanz*) of the Irish harps.[465] R. B. Armstrong's book, *The Irish and the Highland Harps*, gives many other references. In our own times, Mr. Arnold Dolmetsch revived the old metal-strung harps and introduced in them the chromatic mechanism.

233. CLARSECH — Ireland, 1734, by John Kelly

Large Irish minstrel harp. Sound-box hollowed out of a solid block of bog oak, ornamented with incised flowery scrolls and colored hexafoils. Back of sound-box covered with a board with two holes. Carved neck with two brass pin plates. Curved front pillar of T-section, surmounted with a carved head, ornamented with scalloped edges, borders, and flowers; inscribed 'MADE BY JOHN KELLY FOR THE REVD CHARLES BUNWORTH, BALTDANIEL, 1734.' Thirty-seven strings, of which thirty-three are attached to the tuning pins on the neck and four to the pins on the front pillar. Original color scheme green, red, and white. The green paint is oxidized and looks black. Height, total, 169 cm. Sound-box, length, 106 cm.; width, upper end, 10 cm.; lower end, 35 cm.; sides, height, top, 13.33 cm.; bottom, 11.5 cm. Vibrating length of strings, shortest, 8.5 cm.; longest, 112 cm. (17.1787)
Fig. 35, p. 197

The exact tuning of Irish harps is not known. R. B. Armstrong gives one on page 52 of his work on *The Irish and the Highland Harps*. This instrument is described and illustrated there on pages 91 f.

Not much is known of John Kelly, who made this instrument, except that he came from the South of Ireland. The Reverend Charles Bunworth, Baltdaniel, was rector of Buttevant, County Cork.[466] According to Richard Ryan,[467] "he was greatly distinguished for his patronage and knowledge of Irish music, and was a remarkable good performer on the Irish harp." Reverend Mr. Bunworth presided between the years 1730 and 1750 at the conventions or meetings of the bards of Ireland, which were held at Bruree, County Limerick. He was elected an umpire or president at these meetings five times.[468]

The instrument came from Canon Galpin strung with gut strings since, owing to its great age, it would not stand the strain of metallic strings; these last require, too, special technique in plucking. Irish harpers plucked the metallic strings of the *clarsech* not with finger tips, as modern players on gut strings do, but with their finger nails, grown long especially for this purpose.

234. CEIRNIN — Ireland, late 18th century

Small Irish portable harp. Sound-box of trapeziform section; the rear and two side walls are hollowed out of a solid block of wood; three oval-shaped sound-holes in the rear wall; the bottom is open. Sound-board fitted below the edges of the side walls and held by triangular fillets. The neck and the curved front pillar are both set off centre toward the right-hand side of the player.

Both sides ornamented with flat carved scrolls. Twenty-five wire strings. Height, total, 85 cm. Sound-box, length, 65.5 cm.; width, upper end, 9.5 cm.; lower end, 19.5 cm.; sides, height, top, 6 cm.; bottom, 13 cm. Vibrating length of strings, shortest, 13 cm.; longest, 77.5 cm. (17.1788)

The Ceirnin was a portable harp used by priests and religious people.[469]

235. TELYN Wales, ca. 1750, made by John Richards of Llanrwst

The Welsh triple-strung harp. A built-up sound-box consisting of a slightly convex, triangular shaped sound-board and nine panels forming the semi-circular truncated cone body. Straight front pillar ending in a scroll. The neck is gracefully curved and joined to the sound-box by a carved cap. The sound-box is varnished a light yellow-brown and trimmed with black mouldings around the edges of the sound-board. Six small sound-holes in the sound-board. Ninety-six gut strings affixed to the brass tuning pins. Stamped 'J. R.' on the harmonic curve. Height, total, 165 cm. Sound-box, length, 120.5 cm.; width, upper end, 12.5 cm.; lower end, 48.5 cm. Vibrating length of strings, shortest, 13 cm.; longest, 154 cm. (17.1789)

Illustrated in Galpin's *Old English Instruments of Music,* 3rd edition, plate vi.

The word *telyn* comes from the old Welsh root implying something stretched,[470] as the strings of a harp. In Wales, plucked instruments of the lyre or harp type were used in early times, but there is no positive data for assigning a definite period. All that is possible to say is that the *telyn* was probably known in Wales before the tenth century, since in the middle of that century Howel Dda ('the Good'), prince of Dehenbarth (South Central Wales), and later king of Wales from 943 to 950, promulgated a code of laws. In this code a definite rank was assigned to the bard of the palace, who received from the king a *telyn* and from the queen a golden ring.[471]

The triple-strung chromatic telyn is of a comparatively late period, about the seventeenth century. The instrument in this Collection belongs to the latter half of the eighteenth century. Its stringing is somewhat unusual.

The first departure from the standard practice is the position of the strings on the right-hand side of the harmonic curve, so that the heads of the tuning pins are located on the left side. This is the reverse of the usual arrangement. The second feature is the arrangement of the strings in three vertical parallel planes. The outer right-hand plane contains thirty-six strings tuned thus: G, G-sharp, A, and then diatonically to f^4 inclusive. The left-hand outer plane contains twenty-seven strings tuned from *b* to g^4 diatonically; therefore the strings of the right-hand outer plane are practically duplicated, the lower ten strings being omitted, because they would be outside the reach of the left hand. This row has one extra string at the treble end tuned g^4.

The middle row has thirty-three strings tuned chromatically. The strings of this row are so disposed that there are seven chromatic strings to an octave instead of the customary five. This permits great variety in tunings, such as seven sharps and seven flats; tunings with some tones duplicated either enharmonically or in unison, if a lesser number of accidentals is required in a given key. The whole range of the telyn covers five complete octaves from G to g^4 inclusive, with all semitones. Fingering was somewhat difficult, because chromatic tones had to be produced by reaching the strings of the inside row through those of the outside rows. Two additional chromatic strings in the middle row in each octave undoubtedly facilitated the fingering.

John Richards was a famous harp-maker of Llanrwst. Especially celebrated among the instruments made by him were those made for the blind Parry, a famous Welsh harper.[472]

236. MINNESINGER'S HARP — Reproduction

A shallow quadrangular sound-box of spruce; the sound-board has four round sound-holes with inlaid ivory rosettes. Curved front pillar. Neck with twenty tuning pegs for gut strings; lower end of the strings fixed by round-headed buttons. Instruments of this type were used in Germany in the fifteenth century. Height, 61 cm. Sound-box, length, 46 cm.; width, upper end, 7.25 cm.; lower end, 9 cm.; sides, height, top, 2 cm.; bottom, 3.5 cm. Vibrating length of strings, shortest, 12.5 cm.; longest, 53 cm. (17.1784)

237. MINSTREL'S HARP — Flanders, 18th century

A shallow quadrangular sound-box with flat sound-board having six groups of small sound-holes. Straight front pillar with rounded inner surface. Gracefully curved neck having thirty-two tuning pegs for gut strings; lower end of strings held by L-headed wooden pins. Double purfling lines around edges. Height, 128 cm. Sound-box, length, 103 cm.; width, upper end, 10.5 cm.; lower end, 20.5 cm.; sides, height, top, 2.5 cm.; bottom, 4.5 cm. Vibrating length of strings, shortest, 13 cm.; longest, 77.5 cm. (17.1785)

238. HOOKED HARP — Germany, 18th century

Quadrangular sound-box of pine wood with two iron brackets on the lower back edge. Flat sound-board with six groups of sound-holes. Straight front pillar, rounded for three-quarters of its length; top part squared and carved with festoons on both sides. Carved, curved neck having thirty-five tuning pegs for gut strings and eleven hooks or crochets for raising a semitone the strings passing over them. The compass is from B to a^4 diatonically, the tones designated by the white painted letters on the neck. Height, 149 cm. Sound-box, length, 123 cm.; width, upper end, 10 cm.; lower end, 30 cm.; sides, height, top, 4 cm.; bottom, 12 cm. Vibrating length of strings, shortest, 10 cm.; longest, 133.5 cm. (17.1786)

The hooked harp was the first attempt in improving the slow method of re-tuning harps with the tuning key. This was accomplished by means of U-shaped hooks inserted into the neck near the C and F strings, and so located that turning of the hooks by hand would shorten the vibration length of the strings and set their pitch a semitone higher. Hooks were placed also near the B-strings, but the process was reversed. These strings were tuned to B-flat and the hooks were so set that the strings would give B-natural. For flatting of those tones the hooks were released. Although the hooked harp could be reset more quickly than the ordinary diatonic harp, yet each string had to be attended to individually and a player could not retune the instrument while playing.

This method was invented in the Tyrol in the second half of the seventeenth century.

239. HARP — France, 18th century, by Holz, Paris

Pedal, single action, in E-flat. Sound-box with flat sound-board of pine wood, body of seven panels of wood, painted black. Sound-board varnished light yellow-brown, decorated in the style of Vernis Martin with painted flowers, musical instruments, bucolic scenes. The neck ends in a large scroll ornamented with gilt gesso work and small painted medallions in the Chinese style. Straight front pillar, fluted and gilt. Thirty-eight gut strings. Pedal-box at the base of sound-box with seven pedals connected by rods within the front pillar to the hook mechanism and acting on the strings by drawing them over small bridge pins. Height, 160 cm. (18.30)

The single-action pedal mechanism was invented in the first quarter of the eighteenth century, ca. 1720. The invention is attributed to Hochbrucker, but this is disputed, and the names of Gaiffre, Simon, J. P. Vetter, and others are also mentioned.

By means of a single pedal the strings of the same tone in all octaves, say all F-strings, can be raised a semitone simultaneously and while playing. With seven pedals the harp could be tuned in many keys, but not rendered completely chromatic. Originally, single-action pedal harps were tuned in the key of E-flat. Later they were set in C-flat.

SUB-SECTION b: PLUCKED CHORDOPHONES WITH A NECK

PLUCKED chordophones with a neck comprise one of the most extensive groups of sound producers. The principal reason for attaching a neck to the resonating body of the instrument is the possibility of a convenient and positive control of the pitch variation of the strings by different methods of stopping. The left hand is usually employed for stopping the strings. The right hand is used for plucking the strings, either directly with the fingers or with a plectrum.[473]

The instruments themselves range from the most primitive ones, like the Russian peasant's *balalaika* (No. 241), to the most highly developed and musically effective, like the lute (No. 242).

Primitive

240. TANBOURICA — Croatia

A pear-shaped body carved out of a solid block of maple. Flat sound-board of soft pine, veneered in the upper part with pearwood; seventeen small sound-holes, one in the centre and four groups of four holes each. Long triangular-shaped neck. Two pairs of copper wire strings, lower-end fastening (two bosses projecting from the lower part of body); oaken inlay at the bottom preventing string from cutting into the soft sound-board. Low movable bridge, nut, wire guard for strings above the nut. Frontal type of string tuning end fastening, sagittal anterior pegs, inserted directly in the neck. Fourteen wire frets inserted in the neck; two short wire frets inserted in the sound-board. Length, total, 60 cm. Body, length, 17.8 cm.; width, 10.5 cm.; depth, 5.5 cm. Vibrating length of strings, 41.5 cm. (17.1757)
Plate VIII

The *Tanbourica*, as used by the Southern Slavs, belongs to a family of instruments similar to the Arabian-Persian *tanbur*. Its alternative name is *primasica*, or the first voice instrument in a choir.[474]

The tuning is:

241. BALALAIKA Russia, 19th century

Triangular body formed of six ribs of spruce with an inserted flat bottom. Sound-board of soft pine with circular sound-hole. Long neck without finger-board, five gut frets. Flat head placed at an angle, with three sagittal posterior pegs. Three gut strings, lower end fastening, low movable bridge, nut. Length, total, 63 cm. Body, length, 24 cm.; width, 31.5 cm.; depth, 8 cm. Vibrating length of strings, 44 cm. (17.1750)
Plate VIII

The *balalaika* is a Russian folk instrument of comparatively recent origin, ca. 1700. Its immediate predecessor was the *domrà*, an instrument of the *tanbur* class borrowed by the ancient Russians from their Oriental neighbors.[475] As the root word of its name implies (in Russian), it is something which no 'decent' person regarded seriously — just a foolish plaything. There are many derisive proverbs about the *balalaika* and its players, the main point of which is that only wastrels take any interest in it.

The instrument acquired a certain status of musical dignity only after a prominent amateur of Russian folk instruments, V. V. Andreiev, with the help of two Russian instrument makers, F. Passerbsky and S. I. Nalinov, developed a whole family of instruments ranging from piccolo to contrabass[476] out of their primitive and twangy prototype. By the brilliant performances, both in Russia and abroad, of his Russian National Balalaika Orchestra, V. V. Andreiev demonstrated that in the hands of musically trained virtuoso players the instrument deserves serious attention.

Some of the instruments were very tastefully decorated. The most prized balalaikas were those built in the craftsmen's shops of Princess M. K. Tenishev, in the village of Talashkino, Russia, and painted by M. A. Vrubel, the famous Russian painter.[477] The tuning of a balalaika of this size (treble) is:

Lutes

LUTES came to Europe from the Orient through the contact of Europeans with the Islamic civilization in Spain and Sicily. In the Orient the lute had already had a long and romantic history. It is this original impulse and the lute's subsequent history in Europe that always create in one's mind and emotions associations with something exquisite, poetical, and romantic, whenever the name 'lute' is mentioned.

Lutes held a very important place in the development of European music. Indeed, before keyboard and bowed string instruments came into general use, the organ and the lute were among the first instruments for which the oldest compositions were written.

At a certain period the lute was regarded as the most perfect of instruments. No musician's education was considered complete unless he knew how to play one. It was used for solo, accompaniment, and ensemble work, thus providing a foundation for both instrumental and accompanied vocal music. The time of its greatest usefulness can be dated from the fifteenth century. About 1600 the lute reached its zenith and then began to decline. In the

FIG. 36. A LUTE PLAYER

FRANCO-FLEMISH SCHOOL. SEVENTEENTH CENTURY

The painting is in the Museum of Fine Arts, Boston, Massachusetts.
No. 195 of the Museum *Bulletin* contains its description by Dr. George Harold Edgell.

second half of the eighteenth century, the rising popularity of the piano and the guitar caused its final disappearance.

A few words about the lute's Oriental predecessors are necessary. Lutes were introduced into Europe by the Arabs. The early Arabian pre-Islamic prototypes of lutes had skin-covered bellies. At the close of the sixth century the lute proper with the wooden belly (hence its Arabic name *al-'ūd*, 'wood') was introduced into Mecca from Al-Hira.[478] Later, the Persian lute (*'ūd farisi*) was adopted by the Arabs. There were, properly speaking, two distinct types of early lutes in Europe which came with the Arabs. In the *Cantigas de Santa Maria* these two types are still to be seen. One of them was the old type of lute, the *barbat*, which, it seems, was made in one graduated piece, with the neck organically connected to the body.[479] The second type, the *'ūd*, which gradually evolved into the 'classical' European lute of familiar shape, had a neck attached to the sound-box.

Al-Kindi (d. ca. 874) tells us that both the belly and back of the lute were made of thin wood, which should be of uniform thinness throughout.[480] The depth of the sound-box was half the width; the widest part of the belly was at the plucking place, which was about 6.75 cm. from the cross-bar. This plucking place was at the tenth part of the vibrating length of the string; hence the distance from the nut to the cross-bar was 74.25 cm.,[481] or about the size of the tenor-lute.

The *Ikhwan al-Safa'* (tenth century) gave the lute's proportions as follows: the length of the body of the lute should be twice its width, while its depth should be half of its width, and the neck one-quarter of its length.[482] A lute of approximately these proportions is represented in European art on the triptych of the Crowning of the Virgin Mary in Sant' Ansano in Florence.[483]

The classical form emerged about 1500. This transformation is credited to the German luthier, Laux Maller, who lived and worked in Bologna.

Typologically the European lute can be defined as a chordophone with a neck, having a bi-partite body with vaulted back and flat belly with a sound-hole (rose); strings held at the fixed end by the cross-bar attached to the belly (sound-board fastening); the frontal type of tuning end fastening with pegs of lateral type. A detailed description follows, point by point.

1. *Body*. The body of the lute was built up of separate ribs. Its shape was described by Thomas Mace as "the *Pearl-Mould*."[484] The number of ribs varied from nine to over thirty, but the best number was considered to be nine. These ribs were shaped and glued together on a wooden mould made in the shape of the internal space of the lute. They were affixed to a thin bottom block and to a large top block, to which the neck was attached later on. The rib joints were reinforced on the inside by strips of parchment or strong paper glued to them.[485] During the process of affixing the ribs together they were nailed at the bottom to the mould; the nails were withdrawn after the glue had set and dried. To conceal these nail-holes and to reinforce the bottom, a special reinforcing strip was glued on the outside, close to the sound-board.

Mace tells us that the materials for the lute ribs were the following (in order of their preference): "The *Air-wood* is absolutely the *Best*. And next to that, *Our English Maple*. But there are very *Good Lutes* of several *Woods*; as *Plum-Tree*, *Pear-Tree*, *Yew*, *Rosemary-Air*, *Ash*, *Ebony*, and *Ivory*, etc. The two last (though most *Costly*, and *Taking* to a common Eye) are the *worst*."[486]

2. *Belly*, or the sound-board, was made of a thin piece of fir, reinforced inside by six or seven slender cross-bars[487] glued to its back. The sound-hole or rose was cut in the sound-board in very beautiful and complicated patterns, seldom repeated.

Quoting Mace again:

Then for the *Bellies*, make choice of the *finest-grain'd Wood* you can, free from *Knots* or *Obstructions*, which you may easily perceive to hinder the *Grain* of the *Belly* for *Running smooth* to your *Eye*, as it were by small Strings or Threads of Wood from the *Bridge* upward, etc.

The *Best Wood* is call'd *Cullin-cliff*; and it is no other than the finest sort of *Firr*, and the choicest part of *That Firr*. I have seen some of *Cyprus very Good*, but none like the *Cullin-cliff*.[488]

The cross-bar was glued to the belly close to its lower end.

3. *Neck*. It was broad and thin, about one inch near the peg-box, gradually increasing in thickness as it approached the body. There was no separate finger-board; the front of the neck was faced with some hard wood, ebony preferably, flush with the sound-board.

Mace defines the length of the neck as follows:

And in the *Neck* observe the *Length* thereof, which you shall know to be *Good* or *Bad*, according to the *Number of Frets It* carries: If it carry less than *Nine*, it is *too short*; and if *more*, it is *too long*; Therefore *Nine* is esteemed the *Best Number* of a *True-siz'd Neck*.[489]

The nut was usually made of ivory, notched for the number of strings it had to carry; that varied considerably. Mace suggested keeping the outside strings "a little less than one quarter of an inch" away from the edges of the neck.

4. *Frets*. In olden times frets were made of gut strings tied on the necks of the instrument by a special fret-knot. Mace gives very thorough instructions for this operation. Since there is an ever-increasing interest in old music performed on contemporary instruments, and since Mace's book is rare and not readily accessible, we shall quote him at length. The instructions for fretting lutes are also applicable to viols, as Mace himself states; it is for this reason that they are of such importance.

The first point to be noticed (a point missed even by serious students) is that frets are of *unequal thickness*. In the following quotation, 'B Fret' is the first fret, the one closest to the nut. (See Fig. 37, p. 224.)

First, to chuse your *B Fret*, so *Thick* as well you may (according to the *Lying* of your *Nutt*, and *Strings*;) For the *Thicker That Fret* is, the more *easily* may you *fit* all the *Rest*: because that in *Fretting*, every next *Lower Fret*, would be some small matter *Smaller*, than the *next above*, (quite through.) Yet *This Rule* is *not* observed by *most*, who are *Careless*; so that oftentimes, their *Instrument Jarrs, and Sounds unpleasantly*.[490]

Affixing frets on the neck was not a simple operation. Attentive study of some old cuts shows that frets are represented by three closely spaced parallel lines, as for instance, Praetorius, plate v, figure 1. By these three lines artists represented double frets. The following quotation from Mace shows the traditional way of fretting both lutes and viols:

The Way to *Tye on a Fret* the *best way*, is Thus; viz. Your *Lute* standing (as it were) before you upon a *Table*, upon *Its Back*, take your *Fret*, and put *It double, under all the Strings*, beginning from the *Basses*, towards the Trebles; then (putting your *Left Hand* under the *Neck*) take *That Middle Double*, and draw it under the *Neck* towards the *Basses*, (holding fast the two *Ends* in your *Right Hand*) till you have brought them together, (viz. the *Middle Nooze*, and the *Two Ends.*)

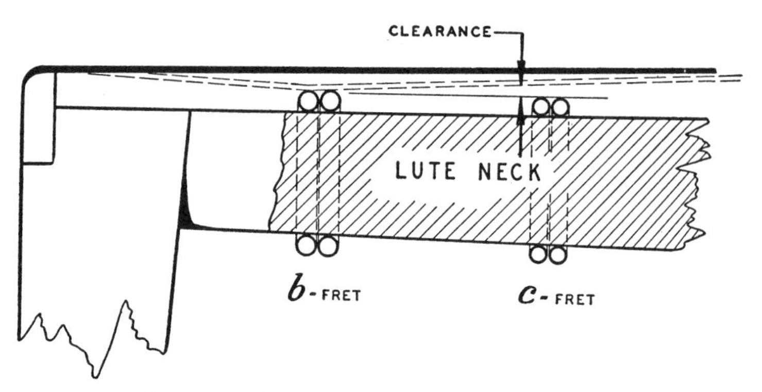

FIG. 37. DIAGRAM OF THE LUTE NECK,
SHOWING FRETS OF DECREASING DIAMETERS

Then take that End next you,[491] which you held in your *Right Hand*, and put it *through That Nooze*, so, that you make *another Nooze of that End*, and then let the *first Nooze go*.

Then again, take but the *other End*, which still remains in your *Right Hand, unused*, and put *It through your last Nooze*, taking the Ends, (in each hand one) *and let All else go*, and (only drawing them straight) your business of *Tying* is over.

This being done, (now comes the *Curiosity*, to *Stiffen, Fasten*, and *Fix This Fret*) I say, take the *Fret* (thus far fastned) and *draw It so close* (by both ends) as you can well, to *stiffen It to the Neck*; then, (holding *both Ends fast*, in your *Left Hand*) with your Right Hand and Left, *force It down so low* (towards *C. D. E. F.* etc.) as you can; then *put It up again* to the *Nutt*, where you'll find it much *too wide* or *slack*; therefore take the *Ends*, (in each hand *One*) and draw *It stiff, and close again*; then (as before) *down* with it, so low as you can, and *up again: Thus do it three or four times*, till at last you find it *stiff*, and so *fast*, that it will *scarce be stirr'd, to Its place of B.* (which is but a very little space).

But here Note, that at last, before you *force it down, to Its place* at *B.* you are (after all stretching) *to Tye it, of another hard Knot*, and then it is *firmly fast*.

And except you serve *This first Fret Thus*, you will always be *Troubled* with *It* in your *Play*.

And if you take notice of *most Lutes* and *Viols*, wheresoever you come, you will find *Them defective in This first Fret*, for want of such a *Care*, as *here* I have directed unto, which is a great *Inconvenience* to the *Instrument*, and the *Musick Thereof*.

I have been the longer about *This*, because I know *it so very Needfull*; and also have taught you to *Tye on All the other by This*; but they will all be *easier to stiffen* than *This*, because they all have more *Room upwards*, in the *Narrow of the Neck*, than *That* has; And besides, they being all *smaller siz'd Strings*, will the *more easily stretch, and ply*, to their *stiffness* and *closeness*.

There is a way which I have lately try'd, and I find it *much Better*, which is, to *Fret a Lute with single Strings*.

My Reason is, because it is not only *sooner done*, and with a *shorter String*; but *chiefly*, it does (assuredly) cause a *Clearer Sound* from the String stopt; which must be granted, if it be considered, that the *String lying* upon This only *Round single Fret*, cannot but *speak Clear*, when as (on the contrary) it lying upon *Two*, (as in the *Double Fret* it does) it cannot be thought to *speak so Clear*, because, that although it *Lye hard and close*, upon the *uppermost* of the *Two*, next the *Finger*, yet it cannot lye so very *close and hard*, upon the *undermost*; so that it must needs *Fuzz* a little, though not *easily discern'd*, and thereby, takes *off* something of *Its Clearness*, especially if the *Fret* be a *Thick-broad-Double-Fret*.[492]

The last paragraph is quoted for the benefit of those purists who insist that the frets should be tied on double.

The number of frets on lutes varied at different periods. But, as Mace states, a properly proportioned lute should have *nine* frets on the neck. On some instruments additional wooden frets were glued on to the sound-board, thus increasing the number of frets to thirteen.[493] But this is a later practice.

There is a very simple and practical procedure for spacing frets on the neck of fretted instruments. This procedure is as follows:

1. Measure exactly the vibrating length of the strings (i.e., between the nut and the bridge).

2. Divide this length into *eighteen* parts and place the first fret one-eighteenth part away from the nut.

3. Measure the distance from the first fret to the bridge; divide this shorter length again into eighteen parts and place the second fret one-eighteenth part away from the first fret.

4. Repeat the same operation with the remaining frets. As a result the frets will be spaced closer and closer as they recede from the nut. Figure 38 shows this very clearly and correctly, as can be ascertained by scaling. Frets placed according to this rule will give a scale very closely approaching the tempered scale.[494]

5. *Peg-box*. Peg-boxes on European lutes followed two Oriental prototypes. In the Orient peg-boxes were attached to the neck in two ways: (a) at an angle of 90°, or very close to it; this was done on both the *'ūd* and the *barbat* types; and (b) obliquely to the neck, as on the *kuwithra* type.[495] In both cases peg-boxes were placed backwards, away from the frontal plane of the instrument.

The principal reason for turning the peg-boxes backwards was to keep instruments in better balance. The bodies of the lutes were of such a flimsy construction that the weight of the neck, peg-box, and numerous pegs would overbalance it, if the peg-box were extended straight.

On later lutes a separate little box with a single peg was attached to the main box just above the nut. It accommodated the highest string, *chanterelle*, which was extremely thin, highly tensioned, and broke quite often.

6. *Strings*. The structural as well as the musical history of the lute could be written in terms of the number of strings. Their constant tendency was to increase in number.

In this connection it should be noted at once that the total number of strings has not corresponded to the similar number of tones.[496] With the exception of the *chanterelle* and sometimes the string next to it, the rest of the strings were doubled, forming a 'choir.' 'Choirs' were tuned either in unison or in octaves. 'Choirs' were also called 'courses.'

All these peculiarities are illustrated in Fig. 38. It represents a detail of an etching reproduced in full on page 234. The total number of strings on this lute is twenty. They are divided into three classes. Counting from the right side of the instrument (beginning with the topmost string), they are:

a. the bass strings; the total number is twelve; they are paired and produce six tones; each pair consists of a thick and a thin string, the thin one being tuned one octave higher than its mate (Nos. 11 to 6 on the tuning diagram).

b. the next six strings are also paired, producing three tones; they are of equal thickness in each pair and tuned in unison (Nos. 3, 4, 5, *ibid.*).

c. the last two strings are single and produce different tones; the extreme left string (the lowest in position on the picture) is the *chanterelle*, the highest tuned string on the lute. On the instrument represented a little separate peg-box is seen above the nut.

The reason for doubling was the increase of sonority and mellowness. Tuning of basses in octaves added a greater richness to the tones of the lower strings, since the fundamental frequency of each thick string was reinforced by its octave (which would be in unison with the second partial of the thick string).

This particular instrument would be tuned thus:

The total number of tones produced is, therefore, eleven, as each paired 'choir' or 'course' produced but one tone.

The number of strings on lutes varied at different periods. The earliest lutes had only four courses.[497] Such an instrument is represented on the relief by Giotto (ca. 1340) on the Campanile in Florence.[498] It has seven strings, three double and the highest single.

Five-course lutes (with nine or ten strings) are represented in the art of the middle of the fifteenth century. Early sixteenth century lutes had six courses (eleven strings). This number of courses can be regarded as the standard one for lutes.

The ever-increasing demands on lutenists for continuo accompaniments forced them to extend the compass of lutes. Finally bass lutes with additional peg-boxes mounted on their long necks and strung with very long bass strings (usually single) were developed. They were known as 'archlutes.' Our Collection has two representatives of this type: No. 243, the *Theorbo*, and No. 244, the *Chitarrone*. The number of strings on instruments of similar type increased to as many as twenty-six.

7. *The Lute Family.* On this point there exists very meager information. The difficulty is increased by the lack of data on the practices of the sixteenth century. Even if the music

Fig. 38. ENLARGED DETAIL OF CHARLES MOUTON'S LUTE

for lute consorts were available, this would not necessarily tell the whole story about the actual instruments or their varieties. Yet it would be, indeed, very strange if the lute should prove an exception to the rule during the period when various types of instruments were built in families.

Again we have to turn to Praetorius for information on the lute family. According to him, it consisted of seven members.[499]

All these tunings are built on the same pattern of intervals between the strings. Taking the tuning of the Alto Lute, G, c, f, a, d′, g′, as the standard, the intervals between the strings are as follows (counting from the highest pitched string downwards):

Between the highest and the 2nd strings, a fourth.
Between the 2nd and the 3rd strings, a fourth.
Between the 3rd and the 4th strings, a major third.
Between the 4th and the 5th strings, a fourth.
Between the 5th and the 6th strings, a fourth.

As will be seen later in connection with the tuning of viols, the same intervals were kept on six-stringed viols. On lutes with more than six strings, any additional strings were tuned diatonically as low down the scale as the number of strings on a given instrument permitted.

8. *Sizes of Lutes.* There is practically no information on this subject. Therefore it would be desirable to establish, at least approximately, what the different sizes of lutes were. The lutes found in the various collections of musical instruments are not always catalogued correctly; sometimes under the name 'lute' are listed instruments of widely varying sizes.

Praetorius in his *Theatrum Instrumentorum* gives the size of the *Chor Laute* (table xvi, fig. 3) as follows: body length, 44 cm.; body width, 31 cm. These dimensions are here scaled and translated into the metric system. (For particulars, see Appendix A.)

Accepting Praetorius' terminology as the basis and the size of the *Chor Laute* as the standard of comparison, it is possible to construct the following table of sizes of the various members of the lute family.[500]

SIZES OF LUTES

Nomenclature	Average Body Size (cm.)		Ratio W:L
	Width	Length	
1. Small Octave Lute[1]	13	21.5	.605
2. Small Treble Lute[2]	21	32.5	.645
3. Treble Lute	26	40	.650
4. Choirist or Alto Lute	29	44	.660
5. Tenor Lute	32	50	.640
6. Bass Lute (Theorbo)	36	56	.645
7. Great Octave Bass Lute (Chitarrone)	40	64	.625

1 Dimensions of lute no. C41 in the Kunsthistorisches Museum at Vienna. Cf. J. von Schlosser, *Sammlung Alter Musikinstrumente* (Vienna, 1920), p. 55, and table vi, fig. 41.

2 Based on the average of the sizes of two instruments: lute no. C39 in the Vienna Collection (*op. cit.*, p. 55), and lute no. 149 of the Berlin Collection (C. Sachs, *Sammlung Alter Musikinstrumente* (Berlin, 1922), p. 180).

There were certain mechanical defects in the construction of the lute. The large number of strings required constant attention and the instrument was difficult to keep in tune. Mattheson's often quoted sarcastic remark that if a lutenist succeeded in living eighty years, at least sixty were spent in tuning, seems not entirely unjustified when one examines the instruments. If lutes should return to favor, our modern mechanical proficiency could be applied to developing an efficient tuning mechanism without sacrificing the aesthetic value of the lute's shape and destroying the balance of the instrument.

Tablatures. The music for lutes was recorded in tablature notation, and not in the usual staff notation. Owing to the fact that the tablatures are difficult to decipher, very little is known of the extensive music heritage still preserved in Europe. Tablature notation consisted of lines corresponding to the number of strings on the lutes (usually six) upon which were noted not the tones, but the actual frets at which a given string had to be stopped. The frets were identified either by letters,[501] as in the English and French tablatures, or by figures, as in the Italian and Spanish ones.

The time values of different tones were designated by notes of the usual type above the tablature lines; these notes gave the rhythmic design of the piece and had no other significance. Completely developed tablatures were 'pricked,' i.e., they indicated by dots which particular finger should be used for plucking a given string. Bass notes were designated below the tablature lines by letters with diacritical marks, although the practice differed at various periods and in different countries.

The principal difficulty in deciphering tablatures is due to the great variety of tunings employed on lutes. If the tuning were given, then the matter of translating the tablature into staff notation would present no particular difficulties. But if the tunings were not given, then the time-consuming and patience-trying method of trial and error has to be used.

The advantage of tablature notation is that it shows the mechanics of stopping the instrument, and, since the composers were also the players, the pieces written for the lute were also conveniently performable. The disadvantage was that it did not give the absolute pitch of the tones recorded, and their musical value was limited to a certain type of instrument tuned and fretted in a given manner. For any other instrument the piece had to be translated into the usual notation.

The following tunings may be found useful by those who would like to play Dowland's accompaniments and Mace's lessons.

The 'Old English Tuning' used by John Dowland (1563–1626) and continued for the theorbo:

The 'Flat French Tuning' of the seventeenth century, which Thomas Mace preferred and used for most of his lute lessons:

The 'New French Tuning,' ca. 1636:

The lowest string is tuned to B-natural. Canon Galpin commented on this: "The B-natural is curious but correct."

For variations in the tuning of lutes special works should be consulted.[502]

Lute-Makers. The importance of the lute as the principal instrument of its own period can be judged by the fact that musical instrument-makers are still called 'luthiers.'

In the fifteenth century Ambrose Heinrich Helt (1414) of Nuremberg, Andres der Bildehouver (1427) of Strassburg and Hans Meisinger (1447) of Augsburg were known as fine lute-makers. At the turn of the century there worked in Bologna the most famous lute-maker of all times, Laux (Lucas) Maler or Maller (d. ca. 1528), known as 'a Stradivari of the lute.' Thomas Mace[503] tells us "... the *Chief Name* we most esteem, is *Laux Maler*, ever written with *Text Letters: Two* of which *Lutes* I have seen (pitiful *Old, Batter'd, Crack'd Things*) valued at 100 l. *apiece.* ... I have often seen *Lutes* of three or *four pounds* price, *far more Illustrious* and *Taking*, to a common Eye." To Laux Maller is credited the transformation of the lute from its Oriental prototype into the classical form of the Renaissance period.

A contemporary of Maller, also a very famous lute-maker, was Hans Frey (d. 1523) of Nuremberg, the father-in-law of Albrecht Dürer.[504]

In the sixteenth century may be mentioned Hans Newslider (1553), Georg Gerle (1569–1586) of Innsbruck, Wendelin Tieffenbrucker (Vendelino Venere) of Padua (d. ca. 1615) and Magnus Tieffenbrucker (d. ca. 1625) known as Magno Diffobruchar, of Venice. Of the French lute-makers, the names of Pierre Lejeune, Jehan Helmu, Philippe Flac, Pierre Le Camus, and Simon should be noted.[505]

In the seventeenth century among German and Italian lute-makers should be mentioned Mattheus Epp (b. ca. 1610) of Strassburg; Thomas Edlinger (ca. 1630–ca. 1690) of Augsburg; Joachim Tielke (1641–1719) of Hamburg, who deserves special mention as a consummate artist in building magnificently decorated instruments; Martin Hoffman (ca. 1650–ca. 1725) of Leipzig, the lute- and viol-maker. The Italian lute-makers were A. Cortaro, the brothers Rochi, G. Sella. French luthiers of the same period were Paul Belami (1612), Doué, praised by Huygens, Claude Colin, Estienne Flament, and Antoine Hudot, all of Paris.[506]

In the eighteenth century, before lutes went out of use, Johann Christian Hoffman (1683–1750), the son of Martin Hoffman and the personal friend of J. S. Bach, was building fine lutes. The archlute-makers were Storino (1725), an Italian; Jauck (1746), a German; and Laurent (1775), a Frenchman.

In the second half of the eighteenth century the lute became extinct.[507]

Thomas Mace's Directions for Playing the Lute

THOMAS MACE'S *Musick's Monument* contains the most interesting and important instruction for playing the lute. We are indebted to him for almost everything connected with the lute and lute playing. For this reason and because his book is one of the rarest works on the lute extant, an extensive quotation will prove of value for the student:[508]

... first set your self down against a *Table*, in as *Becoming a Posture*, as you would chuse to do for your *Best Reputation.*

Sit *Upright* and *Straight*; then take up your *Lute*, and lay the *Body of it* in your *Lap a-Cross*; Let the *Lower part* of *It* lye upon your *Right Thigh*; the *Head erected* against your *Left Shoulder and*

Ear; lay your *Left hand down upon the Table*, and your *Right Arm over the Lute*, so, that you may set your *Little Finger down upon the Belly of the Lute, just under the Bridge, against the Treble or Second String*; And then keep your *Lute stiff*, and *strongly set* with its *lower Edge* against the *Table-Edge*, and so (leaning your *Breast* something *Hard* against *Its Ribbs*) cause it to *stand steady and strong*, so, that a *By-stander, cannot easily draw it from your Breast, Table and Arm.*

This is the most *Becoming, Steady*, and *Beneficial Posture.*

The reason why I order your *Left Hand* to lye upon the *Table*, is for an especial *Great Benefit*; For if first you be thus able to manage the *holding of your Lute with One Hand*, the work will come *easily* on, because the work of the *Left Hand* is the *most Difficult*, and therefore must have *no hindrance*, or *impediment*, but must be *Free.*

And the holding of the *Lute Neck up with It*, (as very many do) takes away the *Chief Strength, Liberty* and *Activity* of *That Hand*; therefore *gain* but this *One Ability* at the *very first*, and it will give you *Ease*, and *Content* ever after, and enable you to do *that which others shall never be able to do*, who hold their *Lutes* by the *Labour* of the *Left Hand.*

This at first will *easily* be *gain'd*, but afterwards *not.*

The 2d. thing to be gain'd is, setting down your *Little Finger* upon the *Belly*, as aforesaid, *close under the Bridge*, about the first, *2d, 3d*, or *4th. Strings*; for thereabout, is its *constant station.*

It *steadies the Hand*, and gives a *Certainty* to the *Grasp.*

The 3d. thing is, (keeping all hitherto in *This Posture*) *span out your Thumb*, amongst the *Basses*, and lay the end of *It down*, upon which you please, but rather upon the *Last, Twelfth*, or *Greatest Bass*; and when you have thus made your *Span* or *Grasp*, view your *Posture* in all respects.

And First, mind if you sit *Comlily, Upright* and *Straight.* 2dly. If your *Lute* be not *sunk down, from its Exaltation*, with the *Heads.* 3dly. That you continue *It stiff, and steadily-strong*, against the *Table.* 4thly. That your *Left Hand*, remain still *upon the Table.* 5thly. That your *Little Finger*, be still *fixt under the Bridge.* 6thly. That your *Thumb End*, lye upon the *last Bass*; I mean the *End of your Thumb*, about *half an Inch* over the *last Bass*, and about *three or four Inches* above the *Bridge.* Lastly, That in *This posture of your Right-Hand, your Right-Hand Wrist, rise up, to a Convenient Roundness*; yet not *too much*, but only to an *Indifferency*, and to keep it from *Flatness*, or *Lying a long*, etc. . . .

And now, supposing you are *perfect* in your *Postures*, proceed to the *striking of a String*, the which first, shall be the *Twelfth*, (the String on which your *Thumb* lyeth.)

And as to that *Work*, it is only (first) keeping your *Thumb straight, and stiff*, and *gently pressing down that String*, (with an *easie strength*) so, as your *Thumb* may only *slip Over it*, viz. *That Pair*, (for you must know, that always the *Pairs* are struck together) and rest it self upon the *next* (or *Eleventh*) *String*, your *Thumb* then standing *ready*, to do the like to *That String*; and so from *String* to *String*, till you have serv'd all the row of *Basses* after the *same manner.*

And when you are able thus, to strike them *Forwards*, try to practise them *Backwards*, which will presently be done, and the *whole duty* (or *work*) of the *Thumb, quite finished.*

But *This* you must *remember*, viz. when ever you *strike a Bass*, be sure, you let your *Thumb rest it self*, upon the *next String*, and *There* let it *remain*, till you have *Use of It* elsewhere.

And this is the only way, *to draw from* a *Lute* (as we term it) the *sweetest Sound, that a Lute is able to yield*; which being perfected, you may conclude, *half the work of your Right Hand accomplished.*

The 4th. thing is, to teach you the *Use* of your *Fingers*, and is *Thus* done.

First, observing still, all your *former Postures carefully*, with your *Thumb* ever *resting* upon some one of the *Basses*, (where you please) put the *End* of your *second Finger*, a *very little* under the *Treble String*, (about three Inches above the *Bridge*) as if you did intend only to *feel your String*, having your *Fore-finger* (at the same time) *close adjoyning* in readiness, (yet not touching your *second Finger*, or the *String*;) then draw up your *second Finger*, from under the String, forcing the

String with a pritty *smart Twitch*, (yet gently too) to cause it to speak *strong* and *Loud*; the which, try to do several times, so long, till at last you perceive (by several ways of *Tryal*) you can draw a *sweet*, *smart*, and *pleasant Sound* from *That String*; and when that is done, strive to do the like with your *Fore-finger*, (your *second Finger* keeping the *same Posture* of *closeness* and *readiness*, as your *Fore-finger* kept.)

Then, try to *divide* your *strokes equally*, betwixt your *Fingers*; beginning first, with your *second Finger*, and then with your *first*: And so endeavour to strike the *Number of four strokes, equally and evenly*; ever observing to begin with the *second Finger*: at which *stroke*, you shall count *one*, then, with your *Fore-finger*, count *two*, your *second Finger* again, count *three*, and the *last*, with your *Fore-finger*, count *four*.

And *Thus* practice to count 1, 2, 3, 4, *often*; and *so long*, till you find you can do them *readily*, *equally*, and *evenly*; and never to *strike twice* together with the *same Finger*. . . .

But in the doing of *This*, take notice, that you *strike not your Strings with your Nails*, as some do, who maintain it the *Best way of Play*, but *I do not*; and for *This Reason*; because the *Nail* cannot *draw so sweet a Sound* from a *Lute*, as the *nibble end* of the *Flesh* can do.

I confess in a *Consort*, it might do well enough, where the *Mellowness* (which is the most *Excellent satisfaction* from a *Lute*) is *lost* in the *Crowd*; but *Alone*, I could never receive so *good Content* from the *Nail*, as from the *Flesh*: However (*This* being my *Opinion*) let *Others* do, as seems *Best to Themselves*.

And that you may learn to *strike a String Clear, and Clean*, take notice, that in *your stroke*, you strive to *draw your Finger a little Upwards*, and not *Slanting*, for that will *endanger* the *hitting* of *another String, together* with *That String*, you intend to Strike *Single*. This is called *Clean Striking*. . . .

And here suffer me to *Tautologize* a little, *viz*. Your *Left-Hand upon the Table; your Lute Firmly Fix'd*; *your self and It, in your True Postures*; and when (but) *This is done*, suppose *your self, half a Lute-Player*; For now you have *little, or nothing* to do more, besides the *bringing up, and ordering of your Left-Hand, and so to joyn their Forces both together*; which you shall presently, and very readily know how to do; as Thus, *viz*.

First, (keeping *your self* still in all your *Exact Postures*, before mentioned) bring *up your Left-Hand from the Table, bended, just like the Talents of a Hawk*; *All*, excepting your *Thumb*, which must stand *Strait*, and *Span'd out*; your *Fingers* also, *all divided* one from the other, in an *Equal*, and *Handsome Order*; and in *This Posture*, place your *Thumb* under the *Neck* of the *Lute*, a little above (B) *Frett*, just in the midst of the *Breadth of the Neck*: all your Four Fingers, in this Posture, being *held close over the Strings* on the *other side*, so that *each Finger*, may be in a *readiness to stop down upon any Frett*.

And now in *This Lively, And Exact Posture*, I would have *your Picture drawn*, which is the most *becoming Posture*, I can *Direct* unto, for a *Lutenist*; and is all I can think upon *Necessary*, as to *Preparation* for *Good Play*.[509] (See the next page.)

242. LUTE — Italy, 17th century

Pear-shaped body formed by two wide and twenty-three narrow fluted ribs of maple with inserted ebony spacers at the junction of the ribs. Adjoining the belly an outside body reinforcement, consisting of two narrow strips which gradually widen at the bottom into a wide, festoon-shaped, reinforcement piece; reddish-brown varnish on the back. Belly of unvarnished fir, decorated with ebony edging, and having a sound-hole with an inset rose of geometrical pattern with an ornamented edge. Front of neck veneered with ebony and inlaid ivory grotesques; back of neck inlaid with black and white herring-bone pattern. Head turned back and set at an angle of 76° to the front plane of the instrument; fourteen lateral pegs with inlaid ivory tips. Strings: seven pairs of gut unisons. Sound-board fixed end fastening; bridge of ebony with inlaid ivory strip;

FIG. 39. A LUTE PLAYER

frontal type tuning end fastening. Broad ivory nut. Nine gut frets. Length, 65 cm. Body, length, 40 cm.; width, 29.75 cm.; depth, 14 cm. Vibrating length of strings, 55.6 cm. (17.1763)
Plate IX and Fig. 40, p. 237

This instrument should be classified as a treble lute (see the table of lute sizes, p. 229).

The stringing is peculiar in that the chanterelle is doubled and tuned in unison as the ordinary courses.

The tuning:

243. THEORBO Italy, 1589, by Magnus Tieffenbrucker

Pear-shaped body formed by eleven broad, slightly convex ribs; inlaid on edge, with a reinforcing piece at the bottom. Sound-board of fir with three geometrically patterned roses. Front of neck veneered with ebony, inlaid with simple trapezoidal figures of cypress wood; back of neck inlaid along its whole length in parallel lines of the same material. Attached to the neck is a lower peg-box with fourteen lateral pegs for unisons. It is set at a very slight angle to the front plane of the instrument and extends upward, supporting the upper peg-box with six lateral pegs for diapasons. Strings: seven pairs of unisons and six diapasons; sound-board fixed end fastening for all strings; frontal type tuning end fastening. Unisons are carried over the notched ivory nut to the tuning pegs in the lower peg-box, diapasons (single) do likewise over the off-set nut inserted in the upper peg-box. Nine gut frets. Label inside, written in large Gothic letters, reads:

'Magn(o?) Diffobruchar
a Venecia 1589'

Length, total, 135.75 cm. Body, length, 52.5 cm.; width, 34 cm.; depth, 13 cm. Vibrating length of strings, unisons, 71.8 cm.; diapasons, 111.3 cm. (17.1764)
Plate IX

1. 'Magno Diffobruchar's' correct name is Magnus Tieffenbrucker. There were two members of this distinguished family of lute- and violin-makers of the same name. The maker of our instrument, designated as Junior (but not necessarily the son of the elder Magnus), worked in Italy between 1589 and 1621.[510] Therefore our instrument, dated 1589, is one of his earliest.

244. CHITARRONE Venice, Italy, 17th century

Pear-shaped body, formed of two wide and twenty-seven narrow fluted ribs of maple with inserted ebony spacers at the junction of the strips. Edge reinforcement similar to No. 242. Reddish-brown varnish on the back of body. Belly of unvarnished fir with ebony lace. Sound-hole covered with parchment rose surrounded by a wide inlaid ebony and pearl border, with small garnets inserted in the centre of pearl inlays. Pearl medallion at bottom with image of a saint; there are traces of painted color (red and green) on this medallion. Front of neck veneered with ebony and inlaid with medallions and grotesques. Upper part above the neck probably restored. Two peg-boxes, the lower with eleven, and the upper with seven pegs. The upper peg-box is supported on

the long neck extension and the necessary clearance for the diapasons is provided by the slight backward inclination of the neck extension. Strings: five pairs of unisons and a chanterelle, and seven diapasons; sound-board fixed end fastening for all strings; ivory nut for unisons, off-set ivory nut for diapasons. Eight gut frets. Length, total, 193.75 cm. Body, length, 63 cm.; width, 41 cm.; depth, 16 cm. Neck, length, 30 cm. Neck extension, length, total, 100.75 cm. Vibrating length of strings, unisons, 78.7 cm.; diapasons, 161.3 cm. (17.1765)
Plate IX and Fig. 41, p. 237

The theorbo and chitarrone served as bass instruments of the lute family. Their tuning shows the register in which they worked. The theorbo was tuned:

No. 243. THEORBO TUNING

Six diapasons of the theorbo were tuned diatonically and played open, without stopping. Seven unisons were tuned the same way as the 'seven course' alto lute. The chitarrone was tuned as follows:

No. 244. CHITARRONE TUNING

Two points should be noted. The downward compass of the chitarrone No. 244 is the same as that of the theorbo. The two first strings (chanterelle and the second one) are tuned to the same tones as the alto lute, but an octave lower, a practice much disapproved of by Mace.

Both the theorbo and chitarrone are 'continuo' instruments. Mace tells us:

> . . . the *Theorboe-Lute is Principally us'd in Playing to the Voice, or in Consort* . . .; [it has] only the *Ground, or Bass, Chiefly to Act in*, which is (in *All Consorts*, or what *Generally is made*) the *Slowest Part of Motion*. . . .[511]

Commenting upon the long diapasons, Mace called them "*Great Inconveniences*" in any quick movements.

> For if you meet with a *Lesson* which runs much with *Quick-Proportion'd Time*, upon *Those Long Basses*; you will find *That Great Inconvenience* before mentioned; which is, That the *Former-Struck-Bass* will *Sound so Strong, and so Long, that the next immediately following, will be so harsh*, (*they Two Snarling together as I may say*) *that it will be as Bad, as False Dischording-Composition, and very Confounding*.[512]

A definite reference to the use of the chitarrone as an orchestral instrument is seen in the fact that Monteverdi used several of them at the performance of his opera *Orfeo* in 1607.[513]

FIG. 40. LUTE
(No. 242)

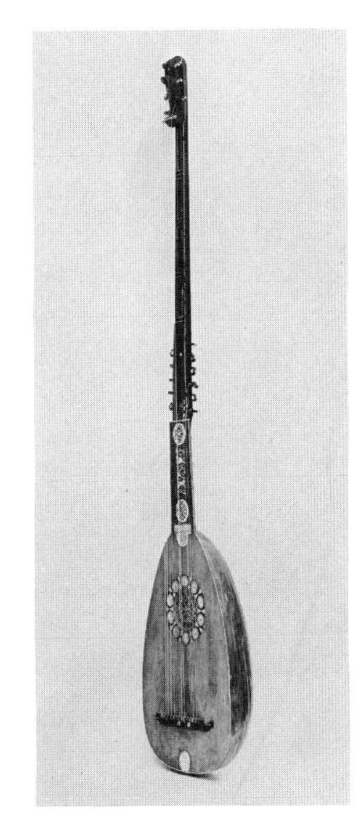

FIG. 41. CHITARRONE
(No. 244)

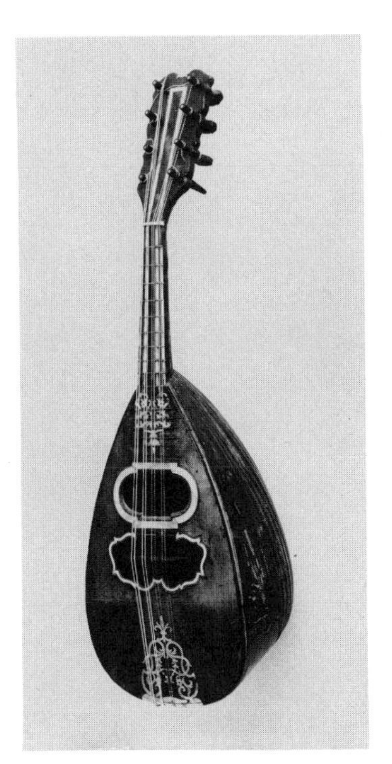

FIG. 42. MANDOLINE
(No. 248)

FIG. 43. CITTERN, OR ENGLISH
GUITAR (No. 251)

Instruments of the Lute Type

245. PANDURINA — Italy, 1756 (?), by M. A. Bergonzi

Small pear-shaped body formed of eleven ebony ribs with ivory spacers at junction of ribs. Reinforcement piece at the bottom. Sound-board of unvarnished fir with rose, inlaid at edges and around sound-hole with ivory and ebony. Front of neck veneered with engraved ivory with nine inlaid frets of ebony; back of neck inlaid with ivory strips. Peg-box, with ten lateral pegs, is carved out of the same piece as the neck; it has at the back an inlaid carved ivory piece; incurved end with a carved grotesque mask. Strings: five pairs of unisons: sound-board fixed end fastening; ivory tipped bridge; frontal type tuning end fastening. Length, total, 53 cm. Body, length, 23.5 cm.; width, 14.75 cm.; depth, 8.5 cm. Vibrating length of strings, 28.7 cm. (17.1761)
Plate IX

246. MANDORA — Belgium, 1771

Pear-shaped body, formed of fifteen ribs of maple varnished deep red-brown. Reinforcement plate at the bottom. Sound-board of pine with rose. Short neck with inlaid ivory edges and traces of six frets. Peg-box, with twelve lateral pegs, curved back ending in a re-curved head inlaid with ivory. Strings: three pairs of gut and three pairs of spun strings; sound-board fixed end fastening; ivory inlaid bridge; ivory nut; frontal type tuning end fastening. Label inside, very faint, reads in part: 'Fait par . . . à Liège, l'an 1771.' Length, total, 57.5 cm. Body, length, 27 cm.; width, 17.5 cm.; depth, 8.5 cm. Vibrating length of strings, 31.5 cm. (17.1762)
Plate IX

The pandurina and mandora, although regarded as belonging to the lute type, were evolved not from the *'ūd*, but from another Oriental instrument, the *qūpūz*.[514] The essential structural difference between them is that in the lute type the neck is attached to the body, while in instruments of the *qūpūz* type the neck is an organic continuation of the body.[515]

There is a confusion of the terms 'mandora' and 'mandola.' In this study the term mandora designates a descendant of the *qūpūz* type; whereas the 'mandola' belongs to the mandoline family. The essential typological difference between the two is that the mandora group of instruments has gut strings of the sound-board fastening type; the mandoline group has wire strings of the lower end fastening type.[516]

247. MILANESE MANDOLINE — Genoa, Italy, 19th century

Pear-shaped body, formed of eleven ribs of alternating dark (palisandre) and light (maple) wood. Thin ornamental reinforcing plate at the bottom. Sound-board of fir with edge inlaid black and white; reinforced inside with two cross-bars; open oval sound-hole with decorations around it. Ebony finger-board with nineteen metal frets. Peg-box, integral with neck, six lateral pegs; head carved in flower and two leaves. Strings: three gut and three spun-silk strings; sound-board fixed end fastening; ebony bridge. Length, total, 57 cm. Body, length, 29.75 cm.; width, 20.75 cm.; depth, 10.5 cm. Vibrating length of strings, 30 cm. (17.1759)
Plate IX

The Milanese mandoline has nothing to do with the real mandolins except in name. Its ancestors are instruments of the mandora type. It appeared in the seventeenth century.

Originally it had six pairs of unisons, but in the eighteenth century it was single strung. Played without a plectrum.

248. MANDOLINE Naples, Italy, 1790

Neapolitan type. Deep pear-shaped body, made of two broad, wedge-shaped pieces and twenty-seven narrow, slightly concave ribs of maple. Very broad reinforcement plate at the bottom. Dark brown varnish. Sound-board of varnished pine, lower third bent slightly backwards; decorated with inlaid mother-of-pearl and tortoise-shell designs at the top and bottom. Oblong sound-hole (open) with pearl decorated edge. Below sound-hole, ornamental tortoise-shell plate for the ebony bridge. Neck veneered with tortoise-shell and pearl. Peg-plate bent back, decorated likewise; has six sagittal posterior pegs. Strings: four double metal strings, lower end fastening (four ivory buttons). Seventeen metal frets, inserted in the neck (ten) and in the sound-board. Label inside reads:

'Gio : Battista Fabricatore fecit
An. : 1790. in. S. M. dell'Ajuto
Napoli'

Length, total, 57 cm. Body, length, 28.5 cm.; width, 17.75 cm.; depth, 14 cm. Vibrating length of strings, 30 cm. (17.1758)
Fig. 42, p. 237

249. MANDOLA Italy, 17th century

Tenor mandoline. Pear-shaped body, formed of seventeen ribs of alternating light (maple) and dark (palisandre) wood. Wide reinforcement piece at the bottom. Sound-board of soft pine has sound-hole with edge of pearl inlay and is covered by a geometrical rose; top and bottom decorated with pearls. Below sound-hole of tortoise-shell, plate edged with thin ebony strips and wide ivory inlay for protecting sound-board from plectrum scratches. Front of neck inlaid with ebony and ivory strips. Back of neck and of peg-box inlaid with strips of ebony and ivory. Peg-box with twelve lateral pegs bent gracefully backward; square head with pearl and ebony inlay. Strings: six pairs of metal strings (the first three of brass, the last three of steel; lowest string spun, lower end fastening, ivory buttons); passing over ivory bottom saddle; ivory-tipped movable bridge and ivory nut; thirteen metal frets, six of which are on the sound-board. Length, total, 76.5 cm. Body, length, 40 cm.; width, 28 cm.; depth, 14.5 cm. Vibrating length of strings, 44.7 cm. (17.1760)

Citterns

THE *Cittern* is a pear-shaped instrument with vertical ribs and flat back. The strings are of metal, of the lower end fastening type attached by a looped end to the buttons or knobs in the bottom, and pass over the movable bridge and the nut. The tuning end fastenings are of the frontal type, but the mechanisms to which the strings are attached vary. The strings are strung in pairs and played either with plectrum or simply by the fingers.

The instrument was known during the Middle Ages.[517] Dr. Curt Sachs is of the opinion that the mediaeval cittern, or citole, was developed from the fiedel of the tenth to twelfth centuries.[518] The number of paired strings varies from four to six; larger sized ones had as many as fourteen paired strings.

The instruments of this Collection are of the eighteenth century, built when the cittern was known as the *English guitar* and was at the height of its popularity.

250. ENGLISH GUITAR England, 18th century, by J. Preston

Cittern. Pear-shaped body of red-brown varnished maple. Sound-board with rose; round sound-hole surrounded by yellow lines. Vertical ribs, back flat except the upper part, which inclines toward the neck. Ebony finger-board with twelve brass frets and four holes for the capotasto. The peg-box of the usual type is replaced by Preston's 'machine.' The neck ends with scroll bent backward to provide clearance for the tuning-key and is surmounted by a small head. Strings: six courses, two lower ones of spun wire and four higher ones of steel in pairs, making ten strings altogether; lower end fastening (small brass pins in the bottom); shallow movable bridge, ivory nut; frontal type tuning end fastening; looped ends of strings attached to movable hooks. The machines engraved 'Preston, Inventor,' and the letters C, E, G, C, E, G, giving the tuning of the strings. The back of the neck is stamped with the monogram 'J.R.P.' and 'Preston, Maker.' Length, total, 69 cm. Body, length, 33.75 cm.; width, 29 cm. Ribs, height, 7.2 cm. Vibrating length of strings, 44 cm. (17.1747)
Plate IX

251. ENGLISH GUITAR England, 18th century, by Lucas, London

Cittern. Shallow, flat body of curved outline. Back and ribs of maple, sound-board of soft pine. Sound-hole covered with a stamped brass rose with musical instruments interwoven in the pattern. Dark brown varnish. Finger-board of stained boxwood, ornamented with engraved pearl and ebony inlays, with fifteen brass frets; four holes for the capotasto. Head has Preston's machine with ten hooks; scroll with square ivory and pearl inlaid end. Strings: five pairs of metal strings, lower end fastening (ivory buttons in the bottom). Ivory tipped bridge, ebony nut. Label inside, much glued over and only partly readable:

'Lucas . . .
Guitar and . . .
Golden Square, London'

Length, total, 67.5 cm. Body, length, 32 cm.; width, 29.75 cm. Ribs, height, 7.5 cm. Vibrating length of strings, 41 cm. (17.1746)
Plate IX and Fig. 43, p. 237

252. PORTUGUESE GUITAR Portugal, late 19th century, by José Paulo Ferreira, Lisbon

Cittern. Shallow body with flat back and ribs made of beechwood; sound-board of soft pine with inlaid edge and sound-hole surrounded by inlaid circles. Finger-board of hard wood with seventeen brass frets. Head with a machine similar to Preston's, but with the screws disposed fan-wise and having knurled knobs for adjustment; scrolled ends. Strings: six pairs of metal strings, lower end fastening (twelve pegs screwed into an ornamental brass plate at the bottom); ivory bridge with wooden lining below, ivory nut; frontal type tuning end fastening (looped ends attached to the hooks of the machine). Body reinforced inside with wide linings, cross-bars on the back and on the sound-board. The instrument throughout is constructed with unusual solidity. Printed label inside. Length, total, 68 cm. Body, length, 31 cm.; width, 28.5 cm. Ribs, height, 6–7.5 cm. Vibrating length of strings, 41.8 cm. (17.1800)

253. SYRON London, England, 1757

Archcither, Archicistre. Large form of the English guitar. Deep body of curved outline, with flat back and ribs of maple. Sound-board of spruce, tapered back in its lower part; sound-hole covered with a rose. Finger-board of ebony with thirteen brass frets; three five-pointed stars of inlaid ivory. Head consists of two peg-boxes, the lower one with eleven lateral pegs and the upper one with five lateral pegs. Strings: all strings of the lower end fastening type; five metal unisons and one single are attached to the ivory buttons at the bottom and pass over the ivory saddle; five metal diapasons are attached to the brass screws in the bottom. Wide ivory-tipped ebony bridge; ebony nut for unisons and ivory nut for diapasons. Label inside:

'REMERUS LIESSEM
fecit Londini 1757.'

Stamped on the back: 'R. Liessem.' Length, total, 89.5 cm. Body, length, 35.5 cm.; width, 31 cm. Ribs, depth, 8.75 cm. Vibrating length of strings, unisons, 43 cm.; diapasons, 63.3 cm. (17.1749)
Plate IX

Guitars

THE *Guitar* is distinguished by its flat, high-ribbed body, with gracefully incurved sides and round sound-hole; fretted neck; flat peg-board, tilted slightly backward, with sagittal posterior pegs; strings, originally all of gut, are of the sound-board fastening type at the fixed ends, and frontal fastening type at the tuning ends. The guitar is played by hand, without a plectrum.[519]

The origin of the guitar has not been ascertained. It is known that there are guitar-like instruments on the Egyptian and Hittite monuments.[520] Here the chain breaks. In mediaeval Spain the guitar reappeared and developed as an indigenous instrument. At least, contemporary writers discriminate between *guitarra latina* and *guitarra morisca*,[521] or the Latin guitar of familiar shape and the Moorish guitar with the lute-like, pear-shaped body and long neck.

The Spanish guitar appears to have evolved from the *vihuela*. There were three kinds of *vihuelas*: [522] (1) *vihuela da arco*, or bowed vihuela, an important link in the evolution of the viol, (2) *vihuela da mano*, or the vihuela played by hand, from which evolved our modern guitar, and (3) *vihuela da peñola*, or the vihuela played with a quill, or plectrum, a probable ancestor of the *chitarra battente*, No. 258.

The number of strings on the guitar varied at different periods. The old guitars were double-strung. In the middle of the eighteenth century they became single-strung.[523]

More specifically, the number of strings on guitars varied from four to seven. There is no definite sequence of increase in the number of strings as time goes on. Thus in the middle of the sixteenth century there were four-, five-, six-, and seven-stringed guitars.[524] The most persistent type was the five-stringed Spanish guitar, which can be regarded as the standard type for certain periods.

It often happened that some people, not knowing the historical facts, 'improved' guitars by adding more strings, and thought of themselves as innovators. Thus J. A. Otto, an instrument maker in Weimar, added a sixth string to the guitar upon the request of J. G. Naumann, ca. 1800.[525] Since then the six-stringed guitar has become the standard. The seven-stringed instruments became the accepted type in Russia after Andrei Osipovich Sykhra, the harp virtuoso of Vilna, reintroduced this number of strings in the last decade of the eighteenth century. His enthusiasm and skill in playing were responsible for the wave of popularity of seven-stringed guitars in Russia in the early nineteenth century.[526]

254. GUITAR Portugal, late 19th century, by Jeronymo José Dos Santos, Lisbon

Treble. Small flat body with incurved sides, made of artificially mottled wood. Sound-board of pine with a round open sound-hole. Finger-board of walnut with seventeen brass frets. Peg-board integral with neck, veneered in front, with four sagittal posterior pegs. Strings: four strings, two gut and two spun silk, sound-board fastening type (buttons). Ebony bridge. Printed label inside. Length, total, 46 cm. Body, length, 21 cm.; width, 12 cm. Ribs, height, 3.5 cm. Vibrating length of strings, 30.3 cm. (17.1751)
Plate IX

The treble guitar is called the *machête de braço*, also the *requinta* in Portugal.

255. GUITAR Italy, 1785, by Carlo Bergonzi, Cremona

Alto. Flat body with incurved sides, back and ribs of maple varnished light yellow. Sound-board of spruce with open round sound-hole encircled by ebony and pearl inlay; black edge and guard plate. Finger-board of ebony let into the neck flush with the sound-board, with seven brass frets; seven frets of whale-bone glued to the sound-board. Peg-board curved in outline with six sagittal posterior pegs; made of pear-wood; tilted back slightly. Strings: six strings, three gut, three spun silk, sound-board fastening type (fixed ends made fast by loops threaded through the holes in the bridge projection). Ebony bridge with ornamental ends. Ivory nut. Label, inside, reads:

'Carlo Bergonzi fece
in Cremona l'anno 1785.'

Length, total, 53.75 cm. Body, length, 29 cm.; width, 21.75 cm. Ribs, height, 5.75 cm. Vibrating length of strings, 30.5 cm. (17.1752)
Plate IX and Fig. 44, p. 243

Carlo Bergonzi II (d. 1820), the third son of Michel Angiolo Bergonzi, was a mandolin and guitar maker and repairer. The instrument is also called *guitarino*, or small guitar.

256. GUITAR France, ca. 1800, by J. B. Champion, Paris

Flat body with incurved sides, back and ribs of stained walnut. Sound-board of lightly stained pine, edged with ebony and ivory inlay. It extends for 3.75 cm. over the neck. Round sound-hole covered with parchment rose, with ebony and ivory inlay at the edge, encircled by thin concentric alternating strips of ivory and walnut. Neck veneered with walnut in front, flush with the sound-board. Twelve gut string frets. Peg-board curved in outline and slightly tilted back; ten sagittal posterior ivory pegs. Strings: five pairs of unisons (gut), sound-board fastening type (loops). Walnut bridge with ornamental ends of ebony. Ivory nut. Very fine instrument with soft, rich tone. Peg-board is stamped on the front and back: 'CHAMPION.' Length, total, 92 cm. Body, length, 44 cm.; width, 27 cm. Ribs, height, 9 cm. Vibrating length of strings, 64.3 cm. (17.1753)
Plate IX and Fig. 45, p. 243

FIG. 44. GUITARINO, OR ALTO GUITAR (No. 255)

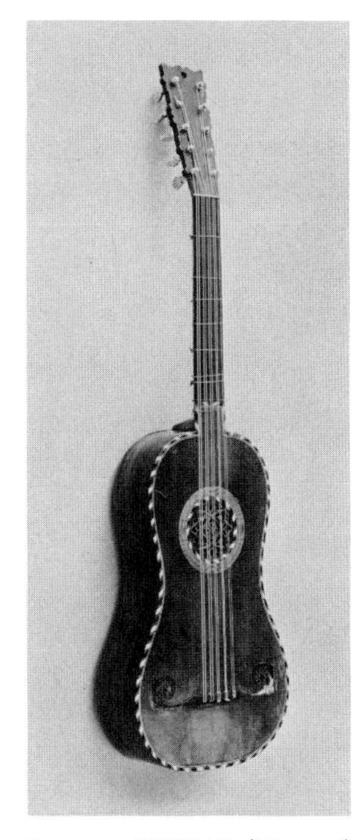

FIG. 45. GUITAR (No. 256)
By Champion

FIG. 46. CHITARRA BATTENTE (No. 258)

FIG. 47. HARP-LUTE (No. 262)

Jean Baptiste Champion (1783–1808), of Paris, probably the son of René Champion de St.-Julien.[527] Credited with adding the sixth string to the guitar.

Five-course guitars were tuned:

257. GUITAR France, ca. 1800

Flat body with incurved sides, back and ribs of stained and varnished walnut. Sound-board of soft pine varnished yellow-brown, with inlaid edge; open round sound-hole encircled with pearl and dark wood inlay. Finger-board of walnut, with seventeen brass frets. Peg-board slightly tilted back, with six sagittal posterior pegs. Strings: six in number; three gut, three spun silk, sound-board fastening type (ebony buttons). Ebony bridge with ivory inlay. Ebony nut. Length, 93 cm. Body, length, 45 cm.; width, 28 cm. Ribs, height, 8.5 cm. Vibrating length of strings, 63.4 cm. (17.1754)
Plate IX

This is the tuning of the 'standard' six-stringed instrument.[528]

258. CHITARRA BATTENTE Italy, 17th century

A guitar played ('struck') with a plectrum. Deep body with incurved sides and convex back. Each rib made of one wide and six narrow strips of walnut, separated by inserted thin spacers of light wood. Back consists of twelve strips extending the whole length and of shorter strips on the bouts, all of walnut, also separated by thin spacers of light wood. Sound-board of pine, bent slightly back below the bridge and extended into the neck about four cm. Finger-board of stained walnut let into the neck flush with the sound-board. Nine brass frets, and five wooden frets glued to the sound-board. Peg-board is curved in outline, integral with neck, bent slightly backward, and veneered with walnut and lemon-wood; ten sagittal posterior pegs of boxwood. Strings: five-course steel wire strings, lower end fastening type (ivory buttons, one for each unison pair); ebony bridge with thin ivory insert; ivory nut.

The outstanding decorative feature of this instrument is the sound-hole. It is circular in shape, with edge inlaid with mother-of-pearl and ebony; it is covered with four-tiered deep rose of intricate design, with a sunburst in the centre and a small garnet on the top of it. Faint traces of gilding and red are still visible. A sonorous, rich-toned instrument. Length, total, 79 cm. Body, length, 39.25 cm.; width, 22.5 cm. Ribs, height, top, 8 cm.; middle, 12 cm.; bottom, 7.5 cm. Distance from sound-board to back, max., 15 cm. Vibrating length of strings, 48.4 cm. (17.1756)
Plate IX and Fig. 46, p. 243

The *chitarra battente* differs from the ordinary guitar in the following points: 1. It is played with a plectrum, not plucked by hand. 2. Its back is convex, comprising a part of an ovoidal surface. 3. The ribs are deeper in the middle bouts, owing to the convexity of the back. 4. The strings are of steel wire, of the lower end fastening type. In the ordinary guitar they are of gut and spun silk, of the sound-board fastening type. 5. It has a real bridge, with a definite cut-off point for each string. The bridge of ordinary guitars is of two types: (a) on the older type of instrument it is really a cross-bar glued to the sound-board; the strings are fastened by a special loop as on the lutes (see No. 256, p. 242); (b) on the later type (such as No. 257, p. 244) the cross-bar serves a double purpose, that of the string fastener (strings held by pins) and the bridge proper. The cut-off point for the string on this double-purpose bar was provided either by a sharp upper lip extending from the cross-bar or by an inserted narrow ivory strip. Historically, as has been pointed out already, the *chitarra battente* probably is a descendant of the *vihuela da peñola* of Spain.

259. LYRE-GUITAR — France, early 20th century

Flat tapering body similar in shape to the ancient lyre. Sound-box mounted on flat rectangular base of mahogany; back and ribs of polished mahogany. Sound-board of spruce with two fretted sound-holes; ornamented at edges with inlaid ebony purfling. Neck of mahogany; ebony finger-board with thirteen brass frets. Head with six sagittal posterior pegs; the two horns of the body and head are braced together by brass rods with ornamental acorn ends. Strings: three gut and three spun silk, sound-board fastening type (buttons with inlaid pearl heads). Ebony bridge, ivory nut. Length, total, 78 cm. Body, length, 37 cm.; width, 33.5 cm. Thickness, 11 cm. Vibrating length of strings, 60 cm. (17.1768)

260. HARPOLYRE — France, ca. 1820

Three-necked guitar. Guitar-shaped body (in lower part) with slightly curved back of polished mahogany. Ribs of mahogany. Sound-board of pine; three sound-holes with marquetry inlay around the edges. The upper part of the body has three extensions, to which are affixed three necks, the middle one being shorter than the side necks. Head-board, veneered with mahogany on both sides, slightly inclined with respect to the necks, of ornamental arched outline with worm and worm-wheel peg adjusting mechanism fixed at the back, ends of pegs passing through clearance holes and extending in front about 15 cm. Right-hand and left-hand necks have finger-boards flush with sound-board and are furnished with fifteen brass frets each. The middle finger-board extends over the sound-board almost to the sound-hole and has nineteen frets. Strings: sound-board fastening type; three groups fastened by buttons to a long ebony cross-bar with three ivory bridges inserted in it; three ivory nuts in their respective necks. Number of strings: right-hand neck, eight spun silk; middle neck, three gut, three spun silk; left-hand neck, seven spun silk. Short steel rest at bottom. Length, total, 102 cm. Body, length, 44 cm.; width, 43.25 cm. Ribs, average height, 10 cm. Vibrating length of strings, right-hand and left-hand, 70 cm.; middle, 62.3 cm. (17.1755)

261. HARP-LUTE-GUITAR — England, early 19th century, by A. Barry, London

Triangular-shaped body with rounded bottom; composed of seven ribs; the middle rib approximately twice as wide as the rest, with narrow sound-hole. Flat sound-board with fretted sound-box. Broad finger-board varnished black with twelve thin ivory frets. Neck and two peg-boxes carved entirely out of one piece of maple, with clearance for the left-hand thumb provided by carving the back of neck thinner on the right-hand side. Lower peg-box with seven lateral pegs is slightly inclined toward back; upper peg-box, also inclined, is brought slightly forward for proper alignment of diapasons. Strings: seven melody (three gut and four spun silk) and four diapasons, sound-board fastening type (looped ends threaded through holes in the cross-bar). Ivory nuts in

each peg-box. Body and sound-board varnished light chocolate-brown with a greenish tint. Sound-board decorated with gilt laurel wreath with ribbon end inscribed: '*LIGHT INVR. BARRY MAKER.*' Length, total, 93.5 cm. Body, length, 44.75 cm.; width, 35.5 cm.; thickness, 15.5 cm. Vibrating length of strings, open, 62.6 cm.; stopped, 44.5 cm. (17.1770)
Plate VIII

This instrument and the one following are the invention of Edward Light (ca. 1747–ca. 1832), the organist of Trinity Chapel, St. George's, Hanover Square, London. Light himself made no instruments. They were made for him by A. Barry of 18 Firth Street, Soho, London.[529]

The harp-lute-guitar, as its name shows, is a hybrid instrument, combining the features of the harp, lute (theorbo), and, to a lesser degree, those of the guitar. Its tuning was in E-flat major (i.e. in the tonality of the old single action pedal harp):

written nominally in C-major, treble clef (i.e., major sixth higher):

This tuning was used for solo playing. When played with the piano, the instrument was tuned in D-major; the accompaniment on the piano had to be written one tone higher, since the piano is in C. Thus, if a piece for the harp-lute-guitar was in C, the accompaniment had to be in D, etc.[530]

The strings used on the instrument were the same type as those used on the harp, C and F being colored red and blue (or black), respectively.[531]

The tone is full, rich, and mellow. With mechanical improvements of construction, instruments of this type could be made musically useful, since their tone is superior to that of the guitar.

262. HARP-LUTE England, ca. 1810, probably by A. Barry, London

Trapeze-shaped body with rounded bottom; composed of seven ribs; the middle rib twice as wide as the rest, with narrow sound-hole. Flat sound-board, round sound-hole with gilt cross and rays. Short neck with clearance for left-hand thumb similar to that of No. 261; surmounted by harmonic curve; thin pillar bracing the harmonic curve. Short finger-board with three ivory bridges in step formation; eight ivory frets. Inclined cross-bar on the neck above finger-board with seven holes for strings. Three loops on the harmonic curve for lowering pitch of strings. Small stop on the neck between the first and second frets. Strings: seven stopped (five gut and two spun silk), five diapasons; sound-board fastening type (looped ends); steel tuning pins with squared heads, sagittal posterior type. Instrument varnished black all over; decorated with gilt stripes and scrolls. Gilt label on the neck in front, reading:

'LIGHT LONDON
Foley Place'

Length, total, 85.5 cm. Body, length, 42 cm.; width, 35.5 cm.; thickness, 14.5 cm. Vibrating length of strings (see statement below). (17.1769)
Plate VIII and Fig. 47, p. 243

The stringing of this instrument is unusual. It is tuned in E-flat as is the previous instrument. The written notes are:

The twelfth string was tuned to c³ (e″-flat in actual sound). The actual scale was a major sixth lower. When played with the piano the instrument was not retuned lower, as was the previous one, but the piano accompaniment was transposed to suit.[532] The stopped strings, before being attached to the tuning pins, have to pass through holes in the inclined cross-bar on the neck; by this method they are brought closer to the neck and additional friction is provided to keep them in place. Three nuts below this cross-bar, located stepwise in three different planes, give the following vibrating lengths to the strings: g′, a′, 40.2 cm.; b′, c″, e″, g″, 38 cm.; c³, 34 cm. The diapasons are attached directly to the tuning pins; the longest one, g, is 64.7 cm.

SECTION B: STRUCK STRINGS

Struck chordophones are instruments of which the primary vibrating element, a string or strings, is set in vibration when struck by some device. Directly controlled instruments of this type, although less used at present, still retain their hold on life. In Hungary, the *cimbalom* is regarded as a national instrument; it is played with two hammers held by the player in his hands. Instruments of this type, when played by a capable performer, produce very pleasing sounds, with a peculiar individuality of tone color which cannot be duplicated on other instruments.

72. TAMBOURIN À CORDES

String drum. (See Plate I. For description see page 73.) (17.1781 a & b)

263. DULCIMER — England, 19th century, by John Grey & Sons, Ltd., London

Dulcetta. Trapezoidal box, sides inlaid in bands. Sound-board varnished black; two sound-holes covered with red flannel. Twenty-one sets of quadruple strings attached on the right side to eighty-four tuning pegs. Two strings of each of these sets are made of one V-shaped wire, the free ends being attached to the tuning pegs and the bottom of the V hooked to a small iron pin on the left side. There are two slotted strips of wood placed over the sound-board. The strip close to the tuning pins supports eleven small movable bridges with tongs fitting into the slot to provide clearance. The other strip supports ten similar bridges, its location being so selected as to divide the vibrating lengths of the string in the ratio of two to three (which gives the ratio of a fifth). A tuning key, No. 263 b, is exhibited with the instrument. Trade Mark: *Dulcetta.* Length of sides, short, 46 cm.; long, 82 cm. Width, 38 cm. Height, 7.3 cm. Vibrating length of strings, shortest, 20 cm.; longest, 58 cm. (17.1780 a)
Plate VIII

The dulcimer (from modified *dulce melos*, 'sweet-toned') is closely related to the psaltery (p. 211), the essential difference being that the dulcimer is a *struck* instrument, played with two light hammers or wooden rods, and a psaltery is a *plucked* instrument. As Canon Galpin points out,[533] the early history of the dulcimer is obscure, owing to the close resemblance between psaltery and dulcimer, except in their manner of playing. In early days, when the psaltery was plucked with long *plectra*,[534] it could be easily struck with them also. Dr. Curt Sachs, commenting on this point, states[535] that down to 1300 only one stick or plectrum was used; after 1300 psalteries were played with two thin sticks which served both for plucking and for striking. The emergence of the dulcimer as a distinctly recognized instrument can be dated at about 1400.[536] But the significance of the difference between the methods of playing was fully appreciated only after the invention of the pianoforte.[537]

The psaltery was the ancestor of keyboard instruments of the plucked type (spinet, virginal, harpsichord). The dulcimer was the ancestor of the struck type, of our modern pianoforte but not of the clavichord. On the last point please read the introduction to the struck keyboard chordophones on p. 332 ff.

264. KEYED GUITAR England, early 19th century

Pear-shaped body with back and ribs of maple; varnished light yellow-brown. Sound-board of spruce with sound-hole covered with stamped brass rose inserted in ivory ring. Ink lines around sound-hole and at the edges of sound-board. Finger-board of ebony with twelve brass frets and three holes for the capotasto. Head with Preston's tuning machine and curved end with inlaid square end. String: two single bass strings of spun silk and four pairs of steel wire unisons; lower end fastening type (small brass pins in the bottom). Ebony bridge; ivory nut. At the lower end Smith's patent box, consisting of two extension arms carrying the oval-shaped box with six keys and hammer mechanism. Key-box stamped 'Smith Patent Box' over the Royal Arms, below which is stamped 'London.' Length, total, 71.75 cm. Body, length, 39.75 cm.; width, 30.5 cm. Ribs, height, 8 cm. Height, total (key-box included), 14.5 cm. Vibrating length of strings, 44.7 cm. (17.1748)

SECTION C: BOWED

BOWED chordophones are instruments of which the primary vibrating element, a string or strings, is set in vibration by friction caused by a bow. Forms of the bow vary; the most fundamental type is a bunch of hair affixed to a holder; but it may also take the form of a wheel, as on hurdy-gurdies. Various theories of the origin of the bow will be examined in the section on bows.

General Considerations. In the history of the development of European music three groups of instruments had the greatest influence: keyboard instruments, lutes, and bowed chordophones. In the fourteenth and fifteenth centuries organs and lutes were the favorite instruments. In the sixteenth century began a rapid evolution of keyboard chordophones (clavichords, spinets, virginals, harpsichords); the same century also witnessed the development of bowed chordophones into three closely related, yet distinct families: viols (*viole da gamba*), lyras (*lira da braccio*, *lira da gamba*), and violins (*viole da braccio*). In a certain sense, each of these families represented a culmination of earlier tendencies. The violin family alone survived the changes of musical styles and changes in the social order which came at the end of the eighteenth century. It is only quite recently (ca. 1900) that the revival of interest in old music and the well founded arguments of some scholars[538] that it should be performed on the instruments for which it was originally written, made the viol family once more a living entity.

Unfortunately, the history of bowed string instruments is full of uncertainties.[539] The instruments themselves are very fragile, so that none of the earlier types has survived. Objective materials extant are pictorial and sculptural images, illuminated manuscripts, and some meagre descriptions. Some of the instruments are known only by name.[540] The internal construction of the earlier types is now practically unknown. Thus, organologists are unable to trace where and when such important details as the bass-bar and the sound-post originated.

This lack of definite knowledge of earlier types is not surprising, because the scientific study of the history of musical instruments is a late nineteenth-century development. Our ancestors in the seventeenth and even in the eighteenth centuries were in a better position to know more of the old instruments and traditions, but, with few exceptions,[541] they have not transmitted to us their heritage. Many valuable old instruments, books, manuscripts, were irretrievably lost.[542]

There are many points about viols which require a more detailed investigation.[543] There is a lack of positive knowledge as to the origin of the violin. If this is true of instruments many of which are in museums and private hands, how much less certain is our knowledge of earlier types.

Extensive investigation has convinced the writer that it is a futile task to trace the genealogical descent of viols and violins from any particular primitive instrument.[544] Nor is it possible to draw a genealogical chart of the evolution of instruments with only their names placed on a piece of paper. Two instances might help in clarifying these statements.

1. *Generic similarity of two families is not sufficient guaranty of their genealogical relation.* For a long time viols were thought to be the predecessors of violins. There are some justifications for this view. Both viols and violins are bowed chordophones with tripartite bodies, having bass-bars and sound-posts; both have the frontal type tuning heads with lateral pegs; the fixed ends of strings on both are of the lower end fastening type. But examination of specific details (see p. 292) points to a different conclusion, which is also supported by historic facts. This question will be discussed fully in the section on violins.

2. *A statement that the Italian* lira da braccio *is a predecessor of the violin is correct,*[545] *but it needs qualifying.* The body of the *lira da braccio* is, practically, that of the violin,[546] but the head of the former is of the occipital type with anterior sagittal pegs. This type of head belongs to a different line of evolution and has little to do with the evolution of the violin.

These two examples show that the names of instruments cannot be placed on a genealogical chart without qualifications. If the additions of such qualifications were attempted, then only a three-dimensional model with many complex lines of relationship would do justice to the whole problem of the evolution of bowed chordophones.[547]

Fortunately, the problem can be simplified if the evolution of important details and of the playing technique are considered, rather than the evolution of complete instruments.[548] Viols and violins are the culmination and synthesis of many details and practices developed on various instruments, some of which were plucked and not necessarily bowed.[549] Although the types of instruments known to us are many, certain typological details, such as bodies, heads, string fastenings, etc., are few in number. Some of these details have shown a remarkable vitality and persistence, while the instruments and even the instrumental types have changed or disappeared altogether.[550] These general ideas will be amplified later on.

Probable Origins of Bowed Chordophones in Europe

THE classical Mediterranean civilization of Greece and Rome knew no bowed string instruments; such is the opinion held by scholars at the present time.[551] Therefore, it is probable that the bowed instruments were brought to Europe from Asia by the invading and immigrating tribes. It seems that the bowed instruments penetrated Western Europe in three places: (1) the North (Finland, Esthonia, Scandinavia); (2) the Near East (Asia Minor and Byzantium); and (3) the South West (Spain during the Moorish conquest); and, possibly, Sicily in the South. There remains one more path of entry,[552] namely, through the Caucasus and the southern plains of Russia, but there is no reliable data with respect to this last upon which an organologist could base any conclusions.

Three distinct types of bowed instruments correspond to these places of penetration. They can be indicated, roughly, as follows:

1. The *bowed-harp*[553] and an instrument closely related to it, the *crwth* (No. 291). This type and the *rotta* (No. 225) undoubtedly had some influence on the development of the *fiedel*. The fiedel type can be described, in the most general terms, as a bowed instrument with tripartite body having a neck attached to it; a polygon or a leaf-shaped head with sagittal pegs; and, either the frontal or the occipital type of string fastening. This group of instruments is the most probable ancestor of the viol family.

2. The *lyra* (No. 265). Between Constantinople and Western Europe there was a considerable trading activity which included also the export of musical instruments.[554] The lyra type had a head with sagittal pegs and occipital string fastening;[555] but its distinctive feature was a pear-shaped body with the neck organically connected to it; in this it has a typological kinship with the *rebec*. This group influenced the development of the *lira da braccio*.[556]

3. The *rebec* (No. 266) is the instrument which developed, most probably, from the lyra and the Moorish *rabab*.[557] The most important typological detail borrowed from the *rabab* is the frontal type fastening for the tuning end of the strings and lateral pegs; the lower end fastening for the fixed end of the strings was the same on the lyra and the *rabab*. The boat-shaped body of the Moorish *rabab*, although used in Spain for several centuries, had but little effect on European instrumental types of later periods.[558] The typological details just enumerated were introduced later in the design of both viol and violin.

An intermediate group of instruments and, finally, our standard instruments of the viol and violin family were developed from these three groups of instruments through the process of combining different details. For instance, the body of the European rebec was borrowed from the lyra group. The head of the rebec with lateral pegs grafted on the tripartite bodies of the fiedels produced the viol type. The same type of head, replacing the leaf-shaped head with sagittal pegs and the occipital string fastening of the Italian *lira da braccio*, which had already developed a body closely approaching that of the violin family, produced our modern violin.

These are the main lines of development of the European bowed chordophones. More detailed consideration of their evolution will be given in the introductions to the family groups and in the notes on individual instruments.

Two Fundamental Methods of Stopping Strings on Bowed Chordophones

THERE are two fundamental methods of stopping strings on bowed chordophones: (a) *without a finger-board*, and (b) *with a finger-board.*

The second method is later and more familiar to us. The strings are stopped by firmly pressing them with the finger-tips against a finger-board. The fact of importance deserving mention in this connection is that the viol family has fretted finger-boards; the violin family has no frets.

The first method is less known in all its varieties. There are three ways of stopping strings without a finger-board.

1. The finger-tips merely touch a string at the nodal points and produce partial tones called *harmonics* of an open string.[559] An instrument having no finger-board and played exclusively by this method is the *tromba marina*, No. 292.

2. The finger-tips are laid on the strings firmly, not allowing production of partial tones; this method is used on some Oriental instruments and those of the Southern Slavs.[560]

3. The strings are supported by nails in a manner similar to that of the tangents on clavichords, forming temporary 'bridges.' This last method of stopping strings is dealt with extensively in the book *The Bowed-Harp* by Dr. Otto Andersson.[561]

This difference in the stopping of the strings is of fundamental importance. It is recognized in the general classification by the introduction of the two following sub-sections a and b.

SUB-SECTION a: BOWED CHORDOPHONES WITHOUT A FINGER-BOARD

Primitive Types

265. LYRA — Greece, end of 19th century

Pear-shaped body made of a solid piece of wood, with integral neck and head, and vaulted back. Sound space hollowed out and covered with pine sound-board with two semi-circular sound-holes. Three gut strings attached by wire loops to a boss at the bottom; movable bridge; two outer strings are attached in front directly to the sagittal posterior pegs, the middle string being guided by a small slotted peg. At the back of the head there are reinforcing bosses providing extra stock for tuning peg-holes and supporting trefoils of the head-board. Roughly made, unvarnished

instrument, used by peasants. Length, total, 44 cm. Width, 14.5 cm. Thickness, 6.5 cm. Vibrating length of strings (approx.), 23.5 cm. Bow description, p. 348. (17.1705 a)
Plate X

The lyra is a Greek folk instrument derived from the pear-shaped *rabab* of the Islamic peoples.[562] Dr. Henry G. Farmer states[563] that, probably, the earliest Arabic reference to the prototype of the lyra is that made by Ibn Khurdadhbih (d. ca. 912), who said that the Byzantines had a wooden instrument of five strings called a *lura* which was identical with the *rabab* of the Arabs. The date of this reference is some time before 893. This places five-stringed instruments in the ninth century, and seems to point to the Levant as the place of origin of this type.

An instrument of the lyra type is represented on the famous Carrand Casket,[564] at Florence, an ivory piece of Italo-Byzantine workmanship, assigned to the ninth century.

As has been mentioned before, there was a considerable trade exchange between Byzantium and Western Europe and musical instruments were among the exports. One of the most interesting sources of study of the early lyra is the sculptured group of twenty-four elders of the Apocalypse on the tympanum of the south portal of the abbey of Moissac.[565] Instruments of two types are represented there:

1. *One-stringed lyra* (held by eighteen elders). Instruments differ in shape, some long, some somewhat narrow with lozenge-shaped bodies, and some a little shorter and less angular.

2. *Five-stringed lira da braccio* (held by three elders). Instruments have pear-shaped bodies, carved tail-pieces, bridges, and occipital string fastening.[566]

The playing position of both types of instrument is against the left shoulder: two elders hold the one- and the five-stringed lyras in such a position. Another interesting feature of the instruments is the variety of shapes of sound-hole; the basic types, except the f-holes of violins, can be found on the Moissac tympanum sculptures.

The lyra type developed along two lines. One of them resulted in the early Renaissance *lira da braccio*, a five-stringed instrument with tripartite body.[567] Later this type developed into the Italian *lira da braccio*, an instrument with seven strings: two bourdons and five stopped on the finger-board.[568] The leaf-shaped head and the occipital string fastening remained the typological feature of these instruments to the end of their existence; the Italian *lira da braccio* was the last type of the European bowed chordophone to retain it.

Another line of development resulted in the rebec, an instrument with pear-shaped body and a head with lateral pegs. For details see the statement under the next instrument. Instrument No. 265, unfortunately, lost its characteristic sound-post, which should have a notch fitted into the leg of a bridge extending beyond the sound-hole.

SUB-SECTION b: WITH A FINGER-BOARD

266. REBEC Reproduction of the 17th-century type

Pear-shaped body made of a solid piece of poplar tree wood, with an integral neck and peg-box; vaulted back. Sound space hollowed out and covered with pine sound-board with two *f*-holes. Finger-board of stained oak glued to a raised step on the neck. Three gut strings fixed to a leathern

tail-piece, hooked to a boss at the lower end. Movable bridge and nut. Frontal type tuning end string fastening, lateral pegs. Sound-post. Although it has but a small resonating space, the instrument possesses a powerful tone. Length, total, 56 cm. Width, 14.5 cm. Thickness, 6.5 cm. Length of sound-space (approx.), 24.5 cm. Vibrating length of strings, 32.25 cm. (17.1706)
Plate X

The rebec is an important link in the evolution of the violin. The ancestry of the rebec is obscure. There are two possibilities. One of them is that the rebec had an Oriental prototype having the same typological characteristics, that is, a pear-shaped body and a head with lateral pegs.[569] Another possibility is that the rebec developed in Europe as a hybrid, borrowing its body from the lyra and its head from the Moorish *rabab*.

The last named instrument differs from the Levantine *rabab* in two important particulars. Its body is long, narrow, boat-shaped; tuning pegs are of the lateral type affixed to a head which is bent back.[570] This instrument penetrated into Europe through Spain and was used there, as is shown on the miniatures in the *Cantigas de Santa Maria*[571] of the thirteenth century. It is also probable that it was used in Sicily, where it would have been brought by the Mohammedan conquerors in the ninth century.

Therefore, it is not improbable that it was in Italy that the two types, the Byzantine lyra and the Moorish *rabab*, were combined to make the rebec.

The history of the rebec can best be traced by sculptural and pictorial representations. In the early period of its existence, the rebec can be found on the portals of churches, in the hands of heavenly musicians; there is no intimation of a lowly status. But approximately in the middle of the fifteenth century the rebec lost caste, and with the rise of viols, and later, violins, it became the instrument of mendicants and village musicians.

Instrument No. 266 is tuned:

that is, the same way as the first three strings of the violin. It is played unfretted. Its principal use is for dance and festival music.[572]

267. REBEC KIT — Italy, ca. 1700

Pochette. Narrow, elongated body of pear wood with five-ribbed back. Arched belly with two sound-holes shaped like the figure 3. Neck of pear wood with peg-box. Tail-piece of boxwood, affixed by ivory tail-pin to the lower block through hole in the belly (not at the bottom!). Four gut strings; movable bridge of standard type, but with narrow base; ivory nut. Lateral pegs. Sound-post. Length, total, 41 cm. Body, length, 21.5 cm.; width, 4.5 cm.; thickness, 3 cm. Vibrating length of strings, 22 cm. (17.1709)
Plate X

The kit or *pochette* is a small string instrument, used formerly by dancing masters, and carried by them in their coat pockets. Tuning:

268. KIT Germany, 1753

Violin form. Body (back and ribs), neck and peg-box carved out of solid piece of maple. Belly of soft pine with *f*-holes. Both back and belly are highly arched. Finger-board of ebony. Tail-piece attached to ivory tail-pin. Four strings; movable bridge, pegs of simplified violin pattern. Bass-bar and sound-post. Light yellow varnish. Label inside, reading:

'*Christ. Phil. Blumenhagen*
Fecit A° 1753'

Length, total, 40 cm. Body, length, 16.25 cm.; width (lower bouts), 8.25 cm.; thickness, 3.75 cm. Vibrating length of strings, 24.75 cm. (17.1710)
Plate X

269. HUSLA Germany, 18th century

Elongated body with incurved sides and flat back. Belly of soft pine highly arched, formed by a part of cylindrical surface with rectilinear generator. Ribs of maple, formed of four pieces, shallow in the upper part and wide in the lower part. Two narrow parallel rectangular slits on the belly serve as sound-holes; in the upper part of the belly a crude rosette, partly covered by finger-board. Neck of oak, integral with leaf-shaped peg-board. Finger-board of maple. The bottom joint of lower bouts reinforced by thin rectangular strip fastened by two button-headed pins; the pin close to belly serving as a tail-pin for tail-piece, three gut strings, movable bridge, nut. Tuning pegs of sagittal posterior type with arrow-shaped heads; strings fastened in front. Sound-post, no bass-bar. Edges of belly, sound-slits, and rosette are embellished with zig-zag and dot pattern burned in wood. A roughly made peasant instrument. Length, total, 62.5 cm. Body, length, 40 cm.; width, upper half, 15 cm.; width, lower half, 19 cm. Ribs, height, upper half, 2.5 cm.; height, at bottom, 9.75 cm. Vibrating length of strings, 34 cm. (17.1707)
Plate X

The *husla* is the old Slavonic instrument used by the Western and Southern Slavs. This instrument comes from the district in Prussia (Niederlausitz) where the Wends or Sorbs live. According to Dr. Georg Kinsky,[573] the *husla* was used there until the first half of the nineteenth century. The instrument had also a wide distribution among the Slavs living on the Balkan peninsula.

The word *husla* comes from the old Slavonic root *gusti*, meaning 'to emit a droning sound, to resound'; from this root word came many names for the stringed instruments of several Slavonic nationalities. Thus, the Russian *gudok* (a bowed chordophone), also *gusli* (a plucked string instrument, like a psaltery), much sung about in the Russian *byliny*, or folk-poems.[574]

270. RUSTIC VIOLIN England, 19th century

Rudely made instrument constructed from a cigar box by a blind man. Long rectangular box with two long slits for sound-holes; tail-piece and finger-board. Four gut strings. Ink label, 'made by E. Clifford, 3 Joiners Place, Dockhead, Bermondsey, S. E.' Length, 58 cm. Width, 11 cm. Thickness, 3.5 cm. (17.1727)
Plate VIII

Viols

THE name 'viol' in its Italian form, *viola* (pl. *viole*), designates many ancient instruments. Among them the most important is the *viola da gamba* (leg-viol), which is the generic name for a whole family of instruments, and the *viola da braccio* (arm-viol), formerly the generic name for instruments of the violin family.[575] There are also the *viola d'amore* (love-viol, with sympathetic strings), the *viola da bardone* (baryton), the *viola bastarda* (lyra-viol), and the *viola da spalla* [576] (shoulder-viol).

In this study the term 'viol,' alone or with the specific designation of its place in the consort of viols,[577] such as the bass viol, will always refer to the *viola da gamba* family of instruments.

Historically, viols held first place among the bowed instruments in the latter part of the fifteenth, during the entire sixteenth, and most of the seventeenth centuries. For this reason considerable attention will be paid to viols and viol playing practices.

Nomenclature and Sizes

A PROPER nomenclature of viols is somewhat uncertain, since very few writers on the subject agree. In this instance confusion is caused mainly by the stressing of the musicological aspect of the problem. The fact that not more than four different tunings of the voices of consort viols are given in old works [579] caused some writers to assume that there were only four, or, at the most, five sizes of viols.

But when the problem is examined organologically, then it is the typological and structural details that determine which instruments do or do not belong to a given family. Then the number of members of the viol family increases to *nine*.[580]

The nomenclature of viols adopted here is based on that of Praetorius, Dr. Georg Kinsky, and Mr. Gerald R. Hayes.[581]

THE VIOL FAMILY [582]

(*Viole da Gamba*)

(Dimensions in centimeters)

Name	Nut to Bridge	Body Length	Widths: Upper Bouts	Widths: Lower Bouts	Rib Height
1. The High Treble	31	31.5–33.5	16	19.75	6.5
2. The Treble	36	35–37	17.5	21.5	7
3. The Alto	40.5	38–40	19	24	8
4. The Small Tenor	48	42–46	22	27.5	9
5. The Tenor	54	48–52	24.5	30.5	10
The Small Bass: 6. The Lyra-Viol	58–60	56–60	27	33.5	11.5
The Small Bass: 7. The Division Viol	64–66	62–65	29	36	12
8. The Full Consort Bass	72	66–71	31	38.5	13
9. The Violone (Contrabass)	104	100	48	60	20

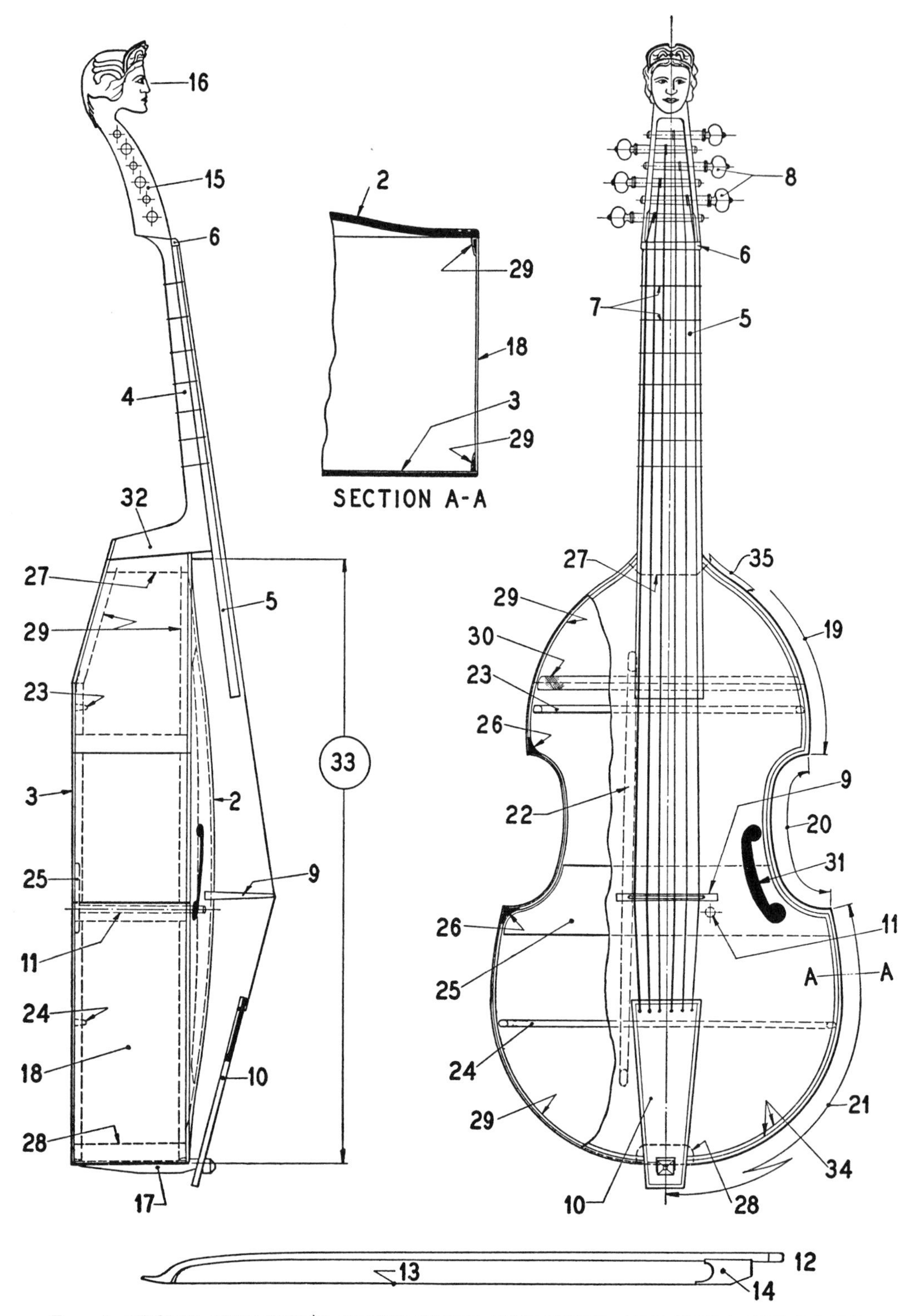

FIG. 48. FRONT ELEVATION, RIGHT-HAND SIDE VIEW, AND THE BOW OF THE BASS VIOL; WITH REFERENCE NUMBERS FOR THE PARTS

A study of the sizes of the instruments from No. 2 to No. 8 inclusive will give a fair idea of viol proportions in accordance with the best English practice. This table is applicable to the standard type of viol body, Fig. 50, p. 258. The sizes of English instruments were different from those in Germany (see Appendix B). Since English composers, players, and viol-makers had a fine reputation abroad, their lead was followed by other countries. Smaller sized instruments were more convenient to hold, and, the distances between the frets being shorter, they were easier to play.

Instrument No. 1, the High Treble Viol, is an eighteenth-century instrument. The contrabass viol (*violone*, No. 9) was not a regular member of the consort of viols.

Nomenclature of Parts

THE following nomenclature of parts is borrowed from *The Division Viol* by Christopher Simpson.[578] It is supplemented by the modern names of parts corresponding to those of the violin family. See Fig. 48.

NOMENCLATURE OF PARTS

No.	English	Latin	French	Italian
1.	A Viol	Chelys	Une Viole	Una Viola
2.	The Belly of the Viol	Umbo	La Table	La Tavola
3.	The Back	Tergum	Le Fond	Il Fonda
4.	The Neck	Iugum	Le Manche	Il Manico
5.	The Finger-board	Canon	La Touche	La Tastiera
6.	The Nut of the Finger-board	Chordotomus; Magas superior	Le Sillet	Il Capotasto
7.	The Frets	Intervalla; ligulae	Les Touches	I Tasti
8.	The Pegs	Collabi	Les Chevilles	I Piroli
9.	The Bridge	Ponticulus; Magas inferior	Le Chevalet	Il Ponticello
10.	The Tail-Piece	Retinaculum; Cauda	La Queue	La Coda
11.	The Sound-Post	Sustenaculum intestinum	L'Ame	L'Anima
12.	The Bow	Arcus; Plectrum	L'Archet	L'Arco
13.	The Hairs of the Bow	Setae	Les Creins	I Crini
14.	The Nut of the Bow	Isthmus; Asserculus; Setis obstans	La Hauste	La Alza

No.	English	No.	English	No.	English
15.	The Peg-box	22.	The Bass-bar	29.	The Linings
16.	The Figure-head	23.	The Upper Cross-bar	30.	The Linen Reinforcement Strip
17.	The Hook-bar	24.	The Lower Cross-bar	31.	The Sound-hole
18.	The Ribs	25.	The Cross-strip	32.	The Neck Bracket
19.	The Upper Bouts	26.	The Corner Fillet	33.	The Length of Body
20.	The Middle Bouts	27.	The Upper Block	34.	The Purfling
21.	The Lower Bouts	28.	The Lower Block	35.	The Shoulders

A Detailed Description of Viol Design

Outline of the body. One of the difficulties in the study of viol design is the variety of shapes and outlines given to their bodies at different periods and in different localities. Some of them are grotesque. Among many shapes there are five types of bodies which are of significance in the history of the evolution of the viol.

1. *The fiedel type*, Fig. 49. This type of body is the fundamental one and goes as far back as the thirteenth century.[583] The middle incurvations are very slight, the back is either flat or slightly curved, the belly is slightly curved. The dotted line shows the middle bout of the next type, which may be regarded as perpetuating the fiedel type.

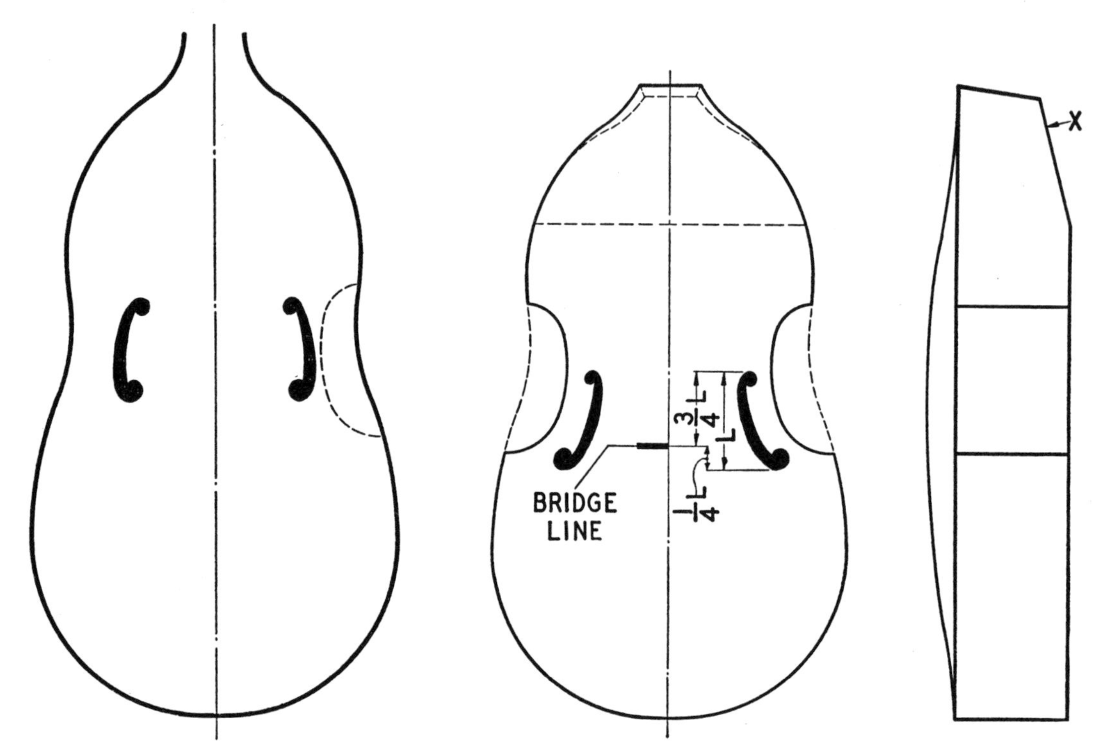

Fig. 49. THE FIEDEL TYPE OF THE VIOL BODY

Fig. 50. THE STANDARD TYPE OF VIOL BODY

2. *The standard type*, Fig. 50; also Fig. 48, p. 256. This type represents the culmination of the evolution of the viol body. It is the shape which is associated with viols in the same way as the standard form of the great Cremonese masters is associated with the violin. The fundamental outline is that of the early fiedel type, as can be seen by comparing Figures 49 and 50. The middle bouts serve the functional purpose of providing clearance for the bow. The back is flat, but has a slanting plane near the neck bracket marked by the letter 'X.' The ribs of the upper bouts slope slightly toward the back, so that the back is somewhat smaller than the belly (the difference is shown by the dotted line). The sound-holes are C-shaped.

3. *The guitar-fiedel type*. This type is represented on page 309, Fig. 56. It differs from the fiedel type by deep middle incurvations and, in some instances, by a more elongated body. It can be traced back to the twelfth century.[584] The guitar-fiedel type of viol body stands

as a connecting link between the viol and the violin, since the fundamental outline of the violin is of the same type (see page 290, Fig. 53).

Actual instruments of this type may be found in the Modena Museo Civico, Italy; the Brussels Collection, Belgium;[585] the Vienna Collection;[586] one by Hans Vohar (?) is described by Mr. Gerald R. Hayes.[587]

4. *The modified guitar-fiedel type*, Fig. 51. This type of body is interesting not only be-

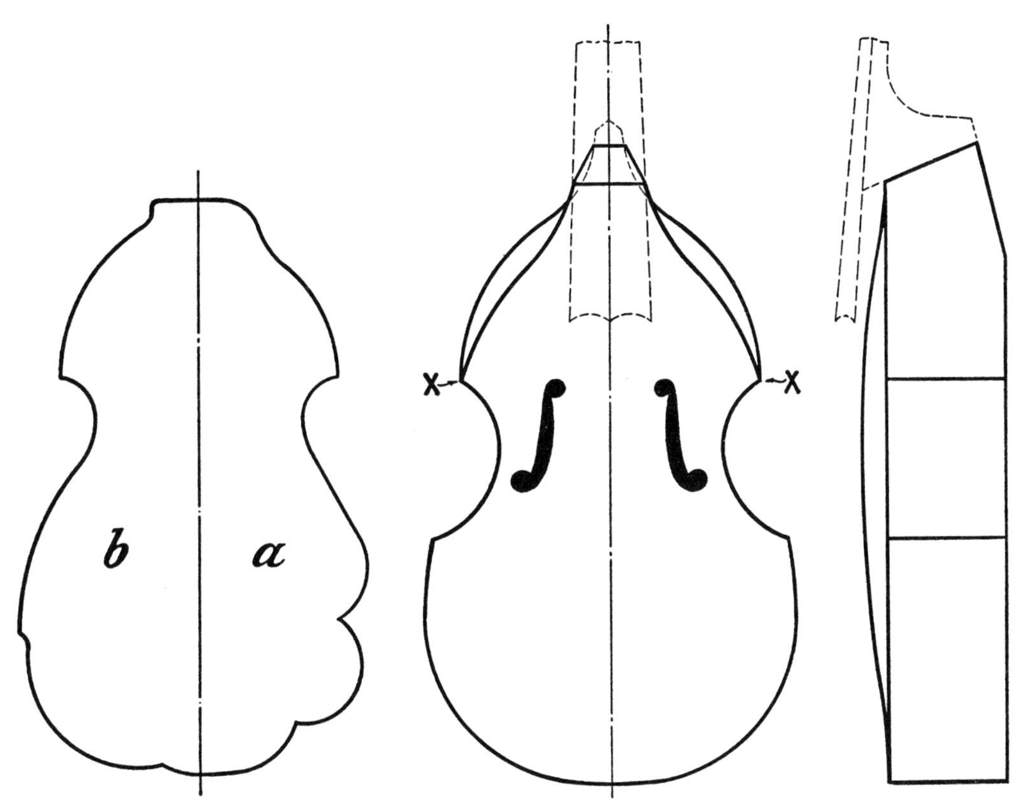

FIG. 51. THE MODIFIED GUITAR-FIEDEL TYPE OF VIOL BODY

FIG. 52. THE SLOPING RIB TYPE OF VIOL BODY

cause it was used for the *viola da gamba* family (Fig. 51 a), but because it also applied to the *baryton* (Fig. 51 b; also Plate XII, Fig. 283) and the philomele.[588] The incurvations in the lower bouts vary in depth and number. There are instruments of this type in the former Heyer Collection,[589] now in the Neues Grassimuseum of the University of Leipzig; also in the Claudius Collection, Copenhagen.[590]

5. *The sloping rib type*, Fig. 52. In types 1, 3, and 4 the ribs are perpendicular to the belly and back; in the standard type the ribs are perpendicular in the lower and middle bouts, but the upper bouts have ribs perpendicular in the lower part and slanting toward the back in the upper part, as already mentioned. But there is a type, Figure 52, which is distinguished by the following characteristics: (a) the shoulders begin to curve immediately at

the corners, 'x'; (b) the belly is shorter than the back and differs from it in outline; (c) the ribs that join the back and belly slope toward the front plane of the instrument at the upper bouts. On some instruments this feature is exaggerated and gives them an awkward and almost repulsive appearance. There are instruments of this type in the Bologna Museo Civico, in the Vienna Collection,[591] and in the Brussels Collection.[592] Gotfredsen's viol No. 272 (page 276) belongs to this type, but the ribs slope toward the front very little, almost imperceptibly.

The *lira da gamba* and later the violin had their influence on the design of the viol body. The outline was modified to resemble the violoncello. Christopher Simpson gives a picture of this type of viol and comments on its sonority.[593]

The Belly. Arched; made of fine, evenly grained pine or spruce. On the better constructed instruments it was carved out of a solid piece of wood. But, as Christopher Simpson remarks,[594] viols of violin shape had "the Bellyes . . . digged out of the Plank," which implies that on some viols the bellies were made by a different process.[595]

The Back. Made of a thin, flat piece of maple. The upper slanting part had a bending line inside, cut into the stock by a blunt tool; over this bending line was glued a strip of coarse linen (page 256, Fig. 48, No. 30).

Since a thin, flat piece of wood offers poor resistance to bending stresses, the backs of viols are reinforced by cross-bars (page 256, Fig. 48, Nos. 23 and 24); the cross-strip (*ibid.*, No. 25) is located so that the sound-post is placed on it.

The edges of both the belly and the back are flush with the ribs.

The Ribs. Deep ribs are the distinguishing feature of viols of all sizes, from the smallest to the largest. They are made of maple, thinner than those used on instruments of the violin family of a corresponding size.

The Linings. Thin and narrow strips of pine glued to the ribs, at the belly and back joints and following the outline of the ribs to provide an increased gluing surface and rib reinforcement. On some instruments the back was joined to the ribs by coarse linen strips, an inferior construction.

The Corner Fillets. The corner joints of the ribs are held not by large corner blocks as in violins, but by small radius fillets. (See page 256, Fig. 48, 26.) This type of joint is less stiff than the violin type.

The Sound-Post. A round stick of fine-grained spruce, the same as in the violin family.

The Bass-Bar. Owing to the lower pitch to which viols were tuned and the lighter strings with which they were furnished, the bass-bar is more slender in design as compared with the modern highly-tensioned members of the violin family.

General Remarks about Viol Body Construction

EXAMINATION of the inside construction of the body of a viol shows that viols were built more delicately than violins and violoncellos. With the belly, back, ribs, corner joints, and bass-bar less stiff than the same members on instruments of the violin family, viols respond to the slightest touch of the bow. Yet the tone color produced by them has less of the crystalline brilliancy of the violin, which in unskillful hands degenerates into unpleasant harsh squeaks; the tone of the viols cannot be forced beyond a certain point, because their bodies are not adapted to respond to harsh attacks. This does not mean that viols lack resonance; quite the reverse is true. But viols, even when forced, never sound vulgar. The delicacy of their body construction should serve as a reminder that viols should not be tuned to our standard pitch.[596]

The Head. Has lateral pegs and a carved figure-head, human or animal, sometimes grotesque. Some of the figure-heads were fine works of art, full of expression and character.[597] Outside surfaces were embellished sometimes with low relief carvings.

The Finger-Board. Except for its width (to accommodate a larger number of strings), it has no special features.

The Tail-Piece and the Hook-Bar. The strings are fastened at the lower end to the tail-piece (page 256, Fig. 48, 10) somewhat similar to that of the violin. But the tail-piece is held, not by a gut string loop fastened to a tail-pin, as in a violin, but hooked on the hook-bar extending to the front of the belly (Fig. 48, 17). The hook-bar is glued to the bottom rib and fastened by screws to the bottom-block. The tail-piece is held in place by the hook in the hook-bar and the tension of the strings, an effective and adequate construction.

The Neck and the Frets. The neck of a viol differs considerably from that of the violin. It is not only wider, owing to the larger number of strings, but much thinner and flatter. On the violin a player has to envelop the neck with his left-hand thumb to guide the hand in position shifts; on the viol the thumb is pivoted on the neck by its tip and the presence of frets would hinder the freedom of movement of the left hand if one were to attempt to hold the viol violin-fashion. Many fine instruments were ruined because their necks were changed into the rounded shape used on violins and the finger-boards narrowed.[598] This brought the strings closer together and made the stopping more difficult; the frets do not hold on such necks as well as they do on a properly shaped viol neck.

All members of the viol family had fretted necks. The frets were made, as a rule, of gut strings, tied on doubly or singly and fastened by a special fret knot; on some instruments, as on our No. 273, frets were made of metal and permanently inserted in the finger-board, an inferior practice, since it prevents the correction of mistakes in placing the metallic frets.

The standard number of frets is seven; they are placed a semitone apart. Sometimes an octave fret is added; it is located opposite the middle nodal point of the string.

The rule given on page 225 of the lute section for placing the frets on lutes is also applicable to viols. Thomas Mace's directions should be implicitly followed. The string-stretching operation, which Mace insists on performing several times, is essential for securing a tight fret which cannot be displaced during the performance. But viol frets should be made somewhat thicker than lute frets.[599] The final placing of frets is done by ear, or the frets are 'tuned.' The gut string frets give a better, 'living,' tone.

The Strings. The standard number of strings on consort viols is six. There are two exceptions to this rule. The smallest viol, the high treble or *pardessus de viol*, had five strings; but, strictly speaking, this instrument was not a regular member of the viol consort. Some bass viols had seven strings.[600]

Since viols were tuned to a lower standard of musical pitch, their strings were stressed less than those of modern violins. For this reason, viol strings were smaller in diameter.

The Bridge. A correctly shaped viol bridge differs from that of the violin and of the violoncello. In addition to the difference in general outline, the viol bridge is less curved at the top. This facilitates the playing of chords, but requires more careful bowing. The violist's difficulty in this respect is the reverse of that of the violinist: it is more difficult for a viol player not to touch two adjoining strings.

Thomas Mace [601] gives the rule for placing the bridge on a viol with respect to its C-holes. He says:". . . the *Best Place* for the *Bridge*, is to stand *just* in the 3 *Quarter Dividing* of the *Open Cuts Below*; though *Most, most Erroniously* suffer them much to stand too *High*, which is a *Fault*." [602]

By "the 3 *Quarter Dividing* of the *Open Cuts Below*" Mace means that the bridge should be placed at a point one-quarter of the whole length of the sound-holes ('*Open Cuts*') counting from the bottom line of the sound-holes.[603] See Fig. 50, page 258.

Decorative features. Viols were very much loved in the old days. Titled and wealthy patrons ordered instruments which were richly carved and inlaid; the backs and ribs were made, sometimes, of two different kinds of wood, of contrasting colors. Some of the most remarkable instruments were built by Joachim Tielke, a celebrated luthier of Hamburg, Germany.[604]

Tone Color and Playing Technique

THE revival of interest in viols and viol music presents many problems, the most important of which is the proper style of performance. With the passing of the old school players and the consequent long period of neglect of the viol, there was a break in the continuity of tradition and a loss of the experience accumulated in previous centuries by many generations of viol players.

The great majority of people who take up viol playing are trained in the violin-violoncello school. There is a 'superiority complex' among the people who play these very difficult instruments and a justifiable pride in their accomplishment. But, unfortunately, this interferes with an understanding of the essential difference between the violin and the viol style and technique of playing. The superiority of the violin technique is taken for granted without a painstaking examination of all the factors involved. The natural tendency is to superimpose the violin technique upon viols. The result is a complete distortion of the true character of the viol style of playing. After all, the style involves not only such purely musical requirements as a proper tempo, phrasing, dynamics, correct execution of ornaments, etc., but also the technical factors and the manner of playing affecting one of the most important things of all: the tone color.

From a violist's standpoint the violin-violoncello enthusiasts who play viols commit the following 'crimes':

1. Play viols unfretted. 2. Bow with the violin-violoncello bow held overhand. 3. Hold smaller sized viols under the chin. 4. String viols with violin-violoncello strings (which are too heavy for viols). 5. Tune viols to the present standard pitch (which is about one half-tone too high).

Viols played this way lose their characteristic tone color. One may ask a pertinent question. Why should instruments be revived which differ but little from violins in tone color and sound inferior to them? The answer is, of course, that viols played in the manner of violins are not viols.[605]

The most vexing question is whether viols should be played fretted or unfretted. The opponents of fretting point to the fact that frets are 'the old-fashioned device of inferior players who cannot play unfretted instruments in tune'; that the frets constantly shift and make viols sound out of tune; that they interfere with the freedom of playing and are impracticable for solo work.

One fact cannot be denied; namely, that unfretted viols lose their characteristic tone color and resonance, while the difficulties of fingering are increased; these questions will be discussed in detail later on.

Frets are 'old-fashioned,' but they cannot be dismissed lightly, since not only the tone color but also the fingering is affected by their presence or absence. So this question can be settled only after the basic facts of both violin and viol fingering technique have been considered.

The shifting of frets can be remedied by a proper method of putting them on, and, fortunately, Thomas Mace made it very clear how this should be done.[606] And since the frets are adjustable, they can be so placed as to make the instruments sound in tune.

Finally, interference with the freedom of playing is largely a matter of habit. Those who actually have played fretted viols say that the frets help rather than hinder playing.[607]

For convenience, various problems in connection with the correct playing of the viol will be considered in the same order as the above-mentioned objections of violists.

1. *Frets.* The frets, as has been brought out, affect (a) the tone color and (b) the fingering technique of the instrument.

(a) *Tone Color.* If such factors as the body construction, the size and tension of strings, location of the bridge and the sound-post, etc., remain the same, the tone color of a bowed instrument is vitally affected by the method of stopping the strings. On violins the difference in tonal qualities of the strings played open or stopped is so considerable that the sharp and powerful sonority of the open tones excludes them from being employed in playing; as a rule violins are played with the strings stopped against the finger-board.[608] The superior resonance of the violin body necessitates the adoption of this method of playing.

In the case of viols it is different. Their bodies are so constructed that the edge is taken off the excessive sonority. With the necks fretted, the difference between the open tones of the strings and the tones of the strings when stopped against the frets is negligible. The frets on viols serve the same purpose as the nut; that is, they provide a definite cut-off point on a string and serve as temporary nuts. Violists use both open and stopped tones in their playing; the choice of either is made from the standpoint of the convenience of fingering. This, with the additional factors to be considered shortly, gives to viols their distinctive and individual tone color.

(b) *Fingering Technique.* The fingering technique of an instrument is determined primarily by the number of strings and the tuning intervals between the strings. Violin fingering is very simple and uniform. One and the same sequence of fingering is repeated in different positions, so, knowing the fingering in the first position, one knows it in the other positions. The difficulties arise from the necessity of correct placing of fingers in shifts of position and from the fact that in the higher positions the fingers have to be placed closer and closer with the shifting of the hand nearer the bridge; but this does not affect the sequence of the finger placing.

Here is the way a violinist fingers the diatonic scale in the first position.

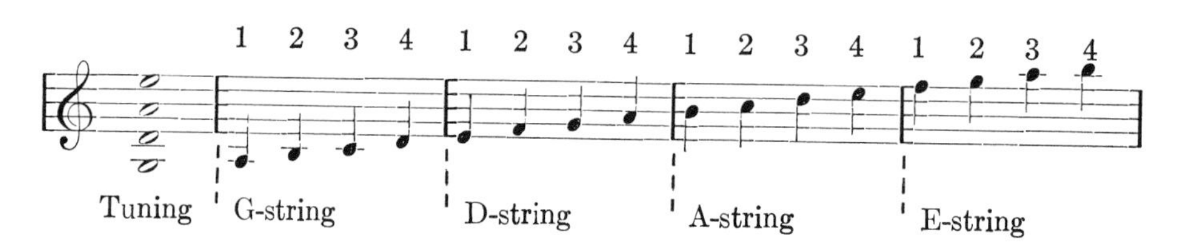

Fingering of Violin in the First Position

THE figures above the notes represent the index, middle, ring, and little fingers, respectively.

Please note that the tones *d′*, *a′*, and *e″* are played not, as one would expect, on their respectively tuned open strings, but on those tuned a fifth lower. That is, *d′* is played on the G-string, *a′* is played on the D-string, and *e″* is played on the A-string. On a given string the violinist fingers four tones a fourth apart between the extremes. For this he uses all four fingers. The same sequence of fingering is repeated on the next string, and, as stated already, the same fingering as that of the first position is repeated in the higher positions. The resulting fingering technique is very uniform; the small number of strings (four) is easier to handle. The well known difficulty in playing chords on the violin is caused, not so much by the wider intervals and the necessity for precision in stopping, as by the greater curvature of the bridge, the highly tensioned strings, and the stiff bow.

Viols have a greater number of strings (six). The strings are tuned to the same intervals as lutes,[609] that is, in fourths, with the major third between the third and the fourth strings. Frets influence the fingering of viols because it is possible to play both open and stopped tones. This affects both the fingering of scales and the playing of chords.

For a description of viol fingering, we quote an authority on the subject, the English composer and violist, Christopher Simpson.[610]

§7. *How the Viol is Tuned, and applyed to the Scale of Musick*

We now suppose you to understand Song, and consequently the Scale of Musick; which known, the Tuning of your Viol appears in such order as you see the six Semibreves which stand one over another, in the first part of the following scale:

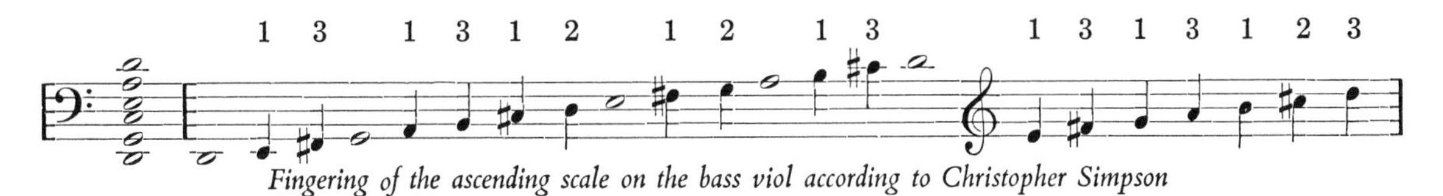

Fingering of the ascending scale on the bass viol according to Christopher Simpson

where note, that all the degrees arising above the highest of those Semibreves, are express'd on the Treble or highest String, by stopping it still lower and lower towards the Bridge.

Your Viol being tuned according to the six Semibreves, your next business is, to play those other Notes, which you see ascend and descend by degrees, over which I have set Figures to direct you with what Fingers to stop them; 1, 2, 3, 4, is set for first, second, third, and fourth Finger. *Those which have no figures over them, are played on the open Strings.*[611]

§8. *How the same Notes may be play'd upon different Strings*

You must know that sometimes Notes are play'd, not on those Strings to which they seem properly to belong; but for ease or better order of Fingering, are play'd upon some other String:

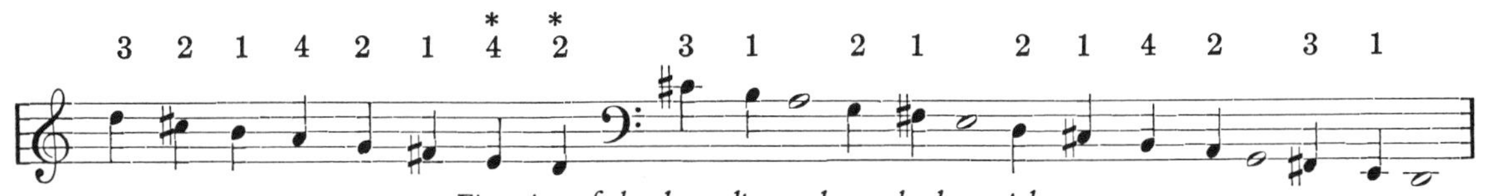

Fingering of the descending scale on the bass viol

An Instance whereof you have in those two Notes marked with little Stars over their Figures; which Notes, are play'd upon the second String; though, a little before, Notes standing in the same places were played upon the Treble or first String: and therefore, when any difficulty shall occur in Fingering, you are to consider how the same Notes may be express'd with most ease and convenience to the Hand.

On the basis of the preceding data, the most essential characteristics of the fingering technique of viols, as related to the tuning and frets, are as follows:

(1) Intervals to which viols are tuned determine their fingering technique. It is less uniform and more complex than the fingering technique of violins. For ordinary fingerings on viols only the first three fingers are used; the fourth (little) finger is used for alternative fingerings and 'extension' stopping.[612] (2) Viol players take advantage of the presence of frets and use both open and stopped tones at their discretion.[613] (3) Closer intervals between the strings on viols and the possibility of using the open tones simultaneously with stopped tones, coupled with other factors,[614] facilitate the multiple stopping and playing of chords.[615]

Therefore, the presence or absence of frets on viols cannot be settled by such phrases as 'old-fashioned,' 'devices of inferior players.' It is hoped that it has been clearly shown that frets are organic fixtures on viols, functionally connected with the tone color and fingering technique. If the old music written for viols is to be revived and performed correctly, with scrupulous regard for the tonal qualities, then viols must be played fretted.[616]

2. *The Bowing Technique.* The importance of correct bowing technique as related to the quality of tone produced on string instruments is so well known that it is surprising that there should be any argument as to how viols should be bowed. If tone color is the primary criterion then viols should be bowed viol-fashion.

All viols, from the smallest *pardessus* to the largest *violone*, are bowed in the same manner.[617] We cannot do better than quote a recognized authority on the subject, Mr. Arnold Dolmetsch. He describes viol bowing technique as follows:

> The arm and wrist are under the bow, in an easy and natural position, in no way weighing on it. The accented stroke being naturally *foreward*, begins at the point of the bow, where the pressure of the fingers is least strong. The conditions being reversed with the unaccented backward stroke, it follows that everything concurs to promote evenness of tone. This bowing is easy to learn; far more so than violin-bowing.[618]

Mr. Dolmetsch contrasts this with the violin-bowing most illuminatingly:

> The bow of the violin or violoncello being held under the hand, the wrist and arm are higher than the bow, and their weight is upon it. The accented note being played with a down bow, which begins right under the hand or very near it, feels the full strength of the arm and wrist in addition to their weight; the up-bow note, which begins at the point of the bow, receives no benefit from this weight, and only a small fraction of their strength. Thus in the violin everything concurs in giving preponderance to the down stroke. Skilled players endeavour, and succeed after long practice, in equalising the strokes and gaining a full command of the tone; but they are working against nature, and cannot do it with the ease and repose of the viol player, who has everything in his favour and does these things without effort.

As to the quality of bowing, Thomas Mace admonished in the *Musick's Monument*:

> A Good Stroak above All Things. Now being Thus far *ready for Exercise*, attempt the *Striking of your Strings*; but before you do *That*, Arm your self with Preparative *Resolutions to gain a Handsom-Smooth-Sweet-Smart-Clear-Stroak*; or else Play not at all. *For if your Viol be never so Good*, if you have an *Unhandsom-Harsh-Rugged-Scratching, Scraping-Stroak*, (as too many have) your *Viol* will seem *Bad*, and your *Play Worse*.[619]

3. *The Holding Position.* All viols, from the smallest to the largest, are played in a vertical position. Except the violone, which is played by a player in a standing position because of its large size, all viols are played on or between the knees of the sitting player. The larger sizes are supported by the legs. Hence the name of the family, *viole da gamba*, leg viols.[620]

The vertical position of the instrument is, really, contingent upon the way the bow is held. Since it is held underhand in playing viols of all sizes, the proper and the most convenient holding position is the vertical one. To become convinced, one has only to try playing the violin with a bow held underhand. It will become immediately obvious why small viols should be held vertically.

The form of the neck of the viol and the position of the left hand with respect to the neck also demand a vertical position. As already stated, on viols the left-hand thumb supports the instrument only by its tip and does not envelop the neck, the necks of viols being wide and thin.[621]

Some of the fine old instruments were disfigured by making the neck shorter, narrower, and rounder. This was done to accommodate violinists and violoncellists, who are used to the shape of the necks of their respective instruments. This is an inexcusable barbarity, not a sign of progress, as it changes the true character of the viol and, really, adds a new family of bowed instruments of questionable merit.[622]

4. *The Stringing of Viols and the Pitch.* In describing the structure of the viol, the fact that it is more delicate than that of the violin was emphasized. Viols were tuned to a lower standard of musical pitch and their structure was designed for that standard.[623] Their strings, being longer and less tensioned, were also smaller in diameter than the strings of violins.

The question of pitch and its influence on tone color is discussed in Appendix B. It is suggested here, for practical reasons, that viols be tuned to a lower pitch having a definite interval relationship with the present standard, A_{49}–440; the interval suggested, a half-tone lower, would bring the standard of pitch to $A\flat_{48}$–415.3.

5. *The Viol Bows.* See page 349.

6. *Tone Color.* The tone color of properly constructed viols, properly strung and fretted, properly held, fingered, and bowed, differs considerably from that of violins and even from that of viols played in the violin-violoncello fashion. It is less assertive than the tone of violins, yet resonant and clear; there is a reedy, almost nasal tinge in it, not devoid of melancholy, yet noble and dignified. Viols sound more poised, less nervous than violins. They are ideal instruments for chamber music and amateur ensembles in schools and colleges, since, if played fretted, viols take less time to learn to play well.[624]

Summary

1. Viols constitute a homogeneous and well developed family, with properly graded sizes of instruments suitable for music written in a polyphonic style.

2. Viols are played with frets, which are organic fixtures of the instruments, influencing the tone color and the fingering technique.

3. Viols are held in a vertical position on or between the knees; they are bowed with viol bows held underhand.

4. Viols should be strung with thinner strings than those used on the violin family.

5. Viols should be tuned to a pitch a half tone lower than the present standard.

History

THE history of the evolution of the *viola da gamba* family and of its musical usage can be divided approximately into three periods.[625]

1. The first period, down to the beginning of the sixteenth century. The instruments were gradually developed to a comparatively high degree of perfection. At the end of that period music written for viols had been composed for trios and quartets.[626]

2. The second period, the sixteenth and the first half of the seventeenth centuries, witnessed the final perfecting of the instruments. Music for viols reached its highest expression

in the works of English and Spanish composers. This period could be called a period of ensemble playing.

3. The third period, beginning roughly in the middle of the seventeenth century and continuing to the close of the life of viols as active instruments, was a period of the gradual decline of ensemble playing and of the emergence of the bass viol as a virtuoso solo instrument. In a certain sense it could be called the period of the French violists and composers.

In the second half of the eighteenth century viols went out of use. The modern attempts to restore them to active use do not belong to the subject matter of this study.

Before beginning a detailed study of the development of the viol family, its general characteristics should first be defined. The probable ancestor of the viol can then be traced by finding the related instruments which possess at least some of these characteristics.

The essential typological characteristics of the viol family are the following:

1. *Body.* Tripartite type; preferably with a flat back, deep ribs, and sloping shoulders.

2. *String fastening.* (a) *Tuning end* (head) of the frontal type with lateral pegs; (b) *fixed end* of the lower end type with the string holder (tail-piece) affixed to the lowest part of the ribs; other types are not excluded, if the rest of the characteristics show that the instruments are related to the viol family.

3. *Tuning and stopping technique.* Strings should be tuned in fourths; necks should be fretted; both open and stopped tones used.

4. *Bowing.* The bow is held, preferably, underhand above the palm.

5. *Holding position.* Vertical, on or between the knees.

The number of strings, although very important typologically, is not an indispensable criterion. The standard number of strings on viols is six. But some viols were built with seven, five, four, and even three strings.[627] Their construction in other respects was such that they could be classified only as viols.

The First Period, to 1500

(1) *The Eleventh Century and before.* The earliest bowed instrument which can be regarded as belonging to the line of the evolution of the viol is the three-stringed bowed rotta (Fr. *crouth*) represented in the hands of the crowned musician in the manuscript of the Abbey of Saint-Martial de Limoges, now in the National Library, Paris. The instrument is held on the left knee in a vertical position, stopped by the left hand, and played with the bow held in the right hand.[628] If the bowed rotta should be accepted as the probable ancestor of the viol, this would open up some interesting possibilities of investigation in connection with that group of instruments, the bowed harps, whose importance was proved by Dr. Otto Andersson.[629]

(2) *The Twelfth Century.* The bowed rotta is sculptured on the capital of the church of Saint-Georges de Bosherville.[630] It is held vertically between the knees, bowed with an underhand bow, and the body has small incurved middle bouts. Another interesting sculpture (*bas-relief*) is in the Museum of Cologne.[631] It is a large three-stringed rotta with sloping shoulders and guitar-shaped body; lower end string fastening; the peg-board string fastening is, it seems, of the frontal type with posterior pegs. Both instruments show an unmistakable affinity to the viol.

The most interesting picture of the bowed rotta is found in the Bible of Saint-Étienne Harding at Dijon.[632] It has a guitar-shaped body with sloping shoulders, three strings, held vertically gamba-fashion and bowed with a bow held underhand. It is played with the organ accompaniment, the organist playing the tones D and F as shown by the letters above the slide keys. An instrument similar to it is found in the cathedral of Troyes (described below), and also in the Harleian Ms. 2804 in the British Museum in London.[633]

(3) *The Thirteenth Century.* The miniatures of the *Cantigas de Santa Maria* in the Codex of Alfonso el Sabio (Alfonso X) King of León and Castile, who reigned between 1252 and 1284, are the most precious source of information for the music and musical instruments of Spain in the thirteenth century. One of the miniatures [634] represents two *vihuelas da arco.*

A study of both shows that they were four-stringed instruments with oval-shaped bodies (two- or three-partitioned?), lozenge-shaped peg-boards with sagittal pegs and occipital (?) string fastening played in a vertical position with the bow held underhand.

Laurent Grillet reproduces the bowed rotta found in the cathedral of Troyes.[635] It is a guitar-shaped instrument with elongated middle part, presumably five-stringed (judging by the number of pegs); it is held on the left knee in the same position as the instrument of Limoges Abbey already mentioned; the bow, unusually long, is held underhand, with the thumb stretched out and pressed firmly against the stalk of the bow. A probable descendant of this type is the guitar-shaped type of viol.

(4) *The Fourteenth Century.* Very little data is available on this. The most interesting is the Manessian manuscript written in the early fourteenth century in Switzerland.[636] It has pictures of Minnesinger fiedels, which Miss Kathleen Schlesinger regards as the immediate predecessors of the viol.[637] There is much to commend this view; opposed to it is the fact that the holding position of the instrument, when shown being played, is invariably a horizontal one. The instrument is held across the breast against the right shoulder. This would indicate, it seems, that the Minnesinger fiedels belong to the line of evolution of the *lira da braccio*, rather than that of the viol.

(5) *The Fifteenth Century.* A large viol is pictured on the Ghent Altar by Hubert and Jan van Eyck,[638] some time between 1420 and 1432. Although it is represented only in part, the most essential details are quite clear. The body is an elongated rectangle with straight sides and semicircular ends, no middle bouts; C-holes have the eyes turned inward. The bridge is located very high and the tail-piece is unusually long. The head is oval in shape with anterior sagittal pegs and occipital string fastening.

In the second half of this century, it seems, viols began to be furnished with heads having lateral pegs. The viol pictured in B. Ramos de Pareja's *De Musica Tractatus* (1482) has not only lateral pegs, but even a well developed scroll of the type usually associated with violins.[639] It has six strings. The body has peculiar incurvations at the top and bottom and well-formed middle bouts. At the turn of the century viols began to assume their final form and proportions. All essential typological elements were already incorporated in their design. Although there was a considerable experimentation not only with the outlines of the body (some of them decidedly fantastic), but also with the instrumental types, such as the lute-viols without bridges,[640] nevertheless, the standard type of body (see p. 258) began to emerge.

The names of two viol-makers may be mentioned. They were Hans Frey (1450–1523) of Nuremberg, Germany, the famous lute-maker who also made viols; and Giovanni Cellini (ca. 1460–ca. 1527–28) of Florence, who, according to the testimony of his famous son, Benvenuto, made some very beautiful musical instruments, among them viols.

The Second Period, 1500–1650

THIS is the most creative period in the life of the viol and music written for it. The typological details of the instrument were already evolved in the previous period. Further evolution was a matter of refinement of detail; finding of practical forms, proportions, and sizes for the instruments of the viol family;[641] and the addition of such new members as the evolution of music and musical usage, as well as the refinement of musical taste, dictated.

In the second period, books devoted to musical instruments and instrumental technique began their appearance. Among them may be mentioned Virdung's *Musica getutscht* (1511), Hans Judenkünig's *Ain schone künstliche Underweisung* (1523), Martin Agricola's *Musica Instrumentalis Deudsch* (first edition, 1528–29, second, 1545), Gerle's *Musica Teusch* (1532), Lanfranco's *Scintille di Musica* (1533), Ganassi's *La Fontegara* (1535) and *Regola Rubertina* (1542–43), Ortiz's *Trattado de Glosas . . . en la Musica de Violones* (1553), Bermudo's *Declaracion de Instrumentos* (1555), Zacconi's *Prattica di Musica* (1596), Cerreto's *Della Prattica Musica* (1601), Ferrabosco's *Lessons for 1. 2. and 3. Viols* (1609), Cerone's *El Melopeo* (1613), Praetorius' great works *Syntagma Musicum* (1618–20) and its supplement, *Theatrum Instrumentorum* (1620), and Mersenne's *Harmonie universelle* (1636–37).

The evolution of the viol in the second period can be traced briefly by representations on Matthias Grünewald's Isenheim Altar picture (1515). A fully developed bass viol with unusually deep middle bouts is represented. The bouts reach the finger-board.[642] An interesting instrument can be found on Hans Burgkmair's *Triumph of Maximilian* (1515), somewhat similar to that of B. Ramos de Pareja's viol mentioned above.[643]

Hans Baldung Grien's allegoric picture (1525) in the Munich Pinakothek gives a tenor viol which, except for its proportions, has all the essential details of later instruments. It differs but slightly from the viol on Tintoretto's picture, *Musizierende Frauen* (ca. 1550), in the Dresden Gallery of Paintings.

Jost Amman's woodcuts, *Drei Geiger* (1568), and groups of musicians on two others, picture bass viols (*Gross-Bassgeige*) of a very large size.[644]

In 1620 appeared Praetorius' *Theatrum Instrumentorum seu Sciagraphia*. This is the best record there is of contemporary instruments. It gives not only their pictures, but, what is far more important, the scale of measurement, so that it is possible to scale the sizes of some of the instruments with a great degree of precision.[645] The viols represented by Praetorius are already fully developed standard pattern instruments.

In connection with the sizes of viols as given by Praetorius and the sizes of viols as used by the English viol players, there exists a serious technical problem. It can be mentioned here that Praetorius' viol sizes are larger than those of the English series as given in the table of viol sizes on page 255. The nomenclature of viols in England and other European countries differs from that of Germany. The whole problem is complicated still more by the existence of the so-called 'lower' tunings of viols and the changing standards of musical pitch. It seems that English viol players at some time about the year 1600 adjusted the sizes of the instruments, bringing them into conformance with the higher pitch, but retaining the 'higher' tunings. Their lead was followed by viol players in other countries. The whole problem is very obscure and complex.[646]

Sometime before 1600, however, the viol family reached its final perfection. Full credit therefore should be given to the English viol-makers, than whom, according to Thomas Mace, there were "no better in the world." The bass viol by Henry Jaye of Southwark, built in 1611, can serve as an outstanding example of a finely proportioned instrument exquisitely wrought by an artist-craftsman.[647]

Examination of the early seventeenth-century instruments shows that viols of reputed makers were as highly developed as Cremona violins and their proportions just as carefully worked out. (See Appendix C.) The quality of workmanship (we speak of fine plain instruments, not of the overdecorated examples) cannot be improved upon. How false, then, is the idea that viols were imperfect predecessors of violins.

In the early seventeenth century a peculiar method of solo playing on viols was developed, 'divisions on a ground'; it is more fully explained on page 279. The playing of divisions required technical dexterity of a very high order. Special viols, 'division viols,' were constructed for this purpose. They were bass viols of smaller size, with a shorter string-length and more convenient for rapid passage work.

Another interesting development of the same period was the playing of viols in the 'lyra way.' This required instruments especially adapted for multiple stopping and chord playing. This requirement was met by lyra-viols, which were bass viols of a still smaller size, the smallest practicable instruments which could be tuned within the range of the bass viol tuning. Lyra-viols are discussed on page 277.

Among composers of music for viols during the second period, the following are outstanding:

The Spanish School. Francisco de Peñalosa (ca. 1500).
Antonio de Cabeçon (ca. 1550).
Diego Ortiz (ca. 1550).

The English School. William Lawes (d. 1645).
John Jenkins (1592–1678).
Christopher Simpson (d. 1669).
and the lesser lights:
John Coperario (Cooper, d. 1627).
Alfonso II Ferrabosco (d. 1628).
Matthew Locke (d. 1677).
Deering.
Thomas I and II Lupo.
Mico.

The French School. André Maugars (b. ca. 1600).
Hottman (d. 1663).

Viol makers of the second period are fairly numerous, especially those of Italy:

England. Thomas Aldred (ca. 1560–1600) of Holborn.
John Ross (Rose, Rosa, ca. 1562–98) of London (Bridewell).
Bolles (ca. 1600–20) of London.
Gillis York (1610) of Northhampton.
Henry Jay (Jaye, Jaie, ca. 1611–ca. 1676) of Southwark (London).
Henry Smith (ca. 1633) of London.

France. Caspar Tieffenbrucker (Duiffoprugcar, 1514–70) of Lyons.

Germany. Ernst Busch (1612–44) of Nuremberg.
Jacob Stainer (1621–83) of Absam, Tyrol; better known as a violin-maker of the first rank.

Italy. Bastiano da Verona (ca. 1500).
Fra. Pietro Dardelli (ca. 1500).
Maestro Lorenzo (ca. 1500) of Pavia, who made organs, lutes, viols, and clavichords.
Johannes Andreas (1511) of Verona.
Peregrino di Zanetto Michelis (ca. 1520–1603) of Brescia.
Francesco Linarolo (ca. 1530) of Venice.
Johannes Maria (1540) of Venice.
Gasparo da Salo (Bertolotti, ca. 1542–1609) of Brescia, who is regarded by some as the first violin-maker.
Francesco II Bertolotti (1565–1614) of Brescia.
Cesare Bonoris (1568) of Mantua.
Ventura Linarolo (1577–91) of Venice.
Antonio Siciliano (Ciciliano, 1630–60) of Venice.

Holland. Jan Boumeester (1637–89) of Amsterdam.

The Third Period, after 1650

THE third period witnessed the gradual decline of ensemble playing and the neglect of the smaller sizes of viols; the only exception to the last tendency was the rise in popularity of the smallest-sized viol, the *pardessus de viol*, which was not among the consort viols of the classical period. It became very popular among ladies of French society in the eighteenth century.

The bass viol was the last instrument of the viol family to disappear from use. It is a curious fact that in books on the instrumentation of the nineteenth century and later it is called by the generic name of the whole family and is known as the *viola da gamba*.[648]

The principal reason for the decline of the viol was the growing popularity of the violin. Changing tastes and social customs demanded performances in large halls and more sonorous instruments. Viols, which are chamber music instruments, could not compete with their fashionable rivals, although the fight between violists and violinists became very bitter.[649]

The bass viol, before it disappeared from use, had a career as a brilliant solo instrument. In France there arose a remarkable school of composer-players, among whom André Maugars (b. ca. 1600), Hottman (d. 1663), and Saint-Colombe (1630–90) can be regarded as the founders. Later came de Machy (1685), Jean Rousseau (1687), the author of *Traité de la Viole*, Marin Marais (1656–1728), who was regarded as an acknowledged master,

J. B. Forqueray (1670–1745), Caix d'Hervelois (1670–1759). The last prominent bass viol player of the old school was Karl Friedrich Abel (1725–87).

The names of viol makers of the third period, and especially their nationalities and the periods of their lives, reveal the shifting of interest in the instruments. In the second period the most numerous group of viol-makers were Italians; in the third period there are very few, indeed, showing clearly that violin-making, which reached its zenith with the appearance of Stradivari (1644–1737), became the principal occupation of Italian luthiers. The English still held their ground. The French had some brilliant representatives who continued the traditions of the English school. The Germans formed the most solid and substantial group of the closing period.

England. John Shaw (1665–98), London.
William Addison (ca. 1670), London.
Thomas Cole (1672–90), Holborn (London).
Barak Norman (ca. 1678–1740), London.
John Baker (1688–1720), London, South Kensington.
Nathaniel Cross (1700–51), Aldermanbury (London).
France. Claude Pierray (1698–1726), Paris.
Louis Guersan (ca. 1713–ca. 1781), Paris.
Claude Boivin (1730–54), Paris.
Feyzeau (1740), Bordeaux.
Benoît Fleury (1751–91), Paris.
Germany. Johann Jacob Epp (1639–69), Strassburg.
Joachim Tielke (1641–1719), Hamburg.
Thomas Edlinger (1656–90), Augsburg.
Georg Aman (1671–1717), Augsburg.
Christoph Mener (1677–85), Danzig.
Martin Hoffman (1653–1719), Leipzig.
Paul Alletsee (1698–1738?), Munich.
Johann Christian Hoffman (1683–1750), Leipzig.
Austria. Daniel Achatius Stadlman (ca. 1680–ca. 1744), Vienna.
Italy. Vincenco Ruggeri (Rugieri, 1690–1735), Cremona.
Holland. Pieter Rombouts (1703–35), Amsterdam.

Viols from the earliest time of their existence were regarded as noble instruments and never lost their standing in the esteem of the upper classes.

The portrait of Madame Henriette of France, the daughter of Louis XV, painted by J. M. Nattier,[650] representing her with a bass viol, is a proof that viols were considered proper instruments for royalty. Going further back into history, Henry VIII of England composed some fine pieces for viol consorts. Viols held their place in the intimacy of home, at church, and at court functions.

Skill in the playing of the viol was at one time regarded as an accomplishment as necessary as the possession of good manners. The viols were used as solo instruments, for voice accompaniment, in different combinations of instruments of their own type (the whole consorts), and in combination with other instruments (broken consorts). The music written for consort playing required moderate technical proficiency, easily attainable by a musical amateur.[651] This was helped by the frets, which were an organic feature of the viol and not merely a condescension to lack of skill. To compensate, viol music required a high degree of musical intelligence and musicianship. At a later period, the viol music written for solo concert performances also required the highest technical skill.

Viols were kept in a specially constructed piece of furniture, the 'chest of viols.' The same expression also referred to a set of instruments, in the sense that a 'violin quartet' meant a set of two violins, a viola, and a violoncello.

The following advertisement printed in *Tripla Concordia* (a collection of airs) in 1667 gives some curious facts about the chests of viols.[652]

There is two Chests of Violls to be sold, one made by Mr. John Ross, who formerly lived in Bridewell, containing two trebles, three tenors, and one bass: The chest was made in the year 1598. The other being made by Mr. Henry Smith, who formerly lived over against Hatton House, in Holborn, containing two trebles, two tenors, two basses: The chest was made in the year 1633. Both chests are very curious work.

Our good friend, Thomas Mace, gives such excellent information about the proper procedure for selecting a full equipment for a 'ready entertainment' that we cannot resist quoting him.

Your *Best Provision*, (and *most Compleat*) will be, a *Good Chest of Viols*; *Six*, in *Number*; viz. 2 *Basses*, 2 *Tenors*, and 2 *Trebles*: All *Truly*, and *Proportionably Suited*.

Of such, there are no *Better* in the *World*, than *Those of Aldred*, *Jay*, *Smith*, (yet the *Highest in Esteem* are) *Bolles*, and *Ross*, (one *Bass* of *Bolles's*, I have know *Valued* at 100 *l*.) *These* were *Old*; but We have *Now*, very *Excellent Good Workmen*, who (no doubt) can *Work* as well as *Those*, if They be so well Paid for *Their Work*, as *They* were; yet we chiefly *Value Old Instruments*, before *New*; for by *Experience*, they are found to be far the *Best*. . . .

Now, suppose you cannot procure an *Intire Chest* of *Viols*, *Suitable*, etc. Then, *Thus*.

Endeavour to *Pick up* (*Here, or There*) so many *Excellent Good Odd Ones*, as *near Suiting* as you can, (every way) *viz*. both for *Shape*, *Wood*, *Colour*, *etc*. but especially for *Scize*.

And to be *Exact* in *That*, take *This Certain Rule*, *viz*. Let your *Bass* be *Large*. Then your *Trebles* must be just as *Short* again, in the *String*, (viz.) from *Bridge*, to *Nut*, as are your *Basses*; because they stand 8 *Notes Higher* than the *Basses*; Therefore, as *Short* again; (for the *Middle* of *Every String*, is an 8*th*.) The *Tenors*, (in the *String*) just so long as from the *Bridge*, to *F Fret*; because they stand a 4*th*. *Higher*, than your *Basses*; Therefore, so *Long*.

Let *This Suffice*, to put you into a *Compleat Order* for *Viols*, (either way;) Only *Note*, That the *Best Place* for the *Bridge*, is to stand *just* in the 3 *Quarter Dividing* of the *Open Cuts Below*; though *Most*, *most Erroniously* suffer them much to stand too *High*, which is a *Fault*.

After all *This*, you may add to your *Press*, a *Pair* of *Violins*, to be in Readiness for any *Extraordinary Jolly*, or *Jocund Consort-Occasion*; But never use Them, but with *This Proviso*, viz. Be sure you make an *Equal Provision* for Them, by the *Addition*, and *Strength* of *Basses*; so that They may not *Out-cry* the *Rest* of the *Musick*, (the *Basses* especially) to which end, It will be *Requisite*, you *Store* your *Press* with a *Pair* of *Lusty Full-Sciz'd Theorboes*, always to strike in with your *Consorts*, or *Vocal-Musick*; to which, *That Instrument* is most *Naturally* Proper.

And now to make your *Store* more *Amply-Compleat*; add to all *These* 3 *Full-Sciz'd Lyro-Viols*;

there being most *Admirable Things* made, by our *Very Best Masters*, for *That Sort of Musick*, both *Consort-wise*, and *Peculiarly* for 2 and 3 *Lyroes*.

Let *Them* be *Lusty*, *Smart-Speaking Viols*; because, that in *Consort*, they often *Retort* against the *Treble*; *Imitating*, and often *Standing instead of That Part*, *viz.* a *Second Treble*.

They will serve likewise for *Division-Viols* very Properly.

And being *Thus Stor'd*, you have a *Ready Entertainment* for the *Greatest Prince* in the *World*.[653]

We shall finish our discourse on viols with another quotation from Mace.[654] His language is quaint, but the sentiment remains true and necessary for our insane times, so lacking in opportunities for a noble emotional release. Viols are the instruments for amateurs. An intelligent enthusiasm for them could be a powerful incentive for the development of our musical culture.

We had for our *Grave Musick*, *Fancies* of 3, 4, 5, and 6 *Parts* to the *Organ*; Interpos'd (now and then) with some *Pavins*, *Allmaines*, *Solemn*, *and Sweet Delightful Ayres*; all which were (as it were) so many *Pathettical Stories*, *Rhetorical*, and *Sublime Discourses; Subtil*, and *Accute Augmentations; so Suitable*, *and Agreeing to the Inward*, *Secret*, *and Intellectual Faculties of the Soul and Mind*; that to set Them forth according to their *True Praise*, *there are no Words Sufficient in Language*; yet what I can best speak of Them, shall be only to say, *That They have been to my self*, (*and many others*) *as Divine Raptures*, *Powerfully Captivating all our unruly Faculties*, *and Affections*, (*for the Time*) *and disposing us to Solidity*, *Gravity*, *and a Good Temper; making us capable of Heavenly*, *and Divine Influences*.

'Tis *Great Pity Few Believe Thus Much*; but Far Greater, that so *Few Know It*.

271. HIGH TREBLE VIOL — Paris, France, 1752

Pardessus de Viole. Standard pattern. Flat back of maple, inlaid purfling at edges and three thin vertical lines of inlaid ebony; *Fleury* stamped on the button. Ribs of composite construction, two strips (light) of maple, the middle one (dark) of walnut. Arched belly of soft pine purfled at edges; inlaid ebony heart below the finger-board; C-holes. Neck and peg-box of single piece of maple, with cherub's head; peg-box embellished with incised lines and stamped circular figures. Finger-board of maple, veneered with ebony. Hook-bar of ebony at the bottom holding ebony tail-piece. Movable bridge (violin type). Five strings attached to five lateral pegs of box-wood. *Inside construction*: top block integral with neck; cross-strip 5 cm. wide and 3 mm. thick, glued to back; rough linen reinforcing strips on rib-joints and on the bend line of back; no cross-bars on the back; bass-bar and sound-post. Eight gut frets on the neck. Light yellow varnish. Printed label inside:

'Benoît Fleury rue des Boucheries
Faubourg St. Germain à Paris, 1752'

Length, total, 59 cm. Body, length, 32.75 cm.; width, upper bouts, 15.5 cm.; middle bouts, 11 cm.; lower bouts, 19.5 cm. Ribs, height, 6 cm. Vibrating length of strings, 30.5 cm. (17.1712) Plate XI

The high treble viol was the youngest of all the viols, being introduced in the eighteenth century. Its five strings are tuned:

It is held in the true viol position, i.e., vertically, between the knees (on both knees and slightly between them, to be exact), and bowed with the bow held over the palm. In the eighteenth century it became fashionable in France among ladies of society.[655]

Lütgendorf[656] gives Benoît Fleury's years of activity as 1751–91; he was admitted to the guild of instrument makers as a master in 1755. This instrument is mentioned by Lütgendorf, but its year is erroneously given as 1764.

272. SMALL TENOR VIOL — Copenhagen, Denmark, 1752

Haute-Contre de Viole. Sloping rib type. Flat back of maple. Ribs of maple. Belly of soft pine, in two pieces, highly arched, with C-holes. Neck with peg-box of maple, with a lion's head at the top. Finger-board of boxwood veneered with ebony. Hook-bar and tail-piece of ebony. Six strings attached to six lateral pegs of boxwood. *Inside construction*: back reinforced by two cross-bars, the cross-strip 4.3 cm. wide and 3 mm. thick, the bend line of the back reinforced by a rough linen strip; regular rib linings at the back and belly joints, circular fillets at the corners (instead of corner blocks as in violins); bass-bar and sound-post. Eight gut frets on the neck. Light yellow varnish. Two labels inside:

1. The original maker's label (printed),
   'Jesper Gotfredsen
   Fiolin-Mager; Kiobenhavn 1752'
2. The repair label (in ink),
   'Repareret Af Jesper Gotfredsen
   Instrumentmager; Kiobenhavn
   Anno 1771'

Length, total, 82 cm. Body, length, 43.75 cm.; width, upper bouts, 21 cm.; middle bouts, 15 cm.; lower bouts, 25.5 cm. Ribs, height, 9.25 cm. Vibrating length of strings, 47.2 cm. (17.1715)
Plate XI

The small tenor was used in consort playing of parts which would correspond to the first tenor in a vocal choir. As Mr. Gerald Hayes pointed out,[657] the sizes of viols were adjusted very finely so that each part in the consort music would have its personal tone color. This is essential in the performance of old music, in which each part had equal importance with the rest, and none was exclusively favored.

This instrument would be tuned:

273. LYRA VIOL — England, ca. 1665, attributed to Addison, London

Standard pattern. Flat back of maple, in two pieces with purfling. Ribs of maple. Belly of soft pine, slightly arched, with two C-holes. Neck of maple with peg-box and carved head of blindfolded woman at the top. Finger-board of maple, veneered with ebony; twenty German silver frets inserted in it. Hook-bar of maple, affixed to the bottom block by two turned pins with heads; tail-piece of maple veneered with ebony. Six strings with movable bridge (violoncello type). *Internal construction* (as found before restoration): back reinforced by two cross-bars and cross-strip 8 cm. wide and 6 mm. thick; the bend line of back reinforced by rough linen strip; regular

lining at the joint of ribs and belly, but the joint of ribs and back formed of rough linen strip glued to both; circular fillets in corners; the ends of both cross-bars supported by small brackets glued to the ribs and cross-bars. Bass-bar and sound-post. Dark reddish-brown varnish. No maker's label. Restored by Messrs. John A. Gould & Sons in 1936. *Note on restoration.* The back was warped, cracked, and the joints opened. The reinforced linen joint of back and the ribs was found inadequate for keeping the instrument in shape, so the regular linings were glued to the ribs; old cross-bars were replaced by newer and stronger ones. The instrument after restoration gives a tone of fine quality. Length, total, 103 cm. Body, length, 56.5 cm.; width, upper bouts, 26.75 cm.; middle bouts, 19 cm.; lower bouts, 32 cm. Ribs, height, 11 cm. Vibrating length of strings, 60 cm. (17.1718)
Plate XI

The lyra-viol or *viola bastarda* is the smallest-sized bass viol. A more correct way of speaking would be to refer to this instrument as 'the viol used Lyra-way.' [658] This alludes to the multiple stopping and chord playing for which the lyra-viol is especially adapted. Its bridge is somewhat flatter than that of the ordinary viol. The shorter string length gives more closely spaced frets; the neck, slightly more narrow than that of the division viol, permits easier manipulation.

The name, 'lyra-viol,' implied the close affinity in its manner of playing with that of the lira family of instruments.[659] The alternative name, *viola bastarda,* according to Dr. Curt Sachs [660] meant that the lyra-viol served as a connecting link between the *viola da gamba* and the *lira da gamba,* with a closer affinity to the former.

The old English lyra-viols had sympathetic strings applied to them about 1600. These were discarded by the middle of the seventeenth century and are not characteristic of the instrument. More of this in the section on instruments with sympathetic strings.

The lyra-viol holds an exceptionally important place in the viol family, since it helps to unravel the confusion of names, sizes, tunings, etc., which exists with reference to the rest of the viols. It is the only instrument which retained its name, relative position in the viol family, its musical usage, and tunings. The only aspect which changed was its size. This supports the contention that the sizes of viols in the sixteenth and seventeenth centuries differed, and, incidentally, justifies Jean Rousseau's assertion that the English reduced the sizes of viols.[661]

The general proposition just stated is supported by a mass of evidence. Both in England and in Germany the lyra-viol holds the same relative place in the viol family. In England the instrument is placed between the tenor and the division viol; its body is longer and wider than that of the tenor (see table of sizes, p. 255). In Germany, as Praetorius stated, the *viola bastarda* "is a type of the *Violn de Gamba,* and it must be tuned as the tenor of the Violn de Gamba (instead of which it can be used in case of need). But its body is somewhat longer and larger." [662] Therefore Praetorius' *viola bastarda* should be placed between the tenor and the *Kleine Bass-Viol,* which in the German series of viols corresponds to the small bass (division viol) of the English series. For particulars see Appendix B.

The musical usage of the instrument was similar in Germany and in England. Praetorius stated that "a good master will venture to play (on the *viola bastarda*) *madrigals;* . . . (in playing) fugues and *Harmony* he can go through and through with all ease and through all the voices; he selects [things to play] sometimes above in the treble, sometimes below in the bass, sometimes in the middle, in the tenor and alto." [663]

Thomas Mace has been quoted on page 275. Repeating for convenience: he said that the lyra-viols "in *Consort*, they often *Retort* against the *Treble*: *Imitating*, and often *Standing instead* of *That Part*, viz. A *Second Treble*."

The tunings of the lyra-viol were less standardized than those of other viols. They were selected in conformance with the tonality of the piece of music played. Since the music for the lyra-viol was written in tablature notation,[664] this variety in tunings facilitated performance.

The early tunings of the lyra-viol are given by Praetorius[665] in *De Organographia*, as follows:

1.	*D*	G	*c*	*e*	*a*	*d'*
2.	*C*	G	*c*	*e*	*a*	*d'*
3.	*AA*	E	*A*	*e*	*a*	*d'*
4.	*AA*	D	*A*	*d*	*a*	*d'*
5.	*AA*	D	G	*d*	*g*	*d'* [666]

The first is the ordinary viol tuning; the second is the ordinary tuning with the lowest string tuned a tone lower.[667] The third and fourth are given by Alfonso II Ferrabosco [668] in *Lessons for 1. 2. and 3. Viols*. So Praetorius' tunings follow the English practice of the early seventeenth century.

So far both the English and the German practice have not differed. It is only when the dimensions of the instruments are studied that the difference in sizes appears and confusion begins.

The Table of viol sizes, page 255, and the diagram, Plate XVI, should be consulted. Praetorius' *viola bastarda* represented on table xx, figure 4 of the *Theatrum Instrumentorum* (page 362 of this study), scales two feet seven inches (Brunswick), or 73.7 cm. An instrument of this size is larger than the largest consort bass of the English series of viols. Since Praetorius stated that the body of the viola bastarda of his time was "somewhat longer and larger" than that of the German tenor viol, the estimated size of the latter would be about 68–69 cm. or the average size of the English consort bass.[669]

The English lyra-viol (*viola bastarda*) is a much smaller instrument. In the seventeenth century it measured (average) about 56.5 cm. or about 17 cm. less. As can be clearly seen on the diagram, Plate XVI, there are the division viols and a whole class of consort basses (called 'tenor viols' in Germany) between the English lyra-viol and Praetorius' *viola bastarda*. For these reasons the size of the lyra-viol becomes the pivotal point in the argument that the viol sizes in England and in Germany differed [670] and that the English violists 'reduced' the sizes of viols.

Summing up: The lyra-viol (*viola bastarda*) in its musical usage held the same place in England and in Germany with respect to the viol family, and also kept its name and its relative position in the series of viols. For this reason, as soon as the exact size of Praetorius' *viola bastarda* is ascertained, the discrepancy in the absolute size between the English and the German instruments becomes obvious and indisputable. The differences in size of the other instruments in the viol family are more difficult to uncover, since viols retained their sizes and tunings, but changed names in England and retained their names in Germany. Appendix B is devoted to a detailed discussion of this important and complicated subject.

274. DIVISION VIOL — England, London, 1713

Flat back of maple in two pieces, inlaid with double-line purfling, ornamental knots, and the double interlaced monogram BN. Ribs of maple. Slightly arched belly of soft pine with double-line purfling at the edges, inlaid floral design below the finger-board with medallion stamped BARAK NORMAN — LONDON — FECIT; two C-holes. Finger-board of maple veneered with ebony. Neck ending with peg-box and scroll, instead of a carved head. Hook-bar of ebony, holding tail-piece veneered with ebony. Six strings fixed to six boxwood pegs; movable bridge. *Inside construction*: top block separate from the neck bracket; back reinforced with two cross-bars and cross-strip 9.8 cm. wide and 5 mm. thick; bass-bar and sound-post. Eight gut frets on the neck. Light yellow varnish. Printed label inside:

'Barak Norman
at the Bass Viol in
St. Paul Church-y:
London Fecit
1713'

Also the repair label of Messrs. John A. Gould and Sons, Boston, Mass., 1936. Length, total, 120.5 cm. Body, length, 68.5 cm.; width, upper bouts, 30 cm.; middle bouts, 22 cm.; lower bouts, 37 cm. Ribs, height, 13 cm. Vibrating length of strings, 68 cm. (17.1716)
Plate XI

Although this viol could be classified as a Bass Viol, because of its dimensions, yet a few details show that it was intended for playing divisions. The vibrating length of the strings is closer to that of division viols, the neck is somewhat narrower than one usually fitted on bass viols of the same number of strings (six), and the whole appearance of the instrument shows that it was intended for brilliant solo work.

Divisions are defined by Mr. Gerald Hayes as follows: "In its essence the name 'Divisions on a Ground' implies that, between two long notes on one instrument, another instrument plays a series of shorter notes, beginning and ending upon the notes of the ground or upon a recognized consonance with them." [671]

Christopher Simpson, the author of *The Division-Viol, or, The Art of Playing Extempore upon a Ground*,[672] tells us that:

A VIOL in the hands of an excellent Violist may (no doubt) be recon'd amongst the best of Musical Instruments. To Play *ex tempore* to a Ground is the highest perfection of it. . . .[673]

§2. . . . A Viol for Division, should be of something a lesser size than a Consort Bass; that so the Hand may better command it: more or less short, according to the reach of his fingers, who is to use it; but the ordinary size, such as may carry a String of thirty Inches [674] from the Bridge (duely placed) to the Nut. The Sound should be quick and sprightly, like a Violin; and Viols of that shape (the Bellyes being digged out of the Plank) do commonly render such a Sound.

It must be accomodated with six Strings; and with seven Frets, like those of a Lute, but something thicker. If also you fasten a small Fret, at the distance of an Octave from the open Strings (which is the middle betwixt the Nut and the Bridge) it will be a good Guide to your Hand, when you stop that part of the Finger-board.[675]

The Strings a little bigger than those of a Lyra-Viol; which must be laid at the like nearness to the Finger-board, for ease and convenience of Stopping.

The Bridge, as round as that of a Consort Bass; that so each several String may be hit with a bolder touch of the Bow.

The Plate, or Finger-board, exactly smooth and even. Its length, full two parts of three, from the Nut to the Bridge. It must also be of a proportionate roundness to the Bridge; so, that each String may lye at an equal nearness to it. . . .

§3. *What kind of Bow.*

A VIOL-BOW for Division, should be stiff, but not heavy. Its length (betwixt the two places where the Hairs are fastened at each end) about seven and twenty Inches.[676] The Nut, short. The height of it about a fingers breadth, or little more.

§4. *How to hold or place the Viol.*

BEING conveniently seated, place your Viol decently betwixt your knees; so, that the lower end of it may rest upon the calves of your legs. Set the Soles of your feet flat on the floor, your Toes turn'd a little outward. Let the top of your Viol be erected towards your left shoulder; so, as it may rest in that posture, though you touch it not with your hand.

§5. *How to hold and move the Bow.*

HOLD the Bow betwixt the ends of your Thumb and two foremost fingers, near to the Nut. The Thumb and first finger fastned on the Stalk; and the second fingers end turned *in* shorter, against the Hairs thereof; by which you may poize and keep up the point of the Bow. If the second finger has not strength enough, you may joyn the third finger in assistance to it; but in Playing Swift Division, two fingers and the Thumb is best.[677]

Holding the Bow in this posture, stretch out your arm, and draw it first over one String and then another; crossing them in right angle, at the distance of two or three Inches from the Bridge. Make each several String yeild a full and clear sound; and order your knees so, that they may be no impediment to the motion of your Bow.

§6. *The posture of the Left Hand.*

WHEN you are to set your fingers upon the Strings, you must not grasp the Neck of your Viol, like a Violin; but rather (as those that Play on the Lute) keep your Thumb on the back of the Neck, opposite to your fore-finger; so as your Hand may have liberty to remove up and down, as occasion shall require.[678]

Barak Norman (1678–1740) is regarded as one of the most outstanding among English viol and violin makers. He was, probably, a pupil of Thomas Urquhardt. In 1715 he took Nathaniel Cross as a partner. His viols have an individual outline which makes them easily recognizable. The purfling was of very elaborate pattern, with decorative knots and his characteristic double diagram on the back and the burned-in trade-mark on the belly, also surrounded by purfled knots. He is also reputed to be the first maker in England to construct a violoncello. His violins followed a Brescia model.

275. BASS VIOL Paris, France, ca. 1708, attributed to Claude Pierray

Standard pattern. Flat back of maple in two pieces; no purfling. Ribs of maple. Moderately arched belly of soft pine in two pieces, double purfling; two C-holes. Neck of maple (not original) with the original peg-box varnished reddish-brown. Hook-bar of ebony holding boxwood tail-piece with inlaid edges. Movable bridge with scalloped top, stamped 'Chanot.' Seven strings attached to seven lateral pegs of boxwood having small ivory buttons inserted in heads. *Inside construction*: back reinforced with cross-strip 9.25 cm. wide and 7 mm. thick and two cross-bars (the original ones were replaced by extra strong bars to prevent warping of the back); bass-bar of generous proportions, sound-post. Eight gut frets on the neck. Dark black-brown varnish on the body. No maker's label. The repair label of Messrs. John A. Gould & Sons, Boston, Mass., 1936. Length, 124 cm. Body, length, 69 cm.; width, upper bouts, 32.5 cm.; middle bouts, 23.5 cm.; lower bouts, 40 cm. Ribs, height, 14 cm. Vibrating length of strings, 72 cm. (17.1717)
Plate XI

The seven-stringed bass viol is the highest development of this member of the *viola da gamba* family. Its introduction is attributed to M. de Sainte-Colombe,[679] ca. 1680, but it was a revival of a practice which was in existence much earlier.[680] The tunings of bass viols are as follows:

Six-stringed instruments (both divisions and bass viols):

Seven-stringed bass viols:

Claude Pierray (1698–1726) was one of the best representatives of the old school instrument-makers of Paris.

276. BASS VIOL England, late 18th century

The shape of the body approaches that of the violoncello; made of thin copper sheets, the edges of the back and belly raised, rounded, turned, and soldered to the ribs. Both the back and belly are arched. Neck, neck-bracket, and peg-box of wood, encased in copper sheathing made of separate parts soldered together. Reinforcing apron on belly for bracket support. The scroll of copper, joined to the sheathing and embellished with raised bosses; a small silver disc on the scroll front with the word '*EUTHERPE*' engraved on it. Ebony finger-board. Long ebony tail-piece attached by the gut string to the end-pin (there is no spike or foot, as on the violoncello or double bass). Four strings attached to four boxwood pegs. Movable bridge. Bass-bar and sound-post of wood. Length, total, 108 cm. Body, length, 75 cm.; width, upper bouts, 37 cm.; middle bouts, 25.5 cm.; lower bouts, 45 cm. Ribs, height, 14.75 cm. Vibrating length of strings, 72.5 cm (18.656)
Plate XIV

This instrument, made of copper — an unusual material — is of special interest as one of the last relics of old church orchestras in England. It was played for many years in the church in Bosham, Sussex, before it was finally superseded by the organ about ninety years ago. The instrument is neither a viol nor a violoncello: it is the 'Eutherpe.'

277. ALTO VIOL London, England, 1786

Long, shallow model, influenced by violin type. Flat back of maple, in two pieces. Ribs of maple, apparently cut down. Belly of pine with raised edges and purfling; scimitar-shaped sound-holes; rosette with the three feathers of the Prince of Wales under the finger-board. Back fitted flush with ribs, belly with overhanging edges as in the violin. Neck and peg-box of pearwood, the head bent back and ending in a square similar to that of the English guitars. Finger-board of ebony. Tail-piece of ebony, with slanting top; attached in violin fashion is an end-pin. Five gut strings pass over the violin type bridge (original one lost). Five box-wood pegs. *Inside construction*: corner blocks as in a violin; two cross-bars and a wide cross-strip glued to the back; deep bass-bar; sound-post. Grayish-brown varnish. Ink label inside:

'MADE BY
RICHARD DUKE
LONDON. 1786'

Length, total, 69.5 cm. Body, length, 41.5 cm.; width, upper bouts, 18.5 cm.; lower bouts, 22 cm. Ribs, height, 3.5 cm. Vibrating length of strings, 39 cm. (17.1713)
Plate XI

There were two English makers by the name of Richard Duke, father and son. The elder, who worked between 1750 and 1780, was regarded as a maker of fine instruments.[681] The son's work was somewhat inferior to that of his father. Our instrument, since it is dated 1786, is the work of Richard Duke, the son.

It is a very interesting instrument, which, while keeping certain earmarks of the viola (flat back with inside reinforcements, sloping shoulders, etc.), shows a decided originality in its departure from the standard pattern in the use of a cittern-like head, and its discreet suggestion of violin corners. The ribs were cut down and the back straightened at a later date.

278. SMALL TENOR VIOL Germany, 18th century, attributed to Elsler

Flat back of maple, in two pieces. Ribs of maple. Belly of pine, slightly arched, purfled; two flame-shaped sound-holes. Narrow neck with peg-box adorned with grotesque man's head. Finger-board of stained boxwood. Tail-piece of ebony, embellished by three inlaid ivory discs, fixed by the gut-loop to the tail-pin. Five strings. *Inside construction*: Corner fillets of large radius; two cross-bars and cross-strip, 6 cm. wide and 3 mm. high, glued to the back. Bass-bar and sound-post. Dark reddish-brown varnish. Length, 74.5 cm. Body, length, 44 cm.; width, upper bouts, 21.7 cm.; middle bouts, 13.7 cm.; lower bouts, 27.5 cm. Ribs, height, 7.2 cm. Vibrating length of strings, 40.3 cm. (17.1714)
Plate XI

This instrument is an example of the transitional type, when violin practice began to influence the design of the viol. The neck is made shorter and rounded, violin-fashion, so that the thumb can envelop it; such a neck is too short for the placing of the standard number of frets (seven). The instrument was obviously meant to be played as an orchestral viola.[682]

279. CITHER VIOL — Paris, France, 1721

Viole d'amour. Deep model. Standard viol pattern. Flat back of maple. Belly of soft pine, slightly arched, two C-holes. Ribs of maple. Neck of maple with a long peg-box ending in cittern-like head with inlaid square end. Finger-board of stained boxwood. Tail-piece affixed by a brass wire to the tail-pin. Ten strings: two lowest of brass wire strung singly; the remaining eight are of steel wire and strung in pairs, thus making a total of six 'choirs.' Ten ebony pegs. Movable bridge, ivory nut. *Inside construction*: corner fillets of small radius; cross-strip, 4.5 cm. wide and 2.5 mm. thick, glued to the back. Bass-bar and sound-post. Dark brown finish. Ink label inside:

'François vailleu
rue Debussy 1721
A Paris'

Length, total, 71 cm. Body, length, 32 cm.; width, upper bouts, 15.5 cm.; middle bouts, 11 cm.; lower bouts, 18.75 cm. Ribs, height, 6.5 cm. Vibrating length of strings, 32 cm. (17.1723)
Plate XI

This is a very unusual instrument. The body construction and size is that of the high treble viol (*pardessus de viol*); but the stringing is very peculiar. The peg-box has ten pegs; there is no clearance under the finger-board; the notches on the nut indicate very clearly how the instrument should be strung: the two lowest strings are single and the rest are double, so that the total number of tones available is six. The instrument is in its original condition,[683] and therefore can be taken as one of the proofs of the existence of instruments with metallic strings, which, according to Jean Rousseau, de Brossard, and Mattheson, were called *violes d'amour*, but had no sympathetic strings. This question is discussed more fully in the note on the *viole d'amour* under No. 281.

280. SULTANA — Dublin, Ireland, 1794

Cither Viol. Body of a modified viol type. Back of one piece of maple, highly arched, with ink line purfling, stamped on the button: 'No. 1954, PERRY, DUBLIN.' Ribs of maple. Belly of pine, highly arched, with ink-line purfling and sound-holes of the flame type. Both back and belly have overhanging edges. Neck and peg-box of maple, ending in a cittern-like head with a square end inlaid with pearl and ebony. Finger-board of stained walnut, inlaid with ivory lining. Tail-piece of black stained boxwood, with ivory inlay; affixed to the ivory tail-pin by U-shaped bent wire fastened to a silver reinforcing piece, the ends of the wire formed into rivet heads. Five double strings, four lower ones of spun silk, six higher ones of steel wire held in the tail-piece by small ivory buttons. Movable bridge with ebony top, ivory nut. No regular peg-box, instead a very solidly constructed machine head with the worm-wheels concealed inside. Internal construction of the violin type. Fine, solid workmanship. Printed label inside:

'Made by
THOMAS PERRY and WM. WILKINSON
Musical Instrument Makers
No. 6 Anglesea Street
No. 1954 Dublin 1794'

Length, total, 71 cm. Body, length, 35 cm.; width, upper bouts, 18.25 cm.; middle bouts, 12.25 cm.; lower bouts, 22.5 cm. Ribs, height, 4.25 cm. Vibrating length of strings, 33.3 cm. (17.1725)
Plate XIV

In the catalogue of the Music Loan Exhibition held at Fishmongers' Hall, London, in 1904, there is the statement that this instrument is not a true viol, but that it embodied the ideas of an Italian musician living in Dublin, with whom Perry was acquainted, and was styled by them a Psaltery.[684]

Bowed Chordophones with Sympathetic Strings

THE principle underlying the action of sympathetic strings is simple. If two strings are tuned in unison, or if one of them is tuned to some harmonic overtone of another string, then the sounding of one string will induce the other to respond in 'sympathy.' Hence the name for this phenomenon, a sympathetic vibration. A string or strings in which such vibrations are induced are called sympathetic strings. The phenomenon is more pronounced on long, low tuned strings; metallic strings respond better than gut strings. The best material for sympathetic strings is a high grade of drawn steel wire. For their successful operation sympathetic strings should be tuned with the utmost precision, otherwise the force of response will be weakened or they will fail to respond altogether.

The application of sympathetic strings to bowed instruments was known in the East several centuries before it was practised in the West. Several types of Eastern instruments have sympathetic strings such as the *čikārā*, *sāraṅgī*, *sāz*, *tad*, *tayuç*, and a more modern one, the *esrāj*.[685]

In Western Europe the credit for the introduction of sympathetic strings belongs to the English. Praetorius, in his description of the viola bastarda, states explicitly that in England steel or wound brass strings were used on this instrument in addition to ordinary bowed strings.[686] The English themselves credit Daniel Farrant, a viol-player in the King's Music under James I, as the inventor of this device, shortly after 1600.[687] John Playford, writing in 1661, stated: "Of this sort of *Viols*, I have seen many, but *Time* and *Disuse* has set them aside." [688] It might be that Farrant applied sympathetic strings without being influenced by knowledge of such a device on Eastern instruments. But more probably he adapted the Eastern invention to the lyra-viol, since the English East India Company was founded at the end of the sixteenth century [689] and was granted royal charter by Queen Elizabeth on December 31, 1600. Undoubtedly, some specimens of Eastern instruments reached England at that time.

Later, instruments with sympathetic strings reappeared in Germany and several instruments came into existence such as the *viole d'amour*, *violon d'amour*, *basse de viole d'amour*,[690] *pochette d'amour*,[691] and *baryton*.

Sympathetic strings impart to bowed instruments a peculiar tone color which was aptly described as 'argentine' or 'silvery.'

281. VIOLE D'AMOUR Hamburg, Germany, 1670

Viol type body, shallow model. Flat back of maple, in two pieces. Ribs of maple. Belly of pine, highly arched between middle bouts; inlaid purfling, flame type sound-holes. Neck of maple with a clearance groove for sympathetic strings. Peg-box integral with neck, slightly tilted toward right, surmounted with blindfolded Cupid's head; back of the peg-box carved and gilded; bored for twelve lateral pegs. Hook-bar of ivory. Tail-piece of ebony, with the top cut slantwise. Two sets of strings affixed as follows: 1. Five playing strings are held by ivory buttons inserted in the tail-piece; they pass over a movable bridge, over the nut and are fastened to five lower pegs. 2. Seven sympathetic strings of thin steel wire are fixed by ivory buttons to an inclined cross-bar glued to the belly and pass through a narrow slit in the bridge, under the finger-board through the neck clearance space, over the auxiliary ivory nut below the main nut (which also has a clearance), and are affixed to the upper seven pegs. *Inside construction*: Two cross-bars glued to the back; small straight corner fillets; bass-bar and sound-post. Dark brown varnish. Printed label inside:

'JOACHIM TIELKE
in Hamburg, an. 1670'

Length, total, 75 cm. Body, length, 38.25 cm.; width, upper bouts, 19 cm.; middle bouts, 13.25 cm.; lower bouts, 23.75 cm. Ribs, height, 4.5 cm. Vibrating length of strings, playing, 36.2 cm.; sympathetic, 36.4 cm. (17.1719)
Plate XII

The *viole d'amour* (Italian *viola d'amore*) is a hybrid instrument. Its body is about the size of the alto *viola da gamba*, with a slope toward the neck bracket as on the viol; it is reinforced by cross-bars and a cross strip. The ribs are higher than those of the viola, but not so high as those of the regular viol; the average size is between 5 to 7 cm. The body outline is usually rather elaborate; the sound-holes are of the 'flame' type. The peg-box is very long, because it has to accommodate additional pegs for the sympathetic strings; it is surmounted by a carved figure-head representing, usually, a blindfolded Cupid. The number of bowed strings varies from five to seven; the finger-board is made to suit the number of strings. In all these details the *viole d'amour* is akin to the viol.

But the *viole d'amour* is played in the same manner as the violin. It is held against the left shoulder under the chin; the left-hand thumb envelops the neck, which is rounded as on the violin. There are no frets. The bow is similar to that of the violin.[692] Therefore, the bowing technique is also similar. In these details and practices the *viole d'amour* is akin to the violin.

The manner of affixing the sympathetic strings can be found in the descriptions of the instruments; on all instruments the finger-board or the neck, or both, are hollowed out to provide a clearance for them.

The term *viole d'amour* includes instruments of two types. Contrary to a generally prevailing impression, the *viole d'amour* is not necessarily furnished with sympathetic strings. Jean Rousseau [693] tells us that " . . . l'on voit encore aujourd'huy une espèce de Dessus de Viole monté de chordes de laton, qu'on appelle Viole d'Amour: mais il est certain que ces chordes font un meschant effet sous l'Archet, qu'elles rendent un Son trop aigre; c'est pour cela que les François ne se sont jamais servy de pareilles chordes, quoy que quelques-uns en ayent voulu fair l'essay. . . ."

S. de Brossard[694] and Mattheson[695] also describe instruments with directly bowed metallic strings and without sympathetic strings which they call *viole d'amour*. This practice of replacing the gut strings in the bowed instruments with those of metal goes as far back as the time of Praetorius (1619), who tells us that violins were furnished with brass or steel strings which " . . . ein stillen und fast lieblichen Resonanz mehr, als die andern, von sich geben." [696]

The more usual type is, of course, the *viole d'amour* with sympathetic strings. It was not a later type, since there is the testimony of Daniel Speer, whose work, like Rousseau's, was published in 1687,[697] that the *viole d'amour* was already furnished with sympathetic strings. Therefore, the two types were contemporary.

The number of sympathetic strings varied, but usually it was either six or seven.[698] A more developed type of instrument and of a larger size was the *English Violet*,[699] with seven bowed and fourteen to fifteen sympathetic strings.

The tunings of the *viole d'amour* are extraordinarily numerous.[700]

Instrument No. 281 with its five strings would be tuned: [701]

Instrument No. 282 with its six strings would be tuned as shown below; the A is added in brackets to indicate the tuning of the seven-string instruments:

The tuning of sympathetic strings is entirely arbitrary. The most logical tuning with a limited number of strings would be to tune them in unison with the bowed strings.[702]

Of all the viols, the *viole d'amour* is the only instrument which has never completely disappeared from orchestral usage or as a solo instrument. In operatic repertoire it is used in *The Huguenots* (1836) by Giacomo Meyerbeer, *Louise* (1900) by Gustave Charpentier, *Le Jongleur de Notre Dame* (1902) by Jules Massenet, and *Madame Butterfly* (1904) by Giacomo Puccini. In symphonic repertoire it is used in the *Sinfonia Domestica* (1904) by Richard Strauss. Paul Hindemith wrote a *Concerto* (1928) for the *viole d'amour*. Our own Boston composer, Charles Martin Loeffler, wrote *Le Mort de Tintagiles* (1905) for symphony orchestra and a *viole d'amour* solo.[703]

Joachim Tielke (1641–1719) was one of the most consummate craftsmen-artists and made many richly decorated instruments, among them some magnificently decorated bass-viols. Our *viole d'amour* is a simple but well made instrument and one of the earliest *violes d'amour* in existence.[704]

282. VIOLE D'AMOUR Italy, 1696

Long model with complicated curved outline. Flat back of maple. Ribs of maple, made of five pieces (two upper bouts, two middle bouts, and a bottom piece). Belly of pine, highly arched (especially under the bridge), purfled at edges; three sound-holes, two flame-shaped ones on both sides of the bridge and a small, comma-shaped one under the finger-board. Short neck with clearance groove for sympathetic strings. Finger-board of ebony. Peg-box without bottom, having only two cheeks; surmounted by a scroll (not original); bored for thirteen pegs. Tail-piece of stained walnut, top cut slantwise, with an ivory reinforcing strip; held by a thick gut-string loop attached to the ebony tail-pin. Two sets of strings affixed as follows: 1. Six playing strings, held by the tail-piece, pass over a movable bridge and an ivory nut to the lower tuning pegs. 2. Seven sympathetic strings of thin steel wire, held by small ivory buttons in the bottom, pass over ebony saddle, over ivory tipped clearance slit in the bridge, through clearance space under the finger-board, over auxiliary boxwood nut under the main one, to the upper tuning pegs. *Inside construction*: three cross-bars and cross-strip 4 cm. wide and 3 mm. thick, glued to the bottom; at the lowest incurvation the joints of the middle bouts and the lower rib are reinforced by large blocks, one on each side; bass-bar and sound-post. Dark reddish-brown varnish. Ink label inside, hardly legible, reading:

'Giovan Grancino
Milano, 1696'

Length, total, 83.5 cm. Body, length, 43 cm.; width, upper bouts, max., 19.75 cm.; middle bouts, min., 12.25 cm.; lower bouts, max., 25.25 cm. Ribs, 6.25 cm. Vibrating length of strings, playing, 38.8 cm.; sympathetic, 39 cm. (17.1720 a & b)
Plate XII

283. BARYTON — Berlin, Germany, the second half of the 19th century

Deep body of complicated curved outline (modified guitar-fiedel type). Flat back of maple, made of one large piece. Ribs of maple: the ribs of the lower bouts fixed to a solid block of maple composing the outer portion of the bottom block. Slightly arched belly of pine, with a double purfling at the edges; four comma-shaped sound-holes; an oval rosette below the finger-board. Neck and peg-box made of one solid piece of maple; the neck with a wide opening, providing the clearance for the sympathetic strings; peg-box with the rear wall pierced with four ornamental openings, surmounted with a winged Cupid's head; bored for nineteen pegs. The opening of the neck covered over in front by a wide board, forming the support for the finger-board located at the left side of neck; the right-hand side of this board embellished by the open fret-work and double purfling. Finger-board of ebony with nine frets of walnut, inlaid flush. Ebony hook-bar affixed to the bottom block. Tail-piece of ebony with open fret-work. Movable bridge with widely separated legs providing clearance for sympathetic strings. Twelve ebony blocks affixed to the belly along an inclined line, and one block off to the right. Two sets of strings affixed as follows: 1. Six playing strings, three of spun silk, three of gut fixed to the tail-piece, passing over a movable bridge, over ebony nut with a narrow ivory insert and fixed at the upper end to six tuning pegs located on the left side of instrument. 2. Thirteen sympathetic strings of thin steel wire affixed to small iron pins in the bottom block, passing over the ebony saddle, and over ebony blocks (one for each string) serving as auxiliary bridges; under the neck supporting board so that they are accessible from the rear; over a wide nut fixed to the bottom wall of peg-box, to the pegs. *Inside construction*: Very wide top block providing a flat surface for holding the neck bracket. The lower block, consisting of two parts: the above-mentioned maple block and reinforcing block of pine. Corner joints of ribs reinforced by pine blocks. Back heavily reinforced as follows (counting from the top): (a) cross-bar with two corner pieces; (b) cross-strip 3 cm. wide and 6 mm. thick; (c) cross-bar in the middle bout; (d) cross-strip (under the sound-post) 5 cm. wide and 6 mm. thick; (e) cross-bar slightly below the joint of the middle and lower bouts. Bass-bar and sound-post. Printed label inside, reading:

'Adolphe Gutche
Lauten und Geigenmacher
in Berlin 18'

Length, total, 128 cm. Body, length, 61.5 cm.; width: upper bouts, 29.25 cm.; middle bouts, 20.75 cm.; lower bouts, 37.25 cm. (max.). Ribs, height, 12 cm. Vibrating length of strings, playing, 62.2 cm.; sympathetic (max.), 87.8 cm.; (min.), 51 cm. (17.1721)
Plate XII

The baryton is also known as the *viola di bordone.*[705] Its body size and the vibrating length of the strings place the baryton in the small bass group.[706] The instrument was invented in Germany in the seventeenth century and was played there as late as the middle of the nineteenth century.[707] Even in Germany it had a moderate use. The principal claim of this instrument for distinction is that Joseph Haydn wrote 175 compositions for the baryton. This was because his patron, Prince Nikolaus Joseph Esterhazy (1714–90), was a skilful performer on the instrument.[708]

The bowed strings of the baryton were tuned the same as those of the bass viol, viz., *D*, *G*, *c*, *e*, *a'*, *d'*. The metallic strings were tuned diatonically from E up; they served as sympathetic strings and also could be plucked by the thumb, since, as stated in the description above, those strings are accessible from the rear. Dr. Curt Sachs [709] pointed out that the difficulties of handling the instrument when plucking the metallic strings,[710] and of keeping so many strings in tune, were out of proportion to whatever artistic value the instrument may have had. This is undoubtedly true, and might account for the lack of the baryton's popularity among viola da gamba players. Yet the baryton had a fine tone according to contemporary evidence.[711]

The baryton is regarded sometimes as the bass of the *viole d'amour*, but this does not seem to be an entirely correct classification. It is true that the metallic strings act as the sympathetic strings do on the *viole d'amour*, but the thumb-plucking technique puts the baryton into a somewhat different category. The true bass of the *viole d'amour* is the lyra-viol (*viola bastarda*) with sympathetic strings.[712]

284. HARDANGERFELE — Norway, 1838

Hardanger Viol. Body of violin type. Back of maple, belly of pine; both are very highly arched. Two f-holes. Finger-board and tail-piece inlaid with walnut and bone checkered patterns. Neck and peg-box of maple; peg-box is bored for eight pegs, ends with small violin-type scroll. Two sets of strings: (1) four playing strings of gut; (2) four sympathetic strings of thin steel wire passing under the finger-board through clearance space in the neck. Movable bridge with two vertical notched brass pieces, permitting the change of tension of sympathetic strings. Bass-bar and sound-post. Ink label inside, hardly legible, reading:

'Jorg (?) Knudsen
Fiolinmager (?) . . . . (?)
1838'

Length, total, 56 cm. Body, length, 34 cm.; width, upper bouts, 14.5 cm.; middle bouts, 9.5 cm.; lower bouts, 17.5 cm. Height, ribs, 3.3 cm.; from back to belly (outside), 7.5 cm. Vibrating length of strings (both playing and sympathetic), 27 cm. (17.1722 a)
Plate XIV

The Hardanger viol is the folk instrument of the Norwegian peasants.[713] Its invention is credited to Lars Klark, about 1670. The instrument is tuned:

Violins

VIOLINS or *viole da braccio* (arm viols) constitute the second great family of bowed chordophones. The word violin is derived from the Italian *violino* which is the diminutive of the word *viola*. Generically, the term *viole da braccio* included all instruments of the violin family, even those which could not be held over the arm because of their size, such as the violoncello.[714] Monteverdi's term used in the score of *Orfeo* (1607) for designating the violoncello was the *basso de viola da braccio*.[715] In 1687, when Daniel Speer was writing the term, *viola da braccio* already designated the viola (the alto violin) only, as if to remind us that the violin family developed from its alto member.[716]

The Violin Family

A COMPLETE family of instruments should have at least four members: the treble, the alto, the tenor, and the bass. Since the lower instrumental register is not limited by the compass of the human voice, the fifth member, the contrabass, is usually added. Organologically, the members of the family should be designed on the same pattern. The viol family is a fine example of such a consistently developed group. Not only are all the voices adequately represented, but some, as the treble, the tenor, and the bass, have two or even three sizes.[717] The sizes are finely adjusted over the whole playing range. The bodies are uniformly designed.[718] All viols are held in a vertical position; the necks are fretted; the tuning intervals are uniform (except in the lyra-viol); the bows are held the same way on all viols; the fingering technique is uniform. This permits players to change from one instrument to another and play after short practice.

The violin family as it is used in modern orchestras and quartet ensembles, if examined critically, is strangely incomplete and unbalanced. Its treble instrument, the violin, is generally acknowledged to be the queen of musical instruments. In the opinion of enthusiasts, when at its best it approaches the ideal as closely as does any of the inspired creations of man. The alto instrument, the viola, is the ailing member of the family. Too large for convenient handling in playing, it is, at the same time, too small and shallow for producing a sonorous and adequate tone. Its proportions are not so firmly established as those of the violin, so there is no general agreement as to what are the best dimensions for a viola. Attempts to improve it have been made but none has gained acceptance.[719]

There is no true tenor voice in the violin family, although at one time there was one in existence and parts were written for it.[720] This is a strange deficiency, since the true tenor

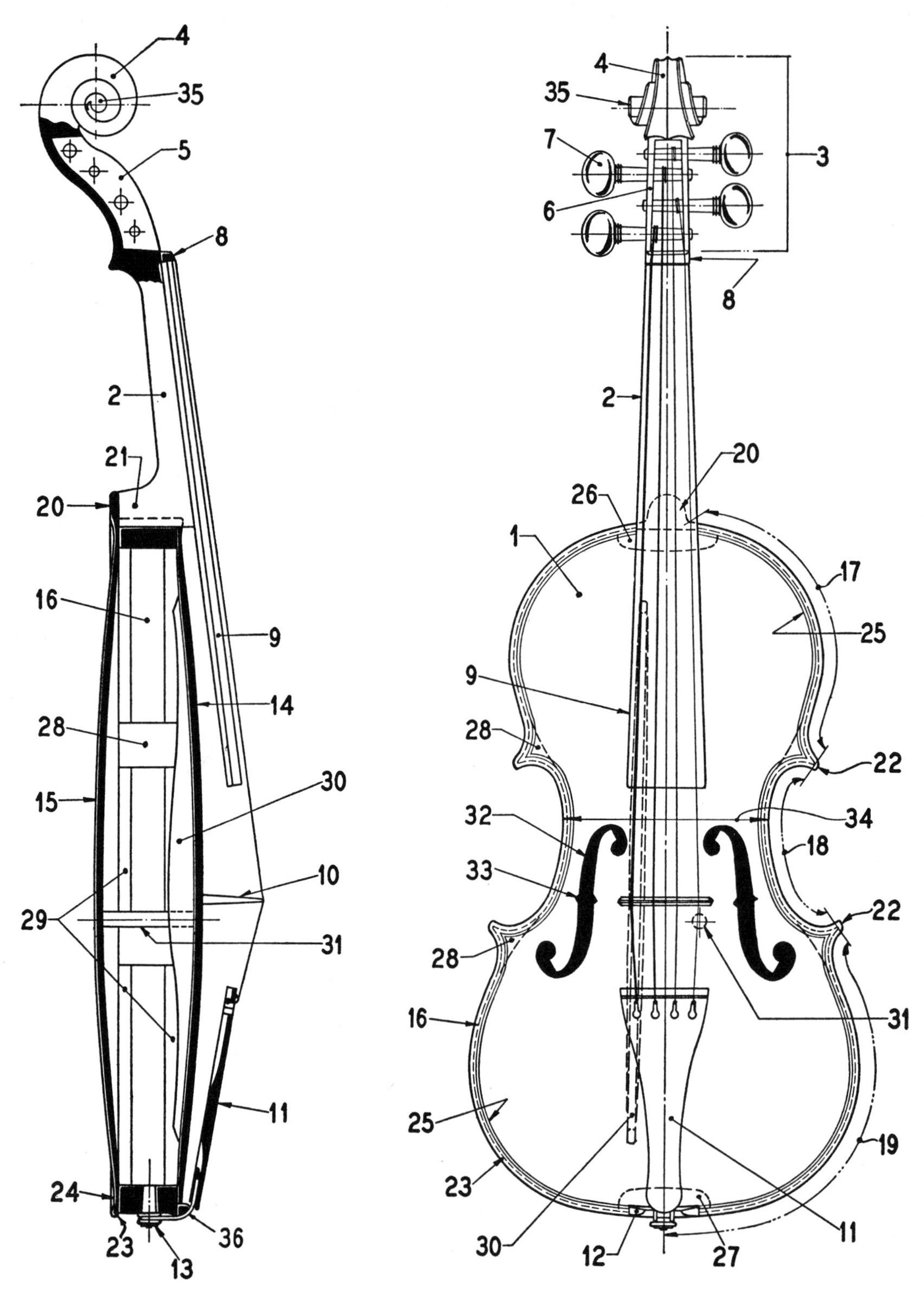

Fig. 53. FRONT ELEVATION AND SECTION OF THE VIOLIN; WITH REFERENCE NUMBERS FOR THE PARTS

tone color cannot be adequately replaced by either violas or violoncellos. The tenor parts are too low for violas and too high for violoncellos. Classical and modern composers learned how to overcome this deficiency by a clever disposition of voices, but the tone color which only the tenor violin could supply is absent now in the most important and basic group of instruments of our contemporary music.

The violoncello is an excellent instrument, properly proportioned, with full and sonorous voice; in the hands of virtuoso players it ranks almost as high as the violin for solo playing.

The double bass is, really, not a member of the violin family, but a much coarsened and degraded violone, a large member of the viol family.[721] There is no consistency in the holding position nor in the playing technique. Violins and violas are held under the chin; violoncellos are held in a vertical position. Violins, viols, and violoncellos are bowed with the bow held overhand, but the double basses are still bowed viol-fashion with the bow held underhand.[722] The fingering technique of violins and violas is the same, owing to the similarity of holding position, although the transition from one to another is not so easily accomplished as that on viols. The violoncello has a different technique of fingering, owing to the difference in holding position and the size of the instrument. It has also a peculiar 'thumb technique,' borrowed from the tromba marina. No interchange is possible from the violoncello to either violin or viola and vice versa.

The double-bass is tuned in fourths, and, consequently, is fingered differently from the rest.

As we shall see later in studying its history, the violin family had many more members. It is a serious question if in our desire for simplification and practical adjustments we have not lost something worth while.

Nomenclature of Violin Parts

1. The Body (or Sound-box)
2. The Neck
3. The Head
4. The Scroll
5. The Peg-box
6. The Peg-box Cheek
7. The Tuning Peg
8. The Nut
9. The Finger-board
10. The Bridge
11. The Tail-piece
12. The Saddle
13. The End-pin (or Tail-pin)
14. The Belly
15. The Back
16. The Ribs (or Sides)
17. The Upper Bouts
18. The Middle (or Centre) Bouts
19. The Lower Bouts
20. The Button (or Neck Plate)
21. The Neck Bracket
22. The Corners
23. The Edge
24. The Groove
25. The Purfling
26. The Neck Block
27. The End-pin Block
28. The Corner Block
29. The Linings
30. The Bass-bar
31. The Sound-post
32. The F-hole
33. The F-hole Notch
34. The Waist
35. The Scroll Eye
36. The Tail-piece Loop

History

The history of the violin was unnecessarily complicated by the tendency of earlier writers on the subject to consider all bowed instruments as the probable ancestors of the violin. Especially confusing was the opinion that the viol family was the immediate predecessor of the violin family and that the violin developed from the treble viol, the viola from the tenor viol, and the violoncello from the bass viol. This led to a misconception of the true character of the viol and added many irrelevant issues.

New vistas in the historical aspect of the evolution of the European bowed chordophone were opened by a vigorous and highly original monograph, *Die Italienische Lira da Braccio*,[723] published by Major Alexander Hajdecki in 1892. Major Hajdecki's principal thesis was that the violin could not develop from the viol family; that the true ancestor of the violin was the Italian *lira da braccio*, which had a body comparable in size and general outline to our modern orchestral viola.[724]

Major Hajdecki stated his views forcefully and somewhat uncompromisingly. Some of them cannot be held today;[725] later views on the problem of the violin's origin are less dogmatic.[726] The position held in this study is a middle path between two extreme views, one of which adheres to the theory that the violin family developed from the viol family and another which maintains that there is nothing in common between them. The term 'viol,' as we have seen before, includes many types of body design. The guitar-fiedel type (see page 309) can be regarded as a connecting link between two families, the *viole da gamba* and the *viole da braccio*.

Since Hajdecki's views, so necessary for a balanced conception of the whole subject, have not penetrated to some quarters,[727] partly because of the fact that his book is rare and not well known in the English speaking world, it is desirable to restate the main arguments, bringing them up to date. For convenience the differences between the viol and the violin are put in tabular form.[728]

COMPARATIVE SUMMARY OF DETAILS OF THE VIOL AND VIOLIN FAMILIES

Viols	*Violins*
Structural Typology	
1. Outline of body oval in shape, with rising shoulders blended into the neck bracket; curves of the upper and lower bouts in joining those of the middle bouts have no extending corners. The middle bouts cut into the body moderately.	1. Outline of body of the figure-eight type; shoulders in one continuous curve to which the neck bracket is tangent; curves of the upper and lower bouts in joining those of the middle bouts form extending corners. The middle bouts cut deep into the body.
2. Convex belly with plain edges fitted flush with ribs.	2. Convex belly with slightly raised edges overlapping the ribs.

Viols	*Violins*
3. Flat back with slanting upper part; wide cross-strip glued to inside of back upon which the sound-post rests; larger sizes have additional cross-bars reinforcing back.	3. Convex back with no extra reinforcements.
4. Deep-ribbed body in all members of the family, from the highest pitched one to the lowest. Bodies of very thin construction.	4. Shallow-ribbed bodies in violins and violas; deep-ribbed body in violoncellos and double basses built on the violin pattern.
5. The ribs at the junction of upper and lower bouts with middle bouts are fastened inside by fillets of small radius.	5. The ribs at the junction of the upper and lower bouts with the middle bouts are fastened inside to the corner blocks.
6. The neck is broad and thin, with the back slightly rounded; it is about 25% longer than that of the violin family.	6. The neck is narrow and thick, with half-round back.
7. Peg-box usually ends with carved head of individual pattern, representing humans or animals; sometimes ends in a scroll.	7. Peg-box ends in a scroll.
8. Tail-piece is attached to a hook-bar fixed to the bottom; no saddle.	8. Tail-piece is attached by a gut loop to the end-pin; belly is reinforced by ebony saddle to prevent the loop from cutting into the soft wood of the belly.
9. The sound-holes are C-shaped or of fancy shapes. Sometimes a rosette is added.	9. The sound-holes are f-shaped.
10. The strings are six in number. Later, smaller instruments had five strings and the bass viol seven strings.	10. The strings are four in number.
11. The strings are light and under moderate tension.	11. The strings are heavier as compared with those of the viols and are under considerable tension.

Tuning and Playing Technique

12. Tuned in fourths with a major third in the middle.	12. Tuned in fifths.
13. All members of the family are held in a vertical position, on or between the legs (hence the name of the family: *viola da gamba*, leg viol).	13. A violin is held in a horizontal position with the lower end resting on the left shoulder under the chin; the violoncello is held in a vertical position between the knees, supported by a steel spike resting on the floor.

Viols	*Violins*
14. Finger-board is fretted; this affects the quality of tone; it has almost the same sound as that of open strings: the tone is noble, yet somewhat subdued.	14. Finger-board is without frets; open strings are not used, since their tones differ considerably from stopped tones; tone color is assertive and brilliant.
15. Left-hand thumb serves as a pivot for the hand and merely touches the back of the neck.	15. Left-hand thumb envelopes the neck, guiding the hand in position shifts.

Bows and Bowing

16. Bows are straight, shorter and lighter than violin bows.	16. Bows have pronounced negative camber when hair tension is released.
17. Bow is held above the palm of the hand, two or three inches away from the nut.	17. Bow is held below the palm of the hand, close to the nut.
18. The order of the bow strokes is the reverse of that for the violin family; they are attacked on the up-bow.	18. The strings are attacked on the down-bow.

Not all of these details are of equal importance; the most essential ones are 1, 3, 4, 6, 10, 11, 12, 13, 14, 16, 17, 18. Yet all of them make clear that the origin of the two families is different.

Additional arguments advanced by Major Hajdecki which still remain valid are as follows:

1. The term *viola* comprises two different things: gambas and violins.[729]

2. *Viole da gamba*, which were called just 'viols,' appeared (in Italy?) in the middle of the fifteenth century; *viole da braccio* (violins), called briefly in Germany *Geigen* and in Italy *i violini*, came into existence in the beginning of the sixteenth century.

3. Violins are not the descendants of viols, because:

(a) They are specifically different in their technical details. (b) Violins did not supersede viols as a new product, but were developing side by side with them during two hundred years and at the end of the existence of the viol had to fight for recognition.[730] (c) Viols achieved, in this parallel development, a perfection in construction equal to that of the violin; they had a musical usage *sui generis*; they preserved the individuality of their life purpose, and therefore have not stood with respect to violins as in the relation of parent to child. (d) The historical development of the two instrumental types was diametrically opposite: the natural evolution of viols was from the fundament to the crown (the bass viol as the progenitor); with violins it was a building up from the small size.[731]

4. The *lira da braccio* is the mother of our violin, because:

(a) Its outer appearance corresponds to that of the violin. (b) The tuning is, practically, the same as that of the violin. (c) It disappeared shortly after the violin became a recognized entity.[732] (d) The *viola da braccio* (violin) was at first called 'lira.' [733]

However important knowledge of the immediate ancestry of the violin is, many obscure problems remain. It is still not possible to answer with certainty such important questions as where the violin first made its appearance,[734] or the date of its origin.

But the task of tracing that which can be ascertained with a tolerable degree of accuracy is made easier by the narrowing of the field of discussion, since viols and their predecessors should be no longer considered as directly related to violins.[735]

There are two principal aspects of the evolution of the violin. One is the evolution of the body. It is closely connected with the acoustical aspect. Another is the evolution of the head, the neck, and finger-board. This is related to the playing technique.

The body of the violin was borrowed from the *lira da braccio*; but the head and the finger-board technique were taken from the rebec.[736] Therefore, instruments belonging to the lines of evolution of both of these types were the soil where the constituent elements of the violin germinated and developed until the time when many of them were synthesized in the violin.[737]

The essential typological characteristics of the violin family can be described as follows:

1. *Body*. Tripartite type; vaulted (convex) back; shallow ribs in the violin and viola; deep ribs in the tenor and violoncello; the edges of the back and belly overlap the ribs. The sound-holes are of the f-shaped type.

2. *Head*. Peg-box surmounted with a scroll or volute, very seldom by a carved figure-head.

3. *String-fastening*. (a) *Tuning end* (head) of the frontal type with lateral pegs; (b) *fixed end* of the lower end type with the string-holder (tail-piece) fastened by a gut-string loop to an end-pin inserted in the lower end block through the rib.

4. *The number of strings*. The standard number is four. On instruments directly related to the violin such as rebecs, three; on the *lira da braccio* (except the bourdons) the stopped strings numbered five.

5. *Tuning and stopping technique*. Strings are tuned in fifths; necks are not fretted; only stopped tones are used.

6. *Bowing*. The bow is held overhand, below the palm.

7. *Holding position*. Violins and violas are held against the shoulder in a horizontal position; the tenor and violoncello are held in a vertical position.[738]

The Probable Time of the Origin of the Violin

As has been already stated, this is highly uncertain. The earliest representation of an instrument which has all the typological characteristics enumerated above is the *viola da braccio* in the fresco by Gaudenzio Ferrari on the cupola of the church of Santa Maria dei Miracoli, Saronno, Italy.[739] It was painted in 1535–36. Allowing fifteen to twenty years for the lapse of time between the appearance of a new instrumental type and the time of its representation on this fresco, the probable date of the emergence of the violin could be placed at about 1515–20, or in the first quarter of the sixteenth century. This is an earlier date than the one usually assigned, 1540–50, and is based on reliable objective evidence.[740]

The evolution of the violin can be divided into two periods. The first period is the history of the development of separate details and of the fundamentals of playing technique which were later incorporated in the violin. The second period is the development of the violin itself, culminating in the creations of Antonio Stradivari and Giuseppe Guarneri (Joseph Guarnerius del Gesu). Certain changes in the structure of the classical model made in the beginning of the nineteenth century, which produced the violin as we know it today, cannot be designated as a period in the history of the violin. More of this later.

Evolution of the body. The basic form of the violin which is acoustically effective is the shape of the space inside the sound-box; it is guitar-shaped.[741] The corner-blocks are not absolutely essential, as the Chanot cornerless violins prove (see No. 289). Therefore, it is important to find how far back this guitar-shaped form can be traced. Surprisingly enough, this is one of the oldest forms, since it may be found on the ancient Hittite monuments dating 1000 B.C., where plucked guitar-shaped instruments are represented.

In Western Europe this form appears on bowed instruments of the twelfth century.[742]

In the thirteenth century an instrument with slightly incurved middle bouts, held in a horizontal position against the right shoulder, is represented on the psaltery in the Munich State Library.[743]

Instruments of similar type are found in the Manessean Mss. (fourteenth century), and have already been commented on in connection with the viol. Representations of instruments played violin-wise are fairly numerous in the fifteenth century. A typical representation can be found on the side panels of Hans Memling's triptych.[744] The emergence of a form of body already resembling that of the violin may be placed in the last decade of the fifteenth century.[745] Francesco Francia's (ca. 1490) angel playing a *lira da braccio* can be seen on the picture *The Enthroned Madonna*, now in the State Hermitage at Leningrad.[746] The appearance of a definite violin form should be placed after 1500, and not later than 1520, as has been stated in connection with Gaudenzio Ferrari's fresco in Saronno.

Evolution of the head. The *lira da braccio* retained to the last its flat leaf-shaped head with sagittal pegs and occipital string fastening, although, as pointed out by Dr. Curt Sachs, there is an example of the seven-stringed *lira da braccio* with lateral pegs and peg-box with a scroll.[747] So the last named typological characteristic is common to all three basic families of the bowed chordophones, since examples of viols and *lira da braccio* are found with a violin scroll.

The head with lateral pegs comes from the Arabian *rabab*, and can be traced to the Arabian influence in Sicily and the Moorish influence in Spain. The *Cantigas de Santa Maria* have *rabab* players represented in miniatures.[748] The earliest appearance of the scroll can be traced, not on violins but on viols, sometime at the end of the fifteenth century.[749]

Evolution of tunings. Members of the violin family are fretless and are tuned in fifths. The tuning in fifths can be traced positively as far back as the thirteenth century. Hieronymus of Moravia gave the following tunings for five-stringed vielles.

The first tuning (ecclesiastical):

The second tuning (secular, with all five strings stopped over the finger-board):

This tuning is interesting, as it gives practically the same tones (given here in the violin clef) as those of the first three strings of the violin; the last interval being the fourth.

The third tuning:

It gives a tuning (designated here in the alto clef) identical with that of the first three strings of the modern orchestral viola.

The next step before the final emergence of the violin-viola tunings can be seen in the tunings of the *lira da braccio* given by Giovan Maria Lanfranco in 1533.[750] Its seven strings were tuned as follows:

It is not difficult to perceive that the last five notes (disregarding g′) give the tuning of the violin (*g*, *d′*, *a′*, *e″*). The first six notes (disregarding the octave duplications of d and g) give the sequence *d*, *g*, *d′*, *a′*, which differs only by its first tone from that of the viola: *c*, *g*, *d′*, *a′*.[751]

Finally, the three-stringed rebecs of Martin Agricola's time (1528–1529) were tuned thus:

As has been pointed out by many writers, the rebec comes closer to the violin in a musical sense than any other instrument which preceded the violin. The tunings of the rebec as given by Martin Agricola prove this contention: the treble and alto-tenor rebec tunings are those of the first three strings of the violin and the viola respectively; the bass rebec tuning is that of the tenor violin.

So the two principal lines of evolution, the *lira da braccio* and the rebec, came together. Although very different instruments in their musical usage, spirit, and even their standing in society,[752] nevertheless both had the necessary elements for the structural and musical synthesis which created the violin family.

The Evolution of the Violin Family

The first and basic instrument of the violin family was the viola and not the violin. There are several reasons for this contention. The first one is the size of the instruments. Praetorius' *lira da braccio* represented on table xx of *Sciagraphia* (fig. 5; reproduced on page 362 of this study) scales one foot seven and a half inches (Brunswick) or 46.4 cm. in body length, the same as the *Tenor-Geig* on table xxi.[753] This gives us a standard of comparison with actual instruments preserved in museums. The *lira da braccio*, no. 1443 of the Brussels Collection, has a body length of 46.5 cm.; that of Ventura Linarolo, made in Venice in 1580 and now no. 108 in the Vienna Collection, is 47.5 cm. long; that of the Berlin Collection, no. 2578, is 47 cm. long. It should be stated that some of these instruments are not in their original condition, the necks and heads having been replaced by those of a later pattern; but the bodies are, it seems, still intact.[754] Even the smallest-sized *lira da braccio*, which was found by Major A. Hajdecki and served as the basis of his conclusions, had a body length of 38.7 cm., which is the size of a small viola.[755] As already pointed out, this is rather an exception; therefore, it seems probable that the first four-stringed instruments of the violin family had bodies of from 45 to 48 cms. in length. Gaudenzio Ferrari's fresco also indicates a large-sized instrument.[756]

The nomenclature of the violin family in the sixteenth century is very indefinite. Although the terms *violon* and *joueur de Violon* can be traced in Lorraine documents as early as 1490, it is not certain that they meant the violin in our sense.[757] The first instruments with four strings, as already stated, were probably called *lira*, as the following testimony of Vincenzo Galilei indicates. In the *Dialogo . . . della musica antica, et della moderna*, published in Florence in 1581, he states: "*Viola da braccio*, which not many years ago was called *lira*." [758] The oldest definite description of the violin is found in the treatise of Philibert Jamb-de-Fer,[759] *Epitome musical de tons, sons et accordz ès voix humaines . . . viols et violons*, published in Lyon in 1556. But even after this date the nomenclature remains unsettled. As late as 1597 Giovanni Gabrieli in *Sacrae Symphoniae* designated as 'violino' a part written in the alto clef and within the compass of the viola.[760] Therefore, the sizes and nomenclature seem to support the contention that the viola was first in appearance among the members of the violin family.

Finally, the tunings of the *lira da braccio* seem to point to the same conclusion. As already stated, they were of such wide range as to include both the violin and viola tunings. Therefore it is probable that a four-stringed instrument with a body size of a large viola would be tuned to the lower tunings of the viola in preference to the higher tunings of the violin. As a matter of fact, organological considerations force this conclusion.[761] The general conclusion from the foregoing premises is that the term *viola da braccio* was used at first in a specific sense to designate the alto violin and later was used in a generic sense to designate the entire violin family. See Appendix E for particulars.

At the turn of the century (1600) the evolution of the violin family must have been very rapid. In 1592 Lodovico Zacconi gave tunings of four-stringed instruments which, considered in connection with their terminology, are startling. He discriminates between *violino* and *viole da braccio*; but, since his text is not very clear, it is not possible either to affirm or deny whether by *violino* he designated the four-stringed violin or a rebec.

Mr. Gerald R. Hayes by comparative study of the statements of Zacconi and Cerone [762] came to the conclusion that the tunings of the violin family in 1592 would be as follows:

Three interesting points should be noticed. The first is that the *viola da braccio* with the viola tunings is called a soprano (treble) instrument; this is of importance in the discussion of Monteverdi's terminology of stringed instruments. The second point is that Zacconi gives the tunings of the true tenor; this is one of the proofs that there was such a member in the violin family. The third point is the tuning of the bass *viola da braccio* one tone below that of the violoncello; it was so tuned in England and France in the seventeenth century.[763] This lower tuning conforms better with the larger size of the earlier violoncellos.[764]

Monteverdi's opera *Orfeo* had its first performance in 1607. Monteverdi gave a list of the instruments and also added many directions as to the particular instruments to be used in specific instances throughout the score.[765] A study of these directions, the clefs, the sounding compass of parts assigned to the stringed instruments, the relative position of those parts on the staff (high or low), their rhythmic divisions, etc., yields rich material and suggests certain conclusions about the instruments. Unfortunately, specialists do not agree on certain doubtful points. Therefore it is desirable to consider anew the problem of Monteverdi's instrumentation.

A study of the original score, which is now available in a facsimile edition,[766] shows that the instruments of the violin family listed below were used in the performance of *Orfeo*. Most of them were explicitly prescribed by Monteverdi himself; uncertainty of nomenclature has caused confusion as to the exact nature of some of these instruments. The tenor violin is suggested here as the most suitable instrument for the performance of certain middle parts.

1. *The violino piccolo alla francese*.[767] The most feasible hypothesis as to its exact nature was advanced by Mr. Andreas Moser.[768] According to him it was a small-sized violin, tuned *c′*, *g′*, *d″*, *a″*; the parts were written in the score an octave lower than the actual tones.[769]

The compass of the parts of the first violino piccolo (the actual tones) is *d''* $-e_{\flat}^3$; that of the second one is *c''*–d^3.

2. *The violino ordinario da braccio.*[770] It would seem that this term should not cause any confusion, yet there is a theory that the *violino ordinario* was an alto violin, the viola of our orchestras.[771] In this study it is regarded as an ordinary soprano violin tuned *g*, *d'*, *a'*, *e''*. In the original score the parts are designated either in the soprano or the treble clef for the first and second violins, and in the mezzosoprano clef for the third violins.[772] The compass of parts for the first violin is *f'*–*b''*; that for the second violins is *d'*–*a''*; and that for the third violins is *d'*–*c''*.

3. *The viola da braccio.*[773] Monteverdi used this term in the generic sense, without stating specifically in the score directions which particular instrument he had in mind. But a study of the parts along the lines suggested before shows that by the *viole da braccio* he meant the violin, the viola, the tenor violin, and the violoncello. Our attention will be confined to the last three instruments.

4. *The soprano*[774] *de viola da braccio.* The viola. It was tuned *c*, *g*, *d'*, *a'*, the same as our orchestral viola, but its size was much larger.[775] The parts are usually written in the alto clef, although the tenor clef is used in some cases.[776] The compass of parts for the first alto is *b*–*d''*; that for the second alto is *g*–*a'*.

5. *The tenore*[777] *de viola da braccio.* The tenor violin. The most probable tuning would be *F*, *c*, *g*, *d'*. The parts are written in the tenor clef; in some instances the baritone clef is used. The compass of parts for the first tenor is *c*–*g'*; that for the second tenor is *c*–*e'*.

6. *The basso*[778] *de viola da braccio.* The violoncello. The most probable tuning would be *C*, *G*, *d*, *a*, or that of our standard violoncello. The parts in *Orfeo* are written in the bass clef. The compass of parts is *G*–*d'*.

The bass string parts having a compass of *D*–*d'*, although within the compass of the four-stringed violoncello, were played, it seems, by the bass and contrabass viols, both of which are specified in the score. (See Appendix E.)

Certain interesting conclusions can be made on the basis of this data. They are briefly summarized here.

I. The bowed string section of Monteverdi's *Orfeo* orchestra was composed as follows:

A. The violin family (*viola da braccio*).

1. The high soprano violin (*violino piccolo alla francese*).
2. The soprano violin (*violino ordinario da braccio*).
3. The alto violin (*viola*).
4. The tenor violin.
5. The bass violin (violoncello).

B. *The viola da gamba family.*[779]

1. The bass viol (*basso da gamba*).
2. The contrabass viol (*contrabasso de viola da gamba*).

II. In the score of *Orfeo* Monteverdi limited the lowest tone of the instruments of the violin family to that of the open tone of the third string (counting from the treble) and did not use the lowest string.

III. In the score of *Orfeo* Monteverdi never wrote above the first position on any instrument of the violin family.

IV. The extreme sounding compass of the instruments of the violin family in *Orfeo* did not exceed two octaves.[780]

Praetorius wrote only a few years after Monteverdi composed his *Orfeo* (1607, 1618–19), yet he made an astounding statement about the violin family: "... since they (violins) are known to everybody ... there is no necessity to enlarge and write more about them." [781]

The nomenclature of the violin family in the time of Praetorius was very complex, overlapping, and unstandardized, especially with respect to the smaller sizes of instruments; it is given in Appendix E.

A study of the violins of Praetorius' time would be incomplete without finding the dimensions of the instruments. In Table I are given the simplified names, also the Brunswick and metric sizes. The sizes were scaled to the nearest quarter of an inch (Brunswick).

TABLE I

SIZES OF INSTRUMENTS OF THE VIOLIN FAMILY

(Praetorius, *Theatrum Instrumentorum*)

TABLE XXI	NOMENCLATURE	LENGTH OF BODY		VIBRATING LENGTH OF STRINGS	
		Brunswick Feet and Inches	Cm.	Brunswick Feet and Inches	Cm.
1.	The Pochette (The *Geig* an octave higher)	0′–9″ (appr.)	21.5	0′–9.5″	22.6
3.	The Violino Piccolo (The treble *Geig* a fourth higher)	0′–11.25″	26.8	0′–9.5″	22.6
4.	The Violin (*Rechte Discant-Geig*)	1′–3″	35.7	1′–0.5″	29.7
5.	The Alto-Tenor Violin (*Tenor-Geig*)	1′–7.5″	46.4	1′–3.25″	36.3
	The Violoncello (estimated)	..	80.0	..	..
6.	The large Quint-Bass (*Bas-Geig de bracio*)	3′–0″	85.6	2′–7″	73.7

The *violino piccolo* of Praetorius is a very small instrument, smaller than a one-quarter size violin,[782] tuned *c′*, *g′*, *d″*, *a″*, or a fourth higher than the standard violin and an octave higher than the viola. The size of the violin (*rechte Discant-Geig*) is commented on in Appendix A, p. 355. The alto-tenor violin is much larger than the grand model violas of Stradivari. Its body size is more comparable to that of the *viola pomposa* of J. S. Bach's time, from which it differed only in the number of strings.[783] The size of Praetorius' violoncello had to be estimated, since the instrument represented on table xxi, fig. 6, is a five-stringed instrument, which should be classified differently. It is usually mistaken for the violoncello, since the name, *Bas-Geig de bracio*, on table xxi can be regarded in the specific sense. But its body size is about ten centimetres longer than the standard violoncello and about five

1. 2. Kleine Poſchen / Geigen ein Octav höher. 3. Diſcant-Geig ein Quart höher.
4. Rechte Diſcant-Geig. 5. Tenor-Geig. 6 Bas-Geig de bracio. 7. Trumſcheit.
8. Scheidtholtt.

Fig. 54. PRAETORIUS, TABLE XXI

1, 2. Small Pochettes, one octave higher. 3. Discant Violin, a fourth higher. 4. Ordinary Violin. 5. Tenor Violin (a large sized Viola). 6. Quint-Bass Violin (see p. 301, and Note 784). 7. Tromba Marina. 8. Scheitholt.

centimetres longer than the assumed size of the early seventeenth-century violoncellos. Hence the name is interpreted in the generic sense and the instrument is regarded as the quint-bass.[784]

Some additional members of the violin family. During the process of the evolution of the violin family some interesting instruments were developed which will be briefly mentioned here.

The *violino piccolo* of Bach's time was a larger instrument than that of Praetorius. More likely it was the three-quarter violin tuned a third higher than the standard violin.[785]

The *quinton* was a five-stringed violin tuned thus:

Its purpose was to facilitate the playing of upper tones. With the development of position technique, both the *violino piccolo* and the *quinton* went out of use. Undoubtedly some characteristic tone colors were lost also.

The *quinton* is very often confused with the *pardessus de viole*, which also has five strings. These instruments belong to different families: the *quinton* is a true violin, and the *pardessus de viole* (the high treble) is a viol.

The *viola pomposa* was a five-stringed instrument with a body length of from 45 to 47 cm., that is, about the size of Praetorius' *Tenor-Geig*. Its probable tuning was:

So tuned, it could have served as an alto voice for a *quinton*. Actual instruments can be found in the European museums.[786]

The *viola da spalla* (the shoulder viol) was a portable four-stringed violoncello of small size, held across the breast by a strap over the right shoulder (and not against the shoulder). In the first half of the eighteenth century it was used in processions as the bass instrument. According to Mattheson,[787] it served for accompaniments and had a strong, penetrating tone, so that no other instrument could play the bass part so incisively. Tuned like the violoncello.

The *viola di fagotto* (the bassoon-fiddle) was a larger sized *viola da spalla* with wire-spun strings, which tended to produce a rattling sound reminding one of a double-reed instrument. Hence its name. Used in the seventeenth and eighteenth centuries.

The *tenor violin.* A four-stringed instrument. A correctly proportioned tenor violin has a body length of about 52 cm., and the vibrating length of the strings is about 50 cm., or the size of a child's cello. The instrument should be tuned an octave below the violin.[788]

The playing position and the fingering technique is the same as on the violoncello.

The *violoncello piccolo*. This instrument is called for in some of J. S. Bach's scores.[789] It is confused with the *viola pomposa*, since both have five strings, but the *violoncello piccolo* is a larger-sized instrument (a body length of about 60 cm.) tuned:

J. S. Bach used it as a solo instrument, since the standard violoncello of his time was a large-sized instrument and the violoncellists did not possess the necessary technique, especially for playing in the upper register.

The *bass and the contrabass violins*. Instruments of the violin pattern and larger in size than the violoncello were very seldom built. One of the probable reasons is the expense and difficulty of carving the back of so large a size as is required for these instruments. The deeper-voiced bowed chordophones were constructed along the lines of viols, sometimes with the sharp corners of violins and f-holes instead of C-holes. But such instruments are not true violins.

285. VIOLIN Antwerp, Belgium, attributed to Matthys Hofmans, ca. 1730

Amati model. Two-piece back of maple marked by a curl of medium width, that of the sides being smaller; of the upper bouts, plainer; purfled; edge of button trimmed with ebony. Ribs of maple. Highly arched belly of spruce, with fine, even grain; purfled; two f-holes. Standard type neck of maple; original scroll. Ebony finger-board, tail-piece, and saddle. Standard small fittings. Four strings. Standard inside fittings. Red-brown varnish. Printed label (not original, although an old one) reading:

'*Mathias Hofman*
Me fecit Antwerpen'

Length, total, 59.5 cm. Body, length, 35.6 cm.; width, upper bouts, 16.6 cm.; middle bouts, 10.6 cm.; lower bouts, 20.2 cm. Ribs, height, average, 29 mm. Arching, belly, 17.5 mm.; back, 13 mm. From the f-hole notch to the top, 19.3 cm. Vibrating length of strings, 32.8 cm. (37.1153)
Fig. 55

The attribution of this violin to Matthys Hofmans of Antwerp is attested by Messrs. William E. Hill and Sons, London, England. In their certificate the name is spelled "Matthys Hofman." The correct spelling is Matthys Hofmans.[790] Lütgendorf gives Hofmans' period of activity as 1689 to 1740.

The story of the violin has been told so many times that it would be useless to cover the same ground once more.[791] But there are some aspects of the violin which are either omitted or glossed over. The modern violin is not a creation of the classical masters such as Gasparo (da Salo) Bertolotti, Giovanni Paolo Maggini, the Amati family, Antonio Stradivari, and Giuseppe Guarneri (del Gesu), but it was modified in its outer aspect and changed in its internal construction.

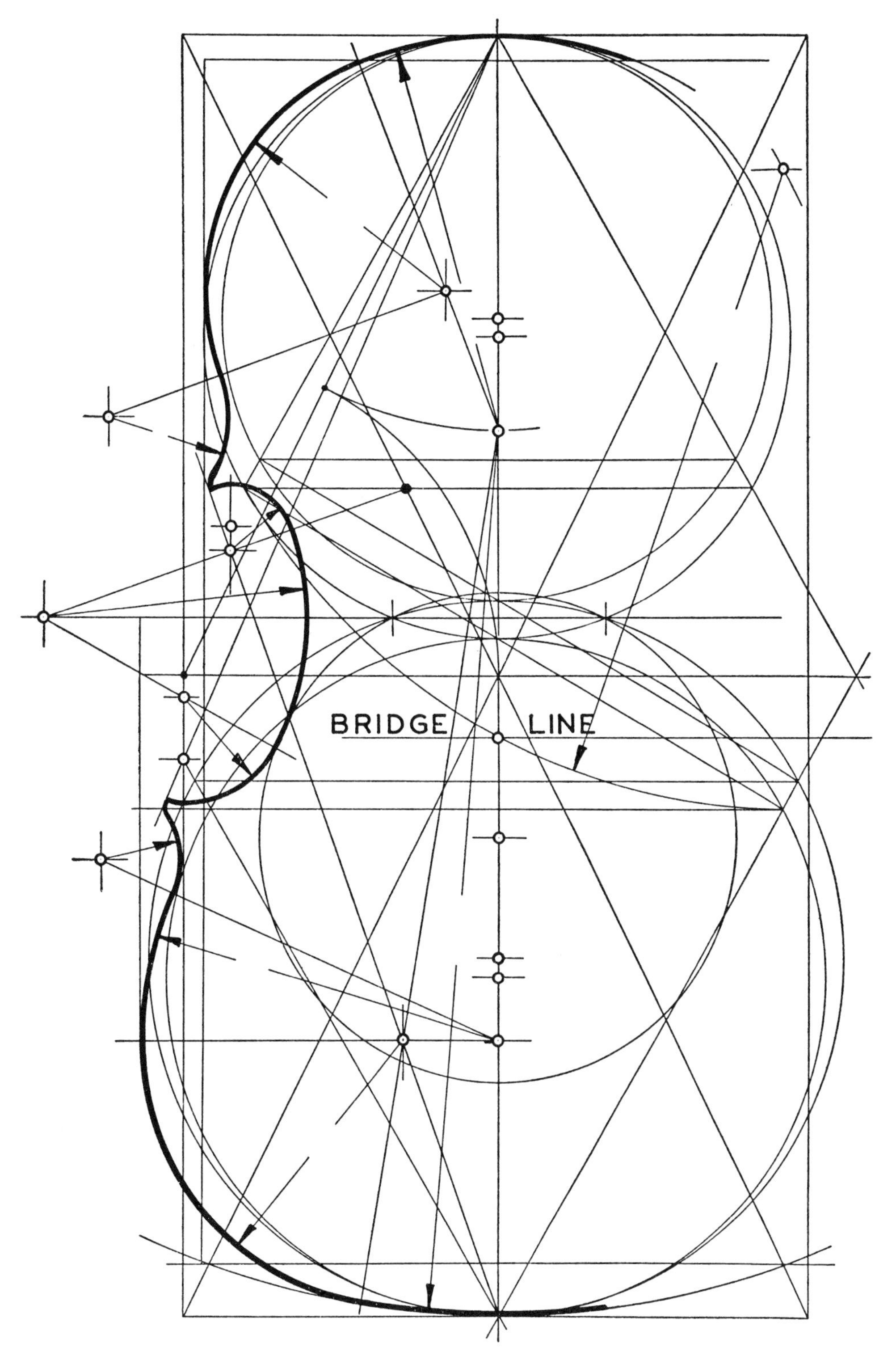

Fig. 55. A COMPLETE GEOMETRICAL ANALYSIS OF THE OUTLINE OF THE AMATI MODEL VIOLIN (No. 285)

The outward modification was the change of form and length of the neck. The violin of the old masters had its neck either parallel or slightly inclined with respect to the front plane of the instrument, and the necessary angle of the finger-board was given by inserting a wedge between the neck and the finger-board. Therefore the thickness of the neck varied, increasing toward the body. In addition, the neck of old violins was from $^3/_{16}$ to $^1/_4$ inch shorter, which made position shifts somewhat awkward. So the old neck was replaced by the modern longer form of more uniform thickness and inclined toward the back; the scroll was skilfully engrafted on the new neck. It is not known who was responsible for this improvement.

The second change, more serious, was forced by the changing standard of pitch, and was made sometime early in the nineteenth century, perhaps simultaneously with the reconstruction of the neck. This was the replacing of the bass-bar of the old masters by a larger and stiffer one. The belly had to be taken off (a very serious thing; sometimes despite every precaution the ribs were damaged), the old bass-bar chiselled off, and the new bass-bar fitted. This is a very delicate operation, requiring the utmost skill and fine judgment of an artist, as it affects the tonal qualities of the violin.

There were some minor, yet essential, changes. The angle of the old finger-boards was less steep, and therefore the bridge was not so high and the strings were laid closer to the belly. The bridge was also flatter, and this, combined with less tensioned strings and the old-type bow, which was better adapted for spanning several strings simultaneously, facilitated the playing of chords.

Such essential changes affected not only the tonal qualities of the violin, but also changed its character. The tone became more brilliant, more assertive, better adapted for larger halls; but it lost much of its mellowness and warmth. A more curving bridge, stiffer strings, and the modern Tourte bow converted the violin into a melodic instrument and impaired its ability to play classical music, in which multiple voice writing was a more organic feature.

Modern violin music is written mostly for the exhibition of brilliant virtuoso technique, and multiple stopping is added to give a player an opportunity to demonstrate that he can overcome (more or less successfully) almost insurmountable difficulties, and not because of any particularly compelling inner necessity on the part of the composer.

The modern violin, it should be acknowledged quite frankly, is essentially a melodic instrument, not adapted organically to many-voiced music, and therefore different in spirit from its older classical prototype.[792]

286. VIOLA Germany, Tyrol, last quarter of the 18th century

One-piece maple back, purfled. Ribs of maple. Belly of two pieces of spruce, finely arched, with two f-holes and purfling. Standard type neck and scroll. Ebony finger-board and tail-piece. Standard small fittings. Four strings. Tuning pegs of boxwood of the old-fashioned viol type. New bridge. Standard inside fittings. Yellowish-brown varnish. No identifying label. Length, total, 62.5 cm. Body, length, 38 cm.; width, upper bouts, 18.25 cm.; middle bouts, 12.25 cm.; lower bouts, 22.75 cm. Ribs, height, 3.5 cm. Vibrating length of strings, 34.4 cm. (17.1730)
Plate XIV

The viola is the alto instrument of the violin family. Its name in English is somewhat confusing, since the term 'viola' is the generic term designating both of the great families of bowed instruments, the viols (*viola da gamba*) and the violins (*viola da braccio*). It is correctly called the 'alto' in several languages: *Alto*, in French, Italian, and Spanish; *alt*, in Dutch and Russian; *altowka* in Polish. The size of the viola is not standardized. The reason is that in the modern string quartet the viola has to take upon itself not only the alto but also the tenor voice, and no satisfactory size for it has been found. The violin family, as already mentioned, is not complete. Several attempts have been made to remedy this defect, but none of them has gained acceptance. It is a serious question whether an extension of the compass of the violin, the viola, and the violoncello, especially upward, and the consequent elimination of the small sized violin and of the tenor, is a gain or a loss. An extension of the compass is not necessarily an extension of the tone color. Some people find this idea difficult to understand. It is true that the violin has a very extended compass in the upper register, so that it covers the same tones as any of those produced by the smaller sized sopranino violins. It is also true that the tenor voice is assigned at present to the viola in its higher position and in its lower position is given to the violoncello, so that all the tones are played and, on the surface, there is no loss. Yet this is only a quantitative solution of the problem. The qualitative aspect or tone color still remains neglected. Both the sopranino and the tenor violins have an individual tone color, especially the tenor.[793] Therefore, the practical gains, such as a smaller number of instruments, smaller number of parts, etc., are bought at the price of artistic loss. Restoration of the tenor violin would help in settling many practical problems and enhance the artistic value of the violin family.

287. VIOLONCELLO — Brussels, Belgium, first half of the 18th century, by Egidius Snoeck

Five-string model. Back of two pieces of maple. Ribs of maple. Belly of two pieces of spruce, two holes. Peg-box integral with neck, of somewhat narrow pattern and with large scroll. Five tuning pegs with unusually large heads. Finger-board and tail-piece of ebony. Standard bridge. Standard inside fittings. Tail-rest of turned piece of wood with long steel spike. Reddish-brown varnish. Printed label inside, reading:

'Marcus Broché à Bruxelles
au Roy David l'An 17[20?]'

Length, total, 120.25 cm. Body, length, 72.5 cm.; width, upper bouts, 33.25 cm.; middle bouts, 23.75 cm.; lower bouts, 41.25 cm. Ribs, height, 11.5 cm. Vibrating length of strings, 68 cm.
(17.1731)
Plate XIV

Five-stringed violoncellos were an experimental type and had a short life. With the development of technical skill in position playing, this type of stringing for violoncellos was discarded.

This instrument would be tuned:

'Marcus Broché' is really Egidius Snoeck, who worked in the early eighteenth century.

The origin of the violoncello is even more obscure than that of the violin. The old theory that the *viola da gamba* (the bass viol) was the parent of the violoncello is not in favor today, mostly owing to Alexander Hajdecki's important contribution and the influence exercised by Arnold Dolmetsch's school of thought.[794] But, it seems, one should be careful not to assume tacitly that Major Hajdecki, by proving that the Italian *lira da braccio* was the ancestor of the violin, has proven thereby that the viol family as a whole had nothing to do with the violin family as a whole; nor should another, seemingly logical, assumption be made, namely, that the *lira da gamba*[795] was the parent of the violoncello. The *lira da gamba* is too different in spirit and musical usage from the violoncello to have been its progenitor. The true ancestry of the violoncello is still an open question.

One possibility is that the violoncello had no ancestor and was built on the violin pattern[796] to extend the violin tone color into the lower register. This implies a spontaneous creation by some person, a rare occurrence; a more probable process would be the evolutionary one. There are certain facts which support the latter view and suggest the probable line of development of the violoncello.

One of them is the tuning of the viol with four or even three strings. Again students are indebted to Mr. Gerald R. Hayes[797] for research on this question. In Ganassi's *Regola Rubertina* (1542–43) there are rules for tuning the viol with a reduced number of strings. Ganassi stated that it is more convenient, when playing compositions limited to the diatonic system, to take off the two highest strings of the viol and use only the remaining four.[798] The intervals between the strings were, in this case, a third between the lowest string and the next higher one, and fourths between the two remaining strings.

But it is the tuning of the viol with only three strings which is of special interest. According to Ganassi the intervals were fifths: "this tuning can be employed by players of the *viola da brazo senza tasti*, since it is tuned according to their practice."[799] However important these remarks of Ganassi might be for an historian of music, they would indicate only a quaint practice during a certain period. But these remarks acquire a significance when certain curious instruments now preserved in the Museo Civico at Modena are examined. Fig. 56, taken from the photograph in possession of the Metropolitan Museum of Art in New York and reproduced here with the courteous permission of the Museum authorities, shows instruments with three and four strings.

The four-stringed instrument, it seems, preserved its original state, as can be judged by the type of scroll, pegs, the shape and position of the sound-holes, which are spaced rather close and have the eyes turned inward. By these earmarks it can be dated about the middle

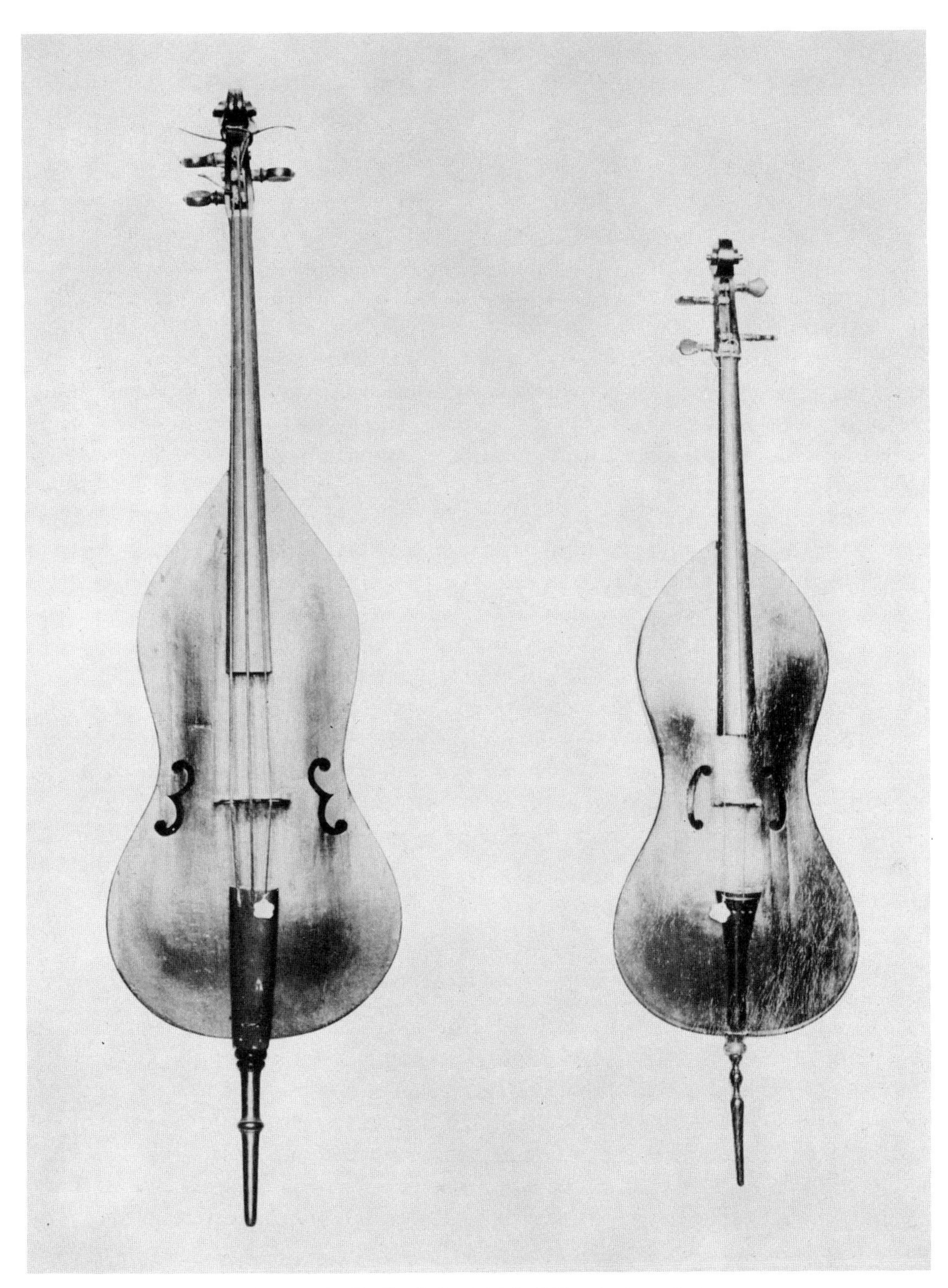

Fig. 56. THREE- AND FOUR-STRINGED VIOLS
Museo Civico, Modena, Italy

of the sixteenth century.[800] The three-stringed instrument appears to have been originally built as a six-stringed *viola da gamba.*[801] The body is wider at the middle bouts; the sound-holes are widely spaced to accommodate a greater number of strings; the scroll and the pegs are obviously of a later period than the body of the instrument.

These two instruments, it appears, were adapted to the type of practice described by Ganassi.[802] Therefore there arise some interesting possibilities. One of these is that the intermediate link between the bass viol and the violoncello might have been a viol with fewer strings than the standard number of six. Since three-stringed viols were tuned in fifths, it is probable that they were played fretless. This surmise is based on Ganassi's obscure warning, reminding his readers about the rule for playing the viol beyond the frets.[803] But in any case, whether they were played fretted or fretless, the viols with a small number of strings and tuned in fifths disclosed to players the advantages of fingering inherent in such a system. Some of them might have made suggestions to instrument-makers, and the violoncello was born.

This theory goes somewhat against the view, which is gradually gaining acceptance, that the viol was not an ancestor of the violin. This is true of the individual case, and it is highly improbable, as has been already shown, that the treble viol was a predecessor of the violin. But it must be emphasized once again that the broad generalization that the *viola da gamba* family as a whole had nothing to do with the *viola da braccio* family as a whole is only a tacit assumption. Such an inference would be too broad.[804]

An examination of the proportions of the violin, the violoncello, and some viols discloses an additional fact. The average ratio of the length of body to the height of the ribs works out as follows:

Instrument	R = Length of body: Height of ribs
The Violin	11.00:1
The Viola	10.00:1
The Violoncello	6.25:1
The Treble Viol	5.12:1
The Tenor Viol	5.00:1
The Bass Viol	5.30:1

It is obvious that the violoncello is closer in this particular ratio to the viol family than to the violin.[805]

From all the facts adduced, the theory here advanced of the origin of the violoncello acquires at least a certain degree of probability.

Strangely enough, the violoncello had to struggle hard against its well liked and established rival, the bass viol. It is only in the second half of the eighteenth century that the violoncello gained a secure position in the musical world. The Italians were the first to recognize its value as a solo instrument, and Domenico Gabrielli's *Ricercari* for the violoncello (1689) can be regarded as the foundation stone of the music written for this instrument.[806]

The subordinate position of the violoncello in the early years of its existence reflected itself even in its construction. The first violoncellos were of a larger size than the standard model developed by the violin-makers of the classical period.[807] It should be remembered that these larger instruments were better adapted to the work they had to do, since the early violoncellos were used for strengthening the continuo and for the doubling, an octave higher, of the contrabass parts.[808] For solo work smaller and more flexible instruments were used, such as the violoncello piccolo of J. S. Bach.[809] The standard violoncello model (75 cm. body length) is a compromise size, sufficiently sonorous and solid in tone to support the double-basses, when necessary, and supple and flexible for solo playing.

288. DOUBLE BASS — England, 19th century

Three strings. Outline of viol type. Back of two pieces of maple, flat in lower and middle bouts, then gradually tapering toward the neck bracket. Belly of two pieces of large grained pine, arched, two f-holes, purfling. Both back and belly with overhanging edges. Finger-board of walnut, stained black. Ebony tail-piece. Normal type bridge. Neck and head of one piece of maple. Machine head with three tuning screws. Rest-pin with a steel spike. *Inside construction*: corner blocks of normal violin type; cross-strip 20 cm. wide and 8 mm. thick, glued to the back opposite f-holes; bass-bar and sound-post. Light yellow-brown varnish. Length, total, 184.5 cm. Body, length, 113 cm.; width, upper bouts, 52.5 cm.; middle bouts, 37.5 cm.; lower bouts, 65 cm. Ribs, height, 20 cm. Vibrating length of strings, 107 cm. (17.1732 a & b)

The violin family, as has been already stated, has no contrabass voice; the double bass of our symphony orchestra is a modified member of the viol family. Although the modern double basses are built sometimes with violin corners, convex back, f-shaped sound-holes, and violin scroll, they retain sloping shoulders and have a muffled tone which indicates their origin.

The first pictorial image of a true contrabass is found, according to Dr. Curt Sachs,[810] in the *Turnierbuch* (1566). Two years later, Amman[811] pictured *Drey Geiger* in the *Eygentliche Beschreibung Aller Stände* (1568).

Praetorius described two large instruments which he included in the viol family.[812] The first one (table vi, 4, reproduced here on p. 354) he called the *Violone*, or *Gross Viol-de-Gamba Bass*. It has six strings and its dimensions are:

Entire length, 191.5 cm. (6 feet, 8½ in. Brunswick.)
Length of body, 114 cm. (4 feet, Brunswick.)

The body length is only one centimetre longer than the average body length of the modern instrument.[813] Praetorius' second instrument, the *Gross Contra-Bas-Geig*, or the *Violn de Gamba SubBass* (table v, 1), is very large in size. Its entire length, including the rest-pin, measures 239 cm. (7 feet, 4 in., Brunswick), or only 23 cm. less than the 'giant' instrument in the Victoria and Albert Museum in London, England.[814] The body length of Praetorius' instrument is 4 feet, 10 in. (Brunswick), or 140 cm.

Commenting on the use of such large instruments, Praetorius[815] makes a statement which is of great interest in the history of instrumentation.

There have been also built in recent times two quite large *Violn de Gamba SubBasses*, whose outlines are found in Table V, with which one may use the other large Contrabasses as the Tenor

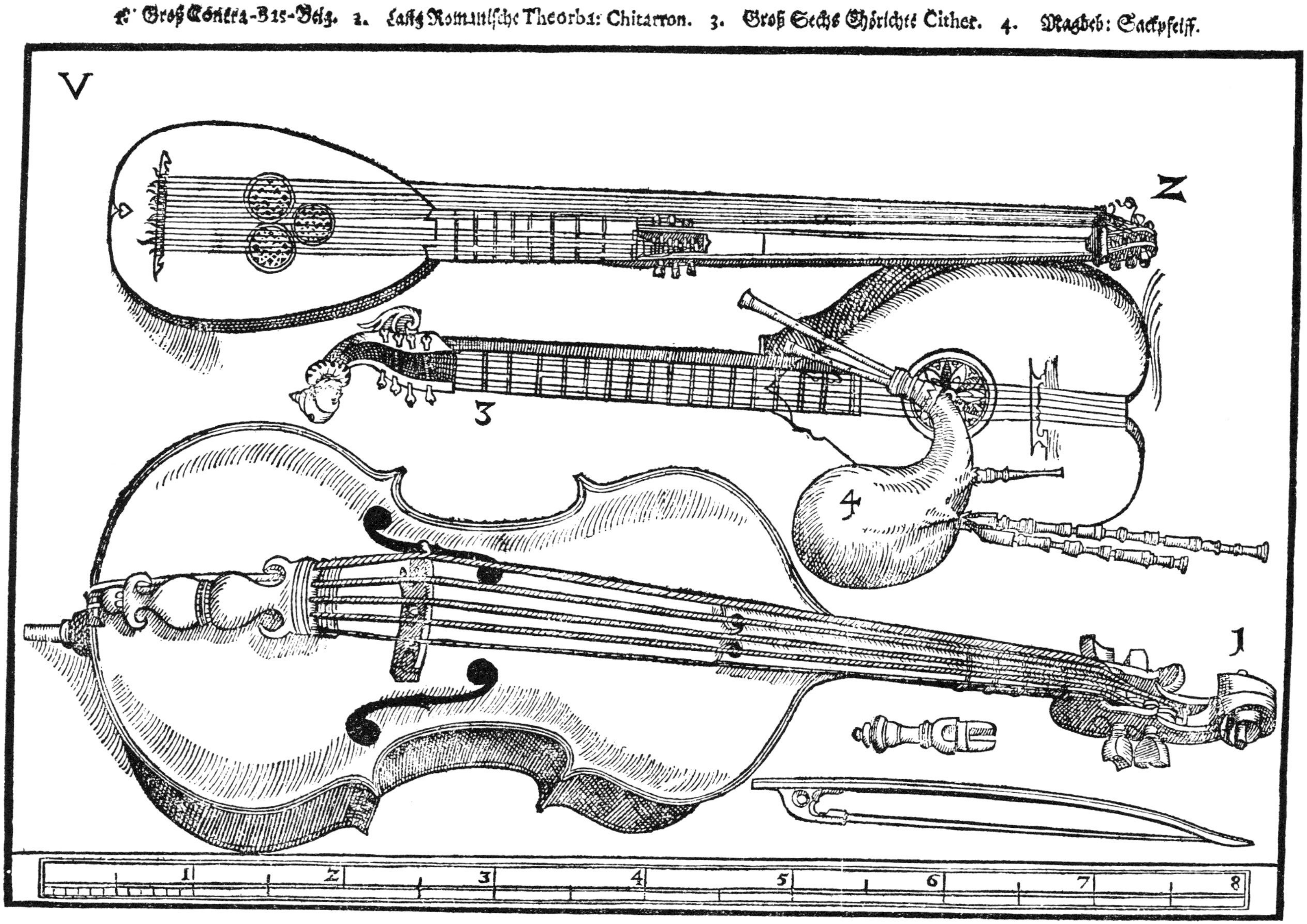

1. Groß Contra-Bas-Geig. 2. Lang Romanische Theorba: Chitarron. 3. Groß Sechs Chörichte Cither. 4. Magdeb: Sackpfeiff.

V

Z

3

4

1

1 2 3 4 5 6 7 8

Fig. 57. PRAETORIUS, TABLE V

1. Great Contrabass *Geig*. 2. *Chitarrone;* long Roman Theorbo. 3. Great Cittern with six sets of strings. 4. Magdeburg Bagpipe.

and Alto voices, and the small *Viol de Gamben Bass* as the Discant.[816] For them I have composed in my humble way, a *Concert* with different choirs (*Lauda Hierusalem Dominum*) with 17 and 21 voices which will, with God's help, appear shortly in *Polyhymnia Nona*: wherein the five voices of that choir must all be played on bowed instruments in an *Octava inferiore*. Therefore, this choir with so many large bowed instruments should be equivalent to an organ, when one accompanies on the manual a third and fifth lower in depth (using) the large *Principal* or *Gedactenflöte* of 16 feet; only these last, as I have found, buzz and grumble too much. So it is incomparably more pleasant and sweet to use the ordinary *Violn de Gamba* for the upper and middle voices and quite large sub-basses in the lower octave as the bass voices, so that they would be heard from a distance as the deep low-bass and sub-bass of the organ.

Here is an example of the perfect coördination of the means for achieving a desired effect. This effect could not be duplicated now, since there are no instruments of such a large size in playing condition for the lowest voice.

The double bass is an instrument which throughout its long history never became stabilized. This is true not only of its body design, but also of the number of its strings and its tunings. At present new body designs are being put on the market; the downward compass of the double bass is not finally settled.[817]

The number of strings varied from three to six.

The three-stringed double basses were tuned either in fourths: [818]

or in fifths:

The four-stringed double basses are tuned in fourths:

This is the standard tuning of the orchestral double basses used in symphony orchestras today.[819] There are four-stringed instruments with an extra long fourth string, which is tuned down to *CC* when played open. The tones *DD*-flat, *DD*, *EE*-flat, and *EE* are stopped by a special mechanism provided with a locking arrangement which can hold the fourth string on the tone *EE* as long as required. When so locked, the instrument can be played in the same way as the ordinary double bass; the lower tones are instantly available, since a pressure on the *EE*-flat lever automatically releases the lock. According to Dr. Richard Strauss,[820] this arrangement was invented by a German musician, Max Poike.

The five-stringed double bass is used in some orchestras[821] at the present time. The lowest string is tuned down to *CC* or *BBB*; the rest of the strings are tuned in the same way as those on the standard instrument.[822]

Tuning of the double bass in fifths is impracticable. The regular violin technique of fingering cannot be used, owing to the wide stretches required in stopping the long double bass strings.[823] Only a few exceptional players possess hands large and powerful enough to manipulate the double bass tuned in fifths.

The six-stringed double bass is tuned variously, but one of Praetorius' tunings[824] is an octave lower than that of the bass viol.

289. VIOLIN — France, 19th century

Cornerless type. Body of guitar form, without corners, with very narrow middle bouts. Back and ribs of maple. Belly of close grained spruce with elongated S-holes. Both back and belly with slight arching, purfling, and edges fitted flush (no overhang, as on standard violins). Violin-type neck, with peg-box and scroll of standard pattern. Finger-board and tail-piece of boxwood stained black. Three-quarter size violin bridge. *Inside construction*: top and bottom blocks; bass-bar and sound-post. Four strings. Reddish-brown varnish. Length, total, 58 cm. Body, length, 34.25 cm.; width, upper bouts, 14.5 cm.; middle bouts, 8 cm.; lower bouts, 17.25 cm. Ribs, height, 3.25 cm. Vibrating length of strings, 31.2 cm. (17.1728)
Plate XIV

This instrument has very narrow middle bouts as compared with violins of the standard pattern. Otherwise in shape of body it follows the Chanot type of cornerless violins. The tone of this instrument is better than that of some mediocre violins made by mass production methods, but not sufficiently distinctive to justify the deviation from the standard type.

290. MUTE VIOLIN — England, 19th century

Anchor-shaped frame, without sound-box. Spine-bar, neck, peg-box, and scroll carved out of a solid piece of maple. Chin-rest formed by a separate piece. Ebony finger-board and tail-piece. Bridge with many extra holes for dampening of vibrations. Four strings. Yellow-brown varnish. Stamped 'Baker, Brighton.' Used for practising. Length, total, 58 cm. Width, under the bridge, 4.5 cm.; chin-rest, 14.5 cm. Height, total, 7.5 cm. Vibrating length of strings, 31 cm. (17.1726)
Plate X

Independent Forms

291. CRWTH (pronounced Crooth) — Dolgelly, Wales, 19th century, by Owen Tudwr

Flat, shallow body with the yoke supporting the neck. Sound-box, yoke, peg-board, and neck carved out of one solid piece of maple. Sound-board of spruce with two circular sound-holes. Finger-board of maple, stained dark brown. Tail-piece with a slant top, hooked by a copper wire to the tail-pin. Bridge of peculiar construction (see drawing); the long leg of the bridge is inserted into the right-hand sound-hole and touches the back. Six gut strings: two open strings located outside the finger-board and four stopped. A nut at the top of the finger-board for the stopped strings. Anterior tuning pegs of steel, plain pattern, with a flattened front end, no holes for strings. The occipital fastening for the tuning end of the strings (see enlarged section on the drawing); clearances for strings cut out in the peg-board to eliminate the sharp angles. *Inside construction*: entire

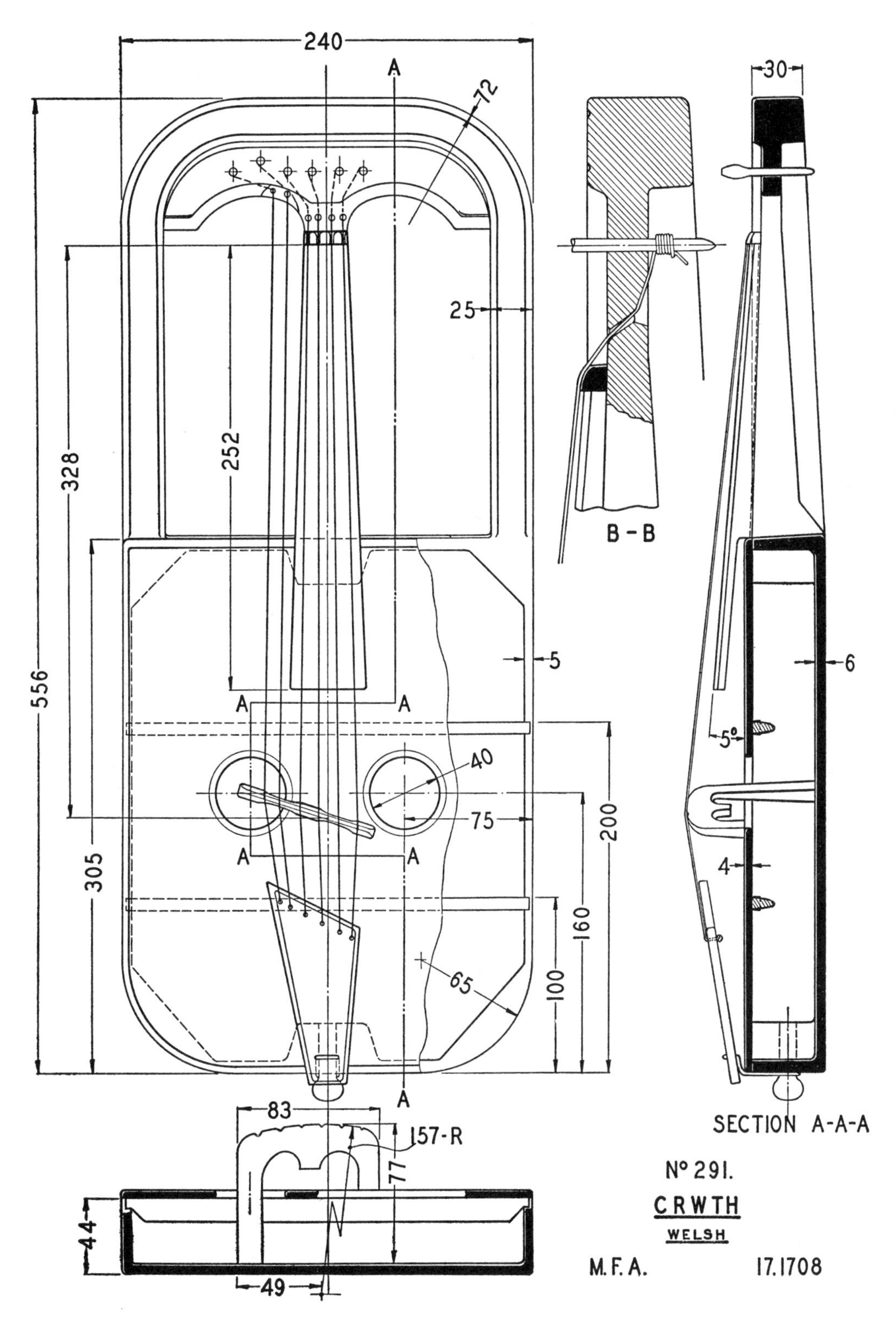

FIG. 58. WELSH CRWTH (NO. 291)

Front elevation and sections. Section B-B shows the 'occipital' (back of the head) method of string fastening.

block cut from the solid; two cross-bars glued to the belly fitting into the notches cut in the sound-box walls. Dark, greenish-brown varnish. Ink label reading:

'Owain Tudwr. Dolgellau
in gweneuthurwr. y
Crwth hwn'

(17.1708)
Plate X and Fig. 58

This instrument was made by an old man, who, according to Canon Galpin, "remembered the instrument as it was in his younger days, and took great pleasure in its reconstruction." [825]

The crwth may be regarded, in a certain sense, as one of the national instruments of the Welsh people, since it survived in Wales until the early part of the nineteenth century. Derivation of the word *crwth* is complex,[826] but the most probable one is that from the ancient Irish *crot* or *cruit*, the Anglicized form of which is *crowd*.

The origin of the crwth is uncertain. Some writers maintain that it descended from the Greek lyra or *chelys*;[827] some from the Greek cithara.[828] More recently, Dr. Otto Andersson brought forward a theory of its relation with the Northern bowed-harp.[829] Still more interesting is his suggestion that the instrument may have been indigenous to Ireland, and that from there it may have been spread by Irish missionaries through the British Isles and Europe.[830] As far back as 1881 J. F. W. Wewertem emphasized the fact that the priests and monks of Celtic origin who brought Christianity to Germany in the sixth and seventh centuries also carried with them musical instruments, among them the crwth.[831] The cultural influence of the Celtic Church has already been mentioned (see Note 552, p. 422) in connection with the probable paths of entry into Europe of bowed string instruments. Professor Arthur Kingsley Porter's well documented narrative of the Coptic influences in Ireland suggests an Oriental origin for the Irish cruit and therefore for the Welsh crwth and for the Northern bowed-harp.[832]

It is safe to maintain that the crwth was played with a bow as early as the first part of the eleventh century.[833] Before this period, objective evidence is lacking, and it is generally assumed that the crwth in the earlier stages of its development was a plucked instrument.

The earliest representation of the crwth in its traditional form was discovered by Mr. Edward Heron-Allen.[834] It is a four-stringed instrument on the seal of Roger Wade (1316). In shape it differs but little from the instrument in our collection. The open strings were added to the crwth, probably during the fifteenth century.

The tuning of the crwth is not certain. According to Daines Barrington,[835] about 1775 it was tuned like this:

William Bingley's often quoted nineteenth-century tuning is given here with a correction suggested by Canon Galpin:[836]

This tuning is usually given with the stopped strings tuned an octave higher; this is too high, because the average length of the strings of the crwth is approximately equal to that of the viola.

The crwth sounds like an alto viol, but more muffled. Since the bridge is very slightly curved, the crwth is adapted for playing chords. Very little is known of the music for the crwth.[837]

As far as is known, there are only three or four genuine crwths in existence. One is in the Welsh National Library at Aberystwyth.[838] Another is in the Corporation Museum at Warrington, Lancashire. The third is at the Victoria and Albert Museum at South Kensington.[839] To these three instruments may be added one preserved in the Collection of the Gesellschaft der Musikfreunde in Vienna, Austria.[840]

292. TROMBA MARINA — Italy, second half of the 17th century

Marine Trumpet. Nun's Fiddle. Monochord with fifty sympathetic strings. Long, hollow sound-box; back of five ribs of pine; open at the bottom. Sound-board of pine extending almost the entire length of the sound-box; the opening at the top providing access to the tuning pegs of the sympathetic strings and covered by a sliding door with open fret-work. Solidly constructed neck with integral peg-box, scroll, and 'top block' at the lower end. Single thick gut-string held by a large knot inside the sound-box at the lower end and fixed to a tuning pin at the upper end. Tuning pin of wrought iron with a square head and a ratchet-wheel affixed to it; pawl held by spring against the ratchet-wheel and fixed to a plate let into the left cheek of the peg-box, providing the bearings for the tuning pin. Ebony saddle-block at the bottom with a groove for the string. A trembling bridge of maple. Ebony nut. Narrow vertical strip of paper glued on the neck front with small cross-strips of white paper pasted over it for indication of the nodal points of the string. *Inside construction*: 'top block' recessed for clearance space for the tuning pegs of the sympathetic strings; oak bridge, with a thin brass strip with spacing notches; similar bridge below. Sound-board is reinforced by a wide bottom panel and four cross-strips, all fitted into recesses in the side ribs; bottom edges of ribs reinforced by oak mouldings. The sound-board reinforced inside at the bottom by oak moulding, serving also as a pin-board for small brass pins holding the fixed ends of the sympathetic strings. (17.1733 a & b)
Fig. 59

The *tromba marina* is one of the rarest instrumental types. Although now a museum curiosity, its significance in the development of the playing technique of modern bowed instruments can be appreciated by these facts:

1. 'Harmonics' used in solo and orchestra playing were borrowed from the *tromba marina*, which used harmonics only.
2. The 'thumb technique' of violoncellos was also borrowed from the tromba marina.
3. The 'machine head' of modern double-basses, guitars, and mandolins was suggested by the ratchet-wheel mechanism of the tromba marina.

Our instrument is remarkable for its unusually large number of sympathetic strings (fifty), and its fine design and workmanship. It was found in an old farm-house in Cheshire, where it had been kept for many years.[841]

The instrument is played in an inclined position, with the neck held over the left shoulder.

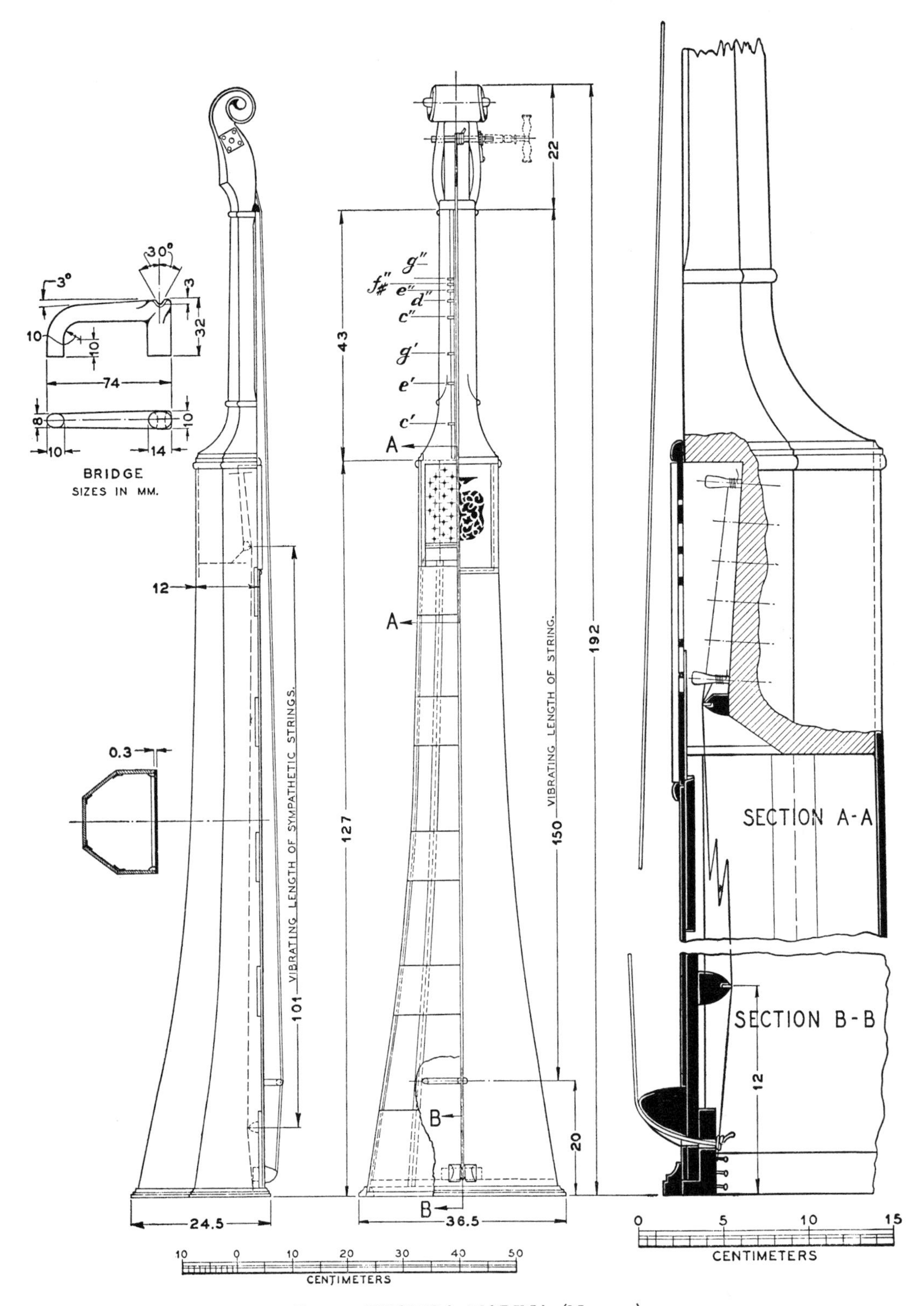

FIG. 59. TROMBA MARINA (No. 292)

Front elevation (the sound board on the right-hand side is not drawn to show the inside construction), right-hand view and partial sections (enlarged).

The string is just touched by the left-hand thumb at the nodal points and the sounds produced are 'harmonics' (more correctly, 'partial tones,' since each is a compound tone consisting of harmonics and partials; see definitions 2, 3, 4, and 9, p. 42 f). The bow is held in the right hand, double-bass fashion, and applied to the string close to the nut and always *above* the point where the string is touched by the thumb.[842]

The most peculiar part of the sound production on the *tromba marina* is its trembling bridge. (See detail, Fig. 59.) Its short leg is placed directly under the string and held stationary by powdered rosin.[843] The long leg, when the string is attacked by the bow, produces a rattling noise by striking itself against the sound-board. Experiments with the Museum's instrument brought out several facts not usually mentioned. The trembling of the long leg of the bridge produces two effects. The first is similar to the percussive action of the snare on the snare drum.[844] The second is similar to the function of the bridge on any string instrument, but with this difference. The sound produced acquires the tone color reminding one of that of the classical natural trumpet. The bridge has to be properly fitted, and produces its optimum effect only at a particular position. When the bridge is shifted out of this position, it produces only a percussive rattle but no trumpeting sound; also, the string sounds its open tone and 'harmonics' in a dull, lifeless fashion. Yet when the bridge is properly placed and the string tension is delicately balanced with respect to the mass of the bridge, then the sounds become surprisingly clear and loud; the timbre becomes so similar to that of the trumpet and the whole effect is so startling that it must be heard to be believed.

The quality of fit between the contacting surfaces of the trembling bridge and the soundboard has a considerable influence upon the intensity of the sounds produced and the richness of their tone color. The number of higher partial tones having the trumpet quality, as well as the ease of their production, is also affected by the smoothness and precision of the fit. For the best results the string should be bowed at the nodal point immediately above the one being touched by the thumb; when bowed close to the nut, the sounds are not as clear and incisive.

The tones playable on our *tromba marina* and having an acceptable 'trumpety' quality of tone, with the string tuned to *C*,[845] are as follows:

The open string sounds with a snarling resonance; the b′-flat, as on the trumpet or horn, is out of tune with the tempered scale; the safe limit on the Museum's instrument is c″; above that the nodal points come too close together and the sound loses its force and its trumpety quality. J. B. Prin's instrument described in his memoir (see Note 843) had a much longer string, measuring 173.2 cm. (5 feet, 4 inches, *pied du Roi*, or the Paris foot; 1 inch equal to 27.07 mm.), as compared with the 150 cm. of the Museum's instrument. On a longer string the emission of higher harmonics would be, undoubtedly, more certain. The sympathetic strings are tuned in unison with the pedal tone.[846]

293. BOW MELODEON Germany, Nuremberg, 1879

Bowed Zither. Shallow sound-box of modified viol form. Back of two pieces of maple. Ribs of maple. Belly of pine with two narrow f-holes, purfled. Both back and belly with overhanging edges as on violins. Neck and peg-plate of maple. Ebony finger-board with twenty-nine brass frets. Three ivory pegs at the back, serving as supporting points of instrument on a table. Five strings: the two higher ones of steel wire, the lower three of spun silk. Frontal type of string tuning end fastening; anterior pegs of round steel with square ends. *Inside construction*: no corner blocks (owing to the peculiar outline of body): sound-post; bass-bar on the left side (opposite to that of violin) owing to the higher strings being located on the right side of the instrument. Printed label reading:

'Ferdinand Sprenger
Instrumentenmacher in Nurnberg
(vormals Carl Sprenger) 1879– '

Length, total, 61 cm. Body, length, 34 cm.; width, upper bouts, 19.75 cm.; middle bouts, 10.5 cm.; lower bouts, 17 cm. Ribs, height, 3.5 cm. Vibrating length of strings, 39 cm. (17.1724)
Plate VIII

This peculiar instrument is placed on a table before the player so that the finger-board will be at his left and the sound-box at his right. The strings are stopped by the left hand and, for the player's convenience, the melody string is placed nearest to him. This results in an arrangement opposite to that of the violin. The tuning of its five strings combines the tunings of both violin and viola, having the highest string tuned like that of a violin and the lowest like that of a viola. The instrument was invented by Johann Petzmayer in Munich in 1823. Although many attempts have been made to improve it, the bow melodeon remains an inferior tone producer.

DIVISION II: INSTRUMENTS CONTROLLED BY A KEYBOARD

KEYBOARD chordophones belong to a division of musical instruments in which sounds are produced by a mechanism operated by a keyboard. Such mechanisms may vary from a simple key with a tangent, as on the clavichord, to the complex arrangement of the double escapement mechanism on the modern piano.

The strings of keyboard chordophones are set in vibration by plucking (virginal, spinet, harpsichord); by striking (clavichord, pianoforte); by bowing (*Geigen Clavicymbel*); by an air stream (*Anemochord* or *Aero-clavichorde*).

Of these four methods of vibrating the strings of keyboard chordophones, plucking and striking are the most widely used.

The historical development of keyboard instruments has been excellently treated in special works devoted to this subject.[847]

SECTION A: PLUCKED KEYBOARD CHORDOPHONES

THE principle of the string plucking mechanism on plucked chordophones is very simple. Essentially, it consists of a key, jack, and jack-guiding element. These last vary on different

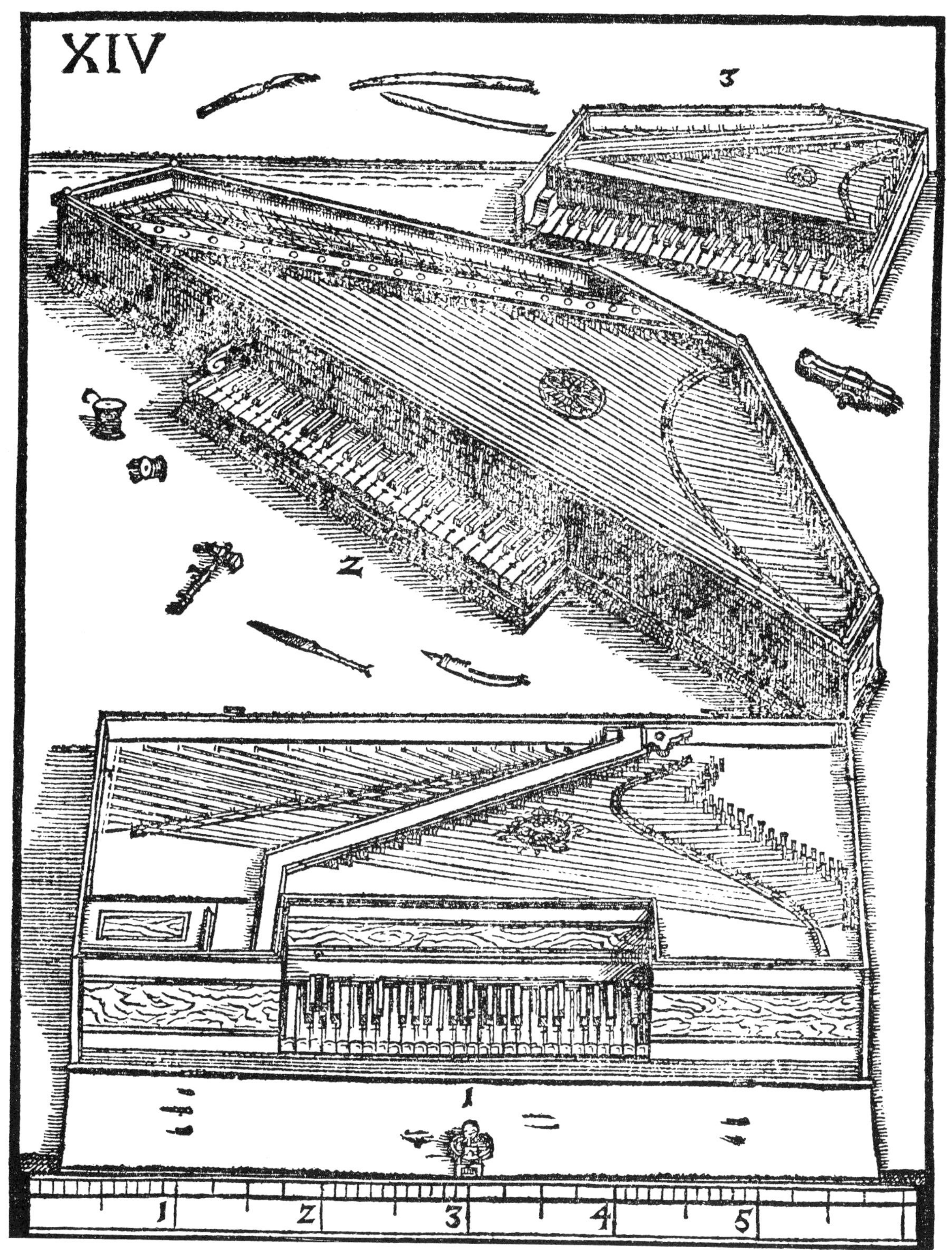

1. 2. Spinetten: Virginal (in gemein Inſtrument genant) ſo recht Chor-Thon.
3. OctavInſtrumentlin.

FIG. 60. PRAETORIUS, TABLE XIV

1, 2. Spinets: Virginal (commonly called an *Instrument*) tuned in the regular *Chor-Ton* pitch. 3. Little Octave Instrument.

instruments. For instance, on the virginal No. 295, the guiding element consists of the bar with slots for jacks cut in it. This bar is fitted flush with the sound-board and is sufficiently thick to guide the jacks properly. The harpsichord has two jack-guiding elements, one stationary, another movable.

Figure A represents the mechanism of harpsichord No. 298. Figure B shows the upper part of the jack in section and the relative position of the string and the quill.

The most important part of the plucking mechanism is the jack. Its body is formed of a

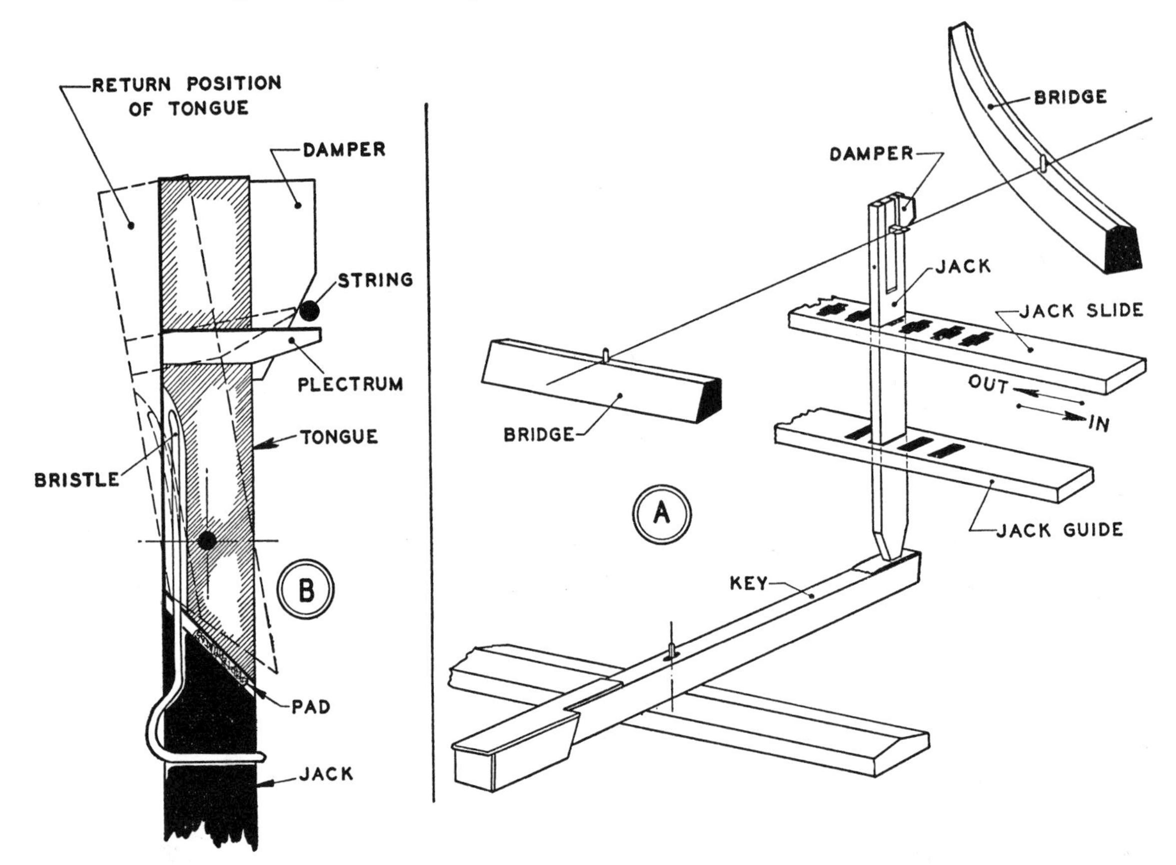

Fig. 61. MECHANISM OF THE HARPSICHORD

thin rectangular strip of wood, in the upper part of which is inserted a tongue mounted on a thin wire axis; this tongue can, therefore, swing out of its normal position. In the tongue is inserted a plucking member (plectrum) usually made of crow quill or leather. In the upper part of the jack are also inserted two dampers of felt cloth (see Fig. A; one of the dampers is omitted for clarity). The tongue is held in place by a stiff boar's bristle acting as a spring.[848]

The action of the plucking mechanism is simple. When the key is depressed, it lifts the jack and forces the quill past the string; the string is plucked by the quill and continues to vibrate. When the key is released the jack falls down of its own weight; [849] the quill touches the vibrating string again and forces the tongue back, so that the jack can pass by the string.

Immediately after passing the string, the tongue is forced by the bristle spring to resume its plucking position. After the jack returns to its initial position the damper stops the residual vibration of the string. The action of the jack mechanism is very rapid and permits the easy execution of trills and complicated embellishments.

The secondary contact of the quill with the string on the downward stroke of the jack produces a slight jarring noise which some purists accept as one of the essential characteristics of harpsichord tone. Some, however, think it a nuisance, and try to avoid it by perfecting the plucking mechanism.[850]

The quality of tone produced by plucked keyboard chordophones is very pleasing. It is governed somewhat by the kind of material used for the plectrum in the jack tongues. Crow quills give a brilliant and somewhat metallic tone. Leather gives a less brilliant tone, but its quality is preferred by some people.

The principal defect of plucked keyboard chordophones is the difficulty of controlling the dynamics of a given set of strings. This limitation is inherent in the principle of the plucking mechanism; the player can make only slight changes in the intensity of tone. The changes of speed or force in operating the keys affect either the quality of tone or its dynamic intensity only within narrow limits. So spinets and virginals, which have but one set of strings, become somewhat monotonous after a while, however charming they may sound at first.

Makers and players have corrected this defect by creating a more highly organized instrument, the harpsichord, which is really a combination of several individual spinets of various sizes. On the more highly developed harpsichords there are several sets of strings (stops), which are nominally referred to as four-foot, eight-foot, twelve-foot, and sixteen-foot stops. The eight-foot stops are usually made in two unison sets. So the dynamic monotony of one set of strings is enriched by combinations of different stops or registers, somewhat on the same lines as on the organ.[851] The art of playing the harpsichord, discussed in detail under No. 298, consists in the complete utilization of the rich tonal and dynamic resources of the instrument. Not without reason was it called by contemporaries the 'lordly harpsichord.'

294. SPINET — Venice, Italy, ca. 1550, attributed to Giovanni Domenico

Rectangular case with projecting keyboard; on stand. Compass from C to f^3; the lowest octave short (C on E). Case painted light pink with green stripes lined red; crudely painted medallion of St. Cecilia at the organ, on inner side of the cover; also a cupid bearing a scroll inscribed 'Sancta Cicilia' [*sic*]. The keys, thirty naturals with boxwood facing and arcaded fronts; twenty sharps of stained boxwood. Sound-board of pear (?) wood with a sunken, three-tiered rose of parchment, beautifully done. Two bridges of birch, one near tuning pins curved, the other straight. Fifty jacks of maple; crow quill plectrums. Triangular compartment in the outer right-hand corner for the tuning key and extras. Case, length, 153 cm.; width, 41 cm.; height, 19.5 cm. Vibrating length of strings, min., 12 cm.; max., 133 cm. (17.1791)

295. VIRGINAL — Antwerp, Belgium, 1610, by Andreas Ruckers the Elder

Rectangular case on stand, with top and front drop covers. Compass from C to c^3; the lowest octave short (C on E). Case painted cherry red in two tones; dark outside border, light inside with

FIG. 62. VIRGINAL (No. 295)
By Andreas Ruckers, 1610

FIG. 63. CLAVICYTHERIUM (No. 296)
Italian, c. 1600

red lines. Inside is decorated with block-printed paper of the Flemish School, glued on the sides of the case and on the front drop cover. Watered paper is also glued to the inside surface of the top cover; within paper border is the Latin motto, 'OMNIS SPIRITUS LAUDET DOMINUM.' The keys: twenty-seven naturals with ivory facings, eighteen ebony sharps. Sound-board of soft pine decorated with painted fruits and flowers; the date, 1610, painted in red; pierced medallion with an angel playing an Irish harp and the letters 'A.R.' Two bridges of birch; one straight, the other partly straight and partly curved and located near the tuning pins at the right. Adjoining the

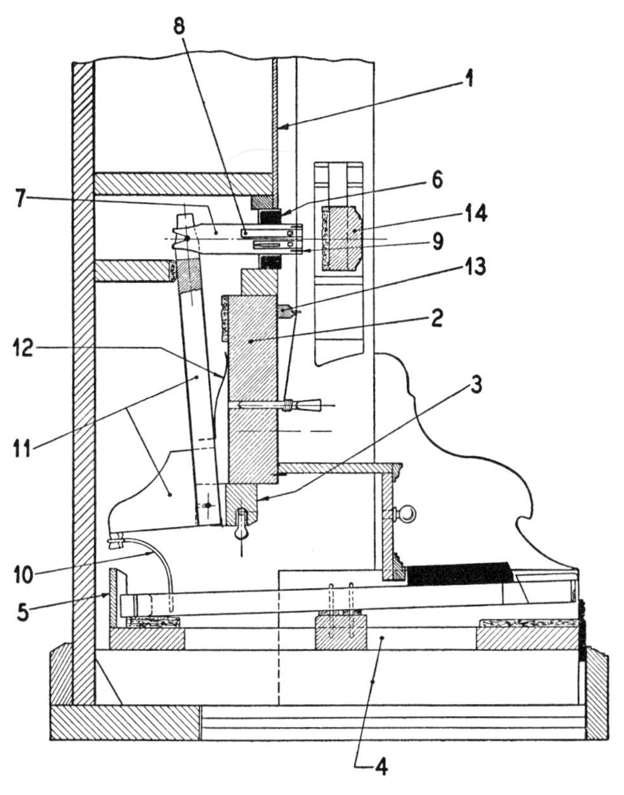

Fig. 64. CROSS-SECTION OF THE CLAVICYTHERIUM (No. 296)

1. Sound-board. 2. Wrest-plank. 3. Jack lever rail. 4. Key-frame. 5. Slotted key-guide. 6. Jack guide. 7. Jack. 8. Tongue. 9. Damper. 10. Lifter. 11. Jack lever. 12. Jack lever spring. 13. Bridge. 14. Jack rail.

straight part of the second bridge is a slide (later addition) with twenty-seven projecting wire loops. Forty-five jacks of maple with crow-quill plectrums. The jack rail inscribed: 'ANDREAS RUCKERS ME FECIT ANTVERPIAE.' Small compartment for tools and extras on the left of the keyboard. Case, length, 130.5 cm.; width, 45.5 cm.; height, 21.5 cm. Vibrating length of strings, min., 14 cm.; max., 112 cm. (17.1792)
Fig. 62

The Ruckers family of Antwerp was master of the harpsichord-making craft from 1579 until after 1667. This virginal, dated 1610, was built by Andreas Ruckers the Elder (1579–

ca. 1652) in the year when he became a Master. It is placed as no. 1 on the list of his instruments in Grove's *Dictionary of Music and Musicians*, iv, p. 479.

296. CLAVICYTHERIUM — Italy, ca. 1600

The Upright Spinet. Vertical case with wing-shaped top side. Compass from C to c³; the lowest octave short. Case painted black; white moulding around front edge. The keys: twenty-seven naturals with boxwood facing and arcaded fronts; eighteen sharps of oak, stained black with decorative ivory wedge inlaid on the top. Sound-board of soft pine with three pierced sound-holes decorated with parchment roses. Ninety tuning pins below the sound-board. Forty-five jacks with double tongues plucking two strings simultaneously. Jack rail placed vertically in the front of jacks. Case, height, 111 cm.; length, 70 cm.; width, 32 cm. Vibrating length of strings, min., 6 cm.; max., 74.5 cm. (17.1795)
Figs. 63, 64

The clavicytherium (keyed harp) or upright spinet is one of the earliest forms of the plucked keyboard instrument and is illustrated in Virdung's *Musica getutscht* (1511). Fig. 64 represents a cross-section of the operating mechanism of the Museum's instrument.

The action of this mechanism is very simple. When the key is pressed down, the lifter (10) rocks the jack lever (11), which pushes the horizontal jack (7) past two strings; when the pressure on the key is released the jack is returned to its initial position by the pressure of the spring (12) on the lever. Travel of the jack is limited by the jack rail (14).

297. SPINET — London, England, ca. 1750, by Baker Harris

Harp-shaped case with projecting keyboard; on a stand. Compass from E to g³. Case of inlaid mahogany with brass-hinged cover. The front board inscribed 'BAKER HARRIS fecit.' The keys: thirty-one naturals with ivory facing and arcaded fronts; twenty-one ebony sharps. Sound-board of spruce. Fifty-two tuning pins in the front. Fifty-two jacks of pearwood with single damper and a tongue located to one side of the centre line. Case, length, 112 cm.; width, 56 cm.; height, 14.5 cm. Vibrating length of strings, min., 5.5 cm.; max., 95.5 cm. (17.1793)
Fig. 65

298. HARPSICHORD — London, England, 1798, by Joseph Kirkman

Two manuals. Long wing-shaped case of inlaid walnut, on a stand. The name-board and inside walls of the case near the manuals veneered with inlaid satinwood. Compass from FF to f⁴ (six octaves, including the four-foot stop). Three sets of strings: four-foot (octave) stop and two eight-foot unisons. Bass strings of brass wire; middle and high register strings of thin steel wire. The keys: thirty-six naturals with ivory facings and twenty-five ebony sharps on each manual. Sound-board of fine grained spruce, the grain running parallel to the long side of the case; sound-hole with pierced and embossed brass rose. Two graduated bridges of birch on the sound-board with low and narrow end at the treble strings increasing gradually in size. Two hundred and forty-four steel tuning pins on the wrest-plank. There are four sets of jacks, sixty-one jacks in each set. The lute stop is operated from the upper manual. The first unison or cymbal stop is operated from both manuals. The second unison stop and the octave (four-foot) stop are both operated from the lower manual only. The jacks are of pearwood; lute and octave stop jacks have one damper each, unison jacks have two dampers each. The oak wrest-plank has a slot for the lute stop jacks. Two graduated bridges of birch on the wrest-plank. The buff slide in the front of the eight-foot

FIG. 65. SPINET (No. 297)
By Baker Harris. London, c. 1750

FIG. 68. MANUALS AND STOPS OF THE KIRKMAN HARPSICHORD

string bridge, with pieces of buff-leather attached for muting the first unisons. The Venetian swell consists of slats mounted on a hinged frame, thereby giving access to the strings. The 'machine' stop is attached to the left side wall and is covered by a projecting rectangular cover. There are six ivory knobs (stops) and two foot pedals for controlling the registration and expression. Five knobs are located on the name-board (see Fig. 68 for detailed description). The sixth knob is located on the left side wall (24, Fig. 67) and controls the engagement of the 'machine.' The left foot pedal controls the 'machine' when the latter is engaged by the sixth knob. The right foot pedal raises the Venetian swell slats. The name-board inscribed:

'Josephus Kirkman Londini fecit 1798
No 19 Broad Street, Soho.'

Case, length, 250.5 cm.; width (not including 'machine'), 94.5 cm.; height, 32 cm. Vibrating length of strings, four-foot, min., 6.5 cm.; max., 111 cm.; eight-foot, min., 12.5 cm.; max., 190.5 cm. (17.1794)
Figs. 66, 67, 68

Joseph Kirkman was the son of Abraham Kirkman and the grand-nephew of Jacob Kirkman, the founder of this famous firm of harpsichord makers. He joined the firm in 1789 and managed it from 1798, the year our instrument was built. Kirkman harpsichords were popular with those of Burkat Shudi, from which they differed only in the order of stops.[852] In quality and workmanship the instruments of both makers were equal. Our instrument is a fine example of English harpsichord-making at its best. It is in playing condition and possesses an extraordinarily rich and full tone.[853]

Fig. 66 represents its outer aspect and Fig. 67 is a cross-section of the keyboard mechanism.

The cross-section shows clearly how the first unison jacks (7) are operated from both the upper and the lower manuals: the thin extension legs of the jacks touch the lower keys and therefore can be lifted independently of the upper keys. It should be noted that the jacks are not attached to the keys, but merely rest on them. Another structural feature of importance is the stationary jack racks (11 and 14, Fig. 67) which guide the lower part of the jacks; while the jack slides (12 and 15) all guide the upper part of the jacks, each one independently of the rest. The jack slides bring the quill plectrums of all jacks of a given stop (register) to their proper position for playing, or move them away from the strings so that the whole stop will be disengaged.[854] The jack slides are controlled by crank levers to which are attached the ivory knobs (also called 'stops') mentioned in the technical description.

Since there is no complete description of harpsichord registration on the mechanical side extant at present, this important procedure will be described in detail.

The stops on the name-board are disposed as shown in Fig. 68.

The left-hand group of three stops located above the upper manual consists of the buff (harp), the lute, and the octave (four-foot) stops. The right-hand group of two stops consists of the first unison (cymbal) stop and the second unison stop. All stops are counted from the left to the right.

The buff stop controls the tone color of the first unison strings only; it changes the metallic timbre of open strings into one similar to that of gut strings. This is done by bringing

FIG. 66. HARPSICHORD (No. 298)
By Joseph Kirkman. London, 1798

pieces of buff-leather or felt mounted on the slide attached to the bridge in contact with the first unison strings. These leather pieces touch the strings very near the bridge pins, shorten the duration of vibrations of the strings, and dampen some of the overtones; the pitch remains unaffected. The resulting tones give a fair imitation of the sound of gut strings. This buff stop is also called by some the harp stop.

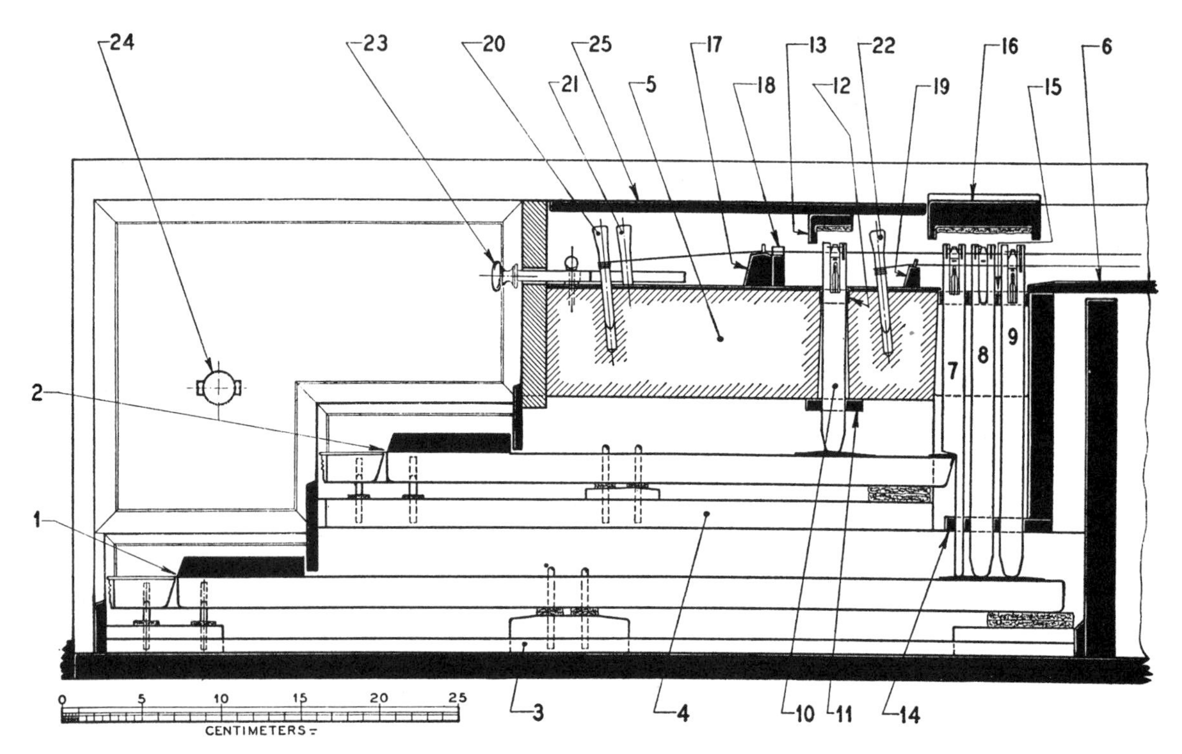

FIG. 67. A CROSS-SECTION OF THE MECHANISM OF THE KIRKMAN HARPSICHORD (No. 298)
1. Lower (forte) manual. 2. Upper (piano) manual. 3. Lower key-frame. 4. Upper key-frame. 5. Wrest-plank. 6. Sound-board. 7. Jack, first unison stop (eight-foot). 8. Jack, second unison stop (eight-foot). 9. Jack, octave stop (four-foot). 10. Jack, lute stop. 11. Lute stop jack guide. 12. Lute stop jack slide. 13. Lute stop jack rail. 14. Jack guide, unison and octave stops. 15. Jack slides, unison and octave stops. 16. Jack rail. 17. Bridge, eight-foot strings. 18. Buff (harp) stop slide. 19. Bridge, four-foot strings. 20. Tuning pins, first unison strings. 21. Tuning pins, second unison strings. 22. Tuning pins, four-foot strings. 23. Stop (the knob on the slide-operating lever). 24. Machine stop. 25. Cover.

The lute stop controls the set of jacks operated from the upper keyboard and located close to the bridge. The distance from the bridge pin to the centre of the quill point is only 1.5 cm. at the highest string in the treble and 7.2 cm. at the lowest in the bass. Compare these distances with those of the second unison stop given below. The lute stop derives its name from the special effect, beloved by lutenists, which consisted of plucking the lute strings close to the bridge, thus producing a peculiar tone color. The lute stop can be played 'open' (without the buff) or with the buff stop engaged. The addition of the buff stop produces a new tone color on the lute stop.

The octave (four-foot) stop is played from the lower keyboard. In the harpsichord it represents the strings of the octave spinet and adds the tone color of that instrument to the other tonal resources of the harpsichord. Played alone, or in contrast with the eight-foot unison stop, it provides the harpsichord with a brilliant upper register. When played with the rest of the stops it reinforces the upper overtones of the longer strings and enhances the richness and fulness of tone of the harpsichord.[855]

The first unison stop is operated from either the upper or the lower keyboard. In both cases it can be played with or without the buff stop. It may be played in conjunction with the lute stop. When so played, the first unison strings are plucked by two sets of jacks operated simultaneously from the upper keyboard.

The second unison stop is operated from the lower keyboard. The distance from the bridge pin to the centre of the quill point is 6.7 cm. in the treble and 20 cm. in the bass. These figures give the average normal plucking distance of harpsichord strings.

The machine stop is operated by the left-foot pedal and is engaged or disengaged by the stop (No. 24) located on the left-hand side of the case. Its mechanism is enclosed inside a separate cover affixed to the left-hand wall outside of the case, spoiling the otherwise impeccable appearance of the instrument. Essentially, the machine stop consists of a slide which engages simultaneously the slots in the brass strip extensions of the octave, the first unison and the lute jack slides; the machine stop slide is pivoted and works against the spring. With the pedal in the 'off' position the octave and the first unison stops are engaged. When the pedal is pressed down with the left foot, the lute stop is engaged, and both former stops are disengaged simultaneously. The action of the mechanism, once it is engaged, is satisfactory, but difficulty is experienced in shifting the slide and catching three slots. This can be done only in a certain position, and the whole contraption has proved to be rather useless.

The Venetian swell was originally invented by Burkat Shudi and patented by him in 1769; later, after the expiration of the patent, it was applied to Kirkman harpsichords. Fig. 66, p. 329 shows the swell lifted up and displaying a part of the operating mechanism. It is worked by the right foot pedal. Although the swell provides a crescendo effect, it does so only in a limited way, and is not an essential addition to the resources of the harpsichord.

The harpsichord can be completely silenced by moving all quill plectra out of engagement with the strings.

Each stop can be engaged singly, with the rest of the stops silent.

A fine harpsichord player can produce a variety of dynamic levels and of tonal colors on a fully equipped instrument by playing on a single stop, doubling up the unisons, using single stops in contrast with several others (the double keyboard permits this): using, for instance the four-foot stop in contrast with the eight-foot stop; selecting different parts of the keyboard (say, the low tones of the four-foot stop and the high tones of the eight-foot stop; both have different tone colors even if played in unison); using the lute and the buff stops. Finally, by using the harpsichord's equivalent for the full organ, the *grand jeu* effect is brought into play.[856]

This discussion shows clearly the many resources which are at the disposal of a harpsichordist. The performance of harpsichord music requires not only technical dexterity but also poetic and artistic imagination in selecting proper tonal colors in registration.[857] In this, harpsichord playing has much in common with organ technique.

Compared with the piano, the harpsichord delivers its dynamic effects in 'quanta' and on different planes of tonal color; it has the power of colorful and dramatic contrasts.[858] The piano is superior to the harpsichord in its ability for continuous dynamic gradation; it is the harpsichord's equal in the power of dramatic contrasts; but all its effects are produced on the same plane of tonal color. Tone contrasts on the piano are obtained by different intensities and shades of the same color rather than the startling contrasts of entirely different tonal colors as on the harpsichord. In agility the harpsichord is superior to the piano.

Harpsichord music loses much of its charm when transcribed for the piano. Complicated embellishments and trills, so graceful and easy on the harpsichord, sound clumsy and heavy on the piano. The variety of registration which is so characteristic of the harpsichord, and which imparts polychromic tonal effects to its music, is entirely lost on the piano. The differences between harpsichord music as played on the harpsichord and on the piano is that between a painting in full color and a monochromatic etching or a photograph.[859] The effect is much worse when harpsichord music is 'edited' and 'adapted' for the pianoforte and the embellishments are omitted. Such a practice is a sacrilege. It should be realized that embellishments are organically interwoven with the main structure, and constitute one of the charming peculiarities of the period. After all, does not the fact that harpsichord music is not suitable for the piano reveal that the piano has the defects of its qualities? Tone color values are not transferable from the harpsichord to the piano.

The problem of transcribing harpsichord music for the piano can be approached correctly only after the difference of character of each instrument is taken fully into consideration. The answer to this problem is complicated by the related problem of the interdependence of a composer's inspiration and his means of expression. Although the inspiration of composers is not governed by instrumental types, the form of expression into which inspiration is moulded is decidedly affected by the instruments at their disposal.[860] Recognition of this fact would bring a better understanding of the proper use of instrumental means in the interpretation of music of the past ages. At present, the way to do justice to the art of music is to perform the creations of the masters of the past on the instruments for which they were written.

SECTION B: STRUCK KEYBORD CHORDOPHONES

THERE are two basic types of struck keyboard chordophones: the clavichord and the pianoforte.

The striking mechanism of the clavichord is very simple. It consists of a flattened out piece of metal called a 'tangent' affixed to the key. When the key is depressed, the tangent strikes the string from below and sets it in vibration. The principle of the production of vibration of a given pitch on the clavichord string is unusual and differs from the rest of the keyboard instruments. Fig. 69 represents the mechanism of the clavichord.

The essential difference in principle is that the pitch of tone produced on the harpsichord, the piano, etc., is predetermined and, once set, remains constant and outside the player's control. Strings on these instruments are stretched over two bridges and the vibrating length of the strings is equal to the distance between the two points of contact of the strings and bridges.

The strings on the clavichord are stretched between the hitch pins and the bridge, so there is only one definite cut-off point on them.[861] The hitch-pin end of the strings on the clavichord is interwoven with the damper cloth called the 'listing.' It is not possible to sound a string on the clavichord or to determine its pitch when it is left free of contact with the

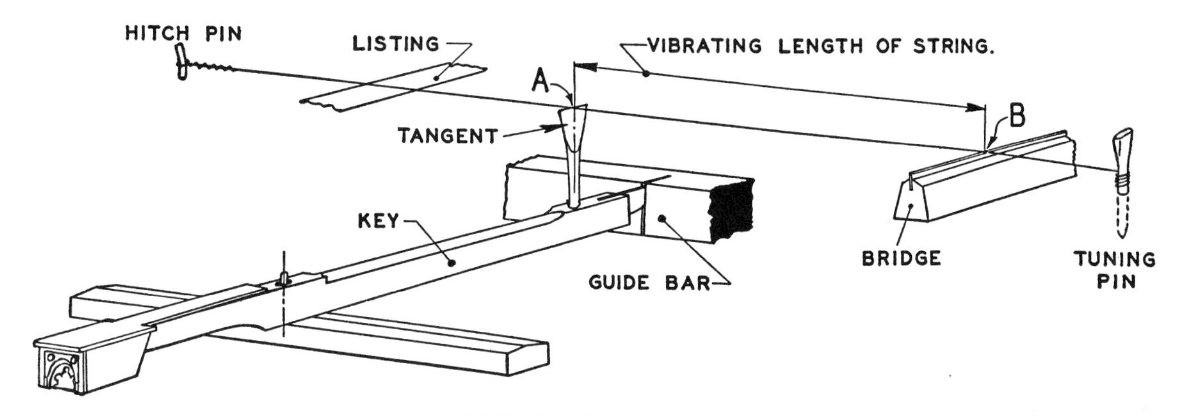

Fig. 69. MECHANISM OF THE CLAVICHORD

tangent, since the listing stops vibrations. The string on the clavichord produces sound only after it is struck by the tangent and as long as it is supported by the tangent. The pitch of the string is determined by its initial tension and the distance from the point of contact of the tangent with the string (Fig. 69, point A) to the bridge (point B). The moment the tangent is removed from contact with the string, the listing stops its vibration.

In other words, the tangent serves as a temporary bridge supporting the string from below and is operated by a key at the will of the performer. The vibrating length of the string on the clavichord is equal to the distance between points A and B and is determined only by the actual contact of the tangent and the string. Hence, certain peculiarities of the clavichord arise. First, it is possible to play out of tune on the clavichord, if the keys are fitted loosely. Then the lateral displacement of the tangent with respect to the bridge will cause the pitch to be higher or lower.

Secondly, since the pitch of a given string is determined by the location of the point of contact A, it is possible to produce several sounds on the same string by striking it with tangents fixed to different keys. In other words, the pitch of the strings on a clavichord is not a constant, but a variable magnitude, depending upon the location of the point of contact A as determined by the location of the tangent with respect to the bridge.

On this principle is based the construction of the 'fretted' (German, *gebundene*) clavichords, on which as many as four different tones were produced on the same string (see text under No. 299). This was done by arranging the tangents on four adjacent keys so that they would strike the same string. Of course, it is obvious that only one tone could be sounded at a time, and chords requiring the simultaneous production of tones by these keys could not be played at all.

Thirdly, since the tangent is practically under the immediate control of the player, he can produce a charming effect, *Bebung* (vibration), similar to the vibrato of a violinist or a good guitar player. This effect is produced by variations of pressure on the keys without completely releasing them and can be applied effectively only to tones sustained for a long time. The *Bebung* can be produced only on the clavichord.

The origin of the clavichord is uncertain. There is a tradition which ascribes the invention of the clavichord to the monk Guido d'Arezzo, who lived early in the eleventh century. It developed, allegedly, from the monochord,[862] which was used by learned monks to demonstrate the Pythagorean theory of the intervals of the musical scale by means of movable bridges. The constant necessity of shifting these bridges suggested, first, a multiplication of strings, and, eventually, the application of a keyboard mechanism.

This theory seems plausible. It is supported by some older writers and by the fact that the monochord was the earliest name of the clavichord; this name was still in use as late as the sixteenth century.[863] But there are certain considerations which suggest a more probable theory of the origin of the clavichord.

The principle of a 'fretted' clavichord is similar to the method of stopping strings on the bowed-harp described by Dr. Otto Andersson.[864] On the bowed-harp the fingernails serve as 'tangents' and support the string from below; several tones are produced on the same string by successive stopping of it by four fingers. The analogy is complete and cannot be disregarded, since this method of stopping strings is, probably, one of the oldest known.[865] If the names of instruments can be used for supporting various theories of the origin of musical instruments, then the names of the clavichord in the Romance languages, *manicordo* (Italian), *manicordio* (Spanish), and *manicorde* (French), meaning 'hand-stringer,' become significant. It seems that they are not corruptions of the word monochord, as is usually explained, but rather exact descriptions of the original method of stopping the strings. The writer is inclined to think that the hurdy-gurdy theory of the origin of the clavichord,[866] uncouth though it may appear to some, has merits which should make it preferable to the somewhat artificial and 'learned' theory of its origin from the monochord. More on this point under No. 305.

The history of the clavichord is divided into two periods. The first period, which lasted until the middle of the eighteenth century, was the reign of the 'fretted' or *gebundenes* clavichord. The ever-increasing application of chromatic tones in music and the greater freedom of modulation required instruments on which all tones should be available without any restrictions. So in the second quarter of the eighteenth century (possibly earlier) clavichords were built 'fretless' or *bundfrei*, with each key striking its own string. The typology of the clavichord is based on keyboard range, constructional details, etc., and is given by Dr. Curt Sachs in his catalogue of the Berlin Collection.[867]

The history of the pianoforte is outside the scope of this study.[868] The invention of the pianoforte is credited to Bartolomeo Cristofori about 1709. His *Gravicembalo col piano e forte* was described in a Venetian journal in 1711. The earliest surviving instrument built by him (in 1720) is now at the Metropolitan Museum of Art, New York City.

299. CLAVICHORD — Genoa, Italy, 1568, by Onesto Tosi

Gebundenes Clavichord. Fretted type. Rectangular case with projecting keyboard. Compass from C to c^3; the lowest octave short (C on E). Case painted dark green outside and decorated inside with crude paintings of Orpheus and Eurydice. The keys: twenty-seven naturals with boxwood facings and beautifully carved arcaded fronts; eighteen sharps of stained boxwood. Sound-board of pine, inclined toward the tuning pins; three straight bridges. Twenty-two sets of double strings attached to forty-four iron tuning pins. Two bridges close to the hitch pins serve a structural purpose only. Small drawer underneath the keyboard for extras. Case, length, 117 cm.; width, 29 cm.; height, 15 cm. Keyboard projection, length, 66 cm.; width, 11 cm. (17.1796)
Fig. 70

As stated in the technical description, this clavichord is strung in pairs, so there are twenty-two 'choirs.' Since the order in which these strings are struck is of interest as an example of the sixteenth-century practice, the table below lists in detail all the strings, the keys striking them, and the tones produced. The keys are numbered to correspond to the diatonic scale [869] up to C_{28}, and to the chromatic scale from C_{28} upward.[870]

String No.	Key No.	Tones Produced	String No.	Key No.	Tones Produced
1.	1	C_{16}	12.	12, 13	$D\sharp_{31}$ E_{32}
2.	3	D_{18}	13.	14, 15	F_{33} $F\sharp_{34}$
3.	5	E_{20}	14.	16, 17, 18	G_{35} $G\sharp_{36}$ A_{37}
4.	2	F_{21}	15.	19, 20, 21, 22	$B\flat_{38}$ B_{39} C_{40} $C\sharp_{41}$
5.	4	G_{23}	16.	23, 24, 25	D_{42} $D\sharp_{43}$ E_{44}
6.	6	A_{25}	17.	26, 27, 28, 29	F_{45} $F\sharp_{46}$ G_{47} $G\sharp_{48}$
7.	7	$B\flat_{26}$	18.	30, 31, 32	A_{49} $B\flat_{50}$ B_{51}
8.	8	B_{27}	19.	33, 34, 35	C_{52} $C\sharp_{53}$ D_{54}
9.	9	C_{28}	20.	36, 37, 38, 39	$D\sharp_{55}$ E_{56} F_{57} $F\sharp_{58}$
10.	10	$C\sharp_{29}$	21.	40, 41, 42	G_{59} $G\sharp_{60}$ A_{61}
11.	11	D_{30}	22.	43, 44, 45	$B\flat_{62}$ B_{63} C_{64}

A study of the table shows that the lower octave is 'short,' since the second string (D_{18}) is struck by the third key, which appears on the keyboard as F-sharp, the third string is struck by the fifth key, etc., so that the keys which appear to the eye at the bass end of the keyboard as:

F♯ G♯ B♭
E F G A B

really sound as:

D E B♭
C F G A B

FIG. 70. CLAVICHORD (No. 299)
By Onesto Tosi. Genoa, 1568

which is, of course, the typical short octave. Beginning with string no. 12 the clavichord is 'fretted,' that is, several keys strike the same string, so that a corresponding number of sounds are produced on that string. Thus strings nos. 12 and 13 are struck by two keys each, nos. 14, 16, 18, 19, 20, and 21 by three keys each, and nos. 15, 17, and 20 by four keys each.

This clavichord is identical in its essential features with no. 1 of the former Heyer Collection,[871] built by Dominicus Pisaurensis in 1543; it has the same number of keys (45), of strings (22), and the strings are struck by the same keys. Therefore it seems possible to conclude that both instruments represent one of the standard systems of clavichord fretting in the middle of the sixteenth century.[872]

300. CLAVICHORD — Dresden, Germany, 1764, by Horn and Mack

Bundfreies Clavichord. Fretless type. Rectangular case with recessed keyboard, on stand. Range EE to f^3. Walnut case painted black; pine cover (not original). The keys: thirty-seven naturals, of boxwood with tips stained black; twenty-six sharps, of ebony with inlaid ivory tops. Sound-board of pine; bent bridge of birch. Sixty-three sets of double strings attached to one hundred and twenty-six tuning pins; the seven lowest 'choirs' are each strung with one thick wound string and one plain thin brass wire. Small compartment for extras. Case, length, 171.5 cm.; width, 52 cm.; height, 20 cm. (17.1797)

The instrument is a fine example of a typical clavichord of the second half of the eighteenth century. The stringing of the lowest seven 'choirs' with strings of different diameters, the thin string of each set tuned an octave higher, is similar to the old practice used on the lutes. See p. 226.

301. PIANOFORTE — London, England, 1770, by Johann Christoph Zumpe and Gabriel Buntebart

Square type. Rectangular case with recessed keyboard, on stand. Compass G to f^3. Mahogany case with black lines; cover with brass hinges. The keys: thirty-five naturals with ivory facings; twenty-four ebony sharps. Sound-board of pine, very short, placed at the right of the key mechanism; bent bridge of birch. Three levers at the left; two levers (the left and the middle) operate the dampers, the third lever (the right) operates the buff stop. Inscribed on the name-board:

'JOHANNES ZUMPE
ET BUNTEBART' — 'Londini Fecerunt, 1770
Princess Street, Hanover Square'

Case, length, 128 cm.; width, 47 cm.; height, 17.5 cm. (17.1798)

This small instrument is one of the earliest specimens by Zumpe, who settled in London about 1760.[873] The construction of the case with its short sound-board and space provided for the key mechanism, very thin steel strings, and the feeble tone produced by the simple key mechanism make it seem like a modified clavichord rather than a pianoforte.[874] For additional data on this famous maker consult *Early Keyboard Instruments* by Philip James.

302. WORKBOX PIANO — Berlin, Germany, ca. 1810, by Vollmer

Octagonal case on stand. Compass c to f^3. Case of mahogany on gilt legs; a mirror inside. Workbox with two large spools on the top. Piano mechanism concealed in the drawer. A genouillère for operating the damper mechanism. The keys: twenty-five naturals with ivory facings; seventeen ebony sharps; the keys are undersized and playable by a small hand only. Case, length, 59.5 cm.; width, 47 cm.; height, 25.5 cm. Total height, 87 cm. (17.1799)

303. UPRIGHT PIANO — Berlin, Germany, middle of the 19th century

Lyre-shaped case. Compass DD to g^4. Rectangular lower case of mahogany on four turned legs; lyre-shaped upper case of mahogany, with seven wooden gilt rods representing lyre strings, backed with blue brocaded cloth; two round candle brackets. The keys: forty-six naturals with ivory facings; thirty-two ebony sharps; the key facings are 15.5 cm. long. Five lowest strings are single, the rest are double. Three genouillères: the left one shifts the keyboard mechanism for striking one string (*una corda* effect); the middle operates the bassoon stop (*Fagottzug*); the right lifts the damper off the strings; the highest twelve sets of strings have no dampers. White enamel plate on the name-board is inscribed:

'J. C. SCHLEIP in BERLIN'

Case, length, 119 cm.; width, 60 cm.; height, 205 cm. (17.3142)

The genouillères (knee levers) are located underneath the case, where they may be conveniently operated by both knees. These levers were invented by John Andreas Stein.[875] The bassoon stop consists of a long horizontal bar, to which a piece of parchment paper is glued in such a way that a lower part of this paper hangs loose in the vertical plane. When the stop is engaged the paper is interposed between the strings and the hammers; a rattling effect, somewhat resembling the tone of a bassoon, is produced. This stop was popular at one time in Vienna and in Germany. On this instrument the bassoon stop has a compass of DD–g''.

315. ORPHICA — Austria, after 1795

Harp-shaped instrument with strings on a horizontal plane. Compass from c to c^4. Case of pine veneered with mahogany. Sound-board of spruce with bridge of birch. The string frame consists of a straight extension arm in front and a curved member in the rear, conjoined at the extreme left. A keyboard of forty-nine keys (four octaves) on a removable frame; primitive key action (*Prellmechanik* in German; cf. Curt Sachs, *Sammlung Alter Musikinstrumente*, Berlin, 1922, p. 73, fig. 2) without escapement; no dampers. The instrument is strung with a single string for each tone. Eight lower strings of brass wire; the rest are of steel. Length, 127.5 cm.; width, 39.5 cm.; height, 11 cm. Vibrating length of strings, lowest, 58.5 cm.; highest, 7 cm. (21.14)

The orphica was invented by Carl Leopold Röllig in 1795 in Vienna, Austria. The instrument was sometimes played suspended by a ribbon across the shoulder like a guitar, and used for serenades. It had but a short life.[876]

SECTION C: BOWED KEYBOARD CHORDOPHONES

INSTRUMENTS of this type are somewhat unusual. There are two basic types: (1) the hand-bowed type, represented by the *nyckelharpa*, No. 304; its bow is pictured on Plate XV, fig. 304-b; (2) the mechanically-bowed type, a typical representative of which is the hurdy-gurdy, No. 305. The history and peculiarities of construction of the latter instrument are given on pp. 340–341.

304. NYCKELHARPA — Sweden, first half of the 19th century

Keyed Viol. An elongated oval body with very small middle bouts, carved with its neck and peg-board from a solid block of pine. Highly arched belly of pine, with two large oval sound-holes and one small heart-shaped hole beneath the key-box. The key-box is attached to the neck and contains twenty-three keys with tangents. Fourteen posterior sagittal pegs, of which eight are inserted in the peg-board and six in the neck; the peg for the chanterelle string has an extra large and long head for convenience in tuning. Four playing strings, three of which are of gut and one (bass) of wound wire; the chanterelle is stopped by nineteen keys; the second melody string is stopped by four keys; ten sympathetic strings of thin steel wire. Tail-piece of maple, stained black, with a long stem ending with a hook which holds it at the lower end of the sound-box; the tail-piece is prevented from shifting by a gut loop attached to the end-piece carved integral with the body. The upper wall of the key-box is provided with holes for strings serving as a primitive nut. The bridge of maple has a peculiar shape, very slightly curved at the top. The sound-post has square ends and cylindrical middle part; loosely fitted against the belly, but mortised into the back and held in position by a wedge inserted in the hole in the back. Gayly colored, hand-woven, woollen belt for holding the instrument is attached by two leather loops. Length, total, 83 cm. Body, length, 50 cm.; width, middle bouts, 13.5 cm.; lower bouts, 17 cm. Ribs, height, min., 4.5 cm.; max., 9 cm. Vibrating length of strings, average, 38 cm. (17.1734)
Plate VIII

305. HURDY-GURDY — Paris, France, late 19th century

Vielle à roue en forme de viol. Viol-shaped body (guitar-fiedel type) of maple, including the belly; the back and ribs plain; the belly edged with black and white inlay; C-shaped sound-holes. Peg-box of maple with carved human head, attached to the belly. Key-box of maple attached to the belly and to the peg-box; hinged cover, of birch veneered with ebony, attached to the key-box. Six sagittal anterior pegs of oak stained black. Twenty-three keys of pearwood inserted in the key-box, each key having two tangents: thirteen naturals with plain heads stained dark-brown, ten sharps with ivory heads. Six strings, occipital fastening; two chanterelles passing over a nut close to the peg-box through the clearance between the key-box and its cover, over the bridge and attached to the tail-piece; *trompette* string passing over the auxiliary nut on the right side of the key-box, over the small bridge (lost) and attached to a small ivory bracket on the rib at the lower end; a *mouche* string passing over the same nut and over the right side auxiliary bridge on the belly; attached at the lower end to the same bracket. The *petit bourdon* and *gros bourdon* strings on the left side passing over another auxiliary nut, over the left side auxiliary bridge, and both fixed to the small ivory bracket on the rib. Rotary friction wheel of maple mounted on the steel axle with crank and ivory crank handle: all the strings are vibrated by this friction wheel. Tail-piece of maple veneered with ebony, permanently fixed to the end block. Long ivory peg in the tail-piece for the auxiliary string controlling the *trompette* string. Small vertical ebony peg inserted in the belly (used for hitching the *trompette* string). Half-cylindrical wheel guard veneered with ebony and set between two ebony brackets on the belly. Three turned mahogany pins in the ribs for the holding strap. *Inside construction:* top and end blocks of pine; two cross-bars on the back; the sound-post, forked at the upper part, placed directly under the main bridge. Light yellow varnish. Stencilled inside the cover: 'Bouvet (?) paris.' Length, total, 63 cm. Body, length (measured on the belly), 48.5 cm.; width, upper bouts, 21 cm.; lower bouts, 26.5 cm. Ribs, height, top, 10 cm.; bottom, 11 cm. Friction wheel, diameter, 14.2 cm. Vibrating length of strings, 31 cm. (17.1735)
Plate VIII

The hurdy-gurdy is a mechanically bowed keyed chordophone. Its 'bow' is the friction wheel, which has a finely polished circumference rubbed with rosin. The rotating crank-handle actuates the friction wheel, which presents an endless bowing surface to the strings. There are six strings on the hurdy-gurdy. Two of them are stopped by tangents fixed to the keys and are therefore melody strings, the chanterelles; four others are drone strings issuing only one tone each. Of these the *trompette* string is of especial interest. It is so named because at one time it had a bridge called a *trompillon* or *coup de poignet*, which was constructed on the same principle as that of the *tromba marina*. An auxiliary string was tied to the *trompette* string between the trembling bridge and the rib bracket; the other end of the auxiliary string was attached to a tuning peg inserted in the tail-piece. The purpose of this arrangement was to control the trumpeting effect of the trembling bridge.[877] In the belly of our instrument (No. 305) is inlaid a thin ivory plate 23 by 35 mm. on which the foot of the *trompillon* should rest to produce its trumpety effect; this also follows the old *tromba marina* practice (see p. 319 of this study). The *trompette* could be disconnected by hitching it to the small peg mentioned in the technical description.

The tuning of the hurdy-gurdy is very peculiar:

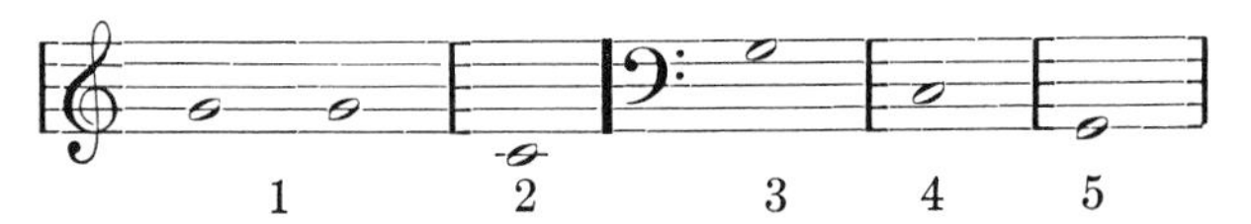

The tunings are respectively: (1) the chanterelles, (2) the *trompette*, (3) the *mouche*, (4) the *petit bourdon*, and (5) the *gros bourdon*. The full stringing of the hurdy-gurdy is used only in dance music and such pieces as the musettes, and then only if the modulations are confined to the tonic and the dominant; otherwise the *trompette* and the *bourdon* strings are disconnected.[878]

The history of the hurdy-gurdy is interesting. Its ancestor, the organistrum, is an instrument of a very respectable antiquity, for it dates back to at least the first half of the tenth century of our era. At that time the second abbot of Cluny, Odo (d. 942) described it in his tract *Quomodo organistrum construatur*, which was printed in Martin Gerbert's *Scriptores Ecclesiastici de Musica Sacra potissimum*.[879] The organistrum was a large instrument which required two players, one for stopping the strings and another for rotating the crank. The earliest representation is on an eleventh-century bas-relief from the abbey of St.-George of Boscherville, Normandy.[880] There are two sculptural representations from Santiago de Compostella, one formerly on the archbishop's palace,[881] another on the *Portica della Gloria* of the cathedral.[882] Both belong to the twelfth century. The early instruments had three strings. Their tuning is not known, but it is probable that the outer strings were tuned in octaves and the middle one a fourth or a fifth above the lower string. The stopping mechanism for strings in the twelfth century consisted of rotating rods, with the low flat bridges which acted as a *capotasto*, and all three strings were stopped simultaneously.[883] The thirteenth-century mechanism consisted of sliding keys with tangents touching only two strings.[884]

In Sebastian Virdung's *Musica getutscht* (1511) the number of strings is represented as four. Some time in the later sixteenth century the number of strings was increased to six.[885] In the fifteenth century, it seems, the organistrum lost caste, and, in a much decreased size, became an instrument of the wandering musicians. Praetorius refers to it rather contemptuously as an instrument of peasants and *Umblaufenden Weiber*. The hurdy-gurdies shown by him on table xxii of the *Theatrum Instrumentorum* are of two types: one has a finger-board and four strings; another is of the usual type with keys and five strings.[886]

In the middle of the eighteenth century the hurdy-gurdy became a favorite instrument of the French court ladies and gentlemen. The queen consort of France, Marie Leszczynska (1703–1768), was a proficient player on the *vielle à roue*.[887] The vogue did not last long. In the present time, the hurdy-gurdy survives in Southern France and in the rural districts of other European countries.

Some scholars maintain that the mechanism of the clavichord was suggested by the tangents on the keys of the hurdy-gurdy. It is possible to extract feeble sounds from hurdy-gurdy strings by striking them with the tangents while the wheel remains stationary. The principle of stopping the strings on the hurdy-gurdy by tangents is similar to that of stopping the strings of the bowed harp by nails which serve as tangents. The persistence of the name *manicordo* (hand-stringer) in Romance languages for the clavichord, and the obvious similarity in the principle of stopping the strings on the hurdy-gurdy and the clavichord with that of the bowed harp, tend to support the theory that the clavichord is a descendant of the organistrum (symphonie) and not of the monochord.[888]

DIVISION III: INSTRUMENTS CONTROLLED BY AUTOMATIC OR AUTONOMOUS MOTION

306. AEOLIAN HARP — England, late 19th century

Long rectangular sound-box of wedge-shaped cross-section with cover; made of pine throughout, except for the two bridges of ebony; round sound-hole in the middle of the belly. Twelve gut strings fixed to small iron hitch-pins on the right side, passing over two movable bridges, and fastened on the left side to twelve iron tuning pins. A removable cover of pine on four legs with iron dowels; the cover is parallel with the bottom of the sound-box and forms a wedge-shaped air passage. Length, 91 cm. Width, 12 cm. Height with cover, 7 cm. Ribs, height, front, 3 cm.; rear, 5 cm. Vibrating length of strings, 79 cm. (17.1779)

The Aeolian harp produces its magic sounds by being exposed to an air draft. Our instrument is intended to be placed on the window sill, so that the air would pass only through the opening between the sound-board and the cover. Although its strings are tuned in unison (usually to G), yet, owing to inequalities of structure and the varying of the intensity of the air current, the sounds produced are different partial tones of the strings. The harmonies produced are composed of the tones of the natural scale of sounds. The phenomenon is similar to the singing of telegraph wires and was explained only comparatively recently.[889] The tones of the Aeolian harp are very delicate and ethereal; no other instrument can imitate these evanescent tones.

The history of the Aeolian harp can be found in Dr. Curt Sachs' *Real-Lexikon*.[890] The classification of the Aeolian harp is always a problem. Structurally it belongs to the psalterium-zither type of chordophone. But its sound production does not fall into any usual division: it is not a directly controlled instrument, it has no keyboard nor any automatic mechanism. For this reason it is classified in this study as a chordophone controlled by an autonomous motion of the air.

CLASS V: ELECTROPHONIC INSTRUMENTS

ELECTROPHONIC instruments are a development of the twentieth century. They are not represented in our Collection. Canon Galpin gave a detailed classification of the instruments of this class so far invented in his *Textbook of European Musical Instruments* (p. 36 and pp. 245 ff.).

CLASS VI: ACCESSORIES

CLASS VI: ACCESSORIES

Bows

ORIGIN of the bow is one of the most controversial problems in organology. Sometimes one is inclined to think that this subject belongs more properly to ethnology and the history of the primitive races of mankind. At present there are several theories concerning the subject. Two of them attempt to settle the question as to whether it originated in Northern Europe or in the East, and, if possible, to ascertain when it came to mediaeval Europe. The third theory, advanced recently by Dr. Curt Sachs, suggests that, owing to the uncertainty of objective data, the questions where and when are irrelevant; that the origin of the bow is not a chronological and technical problem, but an ethnological and psychological one.[891] Of the earlier theories, the Northern and the Eastern, it is the second that seems to be the more plausible. Dr. Otto Andersson in his book, *The Bowed-Harp*, put forth some new arguments in favor of the Northern origin of the bow.[892] The Northern theory would be valid only under two conditions: (1) That the population was indigenous to Northern Europe and not immigrant; (2) that the bow originated in Northern Europe before it did in Asia. The first proposition is not provable. It is more likely that the Northern European aborigines came there by one or more of several possible routes, not improbably from Asia. For the second contention there is no objective data of any kind, either for Northern Europe or Asia. Therefore, pending some new archaeological discoveries, it seems that Dr. Sachs' suggestion is the best way out of the difficulty. Those interested in investigating this question further are referred to the standard works on the subject.[893]

The bow consists essentially of three elements: the 'stick,' the 'hair,' and some sort of adjusting device. The hair is well rosined to increase friction with the strings. Roughly, there are two fundamental types of bows: (1) the older type with a stick of positive curvature, and (2) the modern Tourte bow with a stick of negative curvature. The older type originated, it seems, in the hunter's bow; the hair was tensioned by the elasticity of the bent stick. In more highly developed types, various adjusting devices were used for controlling the degree of tension. An important feature of bows with positive curvature is the possibility of varying the tension of the hair during playing. For instance, in the case of the instruments of the violin family held under the chin, such a bow is held between the first two fingers, placed on the stick, and the thumb, which is placed beneath, either directly on the hair close to the frog or partly on the hair and partly on the frog. This way of holding the bow is represented in the picture of St. Cecilia, Plate XIII. The initial tension is set so that when the thumb pressure is removed the hair becomes less tensioned and easily envelops several strings, which is of advantage in multiple stop playing: the instruments sound more naturally and pleasantly.

Giuseppe Tartini (1692–1770) introduced a bow with a straight stick (zero curvature) and made improvements in various details. About 1770 the German violinist, Wilhelm Cramer, changed the design of the head, making it in the shape of a square, and lightened the frog by cutting out some material on both sides. This unbalanced the bow. Giovanni Battista Viotti attempted to remedy this defect by making the head smaller. Finally, ca. 1780 (Vidal gives the date as 1785–90), François Tourte (1747–ca. 1835), after many years of experimenting, developed the modern bow, and brought it to such a degree of perfection that he is quite deservedly regarded as the 'Stradivari of the art of bow-making.' Tourte bows are distinguished by their exquisite form and perfection of workmanship. Tourte established the standard sizes for the bow: 75 cm. for the violin, 74 cm. for the viola, and 72–73 cm. for the violoncello; selected the best material for the stick, making it of Pernambuco wood (*Caesalpinia brasiliensis*); worked out the standard form of the head by experiments, and of the stem of the stick by graduating its thickness[894] and giving it a negative curvature (*cambrure* in French, the camber); besides making many improvements in details.[895] The Tourte bow made possible the modern virtuoso violin technique with its many types of bow articulation. It should be noted, however, that for multiple stops it is inferior to the old type bow.

The hair-tightening devices were very primitive at first, usually of the slip knot type (bow No. 304 b). The more improved type had a movable frog held by a wire loop hitched into the slots cut in the stick[896] and later into the teeth of a metallic crémaillère plate affixed to the stick (bow No. 284 b). The most advanced type consists of a screw inserted into the end of a stick which engages a nut fixed to the frog. It is possible, by rotating the screw button, to move the frog on the stick back and forth and tighten or slacken the hair tension; this type of adjustment was introduced ca. 1700.

The bows are illustrated on Plate XV. The bows with the letter *b* belong to instruments with corresponding numbers.

307. BUMBASS BOW

Thin notched strip of walnut with roughly cut handle and fifteen notches. Length, 59 cm. Height, 5 cm. Thickness, 7 mm. Length of notched part, 39 cm. (17.1736)

The bumbass, also known as the bladder-and-string, the *bass de Flandres*, is a primitive monochord, consisting of a long stick with a string attached to it and 'tuned' with a peg. In the most primitive forms an inflated bladder served both as a sound-box and a bridge. A pair of small cymbals was attached for increasing noise. The string was 'bowed' with a notched bow stick like that described above and served as some sort of a drone bass. For a modern bumbass picture, see the Catalogue of the Claudius Collection of Old Musical Instruments.[897]

265 b. LYRA BOW

Crudely made from single piece of lemon wood. The hair is tightened by a small wooden peg. Length, 53.5 cm. Thickness, 9 mm. Bowing length of hair, 40.5 cm. (17.1705-b)
Plate X

304 b. NYCKELHARPA BOW

One piece bow made of spruce. The stick is flattened on the inside near the head and curved to form the bow. The black horsehair is fastened to the handle with a slip knot for the adjustment of tension. Length, 49 cm. Diameter of stick, 1 cm. Bowing length of hair, 32 cm. (17.1734-b)

284 b. HARDANGERFELE BOW

Round stick of birch with very small head; movable frog made of maple, held by a wire loop. Crémaillère (notched piece of brass) for adjustment of tension. Length, 57.5 cm. Bowing length of hair, 50.5 cm. (17.1722-b)

309. VIOL BOW — England, ca. 1740

Beautifully fluted stick made of mahogany. The frog and the button of ivory; screw and nut adjustment. Eight semicircular flutes extending the entire length and blending into the head flutes; at the frog end are raised lines (20.5 cm. long) in the hollow of the flutings. The head with a long peak is nicely fluted. Length, 68 cm. Diameter of stick, large end, 8 mm.; neck, 6 mm. Bowing length of hair, 57 cm. (17.1742-b)

310. VIOLIN BOW — England, ca. 1800

Cramer type. Round stick of lancewood with very small negative camber; hatchet type head. Ivory frog, cutout at both ends, with ebony slide and German silver ferrule. Ivory button; screw and nut adjustment. Length, 69.5 cm. Diameter of stick, large end, 10 mm.; neck, 7 mm. Bowing length of hair, 58 cm. (17.1743)

311. BASS VIOL BOW — England, ca. 1800

Round stick of oak. Ivory frog and button; screw and nut adjustment. At the frog end the stick is octagonal for approximately 12 cm. The frog has a rounded outside corner and a semicircular cutout for the middle finger. Rather large and clumsy head, with ivory plate partly covering the face of head. Length, 69 cm. Diameter of stick, large end, 12 mm.; neck, 9 mm. Bowing length of hair, 58.5 cm. (17.1744)

312. VIOLIN BOW — England, late 19th century

Tourte type. Round stick of Pernambuco. Ebony frog with mother-of-pearl slide and German silver trimmings. German silver and ebony button. Ordinary commercial bow. Length, 73.5 cm. Bowing length of hair, 63.5 cm. (17.1745)

282 b. VIOLE D'AMOUR BOW — England, late 19th century

Tourte type. Finely made bow of Pernambuco with octagonal stick. Ebony frog inlaid with large mother-of-pearl shields on the sides; mother-of-pearl slide; German silver ferrule. Ivory button. Length, 71.5 cm. Stick, diagonal at large end, 10 mm.; diagonal at neck, 6 mm. Bowing length of hair, 61.5 cm. (17.1720-b)

292 b. TROMBA MARINA BOW — England (?), late 19th century

Round stick with positive curvature, made of oak; screw and nut adjustment. At the frog end the stick is octagonal for approximately 14 cm. Oak frog with rounded outside corner and semicircular cutout for the middle finger. Ebony button. Black horsehair. Length, 58.5 cm. Height (head and frog), 4.5 cm. Diameter of stick, large end, 16 mm.; neck, 11 mm. Bowing length of hair, 42.5 cm. (17.1733-b)

288 b. DOUBLE BASS BOW — England, late 19th century

Straight round stick of oak, curved at the end to form the head. Ebony frog with mother-of-pearl eyes and slide. Button of German silver and ebony. Length, 70 cm. Diameter of stick, large end, 14 mm.; neck, 11 mm. Height at the frog, 6.2 cm. Bowing length of hair, 56 cm. (17.1732-b)

313. STAGE HARP — London, England, early 19th century

Mute instrument with sixteen 'strings,' used as a stage property. The frame of maple, painted black with gold vine and leaves. Four long strings, each of which is fastened to a hitch-pin and passed over three small pulleys making four short strings; four tightening pegs of boxwood. Maker's name nearly obliterated. Height, 46 cm. Width, 33.5 cm. Thickness (frame), 2 cm. (17.1790)

314. PORTION OF A TIBIA — Roman, ca. first century

Cylinder of bone with two holes in front and one in back. Three incised lines around one end. (17.1815)

According to Canon F. W. Galpin, this piece was dredged up from the Tiber in Rome. Information derived from the typewritten catalogue of the Galpin Collection, 1915.

APPENDICES

APPENDIX A

SCALING OF PRAETORIUS' DRAWINGS

PRAETORIUS' *Theatrum Instrumentorum*, published in 1620, is a priceless documentary record of the contemporary practice of musical instrument-making. Its value is much increased because the drawings were made to scale, with the units of measure drawn on each important table. It is safe to assume that Praetorius gave us representations of the standard instruments of his time. Such instruments are not sudden creations, and the writing of the book itself must have taken a considerable time. It is accordingly safe to assume that the instruments pictured by him give us the true forms of those at the turn of the century, i.e., about the year 1600.

Since many of the conclusions in this study are based on knowledge derived from the scaling of Praetorius' drawings, the method used will be given for the benefit of other students.

There are several technical questions in connection with this somewhat delicate operation. Since the drawings of the instruments are small, the impression prevails in certain quarters that no conclusions can be based on such a slender foundation. This opinion can be held only by those who have never made an exact layout drawing and are afraid of draftsman's tools. Skilful wood-engravers and draftsmen can produce drawings well within a limit of error of one sixty-fourth of an inch, i.e., with errors in linear dimensions not more than .015 inch. The scaling of the drawings is a less difficult task, and can be done very closely indeed by one used to the handling of scales and dividers. The only serious question in this connection is how exactly to scale were the drawings made with respect to the actual instruments represented. The exactness in scaling cannot exceed that which the artist who made the drawings put into them. The size of the drawing is not so important. It is the degree of exactness with which it was made. Later we shall see that the artist who made Praetorius' woodcuts was an exceptionally skilful craftsman and that some of his drawings are very accurate.

1. *The unit of measure used by Praetorius.* Praetorius used the Brunswick foot. Its equivalents in terms of modern measures are:

One Brunswick foot = 11.235 English inches = 285.36 millimetres.

One Brunswick inch = one-twelfth of the Brunswick foot = .93625 English inch = 23.78 mm.

Cf. Horace Doursther, *Dictionnaire universel des poids et mesures anciens et modernes*, Brussels, 1840, p. 405.

2. *The process of scaling.* Since all important tables giving pictures of instruments have the scale drawn on them, the first operation is to measure a desired dimension with dividers (a pair of compasses with sharp steel points), and find the size from the scale on the drawing in terms of the Brunswick foot and fractions thereof. Although the scales on Praetorius' tables are small (one foot equals, approximately, one inch), nevertheless no difficulty should be experienced in determining sizes to the nearest quarter of an inch. The second operation is to translate the Brunswick measures into the desired system of measures. The metric equivalents of Brunswick feet, inches, and fractions are given at the end of this Appendix.

3. *Determination of foreshortened sizes.* The exact measurement of lengths on most of the instruments is possible without any compensation for foreshortening. This is based on the assumption

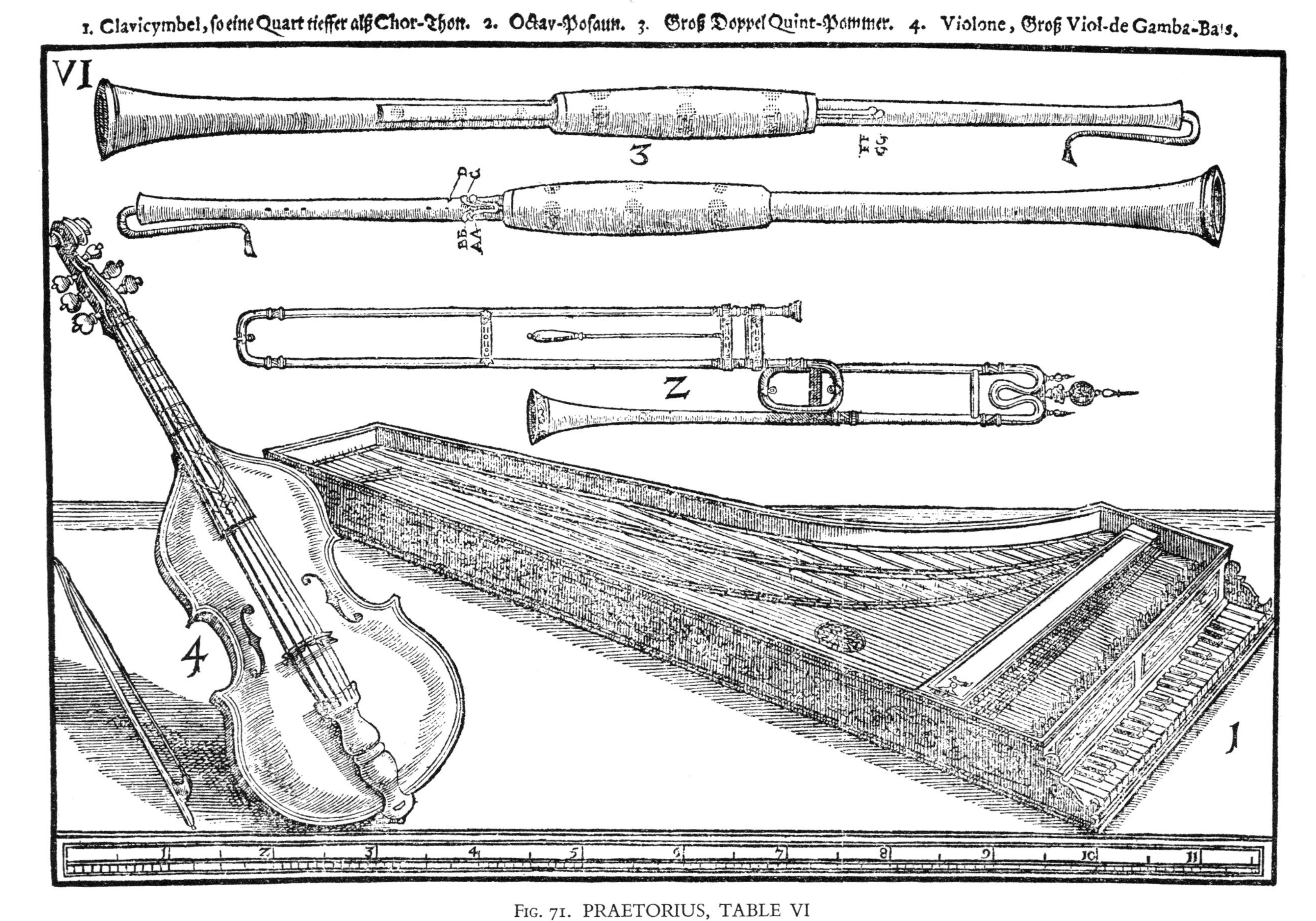

FIG. 71. PRAETORIUS, TABLE VI

1. Clavicymbel (harpsichord), a fourth lower than the Chor-Ton. 2. Octave Trombone (contrabass). 3. Great Double Quint-Pommer. 4. *Violone*, Great Viola da Gamba Bass.

that the projection of Praetorius' drawings is not the exact perspective, but is more akin to the axonometric projection, in which lengths are given without foreshortening.

But with respect to the widths, the situation is different. They were foreshortened in various degrees, and one has to estimate the coefficient of foreshortening and add a certain percentage to the scaled size. Table xvi (lutes, etc.) is drawn either without width foreshortening or with a very small one, about two per cent. But in some cases the widths are foreshortened about ten per cent.

4. *Degree of exactness of Praetorius' drawings.* This can be determined only if a certain instrument can be found which has had its actual size changed but little since the time of Praetorius. Fortunately, such an instrument is available for this determination. It is the violin represented in table xxi, fig. 4, *Rechte Discant-Geig.*

The writer's measurement of the length is 15 Brunswick inches, or 356.7 mm.: the size can be confidently determined, since the outline is very definitely drawn. Dr. Georg Kinsky gives the size of 354 mm. for the same dimension (cf. *Musikhistorisches Museum*, ii, p. 511). The difference is approximately 3 mm. (about 7/64 of an inch), or less than one per cent.

The average length of Cremona violins of the best period is about 355.6 mm. (14 inches). Both the above sizes differ from this average size by less than one-half of one per cent! This is an astonishing degree of exactness, but the objective facts are before us.

Assuming that some important sizes of other instruments can be scaled, say, within three to four per cent, that would give a sufficient degree of exactness for basing any conclusions about the sizes of instruments in the time of Praetorius (about 1600).

5. *Scaling of Viols.* The outlines of such instruments as violins, *lira da braccio* (table xx, fig. 5), etc., are definite enough for scaling their sizes within one per cent. It is not so with viols, which have sloping shoulders blended gradually into the neck bracket.

The measurement of the lengths of the bodies of viols is given in this study from the bottom curve to the plane of the neck extension spanning the clearance between the finger-board and the body of the viol. (See Fig. 48, p. 256, size '33'.) With the experience derived from measuring the actual instruments, one may estimate within three per cent the location of this plane on Praetorius' drawings, and therefore scale the length of the bodies within that limit.

For comparative purposes a few sizes will be given, as determined by Dr. Georg Kinsky and the writer.

1. *Viola bastarda.* Praetorius, table xx, fig. 4, p. 362. The body length as given by Dr. Kinsky (*Musikhistorisches Museum*, ii, p. 492) is 755 mm. The size as determined by the writer is two feet, seven inches, Brunswick, or 737 mm. The difference is 18 mm. or about 2.5 per cent.

2. *Kleine Bass-Viola.* Praetorius, table xx, fig. 3. The body length: Kinsky (*Musikhistorisches Museum*, ii, p. 469, no. 824), 800 mm.; the writer, two feet, nine inches, Brunswick, or 785 mm. The difference is 15 mm., or about two per cent.

3. *Lyra de Gamba.* Praetorius, table xvii, fig. 4. The body length: Kinsky (*Musikhistorisches Museum*, ii, p. 403), 840 mm.; the writer, two feet, eleven and one-fourth inches, Brunswick, or 838 mm.; practically identical, owing to the definiteness of outline of the instrument.

As can be seen, the differences are very small. It seems, therefore, that the scaling of Praetorius' drawings is quite practical, and that conclusions based on such a determination of sizes are valid.

To forestall a possible criticism, let it be said that the shrinkage of paper has been taken into consideration. Undoubtedly the paper on which the original edition of Praetorius' book was printed has shrunk. Dr. A. J. Ellis in his determination of the pitch of Praetorius' organ pipe (*De Organographia*, p. 232) had to calculate the coefficient of shrinkage, because there was no comparative scale drawn on the same page and therefore he had to determine its absolute size.[898]

But in scaling the drawings by means of the scale drawn on the same page, as is the case in all important tables in Praetorius' *Theatrum Instrumentorum*, only their relative sizes, in terms of the

Brunswick measures, are necessary. The absolute sizes are determined by translating the Brunswick measures, scaled directly, into the desired equivalent measure. This is based on the well known principle that in reduction (or enlargement) of sizes in the uniform manner, the ratios and angles remain invariant. Therefore, assuming that paper contracted uniformly,[899] the ratio between the sizes of the instruments and the divisions of scales in Praetorius' drawings remained the same. The relative sizes can be determined, practically, with the same degree of precision as if the drawings had remained unchanged.

For the convenience of readers who would like to scale Praetorius' drawings themselves, two tables of equivalents are given.

TABLE I

METRIC EQUIVALENTS OF BRUNSWICK FEET

Brunswick Measures	Metric Equivalent (*mm.*)
1 foot	285.36
2 feet	570.72
3 feet	856.08
4 feet	1,141.44
5 feet	1,426.80
6 feet	1,712.16
7 feet	1,997.52
8 feet	2,282.88
9 feet	2,568.24
10 feet	2,853.60

TABLE II

METRIC EQUIVALENTS OF BRUNSWICK INCHES AND FRACTIONS

Brunswick Measures	Millimeters
.25 inch	5.945
.50 inch	11.890
.75 inch	17.835
1 inch	23.78
2 inches	47.56
3 inches	71.34
4 inches	95.12
5 inches	118.90
6 inches	142.68
7 inches	166.46
8 inches	190.24
9 inches	214.02
10 inches	237.80
11 inches	261.58
12 inches	285.36

APPENDIX B

SIZES AND TUNINGS OF VIOLS OF THE SIXTEENTH AND SEVENTEENTH CENTURIES

THERE exist several 'persistent problems' in connection with viols which cause endless confusion and exasperation among those who have to deal with them. For instance, let us consider a viol with a body length of 68 cm. An English expert would call it a bass, tune it to *D-d'*, and assign a bass part to it. A German expert, with equal justification, would call it a tenor, yet would tune it *D-d'* and give the bass part, as in the previous case. Why is there this difference in name? But this is not all. There was a period when the same viol was tuned to *D-d'*, called the tenor viol, and played either the tenor or alto parts! This is not a facetious exaggeration, but a matter of fact statement.[900]

Then there is the problem of lower tunings, which showed a 'coy obduracy' to that capable and resourceful investigator, Mr. Gerald R. Hayes. The writer can add his testimony to that of Mr. Hayes, but he is inclined to use much stronger words. The elusiveness of some factors was of such a nature that it seemed as if someone had devised the whole thing with devilish ingenuity to mock and tease unfortunate twentieth-century organologists.

The writer was primarily interested in the problem of sizes and differences in nomenclature. It soon became evident that the whole problem is much wider. Finally this investigation was expanded to include the following:

1. Musical pitch and its variations.
2. The nomenclature of viols.
3. Sizes of viols.
4. Organs and the musical practices of the sixteenth and the seventeenth centuries.
5. The tunings of viols.

Musical Pitch and its Variations

MUSICAL pitch and its variations is primarily a scientific problem belonging to the science of acoustics. Yet it is so intimately connected with various musicological and organological problems that any consideration of musical pitch *per se* becomes irrelevant. Conversely, any intelligent discussion of musical and especially instrumental practices of the past becomes almost impossible unless this subtle factor is kept constantly in mind. Nevertheless it is very rarely taken into account.

The best information about musical pitch of the seventeenth century, as well as some references to the practices of the sixteenth century, is given in Praetorius' *De Organographia*.[901]

Praetorius gives a very interesting description of the conditions in his time. But before quoting him, we should clarify his terminology. In Praetorius' book two principal pitches are suggested: *Chor-Ton* (a'-422.8) and *Cammer-Ton* (a'-475.65): he tells us that in some localities the higher pitch was called *Chor-Ton*.[902] So this difference in terminology should be kept in mind.

The extensive quotation given below is a close, almost literal, translation of two important passages from the second chapter of *De Organographia*:

And, first, be it known that the pitch of organs as well as of other musical instruments often varies a great deal; inasmuch as with the ancients consort playing and playing together on various instruments simultaneously had not become customary, so the wind instruments of various makers differed very much; some were tuned and made high and others low. . . .

The *Chor-Ton* of the ancients was at first about one tone lower and deeper, which still can be found in old organs and other wind instruments. And after that, year by year, it became as high as that which is used at present in Italy and England, and also in the princely choirs of Germany. Although the English pitch for instruments is just a little lower, as is to be perceived in their cornets, shawms, or hoboys (as they call them) which are made there.

Yet there are some people, who are so rash as to suggest raising our pitch a semitone higher still. Although it is not quite proper for me to correct that, yet, according to my estimate, such a height is very inconvenient for singers, especially for the altos and tenors, and is often impossible to achieve. Therefore, it would be better to remain at the above-mentioned pitch; while even the former is very often found to be too high not only for the vocalists, but also for the instrumentalists on string instruments such as *Violini de Braccio* and *Violen de Gamba*, as well as lutes, pandoras, and the like.

Then strings must be exceptional to stand such height. It often happens that the highest strings (*Quinten*) snap when one is in the midst of a song and leave one in the lurch. [Praetorius uses a more robust expression.] Now, in order that the strings might remain in much better tune, these and similar string instruments should be usually tuned about one tone lower, and then, of course, they should be played with other instruments also tuned one second lower. Although this is very difficult for inexperienced instrumentalists, it helps the voices of vocalists and choristers to sing one tone lower.

Therefore, I adhere to the difference which is used in Prague and various other Catholic choirs, where pitches are divided into *Chor-Ton* and *Cammer-Ton* and are used very successfully. Then we ourselves should call the usual pitch to which almost all our organs are still tuned the *Cammer-Ton*, and use it only for amusement at the table and convivial occasions; this would be the most convenient for instrumentalists, either wind- or string-players.

But the *Chor-Ton*, which is about a whole tone lower, should be used only in the churches; first to enable the vocalists, on whom rests the greatest exertion in the churches (especially in Catholic choirs, on account of the many Psalms and the long duration of singing), to come forth so much better with their voices and not to toil until they become hoarse. And next, because human voices in the middle and somewhat deeper (registers) are much more pleasant and charming to hear than when they must, in the higher register, force themselves to shout and scream. Hence, *propter alias etiam multifarias commoditates, suavitem singularem et concentus bene susceptos*, it would be better for all our organs to be tuned and built a tone or a second deeper. But it would be quite impossible to make this change in our German lands, and therefore we must retain the ordinary *Cammer-Ton* (which is called the *Chor-Ton* in most places at present and adhered to for this reason).

Long ago, in England and the Low Countries they voiced and tuned most of their wind instruments about a *tertiam minorem* deeper than our *Cammer-Ton*, so that their F is our D and their G is our E. Likewise the outstanding instrument maker in Antwerpen, Johannes Bossus, voices and tunes most harpsichords and *Symphonien*,[903] as well as the organs made there, in the same pitch.

And it is not without significance that it is possible to give and impart to harpsichords (as understanding instrument-makers know) a more charming and pleasant resonance than when one adheres to the *Cammer-Ton*; how much more pleasant the flutes and other instruments sound in such a low pitch, than in the ordinary pitch, and they bring into hearing quite another kind of art, since they do not bray [904] so hard in the lower pitch.

But such instruments are quite inconvenient for use in choral and instrumental music; and, furthermore, we should adhere to both above-mentioned *Chor-Ton* and *Cammer-Ton*.[905] . . .

This [Halberstadt] organ and similar instruments became a good tone and nearly a tone and a half higher than our present organs which are suitable for choir work, as is shown by the length of the great pipes already mentioned. And it is, therefore, also probable that long before all organs which might have been made of the size already described, as well as all those which were used during the time of Popery for nothing else but choir [work], were tuned in the same pitch or even higher. Finally, the choral organs, which were made a whole fourth higher or a fifth lower with respect to our pitch, were regarded as the most convenient, and were kept at such a pitch.[906] And although some organs are deficient, in that they are not tuned exactly to the described pitch, yet such a defect is not to be attributed to deliberate intention and the diligence of those masters who originally built the old choral organs which are still in use (1619), but it is probably due to their not having at that time worked out a constant chorist- or choir-pitch, as, thank God, is usual now.

Also the organs to which good choristers and screaming voices were appointed to sing and become accustomed, are tuned sometimes a tone higher or lower, and also, after many renovations and voicings, became considerably sharpened above their initial condition.

But otherwise the above-mentioned pitch, namely, one a fourth higher or a fifth lower (with respect to our present usual tone, otherwise called *Cammer-Ton*), is considered as the most suitable, and is found also in the principal cathedral churches. Yet many organs are also found which are a second lower or higher, and not a few are also pitched and built a semitone higher.[907]

In Table I are given the most important pitches which may help in forming an opinion on pitch variations.

TABLE I

VARIATIONS OF MUSICAL PITCH

a'	Name	Year	Authority
377	*A. Schlick's Organ Pipe*	1511	Ellis
396.4	*Tertia Minore* (Praetorius)	1618	Hipkins
421.6	*Mozart's pitch*	1780	Ellis
422.5	*Handel's tuning fork*	1751	Ellis
422.8	*Chor-Ton* (Praetorius)	1618	Hipkins
475.7	*Cammer-Ton* (Praetorius) (a tone higher than *Chor-Ton*)	1618	Hipkins
502.6	*Arnold Schlick, Heidelberg* (also Mersenne's *Ton de Chappelle*, 1636; a fourth higher than Schlick's low organ)	1511	Ellis Hipkins
505.8	*Halberstadt Organ* (tone and a half higher than *Chor-Ton*)	1495	Ellis
563	*Mersenne's Ton de chambre* (approximately a fourth higher than *Chor-Ton*)	1636	Ellis

The history of musical pitch is treated more fully by Dr. Alexander J. Ellis, translator of Professor Helmholtz's *Sensations of Tone*. Dr. Ellis' paper on "The History of Musical Pitch," the most valuable contribution, still valid today in all essential conclusions,[908] was printed in the *Journal of the Society of Arts*, March and April 1880; an abstract in *Nature*, April, 1880, pp. 550–554. A reprint is also extant.

How did such variations of pitch affect the sizes of string instruments? Assuming that the instrument-makers of the sixteenth century were competent (there are plenty of proofs that they were), it would be inconceivable that they should build instruments not adapted to the prevalent contemporary standards of pitch. So, later, studying the sizes of viols we shall see how this problem was handled in practice. But at present the variation in nomenclature should be straightened out first.

Nomenclature of English and German Viols

THERE is a difference in the names of English and German viols. Thus a viol which is called the bass viol in England is called a *Tenor Viola* in Germany, etc. As we shall presently see, the question of divergent nomenclatures goes deeper than the variation in the names of instruments of the same size. These questions arise: Why should the names be different? Why do the Germans adhere to certain names in connection with certain sizes? What is back of this connection, and is it possible to trace it by some incontrovertible objective evidence?

The differences of nomenclature have been emphasized many times. But it was not realized that both English and German nomenclatures are built on the same pattern as to the sequence of voices, if the sizes of the instruments are disregarded for a time. This similarity is shown in Table II.

TABLE II

ENGLISH AND GERMAN VIOL NOMENCLATURE

No.	English	German
1	The High Treble	(*Pardessus de Viole*)
2	The Treble	Diskant-Viola
3	The Alto	Kleine Alt-Viola
4	The Small Tenor	Alt-Viola (Alt-Tenor)
5	The Tenor	Tenor Viola
6	The Lyra-Viol	Viola bastarda
7	The Small Bass (Division)	Kleine Bass-Viola
8	The Consort Bass	
9	The Contrabass (Violone)	Grosse Bass-Viola (*Violone*)

Viols of different voices correspond in both series, except that in the German terminology there is no name for the high treble and the French name is used instead; also there are no names in the German series similar to the Division-Viol and the Consort Bass Viol of the English series. Praetorius and, following him, Dr. Georg Kinsky, use the term *Kleine Bass-Viola,* which would logically correspond to these two instruments.[909]

The position of the Lyra-Viol (*Viola bastarda*) should be noted. In both series it is located between the Tenor and the Small Bass. Praetorius tells us: *Viol Bastarda . . . ist eine Art von* Violn de Gamba, *wird auch gleich also, wie ein Tenor von* Violn de Gamba *gestimmet (den man auch in manglung darzu brauchen kan) aber das* Corpus *ist etwas länger und grösser.*[910]

So it can be considered as established that in all essential points English and German nomenclatures are identical.

Sizes of the English and German Viols

THERE are several references in seventeenth-century books to the large size of sixteenth-century viols.[911] Some of them are obviously exaggerated, but it does not seem possible to reject this testimony as irrelevant.

As already stated, at the beginning of the sixteenth century (1511), organs were tuned to a very low pitch (a′ = 377) and some to a very high pitch (a′ = 502.6). The very high pitch is confirmed by the Halberstadt Organ (1495; a′ = 505.8); also by Praetorius' explicit statement, quoted above, that the choral organs made a whole fourth higher were regarded as the most convenient.[912]

It would be natural to conclude that the larger-sized viols were made for playing with the low-pitched organs, but such a conclusion would not be supported by some facts of sixteenth-century practice. As will be seen later, the same instruments were used, by a very simple and ingenious arrangement, with both the low and the high pitch organs, and the actual pitch at which these instruments were played was, surprisingly enough, very close to, if not identical with, a′ = 440, our present standard pitch.[913] There is the positive testimony of Praetorius' drawings that at least at the turn of the sixteenth century (ca. 1600) viols were of a larger size.[914] Dr. Georg Kinsky published in the catalogue of the former Heyer Collection a table of the sizes of viols.[915] These sizes are based on those of Praetorius. Table III proves this statement.

TABLE III

NAMES AND SIZES OF VIOLS. PRAETORIUS AND KINSKY

Praetorius' Nomenclature	Body Length, cm.		Kinsky's Nomenclature
	Praetorius (scaled)	Kinsky (average)	
Cant	40.5	40	Diskant-Viola
Alt	56.7	56.5	Alt-Viola
Tenor	(68.5)	68.5	Tenor-Viola
Viol Bastarda	73.7	ca. 75	Viola bastarda
Kleine Bass-Viol	78.5	82.5	Kleine Bass-Viola
Gross-Bass-Viol	114	112.5	Grosse Bass-Viola

The size of the Tenor-Viola has to be estimated, since Praetorius gives no drawing of it.[916]

Although the average size of the *Kleine Bass-Viola* of Dr. Kinsky differs from that of Praetorius by four centimetres, the reproduction of Praetorius' instrument is 80 centimetres long (*Musikhistorisches Museum*, ii, p. 469, no. 284; the picture on p. 471). This is only 1.5 centimetres longer than our measurement.

Therefore it can be considered as established that Dr. Kinsky's table of the sizes of viols is based on Praetorius' drawings. Praetorius is a most excellent authority, but his data applies only to a certain period in the history of the viol. The application of this data to a later period should be made with due caution. This can be seen clearly in Tables IV and V.

In Table IV are given the sizes both of the German viols (the average sizes of those given by Dr. Kinsky on p. 437 of the Heyer Catalogue) and of the English viols. Sizes of the latter were selected from the table on p. 255 of this study; they are given so as to facilitate comparisons, but strictly within the limits of that table. Both series are lined up by their names. When the comparison is made, it becomes evident that the German viols are consistently larger than the corresponding English viols.

TABLE IV

ENGLISH AND GERMAN VIOLS COMPARED BY NAMES

English Nomenclature	Body Length, cm.		German Nomenclature
	English	German	
The Treble	36	40	Diskant-Viola
The Alto	40	ca. 48	Kleine Alt-Viola
The Small Tenor	44	56.5	Alt-Tenor-Viola
The Tenor	48	68.5	Tenor-Viola
The Lyra-Viol	56.5	ca. 75	Viola bastarda
The Small Bass (Division Viol)	64 }	82.5	Kleine Bass-Viola
The Consort Bass	68.5 }		
The Violone	100	112.5	Grosse Bass-Viola

1. 2. 3. Violn de Gamba. 4. Viol Baſtarda. 5. Jtalianiſche Lyra de bracio.

FIG. 72. PRAETORIUS, TABLE XX

1, 2, 3. Viols (*Viole da gamba*). 4. Lyra-Viol (*Viola bastarda*). 5. Italian *Lyra da braccio*.
(See Note 916 for identification of viols 1, 2, and 3.)

Several questions arise. Why do the sizes, as related to the same names, differ in England and Germany? Does not this difference point to some important reason, such as the previous existence of a larger series of viols?

It is a very curious fact that the Germans have preserved to our day the nomenclature and sizes of Praetorius, as has already been shown with reference to Dr. Kinsky's table of sizes. Please see Table III above.

Still more curious facts come out when the viols are lined up according to sizes. Table V gives a complete picture of viols both of England and Germany as they are classified at the present time.

TABLE V

ENGLISH AND GERMAN VIOLS COMPARED BY SIZES

English Nomenclature	Body Length, cm. English	Body Length, cm. German	German Nomenclature (Kinsky)
The Treble	36		
The Alto	40	40	Diskant-Viola
The Small Tenor	44		
The Tenor	48	48	Kleine Alt-Viola
The Lyra-Viol	56.5	56.5	Alt-Tenor-Viola
The Small Bass	64		
The Consort Bass	68.5	68.5	Tenor-Viola
		75	Viola Bastarda
		82.5	Kleine Bass-Viola
The Violone	100	112.5	Grosse Bass-Viola

The *Diskant Viola* of the German series, as defined by Dr. Kinsky, has a body size of between 35 and 45 cm.[917] This means that three viols of the English series are included between those limits, namely, the treble, the alto, and the small tenor viols.[918] The sizes of viols in England were adjusted within narrower limits than 10 cm., especially for such small instruments as the treble and the alto viols.

But the lyra-viol is the most typical example of confusion which exists today. The instrument which corresponds to it in the German series, by the logic of musical usage [919] and its location in the series, is the *Viola bastarda*. Its size (ca. 75 cm.) is so large as compared with the English lyra-viol (56.5 cm.) as to put it outside of the consort instruments, the largest of which (the consort bass) rarely exceeds 72 cm. At any rate, the German *Viola bastarda* could be used only as a consort bass, but never as the lyra-viol in the English consort. The actual instrument which corresponds in size to the lyra-viol in the German series is the *Alt-Tenor-Viola* (*Alt-Viola*). But here is another incongruity. The lyra-viol is tuned D-d′; the *Alt-Viola* is tuned either A-a′ or G-g′, according to Dr. Kinsky.[920] The *Kleine Bass-Viola* is too large to be included in the consort and too small to serve as a *violone*.

The comparative study of nomenclatures and sizes of viols permits us to arrive at certain conclusions and to state certain questions as related to both English and German viols.

1. The nomenclatures of English and German viols, when compared without reference to their sizes (Table II), are identical in their musical sequence of voices; this is emphasized by the location of the lyra-viol (*viola bastarda*) between the tenor and the small bass in both series, indicating the similarity of musical usage.

2. The nomenclature of German viols, when referred to the same sizes of instruments (Table V), differs considerably from that of English viols. What is the reason for this difference?

3. The sizes of German viols as related to their nomenclature are those of Praetorius (Table III). The same sizes were adopted as standard viol sizes by Dr. Georg Kinsky.[921]

4. For the same voices the sizes of English viols are consistently smaller than the sizes of German viols (Table IV). This, in conjunction with the discrepancy in nomenclature, should indicate that at a certain period (when?) some adjustment of sizes was made. What was the reason for making such an adjustment?

5. The differences between the sizes and the names of viols suggest the necessity of regarding the sizes of viols from two aspects, absolute and relative.

6. Regarded from the absolute aspect, the average sizes of viols remained constant over a long period, at least from 1575 to the end of their existence.[922]

7. Regarded from the relative aspect, viols of the same size were called differently at various periods and in several countries. Is it possible to establish such periods more definitely?

Logically, the next step should be the study of the tunings of viols as related to their nomenclature and sizes. But before this can be done, it will be necessary to examine certain practices in connection with the organs of the sixteenth and the early seventeenth centuries.

Tonalities of Organs and some Organ-Playing Practices in the Sixteenth and the Early Seventeenth Centuries

THE problem of viol tunings cannot be considered apart from the general musical practices of the sixteenth and early seventeenth centuries. These were determined largely, if not exclusively, by the ecclesiastical music and its principal instrument, the organ.

Choir singers and instrumentalists had to take their pitch from the organ while making music in conjunction with it. Therefore, it should be obvious that organ playing practices and the pitches of organs of that time should yield the solution of some vexing problems and lift the 'cloud of mystery' which still hangs over this obscure subject.

Fortunately, there exists a veritable treasure-trove of information containing many facts about the early sixteenth-century practices of organ playing and Plain Song singing. This is the *Spiegel der Orgelmacher und Organisten* (1511) by Arnolt Schlick, court organist in the Palatinate, who, according to his contemporaries, was *musicus consummatissimus ac organista probatissimus*.[923]

It has been mentioned already that Dr. A. J. Ellis ascertained the pitches of organs in Schlick's time. The passages upon which this finding, as well as many other extremely important facts, is based, are contained in the second chapter of Schlick's book. One is tempted to quote the whole chapter, but only a few excerpts can be given here in translation.[924]

> The organ must be pitched suitably for the choir and conveniently for singing. When such is not the case, then the singers must sing often either too high or too low, and the organist must play with semitones, which is not as yet the accomplishment of everyone. The size of pipe that would be convenient both for the Priests and the choir singers cannot be given definitely, since in singing with others, some men have voices of small, and others of large range. Yet I reckon that when the longest pipe, which gives the great F one tone lower than the great G, measures, from the top to the foot, 16 times the length of the line drawn on the margin,[925] then this pitch must be of a convenient value.
>
> But if the organ should be a fifth lower, then the small C in the pedal (organ) should have that length.

Dr. Ellis followed Schlick's directions, built the special pipe and determined the pitch of the organ with the F-pipe of the length suggested; this pipe gave the pitch corresponding to a′ equal to 377 cycles per second. This is the '*Chor-Ton* of the ancients' referred to by Praetorius.[926] The tonality of this low pitch organ will be referred to as that in A.[927]

The organ called by Schlick 'a fifth lower' had its small c-pipe in the pedal equal in length to the F-pipe of the former organ. This determined its pitch as equal to 502.6 cycles per second, the so-called Cornett-tone pitch.[928] The tonality of this high pitch organ will be referred to as that in D, since it is exactly a fourth higher than the low pitch organ in A.

Schlick preferred the low pitch organ, and gave reasons for his preference. Most of them are of interest only to students of organ history and the Plain Song.[929] For our purposes the following quotation should suffice.

> . . . for rather small organs I would advise using the above designated size multiplied XVI times for the great F below the Gamaut[930] and for the larger organs (using) the largest pipe, once again as long, etc. The reason is that the majority of choir songs which are in the first tone [the church Dorian mode], such as *Salve Regina, Ave maris stella, Gaudeamus, Vita sanctorum*, end *in gravibus*.[931] These and other similar ones can be best intoned for the choir in G. The independent pedal voices (*frey bass contra*) can also be played very well in their proper octave, because the songs have their cadences and endings on great G. It is also possible to lead choir-singing in pedal tones better [on the low-pitched organ] than on the higher-pitched organs (*den andern werken*). Thus, if the above designated songs are played [on the higher-pitched organ] transposed in D, they do not come out as well on the pedals since only a part (*halb*) can be played in octaves; and when choir singing and other low voices begin to go higher, then the organist must take up the playing [of the voices in the pedal] in part on the manual.[932]

The most important point in this quotation is that when the first tone, or the church Dorian mode, was played on the low-pitch organ in A, its 'final' tone was not D, as required by the modal theory,[933] but G. It is only on the high-pitch organ in D that the Dorian mode was played on D, but, as Schlick pointed out, this was inconvenient, since the organist had to play the pedal accompaniment in the next higher octave,[934] and even continue playing on the manual. At that time the music played on the organ was written for as many as seven independent voices,[935] two or three of which had to be played on the pedal; so, as Schlick explained in detail, the crowding of extra voices on the manuals of organs which had only two, caused great inconveniences. He gave several more reasons why low-pitched organs were preferable.

Two interesting conclusions can be drawn from the facts presented. One of them is that the lowest authentic mode, the Dorian, was performed in Schlick's time with the final tones D and G, depending upon which organ, high or low, it was played. As will be seen later, these tones were the fundamental tones of viol tunings.

Another conclusion leads to very important consequences. So it will have to be discussed at length.

Simple arithmetic will show that the tone g′ on the organ in A and the tone d′ on the organ in D are in unison.[936] This means that, since the organs were in a definite pitch relationship (a fourth apart), then, if the tonalities of songs were properly selected, they could be sung either with the low-pitch organs in A or the high-pitch organs in D at the same pitch level and within the most convenient range.[937]

In other words, all church music, that is, both the Authentic and Plagal modes, could be played either on a low-pitch organ in A, or on a high-pitch organ in D, *at the same pitch level* or in unison. This conclusion is based on the clear and precise words of Schlick. In the second chapter of his book he states that the first tone (the first Authentic or Dorian mode) was played in his time with G or D as final tones. The third tone (the third Authentic or Phrygian mode) was played with A or E as final tones, etc. Since Schlick speaks of the transposition of the Authentic modes from one tonal level to the other (in modern terminology this would be equivalent to transposition from one key to another), this invalidates an explanation current in the nineteenth century. Namely, that the organs pitched a fourth higher were built for transposing the Plagal modes so that they would be as conveniently placed for the singers as the Authentic. Assuming, for the sake of argument, that such transposition were plausible this practice would require either two organs of different pitches in the same church, or keyboards on the same organ transposing a fourth. As we shall see, both assumptions are incorrect. More of this in the second part of Note 940.

In the past, due to difference of opinion among musicians as to the proper pitch of organs and many other technical reasons, there existed no explicitly recognized tonality of the musical system. In our own time all keyboard instruments can be regarded as instruments in C, and therefore the basic tonality of our musical system is in C. As shown in Appendix D, there existed in the past musical systems in tonalities other than C. In other words, there existed organs pitched in A, B-flat, B, C, C-sharp, D, E-flat, and even higher. Since the human voice has physical limitations as to its range, the most convenient pitch level for singers was regarded as an implied pitch level. Even with respect to this pitch level there was no commonly accepted standard, as Schlick and Praetorius testified. Schlick suggested what he thought the best implied pitch level by recommending the length of pipes for the low- and high-pitched organs. He confirmed this by his explicit statements as to the tonalities of the modes to be played on both organs. One is forced to the conclusion that in the early sixteenth century (possibly even earlier, and as late as high-pitched organs existed) the organs were treated as *transposing instruments* with respect to the implied tonality of a musical system. As already stated, the resulting effect to the ear was *unison*. In other words, experienced organists could accompany singers at the most convenient pitch for the latter on either low- or high-pitched organs. This was done by a proper choice of tonalities of songs in all the modes, as Schlick thoroughly explained in the second chapter of his book. It should be obvious now why there was no necessity of having two differently pitched organs in the same church. The next problem to be considered is the question of keyboards transposing a fourth. This concerns both the organ and the harpsichord.

Mr. A. J. Hipkins commented that there is no evidence that the keyboards of the early organs, when they had more than one, were arranged for such transposition.[938] The reason for this should now be clear. There was no necessity of having transposing keyboards on the same organ, since the songs were sung on the same pitch level. But the organists who could meet in their practice the organs of various pitches, especially those of the high and low tonalities, had to know two systems of musical notation and play fluently in both. This practice of transposing church modes lasted into the seventeenth century. In 1607 Bernhard Schmid published a book of organ tablatures.[939] On the first page of that book there are given examples in the first tone. They are printed both for the normal tonality in D and also transposed in G. *Primus Tonus transpositus per quartam superiorem* is the explicit direction given by Schmid, and the subscript letters in both examples leave no doubt, since they start on d and on g, respectively.

There also existed Flemish harpsichords with transposing keyboards. They had one peculiarity which, for some reason, was not sufficiently noticed. Mr. Hipkins in describing one of the double keyboard harpsichords with transposing keyboards, built in 1638 by Jean Ruckers, which has reached our times unaltered, states: "The highest note is c^3 in the upper keyboard and f^3 in the lower, the latter being exactly under the former, *the jacks of both touching the same strings*, so that the lower keyboard is a fourth below the upper in pitch." [940]

The only plausible explanation for the existence of harpsichords with transposing keyboards, since there is no harpsichord music requiring such an arrangement, would be that they were used by organists for their private study and practice. The upper keyboard would correspond to the high-pitch organ in D and the lower keyboard to the low-pitch organ in A. This conclusion is based on the positions of the D and G keys: the D keys of the upper keyboard and the G keys of the lower keyboard all pluck the same respective strings; therefore, the lower keyboard transposed a fourth higher and corresponded to the low-pitch organ.[941]

Summary. These basic facts are important for our purposes.

1. Principal tonalities of organs in Schlick's time (1511) were the low pitch in A (a′ = 377) and the high pitch in D (a′ = 502.6). This practice continued into the seventeenth century.

2. Limitations of the human voice do not allow the singing of music at such widely differing pitches.

3. Certain church modes were played in their theoretical tonalities; thus the first tone (the church Dorian mode) was played on D, the third tone (the church Phrygian mode) on E, etc. To bring these tonalities to the most convenient pitch level for human voices, the high-pitch organs in D were built.

4. The keyboards of organs, both pedal and manual, had F as their lowest tone. It was more practical to select the tonalities of church songs in such a way as to utilize the keyboards more completely. For this reason the music of some church modes was transposed a fourth higher (*per quartam superiorem*); thus, the church Dorian mode was played on G, the church Phrygian on A. To bring these tonalities to the most convenient pitch level for human voices, the low-pitch organs in A were built.

5. These transpositions left the modes unchanged: the authentic modes remained authentic and were not changed into the plagal modes.

6. The average singing range of the human voice served as the common pitch denominator for both high- and low-pitch organs. In other words, there existed an *implied pitch* suitable for human voices; evidence exists which permits the assumption that in the early sixteenth century this implied pitch was about 447 cycles per second.

7. Notation of parts in D and in G for the lowest church mode (the Dorian) was therefore *nominal* and not actual. (The same principle is employed at present in the notation of parts for the clarinets in D and in A when both are to play a melody in unison; on paper their parts look different, but in sound they are identical.) In other words, the organs of the sixteenth century and later were treated as the transposing instruments.

8. The actual result in sound of the parts for high- and low-pitch organs written in different notation was *unison*. This conclusion is supported by the existence of harpsichords with transposing keyboards on which the keys, nominally a fourth apart in pitch, plucked the same string.

As we shall see presently, the viol tunings followed this practice.

Tunings of Viols in the Sixteenth and Seventeenth Centuries

BOWED string instruments, like the human voice, have to be 'placed' correctly. Among the most important factors influencing the tone quality of viols is the string tension, which is primarily determined by the standard of musical pitch and tonality of tunings. For a given musical pitch the construction of a viol has to be worked out so that the body and its internal fittings (the bass-bar and the sound-post) shall be suited for the string tension. Any deviation from a certain optimum ratio, which is usually confined within narrow limits, is punished by the loss of quality of tone.

Yet 'unimpeachable evidence' can be found in sixteenth- and early seventeenth-century writings that the tunings of viols differed as much as a fifth. Mr. Gerald R. Hayes pointed out quite correctly that such variations of tunings for consort viols are not possible, if the sizes of the instruments and the standard of musical pitch remain the same.[942]

But as we have seen already, the standard of pitch was a variable quantity. Therefore, it is possible to infer *a priori* that variations of viol tunings were connected with those of musical pitch. As we shall see presently, this was the reason for the variance in tunings and sizes of viols.

Arnolt Schlick, unfortunately, did not mention any stringed instruments which could have been played with organs.[943] But there was a group of writers sufficiently close to his time whose testimony is reliable; they give two sets of tunings for viols. These writers are Martin Agricola (1528) and Silvestro Ganassi (1542), both of whom give the tunings, which will be referred to as 'ordinary' or D-tunings, built on the following pattern:

Treble	d	g	c′	e′	a′	d″
Alto and Tenor[944]	A	d	g	b	e′	a′
Bass	D	G	c	e	a	d′

The 'Ordinary' or D-tunings of Viols

HANS GERLE (1532) gives another set of tunings which will be referred to as 'fifth lower' or G-tunings, since they are, to the eye at least, a fifth lower.[945]

Treble[946]	A	d	g	b	e′	a′
Alto and Tenor	D	G	C	e	a	d′
Bass	GG	C	F	A	d	g

The 'Fifth Lower' or G-tunings of Viols

AGRICOLA, Gerle, and Ganassi wrote in the first half of the sixteenth century and undoubtedly conformed to the practices used in Schlick's time (1511).

Several interesting facts should be noticed. One of them is the intervals between the voices of a given set. In the D-tunings the interval between the treble and the alto-tenor tunings is a fourth; that between the alto-tenor tunings and the bass is a fifth. In the G-tunings the intervals between the voices are fifths.

Another fact of importance is that the alto-tenor and bass voice tunings of the D-set are identical with the treble and alto-tenor voice tunings of the G-set. As will be seen later, this identity of tunings, coupled with the similarity of sizes shown in Table V, permitted a reform in the viol consort demanded by the change of musical pitch at the turn of the century (ca. 1600).

Finally, the tones d, D, and GG in both sets are similar to the 'final' tones of the first authentic church mode (Dorian) and its transposition *per quartam superiorem*.[947]

Almost a century later, in the first quarter of the seventeenth century, another group of writers gave the same two groups of tunings. D-tunings were given by Scipione Cerreto (1601). G-tunings were given by Pedro Cerone (1613) and Michael Praetorius (1618).

Praetorius' testimony is so important for subsequent discussion that it will be given here both in German and in English versions.

Die Violen *de Gamba* haben 6 Säiten, werden durch *Quarten*, und in der Mitten eine Terz gestimmet, gleich wie die sechs-Chörichte Lautten. Die Engelländer, wen sie alleine damit etwas *musiciren*, so machen sie alles bisweilen umb eine *Quart*, bisweilen auch eine *Quint* tieffer, also, dass sie die untersten Säiten im kleinen Bass vors *D*, im Tenor und Alt vors *A*, im *Cant* vors *e* rechnen und halten: Do sonsten, wie oben in der Tabell zu ersehen, ein jedere (nach dem Cammerthon zu rechnen) eine *Quint* tieffer, als nemlich der Bass ins *GG*; der Tenor und Alt ins *D*; der *Cant* ins *A* gestimmet ist. Und dass gibt in diesem Stimmerwerck viel eine anmutigere, prächtigere und herrlichere *Harmonij*, als wenn man im rechten Thon bleibet. — *De Organographia*, p. 44.

In English:

The *Viole da Gamba* have six strings, are tuned in fourths and a third in the middle similarly to the six-choir lutes. Englishmen, when they play in private, sometimes tune them all a fourth, sometimes even a fifth lower, so that they reckon and hold the lowest strings in the small bass from *D*; in the tenor and alto from *A*; in the treble from *e*: otherwise they (the *viole da gamba*) are tuned as may be seen above in the table, each one (reckoning by the *Cammer-Ton*) a fifth lower; namely the bass in *GG*, the tenor and alto in *D*, the treble in *A*. And this tuning gives much more pleasant, magnificent, and majestic harmonies, than the ordinary tuning. [The table referred to is *Tabella Universalis*, p. 25 of *De Organographia.*]

The language of this passage is, admittedly, confusing. Practically every writer who noticed it, 'interpreted' or 'corrected' it to suit his notions of what it should be.[948] For instance, why does Praetorius refer to D-tunings of Englishmen as being lower (than what?) a fourth in the first part and then call G-tunings a fifth lower (presumably lower than D-tunings) in the second part of the same passage? Yet there is a plausible explanation for these seemingly contradictory statements.[949] So this passage should be allowed to remain unchanged.

The problem as it stands now is to explain the relationship of the D and G sets of tunings to the principal pitches of Schlick's and Praetorius' time, to varying nomenclatures and two sets of sizes of viols.

With respect to pitches it was shown that in the early sixteenth century there were two pitches: the high (a′ = 502.6) and the low (a′ = 377), or a fourth lower. In the early seventeenth century the tendency was to find a workable compromise level and to evolve a single standard of musical pitch. In Praetorius' time the principal pitches were the *Cammer-Ton* (a′ = 475.7) and the *Chor-Ton* (a′ = 422.8), only a tone apart. Praetorius suggested that the organs should be tuned to the *Chor-Ton* pitch.[950] This suggestion was, evidently, followed, since the so-called 'classical pitch' which lasted nearly two hundred years was somewhere near 422 cycles per second.[951] With respect to the sizes of viols, it was shown that they should be regarded from two aspects, absolute and relative. Regarded in their relative aspect, viols were divided into two series, one of which, Praetorius' or the German series, was larger than the English series. These series of sizes represented practices of two different periods. A key to the solution of the problem of tunings is the variation of pitch, which was caused by changing musical tastes and the gradual emancipation of secular music from the special requirements of church music. Since conditions as to pitches varied in the time of Schlick and Praetorius, the same sets of tunings of viols evidently had to suit different purposes. For this reason the problem of viol tunings will be considered separately for each period.

Some Viol Practices in the Early Sixteenth Century

SCHLICK's statements about the organ practices of the early sixteenth century provided the clue for the tonalities of the tunings of viols and also for their mutual relationship. At present it is assumed that D-tunings are higher than G-tunings. But in discussing practices of earlier periods nothing should be taken for granted; otherwise insuperable obstacles to understanding will arise.

The problem of tunings is now so hedged in and localized, that only one conclusion is possible with respect to the early sixteenth century. D-tunings were used when viols were played with high-pitched organs and G-tunings with low-pitched organs. In other words, both sets of tunings were nominal and did not represent the actual pitch at which they were played.

Therefore, with respect to the practice of the early sixteenth century, it is possible to speak of G-tunings being lower than D-tunings only in a nominal or relative sense, since actually *both sets sounded in unison.*[952]

To convince oneself, imagine a player sitting at a harpsichord with a transposing keyboard. A certain composition in the Dorian mode could be played either on the upper keyboard or the lower. On the upper keyboard that composition would be played on D; on the lower keyboard on G. In both cases the jacks would be plucking the same strings.

If a viol player were present, he could play his part for this composition from the same tablature without retuning his instrument, since it would be immaterial to him which keyboard the harpsichordist were using at the time of playing. For that matter, the harpsichordist could change from one keyboard to another at will, if he were skilful enough, right in the middle of a measure; still this would not trouble the viol player, since the piece would remain in the same actual tonality. The tones played would be notated differently, depending upon which keyboard was being referred to at the moment.[953] But the actual sounds produced would be the same.

When viols were played with organs, the procedure was similar. A viol player could play either with a low- or a high-pitch organ from the same tablature. Since the pitch of organs was of no importance to the viol players, the tablatures were not even marked with tunings, because they were nominal and not actual realities for the instruments. In actual practice, a viol player coming to play with a high-pitch organ would ask for a tuning note. The organist would press the key sounding D, and the violist, after tuning the lower string to this tone, would tune his viol to the standard intervals by the well known process of tuning by frets. It would be unimportant to the violist what the organist playing the high-pitch organ called the resulting tones, since the tablatures give only the interval relationship and rhythm of a piece of music.[954]

The same viol player could go to a church with a low-pitch organ. Asking for a tuning note, he would get the same tone, but the organist would depress the key G. If the viol kept its tuning and the organs were built exactly a fourth apart, as Schlick suggested, the viol player would find his instrument exactly in tune with the low-pitch organ. He could use the same tablature while playing with either organ.

All this throws a flood of light on the musical practices of the early sixteenth century. We are now in a position to answer some objections against the G-tunings of viols which Mr. Gerald Hayes formulated, with proper qualifications, in his book on viols.[955]

For convenience of discussion they will be stated in a slightly different order. Mr. Hayes' objections are the following:

1. There are no instruments for this pitch.
2. Viol consorts cannot be tuned to the lower pitch.
3. There are no compositions for this pitch.
4. If there were such compositions, parts would not "correspond to the human voice, by which the sixteenth century was wont to cast its instrumental ranges."
5. With reference to D- and G-tunings, "in places and periods where the difference appears the most obvious, there is no suggestion, in the authors responsible for our data, for any such difference." [956]

All these objections are based on certain assumptions. They are correct if one standard of pitch and only one series of viol sizes are assumed. Such a condition existed in the post-reform period in the seventeenth century; but this was not the case at the time when Praetorius was writing. With respect to the early sixteenth century, which can be regarded as a formative period for viol tunings, the existence of organs of two pitches has to be taken into consideration when speaking of viol tunings. The sizes of viols for this period are assumed to be the same.[957]

Mr. Hayes' objections are answered in the same order as they were stated above.

1. There are instruments for this pitch. Anticipating slightly, Praetorius' larger-sized series were actually tuned to G-tunings and at a very high pitch (*Cammer-Ton*, a' = 475.7). More of this later.
2. All this depends on which consorts are meant. The smaller English series cannot be tuned to G-tunings. But the larger German series, as just stated, can be so tuned and were so tuned.
3. For obvious reasons any evidence for the low pitch compositions could not exist as long as viol parts were written in tablature notation and without designation of tunings. Ganassi's reference to transposition a fourth higher is not sufficiently clear to decide whether he meant the actual transposition on viols or merely referred to the fact that with the low-pitch organs viol parts were played, nominally, a fourth higher.[958]

4. Parts for voices and for viols were sung and played at the most convenient range for both. Differences of the organ pitches were accommodated by different notations for organ parts.[959]

5. When there was a necessity to assign a definite tonality to viol tunings, this was done by each author in terms of the only instrument which had a definite pitch, the organ. It is possible to affirm *a priori* that both Martin Agricola and Ganassi were thinking and writing in terms of the high-pitch organs and their keyboards and therefore had the right to refer to viol tunings as D-tunings.

It appears, likewise, that Hans Gerle had a low-pitch organ at his disposal and referred to viol tunings as G-tunings in terms of the keyboard of that organ. The practices in those times varied in different localities. This problem of various notations for viol parts can best be illustrated by taking some simple melody and assuming that it is played by a high-pitched clarinet in D in unison with a low-pitched clarinet in A. In notation their parts would be different and the A-clarinet part would appear a fourth higher. If the A-clarinet were to play the same melody an octave lower than the D-clarinet, the A-clarinet part would look a fifth lower on paper. This example helps one to understand why the notation of tunings should not mislead one. Since for an organist the absolute pitch of parts is immaterial, he can refer to the relative pitch as 'a fourth higher or a fifth lower.' The singers and viol players would find their own pitch level and sing and play in a proper octave. The general effect would be satisfactory, since all parties concerned could play together. The writer hopes that this reasoning will satisfy "a mind that craves precision and Euclidean proof." [960]

Viol Tunings in the Early Seventeenth Century

JUST as long as the early sixteenth-century practice was continued, which meant that there should be two definitely related tonalities of organs with an interval of a fourth, the whole scheme worked. The general drift of secular music away from the church modes, the greater importance assumed by instrumental music, the increasing use of staff notation, and the inconvenience of having parts written in two tonalities, were the principal factors which made the definite recognition of an explicit single pitch level imperative.[961] This process of pitch adjustment was a gradual one, with

TABLE VI

PRAETORIUS' VIOLE DA GAMBA AND THEIR TUNINGS
(1619)

No. in Table XX p. 362	Viols	Body Length (cm.)	Tuning Range: 'Ordinary' or D-tunings	Tuning Range: 'Fifth Lower' or G-tunings
1................	*Cant* (the Treble)	40.5	e–e″ (d–d″)	A–a′
2................	*Alt* (the Alto)	56.7	A–a′	D–d′
	Tenor (the Tenor)	68.5	A–a′	D–d′
3................	*Klein Bass-Viol*	78.5	D–d′	GG–g

the tendency of the low pitches to come up and the high pitches to descend toward a common level. The resulting confusion was very graphically described by Praetorius and caused great inconveniences.[962] One of them was that the tunings and the sizes of the viols required adjustment. All evidence tends to show that the D-tunings for viols were preferred,[963] but, judging by Praetorius' enthusiastic approval of the lower G-tunings, something was amiss. He usually referred to fine tone as a *liebliche Resonanz*, but in speaking of G-tunings he went out of his sober ways and told us that the viols tuned to the latter gave "viel eine anmutigere, prächtigere, und herrlichere *Harmonij*." [964] In order to understand what was involved, one should study Table VI.

In this Table are listed the names, sizes, and two sets of tunings, both mentioned by Praetorius in *De Organographia*.[965]

Although it is not absolutely certain that Praetorius' reference to the *rechte Thon* (ordinary tuning) meant the D-tunings, the principal varieties were only D and G tunings; therefore it is safe to assume that the 'ordinary tunings' meant D-tunings to Praetorius. It should be also taken into consideration that Praetorius stated definitely that the instruments of his time were tuned to the *Cammer-Ton* pitch, as has been mentioned several times.

A comparison of the sizes of instruments with their tunings leads to the conclusion that the viols of such large size, tuned to a high pitch (a′ = 475.7), could not stand the strain of the D-tunings without losing their quality of tone almost completely. But G-tunings would be satisfactory. It should be kept in mind that in the early seventeenth century, when Praetorius was writing, the two sets of viol tunings could be spoken of as 'higher' or 'lower' in the real sense, when the same standard of pitch was referred to. Therefore, it becomes quite clear why Praetorius preferred the lower pitched G-tunings for the viols used in his time. That was one of the practical ways of making an adjustment in the midst of the changing conditions of his period. Without disturbing the accepted nomenclature, Praetorius suggested tuning the viol consort to the set of tunings which were, undoubtedly, well known to his contemporaries. This suited the conservative character of German musicians much better.[966]

But there was another practical, albeit more radical, way of making the adjustment. The honor for doing this belongs to the Englishmen, who were the leading composers, players, and viol makers of that time. They retained the ordinary standard D-tunings, but shifted the whole series of consort viols downward in such a way that the treble became the alto, the alto became the tenor, the small tenor became the lyra-viol, and, finally, the tenor became the bass viol. To fill the gap left in the treble, a small treble viol was added to the consort.[967] With an appropriate sense of the fitness of things, they also readjusted the nomenclature, so that the anomaly of the 'tenor' playing the bass parts would be avoided. It is here that the Dr. Jekyll and Mr. Hyde property of viol sizes,

TABLE VII

COMPARATIVE NAMES, SIZES, AND TUNINGS OF GERMAN AND ENGLISH VIOLS

GERMAN NOMENCLATURE (PRAETORIUS)	BODY LENGTH, CM.		ENGLISH NOMENCLATURE	TUNINGS: 'ORDINARY' FOR ENGLISH VIOLS 'FIFTH LOWER' FOR GERMAN VIOLS
	Praetorius	English		
		36	The Treble	d g c′ e′ a′ d″
Cantus	40.5	40	The Alto	A d g b e′ a′
		48	The Tenor	A d g b e′ a
Alt	56.7	57	The Lyra-Viol	D G c e a d′
Tenor	68.5	68.5	The Consort Bass	D G c e a d′
Kleine Bass-Viola	78.5			GG C F A d g

which confused so many investigators, manifested itself. The same instruments assumed new names and played new parts. Otherwise, things remained the same. This truly remarkable change was possible because the intervals between the voices were either a fourth or a fifth; the interval between the D- and G-tunings also was either a fourth or a fifth, depending upon the aspect from which they were regarded.[968]

Table VII presents a complete picture of this reform. This table compares the nomenclatures, sizes, and tunings of both German and English viols, as referred to the same standard of musical pitch. Both series of viols are lined up by their sizes as in Table V, page 363, but the tunings are added. The same tunings correspond to the same sizes of instruments; they take on different aspects when referred specifically either to the German or to the English viols.

Praetorius' method of tuning large-sized instruments lower and the English method of retaining the ordinary D-tunings, but 'reducing' the sizes of instruments, are therefore equivalent.[969]

If any objective proofs of this adjustment should be required, they are available. The drawings of viols given by Praetorius and reproduced in this study (page 362) are one such proof.[970] These drawings established definitely the sizes of the German viols at the turn of the century (1600).

Another proof is the difference in terminology between the English and the German viols. The German viol nomenclature, like fossilized remains, provides the clue to the late sixteenth- and the early seventeenth-century practices. It should be clear now how this difference arose.

Then there is the definite testimony of Jean Rousseau in his *Traité de la viole* (1687):

> . . . ceux qui font les Viols les ont reduites à une grandeur commode pour les tenir entre les jambes, d'où vient qu'on les appelle Viols de jambe. . . .
>
> Il est vray que les Anglois ont reduit leur Violes à une grandeur commode, devant les François, comme il est facile d'en jouger par les Anciennes Violes d'Angleterre, dont nous faisons une estime particuliere en France.[971]

Rousseau's explanation that the viols were reduced for more convenient holding between the legs is, of course, very naïve. But his testimony of the 'reduction' of sizes should not be dismissed as irrelevant. The most important points in his statement are his crediting to Englishmen this reform and the reference to the reduction of viols to more convenient sizes. Although we know that the absolute sizes of viols were left unchanged, yet from a certain aspect the reform introduced by the English could be regarded as a reduction of sizes, since the smaller instruments were used for the same voices. The time of this reform can be placed somewhere between 1580 and 1610.

The surviving instruments are objective testimony in solid, three-dimensional form. Yet they effectively conceal their identity. Many blunders of identification found in authoritative European publications testify to this. Viols were a standing challenge to musicologists of the late nineteenth and twentieth century. The writer's hope is that this challenge has been met successfully and that new vistas will have been opened for further investigation of some obscure problems of musicology.

APPENDIX C

BASIC PROPORTIONS OF VIOLS

THE exasperating dearth of dimensional information given in some printed works on the sizes of viols (in the Brussels Catalogue, for instance) has proved a blessing in disguise. The writer was forced to rely upon the statistical and graphical methods of dimension analysis. The problem consisted of finding the most important sizes to define the basic proportions both of an individual instrument and of the whole viol family. The most useful sizes of the viol are:

1. Vibrating length of strings (the line 'A,' Plate XVI).
2. Length of the body ('B').
3. Width of the upper bouts ('C').
4. Width of the lower bouts ('D').

All the available sizes were plotted on graph paper. When proper coördinates were selected, the functional relation between the variables was found to be a linear one; in other words, these four sizes were connected by straight lines. In the selection of coördinates the writer followed Thomas Mace's method of defining the sizes of viols in terms of interval ratios.[972] On the axis of abscissas are plotted both the frequency ratio and its inverse, the size coefficient. To explain further: the pivotal instruments of the viol family are the treble and the consort bass viols. Since they are tuned an octave apart, if the frequency ratio of the bass viol is taken as a unit, the frequency ratio of the treble viol is twice that. The sizes are in inverse ratio: if the treble viol is a unit, the bass viol is twice as large.

The actual linear dimensions are plotted on the axis of ordinates; the sizes are in centimetres. Both the statistical averages and the points plotted on the preliminary graph guided location and selection of directions of the lines A, B, C, D, as well as the limits of sizes of various members of the viol family. These limits are clearly shown by vertical lines. The graph, Plate XVI, is applicable to the 'English series' of viols of the standard body type (Fig. 50, p. 258) only if the nomenclature of viols as given on the graph is used. Otherwise it is applicable to the 'German series.' For instance, if Praetorius' instruments were to be reconstructed, their width sizes could be derived from this graph. Another advantage of this graph is that, knowing one of the four basic sizes, the remaining three can be estimated fairly accurately; at least accurately enough to place a viol in a correct group. The writer found it indispensable in referring to the European catalogues. It is, of course, no secret among competent students that these catalogues contain some gross errors in nomenclature and only the sizes can be relied upon.

Now as to the basic proportions of individual viols. The writer had discovered a precise geometrical method of analysis of the outline of the violin before he attempted an analysis of the viol outline. The basic size on the violin is the length of its body; this size is measurable with precision (within one-half of a millimetre) owing to the definite outline. The other important sizes of the violin stand in certain ascertainable ratios with respect to the total length of the body. A complete geometrical analysis of the violin numbered 285 is given on p. 305. Unfortunately, the length of body on the viol is not a definite size, because it has sloping shoulders and a slanting back. (See Fig. 48, p. 256.) In this study the difficulty was obviated by measuring the distance '33' (Fig. 48, where it is encircled), i.e., the distance from the bottom of the viol to the lower plane of the neck bracket. This length so measured is definite, but has no direct relation to the outline of the body.

Therefore, another size was sought as the basic one for the viol: it is the width 'U' of the upper bouts, Fig. 73. This width is taken as a short side of a 'root-four' rectangle of dynamic symmetry.[973] The 'root-four' rectangle is simply a double square. In dynamic symmetry the square root of the number of a rectangle, 'root-two,' 'root-three,' etc., is the ratio of the length of the long side of a rectangle to its shorter side. The 'root-four' rectangle has this ratio expressed by an integer, since the square root of four is two; therefore, the long side of this rectangle is twice as long as its short side. In an ideal case, the width 'L' of the lower bouts is related to the width 'U' of the upper bouts as follows: if the long side 'H' (Fig. 73) of the 'root-four' rectangle is divided by the 'golden

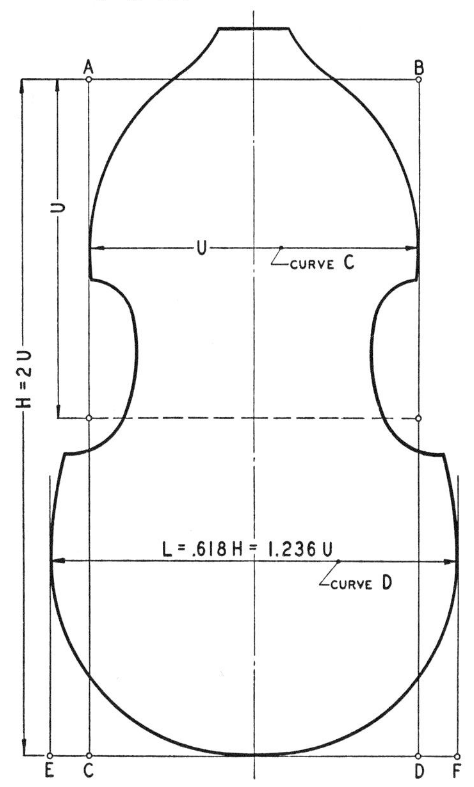

FIG. 73. BASIC PROPORTIONS OF VIOLS

section' into an extreme and mean ratio, then the larger segment, equal to .618 of 'H' or to 1.236 of 'U,' is the width 'L.' The size 'H' has no direct relation to the length of body on a viol. This latter size is determined by other considerations; in general it is slightly shorter than the vibrating length of the strings as shown by the lines 'A' and 'B' on the graph.

The actual instruments, of course, depart from these statistical averages. Yet in some cases the deviation in the width 'L' from this ratio does not exceed one centimetre. In a few cases the ratio is almost exact.[974]

As already stated, Plate XVI represents the 'English series' of viols. Two extreme limits for each voice are given. The division viol comes somewhat close to the lower limit of consort bases, so sometimes it is difficult to assign an instrument to either of those groups without actually examining the instrument in question. Nevertheless, in all ordinary cases this graph can be relied upon. The safest dimension for this determination is the width of the upper bouts (the line 'C'), since it is a definite size. The vibrating length of the strings is a less reliable guide, since the bridge is not always correctly placed on the viols, as Thomas Mace stated. If the bridge is located as Mace suggested, then the ratio between lines 'A' and 'B' and their corresponding lengths works out as shown on the graph.[975]

Two instruments of Praetorius, the *Viol Bastarda* (table xx, fig. 4, of *Theatrum Instrumentorum*, reproduced here on p. 362) and the *Kleine Bass-Viol de Gamba* (table xx, fig. 3) are also represented on the graph. Comparison of their sizes with the average sizes of the lyra-viol and of the consort bass respectively shows better than even a numerical table that there is a quite perceptible difference in sizes between the English and the German series. The size of the lyra-viol (*viola bastarda*) is the pivotal size as shown under No. 273. A complete geometrical analysis of the viol outline is almost as complex as that of the violin shown on p. 305. The writer is now working on a book where this method of analysis, both for the violin and the viol, will be explained in detail. This method is very precise, yet so flexible that it can be used for an exact analysis of any outline of any viol of standard pattern or any violin.

APPENDIX D

THE POLYDIAPASONAL SCALE

THE problem of variations of the standard of musical pitch is one of the most technical and complex questions with which a student of the history of music has to deal. There is a bewildering multiplicity of pitches,[976] and some method had to be found to establish their mutual relationship. Dr. Alexander J. Ellis in his paper on the history of musical pitch estimated the difference in cents, and when one needs to know the precise quantitative difference between several pitches this method is indispensable. Sometimes the problem is of such a nature that the precise quantitative relationship is not necessary and a rough approximation is sufficient. In such a case the difference in pitches is estimated in terms of semitones or whole tones; for instance, Praetorius told us that the *Chor-Ton* (in his terminology) is a whole tone below the *Cammer-Ton*. This method is more comprehensible to a musician, since it deals with a unit which he uses all the time. But even this method gives only a relative relationship between several pitches. It is desirable to find some permanent frame of reference. The method given below has been found useful and practical.

The basic premise is that a given musical system can be assigned some definite tonality. This choice is arbitrary, but once made it gives a fixed point of reference. Our present musical system is regarded as that in C; therefore, such instruments as the organ, piano, or any other keyboard instrument tuned to the American Standard Pitch (a′ = 440 cycles per second) are instruments in C.[977] The transposing instruments can be regarded from two aspects. The generally accepted one is that the French horn in F is in the key of F-major because its natural scale is in that key. The instrument is tuned to the standard pitch, the player has the music transposed for him in the key of F and reads his part directly or has to transpose it if the well-known simplified method of writing the part in the key of C and marking it 'Corno in F' is used. This is a common sense way of handling the problem and works without a flaw only under one particular condition, namely, that keyboard instruments must be in one definite tonality and tuned to some definite standard pitch. The musicologist is confronted with a more complex problem in studying the instrumental practices of the past. One of the stumbling blocks to an understanding is that *in the past there existed musical systems of different tonalities*, and keyboard instruments were tuned in these different tonalities. That is to say, there existed the organ in A, in B-flat, in B, in C, and in D, and even higher. Other keyboard instruments were tuned in the same tonalities, and the wood-wind and string instruments had to be accommodated in some way to that condition.[978] The whole situation was still further complicated because there were several standard pitches for a given tonality. In our own times, until very recently, there were three different standard pitches: the *diapason normal*, *a′* = 435; the American Standard Pitch, *a′* = 440; and the so-called 'high pitch,' *a′* = 452.5, or the Old Philharmonic Pitch, used in England until 1929. This caused and still causes many difficulties.[979]

Certain musicological problems obstinately refused to submit to solution just as long as the idea prevailed in one's mind that the tonality of the musical system in the past was the same as ours, that is, in C, and that only the pitch differed. A more correct approach to the problem is to treat the pitches within the interval of one semitone as belonging to the same musical system. The pitches which differ by more than that interval should be regarded as belonging to a musical system of different tonality.

In order to establish definite reference points, the number of cycles per second of certain tones of the equal tempered scale were selected and regarded as the *diapasons* (i.e., the tuning tones) of the musical systems.[980]

The following *polydiapasonal* scale was constructed, thus:

Tonality of Musical System	A	B-flat	B	C	C-sharp	D	E-flat
Diapason (*a′*).......	370.0	392.0	415.3	440	466.2	494.9	523.3

The number of cycles per second is given here to the first decimal point. The tolerance is plus or minus one-quarter of a tone (50 cents): that is, a pitch either flatter or sharper by not more than that interval with respect to any of these points of reference is regarded as belonging to a tonality chosen as the point of reference. For instance, both the *diapason normal* and the American Standard Pitch belong to the musical system in C. For an exact determination of intervals in cents from their number of cycles per second a special table should be consulted.[981] Below are given the most important historical musical systems and their pitches.

1. *The musical system in A, a′ = 370.0.* Dr. A. J. Ellis selected a′ = 370 as the zero point in his investigation of the history of musical pitch.[982] The most important historical pitch belonging to this tonality is that of the Schlick low pitch organ, a′ = 377. For this reason Schlick's low organ is regarded as an organ in A in Appendix B.

2. *The musical system in B-flat, a′ = 392.0.* Referred to as the 'low chamber pitch' (*tief Cammerton*). Praetorius called this pitch *Tertia minore* (a′ = 396.4) because it was a minor third below his Cammer-Ton (the latter is more frequently referred to as *Chor-Ton*; the reason for the difference in nomenclature is explained in Appendix B, p. 357, and Note 902).

3. *The musical system in B, a′ = 415.3.* Referred to as the 'high chamber pitch' (*hoch Cammerton*). It is Praetorius' *Chor-Ton* (a′ = 422.8); Handel's tuning fork (a′ = 422.5); Mozart's pitch (421.6). This is the tonality of the musical system of the classical period, which lasted from about 1600 until 1810–20. In a performance of music of that period the number of cycles, a′ = 415.3, is suggested as the standard, since it gives a definite interval relationship with our musical system, being exactly one semitone below it. This has many obvious practical advantages. The *viola da gamba* family as well as the old keyboard instruments should be tuned to this pitch. The *viole da gamba* sound better when tuned to this pitch.[983]

4. *The musical system in C, a′ = 440.* The Scheibler pitch; sponsored by the Acoustical Society of America and approved by the American Standards Association on October 15, 1936, as the American Tentative Standard.[984]

5. *The musical system in C-sharp, a′ = 466.2.* Praetorius' *Cammer-Ton* pitch (a′ = 475.7; this number of cycles is determined by Mr. A. J. Hipkins and differs from that as given by Dr. Ellis; cf. *Encyclopaedia Britannica*, 11th ed., xxi, p. 661) is the most important pitch in this tonality. Praetorius explicitly stated in *De Organographia* that all references to the tunings of instruments and voices were made to this pitch. The pitches belonging to this system are usually referred to as a *Chor-Ton* pitch.

6. *The musical system in D, a′ = 494.9.* Referred to as the *Cornett-Ton* pitch since the wind instruments of the *Stadtpfeiffer* (the town musicians in Germany), among them the cornetts, were tuned to this pitch. The most important pitch in this tonality is the pitch of Schlick's high organ (a′ = 502.6), which is precisely a fourth above that of his low pitch organ in A (a′ = 377). Another important historical pitch is that of the Halberstadt organ built in 1495, which had a′ = 505.8.

There were also musical systems pitched still higher, in E-flat and in E. Therefore the extreme fluctuation in tonality of musical systems was between A and E, or the interval of a fifth. Historically and musically, the interval of a fourth was of greater importance, since, as is shown in Appendix B, this interval was determined by two principal tonalities in which some church modes were performed.

APPENDIX E

NOMENCLATURE OF VIOLINS IN MONTEVERDI'S *ORFEO* (1607) AND PRAETORIUS' *SYNTAGMA MUSICUM* (VOLUMES I, II, AND III)

MONTEVERDI and Praetorius were almost constitutionally unable to call the same instrument by the same name. This divergence is undoubtedly a reflection of the prolific creative impulses of their period, when secular instrumental music was beginning to assume greater importance. Although it complicates the task of the investigator, the quest of identity amid diversity is not devoid of fascination. The page references for Monteverdi's nomenclature are those of the Malpiero edition.

Monteverdi's Nomenclature

1. Small violins:
   Violini piccoli alla francese (list of instruments).
   Violini piccioli alla francese (act ii, p. 41).

2. Violins:
   Violini ordinari da braccio (act ii, p. 43).
   Violino (act iii, pp. 84, 96).

3. *Viole da braccio* (violins, violas, and probably tenors are included in this term):
   Viole da brazzo (list of instruments).
   Viole da braccio (act i, p. 14; act ii, pp. 48, 57; act iii, pp. 99, 103; act iv, pp. 125, 137).

4. Violoncello:
   Basso de viola da braccio (act ii, p. 43).
   Basso da brazza (act iii, p. 96).

The *viola da gamba* family is represented by two instruments:

5. Bass Viol:
   Bassi di gambi (list of instruments).
   Bassi da gamba (act iii, p. 107).

6. Violone (the double bass of the gamba family):
   Contrabasso de Viola (list of instruments; act i, p. 14; act iii, pp. 99, 107).
   Contrabasso de Viola da gamba (act iii, p. 103).
   Contrabasso (act ii, p. 48; act iv, p. 137).

Praetorius' nomenclature presents greater complexities. The context in some cases is the only guide as the instrument to which a given name refers. *Kleine Geige*, for instance, is used as a generic name (vol. iii, p. 107; in such cases it is in the plural), and also it may mean either a small violin (vol. ii, p. 26) or the standard instrument (vol. iii, p. 122); in the latter case it is difficult to decide what instrument Praetorius has in mind, because it could also be a small violin. Praetorius' terms are tabulated for the sake of convenience. Roman numerals in parentheses refer to the number of the volume of *Syntagma Musicum*; Arabic figures refer to the page.

It should be noted that in volume iii of the original edition the pages following page 106 are numbered from 127 to 148, or twenty numbers too high. The correct numeration is given here.

Nomenclature of Violins (Viole da braccio) in the Time of Praetorius (1615–19)

No.	Type	Nomenclature
	Family Name	Generic: *Violen, Geigen, Violuntzen* (ii, 43). Specific: (1) *Viole de braccio, Geigen* (ii, 26). (2) ". . . all the *Geigen* which one holds on the arm (the Treble and Bass *Geigen*) were called in common: *Viole da braccio, Vivole da brazzo*" (iii, 122). (3) *Violen de bracio* or Polish *Geigeln* (ii, 44). (4) *Violini* — the small *Geigen* (iii, 107).
1.	Octavino	(1) *Exilent*: very small *Geig* with three strings (ii, 26). (2) *Small Poschen*, the *Geigen* an octave higher (table xxi, fig. 1, 2, p. 302 of this study).
2.	Sopranino or three-quarter violin	(1) Small treble *Geig* (ii, 26). (2) The treble *Geig* a fourth higher (table xxi, fig. 3). (3) Small or treble *Geig* — *Ribechino, Violino, Fidicula* (iii, 122); *Violetta picciola, Rebecchino* (ii, 48).
3.	Soprano (the standard violin)	(1) *Violino, Rebechino*, or *Viol de Bracio* (i, 443). (2) *Vivola, Viola de bracio*; also *Violino da brazzo, Violino* (ii, 48). (3) *Violino* (ii, 26). (4) The ordinary treble *Geig* (*Rechte Discant-Geig*, table xxi, fig. 4).
4.	Alto	(1) *Tenor-Alt Geig, Viola de braccio* (iii, 122). (2) *Tenor Viol* (ii, 26; the tuning given is that of the orchestral viola: *c, g, d', a'*). (3) *Tenor-Geig* (table xxi, fig. 5).
5.	Tenor	The instrument is not represented; its tuning: *F, c, g, d'*, is given under the *Bass-Viol de Braccio* (ii, 26).
6.	Bass (Violoncello)	(1) *Bass-Viol de Braccio* (ii, 26). (2) Ordinary *Bassgeige, Bassviola* (iii, 122).
7.	Gross Quint-Bass	The instrument is represented on table xxi, fig. 6 (reproduced here on p. 302) where it is called *Bass-Geig de bracio*. See page 301 and Note 784 of this study for explanation. The tuning: *FF, C, G, d, a*.

NOTES

NOTES

The pages to which the notes refer are indicated in the margin

P. xxv 1 A. C. Moule, "List of the Musical and other Sound Producing Instruments of the Chinese." *Journal of the North China Branch of the Royal Asiatic Society*, xxxix (1908).

2 F. W. Galpin, "The Whistles and Reed Instruments of the American Indians of the North West Coast." *Musical Association, Proceedings*, pp. 115–138 (March 10, 1903). The classification worked out by Canon Galpin for instruments of this type can be found also in Frances Morris, *Catalogue of the Crosby Brown Collection of Musical Instruments*, vol. ii, *Oceanica and America*, published by the Metropolitan Museum of Art, New York, 1914, pp. 58–59.

P. xxvi 3 Mr. Louis Harap defined musicology as follows: "Musicology is the sum of those collective disciplines relating to music that employ a rigorous technique." Cf. his article "On the Nature of Musicology," *The Musical Quarterly*, Jan., 1937, p. 23. Also cf. P. A. Scholes, *The Oxford Companion to Music*, 1938, p. 601, s.v. 'Musicology.'

4 Cf. Erich M. von Hornbostel and Curt Sachs, "Systematik der Musikinstrumente, Versuch," *Zeitschrift für Ethnologie*, 1914, pp. 553–590.

5 'Organology' is defined in the *Century Dictionary*, 1914, p. 4151 c, (3), as "the study of structure or organization"; this is a broad generic meaning. In a specific sense it is defined in the Supplement, s.v. 'Organology,' (5), as "the science, history, and mechanics of the pipe organ." A definition of organology suggested here is less broad than (3) and more inclusive than (5), namely: organology is the science, history, mechanics, and technology of musical instruments. 'Organology' in the sense suggested is a return to a meaning similar to that in the word 'organography' (Praetorius, *De Organographia*), "a description of musical instruments." Cf. also *A New English Dictionary*, Oxford, s.v. 'Organography.'

6 Georg Kinsky, *Musikhistorisches Museum von Wilhelm Heyer in Cöln, Katalog*: vol. i, Cöln, 1910; vol. ii, 1912; *Kleiner Katalog der Sammlung alter Musikinstrumente*, Cöln, 1913. Curt Sachs, *Real-Lexikon der Musikinstrumente*, Berlin, 1913; *Handbuch der Musikinstrumentenkunde*, Leipzig, 1920 (second ed. 1930); *Sammlung alter Musikinstrumente bei der Staatlichen Hochschule für Musik zu Berlin*, Berlin, 1922. Julius Schlosser, *Die Sammlung alter Musikinstrumente*, Vienna, 1920: this is the third volume of the series published by the Kunsthistorisches Museum in Vienna. *Encyclopédie de la Musique et Dictionnaire de Conservatoire*, pt. ii, vol. iii, Paris, 1927; articles on various instruments; those on the viola da gamba and the harp are especially valuable.

P. xxvii 7 *The Encyclopaedia of Islām.* A Dictionary of the Geography, Ethnography, and Biography of the Muhammadan Peoples. Leiden, 1908–38.

8 Henri Bouasse, *Instruments à vent*, Paris, vol. i, 1929, vol. ii, 1930. His book *Tuyaux et résonateurs*, Paris, 1929, serving as an introduction to the study of the wind instruments, is indispensable. These works require solid mathematical training for a complete understanding; yet some portions can be comprehended by one with an elementary knowledge of acoustics.

9 Albert A. Stanley, *Catalogue of the Stearns Collection of Musical Instruments*, Ann Arbor, Michigan, 1918, second edition, 1921. Even in this work Mr. Stanley states that "this Catalogue is neither a treatise on the phenomena of sound, nor a disquisition on the origin and evolution of musical instruments."

10 Frances Morris, *Catalogue of the Crosby Brown Collection of Musical Instruments*, vol. ii, *Oceanica and America*. New York, 1914. Frances Densmore, *Handbook of the Collection of Musical Instruments in the United States National Museum.* Bulletin 136. Washington, 1927.

11 *Catalogue of the Crosby Brown Collection of Musical Instruments.* vol. i, *Europe*. New York, 1902 and 1904. *The Crosby Brown Collection . . . Catalogue of Keyboard Instruments.* New York, 1903. Canon F. W. Galpin and Mr. A. J. Hipkins, both of England, are responsible for the introductory sections. The classification is that of Canon Galpin.

P. xxviii 12 Francis W. Galpin, *A Textbook of European Musical Instruments*, London, 1937, pp. 26–36.

13 American Engineering and Industrial Standards; The Standard No. Z24.1–1936, *American Tentative Standard Acoustical Terminology*, approved by the American Standards Association, October 15, 1936. Published by the American Standards Association, 29 West Thirty-Ninth Street, New York, N. Y. Price, twenty-five cents.

14 A private national organization supported by contributors from industrial, scientific, and governmental bodies. It supervises, but does not originate, the work of standardization. The principal aim of the procedure is to safeguard the rights and interests of all parties concerned with a given standard.

P. 10 15 *Galpin.* Canon Francis W. Galpin, *Old English Instruments of Music* (London, 1932; first published in 1910), pp. 311 f. Canon Galpin's classification is based on that of M. Victor Charles Mahillon, the curator of the Musée Instrumental du Conservatoire Royal de Musique de Bruxelles, and published in the catalogue of that museum. To M. Mahillon belongs the credit for the fundamental work in the classification of musical instruments. Canon Galpin suggested a more organically developed classification, which was applied by him for the first time for the International Music Exhibition, London, 1900. Afterwards this classification proved its adaptability by being used in the catalogue of the Musikhistoriska Museum at Stockholm, and in that of the Crosby Brown Collection of Musical Instruments, now in the Metropolitan Museum of Art, New York, N. Y.

Since the above lines were written Canon Galpin has published in his *Textbook of European Musical Instruments* (London, 1937) a new classification, in which he introduces some features of the Hornbostel-Sachs classification. The classification of the present study was worked out early in 1936 independently of Canon Galpin's latest one. It should be regarded as an intermediate link between Canon Galpin's classifications of 1910 and 1937.

16 *Curt Sachs.* Cf. E. M. von Hornbostel and Curt Sachs, "Systematik der Musikinstrumente. Ein Versuch," *Zeitschrift für Ethnologie*, 1914, pp. 553–590. This much debated classification is a stimulating and important contribution to the science of organology. There are several interesting features which distinguish it from other types of classification. The numbering of various divisions is according to the Dewey Decimal System. The terminology is carefully worked out. Whenever possible it is used in this study.

P. 11 17 *Lip-vibrated.* These terms were suggested to the writer by Canon Galpin.

P. 17 18 *Membranophones.* Division of 'percussion' instruments into two independent classes is due to M. Mahillon, who called them *autophonic* (self-sounding) and *membranophonic* (membrane-sounding). F. A. Gevaert, in *A New Treatise on Instrumentation* (tr. by E. F. E. Suddard from the French), followed this division. Canon Galpin also adopted it, but suggested the terms 'sonorous substances' and 'vibrating membranes,' respectively. Finally, in the *Real-Lexikon* (p. 195 a), Dr. Curt Sachs pointed out that 'autophonic' might prove misleading, as implying instruments which play themselves, and introduced the term *idiophonic*, subsequently adopted in the Hornbostel-Sachs classification.

Idiophone and the adjective *idiophonic* are from the Greek ἴδιος, own, one's own, and φωνή, sound, tone, and mean 'independent sound,' 'of independent sound'; translating freely, 'sounding one's own (substance).' *Membranophone* and *membranophonic* are from the Greek μεμβράνα, skin, and mean, literally, 'skin-sound,' 'skin-sounding.'

It is a curious fact that the Sanskrit terms for the same divisions are *ghana vādya* and *āvanaddha vadya*. Cf. P. Sambamoorthy, *Catalogue of the Musical Instruments Exhibited in the Government Museum, Madras* (Madras, 1931), p. 2. Dr. A. K. Coomaraswamy has kindly traced one of these terms, *ghana* ('any brazen or other metallic percussion instrument'), to *Harivanisa*, 8688; *vadya* (in the sense of 'instrumental music'), to *Natya-sastra*, xxviii; and *carmaavanadha* ('covered with skin') to *Manava-dharmasastra*, vi, 76.

P. 18 19 *Rank. Encyclopaedia Britannica*, 11th ed., xxv, p. 161 a, s.v. 'Sistrum.' *Encyclopaedia of Religion and Ethics*, ed. by James Hastings, ix. *Catalogue of Reproductions in the Field Museum*, no. 265.

P. 20 20 *Suppressed.* The following works were consulted: Ahmed Djevad Bey, *État militaire Ottoman depuis la fondation de l'Empire jusqu'à nos jours.* Trans. into French by G. Macrides, Paris, 1882. Sir Paul Ricaut, *The Present State of the Ottoman Empire*, London, 1668. Conte L. F. Marsigli, *Stato militare dell'imperio Ottomano*, The Hague, 1732, both in Italian and French.

21 *Bands.* Djevad Bey, *op. cit.*, p. 237.

22 *Commanders.* J. A. Kappey, *Military Music*, London, 1894, pp. 81 f.

23 *Janizary bands.* One of the difficulties in restoring the instrumentation of these bands is the very thorough destruction and dispersion of the property and effects of the janizaries. They were so intensely hated by the populace that, when the order for their destruction was given, their armories were set on fire and the men themselves were hunted like wild beasts. Djevad Bey refers to this indirectly when he says that "... sauf trois ou quatre grands tambours désignés sous le nom de *Kius* et une dizaine de timbales, il n'existe aucun autre instrument de musique." *Op. cit.*, p. 240.

24 *Musicians.* Several European writers give the instrumentation of Turkish bands. The most reliable is Marsigli; yet, curiously enough, he gives only that of the mounted bands, and does not mention the janizary bands as such. The next writer is J. A. Guer, *Moeurs et usages des Turks* (Paris, 1747), ii, p. 255, who gives the instrumentation of the *tabulchana* (drum-band) of a Vizier. G. Kastner, *Manuel général de musique militaire*, pp. 129 f., evidently follows Guer. C. F. D. Schubart, *Ideen zu einer Ästhetik der Tonkunst* (Vienna, 1806), p. 331, gives a different instrumentation. His book is, it

seems, the source from which J. A. Kappey, *op. cit.*, p. 82, and V. C. Mahillon, *Catalogue descriptif du Musée Instrumental . . . de Bruxelles* (Paris, 1909), ii, p. 183, derived their information. Finally, Djevad Bey, *op. cit.*, pp. 237 f., gives the instrumentation reproduced in this study. Raouf Yekta Bey, *Encyclopédie de la musique*, pt. i, vol. iv, p. 2981, obviously follows Djevad Bey; there is a small picture of a janizary band on the same page.

P. 21

25 *Naqqāra.* Persian and Arabian word for a small kettledrum. Cf. C. Sachs, *Real-Lexikon*, p. 268 b.

26 *Marsigli writes. Op. cit.*, p. 54. Translation: The different sounds of all these instruments would be harsh to the ears, if they were not corrected by those of the bass drum; but, when they are all united, their concert is sufficiently pleasing.

27 *Step.* Cf. C. F. D. Schubart, *op. cit.*, pp. 330, 332.

28 *Before him.* Marsigli, p. 51; J. A. Guer, *op. cit.*, p. 256; Djevad Bey, p. 182.

29 *Instruments.* Djevad Bey, *op. cit.*, pp. 178 ff. He quotes the historian Vassif Effendi, who explains the origin of the usage of *tughs* as colors and as distinctive marks of rank.

P. 24

30 *Kappey. Military Music*, p. 82. The writer was unable to check this point more thoroughly. The information is uncertain. Also Michel Brenet, *La musique militaire*, p. 67.

31 *Regiments.* C. F. D. Schubart, *op. cit.*, p. 330. Michel Brenet, *op. cit.*, p. 67, estimates the probable date of the introduction of janizary music in the Prussian Army as about 1750. *Meyers Lexikon*, 7th ed., viii, 1928, p. 470, s.v. 'Militärmusik,' states that formerly the infantry band music was called in Germany *Janitscharen-Musik.*

32 *Vienna.* C. F. D. Schubart, *op. cit.*, p. 331. Also Rosamond E. M. Harding, *The Piano-Forte*, Cambridge, 1933, p. 119. This book has come to the writer's attention since the note on the Jingling Johnny was written. The whole chapter v, "The Influence of Turkish Music upon the Piano-Forte," contains interesting material.

33 *Appearance.* Djevad Bey, *op. cit.*, plate 5, fig. 104, gives a picture of the Turkish instrument (no reference to it in the French text); in Turkish it is called *chaghana.* Cf. H. G. Farmer, "Turkish Instruments of Music in the Seventeenth Century," *Journal of the Royal Asiatic Society*, Jan., 1936. This article is excellent source material, with many references. Reprinted, with additions, in 1937; see Note 65 for reference.

P. 31

34 *Thebes.* F. W. Galpin, *O.E.I.*, 1930, pp. 242 f. In a letter of May 10, 1937, Canon Galpin modified somewhat the statement made on page 243 of that book. "As for the Theban drum, there is no reason for supposing that the string-braces were used for tuning the two heads: it is the ordinary way of affixing the double heads still found in Africa. The tightening of the heads is done by the sun or by a fire."

P. 32

35 *Praetorius. Theatrum Instrumentorum*, table xxiii, no. 2.

36 *Djevad Bey, op. cit.*, plate 5, fig. 96. Marsigli, *op. cit.*, part ii, plate xviii, facing p. 55, pictures several musical instruments. 'A' represents there the bass drum; 'B' and 'C' respectively the large and small drumsticks; with the latter the bass drum was beaten underneath. Instead of a small stick, a kind of broom was sometimes used. Cf. J. A. Kappey, *Military Music*, pp. 82 f.; also F. W. Galpin, *O.E.I.*, p. 248.

P. 33

37 *Real-Lexikon.* Curt Sachs, *Real-Lexikon der Musikinstrumente* (Berlin, 1913), p. 292 a.

38 *Kettledrum.* C. Sachs, *Real-Lexikon*, p. 268 b.

39 *Was used.* C. Sachs, *Handbuch der Musikinstrumentenkunde* (Leipzig, 1930), p. 85.

40 *Minstrels.* Galpin, *O.E.I.*, p. 250.

41 *Escouter.* Jean de Joinville, *Histoire de Saint Louis*, ed. Natalis de Wailly (Paris, 1867), ch. xxxii, p. 98.

42 *Calais.* Jean Froissart, *Oeuvres*, ed. Baron Kervyn de Lettenhove, *Chroniques*, v (1868), p. 217.

43 *Sounes.* Verses 2511–12.

44 *Large kettles.* G. Kastner, *Méthode des timbales* (Paris, 1842?), p. 9; also C. Sachs, *Handbuch*, p. 86.

45 *Hungarian manner.* Galpin, *O.E.I.*, p. 251.

46 *Kettledrums.* One of the best pictures of small Oriental kettledrums is that published by N. C. Mehta in his *Studies in Indian Painting* (Bombay, 1926), pl. no. 38 (in color), representing a Darbar scene. At the top of the picture is shown the *Naubat-Khana*, the salute building, with the band of royal musicians. In the centre, sitting on a dais, is the leader of the band, playing a pair of small kettledrums, only slightly larger than those played by the five musicians around him. One of the players beats with his fists a large kettledrum, the *kūs* or *naubat.* Cf. Notes Nos. 62, 63.

47 *Musical instruments.* J. Schlosser, *Die Sammlung alter Musikinstrumente* (Vienna, 1920), p. 36, no. A29, and illustr. pl. iv, no. 29, represents a pair of Turkish kettledrums made of copper in leather cases with hanging leather straps. They were beaten by two simple drumsticks. Dimensions: height, 20 cm.; diameter of the beating surface, 20 cm. (the outside diameter is, evidently, larger, but is not given).

P. 34

48 *Sardar-naqqāra.* Marsigli, *op. cit.*, pt. ii, p. 54.

49 *Russian sources.* There is a tremendous wealth of material extant, both manuscripts in the libraries and actual instruments in the museums. The principal sources

for the second half of the note on kettledrums were as follows. *Polnoe Sobranie Russkikh Letopiseĭ*, published by the Archaeographical Commission over a period of years. It consists of the complete works of Russian chroniclers, collated, with exhaustive scholarship, from many manuscripts, and represents one of the principal sources of material for Russian history. *Drevnosti Rossiĭskago Gosudarstva*, a magnificently illustrated work on the antiquities of the Russian state, published in 1849–53. P. I. Savvaitov, *Description of Ancient Russian Furniture, Dresses, Arms, and Armor* (St. Petersburg, 1896). A. S. Famintsyn, *Gusli* (St. Petersburg, 1890), and *Domra* (*ibid.*, 1891). N. F. Findeisen, *Schilderungen aus der Geschichte der Musik in Russland von der ältesten Zeit bis zum Ende des XVIII. Jahrhunderts.* This book is in Russian, except the title and explanatory notes on illustrations, which are also given in German. The late N. F. Findeisen (1868–1928) was an outstanding Russian musicologist, and this work, published in 1928 in two volumes, is the pioneer work in the history of ancient Russian music. Recently, A. V. Viskovatov's large work has become available; see Note 68 for reference.

P. 34

50 *Ancient meaning.* N. F. Findeisen, *op. cit.*, p. 222.

51 *Troitzkaia Letopis.* N. F. Findeisen, *op. cit.*, p. 223.

52 *Vargani and nakri. Polnoe Sobranie*, xii, p. 84. This particular reference concerns the siege of Constantinople by the Turks in 1453. *Surni* is *zurna*, an oboe type of instrument. The *vargani* (sing. *vargan*) were military instruments of an unknown type, possibly similar to the 'Jingling Johnny.' *Vargan* at present is the name of the 'Jew's harp' (No. 12), which has a feeble sound and could not have been employed on the battlefield to frighten enemies. N. F. Findeisen, *op. cit.*, p. 225, writes that the context of Russian references in the chronicles implies a noisy instrument "similar to the ancient Egyptian and Roman sistrum."

53 *Nagaras. Nagara* is Bengali for *naqqāra*. Cf. C. Sachs, *Real-Lexikon*, p. 267 a. The Russian text (transliterated) reads *da verbludov sto s nagarami. Polnoe Sobranie*, vi, p. 340.

54 *Two men. Op. cit.*, p. 340. This travel story of intense interest was never completely translated into English. There is a translation in German by Karl H. Meyer, *Die Fahrt des Athanasius Nikitin über die drei Meere.*

55 *Great and small.* N. F. Findeisen, *op. cit.*, p. 225. Also Savvaitov, *op. cit.*, p. 82. The players of the *nakri* were called in Russian *nakrachei*. Cf. N. Karamzin, *History of the Russian State*, x, note 119. In Russian.

56 *Briazalo.* Cf. Findeisen, *op. cit.*, pp. 222 f. "Play beat the *briazalo*" is the reference quoted by him from the *Minea* of 1096.

57 *Nakri. Polnoe Sobranie*, vii, p. 312, under the year 1553.

58 *Very large size.* C. R. Day, *The Music and Musical Instruments of Southern India*, plate xi, p. 139. He gives a picture of a large kettledrum and mentions that "these instruments are sometimes made as much as five feet in diameter." V. A. Smith, *Akbar, the Great Mogul* (Oxford, 1917), p. 90, states that *mahanagaras* in the palaces of Indian potentates were eight to ten feet in diameter.

59 *Different from ours.* Dr. Giles Fletcher, *Of the Russe Common Wealth* (London, 1856), p. 78. This is the reprint of the book published in London, 1591. Dr. Fletcher was an ambassador from Queen Elizabeth to Tsar Theodor Ivanovich in 1588. The Russian historian N. M. Karamzin quoted from this source very extensively. It has the earmarks of careful observation and rather unusual correctness of details, proven by the use of Russian words, sometimes very quaintly spelled, but easily recognizable. 'Shawmes' are Russian *surni.*

60 *The year 1553. Polnoe Sobranie*, vi, p. 310. Another reference, p. 313, is the order of the grand duke (Ivan the Terrible), after the fall of Kazan: "the *gosudar* himself, because of his great joy, ordered to play military *surni*, and to trumpet the trumpets, and to beat *nabati* unceasingly."

61 *Play surni. Polnoe Sobranie*, vi, p. 312. This reference is of importance in showing that *nabati* and *nakri* were kettledrums of distinct types. References to musical instruments in Russian chronicles are very few and correspondingly important.

P. 35

62 *Naubat or kūs.* Djevad Bey, *op. cit.*, p. 240, gives the sizes of large kettledrums, *Kius* (should be spelled *kūs*), as follows: The upper diameter, 120 cm., the lower diameter about 70 or 80 cm., and the height 130 cm. H. G. Farmer, "Turkish Instruments of Music," *Journal of the Royal Asiatic Society*, Jan., 1936, pp. 11 f., gives further particulars.

63 *Salute-building.* The Arabian word *naubat* has a specific meaning when it refers to the large kettledrum and a generic meaning signifying all the instruments composing the orchestra playing in the *naubat-khana.* Cf. C. Sachs, *Real-Lexikon*, p. 269 a. The picture in N. C. Mehta's book on Indian painting, referred to in Note No. 46, gives an excellent idea of how an oriental orchestra looked about 1538. Cf. *Ars Asiatica*, xiii, plate lv.

64 *For the performers.* One of the most magnificent *naubat-khana* is that in Fathpur-Sikri, India, the city built by Akbar. It is described in the Archaeological Survey of India, by Edmund W. Smith, *The Mogul Architecture of Fathpur-Sikri* (Allahabad, 1897), iii, pp. 57 f.,

and plate xc. Unfortunately the photo-etching represents only the main gate with a gallery for the musicians, but gives no idea of the whole structure, which is built in the form of a square measuring 155 feet on the outside and 115 feet on the inside. Within is a court with suites of rooms and in the centre of each side there is a large arched gateway.

P. 35 65 *Tulumbaz.* Two possible derivations: the first is from the Turkish *tulum* = skin, and *baz* = a falcon; cf. *Dictionnaire turc-français* by Kieffer and Bianchi (Paris, 1835–37). The second is from *tabl-i-baz*, the hawking kettledrum; cf. H. G. Farmer, *Turkish Instruments of Music in the Seventeenth Century* (Glasgow, 1937), p. 15. The old Russian spelling is *tulumbaz*; the newer one, *tulumbas*, is the name of the bass drum in the infantry bands.

66 *Mostly for hawking.* Hawking was not its only use. In the army it was used in the same way as the field drum, borne on the left side by infantrymen and on the right side of the saddle by mounted men.

67 *Steel used for armor.* The Russian word is *bulat.*

68 *Violet velvet.* References to the lists of the tsars' properties are borrowed from P. Savvaitov and N. F. Findeisen. Since these lines were written, the source from which these scholars derived their information has become available in the Harvard University Library: V. Viskovatov, *Historical Description of Uniforms and Armaments of Russian Troops*, St. Petersburg, 1841–61. This enormous work in 29 volumes is richly illustrated with numerous plates and contains many valuable references to the old sources, both Russian and foreign. In Russian.

69 *Litavri.* This word is a Russianized version of the Arabic *el-tabl*, a drum.

P. 37 70 *Eunuch's flute.* Christopher Welch, *Six Lectures on the Recorder and other Flutes* (London, 1911), p. 118.

P. 41 71 *Aerophones.* The term has already been used by Thomas A. Edison. See *The Century Dictionary*, s.v. 'Aerophone.'

72 *The bull-roarer.* Cf. C. Sachs, *Real-Lexikon*, p. 341 b, s.v. 'Schwirrholz.' A picture and references are given, as well as the names of similar instruments.

73 *Tubes.* The whole subject is, of course, quite complex. The geometrical shape of the tube and the volume of air confined in the tube and participating in the vibratory activity, etc., have their influence. As a rough approximation the statement is correct.

74 *Factor.* On ordinary musical instruments this causative factor might be the vibration of a substance, membrane, string, stream of air striking against an edge, reed, lip muscles, etc.

75 *Fundamental frequency.* At this stage the definition is quite broad, and a periodic wave or quantity is not necessarily a compound tone produced by a musical instrument. This definition has been borrowed for acoustics from the American Standard Definitions of Electrical Terms. Cf. 'Acoustical Terminology,' p. 5. A musical tone is only a particular case of a periodic wave or quantity.

P. 42 76 *Harmonic series of frequencies.* It is unfortunate that such an important fundamental concept should be left undefined in American Tentative Standard Acoustical Terminology. Definition 6.14, *Just Scale*, of the A. T. S. Acoustical Terminology (p. 16, quoted in this book on p. 5, item 17) contains the term 'harmonic series.' There are at present several meanings attached to this term. It is used to designate (1) the frequencies of a compound tone, which are referred to as 'tones,' 'harmonics,' 'partials,' 'upper partials,' 'overtones'; (2) the scale of compound tones produced by overblowing on natural horns, trumpets, bugles, etc.; this scale is also called 'the natural scale.' It seems that the 'harmonic series' should have a rigidly limited meaning, and that this term or a more complete term, the 'harmonic series of frequencies,' should mean a series of frequencies and nothing else. A suggested definition is expressed here in terms of musical interval relationship, for convenience only. Five explanatory clauses in the note are corollaries of the basic premise that a 'harmonic' by definition is 'an integral multiple of the fundamental frequency.' Two aspects, the simultaneous (chord) and the seriatim (scale) of the harmonic series of frequencies have not been discriminated between explicitly, and this has caused confusion. To eliminate this confusion, two additional terms are suggested, 'the harmonic scale of tones' and 'the natural scale of tones'; the reasons for these additions are given in Notes 80 and 83 of this section.

77 *Basic frequency.* The gong, for instance, produces a very complex tone in which many partials are present which do not bear an integral relation to the basic frequency.

P. 43 78 *Frequencies.* In this study the following corresponding entities having the same interval relationship are identified by the same numerals: (1) members of the harmonic series of frequencies (see note example on p. 42); (2) members of the harmonic scale of tones; (3) members of the natural scale of tones; (4) overtones. There is only one exception: the series of overtones has no member called 'overtone no. 1,' since number one of this series is the basic frequency, which, obviously, cannot be an overtone. Confusion has been caused by the different numeration of partials and upper partials. Cf. Hermann Helmholtz, *On the Sensations of Tone*, 3rd English ed., New York, 1895, p. 22, and especially the note on p. 23, where Dr. Ellis, the translator, warns against referring to an upper partial by its ordinal number, since the latter differed from the ordinal number of the corresponding partial in Helmholtz's notation.

P. 43

79 *Harmonic tone.* This definition is not entirely theoretical. Dr. Dayton C. Miller constructed a set of tuning forks accurately tuned to the pitches of a fundamental frequency of 128 cycles per second and its nine harmonic overtones. According to Dr. Miller, when all ten forks sound simultaneously "one is hardly conscious that the sound is from ten separate sources, the components blend so perfectly into one sound. The tone is vigorous and 'living,' and has a fullness and richness rarely heard in musical instruments." Cf. his *The Science of Musical Sounds*, 1916, p. 212.

80 *Harmonic scale of tones.* The suggested definition is an attempt to state explicitly and in precise terms the second aspect, the scale, implicitly contained in the term 'harmonic series' as used heretofore. The aim of the standard definition should be the elimination of ambiguity and of implicit meanings. A definition should be exclusive and define one thing only. If there are several aspects to a certain concept such aspects should be explicitly stated. A concept of the harmonic scale of tones is implicit in the writings on acoustics and is, really, the basic concept of the Helmholtzian classical acoustics. It is, of course, an idealization of objective reality. Yet, as in the case of a harmonic tone, it would be possible to construct several sets of tuning forks on the same principle as that of Dr. Dayton C. Miller referred to in Note 79 above. The fundamental frequencies of each such set could be made to correspond to the frequencies of some harmonic series, and all these sets would demonstrate a scale of harmonic tones. Theoretically, such a concept as the harmonic scale of tones is indispensable; for this reason it is deemed necessary to introduce it among the definitions.

81 *Frequency.* A fundamental tone is defined in the American Tentative Standard Acoustical Terminology (6.6) as follows: "the fundamental tone of a compound tone is that one of its partials which has the lowest frequency." It is obvious that "the fundamental tone of a compound tone" is a simple tone (the latter is defined in 6.3 as "one which consists of a single frequency"). Therefore the fundamental tone consists of a single frequency, or, simply is a frequency. Hence definition 6.6 of the fundamental tone duplicates unnecessarily definition 1.8 of the fundamental frequency and preempts a term much needed elsewhere.

82 *Manner.* The terminology of overblown tones *regarded as the constituent members of a natural scale of tones* has never been 'legalized.' Owing to the fact that overblown tones have the same interval relationship as the harmonic series of frequencies, they are still referred to as 'partial tones,' 'partials,' 'harmonics,' 'natural harmonics,' and even 'overtones.' In the Acoustical Terminology they are not defined. The scale of overblown tones is referred to as 'the harmonic series,' 'the natural scale,' with the word 'tones' sometimes added. In many cases one is forced to find from the context just what is meant: a chord of partials of a compound tone or a scale of overblown tones. Such looseness of terminology could be eliminated if it were agreed to refer to the components of compound tones as 'frequencies' and reserve the term 'tone' for compound tones. The unqualified term 'tone' would then be a generic term for a compound tone. Qualified terms such as 'fundamental tone,' 'partial tone,' and, in a particular case, a 'simple tone,' if properly defined, would be specific instances of a tone, and no confusion would be possible.

As things stand now, for instance, an overblown French horn tone, which is a compound tone of great complexity, is without a legalized term, since the terms partial (1.11), harmonic (1.9), and partial tone (6.5) *all define a single frequency.* The standard definitions 1.8 (Fundamental Frequency), 1.11, and 1.9 are necessary and sufficient to describe the components of a compound tone. The definition 6.5 reads: "a partial tone is any component of a compound tone." Thus defined, 6.5 becomes superfluous, since it is not used in the Acoustical Terminology in the definition of a compound tone. The latter (6.4) reads: "a compound tone is one which consists of more than a single frequency." This definition should read, "a compound tone is one which consists of more than a single partial tone." Such formulation is not necessary, since the standard definition 6.4 is perfectly adequate. Therefore, the standard definition 6.5 of a partial tone duplicates definition 1.11 and is an unnecessary repetition of the same idea in different words. The term 'partial tone' should be reserved for the overblown tones of wind instruments and 'harmonics' of the string instruments, or a new term officially adopted for such tones.

83 *Natural scale of tones.* A natural scale of tones is a generalized concept of a scale of compound tones, a particular case of which is the harmonic scale of tones. The latter stands in the same relation to the former as an harmonic to a partial. Compound tones constituting the natural scale are the partial tones which, in the most general case, duplicate the interval relationship of the harmonic series of frequencies and have the same ordinal numeration as the latter. The actual natural scales of musical instruments differ. Thus the 'brass wind'

instruments have their partial tones in the same sequence as the harmonic series of frequencies, that is, they constitute a 1, 2, 3, 4, 5, . . . series of tones. Some brass instruments, such as the low-pitched horns, have no tone No. 1, and are referred to as 'half-tube instruments' (see pp. 12 and 13). The clarinets have a peculiarity in that their overblown tones enter into a 1, 3, 5, 7, . . . series, or they produce only the odd numbered partial tones. Such differences are essential in practice and provide the basis for the classification of instruments.

P. 43 84 *The pedal.* Alternate term used for this tone is the fundamental tone. Dr. Bouasse has shown conclusively that the lowest tone of the brass instruments is a 'privileged' tone and not a true fundamental. This question is very technical. The reader is referred to Dr. Bouasse's books, *Tuyaux et résonateurs* (1929) and *Instruments à vent*, i (1929) and ii (1930), all published in Paris.

85 *Qualitative.* A tone color is a subjective *quality* (cf. D. C. Miller, *The Science of Musical Sounds*, p. 58), and is therefore a qualitative characteristic. The fact that it can be scientifically analyzed does not convert it into a quantitative or a numerical one.

86 *Formant.* The suggested definition of a formant is quite tentative.

87 *Tabular form.* This table exhibits the logic of the definitions of acoustical terms used in this study. The point of departure is a compound tone. In the most general case its components are both partials and harmonics. Harmonics are particular cases of partials. Harmonic tones are particular cases of compound tones. Partial tones of natural scales are compound tones. The harmonic scale of tones is a particular case of a natural scale. Both natural and harmonic scales are based on the harmonic series of frequencies. Each definition refers to one entity only.

P. 44 88 *Scale.* The reason for selecting the second partial tone for the determination of tonality is because some brass instruments and the pipes have no pedal tone. In the determination of tonality of an instrument true pitch position as to the octave is not essential, but in finding the tonal position a correct pitch position, with proper qualifications, is necessary. See the rules given in the text.

P. 45 89 *High.* The difficulty of assigning proper voice names for the recorders was commented on by Praetorius. Cf. *De Organographia*, p. 21, note. Also see note 92 below.

90 *Instruments.* Rules given below formulate explicitly conditions necessary and sufficient for determination both of the tonality and tonal position of the wind instruments. Lack of definite rules caused incredible confusion in voice naming. Since acoustical properties, the downward compass extension, and musical notation differ so much, rules are complex and require qualifications.

91 *True tonality.* The adjective 'nominal' requires an explanation. There is a difference between the acoustical pedal tone and the musical pedal tone of an instrument. A maker and acoustician deal with the actual lowest tone of the instrument; for them the maximum length of the tube is of importance. A musician is concerned with acoustics only indirectly, and deals with the tonality of some instruments as follows. In order to eliminate transposition, the acoustical tonality of an instrument is disregarded and the instruments are divided into three groups according to their lower compass limit: (1) those with a *normal* compass in which the lowest tone coincides with the musical tonality of the instrument; e.g., the concert flute having *c'* as the lowest tone is an instrument with a normal compass; (2) those with an *extended* compass, in which the lowest tone is lower than the musical tonality of the instrument; for instance, the oboe descending to *b*-flat or the bassoon descending to *BB*-flat (or *AA*) are such instruments; and (3) those with an *incomplete* compass, in which the lowest tone is higher than the musical tonality of the instrument; the concert flute having *d'* as its lowest tone is an example of such an instrument. Yet a musician regards all these instruments as non-transposing instruments in C. Thus only an instrument with a normal compass has its pedal tone identical with its lowest tone. In this case both acoustical and musical tonalities coincide. In other cases the tone C, being a musical convention and not an acoustical reality, is a *nominal* pedal tone. This convention is applicable to the 'wood-wind' instruments without serious interference with acoustics. On the brass instruments the actual acoustical length of the tube determines the tonality, and the instruments have to be treated as transposing or non-transposing according to the generally agreed upon conventions. Thus the tenor trombone is in B-flat, but its parts are written as if it were an instrument in C. The same is true of the bass tubas.

92 *Lower.* The soprano and the bass recorders are already notated one octave lower, so no transposition is necessary. The English and the German nomenclatures of recorders differ at the present time. On this point see P. A. Scholes, *The Oxford Companion to Music*, p. 785 a.

93 *A fourth higher.* The determination of tonality and tonal position of the flageolet is somewhat complicated. The lowest tone of the flageolet is *g'*. On the keyed flageolet this tone is actual, played with the low G-key. On the keyless flageolet it is 'fictitious' and is played with the bell opening half-stopped. If this lowest tone (*g'*) should be regarded as a nominal C, then the tonality of

the flageolet would be in G. To avoid this, the flageolet is regarded as pitched in C, with *c''* as the nominal pedal tone and extended compass descending to *g'*. The tonal position of the flageolet then becomes equivalent to that of the piccolo flute; therefore it is an octave instrument in C. In technical descriptions of flageolets of this Collection acoustical and not musical tonality is given.

P. 45 94 *Lower.* The pedal tone on the pipe can be played only pianissimo and is difficult to produce in tune. The first practicable tone is the second partial tone. In order to place a pipe in a correct tonal position, a transposition of the second partial tone one octave lower is necessary.

95 *One octave lower.* The rule appears to be complicated at first; in practice it is simple. A clarinetist fingers low F and overblows a twelfth; if the clarinet is in C, the actual tone produced is *c''*. To place the clarinet in a correct tonal position the note representing this overblown twelfth is transposed one octave lower. This establishes the tonal position of a clarinet. The same procedure is followed with clarinets of other tonalities: a twelfth overblown from the low nominal F gives the tonality directly; a corresponding note an octave lower gives the characteristic 'tone.' Cf. *Encyclopédie de la musique*, pt. ii, vol. iii, Paris, 1927, p. 1417. It is curious that the lowest tone of the primitive chalumeau and the earliest clarinet (with two keys) is F.

96 *Instruments.* A methodology of tonal position was developed by Dr. Curt Sachs in 1911. Cf. *Zeitschrift für Instrumentenbau*, xxxi, p. 1216 (1911); also the *Sammlung . . . Berlin*, pp. 193–194; his *Handbuch*, second ed., 1930, p. 251.

97 *Notation.* The characteristic tone is either a pedal tone, or a nominal pedal tone, or the second partial tone. The notation has to be considered, since, when the rule is applied to such instruments as recorders or pipes, the relative pitch of the pedal tone or of the second partial tone is taken as the guide; otherwise some recorders and pipes would be placed too high.

P. 47 98. *Flue.* The 'flue' is the wind-way in the foot of the flue-pipe of an organ. See p. 61 for a picture. The lips of a flute-player form a flexible wind-way or a passage for air on transverse flutes.

99 *Tube.* Cf. E. G. Richardson, *The Acoustics of Orchestral Instruments and of the Organ*, London, 1929, chapter ii.

P. 48 100 *Description.* The embouchure distance is given with a tolerance of plus or minus one half of a millimeter. The joints on old instruments are very seldom in good order. Precise measurements are accordingly difficult.

P. 49 101 *Chromatic tones.* 'Cross-fingering' is a technical term designating a simultaneous movement of certain fingers in opposite directions and stopping of the finger-holes in a non-consecutive order. For instance, on the old flute the tone *d'* is played with all finger-holes stopped, the tone *e'* with the first hole (see Fig. 5 on page 48) open. The logical sequence of opening the finger-holes requires that the first and second finger-holes should be open next. When this happens the tone produced is *f'*-sharp; to produce the tone *f'*-natural the first hole is stopped again and the second hole is left open. The sequence of tones *e'*, *f'*, on the old flute requires 'cross-fingering.' The movement of the fingers in opposite directions is not difficult, as keyboard players demonstrate. On the wind instruments more is involved than merely a pressing down of the keys. The difficulty consists in proper and simultaneous covering of the finger-holes so that no intervening tones will be heard, or, in other words, it is difficult to play 'clean' when cross-fingering is involved. Cf. R. S. Rockstro, *A Treatise on the Flute*, 1890, pp. 189 f., paragraphs 373, 374, and especially 375, where impairment of tone is discussed; only it should be remarked that Mr. Rockstro emphasized the tonal defects of cross-fingered tones too much. Also cf. E. G. Richardson, *The Acoustics of Orchestral Instruments*, for a mathematical theory of cross-fingering (appendix). For a pictorial explanation of 'cross'- or 'fork'-fingering, see C. S. Terry, *Bach's Orchestra*, p. 73.

102 *Performers.* Please read paragraph 195, p. 379, in H. Bouasse's *Instruments à vent*, i. Dr. Bouasse does not mince words in stating plainly that good musicians can play well on 'faulty' instruments. The trouble is not so much with the instruments as with the musicianship.

103 *Instrument.* A 'non-transposing instrument' is a musical term used in connection with those instruments which produce at their true putch the tones as designated by the notes. It should be emphasized that acoustical tonality has nothing to do with the fact that an instrument is treated in notation as non-transposing. See Note 91, p. 389.

104 *Identical.* See under No. 41, p. 55.

105 *Romans.* Cf. *Encyclopaedia Britannica*, 11th ed., x, p. 580.

106 *Italy. Ibid.*

P. 50 107 *Adopted.* The original of this picture was published in: Th. Solnzev, *Drevnosti Gosudarstva Rossiyskago. Kievskiy Sofiyskiy Sobor*, St. Petersburg, 1853; in Russian; plate 53, fig. 11. No description except a short reference that it represents musicians, dancers, and pole climbers.

108 *Literature.* Cf. *Encycl. Brit.*, 11th ed., x, p. 581.

109 *Military instrument.* Cf. *Encycl. Brit.*, x, p. 581; also, C. S. Terry, *Bach's Orchestra*, p. 71.

110 *Bass.* These sizes are estimated; the flutes on

Table IX, figs. 2, 3, 4, and 5 are, it seems, drawn to a larger scale than the rest of instruments on the same table; the factor 0.835 was used to determine the sizes. In this case the usual exactness of Praetorius' drawings is not present. See Appendix A.

P. 50 111 *Nineteenth century.* Cf. H. Macauley Fitzgibbon, *The Story of the Flute*, pp. 44 ff. Also R. S. Rockstro, *The Flute*, see its index, p. 655.

P. 52 112 *Key.* The statement is taken from the Royal Military Exhibition *Catalogue*, p. 44, under no. 100, where our flute is described.

113 *Fingers.* The writer has certain reasons to believe that Dr. Burghley's flute was a modified flute, suggested first by Dr. H. W. Pottgiesser in 1803 in an anonymous article printed in *Allgemeine musikalische Zeitung*. Compare the sketch in Rockstro's treatise, p. 267, fig. 47, ii, and especially the statements about a wider bore and shorter length on p. 268.

P. 53 114 *Adjusted.* Cf. Rockstro's treatise, p. 150, paragraph no. 326, where he quotes Tromlitz (1791) as recommending as many as seven middle joints.

115 *Pin-and-socket joint.* For picture see p. 148, fig. 17 of Rockstro's book.

116 *Invention.* Cf. Rockstro, *op. cit.*, pp. 151 f.

117 *Overblowing. Ibid.*, pp. 155 f., where influence of the stopper's position is explained.

118 *Flute.* Cf. C. Sachs, *Handbuch* (1930), p. 316.

119 *Tenor Flutes.* The nomenclature of flutes and the nomenclature of tonal position do not coincide. Low pitched flutes are difficult to make, and the name of 'bass flute' was applied practically to any flute pitched below the soprano instrument.

P. 54 120 *Hotteterre-le-Romain.* Cf. H. M. Fitzgibbon, *The Story of the Flute*, p. 35; an etching by Picart is reproduced there on p. 36.

P. 55 121 *Quasi-paraboloidal.* Cf. Theobald Boehm, *The Flute and Flute Playing*, D. C. Miller, tr., Cleveland, 1908, pp. 17 ff. On p. 18 Dr. Miller has plotted the actual curve of "an excellent specimen of Boehm & Mendler flute"; the straight taper contraction is plotted on the same diagram. It is not known whether the old flute-makers bored the heads of their flutes slightly conoidal by intent or for a technological reason explained in the text. At any rate, the decrease in size of the bore of the head is more in keeping with the modern practice than the cylindrical head.

122 *Zoeller.* Cf. the Royal Military Exhibition *Catalogue*, p. 31.

P. 57 123 *Contention.* See Note 102 of this section (p. 390).

124 *Mechanism.* In mechanical engineering this process of replacing the skill of individual craftsmen with some mechanical device (jigs, fixtures, dies, etc.) is known as 'transference of skill.' The writer is not advocating a return to the old system, but he feels that opponents of the excessive mechanization of musical instruments have some arguments in their favor.

125 *Principle.* Cf. Boehm, tr. Miller, *op. cit.*, pp. 60 f.

126 *In A.* Cf. C. Sachs' *Real-Lexikon*, p. 1, s.v. 'A-Flöte.' See p. 119, Fig. 23, 4. P. 58

127 *Alto Flute.* The old nomenclature is retained; its pitch is that of a soprano flute.

128 *London.* Cf. Rockstro's *Treatise*, p. 275, para. 513; H. M. Fitzgibbon, *The Story of the Flute*, p. 87 and p. 89, fig. 1. P. 59

129 *Deudsch.* Page 26 of Leipzig reprint of 1896; the 1545 edition of Agricola's treatise is the fourth. P. 60

130 *B-flat.* Cf. C. S. Terry, *Bach's Orchestra*, p. 72, for the pitch of Praetorius' flutes, the true tonalities of which were, of course, one tone lower. Also see Mahillon, *Catalogue . . . de Bruxelles*, i, p. 251.

131 *Fipple flute.* See *Encyclopaedia Britannica*, 11th ed., xx, p. 257. 'Lip distance' alone does not determine the pitch of a pipe, since several other factors, such as the ratio of the cross-section area to its length, affect pitch also.

132 *Embouchure.* This term is somewhat difficult to define. Contrary to the prevalent impression (cf. P. C. Scholes, *The Oxford Companion to Music*, 1938, p. 29, s.v. 'Embouchure'), this term is also used by flutists. A colloquial term, 'lip' ('he has an iron lip'), refers to the lip formation employed in playing wind instruments, not only the brass but also the flutes and reed instruments. Much more is involved, however; the lips not only have to be formed in a certain manner, but certain lip muscles have to be strengthened and developed, so that a player may have perfect control of tone and pitch. A relative setting of lips with respect to the orifice of the flute (this orifice is also called 'embouchure'; the French use this term also for the mouthpiece of brass instruments) is of great importance. On brass instruments the whole question is even more complex. P. 61

133 *Exactly the same.* It seems that a complete coupled system in playing flutes, either fipple or transverse, consists of the following links: (1) the air filling the chest cavity controlled by the lungs and the diaphragm, (2) the mouth cavity, (3) the air stream issuing from the mouth cavity, passing through the 'flue,' and striking the edge, (4) the air eddies at the edge, and (5) the vibrating air column in the tube. The essential difference between the fipple and the transverse flute is that on the former the lips have no control of the air stream and the 'flue' is rigid; on the transverse flute the lips form a flexible 'flue' and the player P. 62

exercises greater control over not only the tonal quality but also the pitch of tone. But this difference is that of degree and not of kind. With so many factors involved in tone production, even such an important factor as the 'embouchure' ('lip') does not reduce the others to insignificance. Trained singers and wind instrumentalists make better recorder players at first than pianists or string players; the latter have to master the art of breath control.

P. 62 134 *Palate.* The *c''*-sharp hole (no. 6) is used as a vent-hole for several overblown tones in the same way as on the transverse one-keyed flute. In many respects the fingering technique of the vertical flute is similar to that of the old transverse flute.

135 *Octave.* The recorder with all finger-holes stopped overblows also a twelfth and a fifteenth. Low-pitched recorders, especially the bass, can produce a chord tone when the lowest hole (stopped by a key) is very slightly opened; sometimes it happens when the key pad is not entirely air-tight; the fundamental and at least the second and the third partials can be heard simultaneously.

136 *Cross-fingered.* The tone *c''*-sharp can be overblown from the low *c'*-sharp with difficulty, since the latter tone is produced by half-covering the d'-hole (no. 1). On some instruments this hole is split into two small holes and *c'*-sharp is produced by covering one of them. The *e'*-hole is also made double on some instruments to insure certainty in producing *e'*-flat.

P. 63 137 *Vent-hole.* 'Pinching' is not the only way to convert the thumb-hole into a vent-hole; just a slight shift of the thumb will produce the same effect. Some players shift the thumb in preference to pinching. The thumb-hole no. 8 when pinched corresponds to the octave key on the oboe and the saxophone and to the speaker key on the clarinet.

138 *The Flageolet Family.* The name 'flageolet' was erroneously applied at one time to the vertical flute. The true flageolet differs from the vertical flute not only in the disposition of its finger-holes but also in the fingering technique. It seems that the parent of the flageolet was the 'klein Flötlin mit vier Löchern' of Martin Agricola. Invention of the flageolet is ascribed to Sieur Juvigny of Paris in 1581. Mahillon's derivation of the flageolet does not seem to be correct. Cf. Christopher Welch, *Six Lectures on the Recorder and other Flutes*, pp. 47 ff. and index, p. 444. Mr. Welch is the first, it seems, who has given a correct classification of fipple flutes.

139 *Hand.* The technique of producing the lowest tone on the short fipple flute by a partial covering of the bell opening was known at least in Agricola's time (1528). See Note 150.

P. 64 140 *Regular playing.* See *Encyclopaedia Britannica*, 11th ed., xxi, p. 634 a, s.v. 'Pipe and Tabor.' It is stated there that the pedal tone ('fundamental note') cannot be produced on the pipe. Pipes in this Collection produce the pedal, but it is useless in playing. See Note 94, p. 390.

141 *Without pedal tone.* More on this in the brass instrument section. See p. 136.

P. 65 142 *Enlarged.* This enlarged hole was patented by Bainbridge in 1803. Royal Military Exhibition *Catalogue*, p. 17.

143 *Effect. Ibid.*, p. 16.

P. 66 144 *French.* Another name for the *flûte douce* is *flûte à neuf trous*, a flute with nine finger-holes. The lowest hole on the smaller-sized recorder is bored in duplicate to accommodate right- and left-handed players. One of them is stopped with wax, so the total number of active finger-holes is eight. This practice was discontinued when the tube of the recorder was made in several parts, so that the position of the lowest hole could be adjusted by rotating the foot-joint. See Note 145 for reference. The nomenclature of the old scores is of interest. Down to about 1760 the name 'Flauto' meant recorder and not flute. Thus, the *Second Brandenburg Concerto* (F major) of J. S. Bach is scored for 'Flauto'; the instrument intended is alto recorder in F. If Bach scored for concert flute, he wrote 'Flauto traverso' or 'Traversa.' C. S. Terry, *Bach's Orchestra*, p. 62.

145 *Virdung.* The reprint of Virdung's book is now a bibliographical rarity. A more accessible reference is C. Welch, *Six Lectures on the Recorder and other Flutes*, pp. 23 ff. On p. 24, fig. 2, is reproduced Virdung's diagram showing the right- and left-handed way of playing the recorder.

146 *Fontanelle.* See under No. 130, p. 116, for reference.

147 *Prattica di Musica.* Published in Venice in 1596.

148 *Octave too low.* Modern notation for the alto and tenor recorders corresponding to the 'canto' and 'tenore' recorders of Zacconi is written one octave higher. Praetorius' notation is the same as the modern one.

149 *Cornett.* See C. Welch, *op. cit.*, p. 42, where he translates Praetorius' relative pitches of recorders. It should be noted that tonalities of recorders as given in the table on p. 66 are acoustical tonalities; in musical notation the cornetts and recorders are treated as instruments in C.

P. 68 150 *Agricola. Musica Instrumentalis*, Leipzig reprint, pp. 29 ff.

151 *Family.* Praetorius, *op. cit.*, p. 34; it is not listed among the recorders, nor mentioned in *Tabella Universalis*.

152 *Handbuch*, 1930 ed., p. 303.

P. 68 153 *Flutes*. Another excellent source of information is *A Practical Method for the Recorder* by E. H. Hunt and Robert Donington, London, vol. i.

P. 71 154 *Picco's Tibia*. See C. Welch, *Six Lectures on the Recorder and other Flutes*, p. 193, where a drawing of the tibia is given.

155 *Little Recorder*. *Old English Instruments of Music*, plate xxix, no. 11.

P. 72 156 *Toontoona*. C. Welch, *op. cit.*, p. 195, fig. 67. Mahillon, i (1893), p. 375, has the same picture but, curiously, reversed. Welch's is correct.

157 *Santa Maria*. Grove's *Dictionary of Music*, third ed., iv, p. 184, plate lx.

158 *Tempest*. C. Welch, *op. cit.*, p. 190.

159 *Collection*. Mahillon, *Catalogue . . . de Bruxelles*, ii, p. 282. The factor .835 was used for Praetorius' instrument. See Note 110.

P. 73 160 *Tountouna*. This is just another spelling. See Note 156.

161 *Brussels Collection*. Vol. i, p. 246, no. 191; vol. iv, p. 218, no. 2354.

P. 77 162 *Octave*. In other words the cylindrical tube instruments have their natural scale, consisting of 1, 3, 5, 7, . . . or the odd series of partial tones; the conoidal tube instruments have a complete series of partial tones, that is, a 1, 2, 3, 4, 5, . . . series.

163 *Closed*. In some cases the closed end is formed by a knot of the reed; but usually the reed is cut below the knot and the top opening filled with wax.

P. 78 164 *Instrument*. The double reed is usually connected to the bore of the instrument by an intermediate member consisting of a conoidal brass tubing; the short, straight tube is called the 'staple,' the medium or long, curved tube, the 'crook.' The reed is fitted over the narrow end of the staple or crook. The oboe reed, because of its small size, is usually fixed permanently to the staple; the latter is furnished with a cork-tipped end inserted into the bore of the instrument. The larger-sized English horn and bassoon reeds are made on the pattern shown in Fig. 15, p. 78, and are detachable.

P. 80 165 *Flutes*. C. Welch, *op. cit.*, p. 18, note, also p. 351.

166 *Sourdines*. The sourdines were described by Praetorius and pictured on table xii (reproduced here on p. 108). The Kunsthistorisches Museum in Vienna has four sourdines, two basses in C (nos. 226 and 227), and two contrabasses in F (nos. 228 and 229), the original sixteenth-century instruments described in the catalogue of the Vienna Collection. See Julius Schlosser, *Die Sammlung Alter Musikinstrumente*, Vienna, 1920, pp. 87 f. and table xli. No other original instruments have reached our times. A copy of the contrabass sourdine is in the Crosby Brown Collection of the Metropolitan Museum of Art, New York (no. 2700, Contrabass Sourdine, *Catalogue*, i, 1902, p. 147). Mahillon's *Catalogue . . . de Bruxelles* has copies of sourdines in vol. ii, pp. 228 ff., nos. 946 to 949 inclusive.

P. 81 167 *Makers*. The clarinet key mechanism is a nineteenth-century development.

168 *Seventeenth century*. See C. Sachs, *Real-Lexikon*, p. 233 b.

169 *Overblowing*. In the *Encyclopaedia Britannica*, 11th ed., vii, p. 485, is the statement that the cromornes do not overblow, because "to obtain an harmonic on the cromorne, the cap would have to be discarded, for a reed only overblows to give the harmonic overtones when pressed by the lips." This is not correct. The covered reed overblows as well as the uncovered directly controlled reed. The cromornes were not overblown merely because there would be a gap between the normal tones and the overblown tones, since the cylindrical pipe overblows a twelfth. As stated in the text, p. 81, the key mechanism used to bridge this gap was not invented when cromornes were played. The overblowing on the covered reed instruments requires considerable air pressure, and not every player possesses sufficiently strong lungs. The stiffness of the reed has much to do with the ability of a covered reed to overblow. See Note 179 below.

P. 83 170 *Harmonie universelle*. Livre v, p. 305.

P. 84 171 *Standard works*. An excellent book on the bagpipe, containing its bibliography, is Dr. William H. Grattan Flood's *The Story of the Bagpipe*, London, 1911.

172 *Cromorne*. *Encyclopaedia Britannica*, 11th ed., xxi, p. 805, s.v. 'Platerspiel.' The Platerspiel is an utricular instrument, that is, one with a distensible air reservoir; the cromorne has a rigid cap surrounding the reed. This constitutes a typological difference.

P. 86 173 *Zalzal*. See H. Helmholtz, *On the Sensations of Tone*, London, 1895, appendix, p. 515, scales numbered 51 and 52; also Grove's *Dictionary of Music*, 3rd ed., New York, 1927, i, p. 195, where several Highland scales are compared.

174 *Another player*. For a picture of Italian *zampogna* players see *The Oxford Companion to Music*, p. 63, plate 13, fig. 5.

P. 87 175 *Grace*. Kathleen Schlesinger, *Encyclopaedia Britannica*, 11th ed., iii, p. 204 b.

176 *Breeding*. Cf. W. H. Grattan Flood, *The Story of the Bagpipe*, pp. 123 f.

P. 89 177 *Hotteterre*. C. Sachs, *Real-Lexikon*, p. 264 b.

P. 91 178 *Musette*. C. Sachs, *op. cit.*, p. 353.

179 *Recorder*. Dr. Percy A. Scholes in *The Oxford Companion to Music*, p. 59 a, states: "It should be noted

that the chanter is exposed to a limitation as compared with the other wood-wind instruments; these obtain their second octave by overblowing, which in the case of the bagpipe, as the mouth is not in direct contact with the reed-pipe, is not possible." In this statement there are two errors. The fact is that the chanters on some bagpipes overblow. Examination of the fingering chart reproduced by Dr. Flood on p. 218 of his book on the bagpipe shows that the second octave beginning with e'' has the same fingerings as the corresponding tones of the first octave; the only correct explanation of such fingering is that the tones of the second octave are overblown. The writer had this overblowing of the chanter demonstrated to him by Mr. Daniel J. Murphy and Mr. Patrick Brown; the latter is an amateur Irish bagpipe maker. Dr. Scholes' explanation of the reason why indirectly controlled reeds do not overblow is not correct. The fact that the lips of a player do not touch the reed on the bagpipe has nothing to do with it. On the Irish bagpipe chanter, the double reed is made quite delicately; the bag is inflated by the bellows; for overblowing a player gives the bag a quick squeeze and pumps the bellows a little faster. Thus both velocity and pressure components are increased and the chanter overblows. See p. 43, item 11, for definition of overblowing. Any pipe with a covered reed will overblow, if the pressure component becomes sufficiently strong. A sudden air shock delivered by such means as a quick compression of the bag helps to establish a regime for the production of partial tones.

P. 91

180 *True nature.* In *Encyclopaedia Britannica*, 11th ed., iii, p. 205 a, there is the statement: "regulators correspond to the sliders on the drone-barrel of the musette." The sliders on the musette, as is stated on p. 89, are used for changing the pitch of the drones so that the latter may be used in two tonalities, or for silencing the drones; pitch regulation is possible within narrow limits. The regulator on the Uilleann bagpipe is a stopped pipe of peculiar construction for which there is no exact counterpart on any other instrument. The name, as was explained by the Irish pipers, comes from the fact that the regulators 'regulate the harmony.' More about the musical use of regulators can be found in Captain Francis O'Neill's *Irish Folk Music*, Chicago, 1910; also W. H. Grattan Flood, *The Story of the Bagpipe*, p. 226, where O'Farrell's *Treatise on the Irish Bagpipes* (1801) is quoted. O'Farrell mentions only one regulator. There were more than one on the elder Kenna's pipe made in 1770 and represented on the plate facing p. 54 of Dr. Flood's book. On the same plate Dr. Flood refers to a regulator as "a chanter fitted with keys"; this is not a safe term to use, since Kenna's pipe has a real chanter fitted with keys. A regulator is a stopped pipe with closed keys, which is used for an harmonic accompaniment and which chants no melodies.

181 *Tone.* Mr. Daniel J. Murphy explained to the writer that the rush is not absolutely essential for tuning purposes, as a piece of wire alone is just as effective; but the rush pulp softens the tone of the regulator.

182 *Speak.* It should be taken into consideration that when the keys on the regulators are closed an equalized air pressure permits the laminae of the double reeds to resume an 'open position' (see p. 78, fig. 15). A sudden opening of a key lets the air out of the tube and therefore from the inside of the reed. The air pressure on the outside of the reed then begins to act and sounds the regulator as long as the key is open. The closing of the key restores the equilibrium of the air pressure, both on the outside and on the inside of the reed, and stops the speaking.

P. 94

183 *Left-hand joint.* The position of the hands on wood-wind instruments is now standardized; the left hand is placed near the mouthpiece and the right hand is held underneath the left hand.

P. 96

184 *Lower octave.* More precisely: the tones an octave higher do not repeat the fingerings of the lower octave; beginning with a twelfth from the nominal low *e*, that is, starting with b', the fingerings are repeated, but the tones are related by an interval of a twelfth.

185 *Chalumeau register.* The chalumeau register on the clarinet derives its name from a primitive instrument which is an ancestor of the clarinet. The tones from f to g' duplicate the tones of the old chalumeau; the low *e* is a later addition. On the clarinet the tones from g' to b'-flat, as stated in the text, are produced with the rear thumb-hole open and form a group related by its own tone color; for this reason, the chalumeau register is, really, limited by f'. Another interesting designation of the clarinet register is given by F. L. Schubert in *Katechismus der Musik-Instrumente*, pp. 30 f. The tones from *e* to b'-flat are called *Schalmeienton*; from b'-natural to c^3-sharp the register is referred to as *Zinkentöne*; above that is the high register. *Zinke* is a cornett.

186 *Clarion register.* The term 'clarino' is used in connection with the high trumpet parts; the first and second trumpeters were known as clarino players; see p. 195 for the nomenclature of trumpet parts. This term was adopted to designate the high register of the clarinet because of its resemblance to the high tones of the trumpet; this happened at a time when the art of trumpet playing was not yet extinct.

187 *High register.* The best way of settling scientifically the extent of various registers would be to determine the formants over the whole playable range of the

clarinet. As things stand now, the number and the limits of various registers are not definitely settled.

P. 96 188 *Size.* More complete enumeration of the members of the clarinet family can be found in Dr. C. Sachs' *Handbuch* (1930), p. 347. The letters in brackets represent the lowest tones of the respective instruments.

189 (*D-flat*). The nomenclature of the clarinets and the nomenclature of tonal position do not coincide, as is the case with the flutes and other instruments.

190 (*DD*). There are two types of the contrabass clarinets: (1) with normal clarinet compass descending to the nominal E (sounds *DD* on the B-flat instrument); (2) with extended compass descending to *BBB*-flat or even to *AAA*, or as low as the double bassoon. The first type is built in Germany, the second in France.

P. 97 191 *Instrument.* See p. 113 for etymology of the word *chalumeau.*

P. 98 192 *Open.* There are two kinds of double holes on wind instruments. The first kind is made to accommodate right- and left-handed players, as already stated in the description of the recorder on p. 68; such holes are bored far apart. The second kind is really a split finger-hole; two small, closely spaced holes replace the finger-hole of normal size; the purpose is to eliminate half-stopping, which is uncertain in its results.

193 *Twelfth. Catalogue . . . de Bruxelles*, ii, p. 206.

194 *Makers.* See W. Altenburg, "Zur Entwicklungsgeschichte des Klarinettenbaues," *Zeitschrift für Instrumentenbau*, xxv, p. 390 b (1905). This is one of the best articles on the history of the clarinet.

P. 101 195 *Tone.* Dr. C. Sachs in the *Handbuch*, p. 345, cleverly remarks that it stands with respect to the clarinets as the viola da gamba to the violin family.

196 *Nominal C.* Since basset horns were usually built in F, the actual lowest tone was *F.* In Mozart's time some soprano clarinets had their compass extended down to the nominal C (sounding *B*-flat on the B-flat clarinet).

P. 102 197 *Ninety degrees.* The Berlin Collection basset horn no. 578 (*Catalogue*, plate 29) has its tube bent at a ninety-degree angle.

198 *Mayrhofer of Passau.* There is a very interesting article by W. Altenburg, "Eine Wiedereinführung des Bassethorns," *Zeitschrift für Instrumentenbau*, xxviii, p. 555 a. The story about a certain maker by the name of Horn as the inventor of the basset horn is, it seems, a fine anecdote.

199 *Length.* See *Encyclopaedia Britannica*, 11th ed., iii, p. 494 a; even this list is by no means complete.

P. 103 200 *Usual type.* The catalogue (1910) of a Bohemian firm lists somewhat similar instruments as "Alt- und Bass-Klarinetten für Theater in Fagottform."

P. 104 201 R. M. E. *Catalogue.* P. 125, no. 266; also see *Encyclopaedia Britannica*, 11th ed., iii, p. 491 b.

202 *Place.* See C. Sachs, *Sammlung . . .*, p. 299, no. 87; *ibidem*, pp. 300 b and 301 a, no. 1051; the picture on plate 29 is erroneously numbered as 1057.

203 *Saxophone.* See Constant Pierre, *La facture instrumentale*, Paris, 1890, p. 50. Also Jaap Kool, *Das Saxophon*, Leipzig, 1931, p. 184, fig. 63.

204 *Not a saxophone.* Jaap Kool, *Das Saxophon*, p. 185. Mr. Kool is the first writer to state that he actually tested Desfontenelles' clarinet. M. Mahillon pointed out long ago (in the *Catalogue . . . de Bruxelles*, iv, pp. 357 f.) that Desfontenelles' instrument was a clarinet; the form of that clarinet was anticipated by the bass clarinet no. 939 of the *Catalogue . . . de Bruxelles.*

205 *Family.* Reproduced on p. 175 of Mr. Jaap Kool's book.

P. 105 206 *Sax.* Cf. *The Musical Times*, lxxiii, p. 1077 (Dec., 1932).

207 *University of Edinburgh.* Cf. F. W. Galpin, *A Textbook of European Musical Instruments*, London, 1937, p. 193, where a reference is made to an article by Mr. Lyndesay G. Langwill.

208 *E-flat.* Cf. his *Manuel général de musique militaire*, Paris, 1848, table xxv, note. Unfortunately the text has only a very brief reference to the saxophone family; as to its technical details there are no particulars.

209 *Factory numbers.* The saxophones built by A. Sax are numbered: (1) the tenor in C, no. 20669 (Ann Arbor, no. 641); (2) the baritone in E-flat, no. 26695 (Berlin, no. 1346).

210 *Consulted.* Second ed. (1936), p. 169; some additional remarks, pp. 491 f.

P. 106 211 *Counter-proposal.* M. Carafa's instrumentation was justified much later by that of the 'symphonic bands,' in which the clarinet family held the same position as the violins in the symphony orchestra. At the time (1845) the problem was the organization of military bands; musical delicacy was out of the question. The demand was for a robust and masculine group of instruments for playing in the open air, for marching purposes, and for attacks in battle. A. Sax had such a band in mind, and his saxhorns provided a sonorous and homogeneous foundation for the military band. For details see Oscar Commetant, *Histoire d'un inventeur au dix-neuvième siècle, Adolphe Sax* (Paris, 1860).

212 *Sax. Ibid.*, pp. 106 f.

P. 107 213 *Instruments.* Cf. Oscar Commetant, *op. cit.*, pp. 522 f., for an enumeration of the principal inventions of Adolphe Sax.

214 *Survive.* Praetorius on p. 40 of his *De Organographia* mentions that such instruments as the sourdines,

the racketts, (some) bagpipes, the cromornes, and the *schryari* give only as many tones as there are finger-holes; all of these instruments have covered, indirectly controlled reeds. This means that such instruments were not overblown. See Note 169.

P. 107 215 *Completely*. Cf. the R. M. E. *Catalogue*, p. 97, where Sir John Hawkins is quoted on a short bassoon or *cervelat* (the sausage bassoon in French), in which "by reason of its closeness, the interior parts imbibed, and retained, the moisture of the breath, the ducts dilated, and broke. In short, the whole blew up." One has to examine the construction of a rackett (*cervelat, Wurstfagott*, the sausage bassoon) to appreciate this remark.

216 *The Sourdines. Sourdine* is a French word. It is spelled *sordone* in Italian and *Sordun* in German. Praetorius spelled it *Sordune*. See pp. 80 f. and Note 166 for further references.

217 *The Tartoelds*. In the Kunsthistorisches Museum at Vienna is a family of most unusual double reed instruments, the tartoelds, consisting of two trebles, two alt-tenors, and one bass. The body of a tartoeld is of yellow brass, cast in the form of a dragon and painted in green, red, and gold. The reed is set on the end of the dragon's twisted tail; the latter is a conical bore counterpart of the crook of the bassoon. The main tube is concealed inside and is coiled like a helical tube in a gas-heater; its bore is, it seems, cylindrical. (The Vienna Catalogue makes a qualified statement: ". . . Roehre, die zylindrischen Verlauf zu haben scheint.") The bell end is shaped like a dragon's open mouth. The tartoeld has seven finger-holes in the front and a thumb-hole in the rear. This set of instruments is unique. Cf. Julius Schlosser, *Die Sammlung alter Musikinstrumente*, Vienna, 1920, p. 85 and plate xl.

218 *Covered reed*. See table xii, fig. 7, reproduced here on p. 108.

219 *Britannica*. 11th ed., ii, p. 917, s.v. 'Aulos.' After these lines were written, Miss Schlesinger published a monumental piece of scholarship, *The Greek Aulos*, London, 1939. The writer is convinced that she discovered a new and vital principle in 'equal measure' and its application to modal music. No serious student of musical instruments should neglect this outstanding contribution.

220 *Valuable*. *Harvard Studies in Classical Philology*, vol. iv, Boston, 1893.

221 *Harmonie universelle*. See this work, ii, p. 298, for a picture of the courtaud; Mersenne spells it 'courtaut.' Mersenne's definition: ". . . qu'il ne soit autre chose qu'un Fagott, ou Basson racourcy, qui sert aussi de Basse aux Musettes" (p. 299). Mahillon, *Catalogue . . . de Bruxelles*, ii, p. 240, under no. 952, lists a courtaud; the instrument pictured is a cromorne or a 'tournebout.'

222 *Bass. De Organographia*, p. 40. Also see Praetorius' table x, figures 8 and 9, on p. 127 of this study, where the sausage bassoons of various sizes are shown.

223 *Praetorius' time*. This is a corollary of the statement made in Note 214 above.

P. 110 224 *Playing*. The French have a special aptitude for bringing out the lyrical, tender, feminine characteristics of instruments. The oboe of old was a strident military band instrument, and not a singer of pastorals, as it became later. Dr. Richard Strauss paid a graceful compliment to the French school of oboe playing in his revision of Berlioz's *Instrumentationslehre*; cf. p. 198, note, of that work.

225 *Generic group*. In the process of classification of any complex field the class from which the division starts is known in the science of logic as the *summum genus*, or highest class. Any intermediate group which stands as a genus with respect to a lower specific division is called a *proximum genus* of its component species.

Therefore, the classification of instruments in this study is brought down to the lowest *proximum genus*. The best exposition of the classification process is given in L. Susan Stebbing's *A Modern Introduction to Logic*, London, 1930. It is this writer's fervent prayer that the authors of books on musical instruments study part iii of her "The Theory of Definitions," pp. 422 ff., and especially its third paragraph, "Classification and Division in relation to Definition." Many a pitfall violating the most elementary principles of classification would then be avoided.

P. 112 226 *Properties*. This statement refers only to the form given to the tube in order to shorten its length and make the instrument easier to handle. Wood-wind instruments, especially such long instruments as the contrabass clarinet and the double bassoon, are formed into different shapes or 'models' in accordance with the ideas of their makers. This is still more true of brass instruments. Although there are several standard shapes, such as a trumpet, a horn, a tuba, a trombone, etc., nevertheless even within these forms there are innumerable variations. One thing cannot be changed in all this bending and twisting of the tubes of the wind instruments. The geometrical shape of the bore must retain the same form as if it were made with a rectilinear centre line. For a strict mathematical definition of this property of tubes, based on a concept of the bore as an envelope of spheres of constant radius of curvature for cylindrical tubes and with variable radius of curvature for conoidal tubes, cf. H. Bouasse, *Instruments à vent*, i (1929), p. 301, para. 154, 'Courbure des tubes.'

P. 112 227 *Families.* For instance, there are two different systems of key mechanism on the modern bassoon: the French system (E. Jancourt) and the German system (W. Heckel). These systems differ so greatly that a bassoonist used to one of them cannot play on a bassoon of the other system.

228 *Series.* The same is true, of course, of the conoidal bore instruments with covered, indirectly controlled double reed, when they can be made to overblow, as is the case on the Uilleann bagpipe chanter.

229 *The oboe family.* The oboe family in this study is a specific and not a generic group. Only the oboes in the strictly technical meaning of the word are included. Such instruments as the English horn and the bassoon are not regarded as members of the oboe family.

230 *Practical reasons.* When there are only two representatives of the double reed instruments which are invariably employed in orchestral scores, the oboe and the bassoon, with the English horn as an occasional visitor, it would be pedantic to insist that they belong to three different families. An organologist, however, deals with so many double reed instruments that a more specific division is imperative.

P. 113 231 *Fourteenth century.* Cf. *Encyclopaedia Britannica,* 11th ed., xix, s.v. 'Oboe.'

232 *It seems.* Praetorius' pictures of shawms of larger sizes show no pirouettes. See table vi, fig. 3, and table xi, fig. 1, reproduced in this study on p. 354 and p. 115 respectively. Also see Note 259.

P. 114 233 *Trompette.* Cf. *Harmonie universelle,* ii, p. 303. Translation: "As to their [shawms] music, it is appropriate for large assemblies, such as ballets (although the violin is now used in their place), for nuptials, for village festivals, and for other public rejoicings, because of the great noise that they make and the grand harmony that they supply, because they have the loudest and most violent sound of all the instruments, if the trumpet is excepted."

P. 116 234 *Feature.* See Georg Kinsky, *Kleiner Katalog der Sammlung alter Musikinstrumente,* Cöln, 1913, p. 154.

235 *Recorder. Op. cit.,* pp. 25 f., fig. 4; the 'box' in this figure is the fontanelle.

236 *Kinsky.* Cf. *Kleiner Katalog,* pp. 146, 153.

P. 117 237 *Berlin.* The Catalogue, p. 272 a, no. 289, and plate 27. Table vi of Praetorius is reproduced in this study on p. 354.

238 *Military instrument.* Cf. F. L. Schubert, *Katechismus der Musik-Instrumente,* Leipzig, 1862, p. 29. It is stated there that the oboe had led the melody in the military bands before the invention of the clarinet, and that band musicians were called oboists. The writer remembers that military bandsmen in Russia were so referred to as late as 1912; they were called in Russian *goboisty*; the oboe is *goboi* in Russian. This undoubtedly came from Germany. Cf. C. S. Terry, *Bach's Orchestra,* p. 100.

239 *Orchestra.* This is one of a very few instances when modern sonority is a subdued refinement of the coarse and powerful tone of an old instrument. Cf. C. S. Terry, *Bach's Orchestra,* p. 102 and especially p. 103. The usual direction of evolution is the 'survival of the loudest.'

240 *In A.* Cf. Georg Kinsky, *Kleiner Katalog,* p. 156. The ordinary soprano oboe was also known as the 'oboe piccolo.' The bass oboe No. 8 is represented in the Crosby Brown Collection and listed in the catalogue as "No. 2351, Oboe. Contra Bass in F." (1902 ed., p. 145; picture).

P. 118 241 *Bore.* Constant Pierre, *La facture instrumentale,* p. 23, describes "un Hautbois baryton" with pear-shaped bell and refers to the similarity of its tone to that of the English horn. Such an instrument is not a true oboe. V. C. Mahillon, *Catalogue . . . de Bruxelles,* ii, p. 261, no. 985, describes a true low pitched oboe, a facsimile of one constructed by C. Denner.

242 *Confusion.* The *fundamentum divisionis* (the basis of division in classification) must be so selected that the resulting groups are mutually exclusive. Violation of this rule results in 'cross-division' or overlapping groups. See L. Susan Stebbing, *A Modern Introduction to Logic,* p. 435.

243 *Seventeenth century.* Cf. *Encyclopaedia Britannica,* 11th ed., xix, s.v. 'Oboe.'

244 *Oboe. Pro*: Hoffmann, *Encyclopaedia Britannica,* 11th ed., xix, p. 951; C. S. Terry, *Bach's Orchestra,* p. 95. *Contra*: C. Sachs, *Real-Lexikon,* p. 276 a.

245 *Pomone.* See C. S. Terry, *op. cit.,* p. 95.

P. 121 246 *Old oboes.* C. Sachs, *Sammlung . . .,* pp. 273–274, fig. 29. W. Heckel builds oboes with this early form of bell.

247 *Oboe basso.* The real oboe in A was known as the 'oboe basso.' See Note 240. The *oboe d'amore* (also in A) has a pear-shaped bell and therefore belongs to a different family.

P. 122 248 *Bore. Catalogue . . . de Bruxelles,* ii, pp. 251, 256.

249 *Fields.* Constant Pierre was the first to suggest that the *oboe d'amore*, the English horn, and the 'baritone oboe' with the pear-shaped bell constitute a family distinct from the real oboe family. Cf. his *La facture instrumentale,* p. 23. In this case the *fundamentum divisionis* is the tone color. The instruments with pear-shaped bell have very characteristic lower tones which set them apart from real oboes; the rest of their register also differs from that of the oboe family.

P. 122 250 *Eighteenth century.* Cf. C. S. Terry, *Bach's Orchestra*, p. 107.

251 *Exist.* English horns with straight tubes, selected at random, are: (1) 'haut-contre de hautbois,' *Catalogue . . . de Bruxelles*, i, p. 236, no. 179; ii, p. 255, no. 977; both instruments have pear-shaped bells and descend to *f.* (2) C. Sachs, *Sammlung . . .*, p. 278, no. 516, plate 26. (3) Miss K. Schlesinger mentions one by Stainsby, Jr.; cf. *Encyclopaedia Britannica*, 11th ed., vii, p. 135. (4) W. Heckel, *Der Fagott*, p. 10, fig. 'a,' a copy of the Berlin instrument no. 249 of Grundmann. The modern instrument is obviously a lineal descendant of this type of English horn. It is doubtful whether the straight tube instrument should be referred to as the *oboe da caccia*. It seems better that the latter term should be reserved for a curved double reed aerophone with conoidal bore and wide flaring bell, as on our instrument No. 142.

P. 123 252 *Rough.* In the Berlin Collection is an *oboe da caccia* of similar design. It is listed in the text of *Sammlung . . .*, on p. 278, as 'Altoboe' no. 581, and represented on plate 26, where it is named 'Engl. Horn.'

253 *Galpin.* Cf. the R. M. E. *Catalogue*, p. 68, where this idea is credited to Canon Galpin. Also see *Encyclopaedia Britannica*, 11th ed., vii, p. 135 a, fig. 2. Dr. C. Sachs objects to this derivation of the term: cf. his *Real-Lexikon*, p. 129 a.

254 *Oboe.* Cf. C. Pierre, *La facture instrumentale*, p. 23.

255 *Oboe d'amore family.* A more important reason, as already stated, is that the tone color of the baritone oboe with the pear-shaped bell is more akin to that of the *oboe d'amore* and of the English horn.

P. 124 256 *Tone color.* Cf. C. S. Terry, *Bach's Orchestra*, p. 110.

257 *Description.* R. M. E. *Catalogue*, p. 94, under no. 210.

258 *Bassoon.* This often repeated tale has been proved false several times. The latest and most competent negative statement is in C. Forsyth's *Orchestration*, appendix.

259 *Real-Lexikon.* Page 135 b. One statement there should be questioned: that the 'Bombart' (the bass pommer) had a pirouette ('Rohrmanschette'). *Contra*: see Note 232 above; also Mahillon, *Catalogue . . . de Bruxelles*, ii, p. 21; C. Sachs, *Sammlung . . .*, no. 642, plate 27; W. Heckel, *Der Fagott*, p. 7, fig. 'a.'

P. 125 260 *Later instruments.* Cf. Lyndesay G. Langwill, "The Curtal (1550–1750). A Chapter in the Evolution of the Bassoon," *The Musical Times*, lxxvii, p. 307, figs. 3a and 3b.

261 *Bassoon-making.* It is curious that Wilhelm Heckel's booklet on the bassoon is called '*Der* Fagott'; on p. 12 is a reference to Praetorius and also the eighteenth century designation of the bassoon in the masculine gender. The grammatically correct form is the prosaic 'das,' a neuter.

P. 126 262 *E-hole.* In this study the finger-holes are numbered from the lowest one upward; they are designated also by the actual tones produced when open, assuming that the rest above a given finger-hole are stopped. The keys are designated by the actual tones produced by an instrument when the key levers are pressed down. This eliminates the necessity of discriminating between the open and closed keys. On this point, cf. Jaap Kool, *Das Saxophon*, pp. 82 ff. Praetorius gave two rules: (1) the instruments on Table X (reproduced here on p. 127) and numbered from 1 to 5 inclusive, have their finger-holes designated by the tones sounded when they are closed; (2) the instruments numbered from 6 to 9 have their finger-holes designated by the actual tones. The explanation of these rules should be sought in the fact that the first series of instruments has open keys and the second one has no keys. In Praetorius' time the keys were always made open; they were called by the tone produced when closed. Thus, the key covering the G-hole when pressed down made the instrument produce the tone F and therefore was referred to as the F-key. The fingers acted as open keys with respect to the finger-holes. This made it possible to keep the designation of tones on keyed instruments consistent. The finger-holes were referred to as being one tone lower. On keyless instruments this convention was not kept and the finger-holes were called by the actual tones produced, i.e., the musical and acoustical designation coincided. When later the closed keys were added to the instruments, the whole scheme became hopelessly confused, since the closed keys produce the actual tone when pressed down, and not a tone which is a semitone or two semitones lower, as do the open keys.

P. 128 263 *Bassoon.* In the same sense as the scale of the flute and the oboe is regarded as the C-scale and the extra tones are treated as an extension of the compass. See Note 91, p. 389. Also W. Heckel, *Der Fagott*, p. 27; L. G. Langwill, "Some Notes on the Bassoon. With Particular reference to its Fundamental Scale," *Musical Progress and Mail*, Aug., 1933. This last reference is taken from the *Catalogue of Books Relating to the Flute*, by Dr. D. C. Miller, Cleveland, 1935, p. 67. The article was not accessible to the writer and Mr. Langwill's conclusions are not known to him.

264 *Way.* The lack of agreement as to what constitutes the fundamental scale of the bassoon ceases to be a matter of argument and becomes serious when the tonal position of the bassoon has to be determined. If it is an instrument in F, an octave below the English horn, as some contend, then its tonal position is that of

the bass instrument; below the tone *F* its tones would then be extension tones. The next logical step would be to treat the bassoon as a transposing instrument and write the parts accordingly; this would have a practical advantage in that the oboists, flutists, and saxophonists could learn to play the bassoon in one or two months. On this point, cf. *Encyclopèdie de la musique*, pt. ii, vol. iii (1927), p. 1417 a. If the fundamental scale of the bassoon is in C, then its tonal position is that of the contrabass. It is so treated in the musical notation of orchestral scores and its parts are written as if it were a non-transposing instrument in C.

P. 128 265 *Time*. Cf. Daniel Speer, *Unterricht der musicalischen Kunst*, 1687, pp. 116 f.

266 *Praetorius*. In the Vienna Catalogue Mattheson is extensively quoted; see p. 46, para. 9.

267 *G-sharp*. Cf. C. Sachs, *Real-Lexikon*, p. 136 a.

268 *Publications*. Dr. D. C. Miller's library has the first volume of Samuel Holyoke's work. See his *Catalogue*, p. 56.

P. 131 269 *Savary's model*. Two instruments of this celebrated maker, the bassoon and the tenoroon, are in the Casadessus Collection, now in Symphony Hall in Boston.

270 *Der Fagott*. However inadequate this booklet is in size, at present it is the only publication devoted to the bassoon. It contains also much valuable and authentic information on many other related instruments.

271 *Music*. P. 168, and appendix, p. 288.

P. 132 272 *Brussels Collection*. *Catalogue . . . de Bruxelles*, i, p. 437; ii, p. 268; the latter is illustrated.

273 *Family*. For the opposite opinion, cf. C. Pierre, *La facture instrumentale*, p. 26.

274 *Paris, 1889*. Cf. C. Pierre, *op. cit.*, p. 26. The writer is in agreement with M. Pierre when on p. 28 he expresses regret that no modern bassoon-maker has constructed a low-pitched bassoon (*Quartfagott*), the tonal position of which would be between the ordinary bassoon and the double bassoon.

P. 134 275 *Thumb*. Cf. W. Heckel, *Der Fagott*, p. 16, fig. 'c.'

P. 135 276 *Instruments*. Examination of the general classification shows that both cylindrical and conoidal tube instruments are divided into symmetrical groups and sub-groups. See p. xii, Section C, Sub-sections a and b.

277 *Valve mechanism*. The British writers had a singularly unfortunate experience with Dr. Schafhäutl's division of the brasses into the whole- and half-tube groups. A detailed technical discussion would be too long and complicated. Only the principal source of errors can be pointed out. It is an incorrect analysis of the specific acoustical properties of the brass wind instruments. This, it seems, is due to failure to discriminate between the musical usage of not employing at times the pedal tone when available and the actual unavailability of the pedal tone on some instruments. Thus, cornets, horns, trumpets, and the higher saxhorns are regarded as half-tube instruments. Since the higher horns (from G upward), the higher trumpets (from F upward), and all the saxhorns produce the pedal tone and are therefore whole-tube instruments, a grouping which does not take this into account results in a cross-division, a logical and classificational fallacy. See Note 242 on this point. The separation of the tubas (the bass and contrabass saxhorns) from the rest of the saxhorns, on the alleged ground that the tubas are whole-tube instruments and the higher saxhorns are half-tube instruments, is highly questionable. As is shown in Note 295, Adolphe Sax constructed a whole family of saxhorns with four valves, ranging from the sopranino in E-flat to the bass in E-flat. This fourth valve is a *Quartventil*, and the only reason for adding it to an instrument is that the pedal tone is easily producible.

278 *Essayé*. *Harmonie universelle*, book v, pp. 249 f. P. 136
Translation: 'It should also be noted that the tone which is ordinarily referred to as the first or the lowest one on the trumpet is not the one which is ordinarily used, and which I have named UT, because it is placed a whole octave lower, in spite of the fact that many trumpeters do not believe this because they either cannot produce it or because they never have tried it.' Also quoted by Werner Menke, *History of the Trumpet of Bach and Handel*, p. 45.

279 *That time*. Cf. *Encyclopaedia Britannica*, 11th ed., ix, p. 892, s.v. 'Euphonium.' Reference: K. E. von Schafhäutl, 'Die Musikinstrumente,' in *Berichte der Beurteilungscommission bei der allgemeine deutschen Industrie Ausstellung in München, 1854*, sect. iv, pp. 169–170.

280 *Family*. In a general classification one has to disregard certain specific differences, however important they may become when finer distinctions have to be made. The points of similarity between the instruments gathered into this much named group are so many and so important that they far outweigh specific differences. Further references to the instruments of this type will be as 'bugles,' in the same general theoretical sense employed by Dr. C. Sachs in the *Real-Lexikon*, p. 62 a, s.v. 'Bügelhörner.'

281 *Three-valve instruments*. The publishers of music P. 137
for bands have to consider average conditions and not exceptions. In bands the brass soprano parts can be played by cornets, trumpets, and flügelhorns, all of which are built with three valves and in B-flat. The sopranino, soprano, and alto bugles with four valves

would require parts written especially for them if their full register were to be utilized.

P. 137 282 *Problem.* In some solos written for the soprano brasses the 'snob value' of the pedal tones is emphasized, and a soloist is required to play a few chromatic tones producible with the valves in the pedal register. Such a procedure is senseless, even from a musical standpoint, since these tones are detached from the rest of the register of three-valved instruments and have none of the artistic value of the trombone pedals. The only advantage in using pedals on soprano instruments is that the lower register in the neighborhood of the second partial tone acquires more solidity and the tones themselves can be played in better tune.

283 *Single horn.* The exacting demands made on horn players in the modern symphony orchestra have forced the first and third horn players to adopt a tonally inferior but more easily blowing instrument; another advantage of the B-flat horn is a greater freedom from 'breaks' and a smarter attack.

284 *Horn in B-flat.* In addition to the three customary valves it has a muting valve, permitting muted tones to be played in tune and without transposition; these four valves are mandatory on the B-flat single horn. The fifth valve is the *Quartventil*, permitting the player to span chromatically the interval between *E* and *BB*-flat.

P. 138 285 *A-flat.* This dividing line is somewhat arbitrary. Some trumpet players have difficulty in producing the pedal tone on the E-trumpet. See Note 350.

286 *Studied.* From a musical standpoint no other instrument needs the pedal tone less than the trumpet. Even at best it is valueless as a tone and too flat to be corrected by the lips. The second partial tone is also too flat on some instruments and cannot be raised. This is true of the trumpets of this Collection.

287 *Mouthpieces.* Among the arguments intended to prove that the presence or absence of the pedal tone is not a reliable guide is this: place a trombone mouthpiece on a trumpet and the pedal tone becomes playable; *ergo*, it is not an inherent property of the tube, but depends upon the type of mouthpiece and ability of a player. It would seem that the trumpet tube with a trombone mouthpiece is no longer a trumpet, since the higher partial tones also decrease in number. Long experience has taught what type of mouthpiece suits best certain types of tubes and a certain type of playing. Theoretically, all tubes should have the pedal tone.

288 *Acoustical unit.* Adolphe Sax understood this point very well when he built the bass trombone in F *à tubes indépendants*; this trombone has seven independent tubes and six valves. The idea was to build the valve trombone without the defects inherent in the combination of valves on the ordinary three-valve instruments. See Note 381 for further references.

P. 139 289 *Clarinblasen.* The 'Clarinblasen' (clarino-playing) in its proper sense designates the lip technique employed in playing partial tones on the low-pitched trumpets in their highest register. As explained by Mr. W. F. H. Blandford, in "The 'Bach' Trumpet," *Monthly Musical Record*, May, 1935, p. 73, the term 'Clarino' found in the scores of old masters denotes the register, not an instrument; it meant the trumpet. In this study the meaning of the term 'Clarinblasen' (or its English equivalent) is extended to describe the ability to produce high tones on brass instruments beyond the range of the average player. See Note 426. In this sense the extended meaning is practically equivalent to Praetorius' 'Falset-Stimme'; cf. his *De Organographia*, p. 12.

P. 140 290 *Limit.* The high trumpet part (in F) of the *Second Brandenburg Concerto* of J. S. Bach is not playable on the B-flat trumpet.

291 *Overtones.* Cf. D. C. Miller, *The Science of Musical Sounds*, p. 202, The Horn. Fig. 152 shows the form of the tone of the horn (D-75 cycles per second); the analysis of this tone shows the presence of an entire series of partials up to thirty.

292 *Register.* This point is discussed at length on pp. 145 f.

P. 141 293 *Almost superfluous.* The first valve horns and trumpets were built with two valves. The reason is that in the third and fourth octave the partial tones of both the horns and the low-pitched trumpets are spaced at close intervals; the largest important interval to be filled with valved tones is a fourth between the third and fourth partial tones. In this interval only one tone (g-sharp) requires the third valve, and even this tone can be played with the first valve, although with some difficulty. If this one tone is sacrificed, the most used range of tones on the horn and the trumpet can be played *chromatically* with two valves only.

294 *Post-horn.* Such instruments as the two-valve cornopean No. 184 and many others in existence show that, perhaps, at the beginning of the introduction of valves the difference between the four-octave instruments (the horns and trumpets) and the three-octave instruments (the bugles and post-horns) was not very clearly understood. As just stated in the previous Note, it is possible to omit the third valve on the horns and trumpets. On the three-octave instruments the most important interval to be filled with the valved tones is a fifth between the second and third partial tones. To produce even a diatonic scale the third valve is necessary to the three-octave instruments. The ancestor of the cornet-à-pistons is the French type post-horn. The

German post-horns are really the trumpets (see remarks under No. 213, p. 198).

P. 141 295 *Four valves.* Cf. Georges Kastner, *Manuel général de musique militaire*, Paris, 1848. The family of saxhorns with four piston valves is represented on plate xx, and the family of saxhorns with three valves is represented on plate xxiii of that book. The four-valve saxhorns form a complete family and range from the high-pitched sopranino saxhorn in E-flat to the bass saxhorn in E-flat. The fourth valve on all these instruments is the *Quartventil*, adding five semitones or a fourth, and not a tricky 'echo' valve. The existence of these instruments for some reason has been overlooked, yet they prove conclusively that all saxhorns are whole-tube instruments. Therefore the division of saxhorns into two groups, the upper saxhorns (half-tube) and the lower saxhorns or tubas, accepted among British writers on instruments, is not correct, unless properly qualified by the statement that it is a musical and not an acoustical division.

296 *Trombone.* The family of saxotrombas is represented on table xxi of the *Manuel général de musique militaire.* The note states (translated): 'Family of saxotrombas. Instruments of new proportions holding a place, for quality of sound, between the Bugle, the Ophicleide and Cornet, the Trumpet and the Trombone.'

297 *Tone.* The only saxtuba known to the writer is now in the Crosby Brown Collection of the Metropolitan Museum of Art, New York, and is listed in its *Catalogue*, i, p. 194 (1902 ed.) as "No. 1109. Bombardon. Bass in E-flat. Brass, with three pump valves. The tube forming the bell makes a large sweep over the head of the player. Inscribed: Adolphe Sax, Paris, No. 13802." The tube is shaped like an ancient Roman *cornu* or *buccina.* The instrument is, undoubtedly, a saxtuba.

298 *Post-horns.* The Crosby Brown Collection has a B-flat tenor cornopean with two valves, no. 2412. The existence of such an instrument proves that the cornet family was developed at least to a tonal position of the tenor.

299 *Low.* As shown on p. 155, trumpets are alto and tenor instruments. Since these trumpets are fatiguing to play, they were seldom used as melodic instruments.

P. 142 300 *Clear.* The high C trumpet is chosen for comparison instead of that in B-flat for convenience in illustrating the tonal position of three-octave instruments. The trumpet players in the Boston Symphony Orchestra use the high C trumpets.

301 *Inferior.* The case of the B-flat trumpet is somewhat similar to that of the B-flat horn. The demands on trumpet players in the modern symphony orchestra are too exacting and breaks are not forgiven. The parts are placed high and are difficult technically. Trumpet parts found in classical scores, with the exception of certain very low tones, may be transposed on modern instruments. The old low trumpets are fatiguing to play and their tones break almost as easily as those of the horn. Finally, the modern idea of blending the tonal palette is better met by the B-flat trumpet, since it blends admirably with the trombone. Acoustically the B-flat trumpet is the soprano valve trombone. So the missing soprano voice of the trombone choir is found once more! If composers and conductors were to exercise their sense of humor, they would see that the modern orchestra is left without a real trumpet. For particulars see Note 345.

302 *Improved.* Three-octave instruments, with the exceptions mentioned below, are not on the same artistic and tonal level as the horns and low trumpets. Their utterances have force and directness, but are devoid of subtlety and nobility. Slide trombones are an exception; when played properly they are serious and noble instruments. Among the conoidal bore instruments there are two which deserve attention because of their fine tone: the tenorhorn (the tenor cornet preferably, especially when played with elongated cup mouthpiece) and the euphonium (the baritone saxhorn with a wide bore; the 'tenor tuba' of the orchestra, not to be confused with the Wagner tenor tuba). The bass tuba is not handled with understanding by some orchestral composers. On this point Mr. Cecil Forsyth, *Orchestration*, p. 159, has many true things to say.

P. 144 303 *Horn Trio.* The quotation is borrowed from Mr. Henry S. Drinker, Jr., *The Chamber Music of Johannes Brahms*, Philadelphia, 1932, pp. 111 f. In the same work is contained the additional testimony of Clara Schumann, who included the *Horn Trio* in her repertoire. On her concert tour she tried, not always successfully, to persuade the prominent local hornists to play the *Trio* on the hand horn. Some of them preferred the relative security of the valve horn to the more difficult technique of the hand horn. See Note 398. On the opposing side, see Berlioz and Strauss, *Instrumentationslehre*, p. 265. Berlioz is only partly correct in pointing out the defects of hand-stopping technique on the horn. His criticism applies only to bad playing, when the tone of the hand horn is forced and the open tones are played too loudly. Likewise Mr. Cecil Forsyth's remarks on p. 77 of his *Orchestration* should be taken with a grain of salt. After all, there was something in the tonal quality of the hand horn which appealed to such musicians as Clara Schumann and Brahms. A modern performance of the *Horn Trio* is a caricature of Brahms' original intentions. The piano of magnificent sonorities is banged 'brilliantly,' the violin screeches at the top of its voice, and the modern wide-bore horn, muffled not too discreetly, competes with the rest. "The tone is rough from the beginning."

P. 145 304 *Cavalry trumpeters.* See *Arban's Method for the Trumpet or Cornet,* Carl Fischer, New York, p. 2. The fourth valve serves also as a correction valve in the low register. C. Sachs, *Real-Lexikon,* p. 399 b, gives a valve arrangement which is very unusual and not typical. Before the present standard valve arrangement became established, the sequence of ½, 1, 1½ tones was also in use; the horn No. 195 of this Collection has a semitone valve as the first valve. The set of Wagner tubas described by Dr. Sachs was, undoubtedly, especially built for players used to the old arrangement.

P. 146 305 *Alto horns.* The highest pitched instrument which can be compared by its tonal qualities with the horn is Červeny's *Primhorn* or *Octavhorn* in F. It is one octave higher than the French horn in F, or in the same tonal position as the alto trumpet in F; therefore an alto instrument. Although built like the French horn with wide bell and played with a French horn mouthpiece, it is not a French horn but an alto horn-tuba. Its tone is pleasant and reminds one of the horn, yet is not a true horn tone. On the opposite end of the register, the B-flat basso horn by its tonal position is a contrabass instrument, but its tonal qualities are distinctly not those of the contrabass. The tubing is so long (576 cm., as stated) and narrow that it is not in good pitch and not sonorous in the low register, where a contrabass instrument should be at its best. If the bore is increased sufficiently to improve the tonal qualities in the low register, the modified horn displays the characteristics of a three-octave instrument; or, to put it bluntly, the horn becomes a narrow bore contrabass saxhorn.

The last statement may seem incredible to some. So the following example is selected because the statement can be checked with the instruments easily available. Few people, even those interested in musical instruments, realize that the French horn in E-flat and the bass tuba in E-flat are both bass instruments. (The same applies to the F-horn and the F-tuba.) The theoretical length of both instruments is the same: 442.2 cm. The partial tones of their natural scale are therefore of the same pitch. Assuming that the bass tuba has only three valves, both instruments descend chromatically to *AA* of the contra octave. This tone is in unison with the lowest tone of the bassoon with the low A extension bell. The bass tuba can play its pedal tone and the horn cannot. Yet from *AA* up to *e'*-flat (the eighth partial tone of the natural scale of both instruments and the limiting tone of the upward reach of the tuba, that is to say for the whole chromatic playing range of the three-valved tuba), the French horn in E-flat duplicates the tones of the tuba, each for each. It is at this point that similarity stops. The tuba has sonorous, full, organ-like tones in the lower register. The horn has rich, beautiful tones in the same register, but they lack sonority and breadth. The greatest difference between the two instruments comes in their upper register. Above the fifth partial tone the tuba begins to sound thin and strained. The horn has its best middle register between the fourth and the eighth partial tones and adds a whole chromatic octave up to *e''*-flat, its sixteenth partial tone. This last mentioned tone is heard every time the E-flat horns play the famous horn trio passage in the Scherzo movement of Beethoven's *Eroica*; in that place the first hornist ascends to *e''*-flat and the second descends to *E*-flat, the second partial tone of his instrument, three octaves lower.

This example proves that an increase of sonority in the lower register can be achieved only by increasing the bore and widening the taper of the tube. When this is done sufficiently, the tone quality and the whole character of the instrument change completely. The writer does not know of any example which illustrates so well the profound difference between three-octave instruments (the tuba in this case) and four-octave instruments (the horn).

306 *Instruments.* The B-flat horn (*alto*) is close to the limit of tolerable impairment of the horn tone. Exceptional players can produce fine tone; the average player has the 'sandy' quality on the B-flat horn. The high C-crook was discarded because it sounded rough.

307 *Tubing.* A change of mouthpiece may affect the specific characteristic of the tube. The emission of the pedal tone may be facilitated or hindered. On this point, cf. F. W. Galpin, *A Textbook of European Musical Instruments,* 1937, p. 220, where a change in the type of mouthpiece on Neuschel's trombone is described (partly quoted here in Note 319 below). An unsuitable mouthpiece, like that fitted into post-horn No. 213, may affect the tone color and may reduce the number of partial tones producible. Nevertheless, if a reasonable limitation on deviation from the best tone color which is characteristic of a given instrument is imposed (this means the mouthpiece cannot deviate too much from the accepted type), then the changes in acoustical characteristics will be very slight. Therefore, the proportion of tubing is the determining factor.

P. 147 308 *Pedal tone.* The low-pitched members of the cornet family have been experimented with, but have proven unsuitable; even wide bore contrabass tubas are not entirely satisfactory at the bottom of their scale.

P. 147 309 *Conoidal.* The term 'conoid' has several meanings. One of them refers to the solids formed by the revolution of such curves as a parabola, or hyperbola, around their axes. Another recognized meaning of a conoid used throughout this study is 'shaped like a cone.' Cf. *The Century Dictionary*, 1914, p. 1201, s.v. 'Conoid.'

P. 148 310 *Instruments.* Cf. C. Sachs, *Sammlung . . .*, pp. 215–216, figures 23 and 24, where the scales (*Mensuren*) of the tubes are graphically compared; relative lengths of the conoidal and the cylindrical portions there shown are not absolute, as can be seen by the relative lengths of the trombone tube represented there.

311 *Semi-spherical.* Only a few old trumpet mouthpieces had an approximately semi-spherical cup. The majority had an ovoidal cup resembling a paraboloid.

312 *Partial tones.* Much valuable information about mouthpieces can be found in a booklet by Vincent Bach, *The Art of Trumpet Playing*, New York, 1925.

313 *Piano.* The writer is thinking primarily of the low-pitched four-octave trumpet.

P. 149 314 *Properties.* There are two types of classification of musical instruments. One, the Mahillon-Galpin type, is based primarily on the playing technique of instruments and secondarily on their structure. Another, the Hornbostel-Sachs type, is based primarily and almost exclusively on their structure. The aerophones disclose nothing of their acoustical properties from their structure until actually tested (assuming that no previous knowledge is available). It seems, therefore, that a correct type of classification, yet to be worked out, should combine both principles, since the strictly structural basis for aerophones permits their classification into cylindrical and conoidal instruments only.

P. 150 315 *Conoidal bore instruments.* Exactly: the cornet-à-pistons has a conoidal-cylindro-conoidal tube; some flügelhorns have the same type of bore, but of different taper. Some flügelhorns have a cylindro-conoidal bore, if the tuning is done by a sliding tube inserted into the mouthpipe as is done on the French army bugle.

316 *Fine.* On this point we have the testimony of M. Gabriel Parès, the bandmaster of the Garde Républicaine band in Paris. Cf. his *Traité d'instrumentation et d'orchestration à l'usage des musiques militaires*, Paris, 1898, p. 93, the end of paragraph 192; also paragraph 194.

317 *Mouthpiece.* There are no 'standard model' conoidal bore instruments. The bore taper is selected by each maker. In addition, several bores are provided for the same type of instrument. Thus a large Bohemian firm manufacturing brass instruments lists three bores for soprano flügelhorns, accommodating each voice in its proper register.

318 *Traditional families.* The 'army trombones' of Červeny belong to the same family group as the saxotrombas. The proportions of the tubes of the two kinds of instruments differ, but not sufficiently to justify their separation into two distinct types.

P. 151 319 *Separate instruments.* These principles seem obvious and elementary, yet their application to actual analysis is not so simple. If one should deal with natural instruments alone, the problem would be complex enough. As M. Gevaert, the author of *Nouveau traité d'instrumentation* (1885), pointed out, the natural horns and trumpets with crooks have the most complex technique. His book proves it, since over ten per cent of the whole is devoted to its exposition. An analysis of Canon Galpin's new redefinition of Dr. Schafhäutl's terms *Ganz-Instrument* (the whole-tube instrument) and *Halb-Instrument* (the half-tube instrument) may show how difficult it is to avoid the pitfalls of cross-division. The following passage is found on p. 220 of Canon Galpin's book, *A Textbook of European Musical Instruments.* With reference to the lip-vibrated instruments it is stated: "A division, too, of these instruments into *Ganz-instrumente* (complete) and *Halb-instrumente* (incomplete) is popular in Germany, but such terms must not be used capriciously. A 'complete' instrument is one which employs the lower octaves of harmonics [partial tones] and has its scale diatonically and chromatically perfected by mechanical means — finger-holes, keys, or valves. The cornetts and ophicleide group are therefore *Ganz-instrumente*, and also the deep tubas with four valves and the seven-cylinder trombones. The bugles, horns, and trumpets are *Halb-instrumente*, because they are not complete in the scale of the lower harmonics. It is misleading to define a *Ganz-instrument* as one that will produce more easily its fundamental harmonic, for that largely depends on the shape and size of the mouthpiece and the ability of the performer. With a tenor trombone in our collection made by Neuschel of Nürnberg in 1557 there are two old ivory mouthpieces, apparently original; one is similar in size and cup to that usually found on a tenor trombone; the other has a deeply conical cup and a broad rim. With the former the fundamental note is treacherous; with the other it speaks at once. But we should not call it therefore a *Ganz-instrument*, because its lowest octave is still incomplete."

There are several specific statements which can be questioned in this quotation. But the writer finds himself most unable to agree with the new definitions of the terms *Ganz-* and *Halb-Instrument.* Canon Galpin's new terms 'complete' and 'incomplete' fill a long felt want for terms which may serve to discriminate the instruments having a complete chromatic scale from the pedal tone ('fundamental harmonic') upward, and those which begin their chromatic scale from the augmented fourth above the pedal tone. But, as we shall see presently, the terms 'complete' and 'incomplete' supplement but do not replace the old German division. In further discussion only the valve instruments will be considered.

The principal difficulty arising from Canon Galpin's new definition of the old German terms is the double *fundamentum divisionis*. Explicitly stated, the *fundamentum* in this definition is a structural basis, namely, the number of valves. A four-valved tuba is a 'complete' instrument because it can play a complete chromatic scale from the pedal tone upward. A three-valved tuba made on precisely the same pattern and therefore having an identical natural scale (including a playable pedal tone) is an 'incomplete' instrument because the elimination of the fourth valve no longer permits one to descend chromatically to the pedal tone. The implicitly assumed *fundamentum divisionis* is the presence or absence of the pedal tone, because it would be useless to add the fourth valve to an instrument having no pedal tone. If a proper sequence of classificational steps is to be maintained, such an important *fundamentum* should not be implicitly assumed. The correct sequence is (1) to ascertain if a tube of given proportions has the pedal tone; this property does not depend upon the number of valves; (2) to classify an instrument as 'complete' or 'incomplete,' depending upon the number of its valves. In other words, the more general characteristic should take precedence over the less general one. The cross-division which results from neglecting to follow this sequence can best be illustrated by the following example. The French horn in F and the bass tuba in F have their second partial tone at precisely the same pitch (*F* of the great octave). Let us assume that the bass tuba in F has three valves (the majority of them are built thus). According to Canon Galpin's definition both instruments are incomplete, because each has only three valves; therefore, they belong to the same sub-group. Yet there is an essential difference between the two instruments: the French horn in F will always remain an 'incomplete' instrument; the bass tuba in F can be furnished with a fourth valve and thus become a 'complete' instrument. Why? Because the bass tuba has the pedal tone and the French horn in F has not. Therefore, though essentially the same instrument, the bass tuba in F may belong to either of two sub-groups, complete or incomplete instruments, depending on a purely accidental structural characteristic. Such is the logical fallacy of cross-division or overlapping classes. It seems to us that Dr. Schathäutl's terms, *Ganz-* and *Halb-Instrument*, should be left as defined by him, since they are indispensable for the acoustical classification of tubes into specific groups. Canon Galpin's division is also indispensable, but should take its proper place on the classificational ladder, that is, when the completeness or incompleteness of the chromatic scale with respect to the pedal tone is considered. The whole argument can be summarized briefly thus: in the classification of the brass instruments the natural scale takes precedence over the mechanically produced chromatic scale. To determine a natural scale a simple tube is all that is necessary.

320 *Aerophones*. The term 'family' is used here in a generic sense. This becomes clear when bugles are examined. There is a difference between the saxhorn and the flügelhorn: the size of taper is different. The saxhorn has a narrower taper than the flügelhorn. Therefore if there is any difference between a saxhorn and a flügelhorn it will be a noticeable, but slight difference in tone color. Otherwise the instruments are exactly alike in their basic acoustical properties. Generically both the saxhorns and flügelhorns are bugles. P. 152

321 *Without pedal tone*. Acoustically the cornet family is the most difficult to describe. During its evolution several important changes were made. The prototype of the cornets is a circular-wound post-horn with a narrow-tapered conoidal bore and deep cup mouthpiece. Nomenclature in French: *cornet, cornet ordinaire, cornet de poste*. When the valves were added to this post-horn, it was changed to resemble the trumpet and became known as the cornopean, and later, the cornet-à-pistons. The early valved cornets had the deep cup mouthpiece of their ancestor. When it was discovered that the trumpet parts could be played more easily on the cornet, the cup of the mouthpiece was made almost as shallow as that of the trumpet, but the backbore and short shank of the cornet mouthpiece were retained. In the early nineteenth century the cornet was crooked down as low as D. See Note 322 for reference. Berlioz states that the pedal tone of the soprano cornet in C is 'bad,' that in B-flat is 'very bad,' and that in A 'still worse'; in the lower tonalities the pedal tone is disregarded completely. The cornet in F starts its scale with the second partial tone, since the valve tones below that are out of tune. The cornet crooked in D starts with the third partial tone, because the ratio of the bore to the length of tubing of the cornet crooked in this tonality is such that the lower register is out of tune. Thus the low-pitched cornet in D had, practically, the same compass as the cornet crooked in B-flat, a minor sixth higher!

The lower-pitched cornets were discarded by the middle of the nineteenth century in favor of more practicable tonalities (see Note 322 below). The cornets have not remained without competitors. The saxhorns and flügelhorns had a better tone than the old-fashioned cornets. So the cornet had the bore taper widened and acquired a pedal tone of good quality. One is at a loss whether to classify some modern cornets as wide-bore cornets or narrow-bore flügelhorns. It can readily be seen that it is rather difficult to assign the cornet to a proper subgroup. In this study, to avoid historical and musical complications, the cornet is regarded as a half-tube instrument without pedal tone. In some cases this is a compromise classification, more correct musically than acoustically. It might be questioned whether such an unstable characteristic as the presence or absence of the pedal tone should be considered in scientific classification at all. The answer to the negative contention is, that running away from difficulties is not a scientific attitude; besides, the complex properties of the brass instruments cannot be intelligently known without ascertaining the behavior of a given instrumental type with respect to the pedal tone; much can be learned from the study of different members of the same family. Note 349 and Note 382 should be consulted in this connection.

P. 152

322 *The Cornet in B-flat.* Berlioz in *Instrumentationslehre,* revised by R. Strauss, 1905, pp. 315, 317, lists eleven cornets in tonalities ranging from C to low D. F. L. Schubert in his *Katechismus* (1862) enumerates a whole series of cornets, from B-flat to low C. It seems that most of these tonalities were somewhat theoretical, especially in the low register. Schubert himself (p. 66) states that the best tonalities of cornets were B-flat, A, A-flat, and G. This sounds more sensible.

323 *The Althorn in F.* The Bohemian manufacturer's catalogue (1910) lists the 'Alt-Cornet,' a cornet made in the form of an althorn and pitched in F or in E-flat. Its tube differs from that of the alto bugle.

324 *The Tenorhorn in B-flat.* The lowest tonal position of the old type cornet which the writer is able to trace is that of the tenor. The Crosby Brown Collection has a cornopean (no. 2412) with two valves, the tenor in B-flat. For a long time makers kept the tenorhorn in the cornet family. A true tenorhorn is a comparatively narrow bore instrument, more adapted for playing in the higher register than the baritone. Like all cornets, it possesses a greater agility than the bugle of the same tonal position. The old bandmasters had three or four tenorhorns in their bands. Except for the first one, they either played with the althorns or doubled the trombones in certain passages. The first tenorhorn played in unison with the solo baritone, but seldom followed it in the lower register, when the latter instrument was used to support the basses. The principal use of the first tenorhorn was to play countermotives, and in the upper register its parts were more florid than those of the baritone. It is fine as a solo instrument. It should not be confused with the tenor bugle, which is also called the tenorhorn. The British persist in applying the term 'tenorhorn' to the althorn in E-flat. It should be stated also that there is a group of Červeny's 'Cornet-Instrumente,' patented by him in 1876, which were built in a circular form and ranged from the sopranino in E-flat to the contrabass in BB-flat. This family should be classed as narrow taper bugles played with a deep elongated-cup mouthpiece; therefore Červeny 'cornets' should not be confused with the cornet-à-pistons. Hence the statement that the true small-bore, narrow-taper cornets were not built deeper in pitch than the tenor is not affected by the fact that there is the contrabass 'cornet' of Červeny. Dr. P. A. Scholes commented (*The Oxford Companion to Music,* p. 832, note 3) that "the muddles of nomenclature in relation to this (saxhorn) family of instruments are diabolic." This is true not only in relation to saxhorns but to the rest of the brasses.

325 *Horn-tubas.* This name is suggested for the family of instruments of which there are at least three sub-families: the Wagner tubas, cornons (Červeny), and cornophones (Fontaine-Besson). All instruments belonging to these sub-families are played with funnel-shaped mouthpieces of the French horn type. The Wagner tubas, as already stated, are played by French horn players, who use the same mouthpieces interchangeably. Another peculiarity of the Wagner tubas is the left-hand valve mechanism to accommodate horn players, who alone of all brass instrumentalists use the left hand for operating the valves. Cornons and cornophones have right-hand valves. To prevent confusion, this group should be recognized as a separate entity.

In the technical description one item is omitted, the generic classification of horn tubas. The reason is that two families, the cornons and cornophones, are extended into the tonal positions above the horn in B-flat *alto.* Červeny builds the alto cornons in E-flat and in F. Cornophones of higher pitch are the alto in E-flat and soprano in B-flat. As already stated, the horns in the alto and soprano tonal positions are no longer four-octave instruments. The compass of cornophones given on p. 16 of Pierre's book confirms this statement. The tenor instruments are more properly classified as three-octave whole-tube instruments; although they ascend (with some difficulty) as high as the twelfth partial tone (this is true of the Wagner tenor tuba, tenor cornon, and tenor cornophone), yet their tone color is more akin to that of the tenorhorn. Only the bass instruments pitched in F and E-flat, and Červeny's contrabass cornon in BB-flat, are four-octave instruments (no pedals). Therefore the horn-tuba family consists largely of three-octave whole-tube instruments; only the bass and contrabass instruments are four-octave half-tube instruments.

P. 152 326 *Cornophones.* Cf. C. Sachs, *Real-Lexikon*, p. 95 b, s.v. 'Cornophone.'

327 *E-flat.* Cf. C. Pierre, *La facture instrumentale*, p. 17, where three cornophones are pictured. Červeny's cornons, to the writer's knowledge, are not illustrated anywhere except in the firm's catalogue.

328 *Six valves.* V. F. Červeny made the bombardon in F with six rotary valves.

329 *Saxhorns.* At present there are no dimensional standards which would permit one to say definitely that a given instrument is a soprano saxhorn. Each maker has his own ideas as to what the proportions of tubes should be. Sometimes bugles of the same tonal position differ in their bores and tapers, and in one case they bear different names. For instance, there are four bugles in B-flat and by their tonal position baritones: (1) a narrow-bore bugle with a moderate taper called tenorhorn (not to be confused with the real tenorhorn of the cornet family); (2) a medium-bore bugle, the baritone; (3) a wide-bore bugle, the euphonium; (4) a still wider-bore bugle, the bass tuba (also called the 'Tenorbass'; the 'baroxyton' of Červeny). All these instruments have the same acoustical properties: all are three-octave whole-tube instruments. They differ only in tone color, which becomes broader and more solid in the lower register as the bore and taper size increases. The best possible statement to make at present is that the saxhorns have a rather narrow taper, the flügelhorns have a medium taper, and the bugle-tuba group has a wide taper.

330 *In F.* There are still higher pitched bugles in B-flat and C, an octave above the soprano instrument; they are too difficult to play and have been discarded.

331 *In B-flat.* The soprano flügelhorn is also called in Germany the 'Diskant-Tuba.' Cf. F. L. Schubert, *Katechismus der Musik-Instrumente*, Leipzig, 1862, p. 63; C. Sachs, *Real-Lexikon*, p. 112 a, s.v. 'Diskanttuba.' The origin of the word flügelhorn is variously explained. The most plausible derivation of the term is given by Schubert (p. 48); according to him the valveless flügelhorn was used as an instrument for signalling the movements of the wing of army units (called *Flügel* in German); hence the name 'flügelhorn.' For another explanation, cf. Arthur A. Clappé, *The Wind-Band and its Instruments*, New York, 1911, p. 41.

332 *In E-flat.* In Germany the althorn is also called the 'Alt-tuba'; cf. F. L. Schubert, *op. cit.*, p. 63. It should be remarked that the old Prussian 'Cornet' is a bugle with a straight conical bell which has a very small flare. Schubert used the terms 'Cornet,' 'Flügelhorn,' 'Tuba' interchangeably for designation of various members of the bugle family. The term 'tuba' is used in England for the lower-pitched bugles only, which are referred to sometimes as the 'British tubas'; since similar instruments are made in other countries the term is a misnomer.

P. 153 333 *Euphonium in B-flat.* The term 'Euphonium' or 'Euphonion' originally referred to the bass ophicleide. F. L. Schubert, *op. cit.*, p. 53, pictures and describes 'das Euphonion' with three valves, pitched in C, B-flat, and A, with a comparatively narrow bore. In German and Russian military bands this instrument, in the middle of the nineteenth century, was used instead of the bassoon. The modern instrument is a wide-bored bugle with four or five valves, the busiest and most useful instrument in the band; an excellent solo instrument.

334 *Bass in B-flat.* Already alluded to in Note 329. F. L. Schubert, *op. cit.*, p. 52, describes it as a large-bore bugle which replaces the tenorbass trombone and is intended to play "the deep tones of the bass tuba one octave higher in the low tenor position." On p. 53 he adds: "it heightens the strength of the deeper basses by its assistance." This practice is similar to that of doubling the string double basses by playing the violoncellos an octave higher. In the Russian army bands this type of instrument was, at one time, officially adopted for its bass section. Nomenclature: the bass in B-flat; the tenorbass; the Primbass; the baroxyton.

335 *Bass tuba in F.* Also called the bombardon. In the Russian army bands the bass tuba in E-flat was called the 'middle bass,' since it played either in unison or, sometimes, an octave above the BB-flat tubas.

336 *In BB-flat.* The largest standard instrument; built in the straight tuba model and the circular model. The latter is built in several forms: (1) the helicon, having a straight bell pointed toward the left or right side of the player; (2) the sousaphone, with a bent bell-joint and bell pointed upward; (3) the modern model (misnamed 'sousaphone'), with a doubly bent bell-joint and an adjustable bell placed in a vertical plane. The circular model carried over the shoulder is not confined to this type; there is a family of helicons also. Beginning with the alto instrument, all of them are made to be carried over the shoulder. See Metropolitan Museum of Art, *Catalogue of the Crosby Brown Collection*, i, 1902, p. 190.

337 *Sub-bass tuba in EE-flat.* This giant instrument is

pitched one octave lower than the E-flat tuba. The first instrument of this type was built by A. Sax for the Paris Universal Exposition of 1855. Cf. *Encyclopédie de la musique* pt. ii, vol. iii, p. 1675, fig. 735, for a picture; the French name is 'sax-bourdon en mi-bemol' or 'sax-horn bourdon.'

P. 153

338 *Sub-contrabass tuba in BBB-flat.* The largest practicable directly controlled instrument that a man can play. The first sub-contrabass tuba in BBB-flat was built by A. Sax in 1855, as was that mentioned in Note 337. It is pitched one octave lower than the contrabass tuba in BB-flat. Here are the dimensions of one built for the Gilmore Band and used at the World's Columbian Exposition in Chicago in 1893: height, 208 cm.; width, 78 cm.; diameter of bell, 80 cm.; initial bore, 2 cm.; bore at the valves, 2.5 cm.; length of air column (approx.), 1110 cm. This tuba descends easily to its second partial tone and is a fine practicable instrument musically. It has two structural defects: (1) there are only three valves without any compensation; (2) the straight tuba model is too cumbersome. The writer is indebted to Mr. F. E. Burgstaller of Carl Fischer, Inc., of Boston for permission to measure and test the instrument.

339 *Four-octave instruments.* Lest there be some misunderstanding, it should be said that the horn players of symphony orchestras, in this country at least, are supposed to master the whole register of their instrument. The high B-flat horn is playable, by practised lips, from the pedal tone of the third valve (*GG*; G_{20} of the contra octave) up to its sixteenth partial tone. The F-horn is playable from *BB* (its lowest F-sharp note played with three valves down); the second horn player is required to hold the tone *C*, one octave above *CC* of the double bassoon, for nine opening bars, *legato*, *forte*, in the first movement of the C-minor symphony of Brahms. This is done on the F-horn with the first and the third valves down, the low G of the F-horn. (Brahms wrote for 'Hörner in C,' of course!) At the other extreme of the compass the first horn player is required to play, without hesitation, the sixteenth partial tone of the horn in E in the second movement of Beethoven's D-major symphony and *piano* at that!

340 *Horn family.* The narrow-bore cornets in the soprano position might be regarded, in a certain sense, as soprano horns, but they are three-octave instruments with an entirely different tone color. The alto instrument, the Primhorn in F of Červeny is, as shown in Note 305, a narrow-bore horn-tuba, also a three-octave instrument. The B-flat horn, it seems, is the limit of true four-octave instruments still retaining the real horn tone. It would be rash to say that an extension of the horn tone into higher tonal positions is impossible, but thus far no one has succeeded in producing real soprano and alto horns.

341 *Within the family.* See pp. 137 f.

342 *B-flat.* No. 199 of this Collection is a real soprano slide trombone. At present several American instrument makers build a 'soprano slide cornet,' a misnamed soprano slide trombone played with a cornet mouthpiece. Why 'cornet'?

P. 154

343 *Trombone in C.* The tenor trombone No. 201 of this Collection is in C. At least one American maker still lists the slide trombone in C.

344 *Tenorbass trombone in B-flat.* F. L. Schubert defines it as a tenor trombone with a large bore; cf. his *Katechismus*, p. 70. The modern instrument has a *Quartventil* operated by a thumb-valve, changing it to a *Quartposaune* in F.

345 *Trumpet model.* Much of the confusion in the brass wind instrument nomenclature arises from the fact that the acoustical designation and the model name of the instrument do not always coincide. As stated in Note 226, the shape into which the tube is bent to form a model is not important, as long as the bore is kept geometrically similar to one with an imaginary straight centerline. As long as this requirement is fulfilled, the acoustical properties of the tube remain unchanged. Therefore, not every instrument in a trumpet shape is a trumpet. A trombone tube bent into a 'trumpet' model does not necessarily become a trumpet. The well known misnomer is the 'bass' trumpet, which really is a valve trombone. So far as the writer knows, no one has investigated conclusively the real acoustical status of the modern high-pitched trumpets. Here is the general logical chain of reasoning applying to the octave, sopranino, soprano, some alto (the tromba contralta of N. A. Rimsky-Korsakov, Note 428; R. Wagner's 'bass' trumpet in E-flat), and 'bass' trumpets:

First comes a structural examination. The tube of a given instrument is found to be two-thirds cylindrical and one-third conoidal; such tubes are briefly referred to as 'cylindrical.' This is the generic structural characteristic of both the trombone and the trumpet tubes. Even the use of a trumpet mouthpiece does not settle conclusively the acoustical standing of the instrument. The actual playing test is necessary. A given cylindrical tube instrument is classified as a 'trombone,' if its natural scale is of the three-octave type, i.e., playable up to the eighth partial tone inclusive, under average practical conditions. If its natural scale is of the four-octave type, i.e., playable up to the sixteenth partial tone inclusive, then the instrument is a 'trumpet.' Let us select the soprano 'trumpet' in B-flat, a modern and widely used instrument. Is it a 'trumpet' in a strictly technical sense?

No! Why? Because its natural scale is of the three-octave type. Therefore its tube is the tube of a soprano trombone; since the instrument has a valve mechanism, it is a soprano valve trombone; having a trumpet mouthpiece, it is a soprano valve trombone with a trumpet mouthpiece. Hence, the modern B-flat soprano 'trumpet' is, acoustically, a soprano valve trombone played with a trumpet mouthpiece. This strictly scientific classification eliminates heretofore existing confusion, since there is a real four-octave tenor trumpet in B-flat playing at the same pitch as the modern trumpet. — For an organologist there are no 'obsolete' instruments; only instruments varying in their type, structure, and different degrees of tonal qualities. — For the lack of a generally accepted alternative term, the modern trumpets are called in this study the trumpets. So there still remains the difficulty of overlapping nomenclature. It could be eliminated by adopting for the modern trumpet the name 'trumpetina,' suggested, with a little malice, in the late nineteenth century by the players who still knew the superior tonal qualities of the real trumpets. (As also their defects, it should be added.) So the trumpets proper will be referred to as the 'real' or 'classical' trumpets. This designation will be applied also to such valved trumpets as retain the tonal position, tonal qualities, and acoustical properties of the old natural trumpets; structurally their tubes should be identical with the latter. The necessity of this qualification will become apparent after reading Note 428 in which the tromba contralta in F is described.

On the basis of the preceding, it is possible to suggest a following broad principle: the structural characteristics are necessary, but not sufficient for proper classification of lip-vibrated aerophones ('brass wind'); their complex acoustical properties have to be considered before an assignment to a proper family or sub-family becomes possible. Please read also Note 418 and Note 424.

P. 154

346 *In F.* These high-pitched instruments are used for playing the high trumpet part in J. S. Bach's *Second Brandenburg Concerto.* See Note 429. The sopranino trumpet in D is built primarily for J. S. Bach and Handel high trumpet parts. It is half as long as the classical trumpet of that period. Tonally it is inferior to its noble predecessor, the name of which it usurps.

347 *Contralta in F.* This instrument, originally conceived (in Russia at least) by N. A. Rimsky-Korsakov, is an alto valve trombone built in the trumpet form and played with a trumpet type mouthpiece. It is not equivalent to the 'bass' trumpet in E-flat of R. Wagner; the latter is played with the trombone mouthpiece. See Note 428 for detailed discussion of the tromba contralta.

P. 155

348 *Saxotrombas.* This name is no longer proprietary. The saxotromba family of A. Sax and the 'army trombone' family of Červeny cannot be classified as valve trombones. The latter still have the same proportion of tubes as the slide instruments, whereas the former two families have the cylindrical portion of their tubes shorter, the conoidal part longer and with a wider taper.

349 *Instruments.* The problem of the pedal tone for the whole family can be settled only by considering the behavior of all the members of the family. A musical tone should have a certain minimum of quality to sound acceptably to the ear. It is possible, after practice, to get out something resembling a pedal tone on the low-pitched trumpet; yet this tone should be more correctly described as an 'unpitched sound.' The old German name for it, *Flattergrob* ('a rough unsteady flutter'), a precise description, cannot be improved upon. Much can be learned about a trumpet crooked in a given tonality by the study of its second partial tone: if this tone is not certain in quality or intonation, the pedal tone is even worse. Not only the second but also the third partial tone of the low trumpets in A, B-flat, and B is out of tune. On the trumpets in C and D the second partial tone sounds rather uncertain. On E-flat trumpets the second partial tone sounds very fine and strong if the mouthpiece has a large throat diameter, as is the case on No. 209; the D valve trumpet in the writer's possession, played with a normal trumpet mouthpiece, produces a barely acceptable second partial tone. The F-trumpet and higher (G-flat and G) have their natural scale beginning with the pedal tone in tune. Berlioz remarked that the pedal tone of these trumpets has an extraordinary fulness of sound. (Cf. Berlioz, *Instrumentationslehre*, rev. by Strauss, p. 301 a, note.) The upper register of the trumpets as given by Berlioz represents an average French trumpeter of the particular period when Berlioz wrote his treatise on instrumentation. According to him they were inferior to the English and German trumpeters. With the recovery of the 'Clarinblasen' technique the upper limit of an average player should be set as the sixteenth partial tone for the alto trumpet in F.

350 *In E.* Berlioz speaks of the second partial tone of the trumpet in E being of mediocre quality; its pedal tone is not musically acceptable. For these reasons it is set in this study as a dividing line in the specific subgroup division of the trumpets.

351 *In D-flat.* The trumpet in this tonality was regarded by Berlioz as possessing the most beautiful tone color.

352 *Opening.* There is another type of primitive horn with an embouchure opening cut in the side. This type

is widely distributed among primitive peoples, especially in Africa.

P. 156 353 *Egyptians*. Cf. C. Sachs' *Real-Lexikon*, p. 371, s.v. 'Sofar.'

354 *St. Eustace*. Cf. *Klassiker der Kunst in Gesamtausgaben*, iv, *Dürer*, third ed., p. 115.

P. 159 355 *Bouasse*. Dr. Bouasse's experiments confirmed the fact that it is possible to produce several more tones below each partial tone, especially in the low register. Therefore Praetorius' 'Falset-Stimme' tones, known also as 'factitious tones' (see Note 399), receive scientific support. Also see No. 165, p. 162.

356 *Chapels*. Quoted by C. S. Terry, *Bach's Orchestra*, p. 37; Mersenne, *Harmonie universelle*, book v, p. 274.

357 *Breath*. Mersenne, *op. cit.*, p. 276.

358 *Lungs*. Cf. C. S. Terry, *op. cit.*, p. 37, where North and Schubart are quoted.

359 *Century*. F. W. Galpin, *Old English Instruments of Music*, 1932, pp. 189 f.

360 *Long ago*. *Op. cit.*, p. 48.

361 *Europe*. Information borrowed from A. Novoselsky, *Sketches on the History of Russian Folk Instruments*, Moscow, 1931, pp. 23 ff. (In Russian.)

P. 162 362 *Intonation*. H. Bouasse, *op. cit.*, p. 376. This means that only a trained singer could play the serpent well. Good breath control is indispensable for playing this instrument in the low register.

363 *Musically faulty*. Two aspects of tones of valved instruments should be considered: absolute (acoustical) and relative (musical). The natural scales produced by a valved brass instrument with the basic length of tubing augmented by the additional lengths of the valve crooks in various combinations are, acoustically, correct scales for each length taken separately. It is only when these natural scales are combined to produce a complete chromatic scale that some of the natural scales are, relatively, sharper than the rest.

P. 163 364 *Fact*. H. Bouasse, *Instruments à vent*, ii, p. 43, para. 3.

365 *France*. Cf. C. Sachs, *Real-Lexikon*, p. 343 b.

P. 165 366 *Pedal tones*. Pedal tones on the key bugle are producible for each length of tubing as the keys are opened; but musically they are useless, and tonally, especially for the shorter lengths of tube, very inferior.

367 *Tune*. This is also true of the low register of the flute. The lower tones (d'-flat and below) of mediocre instruments sound 'out of tune'; the pitch of tone may be correct, but the change in quality of tone color creates the illusion of change of pitch. Some old time flutists objected to the extension of the flute compass below d'.

P. 169 368 *Pedal tones*. The plural 'pedal tones' is correct, since below the pedal tone of the tube with the valves 'off' there are also the pedal tones of the tube extended in length by the valves.

P. 170 369 *Filled in*. This statement should be modified somewhat, if Praetorius' 'Falset-Stimme' tones are added to the low *E* of the seventh position. Modern practice does not allow such artificial tones.

370 *Instruments*. The valves 'off' is one of these combinations; when the valves are used there are six additional combinations.

371 *Two valves*. See Notes 293 and 294.

372 *In C*. The instrument is not an imaginary one; see Note 343. This tonality is selected for two reasons: (1) the note examples for each position can serve as models, if properly transposed, for any tonality; (2) the scale which has as its tonic the tonality of the instrument is not the simplest scale on the slide trombone. In other words, if the slide trombone were to be treated in notation as a transposing instrument, then its nominal C-major diatonic scale would not be the simplest scale for playing, as it would involve difficult shifts of position. The easiest scale, so far as the sequence of shifts is concerned, is the nominal D-major scale. On a B-flat slide trombone the latter becomes a C-major scale. This is the real reason why the B-flat tenor trombone is treated in notation as a non-transposing instrument.

373 *Tone*. High f'' is the goal of every aspiring tenor trombonist.

374 *Far*. In shifting the slide from position to position no two trombonists shift by the same amount while playing the same tone on the same instrument; there always will be some individual differences. Cf. H. Bouasse, *Instruments à vent*, i (1929), pp. 369 f.

P. 172 375 *Mersenne*. Mersenne recorded the fact, but was at a loss to explain it. With reference to the note example of the C-major scale given in the text and played on the tenor trombone in C, the tones *g* and *b* may be played also in the sixth position, and the tone c' in the fifth position. For the complete table of equivalent positions, see R. N. Davis, *The Imperial Method for the Slide Trombone*, pp. 20 and 77. See Note 376 below.

376 *Position*. Skilful trombone playing consists in utilizing the possibility of producing certain tones in several positions, so that the slide will travel a minimum distance for a given musical phrase. This is important in rapid tempo and bravura passages.

377 *Octave*. This was not always so. On some instruments the first valve was the semitone valve, the second was the whole-tone valve, so that the sequence of adding the semitones was 1, 2, 3. The resulting fingering with this sequence is less convenient. For an example of this arrangement see Plate VII, No. 195.

P. 172 378 *Fourth.* In German this valve is called the *Quartventil.*

P. 173 379 *Too sharp.* For details see Arthur Clappé, *The Wind-Band and its Instruments*, chapter iv, pp. 25 ff. See Note 363.

380 *Convenient.* The true partial tone of a tube is one which requires a minimum effort for the lips to sound it. Training one's lips to play flatter and compensate for the defects of the valve mechanism requires rather long practice. To remedy these defects of the valve instruments many compensating mechanisms were invented, some of which automatically introduce the additional lengths of tubing when the valves are used in combination, so that the fingering is not disturbed. This type is the best.

381 The description and pictures of the seven-tube valve trombone can be found in (1) the *Catalogue . . . de Bruxelles*, ii, pp. 463 f., no. 1288; (2) C. Sachs, *Sammlung . . .*, p. 230, no. 3109, plate 24. Referred to in Note 288.

382 *Professor Bouasse.* Cf. Henri Bouasse, *Instruments à vent*, i (Paris, 1929), pp. 304 ff., paragraphs 156 to 159 inclusive, especially p. 308, item 3; also ii (1930), pp. 45 f., paragraph 11. Professor Bouasse's theory deserves serious consideration. At last a scientist of standing, with the capable experimental assistance of Dr. M. Fouché, has paid attention to the objective facts and the deviations from the rigid and much too ideal theories of the classical acoustics of Professor Hermann Helmholtz. Although the works of Professor Bouasse require a considerable knowledge of mathematics, there are many sections which are stated in simple and clear language. The Helmholtzian idea that the brass wind instruments have the partial tones of fixed pitch comprising in their totality a harmonic scale of tones is contradicted by so many facts that it needs a complete restatement. Professor Bouasse has shown that, since the tubes of all actual brass instruments are cylindro-conoidal, the natural scale of tones of such tubes is affected by the properties of both types of tubes. The cylindrical portion of the tube tends to the odd series of partial tones, whereas the conoidal portion has the complete series. This combination tends to produce a somewhat distorted natural scale of tones, which is not always in tune with the theoretical harmonic scale, at least in some of its parts. This deviation is greater in the lower part of the compass. The true fundamental tone of the cylindro-conoidal tubes is not used. The conventional 'fundamental tone' (the 'pedal tone' of this study) is really a 'privileged tone,' the sub-harmonic of a higher partial tone, and not a fundamental tone at all. The partial tones of the natural scale are not only not fixed in pitch, but, on the contrary, they can be varied by the lips, especially in the lower part of compass, within a large interval. There is an upper limit in pitch, above which the partial tone cannot be raised: it either breaks or slips into the next higher one. The variation downward is much greater. On the long tube, narrow-bore instruments the pitch of the second partial tone can be lowered by the lips as much as a fourth and sometimes a fifth (this can be readily demonstrated on the French horn in F; the hunting horn No. 191, as stated on p. 180, descends as low as *AA*). Professor Bouasse's theory explains the strange behavior of the 'fundamental' tone of the usual acoustical theories. Sometimes the proportions of the tube are such that this 'privileged tone' (in Professor Bouasse's terminology) is too flat to be corrected by the lips; in other words, the upper limit of its playability is too flat to permit this tone to enter the natural scale as the number one of the series. Sometimes it is not playable at all, as on the low-pitched French horns. As every maker of brass instruments knows, the new models are developed after considerable attempts by trial and error to find the proper proportions. When the preliminary model is made, one has to be ready for surprises. Some parts of the scale are apt to be out of tune. Sometimes a slight variation in proportions, amounting only to a few thousandths of an inch, corrects the trouble, or, as is more often the case, starts a new series of troubles in some other part of the scale. In some cases several modifications of the new model are required before more or less satisfactory results are achieved. In some cases the trouble is too difficult to correct. For instance, the standing problem in the making of the French horns is the tenth partial tone (the nominal *e''*); it is too flat and has to be 'lipped.' Yet on other brass instruments, when playable, it is in tune. On some instruments (the low-pitched trumpets in D, C, and B-flat basso) the second partial tone is too flat; the B-flat horn basso starts its natural scale correctly on the third partial tone. Many more similar facts could be adduced. The general conclusions can be summarized as follows. (1) The natural scale of brass instruments is dependent upon proportions of tubing, and some of its partial tones are not necessarily in tune with the theoretical harmonic scale of tones. (2) The true fundamental tone is not used. (Cf. H. Bouasse, *op. cit.*, ii, p. 45, paragraph 11.) The pedal tone is not playable on some instruments (the 'half-tube' instruments). (3) The partial tones are not fixed in pitch; the lips can vary their pitch within a certain interval, which in some cases is quite large. The tubes with a longer conoidal part (cornets, bugles, and horns) have greater limits of variation; the tubes with a longer cylindrical part (trumpets and trombones) have smaller limits.

The discussion has proceeded thus far on the assumption that the accepted types of mouthpieces are employed in playing. Variations in mouthpieces have their influence, which is too complicated to be touched here. The writer hopes that Professor Bouasse's books on acoustics of wind instruments will be more widely studied. They are of importance not only theoretically, but also pedagogically.

P. 175 383 *Many tonalities.* See Note 322.

P. 176 384 *Schubventil.* Cf. C. Sachs, *Sammlung . . .*, p. 207, fig. 21.

385 *Piston valves.* Very gradually the rotary valves are beginning to win favor in this country on other instruments. Some bass tubas are built now with the rotary valves.

P. 178 386 *Main tubing.* Cf. C. Sachs, *Sammlung . . .*, p. 207, fig. 22, marked "Wiener Ventil, um 1830."

387 *Reasons.* The pedal tone is not employed in playing. Canon Galpin's classification of similar instruments as 'incomplete' is indispensable in such cases. See Note 319 for a discussion of Canon Galpin's classification.

P. 179 388 *Fourteenth century.* Cf. *Encyclopaedia Britannica*, 11th ed., xiii, p. 702, s.v. 'Horn,' fig. 4; F. W. Galpin, *Old English Instruments of Music*, p. 185; the latter referred to C. Sachs, *Real-Lexikon*, p. 419 a.

389 *C. basso.* Cf. *Encyclopaedia Britannica*, 11th ed., xiii, p. 703, s.v. 'Horn.' The parts are for four horns in C; *e*, being a fifth partial tone, can be produced only on the low-pitched instrument.

390 *Hand.* The horn was not always played with the hand in the bell. In earlier times it was held with the bell turned up. R. Wagner requests horn players to hold the bells upward (*Stürze in die Höhe*) at the end of the overture to the opera *Tannhäuser*; this is only a reversal to the earlier tradition. Professor Henri Kling's censure of this practice is too harsh. Cf. his *Modern Orchestration*, New York, 1905, p. 133 a.

391 *Choked.* Some German-built horns have larger bores as compared with the English- and French-built horns made on the Raoux model. The German horns sound more open. In large orchestras and for playing Wagnerian music they are excellent. For the old classical music a lighter-toned and more flexible Raoux model is preferable. See p. 143 for additional information about hand-stopping technique.

392 *Octavia.* Cf. *Encyclopaedia Britannica*, 11th ed., xiii, p. 704 a.

393 *Raucous.* More so than the modern instrument. The essential improvement on the latter is a more rationally designed tube.

394 *In F.* The explanation is very simple. The proportions and the length of tubing and mouthpiece for this tonality are matched in the best way. For other crooks the whole combination is less suitable.

395 *Cylindrical.* On some horns of better makes the crooks were made with the conoidal bore down to the E-flat crook at least.

396 *E-flat.* For the low-pitched crooks a compounding of crooks was practised to save the cost. See under No. 195, p. 182, of this study.

P. 180 397 *Crook.* See Wilhelm Schneider, *Historisch-technische Beschreibung der musicalischen Instrumente*, Leipzig, 1834, p. 35; also Cecil Forsyth, *Orchestration*, p. 82, text and note.

398 *False.* Frau Schumann contributed the following testimony: "We had studied your trio very well, and the horn player [at Frankfort] was excellent. I do not think he spluttered once, and that says a great deal; though it is true that he played on a ventil-horn. He would not be induced to try a wald-horn." (A letter to Brahms from Coblenz, December 22, 1866. Cf. H. S. Drinker, Jr., *The Chamber Music of Johannes Brahms*, p. 113.) Another interesting detail worth recording. The old time players on natural horns carried crooks on the left forearm, neatly arranged like some sort of grotesque bracelet. The 'clankety-clank' horn crook percussion 'obligato' when the hornist moved or changed the crooks is no longer heard in concert halls.

399 *Staccato.* The tones played below the true partial tone were known as the 'factitious notes'; on this point cf. C. Forsyth, *Orchestration*, p. 110 and example 44. They are the 'Falset-Stimme' of Praetorius. Now this practice is discontinued.

P. 181 400 *Second.* One may compile a table of the length of horns of different tonalities by adding the length of the crooks given on p. 149 of the Royal Military Exhibition *Catalogue* to 246 cm.

P. 183 401 *Figure.* It does not include the length of the shanks, since they add nothing to the acoustical length of the tubing.

402 *Prescribed.* In other words, some composers thought that it was possible to have a chromatic horn in any tonality by changing the crooks alone. The technical point overlooked is that the length of the valve crooks must be in a definite relation to the length of the main tube. Once this length is changed the valve slides have to be either shortened or lengthened. Since these possibilities are limited and crook changes are a nuisance, the horn players preferred to transpose everything on the F-horn.

403 *Existence.* Well built double horns have two sets of valve crooks, the longer one for the F-horn and the shorter one for the B-flat horn. There is a thumb-valve which either subtracts or adds a length of tubing repre-

senting the difference in the lengths of the F and B-flat horns. This valve also shifts the air stream from one set of valve crooks to another, depending upon which particular horn, high or low, a player prefers to use at the moment. Therefore, a horn player has at his disposal two chromatic instruments in one, complete in all particulars, but using a common mouthpiece and a certain common length of tubing including the bell. The change from one tonality to another can be made instantaneously, so that a player may start a phrase on the F-horn, change to B-flat if necessary, and go back again, without disturbing the flow of melody. The double horns have one disadvantage; their tube proportions are designed primarily for the F-horn; when the excess length of tubing is shut off by the thumb-valve and the horn is changed to B-flat, the resulting tubing proportions are not so favorable for the higher tonality. To remedy this defect, the single B-flat horn was introduced, since its tubing could be designed for the best tonal results. Even then the B-flat horn is not an entirely satisfactory instrument.

P. 183 404 *Also.* Some conductors overemphasize accentuation, and require hornists to put more *Schmalz* in their playing. The latter oblige by adopting a mouthpiece with a shallow funnel cup which comes dangerously close to an elongated flügelhorn mouthpiece. The attack and even the tone of the horn then reminds one of a bugle.

P. 184 405 *Manuscripts.* Cf. C. Sachs, *Handbuch,* 1930, p. 282, text and note 3.

406 *Handbuch.* Cf. *Encyclopaedia Britannica,* 11th ed., xxiii, p. 973, s.v. 'Sackbut.' F. W. Galpin, "The Sackbut," published in Musical Association, *Proceedings,* xxxiii, 1906–1907. C. Sachs, *Handbuch,* 1930, pp. 282, 290.

P. 186 407 *Therefore in F.* If *B* is the lowest tone of its seventh position, then the tonality is F, since the second partial tone of the first position sounds F.

408 *Trouble.* Praetorius mentions nothing about trombone pedals.

409 *Years.* Praetorius' second volume of the *Syntagma Musicum* was published in 1619; Dr. Bouasse's *Instruments à vent,* vol. i, in 1929.

410 *B-flat.* The tonality of Praetorius' trombones is given by M. Mahillon in D and in A; cf. *Catalogue . . . de Bruxelles,* i (1893), p. 305. This is repeated in *Encyclopaedia Britannica,* 11th ed., xxvii, p. 304. C. S. Terry, *Bach's Orchestra,* p. 38, pays his respect to this fiction, but on p. 39 disregards it, since the tenor trombone is once more given as in B-flat. It should be remarked that Praetorius gives the lowest tone of the tenor trombone as *E*, and not *e* (see note example on p. 39 of Terry's book), which tone (*E*) is the second partial tone of the B-flat tenor trombone tube in the seventh position, its normal tone for that position. Praetorius gives no D and A tonalities to the trombones of his time. *Tabella Universalis* (cf. *De Organographia,* p. 20, col. v) and the text (*ibid.,* pp. 31, 32) are clear and consistent only when it is assumed that the *Gemeine Rechte Posaun* is the ordinary tenor trombone pitched in B-flat. Cf. Curt Sachs, *Handbuch der Musikinstrumentenkunde,* 2nd ed., Leipzig, 1930, p. 298.

411 *Lowest position.* Table viii, fig. 2 (reproduced here on p. 185), shows the *Quart-Posaun,* the slide of which is marked with the letters of some of the tones produced. The lowest position is marked *AA* and the highest (?) *D*. The tone *AA* is the second partial tone of the seventh position of a trombone pitched in E-flat; if so, then this instrument is really the *Quint-Posaun.* It is necessary to count from the lowest normal tone upward for the following reason. The lowest normal tones of the alto, tenor, and *Quint-Posaun* are given by Praetorius as *B*, *E*, and *AA*; assuming these as the tones of the seventh position, the respective tonalities of Praetorius' trombones come out as the alto in F, the tenor in B-flat, and the *Quint-Posaun* in E-flat. The whole picture is consistent.

412 *Former.* There existed a third type of *Octav-Posaun,* one with the double slide. Cf. F. W. Galpin, "The Sackbut," pp. 11 f., 17. Canon Galpin states that Hans Neuschel, the famous brass instrument maker of Nuremberg, received in 1542 a request from Duke Albrecht of Prussia for a trombone in silver with four slides (double slides). A similar instrument was made in 1612 by Jobst Schnitzer. As Canon Galpin correctly points out, the alleged invention of the French maker Halary was anticipated by more than two centuries.

413 *Old timers.* Two things can be mentioned: the 'Clarinblasen' and 'Falset-Stimme' playing below the true partial tones.

414 *Intervalle enorme. Instruments à vent,* i (1929), p. 308, para. 158, item 1; please read the rest. P. 187

415 *Impossible. De Organographia,* p. 32. The translation is literal; it gives the flavor of Praetorius' style. Transpositions on the primitive lateral hole wind instruments were very difficult and in certain keys impossible.

416 *Point.* Cf. F. W. Galpin, "The Sackbut," Musical Association, *Proceedings,* xxxiii, 1906–1907, p. 21. Here an old funnel-shaped trombone mouthpiece similar to that of the orchestral horn is described. The old time sackbut tone depended largely upon a mouthpiece of this shape.

417 *Santa Maria.* Cf. Grove, *Dictionary of Music,* iv, p. 184, plate lx, no. 7. P. 188

P. 189 418 *Trumpet.* The soprano slide trombone has a cylindro-conoidal bore. Some of the old models of the B-flat soprano trumpets had the same type bore, and therefore did not differ from the soprano slide trombones in any essential points, so far as the geometrical shape of the bore is concerned. The modern B-flat trumpet has a tube beginning with a conoidal 'mouthpipe' (about 23 cm. or nine inches long), after which follows a cylindrical bore, until it begins to expand into the conoidal bell joint. Therefore, the geometrical shape of the modern B-flat trumpet bore is conoidal-cylindro-conoidal. However, the B-flat trumpet bore differs considerably from the cornet bore. Even with this change, acoustical properties of the B-flat trumpet remain the same: it is still a three-octave, whole-tube instrument. Addition of the conoidal part to the bore changes the tone color of the B-flat trumpet, but not sufficiently to place it into a special group. Therefore, the modern B-flat trumpet is a soprano valve trombone. See Note 424 below.

419 *Widor.* Charles Marie Widor, *The Technique of the Modern Orchestra*, London, 1906, p. 86. Higher trumpet tones can be more successfully cultivated on longer, low-pitched trumpets. It should be understood, however, that there are certain practical limitations, such as the necessity for a player to develop a special embouchure which is suitable for the highest register only.

P. 190 420 *Branches.* Cf. Metropolitan Museum of Art, *Catalogue of the Crosby Brown Collection*, 1902, i, p. 191 and plate. The whole family is represented, except the sopranino in E-flat.

P. 191 421 *Holland.* G. Kinsky, *Geschichte der Musik in Bildern*, Leipzig, 1929, p. 150, fig. 7.

422 *Handle.* G. Kinsky, *op. cit.*, p. 150, fig. 8.

P. 192 423 *Knightly art.* Cf. Wilhelm Schneider, *Historisch-technische Beschreibung der musicalischen Instrumente*, Leipzig, 1834, p. 42. Also Werner Menke, *History of the Trumpet of Bach and Handel*, pp. 25, 27 f.

424 *Trombone.* To the arguments considered under No. 199, p. 188, and in Note 418, the following should be added. Typologically a brass instrument belongs to a given family, if the following conditions are satisfied: (1) the geometrical proportions of its tube are similar to the rest of the members of that family; (2) the mouthpiece is of the same type; (3) the natural scale is of the same type (three-octave or four-octave); (4) the tone color is of the same timbre. In the particular case, all these conditions are satisfied by two members of the horn family, the horns in B-flat, *basso* and *alto*. These horns are pitched one octave apart, i.e., their natural scales are one octave apart, tone for tone. Both instruments are true horns. Superficially the trumpet family is analogous to the horn family. There are two trumpets, the low-pitched tenor and the high-pitched soprano, both in B-flat. The length of their tubes corresponds to their tonal position; the tenor trumpet has the tube twice as long as the soprano trumpet. The geometrical shape of the tubes of both instruments is similar (at least on the early models; see Note 418 for the modern deviation); the mouthpieces are identical. Here the similarity stops. Although the soprano trumpet is half as long, it plays at the same pitch as the tenor trumpet. For instance, the famous trumpet call in the *Leonore No. 3* of Beethoven (Philharmonia Scores, No. 18, pp. 30 and 32) is scored for B-flat tenor trumpet. The modern trumpet plays this part without transposition (i.e., at the same pitch). If the modern trumpet were a real trumpet, its natural scale would be an octave higher with respect to the old tenor trumpet in the same way as the natural scale of the B-flat horn *alto* is an octave higher than that of the B-flat horn *basso*. In other words, if the similarly numbered partial tones were played on the modern instrument, the call in question would sound one octave higher. Since this is not the case, the modern trumpet has its natural scale not of the same type as the tenor trumpet; the modern trumpet is a three-octave instrument and the tenor trumpet is a four-octave instrument. In a few words: the modern 'trumpet' is not a trumpet. Then to which family does it belong? There is only one possible answer, the valve trombone family. This acoustical and organological difference explains the difference in tonal qualities between the real trumpet and its modern namesake. Hence the statement in the text that the classical trumpet stands to the modern trumpet as the French horn to the melophone.

425 *Produced.* The most competent history of clarino-playing is written by Mr. Walter F. H. Blandford, the noted English authority on brass instruments. Cf. his letter to the editor of *The Monthly Musical Record*, Feb., 1931, pp. 44 f. Also his articles in the same magazine: (1) "Bach's Trumpets," July, 1931, and (2) "The 'Bach' Trumpet," March–April, May, and June, 1935. The recovery of the clarino-playing technique started in 1871, when Julius Kosleck, a Berlin cornet player, discovered in Heidelberg an ancient trumpet (a buysine, rather) which was allegedly used for playing the high trumpet parts of J. S. Bach's scores. Kosleck's own instrument was a straight trumpet in A, with two valves, and played with an elongated cup mouthpiece almost approaching in shape to that of the French horn. (See Appendix to W. Menke's book on the trumpet for its section.) Mr. Walter Morrow, the English trumpet player of note, developed a trumpet in A similar to Kosleck's. Recently, Mr. Werner Menke designed two-

valve low trumpets in F and in D which duplicate the average proportions of the eighteenth-century instruments. It cannot be too strongly insisted that the real clarino-playing means the production of high pitched partial tones on the long-tube alto trumpets, which are twice as long as the modern 'Bach trumpets' in high D and F. In other words, the clarino tones are the high-pitched register of the low-pitched, long-tube trumpets and not the tones of a high-pitched instrument. The reason for this seemingly pedantic insistence is that the timbre of the classical trumpets in the clarino register, when played with properly developed lip technique, is so superior that no efforts should be spared to recover the old skill.

Bibliography. In addition to the works mentioned in Note 423, the following should be consulted. Daniel Speer, *Grund-richtiger . . . Unterricht der musicalischen Kunst,* Ulm, 1687. J. E. Altenburg, *Versuch einer Anleitung zur heroisch-musikalischen Trompeter- und Pauker-Kunst,* Halle, 1795; reprint, Leipzig, 1911. Hermann Eichborn, (1) *Die Trompete in alter und neuer Zeit,* Leipzig, 1881; (2) *Das alte Clarinblasen auf Trompeten,* Leipzig, 1894. Since Dr. Eichborn is a pioneer in this line of study, his statements should be examined in the light of later findings; W. Menke is heavily indebted to Dr. Eichborn. *Grove's Dictionary of Music,* 1927, v, s.v. 'Trumpet.' Walter Morrow, "The Trumpet as an Orchestral Instrument," Musical Association, *Proceedings,* xxi, pp. 133–147 (June 11, 1895). For a most interesting exchange of opinions on the high-pitched trumpet, the terz-heckelphone, etc., for the high trumpet parts of J. S. Bach's scores see *Zeitschrift für Instrumentenbau,* xxx, pp. 194 f., "Die Höhen Bach-Trompeten"; a rejoinder by W. Altenburg, pp. 227 f.; discussion, pp. 375–378.

P. 192 426 *High tones.* N. A. Rimsky-Korsakov in *My Musical Life,* pp. 120 f., relates that A. P. Borodin, another Russian composer, produced the high tones of the brass instruments with extraordinary ease.

427 *Softly.* The best known example is J. E. Altenburg's often quoted statement about his father's ability to reduce the force of high tones of the trumpet to a mere whisper and yet to retain perfect control. Another player, Cario, had similar fine control; cf. W. F. H. Blandford, *Monthly Musical Record,* June, 1935, p. 98. F. W. Galpin, *Old English Instruments of Music,* p. 205; Werner Menke, *History of the Trumpet of Bach and Handel,* p. 221.

P. 193 428 *Instruments.* Here is again a complication. There are two types of alto valve trumpets in F. The first type is the real trumpet, having the bore and mouthpiece identical with the classical natural trumpet of the same tonality. Its tone duplicates the classical counterpart in the same way as the valve horns built on the Raoux model duplicate that of the natural horns; the principal difference is that both the modern alto valve trumpets in F and the valve horns have a chromatic scale. It is this type of instrument that should play the trumpet parts of classical and romantic composers. N. A. Rimsky-Korsakov introduced another type of valve trumpet, the so-called *tromba contralta* in F. This tromba is really an alto valve trombone in F, played with a modified trumpet mouthpiece, having a larger cup and a shorter backbore than the real trumpet mouthpiece, yet not so large as the alto trombone mouthpiece. In his book, *Principles of Orchestration,* Rimsky-Korsakov says: "The Alto Trumpet (*tromba contralta* in F). An instrument devised and introduced by me for the first time in the score of the opera-ballet *Mlada.* The reason for its introduction: to obtain the low tones (from the second to the third partial tones of the ordinary natural trumpet) which would have greater fulness, clarity, and charm. The three-part combinations consisting of the two ordinary trumpets and the third, the alto trumpet, sound smoother than the three trumpets of the same tonality. After becoming convinced of the beauty and usefulness of the alto trumpet, I continued to employ it in many of my subsequent operas having the wood-winds in three's. *Note.* To prevent the difficulty of acquiring the alto trumpet for the orchestras of the private opera companies, or for casual concert performances, I have avoided giving to this instrument the four lower tones of its compass with their chromatic semitones; because of this the performance of the alto trumpet parts becomes possible on the ordinary trumpet (B-flat or A)." (Translated from the original Russian edition, *Osnovï Orkestrovki,* 1913, p. 29. Compare this translation with the English version, *Principles of Orchestration,* tr. by E. Agate, Paris and London, p. 23.) In the table C, Brass Group (p. 25 of the English ed., and p. 31 of the Russian), the natural scales of three trumpets in B-flat, in A, and in F are shown as being identical as to the serial numbers of partial tones, differing, of course, in their respective pitches. This can mean only one thing: the *tromba contralta* in F of Rimsky-Korsakov is a three-octave instrument, or, in other words, an alto valve trombone played with the modified trumpet mouthpiece, and not the modern valved counterpart of the classical trumpet in F. The following table shows the difference.

Trumpet in F	*c'*	*e'*	*g'*	*c''*	*e''*	*g''*
Partial No.	4	5	6	8	10	12
Actual Pitch	*f'*	*a'*	*c''*	*f''*	*a''*	c^3

Tromba c.-alta in F	*c'*	*g'*	*c''*	*e''*	*g''*
Partial No.	2	3	4	5	6
Actual Pitch	*f*	*c'*	*f'*	*a'*	*c''*

In other words, the trumpet in F transposes its written notes a fourth higher; the tromba contralta in F, a fifth lower. This is due to the difference in bore and in the proportions of the mouthpiece. The tromba contralta is more adapted to playing the lower partial tones. Although it plays in the same tonal position as the alto trombone in F, its tone is more incisive than that of the latter instrument. Again this difference is due to the mouthpiece. (The alto trombone has a real trombone mouthpiece, similar in shape but smaller in size than that of the tenor trombone.) In general, it is possible to state that the tromba contralta is a modern incarnation of the obsolete alto trombone, disguised in the shape of a trumpet, furnished with valves, and played with a trumpet-type mouthpiece. In this form the instrument is more successful than the alto trombone.

In this study the tromba contralta, the soprano, sopranino, and octave trumpets are classified generically as valve trombones (see p. 154). It is feasible to segregate them into a separate sub-family for the following reasons. As a general proposition, the valve trombone duplicates the bore and tube proportions of the slide trombone (the slide of the latter should be imagined in the first position) of the corresponding tonality and is played with the trombone mouthpiece. The modern trumpet introduces a new variation. It duplicates the tube of the slide trombone (at least the early model; see Note 418, p. 413), but uses the trumpet mouthpiece. Therefore the modern trumpet stands between the trombone and the real trumpet in construction and tone color. From this organological classification follow important musical consequences. The real place of the modern trumpet is not to serve as a substitute for the real trumpet, but as a connecting link between the real trumpet and the trombones. Another purpose which the modern trumpet fulfils admirably is to extend (with some modification, of course) the trombone tone color into the higher tonal positions. From the history of the trombone family we know that several attempts were made to add the alto and the soprano voices to the trombone choir, but each time the instruments were made with the slide and played with the trombone-type mouthpiece. As our present experience shows, the modern valve mechanism and the trumpet mouthpiece are more suitable for the shorter trombone tubes, so that not only the alto and the soprano, but also the sopranino and even the octave valve trombones become possible. So it is suggested here that the alto trombone parts of the classical and romantic scores, especially when written rather high for the tenor slide trombone, could be played on the tromba contralta with excellent results. N. A. Rimsky-Korsakov wrote successfully in his operatic scores for the high sopranino trumpets in D and E-flat. In this instance the parts were conceived and written for the instruments, both in the alto and sopranino tonal positions in addition to the customary soprano trumpets, by one of the greatest masters of orchestral tone color and instrumentation, in terms of those instruments and with full knowledge of their qualities and limitations. Properly written for, the modern trumpets sound excellently, especially when their possibilities and limitations are intimately known by the composer. N. A. Rimsky-Korsakov's operatic scores (alas, rather difficult of access in this country) should be studied to learn how to write for the modern trumpets in various tonalities (he writes for E-flat, F, A, B-flat, C, D, and high E-flat trumpets). These are positive achievements. The same cannot be said about the total extinction of the real trumpet. The modern trumpet is akin to, but not the equivalent of, the classical trumpet. The loss of the distinctive tone color of the latter is almost inexplicable in an age of virtuoso mastery of musical instruments, when the individuality of tone color and variety of tonal palette is considered important. The real trumpets should be scored as a separate group, and their parts written along traditional lines; only then can their full effectiveness be realized. If the real trumpets were used in the modern orchestras, some of the works in which they are scored (to cite at random the *Second Brandenburg Concerto* of J. S. Bach, his *B-Minor Mass*, Handel's *Messiah*, Tchaikovsky's *1812 Ouverture Solennelle*, Anton Bruckner's *Ninth Symphony*) would sound more majestic.

P. 193

429 *Difficult.* It seems, *a priori*, that the high tones should be more easily playable on small, high-pitched instruments. In practice the high-pitched wind instruments in general and the lip-vibrated aerophones in particular have several limitations. On the latter, the shorter the tube, the fewer in number and more difficult are the high partial tones. It is true that the lip technique (the so-called 'pressure' and 'no pressure' methods of tone production) has influence on the effort required and the number of tones producible. Nevertheless there are physical limitations of the human organism which cannot be exceeded. On the long, narrow-bored tubes of the horn, the sixteenth and, in some cases, even the twenty-first partial tone is not difficult. On the B-flat soprano trumpet some players succeed in reaching the twelfth partial tone or even higher, but such feats are more in the nature of tricks; the real test comes

when a sustained performance is required. The high trumpet part of J. S. Bach's *Second Brandenburg Concerto* is not playable at its proper pitch on the B-flat soprano trumpet. The writer has noticed several times that the first trumpeters of our finest symphony orchestras sometimes break on the high b''-flat in P. I. Tchaikovsky's *1812 Ouverture Solennelle* (cf. Eulenburg's small score, p. 71, the part marked 'Piston' and played, of course, on the B-flat or C-trumpet; this tone is the eighth partial tone of the B-flat trumpet and the seventh of the C-trumpet). This means that the safe practical limit for the B-flat trumpet should be the eighth partial tone; the same limit should be set for ordinary players on D, E-flat, and F sopranino trumpets. For the octave trumpets (high A-flat, B-flat, and C) the limit should be the sixth partial tone. Beyond these limits the strain in sustained playing becomes so great that health is jeopardized. In the foreign army bands, where the hapless conscripts were forced, at one time, to play high A-flat cornets, many had hernia and some became tubercular. The high F-trumpets are not so difficult, but even they are close to the limit of endurance. One must converse with players who performed the *Second Brandenburg Concerto* on the high-pitched F-trumpet to realize that the lips are strained to the limit and sometimes split. In this connection Mr. John Solomon's letter in *The Monthly Musical Record*, Feb., 1931, pp. 43 f., should be read.

P. 193 430 *Argument.* See Note 425 for reference. Since high-pitched trumpets are so difficult to play in the extremely high register, is it possible to speak of any artistic effect? N. A. Rimsky-Korsakov in *Principles of Orchestration* says: "Similarly to piccolo flute and contrabassoon, the concept of expressive playing is almost inapplicable to the small trumpet (D–E-flat) and contrabass tuba." Compare p. 33 of the Russian and p. 26 of the English text. Translated from the Russian; the English text gives the general impression of N. A. Rimsky-Korsakov's thought but does no justice to his style. The low-pitched trumpets played by properly developed 'Clarinblasen' technique impose no such strain on the performer, while the results are artistically gratifying.

P. 195 431 *Today.* The first and third horn players are given the high parts; the second and the fourth hornists are required to descend to the bottom of the register of the horn. The low C on the horn in C-basso is found in the classic scores and even in Brahms (see Note 339).

432 *Trumpet.* Cf. *Encyclopaedia Britannica*, 11th ed., xxvii, p. 327 a.

P. 196 433 *Valve trumpet.* It should not be thought that these two positions are equivalent to the two valves of the early valve trumpets. The first and the second valve combined lower the pitch three semitones; therefore, three positions of the slide would be necessary as an equivalent. On trumpet No. 210 of this Collection the slide motion is limited; in the second position it comes within one-half inch from the player.

P. 198 434 *Orchestra.* Praetorius, *De Organographia*, p. 33. C. S. Terry, *Bach's Orchestra*, p. 48.

P. 199 435 *Berlin.* Cf. F. L. Schubert, *Katechismus*, p. 59. Also C. Sachs, *Real-Lexikon*, p. 44 b, s.v. 'Berliner Pumpen,' and *Sammlung . . .*, pp. 207–208.

436 *Consulted.* Cf. Percy A. Scholes, *The Oxford Companion to Music*, 1938; *Grove's Dictionary of Music* (1927); the *Encyclopaedia Britannica*, 11th ed.; all s.v. 'Organ.' G. A. Audsley, *The Art of Organ-Building*, New York, 1905, 2 vols. Some references to the works on organs published between 1900 and 1913 can be found in Dr. Sachs' *Real-Lexikon*, s.v. 'Orgel.' Also Émile Rupp, *Die Entwicklungsgeschichte der Orgelbaukunst*, Einsiedeln, Switzerland, 1929; Winfred Ellerhorst, *Handbuch der Orgelkunde*, Einsiedeln, 1936; William H. Barnes, *The Contemporary American Organ, its Evolution, Design, and Construction*, New York, 1937.

P. 200 437 *In unison.* A complete discussion of this fact is given in Appendix B.

438 *Page.* See Appendix B, p. 366.

439 *Publications.* F. W. Galpin, (1) *Reliquary*, July, 1904; (2) *Scientific American*, Nov. 19, 1904; (3) *English Music, 1604 to 1904*, second ed., London, 1911, pp. 355 ff.; the last-named contains fine illustrations, section drawings, and music examples.

P. 203 440 *Michigan.* Cf. its *Catalogue* by Stanley; no. 740, the lap organ by C. Austin; no. 741, the Rocking Melodeon by A. Prescott.

441 *Collections.* Cf. Metropolitan Museum of Art, *Catalogue of the Crosby Brown Collection*, ii, nos. 1194, 1195, 1522. See also *Catalogue . . . de Bruxelles*, iv (1912), pp. 60 ff., no. 2187; some additional information on American makers can be found on p. 62.

P. 207 442 *Simply 'strings.'* In orchestral usage 'strings' usually mean bowed strings, because, with the exception of harps and the pianoforte, other string instruments are very seldom used. In the Hornbostel-Sachs classification chordophones are numbered as class 3, and not class 4, as in the Mahillon-Galpin classification. This is one of the points where the former departs from the time-honored order. In a certain sense such a departure is justified, since chordophones are closely related to membranophones for two reasons: (1) both are played by the same methods, i.e., by plucking, striking, and bowing, and (2) the primary vibrators do not differ essentially, because a membrane can be regarded as a flattened-out string, and, conversely, a string as a rolled membrane.

P. 207 443 *Are adopted.* C. Sachs, *Handbuch*, 1930, p. 159, introduced this method for the identification of the parts of instruments. It was intended only for *composite chordophones*, or chordophones with a neck, but it can be applied to such instruments as zithers, if their playing position is disregarded. Cf. Note 444, below.

444 *Strings are fastened.* This rule has its exception in the harp. For harps, their playing position serves as a guide for the identification of their sides. The front of the harp is where the pillar is located. Strings are placed on the left side of the harmonic curve on the neck (except the telyn, the Welsh harp, on which strings are placed on the right side), and the sides correspond to the hands of a player.

P. 208 445 *Variation of tension.* The E-string of violins has an auxiliary tuning arrangement at the fixed end, permitting a fine adjustment of pitch. This device is an exception not affecting the general principle.

P. 209 446 *The frontal type.* Dr. Curt Sachs (*Handbuch*, 1930, p. 126) used the term 'frontal' as an alternative for *flankenständig* (lateral) in connection with the designation of a specific peg type. In this study the term 'frontal' is used in the generic sense and is applied to the method of fastening the tuning ends of the strings. The frontal type of string fastening represents a typological characteristic independent of the type of pegs used in connection with it. It is used with sagittal pegs, both anterior and posterior, and also with lateral pegs.

447 *Back.* The occipital type of fastening of the tuning ends of strings represents a typological characteristic generically distinct from that of the frontal type. The former type is shown on p. 315, fig. 58, the section B-B, as used on the Welsh crwth. The occipital fastening of strings is still used on some Asiatic instruments, and was used quite extensively on European instruments which were derived from the Byzantine lyra. The earliest identifiable instruments with this type of fastening are, it seems, the lyras in the hands of twenty-four men of the Apocalypse on the tympanum of the abbey of Moissac. The photographs in the possession of the Museum of Fine Arts, Boston, were examined under a powerful magnifying glass; the characteristic holes through which strings were threaded to bring them back of the head are clearly discernible. The sculptures of the tympanum are dated before the year 1115.

The most typical representative of this type of fastening is the *lira da braccio*, an instrument of exceeding rarity found only in the largest European collections. The head of this instrument is a leaf-shaped block of wood, hollowed out in the rear, with anterior pegs; it has a set of five stopped strings and two open strings fixed as described in the text. For the best information on the *lira* family, cf. G. Kinsky, *Musikhistorisches Museum von Wilhelm Heyer*, ii, pp. 383 f. The illustrations on p. 378 give a clear picture of the method of leading the strings from the front; those on p. 421 show the back of the head.

P. 210 448 *Violin playing.* This statement is subject to the following qualification. Violin players do use open strings in very fast passages if it simplifies fingering; but then the string played open has no time to issue its full tone. A constant admonition of conductors to inexperienced string players in amateur orchestras is, "Do not use open strings."

Multiple stops of certain type are played with one or two strings open, bourdon-wise. Their aesthetic value, when played on the modern violin, is a matter of taste. Some people suffer at hearing them played.

449 *Tone of the belly.* E. Heron-Allen, *Violin-Making* (London, 1884), p. 153.

450 *Vibrations in its neighborhood.* Ewald Speth, "Die Schwingungsvorgange in der Geige," *Zeitschrift für Instrumentenbau*, 1929, no. 3, pp. 78 f. On p. 79 is given a sketch of the distribution of vibrations of the different strings on the violin belly.

451 *5000 years.* Cf. F. W. Galpin, *The Music of the Sumerians, . . . the Babylonians and Assyrians*, Cambridge, England, 1937, chapter iii.

P. 211 452 *Not organic.* This classification differs from that of Hornbostel-Sachs. In the latter, chordophones are divided into simple chordophones (zithers) and composite chordophones (lutes and harps). The difference is due, not only to various principles upon which the Mahillon-Galpin and Hornbostel-Sachs classifications are built (the playing technique as the primary basis in the former and the structural basis in the latter), but to a different approach to the classification of the harp. The group of chordophones with a neck corresponds to the lutes of the Hornbostel-Sachs classification, except that it is narrower, since it does not include bowed instruments. The principal difference concerns the question whether the harp should be classified as a composite chordophone. The writer's considered opinion is that the harp should not be regarded as such.

Let us recall the basis for the Hornbostel-Sachs division. According to Dr. Sachs (cf. his *Handbuch*, 1930, p. 128), chordophones are divided into two sub-classes, simple and composite, depending upon whether the dismemberment or elimination of the resonating body renders an instrument unplayable or not. In other words, the simple chordophones or zithers may or may not have a sound-box; this would affect the loudness of the sounds produced, but would not destroy the playability of the simple chordophone. This applies not only to the zither, but also to the harp. It is possible, as the writer's experiments have shown, to construct a harp with a sound-board only and get an acceptable degree of sonority, especially with metallic strings. The playability of such an instrument is not affected by this drastic operation.

Therefore, complying strictly with Dr. Sachs' own definitions, it is possible to classify the harp as a simple chordophone.

Canon Galpin called the writer's attention to the fact that hooked harps, pedal harps, etc., have a mechanism for 'stopping' the open strings located on an extended member (the harmonic curve). Such mechanisms are later accretions and do not affect the generic characteristics of the chordophones without necks. It seems that the primitive forms are the proper basis for the generic typological distinctions.

P. 211 453 *Eleventh century.* C. Sachs, *Handbuch*, p. 135.

P. 212 454 *Along similar lines.* A. S. Famintzyn's book on *Gusli* mentioned in Note 49 is a scholarly discussion of this question. *Gusli* are mentioned in Russian folk songs and ancient *bilini*, but no actual instruments have reached our time.

P. 213 455 *Nineteenth century.* C. Sachs, *Real-Lexikon*, p. 336 b.

P. 214 456 *Hearpe.* Kathleen Schlesinger, *Encyclopaedia Britannica*, 11th ed., xiii, p. 13, s.v. 'Harp'; Galpin, *Old English Instruments of Music*, p. 10.

457 *Musically.* Canon Galpin, *The Music of the Sumerians*, plate v. There is an excellent article on the ancient Indian bow-harp, *vina*, by Dr. A. K. Coomaraswamy in the *Journal* of the American Oriental Society, l (1930), pp. 244 ff.; supplemented by additional notes, *ibid.*, li (1931), pp. 47, 284; lvii (1937), p. 101.

458 *Japan.* Curt Sachs, *Handbuch*, 1930, p. 236.

459 *Sachs. Handbuch*, 1930, pp. 236 f. Also Galpin, *op. cit.*, p. 30 and plate xii.

P. 215 460 *Dr. W. H. Grattan Flood.* Cf. *The Musical Times*, London, March, 1912, in answer to Canon Galpin's article "The Origin of the Clarsech or Irish Harp" in the February, 1912, number of that magazine.

This question was touched upon by M. Marc Pincherle in the *Encyclopédie de la musique*, pt. ii, vol. iii, Paris, 1927, s.v. 'La Harpe,' pp. 1906 f. M. Pincherle points out that the earliest objective evidence of the triangular harp in Northern countries is the sculptured image in the church of Opdal, Norway, thirteenth century (also ascribed to the eleventh century). If so, then it seems that the absence of such evidence of earlier date would oppose Canon Galpin's theory and would be a more serious objection than those advanced by Dr. Grattan-Flood. Archaeological evidence shows that the general movement of cultural influences in Northern Europe was from the West to the East. On this point see Note 552.

461 *Cruit.* For a complete discussion of this question, cf. F. W. Galpin, *Old English Instruments of Music*, 1932, pp. 287 ff. It seems that a considerable amount of unscientific emotion is aroused by the lack of a clear idea as to what is meant by the term 'harp.' The assertion that the instruments on the Irish granite crosses are not harps, but cruits, is a small point. For a strange reason it becomes equivalent in some minds to a denial of the great musical culture of the ancient Irish, which is not the point under discussion. The existence of a musical culture in ancient Ireland and the superior technical skill of the Irish musicians are readily acknowledged by all competent students.

The Irish granite crosses with images of the 'harpers' on them display very clearly the Coptic influences in ancient Ireland. This fact is now firmly established. Cf. Prof. A. K. Porter, *The Crosses and Culture of Ireland*, New Haven, 1931. Also see Note 552 of this study.

462 *Influences.* This possibility was suggested to the writer by Mrs. Georgia Atwood White, an American investigator who has made a serious study of the history of the harp.

463 *Examination of historical material.* Cf. Eugene O'Curry, *On the Manners and Customs of the Ancient Irish* (London, 1873); W. H. Grattan Flood, *A History of Irish Music* (Dublin, 1905); R. B. Armstrong, *The Irish and the Highland Harps* (Edinburgh, 1904). The last-named work not only describes the instruments but also gives a wealth of historical material on Irish musical culture.

P. 216 464 *Trinity College, Dublin.* R. B. Armstrong, *op. cit.*, pp. 55 f.; cf. *Catalogue of the Crosby Brown Collection of Musical Instruments*, New York, 1904, i, *Europe*, p. 21, no. 1706, reproduction in the Metropolitan Museum of Art. It is an interesting fact that the oldest surviving triangular harps are the Irish harps. Some further historical information is contained in Carl Engel's *Descriptive Catalogue of the Musical Instruments in the South Kensington Museum*, second ed., London, 1874, pp. 239 f.

465 *The Irish Harps.* Praetorius, *op. cit.*, p. 56; also table xviii, fig. 2. As R. B. Armstrong pointed out in his book on harps, the image should be reversed; the strings are shown on the right-hand side instead of the left; see Note 444.

466 *County Cork.* R. B. Armstrong, *op. cit.*, p. 91.

P. 216 467 *Richard Ryan. The Worthies of Ireland*, p. 228, as quoted by R. B. Armstrong.

468 *Five times.* Carl Engel, *op. cit.*, p. 240.

P. 217 469 *People.* R. B. Armstrong, *op. cit.*, p. 39.

470 *Stretched.* Kathleen Schlesinger, *Encyclopaedia Britannica*, 11th ed., xiii, p. 13, s.v. 'Harp.' F. W. Galpin, *Old English Instruments*, p. 14.

471 *The golden ring. Encyclopaedia Britannica*, 11th ed., xiii, p. 838, s.v. 'Howel Dda.' Lavignac and Laurencie, *Encyclopédie de la musique*, pt. ii, vol. iii, p. 1910.

P. 218 472 *Welsh harper.* F. W. Galpin, *Old English Instruments*, p. 15. Mr. Ashton Sanborn has called attention to the fact that the harpers shown in ancient Egyptian representations are blind.

P. 219 473 *With plectrum.* The holding of chordophones with a neck so that the strings are stopped with the left hand is not the exclusive method; old pictures representing players of necked instruments show the reverse method of holding them, where the right hand is used for stopping and the left for plucking. The same is true of bowed instruments.

474 *Instrument in the choir.* A. S. Famintzyn, *Domra* (St. Petersburg, 1891), pp. 15 f. gives many pictures of *tanburs*; on pp. 37 f. he describes *tanbouricas* of different sizes and gives their tunings and pictures. This book is an important contribution of a Russian musicologist to the history of Asiatic and Russian stringed instruments.

P. 220 475 *Oriental neighbors.* A. S. Famintzyn, *op. cit.*, pp. 55 f.

476 *From piccolo to contrabass.* Cf. G. Kinsky, *op. cit.*, ii, p. 227, for the tuning of the whole family.

A new member of the balalaika family was added in 1912; the octobass balalaika. The credit for originating it should be given to Colonel Alexei Fedorovich Lvov, the grandson and the namesake of the composer of the Russian National Hymn (*God Save the Tsar*). The octobass balalaika was used for the first time in the soldiers' balalaika orchestra in the Railway Battalion of the Imperial Guard which Colonel (then Captain) Lvov commanded before the World War.

477 *Famous Russian Painter.* S. P. Iaremich, *M. A. Vrubel, Life and Works* (Moscow, 1911), pp. 120, 121, 123, 184. In *Russian Artists*, a series of illustrated monographs, ed. by Igor Grabar. Vrubel was a painter of extraordinary talent, not appreciated during his life, except by a few. In the summer of 1899 he painted several balalaikas as models for the *Kustar'* (craftsman-coöperator) workers in Princess Tenishev's school-shop.

P. 222 478 *Al-Hira.* H. G. Farmer, in *The Encyclopaedia of Islām*, iv, pp. 985 ff., s.v. 'Ud.'

479 *To the body.* H. G. Farmer, *loc. cit.*, p. 985.

480 *Uniform thinness throughout.* H. G. Farmer, *Studies in Oriental Musical Instruments*, London, 1931, p. 97.

481 *Was 74.25 cm.* Dr. Farmer, *op. cit.*, p. 97, gives the size as 75.25 cm.; a slip of the pen, since there are eleven parts to the string and the 'beating place' is located at the tenth part. 6.75 cm. by 11 give 74.25 cm.

482 *Its length.* H. G. Farmer, *op. cit.*, p. 98.

483 *Florence.* C. Sachs, *Handbuch* (1930), p. 220, fig. 83.

484 *Pearl-Mould.* Thomas Mace, *Musick's Monument*, p. 49. This is a more correct description of the lute's shape than 'pear-shaped.'

485 *Glued to them.* Arnold Dolmetsch, "The Lute," *The Connoisseur*, April, 1904, p. 216. This excellent article is continued in the May number. One of the most valuable contributions in popular form to the history, construction, and playing of the lute.

P. 223 486 *The Worst.* Thomas Mace, *op. cit.*, p. 49. Cf. the article by Mr. Arnold Dolmetsch referred to in Note 485. Canon Galpin kindly supplied the following information on 'air-wood.' "It is the handsome wood of the Oriental Plane (*Platanus Orientalis*), a native of South Europe and the East. The wood was cut in thin strips and dried in the open air for cabinet work."

487 *Cross-bars.* Thomas Mace, *op. cit.*, p. 54. "Because the *Belly* being so very *Thin*, and only supported with six or seven *small weak* Barrs. . . ."

488 *Cullin-cliff.* Thomas Mace, *op. cit.*, p. 49. Canon Galpin added: "Cullin-cliff is the wood of the Silver Fir (*Pinus Picea*) which abounds in the forests of Central Europe. It is soft, white, light with little resin and was especially used for the sound-boards of musical instruments. The name, which is a corruption of 'Cologne-cleft,' would imply that it was prepared in the Rhineland for this purpose."

489 *True-siz'd Neck.* Thomas Mace, *op. cit.*, p. 50.

490 *Sounds unpleasantly.* Thomas Mace, *op. cit.*, p. 68. Fig. 37 is drawn to show the reason for a gradual reduction in fret sizes. When a string is pressed against the 'b' fret and assumes the position shown by the dotted line, the 'c' fret should be smaller in size to provide sufficient clearance for the vibrating string.

P. 224 491 *End next you.* This is not quite clear. It does make a difference which end should be put through "*That Nooze.*" It seems that the fret knot shown in Mr. Gerald R. Hayes' book on viols (*Musical Instruments 1500–1750*, ii, *The Viols*, p. 24) is not in accordance with Mace's directions. If the lute is imagined ". . . standing . . . before you upon a *Table*, upon *Its Back* . . ." (i.e., lying upon the table with its bottom toward the beholder and its head away from him), the "End next you" of the double fret is the lower end and not the upper end, as shown on Mr. Hayes' drawing. The second loop ("*Nooze*") should be inserted upward (toward the head of the lute); the upper end is threaded through the second loop, taken into the left hand and drawn straight away ("only drawing them straight"), the right hand tightening simultaneously the lower (looped) end. The fret tied this way is neat and without any twists, since the upper end will be directly in line. Mace's fret is not only self-locking, but also can be loosened by pulling the upper end, if for any reason it is desired to untie the fret knot. The extra knot tied before the final downward shift of the fret into its proper position is absolutely necessary. When this is done the fret is, indeed, "*firmly fast.*"

P. 225 492 *Double-Fret.* Thomas Mace, *Musick's Monument*, pp. 69, 70.

493 *Frets to 13.* Cf. A. J. Hipkins, *Musical Instruments, Historic, Rare, and Unique*, Edinburgh, 1888, plates xii and xv. Also J. Schlosser, *Die Sammlung alter Musikinstrumente*, Vienna, 1920, lutes numbered N.E.48 and N.E.49.

494 *Approaching the tempered scale.* This empirical rule was known to Mersenne (1636). For detailed discussion, cf. Paul Garnault, *Le Temperament, son histoire, son application aux violes de gambe et guitares*, 1924; also his article, "Les Violes," in *Encyclopédie de la musique*, pt. ii, vol. iii, pp. 1763 ff. The comparative tables on p. 1764 show exactly how much the fretted viol scale differs from the tempered scale. Joseph Bacher, *Die Viola da Gamba*, Kassel, 1932, p. 27, gives a graphical method of locating frets, as well as the calculation of coefficients for just, tempered, and empirical tunings.

495 *Kuwithra type.* H. G. Farmer, in *Encyclopaedia of Islām*, iv, p. 987.

P. 226 496 *Number of tones.* The number of open tones of the lute can be determined as follows:

(1) When the total number of strings is odd; this means that the chanterelle is single. Add one to the total number of strings and divide by two; the quotient is the number of tones; thus, the eleven-string lute has six tones: $11 + 1 = 12$; $12 \div 2 = 6$.

(2) When the total number of strings is even. In this case there are two possibilities: (a) the chanterelle is doubled and two strings are tuned in unison (as in lute No. 242); in such a case the number of tones produced is equal to the total number of strings divided by two; (b) the two highest strings are single; in this case the number of tones produced is equal to the total number of strings plus two, divided by two. This last instance is illustrated by Mouton's lute, which has twenty strings, of which the two highest ones are single; $20 + 2 = 22$; $22 \div 2 = 11$; see also the tuning diagram on p. 226. When the total number of strings is even, the construction of the instrument should be examined to determine the number of tones correctly.

497 *Four courses.* Praetorius, *De Organographia*, p. 49.

498 *Florence.* G. Kinsky, *Geschichte der Musik in Bildern* (Leipzig, 1929), p. 42, fig. 5.

P. 228 499 *Seven members.* The tunings of different members of the lute family were taken from three sources: Praetorius, C. Sachs' *Real-Lexikon*, and G. Kinsky's *Musikhistorisches Museum von Wilhelm Heyer*, ii, p. 85; *Small Octave Lute* is assumed here to have only four courses, as the instrument was quite small (cf. J. Schlosser, *Alte Musikinstrumente*, Vienna, 1920, p. 55, and table vi, fig. 41).

P. 229 500 *The lute family.* This table should not be regarded as definitive. So far as the present writer is aware, this is the first attempt to establish the sizes of lutes in conjunction with the nomenclature. As an approximate guide it may prove useful.

501 *By letters.* In the French and English tablatures the open string was designated by a, the first fret by b, the second by c, and so on, d, e, f, g, h, i, and the ninth and the last by k.

P. 230 502 *Should be consulted.* One of the best and most comprehensive books on the subject of lute tablatures is Dr. Johannes Wolf's *Handbuch der Notationskunde* (Leipzig, 1913–19), vol. ii. Thomas Mace's *Musick's Monument* is a source of valuable information. *Encyclopédie de la musique*, pt. ii, vol. iii, pp. 1972–90, has an excellent article on the lute by Mme. Adrienne Mairy and M. Lionel de la Laurencie.

Dowland's and Mace's tunings were added on Canon Galpin's suggestion. He wrote: "I mention this because friends of mine, who are lutenists, are troubled by the fact that they cannot play Dowland's accompaniments and Mace's Lessons upon their instrument *in ordinary tuning*." Dowland's tuning is given by Mace on p. 209 of his *Musick's Monument*. "*The Flat French Tuning*" is given there on p. 83; Mace comments that it is called flat "erroniously" [sic] and should be called "sharp." The "*New French Tuning*" is given by Mace on p. 181, and its date is established by his mention on p. 191 that it was about forty years old. *Musick's Monument* was published in 1676.

P. 231 503 Thomas Mace, *op. cit.*, p. 48.

504 *Albrecht Dürer.* J. Schlosser, *op. cit.*, p. 54.

505 *Should be noted. Encyclopédie de la musique*, pt. ii, vol. iii, p. 1978.

506 *All of Paris. Encyclopédie de la musique, ibidem*; G. Kinsky, *op. cit.*, ii, p. 88.

507 *The lute became extinct.* Mattheson in his *Das*

Neu-Eröffnete Orchester (Hamburg, 1713) was very sarcastic as to the lutes and lute-players of his time. It is difficult to decide whether he felt a greater contempt for the lutes or the lutenists. His remarks are too long to quote here, but they should be read *in toto*. J. von Schlosser quoted Mattheson extensively. Cf. his *Sammlung alter Musikinstrumente*, pp. 45 ff. It is curious that early in the eighteenth century there were already outspoken people, like Mattheson, who saw that the lute no longer met the requirements for greater sonority and convenience of handling.

P. 231 508 *Student*. Mace's instructions should be compared with those for guitar playing of the Tarrega school. A striking similarity of technique will become apparent. Mace's instructions are still valid today.

P. 233 509 *Good Play*. Thomas Mace, *op. cit.*, pp. 71–74. Only a few redundant paragraphs are omitted. *A Lute Player* is the engraving by G. Edelinck from the painting by François de Troy of the lute-player Charles Mouton (b. 1626, lived in Paris 1678–92).

P. 235 510 *Between 1589 and 1621*. Cf. G. Kinsky, *op. cit.*, ii, pp. 269 ff.

P. 236 511 *Motion*. Mace, *op. cit.*, p. 207.

512 *Very Confounding*. Mace, *op. cit.*, p. 208.

513 *In 1607*. Caccini and Cavalieri also used the chitarrone in their opera orchestras. The score of *Orfeo* calls for two chitarroni in the list of instruments; but in the score proper three instruments are required. Thus act i, *Choro*, and act ii, *Ritornello*, both call for "*tre chitarroni*." Cf. *Tutti le Opere di Claudio Monteverdi*, ed. by G. Francesco Malpiero (Asolo, 1926–32), tomo xi.

P. 238 514 *Qūpūz*. C. Sachs, *Handbuch* (1930), p. 216. Cf. H. G. Farmer, *Studies in Oriental Musical Instruments*, p. 73.

515 *Continuation of the body*. There are several Oriental instruments which have this feature. The *barbaṭ* has been mentioned already. Cf. C. Sachs, *Real-Lexikon*, p. 89 a and b, where the *cobza* is pictured.

516 *Lower end fastening type*. Cf. C. Sachs, *Real-Lexikon*, pp. 251 f.

P. 239 517 *Middle Ages*. F. W. Galpin, *Old English Instruments*, pp. 26 f.

518 *Centuries*. C. Sachs, *Real-Lexikon*, p. 82 b; Kathleen Schlesinger, in *Encyclopaedia Britannica*, 11th ed., vi, p. 399, s.v. 'Cittern.'

P. 241 519 *Without a plectrum*. In this study only the old type guitars with gut strings are referred to. The modern instrument with steel wires played with a plectrum is more akin to the *chitarra battente*.

520 *Hittite monuments*. Kathleen Schlesinger, *Precursors of the Violin Family* (London, 1910), p. 446; *Encyclopaedia Britannica*, 11th ed., xii, p. 703.

521 *Guitarra morisca*. Kathleen Schlesinger, *Precursors*, pp. 242–243.

522 *Vihuelas*. Kathleen Schlesinger, *op. cit.*, p. 245. Also *Encyclopaedia Britannica*, xii, p. 703.

523 *Single-strung*. C. Sachs, *Handbuch* (1920), p. 225.

524 *Seven-stringed guitars*. Kathleen Schlesinger, *Encyclopaedia Britannica*, 11th ed., xii, p. 703. A seven-stringed instrument is pictured there: the picture is taken from Juan Bermudo's *Declaracion de instrumentos musicales* (Ossuna, 1555).

P. 242 525 *Ca. 1800*. G. Kinsky, *Musikhistorisches Museum von Wilhelm Heyer*, ii, p. 132.

526 *Nineteenth century*. Cf. A. S. Famintzyn, *Domra*; N. F. Findeisen, *Schilderungen aus der Geschichte der Musik in Russland* (1928–29), vol. ii.

P. 244 527 *St.-Julien*. W. L. von Lütgendorf, *Die Geigen- und Lautenmacher* (1913), ii, p. 124.

528 *Instrument*. The tuning of the guitar differs only in the location of the major third interval from that of the tenor lute as given by Praetorius (see *supra*, p. 228). The third string of the guitar is tuned to *g*, instead of *f*-sharp, thus shifting that interval from its middle position to one between the second and the third string.

P. 246 529 *London*, R. B. Armstrong, *English and Irish Instruments* (Edinburgh, 1908), p. 25.

530 *Etc. Ibid.*, p. 55.

531 *Respectively. Ibid.*, p. 56.

P. 247 532 *To suit. Ibid.*, p. 69.

P. 248 533 *Points out*. F. W. Galpin, *Old English Instruments of Music*, pp. 56 f.

534 *Plectra*. Cf. F. W. Galpin, *op. cit.*, plate xx; the lower left-hand circle represents a psaltery-player with plectra.

535 *States*. C. Sachs, *Handbuch* (1930), pp. 135 f.

536 *About 1400*. F. W. Galpin, *Old English Instruments*, p. 62.

537 *Pianoforte*. Kathleen Schlesinger, in *Encyclopaedia Britannica*, 11th ed., viii, p. 652, s.v. 'Dulcimer.'

P. 249 538 *Scholars*. Among them are Mme. Wanda Landowska and Mr. Arnold Dolmetsch, practical musicians who play ancient instruments. Mme. Landowska is interested primarily in keyboard instruments. Mr. Arnold Dolmetsch encompassed the whole field. In addition, Mr. Dolmetsch contributed much to the continuance and recovery of the technique of building ancient instruments. His keyboard instruments, lutes, viols, violins, recorders, are considered among the best musical instruments of ancient type now built.

539 *Uncertainties*. Cf. Karl Nef, *An Outline of the History of Music*, New York, 1935, p. 132. Speaking of the origin of bowed instruments the author states: ". . . their origin is shrouded in absolute darkness. It is possible,

but not at all certain, indeed, not even especially probable, that we took them from the Arabians." The triple qualification in this statement is an example of the bewilderment of a writer attempting to find factual data in the writings of specialists on the subject. Incidentally, Professor Nef's statement is a deserved criticism (perhaps not intentional) of the failure of some specialists to admit frankly that the objective facts available at present are inadequate to form any feasible theory of the origin of bowed instruments.

P. 249 540 *By name.* For instance, there are still uncertainties about such comparatively recent instruments as the 'violoncello piccolo' of J. S. Bach; cf. C. S. Terry, *Bach's Orchestra*, pp. 135 ff. Monteverdi's 'violino piccolo alla francese' is still a subject of discussion; see pp. 299 f. of this study.

541 *Exceptions.* Among these exceptions Michael Praetorius is the most conspicuous. His work is absolutely indispensable in any organological research.

542 *Irretrievably lost.* There was a mania at one time for destroying old instruments. Many clavichords and harpsichords were either broken up or changed into pianos; viols were mercilessly mutilated and converted into bastard violins, violas, and violoncellos. We have no means of knowing how many valuable instruments were lost.

543 *Detailed investigation.* It is the writer's hope that his investigation of sizes and tunings of viols of the sixteenth and seventeenth centuries contained in Appendix B contributes to the solution of some 'persistent problems' of organology. Their continuing presence became a standing disgrace, reflecting upon the imperfect state of organology as a science.

544 *Primitive instruments.* Nineteenth-century authors writing on the origin of the bowed instruments insisted that they descended either from the Arabian rabab or the Welsh crwth or, even, from the imaginary 'ravanastron' invented by F. J. Fétis in support of the Oriental origin of the bow. (Cf. *Histoire général de la musique*, Paris, 1869–76, ii, p. 292, and p. 293, fig. 46; quoted by Dr. Otto Andersson in *The Bowed-Harp*, London, 1930, pp. 8, 9; also Curt Sachs, *Die Musikinstrumente Indiens und Indonesiens*, Berlin, 1915, p. 111, where Dr. Sachs states that there is no word 'ravanastron' in the Hindu language.) Or that the bow was either of Northern European or of Oriental origin. Again, as Mr. G. R. Hayes pointed out (*Musical Instruments and their Music; The Viols*, p. 168), many writers on the origin of the violin attributed it to some individual discoverer. The simple idea that several individuals or factors can contribute to the same thing seems to have never occurred to them.

545 *Is correct.* The originator of this idea was Major Alexander Hajdecki, whose *Die Italienische Lira da Braccio* has done much to get historical research on bowed string instruments out of its rut. There will be more about this in the section on violins. The adjective 'Italian' is necessary, since it specifically identifies the seven-stringed instrument of which two strings were bourdons.

546 *Violin.* It differed in the geometrical outline; on some instruments the bottom part of the lower bouts had an indentation, the neck had no neck bracket, and there was no corresponding 'button' on the back. Dimensions, of course, differed considerably — the lira being larger than the violin; it was nearer in size to the viola.

547 *Chordophones.* The writer came to this conclusion after several unsuccessful attempts to devise a genealogical chart which would mean something. The lines of relationship cannot be properly represented in two dimensions. P. 250

548 *Complete instruments.* Dr. Curt Sachs is largely responsible for the introduction of this simple yet powerful method of analysis. Organology suffered from lack of definite terminology and still more from the absence of any definite methodology. Dr. Sachs' contributions to both are of fundamental importance.

549 *Not necessarily bowed.* The lute influenced the technique of the viol, bequeathing to it its tuning intervals and frets.

550 *Disappeared altogether.* The lateral pegs of the *rabab* were used on rebecs and later were adopted on viols and violins.

551 *Present time.* See F. W. Galpin, *A Textbook of European Musical Instruments*, London, 1937, pp. 132 f.

552 *Path of entry.* There still remains one more possibility, although it is somewhat conjectural. This would be the eastward travel of cultural influences from Ireland to Western and Northwestern Europe in the early centuries of the Middle Ages. Since it is known that the Coptic influences were strong in the Irish monastic and cultural life (cf. A. K. Porter, *The Crosses and Culture of Ireland*, New Haven, 1931, index, p. 133, under "Coptic influence in Ireland"), it does not seem impossible that musical instruments such as the harp, cruit, and some distant relative of the bowed harp were brought into Ireland from the Orient. Dr. Otto Andersson considered the possibility that the bowed harp might have been indigenous to the British isles and might have gone thence to Norway, then migrated eastward to Esthonia and Finland. (Cf. *op. cit.*, pp. 258 ff., 269.) This coincides with the eastward movement of culture in Northern Europe, also mentioned by Dr. Andersson (*ibid.*,

p. 258). The question of where bowed instruments came from, if they were brought to Ireland before their emigration to Europe, still remains open. The reasoning of some scholars that the crwth was originally a plucked instrument and later became a bowed one is only a temporary stop-gap.

The writer feels that it is too early to assign any definite chronology to the origin of the bow; as to its place of origin, all evidence points to the Orient.

P. 250 553 *The bowed-harp*. The bowed-harp is the generic term assigned by Dr. Otto Andersson to a whole series of bowed instruments found in Northern Europe, Esthonia, and Finland. Although not all Dr. Andersson's conclusions are acceptable, the value of the material collected by him, the 'nail technique' of playing the bowed-harp without a fingerboard, and many interesting questions raised by him, make his work outstanding and one of the most important contributions published recently. For a description of instruments the reader is referred to Dr. Andersson's work, *The Bowed-Harp*, London, 1930.

554 *Instruments*. C. Sachs, *Handbuch*, 1930, p. 177, note 2.

555 *String fastening*. An attentive examination of the photographs of the sculptured group on the tympanum of the church of Saint-Pierre, the Abbey of Moissac, has shown that the five-stringed instruments represented there had strings led back through the holes over the nut. This feature shows itself clearly only on photographs; the photo-engravings are too small and not clear enough. This type of instrument survived until our day almost intact. Cf. F. J. Fétis, *Histoire général de la musique*, ii, p. 141, fig. 18, and C. Sachs, *Handbuch*, 1930, p. 177, fig. 52 (a).

556 *Lira da braccio*. See Note 567.

557 *Rabab*. Cf. *Encyclopaedia of Islām*, iii, p. 1085, 3, in the article *Rabab* by Dr. H. G. Farmer.

558 *Later periods*. The only possible exception would be pochettes or kits (see No. 267 in this study), which had narrow, elongated bodies.

P. 251 559 *Open String*. According to the definition given in *American Tentative Standard Acoustical Terminology* (No. Z24.1-1936), p. 16, 6:7, "a harmonic is a partial whose frequency is an integral multiple of the fundamental frequency." The alternative definition (1.9 of the *American Tentative Standard*) is quoted here on p. 41, item 5. Musical usage of the term 'harmonic' with respect to a tone produced both on the bowed and the plucked instruments by lightly touching a string at a nodal point, becomes therefore inexact. A tone produced by this method is, acoustically, a partial tone. The duplication of terms could be easily avoided if the term 'flageolet tone,' or, simply, 'flageolet,' were used instead. Cf. P. A. Scholes, *The Oxford Companion to Music*, p. 9 a.

560 *Slavs*. Cf. Otto Andersson, *op. cit.*, p. 139.

561 *Andersson. Ibid.*, pp. 112, 113. This 'nail technique,' or, as the writer prefers to call it, the 'tangent technique,' deserves considerable attention. Its similarity to the technique of the clavichord is pointed out in the text, p. 334; also Note 866.

P. 252 562 *Islamic peoples*. Cf. *Encyclopaedia of Islām*, iii, p. 1085, 4.

563 *States. Ibid.*, p. 1085.

564 *Carrand Casket*. See Adolfo Venturi, in *Le Gallerie Nazionali Italiane*, Notizie e Documenti, iii (1897), p. 263, with a plate.

565 *Abbey of Moissac*. This remarkable sculptural group, referred to in Note 555, deserves the most attentive study. The photographs of the original tympanum *in situ* should be examined, since there are photographs of the plaster reproduction available in the local museum. There is an excellent paper by Dr. Meyer Shapiro, "The Romanesque Sculpture of Moissac," in *The Art Bulletin*, xiii, no. 3, pp. 250 ff., and no. 4, pp. 464 ff. The musical instruments alone deserve special study.

566 *String fastening*. The nomenclature of mediaeval instruments is far from being settled. The term *lira da braccio* applied in this instance follows the Dolmetsch school. Cf. Robert Donington, *The Work and Ideas of Arnold Dolmetsch*, 1932, p. 16.

567 *Body*. The writer prefers this name (*lira da braccio*) to that of the fiedel when applied to such instruments as that represented on Hans Memling's triptych now in Antwerp. Cf. Georg Kinsky, *Geschichte der Musik in Bildern*, p. 57, 2, the angel with the bowed chordophone on the extreme right. The evolution of this five-stringed type into the Italian *lira da braccio* was a logical step.

The fundamental typological characteristics which served as a connecting link were: the number of bowed strings (five), the occipital string fastening, the tripartite body of the guitar-fiedel type, and the holding position. The tunings can also be regarded as such a link, as suggested by Dr. Curt Sachs (*Handbuch*, 1930, p. 181).

568 *Finger-board*. The Italian *lira da braccio* is the ultimate development of the lyra type. Very few actual instruments survive, but its representations on paintings are fairly numerous. Cf. Georg Kinsky, *op. cit.*, pp. 142 f. More complete references are given in the section on violins.

P. 253 569 *Pegs*. This conjecture is not very probable. Among seven types of the *rabab* mentioned by Dr. H. G. Farmer in the article in the *Encyclopaedia of Islām*, already referred to, there is no instrument of this type. The name 'rebec' is used too loosely, being applied to instruments of the lyra group. It is true that generically the lyra belongs to the *rabab* group (cf. H. G. Farmer, *loc. cit.*, iii, p. 1085, type 4), but since this group is so numerous, a more specific division is desirable, especially with reference to instruments used in Europe. The dividing line should be the type of peg and the shape of the head. Rebecs have lateral pegs and a head with cheeks somewhat similar to those of the violin. Lyras have sagittal pegs and flat, leaf-shaped (sometimes polygonal) head; in these typological characteristics they are similar to the Levantine *rabab*.

P. 253 570 *Back*. This instrument is represented correctly in many works, among them in F. J. Fétis, *op. cit.*, ii, p. 146, fig. 20; J. Rühlmann, *Die Geschichte der Bogeninstrumente*, i, fig. 8, copied from Alexandre Christianowitsch, *Esquisse historique de la musique arabe*, Cologne, 1863; reproduced also in C. Sachs, *Real-Lexikon*, p. 317 a. Also C. Engel, *A Descriptive Catalogue of the Musical Instruments in the South Kensington Museum*, 2nd ed., London, 1874, p. 143, fig. 108. G. Kinsky, *Musikhistorisches Museum*, ii, p. 328; there are represented photographs of three *rababs* and two rebecs.

571 *Santa Maria*. Grove's *Dictionary of Music*, iii, plate xlvi, facing p. 260. The *Cantigas de Santa Maria* is one of the most important sources of information on Spanish music and musical instruments of the middle of the thirteenth century. For exact references, cf. Kathleen Schlesinger, *Instruments of the Modern Orchestra*, ii, p. 243.

572 *Festival music*. A very interesting suggestion was made by Mr. Robert Donington in *The Work and Ideas of Arnold Dolmetsch*, p. 15, on the possible use of rebecs for achieving special color effects in conjunction with violins in the modern orchestra. Also see G. R. Hayes, *The Viols*, pp. 158 f. Another possibility is that the rebec should be tuned *d′*, *a′*, *e″*. Such tuning is more logical, if the size of the instrument and construction of the body are taken into consideration. This opens an interesting line of investigation. See Note 780, the violin tuning.

P. 254 573 *Kinsky. Musikhistorisches Museum*, ii, p. 583.

574 *Folk-poems*. A. S. Famintzyn, *Gusli*, St. Petersburg, 1890, pp. 1 ff.

P. 255 575 *Family*. In Grove's *Dictionary of Music*, 1928, v, p. 514, there is the following statement: "The viol was made in three principal sizes — Bass (*viola da gamba*), tenor (*viola da braccio*), and treble or descant." Mr. Cecil Forsyth in *Orchestration* (London, 1914 and 1937), p. 300, also states: "The original Viol-family consists of three members, (1) the *Discant-* or *Treble Viol*, (2) the *Tenor-Viol* or Viola da braccio, (3) the *Bass-Viol* or *Viola da gamba*." Both statements are similar and both are wrong. Paraphrasing them in English, they would mean: The viol family consists of three members, the treble viol, the viola (alto violin), and the bass viol. The viol family cannot consist of a mixture of viols and violins. *Viola da braccio* is the generic name of the violin family and under no circumstances should it be confused with the *viola da gamba* family. It is possible to adduce such a mass of testimony on the correct usage of both names that there is no excuse for perpetuating a false terminology. Praetorius is the most explicit in his *Tabella Universalis* (*De Organographia*, pp. 20–30). On page 25 he lists the tunings of the *Viole de Gamba* or *Violen* and on page 26 he lists those of the *Viole de Braccio* or *Geigen*. Tables xx and xxi of *Theatrum Instrumentorum*, reproduced here on pp. 363 and 302, show unmistakably what Praetorius meant by the *Viole da gamba* and *Viole da braccio* (German *Geigen*, or our violins). The testimony of writers of the late sixteenth, seventeenth, and eighteenth centuries with respect to the generic difference of the two families is consistent. The nomenclature of individual instruments was very uncertain (see Appendix E), but the names of families of bowed instruments were never confused. See p. 298 on *viola da braccio* in a specific sense.

576 *Viola da spalla*. Here is another name about which there exists the greatest confusion. See p. 303 for a correct description.

577 *Consort of viols*. 'Consort' was the generic term used for a group of several instrumentalists or several instruments, or the music for such a combination of instruments. For details see *New English Dictionary*, ii, pt. 2, p. 868. Specifically, there were two kinds of consorts: whole consorts, consisting of instruments of the same family, and broken consorts, in which several instruments of different families played together. Our symphony orchestras are 'broken consorts.'

P. 257 578 *Simpson. Chelys, Minuritionum Artificio exornata: . . . The Division Viol, or, The Art of Playing ex tempore upon a Ground*. Authore Christophoro Simpson. Editio secunda. London. M.DC.LXV.II. The last two figures are stencilled and added, it seems, later. Cf. G. R. Hayes, *The Viols*, p. 121, n. 2, for explanation.

P. 255 579 *Old works*. This is an excellent example of the uncertainty with respect to musical instruments when they are studied only in their musicological aspect. Practical violists and viol-makers developed instruments to suit special requirements. See the next note.

580 *Nine*. There are two treble instruments, one alto, two tenors, three basses, and one contrabass in the viol family. Praetorius also counted the *Viol de Gamba Sub-Bass* (*De Organographia*, p. 46) or the *Gross-Contra-*

Bass-Geig which is represented on table v, fig. 1, of *Theatrum Instrumentorum*, among the members of the viol family. This is logical, because even our orchestral double-bass is, really, a member of the viol family. Since very few instruments of this size were ever built, it is deemed inadvisable to include them among viols. In each case an addition to the viol family was made on practical grounds. Thus, the division viol was added for a faster work and its size was smaller than that of the consort bass. The lyra-viol (*viola bastarda*) was made still smaller to adapt it better for multiple stopping.

P. 255 581 *Mr. Gerald R. Hayes.* In Appendix B it is proven that Dr. Kinsky's terminology and viol sizes follow those of Praetorius. It is also shown there that German and English terminologies are practically identical. See Table II, p. 360, and Table III, p. 361, of this study.

582 *The Viol Family.* The names, sizes, and tunings of viols are 'persistent problems' of organology. In the course of studying these and other related problems (see Appendix B), the writer has reached the following conclusions. (1) The names of viols in all the catalogues so far published are applied to them, with a few exceptions, quite arbitrarily, and without any consistent reason with respect to sizes. (2) The average viol sizes of the standard pattern were worked out by old makers within reasonably close limits. (3) Average sizes of viols, regarded in their absolute aspect (i.e., irrespective of the names applied to them), remained constant over a very long period of time, namely from about 1575 until the end of their existence. (4) Average sizes of viols, regarded in their relative aspect (i.e., when a definite name was attached to them), varied at different periods; in other words, the same instruments were called differently and played different parts. (5) This practice just mentioned was not haphazard, but quite consistent, so it is possible to trace it definitely.

These conclusions, as the writer fully realized, are at variance with certain firmly rooted opinions. Therefore a very thorough and detailed study was made of sizes and proportions of viols, and a graph of the sizes was drawn (see Plate XVI), which provided a firm ground for subsequent conclusions. For the finding of average sizes all reliable dimensions of viols of the standard pattern were tabulated and analyzed statistically. It was found that the average basic sizes fell naturally into definite groups and were confined, as stated, within reasonably close limits, in many cases within closer limits than those of the modern orchestral viola. It was also found that the sizes of viols scaled from Praetorius' drawings fitted well within those limits. This was quite an unexpected confirmation of conclusions as to the sizes of viols in their absolute aspect. It revealed also a consistent difference in nomenclature between the English series of viols as presented in this table and that of Praetorius-Kinsky (see Table III, p. 361), or the German series of viols. The comparative studies of names, sizes, and tunings (see Table IV, p. 361, Table V, p. 363, and Table VII, p. 372) brought out a complete and consistent picture of their mutual relationship.

583 *The thirteenth century.* Cf. *Geschichte der Musik in Bildern*, ed. by Georg Kinsky, Leipzig, 1929, p. 45, 3. There is also the English edition. Cf. J. Rühlmann, *Die Geschichte der Bogeninstrumente*, table vii: for the later types, table viii. P. 258

584 *The twelfth century.* Cf. J. Rühlmann, *op. cit.*, p. 119, fig. h. Also Laurent Grillet, *Les ancêtres du violon*, Paris, 1901, p. 122. Grillet assigns the image of the 'rote' player to the thirteenth century.

585 *Belgium.* The writer had access to the collection of photographs of musical instruments belonging to the Crosby Brown Collection of Musical Instruments in the Metropolitan Museum of Art, New York. It is unfortunate that very little is known of the Italian instruments in various local museums in Italy; yet there are some very interesting instruments which should be described. The Brussels Collection instruments are numbered 1407, 1410, 1420, 1421. P. 259

586 *The Vienna Collection.* Julius Schlosser, *Die Sammlung alter Musikinstrumente*, Vienna, 1920, table xvi, fig. 71, and table xvii, figures 73 and 74. The last two instruments have only four strings.

587 *Mr. Hayes. Viols*, plate i and in the text. If this instrument is as old as Mr. Hayes thinks (cf. p. 45), then our opinion of viols should be considerably revised. It looks too modern in some details, especially the F-holes. But if accepted as a genuine, untampered example of the late fifteenth-century work, even as an exception to the general rule, it would support Mr. Vander Straeten's statement that the scroll is a fifteenth-century detail; cf. his *History of the Violin*, London, 1933, p. 25, fig. 26.

588 *Philomele.* Cf. G. Kinsky, *Musikhistorisches Museum*, ii, p. 526, no. 904.

589 *Collection.* Cf. G. Kinsky, *op. cit.*, ii, p. 448, no. 802; p. 451, no. 811; p. 452, no. 808.

590 *Copenhagen.* Cf. *Carl Claudius' Samling af Gamle Musikinstrumenter*, Copenhagen, 1931, p. 210; p. 213, nos. 261 and 264; p. 215, no. 265; p. 223, no. 272; p. 225, no. 280.

591 *Vienna Collection.* Julius Schlosser, *op. cit.*, plate xvii, figs. 72, 75, 76. P. 260

592 *Brussels Collection.* Instruments nos. 1402, 1414, 1424, 1425. Information derived from photographs in the Metropolitan Museum of Art, New York.

P. 260 593 *Sonority.* The plate facing page one of *The Division Viol* represents two viols; the one on the left has a shape very much like that of a violoncello. With reference to this instrument Simpson tells that it is "... better for sound."

594 *Remarks. Op. cit.*, p. 1.

595 *Process.* It seems that the bellies of the instruments of the Vienna Collection referred to in Note 591 were not carved, but shaped by steaming.

P. 261 596 *Pitch.* This is true of instruments of the seventeenth and eighteenth centuries. The sixteenth-century mean pitch is not absolutely certain. See Appendix B, p. 360.

597 *Character.* In *Atlantis*, Nov., 1934, there is an excellent article with pictures illustrating some fine viol heads.

598 *Narrowed.* A narrow neck *per se* is not necessarily an objectionable feature, since the sixteenth-century instruments had rather narrow necks, but on some instruments which were examined by the writer the necks were made too narrow. A characteristic viol neck is as thin as that on the lute, and holds the frets better.

599 *Frets.* C. Simpson, *op. cit.*, p. 1. Quoted on p. 280 of this study. The graduation in sizes of frets is also important. See p. 224, fig. 37.

P. 262 600 *Seven strings.* A seven-stringed *viola bastarda* is represented in a painting by Domenico Zampieri (Domenichino), ca. 1620. Later the seven-stringed bass viol became almost the standard instrument of the soloist. Cf. C. Sachs, *Handbuch*, 1930, p. 195, fig. 65; also G. Kinsky, *Geschichte der Musik in Bildern*, p. 145, 3. Fig. 65 of *Handbuch* shows six (!) strings. Tuning pegs on the right side number four, so the total number of strings should be seven. Kinsky's picture also shows four pegs on the right side, but the number of strings cannot be counted due to the size of reproduction.

601 *Mace. Musick's Monument*, p. 246.

602 *Fault.* Quoted in its context on page 274 of this study.

603 *Sound-holes.* Experiments on viols in this Collection and the geometrical method of laying the correct position of the bridge prove that Mace was right.

604 *Germany.* A fine example of Joachim Tielke's work is the bass viol in the Claudius Collection. Cf. the Catalogue, p. 221, fig. 270, which gives several views of the instrument. Tielke's viols, however, miss something in their body outline. The viols of old English masters, such as Henry Jaye (cf. F. W. Galpin, *Old English Instruments of Music*, London, 1932, plate xvii), some viols of Barak Norman (cf. Curt Sachs, *Sammlung alter Musikinstrumente*, Berlin, 1922, plate 14, no. 168); the viols of Martin Hoffmann (*Musikhistorisches Museum*, ii, p. 452, no. 812) and of Johann Christian Hoffmann (*ibid.*, p. 447, no. 805, and p. 468, no. 819) are more harmonious in their proportions and outlines.

605 *Viols.* This uncompromising position is taken by the Dolmetsch school, with which the writer is in complete agreement. His own experiments on this point convinced him that viols should be played fretted. Chapter v of Mr. G. R. Hayes' *Treatment of Instrumental Music* should be studied attentively; one becomes convinced after hearing a fretted viol played in the proper manner. P. 263

606 *Should be done.* See the lute section of this study, p. 224, for complete instructions for fretting. Lutes and viols had necks of the same cross section, that is, somewhat flat, so the technique of fretting described by Mace for the lute is applicable also to the viol. See page 280 for particulars of viol fretting.

607 *Playing.* Cf. G. R. Hayes, *op. cit.*, p. 40, where he states that the frets in no way interfere with the performance of music in a rapid tempo.

608 *Finger-board.* See Note 448, p. 417.

609 *Lutes.* See p. 228. P. 264

610 *Simpson. Op. cit.*, pp. 4, 5.

611 *Strings.* The italics are mine. P. 265

612 *Stopping.* That is, for playing accidentals when convenient.

613 *Discretion.* Special phonograph records of the unfretted bass viol played by a competent artist show that when chords of three or more tones are struck the exigencies of stopping require that some of them be played open. The difference of tone color and sonority between the open and stopped strings becomes immediately apparent. The result can hardly be called satisfactory. On the fretted instrument the tones of the strings when stopped against the frets have the quality of open tones, so the tone color of the whole scale is uniform and sonorities are equalized. Cf. G. R. Hayes, *The Treatment of Instrumental Music*, pp. 40 f.

614 *Factors.* These factors are the proper 'Appointments' of a viol, such as strings of suitable size, tuned a half tone lower than the present standard; properly shaped (flatter) bridge; the real viol bow, which is less stiff than the violin bow and has less hair.

615 *Chords.* Old musicians called such chords a 'Full Stop.' Cf. Thomas Mace, *op. cit.*, p. 259; also G. R. Hayes, *The Viols*, p. 134.

616 *Fretted.* A waggish musical friend of the writer, after attending a concert of old music played by a very competent violoncellist on an unfretted bass viol, remarked that he had not heard the viol. To the question, "What did you hear?," he answered, "A cellamba!" ('cello plus gamba). P. 266

The tone color of an unfretted viol is not distinctive enough to justify the existence of an instrument which reminds one of something else and is more difficult to play than the violoncello. On this point see Note 624 below.

P. 266 617 *Manner*. The old viol bowing technique survived only among the double-bass players; but even in this case the tendency is to adopt the violoncello type bow and its corresponding technique. The correct manner of holding the viol bow is given in the words of Christopher Simpson on p. 280.

618 *Violin-bowing*. Arnold Dolmetsch, *The Interpretation of the Music of the XVIIth and XVIIIth Centuries* (1915), pp. 446 ff. Quoted by G. R. Hayes, *The Viols*, p. 67.

619 *Worse*. *Op. cit.*, p. 248. The first sentence quoted is a side note. Mace's admonitions are not obsolete; they still apply to some violin and violoncello players of today.

620 *Leg viols*. The proper holding position of viols is argued very ably by Mr. G. R. Hayes in his book on viols; cf. pp. 30 ff., especially pp. 32, 33, 34. *Gamba* in Italian means 'leg.'

P. 267 621 *Thin*. See p. 261 and Note 598, p. 426.

622 *Questionable merit*. Late in the nineteenth century and in the early years of the twentieth century several societies were organized abroad (mostly in France) for the revival of ancient music for old bowed instruments. These groups should be given all the credit they deserve for their pioneering work. Unfortunately, very little was known about viols at that time. The writers on the bowed instruments were doing their research under the misconception that the violin descended from the viol, and assumed that the smaller-sized viols should be played the same way as the violin and the viola (alto violin), with the violin bow and, of course, unfretted.

The existence of mutilated viols with the ribs cut down and the necks rounded and shortened only added to the confusion. Therefore the early modern revival of viol playing continued the degenerate practices of the late eighteenth century, when the viol was going out of use.

So at present there are two schools of viol playing, one of which still continues with its early misconceptions, and another one which is supported by the painstaking scholarship based on the writings of contemporary authorities such as Martin Agricola, Gerle, Lanfranco, Ganassi, Ortiz, Zacconi, Cerreto, Cerone, Praetorius, Playford, Simpson, Mace, and Rousseau.

This divergence of views has not only an academic but also a practical significance. Recently the writer examined some viols made abroad as late as 1935, excellently contructed, but in their smaller sizes adapted for playing under the chin, violin-fashion. The necks were rounded and made shorter so that it would be impossible to fret them properly. When instruments are built adapted for a practice which the best scholarship proves as a mistaken conception, an organologist has a right to question whether such a new family of instruments has any merit or even a reason for existence.

623 *Standard*. Some of the writer's personal friends who play the old viols report unanimously that the instruments 'feel happier' and sound better when tuned to a proper pitch, half a tone lower than our present standard. An important technical point: on some old instruments which passed through the hands of modern repairers the bass-bars are made larger and stiffer to accommodate the viols to the modern high pitch. If the bass-bar is enlarged, the lower pitched tuning does not restore completely the old tone color. The remedy is to restore the bass-bar to its original size and tune the viol to the low pitch.

624 *Play well*. The fretted instrument is easier to play and the viol fingering technique, although less uniform than that of the violin, is admirably adapted to the frets. When the frets are discarded, then to all the difficulties of stopping an unfretted instrument are added those of stopping a greater number of strings; the irregular intervals of the viol tunings then aggravate this difficulty still further.

Therefore, if viol playing is to become popular among amateurs, viols should be built properly and played fretted.

On viols as a chamber music instrument, see G. R. Hayes, *The Treatment of Instrumental Music*, pp. 41 ff.

625 *Three periods*. Such divisions are, of necessity, somewhat arbitrary and not applicable to all countries.

626 *Quartets*. Cf. G. R. Hayes, *Viols*, pp. 86 f.

627 *Three strings*. See p. 309, fig. 56. P. 268

628 *Right hand*. Reproduced in many works. Cf. Carl Engel, *A Descriptive Catalogue of the Musical Instruments in the South Kensington Museum*, 2nd ed., London, 1874, p. 100, fig. 83; J. Rühlmann, *op. cit.*, plate vi, fig. 2; *Encyclopédie de la musique*, Paris, 1927, pt. ii, vol. iii, p. 1755, fig. 930. The facsimile reproduction in G. Kinsky's *Geschichte der Musik in Bildern*, p. 35, fig. 5; also in O. Andersson's *The Bowed-Harp*, p. 235, fig. 86.

629 *Andersson*. *The Bowed-Harp*. All chapter vi on the Welsh crwth.

630 *Bosherville*. L. Grillet, *Les Ancêtres du Violon*, p. 120.

631 *Cologne*. L. Grillet, *op. cit.*, p. 121.

632 *Dijon*. Cf. *Encyclopaedia Britannica*, 11th ed., xx, p. 268, fig. 6. P. 269

P. 269 633 *London*. Kathleen Schlesinger, *The Instruments of the Modern Orchestra*, ii, p. 388, fig. 129.

634 *Miniatures*. Grove's *Dictionary of Music and Musicians*, 1927, iii, plate xlvi, facing p. 260, fig. 1.

635 *Troyes*. Cf. L. Grillet, *op. cit.*, p. 122. See Note 584, p. 425.

636 *Switzerland*. *Die Minnesinger in Bildern der Maneseschen Handschrift*. Insel Bücherei no. 450, Leipzig; fine colored reproduction. Also G. Kinsky, *Geschichte der Musik in Bildern*, p. 47, fig. 4.

637 *Viol*. *Encyclopaedia Britannica*, 11th ed., xxviii, p. 101, s.v. 'Viol.'

638 *Van Eyck*. G. Kinsky, *Geschichte der Musik in Bildern*, p. 56, fig. 2. Also C. Sachs, *Handbuch*, 1930, p. 187.

639 *Violins*. Cf. E. Vander Straeten, *The History of the Violin*, p. 25, fig. 26. The viol represented there is taken from *De Musica Tractatus*, Bologna, 1482, by Bartolomeo Ramos de Pareja. See Note 587, p. 425. The writer is not certain of Mr. Vander Straeten's reference, since he had no opportunity to examine the primary source. The same type of viol is shown on the title page picture of Ganassi's *Regola Rubertina* published in Venice, 1542.

640 *Without bridges*. Instruments of this type are represented without a bridge in many pictures, etchings, and woodcuts. Dr. Curt Sachs calls this type the *Lautenfiedel* (lute-fiedel). Cf. his *Handbuch*, 1930, pp. 185 f., where numerous references are given.

P. 270 641 *Viol family*. The geometrical method of construction and the analysis of the outlines of the viol and the violin developed by this writer show that viol outlines of the standard pattern follow certain well-defined ratios. Dynamic Symmetry and the golden section enter into their construction just as much as into that of the violin. Viols are perfectly developed instruments. See Appendix C for proportions of viols.

642 *Finger-board*. Cf. C. Sachs, *Handbuch*, 1930, p. 189, fig. 60. Viol no. 1429 of the Brussels Collection has a very narrow waist.

643 *Mentioned above*. See Note 639. Cf. C. Sachs, *op. cit.*, p. 189, fig. 61.

644 *Large size*. Cf. C. Sachs, *op. cit.*, p. 190, fig. 63. For Tintoretto's picture, see G. Kinsky, *Geschichte der Musik in Bildern*, p. 113, 2. Jost Amman's woodcuts are reproduced *ibid.*, p. 81, figs. 6 ('Drei Geiger'), 7, 8.

645 *Precision*. See Appendix A.

P. 271 646 *Complex*. For a complete discussion of this question see Appendix B.

647 *Artist-craftsman*. Cf. F. W. Galpin, *Old English Instruments of Music*, 1932, plate xvii, facing p. 90. See also Note 604, p. 426.

P. 272 648 *Gamba*. Beginning with Berlioz' treatise on instrumentation.

649 *Bitter*. Hubert Le Blanc's *Défense de la basse de viole contre les entreprises du violon et les prétentions du violoncel*, Amsterdam, 1740, is one of the most vitriolic attacks on the violin and the violoncello.

P. 273 650 *Nattier*. Fine reproduction in *Masters in Art* series, pt. iii, vol. iii, *Nattier*, Boston, June, 1902. Also G. Kinsky, *op. cit.*, p. 238, 3.

P. 274 651 *Amateur*. Cf. G. R. Hayes, *The Treatment of Instrumental Music*, pp. 41 f., and *The Viols*, pp. 236 f.

652 *Chest of viols*. A 'chest of viols' had two meanings. One of them was the chest proper which was defined as "a shallow vertical press with double doors" (cf. Grove's *Dictionary of Music*, ii, p. 618), or "a large hutch, with several apartments and partitions in it; each partition was lined with green bays to keep the instruments from being injured by the weather." For this quotation and one in the text, cf. Lyn Venn, "The 'Chest of Viols' and Its Music," *The Strad*, 1920, pp. 195 f., 213 f. Also quoted in Grove's *Dictionary*.

Another meaning referred to a group of viols and was equivalent to a consort of viols.

P. 275 653 *World*. Thomas Mace, *Musick's Monument*, 1676, pp. 245, 246.

654 *Mace*. *Ibid.*, p. 234.

P. 276 655 *Society*. Cf. G. Kinsky, *Musikhistorisches Museum*, ii, pp. 429 f. and note 1 on p. 430.

656 *Lütgendorf*. *Die Geigen- und Lautenmacher*, 1913, ii, p. 232.

657 *Pointed out*. *The Viols*, pp. 36 f. Also cf. Thomas Mace, *Musick's Monument*, p. 234.

P. 277 658 *Lyra way*. John Playford's book, published in 1661, was entitled *Musick's Recreation on the Viol, Lyra-Way*. Cf. G. R. Hayes, *The Viols*, p. 128, n. 1.

659 *Instruments*. Cf. C. Sachs, "Die Viola bastarda," *Zeitschrift der internationalen Musikgesellschaft*, xv, pp. 123–125 (1914).

660 *Dr. Curt Sachs*. *Handbuch*, 1930, p. 194.

661 *Sizes of viols*. Rousseau is quoted on p. 373 of this study.

662 *Larger*. Praetorius, *De Organographia*, p. 47. This passage will be meaningless and subject to erroneous interpretation until the sizes of instruments are taken into consideration. See Note 670 below.

P. 278 663 *Alto*. Praetorius, *op. cit.*, p. 47. Cf. G. R. Hayes, *The Viols*, pp. 134 f., on the exacting demands of lyra music.

664 *Tablature notation*. Cf. G. R. Hayes, *The Viols*, p. 126. One of the points seldom mentioned, to the writer's knowledge, in connection with tablature notation is that composers had to know the playing tech-

nique of instruments to perfection to be able to write practical music. The staff notation shifts the responsibility to the player and much impractical instrumental music is written by people whose inspiration outruns their knowledge of instrumentation.

P. 278 665 *Praetorius. Op. cit.*, p. 26, under no. 21, *Viol Bastarda.*

666 *d′*. G. R. Hayes, *op. cit.*, p. 132, gives this tuning (his no. 4) as AA, D, G, d, *a*, d′. The *a* is incorrect. See the tuning no. 5 of Praetorius in the table just referred to.

667 *Lower.* Cf. G. R. Hayes, *op. cit.*, p. 131, note 4.

668 *Ferrabosco.* Cf. G. R. Hayes, *op. cit.*, p. 131.

669 *Consort bass.* Cf. Praetorius, *De Organographia*, p. 47.

670 *Differed.* The sizes of lyra-viols have always been a stumbling-block for organologists. Cf. V. C. Mahillon, *Catalogue du Musée Instrumental du Conservatoire Royal de Musique de Bruxelles*, i (1893), p. 318; correction in iii (1900), p. 46. Dr. Georg Kinsky's comment: *Musikhistorisches Museum von Wilhelm Heyer*, ii (1912), p. 492 (1). Dr. Curt Sachs' sarcastic comments on both: "Die Viola Bastarda," *Zeitschrift der internationalen Musikgesellschaft*, xv, p. 124. It happens that none of these three esteemed scholars is entirely right.

P. 279 671 *With them.* G. R. Hayes, *The Viols*, pp. 117 f.

672 *Ground.* See Note 578 for the exact title. The quotation is from pp. 1–4.

673 *Perfection of it.* 'Swing' is not so modern.

674 *Thirty inches.* This particular measurement and that of the bow, given by Simpson as twenty-seven inches, is a moot point. Mr. G. R. Hayes solved the problem (cf. *The Viols*, p. 37, note 1, and p. 122, note 4) by the assumption that Simpson had a shorter measure in his mind, such as the 'Burgos foot' of Spain. The alternative is that Simpson used the English inch. In this case the vibrating length of the string on the division viol would be about 76.2 cm. Since the length of the body of a viol is about equal to the length of its strings, on the second assumption Simpson's division viol would have a body 72 to 74 cm. long, or approximately that of Praetorius' *viola bastarda.* This fact has interesting implications, one of which is that some musicians might have preferred the old fashioned instruments of the larger series.

P. 280 675 *Finger-board.* This is one of the proofs that the higher 'positions' were used in viol playing. Cf. G. R. Hayes, *The Viols*, p. 76.

676 *Inches.* See Note 674.

677 *Is best.* Thomas Mace in *Musick's Monument*, p. 248, repeats Simpson's directions for holding the bow, but also states: "Yet I must confess, that for *my own Part*, I could never *Use It so Well*, as when I held It 2 or 3 *Inches off the Nut* (more or less) according to the *Length or Weight of the Bow*, for *Good Poyzing of It*: But 'tis possible, that by *Use* I might have made It *as Familiar to My self*, as It was to *Him*."

678 *Require.* J. Rousseau recommends holding the thumb opposite the middle finger. "Le Port de main consiste à la porter vers le haut du Manche ou sont les Touches, en arrondissant le poignet et les doigts, alors il faut placer toujours le pouce sous le doigt du milieu." *Traité de la viole*, 1687, p. 29.

P. 281 679 *Sainte-Colombe.* J. Rousseau, *op. cit.*, p. 24. Quoted by Dr. Georg Kinsky, *Musikhistorisches Museum*, ii, p. 439.

680 *Earlier.* The seven-stringed viol is represented on Tintoretto's painting *Musicirende Frauen* in the Dresden Gallery of Paintings. Cf. G. Kinsky, *op. cit.*, p. 395. Also see Note 600.

P. 282 681 *Instruments.* Lütgendorf, *Die Geigen- und Lautenmacher*, 1913, ii, p. 183.

682 *Viola.* This is one of the examples of the decline of the viol referred to in Note 622.

P. 283 683 *Condition.* This point was very carefully ascertained. There are no indications of any sort that it was ever changed.

P. 284 684 *Psaltery.* Cf. *An Illustrated Catalogue of the Music Loan Exhibition . . . 1904*, London, 1909, p. 149. The reader has a choice of names!

685 *Esraj.* Cf. Curt Sachs, *Real-Lexikon*, Berlin, 1913, for description of these instruments, s.v. 'Esrār.'

686 *Bowed Strings. De Organographia*, p. 47.

687 *After 1600.* Cf. G. R. Hayes, *The Viols*, pp. 127 f., the quotation from Playford's *Musick's Recreation on the Viol, Lyra-Way*, 1661. The reference there is to the Lyra-viol.

688 *Aside.* This passage from Playford refers to the discontinuance of sympathetic strings on the lyra-viol. There is a lack of definite agreement among organologists as to whether a lyra-viol (*viola bastarda*) should be regarded as an instrument with or without sympathetic strings. The German organologists seem to think that their presence is an important typological characteristic.

There is another interesting point in connection with the presence or absence of sympathetic strings on the lyra-viol. Dr. Curt Sachs in his article, "Die Viola Bastarda," already referred to in Note 670, is of the opinion that the bowed instruments with sympathetic strings should have a rose on the belly (". . . ein richtig konstruiertes Sympathiesaiteninstrument Rose und Schlitze braucht," *loc. cit.*, p. 125). When the sympathetic strings were taken off the lyra-viol, the presence of a rose became superfluous. As a matter of fact, it was never necessary, since it is a well known acoustical fact that on the bowed instruments any large opening, such as a rose, interferes with the distinctness of sound. On some later viols, the only reminder of roses formerly cut in the bellies were little embellishments such as the inlaid heart-shaped piece on the viol No. 271 (see p. 275, technical description). Since a rose is not necessarily the sign of a *viola bastarda* (see Note 921 for reference to other viols; the *Lauten-Fiedel* of Virdung and Martin Agricola had them also), can it be taken as one of the identifying marks of a *viola bastarda* in absence of any others? Specifically, can such instruments as viols nos. 165 and 2482 of the Berlin Collection, already questioned for a different reason (their sizes: see Note 921), be regarded as lyra-viols?

P. 284 689 *Sixteenth Century.* Cf. *Encyclopaedia Britannica*, 11th ed., viii, p. 834 a.

690 *Basse de viole d'amour.* Cf. Curt Sachs, *Real-Lexikon*, 1913, p. 35 b, equivalent to *viola bastarda*; also G. Kinsky, *Musikhistorisches Museum*, ii, p. 493. The originator of this term is, it seems, M. Laurent Grillet (cf. his *Les ancêtres du violon*, i, p. 213). According to him, it would be logical to apply the qualification 'd'amour' to all instruments with sympathetic strings. The writer was unable to trace the use of this term to any other source. *Viola bastarda* is a very old term, mentioned first in 1589 (cf. Otto Kinkeldey, *Orgel und Klavier*, pp. 173 f., and p. 312, the note example; cf. also Curt Sachs, *Handbuch*, p. 194). The *viole d'amour* is a late seventeenth-century development. If the historical perspective were undistorted in the nomenclature of musical instruments, the term *basse de viole d'amour* would be given a secondary position.

691 *Pochette d'amour.* Cf. G. Kinsky, *Musikhistorisches Museum*, ii, p. 350, no. 741.

P. 285 692 *Violin.* According to F. A. Weber, it should be longer. Cf. G. Kinsky, *op. cit.*, p. 476, text and note 2.

693 *Rousseau. Traité de la viole*, 1687, p. 22. Quoted by Dr. Georg Kinsky, *op. cit.*, p. 477; also by G. R. Hayes, *The Viols*, p. 216. The cither viol No. 279 of this study is one of the illustrations.

694 *de Brossard.* Cf. *Encyclopédie de la musique*, pt. ii, vol. iii, p. 1781 a, text and note 5.

695 *Mattheson.* Cf. Georg Kinsky, *Musikhistorisches Museum*, ii, p. 477.

P. 286 696 *von sich geben. De Organographia*, p. 48.

697 *Works.* Cf. G. Kinsky, *Musikhistorisches Museum*, ii, p. 477.

698 *Seven.* Cf. *Encyclopédie de la musique*, pt. ii, vol. iii, p. 1784.

699 *English Violet.* Cf. Leopold Mozart, *Versuch einer gründlichen Violinschule*, Augsburg, 1756, p. 4. A facsimile reprint edited by Dr. Bernhard Paumgartner, 1922, is available. Quoted by Dr. G. Kinsky, *op. cit.*, ii, pp. 478 f. There is a fine picture in Kinsky's work, ii, p. 488, no. 851.

700 *Numerous.* Many of them are given by Dr. G. Kinsky, *op. cit.*, ii, pp. 478, 479. The statement itself was made by Leopold Mozart, *op. cit.*, p. 4.

701 *Tuned.* This tuning was given by Mattheson in his *Das neu-eröffnete Orchestre*, 1713, p. 282. Cf. G. Kinsky, *op. cit.*, ii, p. 477; also G. R. Hayes, *The Viols*, p. 216.

702 *Strings.* Cf. Praetorius, *De Organographia*, p. 47. This practice was suggested also by Playford in 1661. Cf. G. Kinsky, *Musikhistorisches Museum*, ii, p. 491, note 1.

703 *Solo.* Charles Martin Loeffler (1861–1935), the distinguished composer and violinist, played the *viole d'amour*. He presented the *viole d'amour* made in the eighteenth century by Tomaso Eberle of Naples to Mrs. Isabella Stewart Gardner. This instrument is now in the Gardner Museum, Fenway Court, Boston. Cf. that Museum's *General Catalogue*, 1935, p. 19.

704 *In existence.* Mr. G. R. Hayes made a reference to an instrument "made by Tiekle (sic !) of Hamburg about 1670." Cf. his *The Viols*, p. 216, note 1. Evidently it is our instrument that is referred to by Mr. Hayes. The date is positively stated on the label as 1670.

P. 288 705 *Viola di bordone.* The name is spelled sometimes as *viola da bardone, viola de paredon (paraton, barydon)*. It has nothing to do with the *viola di fagotto*; the last belonged to the violin family; see p. 303 on this point.

706 *Group.* The average sizes of seven instruments are: length of body, 61.5 cm.; width, upper bouts, 29.25 cm.; lower bouts, 36.5 cm. These sizes show that the body of the baryton is that of a division viol.

707 *Nineteenth century.* Cf. C. Sachs, *Real-Lexikon*, p. 33 a.

708 *Instrument.* Dr. Georg Kinsky gives the best and most complete information on this point. See his *Musikhistorisches Museum*, ii, p. 500, note 2.

709 *Dr. Curt Sachs. Op. cit.*, p. 33 a.

710 *Strings.* These difficulties are not insurmountable. Viol players do not depend entirely on the thumb for supporting the instrument.

711 *Evidence.* Cf. G. Kinsky, *Musikhistorisches Museum*, ii, p. 499.

712 *Sympathetic strings.* See Note 690. The statement is correct only if the *viole d'amour* is regarded as a member of the *viola da gamba* family. For this view the flat back, the deep ribs (but not so deep as those of the true viol), and the tunings would be supporting arguments. Arguments not supporting this statement are the hold-

ing position, the short fretless neck, the violin bowing technique, and the bow of violin type.

P. 289 713 *Peasants.* Cf. G. Kinsky, *Musikhistorisches Museum*, ii, pp. 533 ff., for interesting data. The tunings given here were borrowed from Dr. Kinsky's work.

714 *Violoncello.* Praetorius is very explicit on this point. In addition to his often quoted statement in *De Organographia* (p. 44), he wrote in the third volume of the *Syntagma Musicum* (p. 142): "*Tenor*-Alt-Geig, und alle Geigen welche man Uffm Arm helt, Discant- und Bassgeigen, werden in gemein genennet — *Viole de braccio, Vivole da brazzo.*" It is interesting to note that Praetorius singled out *Tenor-Alt-Geig* from the whole family for a specific reference. See Appendix E for further details. Also Note 575.

715 *Viola da braccio.* See Appendix E.

716 *Alto member.* Mr. Charles Reade was the first to advance this opinion. Cf. E. Heron-Allen, *Violin-Making, as it was and is*, pp. 71 f., note 1, for an extensive quotation from Mr. Reade's article, originally printed in the *Pall Mall Gazette*, Aug. 19, 1872.

717 *Three sizes.* See Table of viol sizes, p. 255. There were two trebles, two tenors, and three basses in a fully developed viol family. The violone was not a regular member of the viol consort in England; yet it is built on the viol pattern and organologically belongs to the viol family.

718 *Uniformly designed.* This refers to the standard type of body. It is, of course, well known that there were many fancifully shaped viols for which no general rule can be established.

719 *Acceptance.* Cf. G. Kinsky, *Musikhistorisches Museum*, ii, p. 539; also C. Sachs, *Handbuch*, 1930, p. 203.

720 *For it.* Cf. G. R. Hayes, *The Viols*, p. 204; also pp. 183 f. for tunings of Praetorius. There were several attempts made to reintroduce the tenor into the violin family. Cf. *Encyclopédie de la musique*, pt. ii, vol. iii, pp. 1792 ff. The name of M. Auguste Tolbecque should also be added. In 1890 he published a brochure wherein was mentioned the absence of the tenor; cf. his *L'Art du luthier*, 1903, p. 25. M. Tolbecque built the tenor and described it in his book.

P. 291 721 *Viol family.* The modern double-bass preserves to our day the size of Praetorius' *Violone* or *Gross Viol-de-Gamba-Bass* (*Theatrum Instrumentorum*, plate vi, fig. 4), which measured 114 cm. in body length. Modern instruments average 112 to 114 cm. for the same size.

722 *Underhand.* Even here the tendency is to hold the violin type bow overhand. Why not be consistent and construct the double-basses on the real violin pattern? (Some double-basses which have a violin outline still have flat backs.)

P. 292 723 *Lira da Braccio.* A. Hajdecki, *Die italienische Lira da Braccio. Eine kunst-historische Studie zur Geschichte der Violine.* Mostar, 1892. Only 300 copies were originally published and the writer is not aware of any reprints. At the time of its writing the enthusiasm of violin worshippers, not to mention the deft fostering of commercial interests, threatened to lead research, or what passed for 'research' in those exciting days, into fictitious channels. Major Hajdecki's book challenged the entire trend of the 'historians' of the violin, and helped considerably to stop much of the nonsense written about the instrument. The battle is not completely won even at the present time.

724 *Orchestral Viola.* The average size of the modern orchestral viola is about 400 mm., but the sizes of violas differ considerably. Some fine violas measure 385 mm. The Italian *lira da braccio* by 'Joan Maria' (cf. G. Kinsky, *Musikhistorisches Museum*, ii, p. 389, text and note 2 for complete discussion) found by Major Hajdecki measured 387 mm. in body length. Two dimensions given by Major Hajdecki, 364 mm. for the large violin and 480 mm. for a Stradivari viola (*Die italienische Lira da Braccio*, p. 29), are quite exceptional.

725 *Today.* Cf. G. Kinsky, *Musikhistorisches Museum*, ii, p. 389, note 2. Also a few small details. But it should not be forgotten that Major Hajdecki was a pioneer and did not benefit from the later researches of other scholars.

726 *Dogmatic.* Cf. C. Sachs, *Handbuch*, 1930, p. 199.

727 *Some quarters.* One is surprised to find in the *Encyclopaedia Britannica*, 14th ed., xxiii, p. 176, the following statement: "*The immediate ancestors of the violins were the viols*, which were the principal bowed instruments in use from the end of the 15th to the end of the 17th century." The italics are mine. This contention was shown to be false by Major Hajdecki as far back as 1892!

728 *Tabular form.* This form, as well as some of the statements, are borrowed from Major Hajdecki's book. They have been brought up to date and supplemented by the results of the later researches of Messrs. Arnold Dolmetsch and Gerald R. Hayes, and by the findings of the writer, based on the personal examination of many instruments.

P. 294 729 *Violins.* Major Hajdecki, as a matter of fact, was the first modern writer to point out that there were *three* fundamental families of bowed instruments: (1) *viola da gamba*, (2) *viola da braccio*, and (3) *lira*. See p. 11 of his essay. Although Julius Rühlmann was writing earlier (1882) about various bowed instruments, including *lira*, he failed to bring out this point with sufficient clearness.

730 *Recognition.* Mr. G. R. Hayes, writing later (*The*

Viols, 1930, p. 175), expressed the same idea independently of Major Hajdecki.

P. 294 731 *Size*. This opinion is common among German organologists. Cf. C. Sachs, *Handbuch*, 1930, pp. 186 f. The violin family started most probably with the alto member. See Note 716.

732 *Entity*. Not quite. The *lira da braccio* was still active in Praetorius' time (1619).

733 '*Lira*.' A reference is made to Sandys and Forster's *The History of the Violin*, 1864, p. 97, by Major Hajdecki on p. 31 of his book. The authority is Vincenzo Galilei (ca. 1533–ca. 1600), *Dialogo . . . della musica antica, et della moderna*, Florence, 1581, p. 147, a book inaccessible to Hajdecki. Cf. G. Kinsky, *Musikhistorisches Museum*, ii, p. 398. But the question is whether Galilei meant the viola (alto violin) or the violin by *viola da braccio*.

P. 295 734 *Appearance*. Many countries made claims for the honor (?) of originating it. The violin came from the 'lower depths,' and for a long time was regarded as a humble instrument.

735 *Violins*. This statement should be qualified to the extent that viols with the guitar-fiedel type of body might be regarded as a connecting link between the two families. See pp. 308 f. of this study.

736 *Rebec*. Praetorius' *italienische Lyra de bracio* shows frets. The instruments from which the *lira da braccio* with seven strings developed were also fretted. The rebec has no frets.

737 *Violin*. The *lira da braccio* kept the leaf-shaped head with anterior pegs and occipital string fastening of the tuning end of strings. This type of head permitted an easier fastening of the bourdon strings, of which the *lira* had two. Yet, as Dr. Curt Sachs pointed out (*Handbuch*, 1930, p. 182, fig. 56), there were *lire da braccio* with lateral pegs.

738 *Position*. The holding position of an instrument varied considerably; but essentially there were only two fundamental holding positions, horizontal and vertical.

739 *Italy*. The writer is aware of the existence of Dr. Karl Geiringer's paper "Gaudenzio Ferraris Engel-Konzert im Dome von Saronno," published in *Kongressberichte*, Vienna, 1927 (cf. Dr. Heinrich Besseler, *Die Musik des Mittelalters und der Renaissance*, Potsdam, 1931, pp. 243, 320), but was unable to find it in the three largest libraries which were accessible to him. At the time of publication the contents of Dr. Geiringer's paper and his conclusions are unknown to the writer.

740 *Evidence*. Gaudenzio Ferrari's fresco can be trusted, it seems, literally. Among the instruments there represented is one which at first glance is so fanciful in outline that one would be inclined to regard it as a fantasy of the artist. Yet Lütgendorf in *Die Geigen- und Lautenmacher*, 1904, p. 163, reproduced the actual instrument, the *Orpheoreon*, now in the Paris Conservatory Collection, which proves that Ferrari painted the instrument with an almost photographic exactness. Another unusual-looking instrument, the Sicilian *pochette*, is also in existence (cf. J. Schlosser, *Sammlung . . .*, no. 116; also Mahillon, *Catalogue . . .*, i, p. 333, no. 243). Therefore, it is safe to conclude that in the case of the *viola da braccio* Ferrari represented the actual instruments and not products of his imagination.

Ferrari's evidence suggests that, perhaps, Ganassi's *viola da brazo senza tasti* (*viola da braccio* without frets) was a violin after all! See Note 799.

P. 296 741 *Guitar-shaped*. The corners and the corner blocks of the violin are structural and not organic features, as is proven by the existence of cornerless violins.

742 *Twelfth century*. Cf. Kathleen Schlesinger, *The Instruments of the Modern Orchestra*, ii, p. 388, fig. 129; also p. 457, fig. 176.

743 *Library*. G. Kinsky, *Geschichte der Musik in Bildern*, Leipzig, 1929, p. 45, fig. 3.

744 *Triptych*. G. Kinsky, *op. cit.*, p. 57, fig. 2.

745 *Fifteenth century*. The *lira da braccio* began this transition about 1490; cf. G. Kinsky, *Musikhistorisches Museum*, ii, p. 383.

746 *Leningrad*. Cf. G. Kinsky, *Gesch. der Musik in Bildern*, p. 111, fig. 3.

747 *Scroll*. See Note 737.

748 *Miniatures*. See Note 571.

749 *Fifteenth century*. See Note 587; also Note 639.

P. 297 750 *In 1533*. Cf. G. Kinsky, *Musikhistorisches Museum*, ii, p. 386. Praetorius gave the same tunings, except that the highest string was tuned to d'' instead of e''; cf. *De Organographia*, p. 26.

751 *a''*. The usual emphasis is on the similarity of the violin tunings to those of the *lira da braccio*. To the writer's best knowledge, no one has noticed that the *lira da braccio* tunings are almost identical with the viola tunings. This is one of the facts which supports the contention that the viola and not the violin was the first instrument of the violin family to emerge.

752 *Society*. The rebec was already declining in popularity and eventually fell into disrepute.

P. 298 753 *Table xxi*. Praetorius also states in the text, "Die kleine Lyra ist der *Tenor Violen de bracio* gleich: Daher sie auch *Lyra de bracio* genennet wird" (*De Organographia*, p. 49). One gains more confidence in Praetorius when he is so remarkably consistent. Table xxi is reproduced here on p. 302.

754 *Intact*. One can be sure of this with respect to the Vienna instrument no. 108; the Berlin instrument, no.

2578, might have been slightly 'improved' in outline when the original neck was replaced.

P. 298

755 *Viola*. See Note 724.

756 *Instrument*. Its size can be estimated fairly closely by comparison with the size of the angels painted on the fresco.

757 *Sense*. It is not positively known what instruments were called by this name.

758 *Lira*. For an exact reference see Note 733.

759 *Jamb-de-Fer*. This is one of the rarest books. Cf. G. Kinsky, *Musikhistorisches Museum*, pp. 510 f.

760 *Viola*. Cf. C. Sachs, *Handbuch*, 1930, p. 200.

761 *Conclusion*. It would be absurd even to attempt to tune an instrument the size of no. 108 of the Vienna Collection (body length 47.5 cm.) to violin tunings. Yet the majority of the *lire da braccio*, as well as Praetorius' instrument, are of this size. Some, as the Vienna *lira da braccio* no. 94 by Giovanni d'Andrea of 1511 (that is, shortly before the emergence of the viola), were even larger (body length 51.5 cm.). The instrument found by Major Hajdecki (body length 38.7 cm.), although comparatively a small one, is still in the viola class.

P. 299

762 *Cerone*. G. R. Hayes, *The Viols*, p. 180.

763 *Seventeenth century*. G. R. Hayes, *op. cit.*, p. 180.

764 *Violoncellos*. They were about 5 cm. longer. See Notes 778 and 807.

765 *Score*. Cf. *Tutti le Opere di Claudio Monteverdi*, ed. G. F. Malpiero, xi, Asolo, 1930. All references in the text and notes of this study are to Malpiero's edition, supplemented in the parentheses by references to the pages of the original edition. The earlier edition is in the series *Die Oper von ihren ersten Anfängen bis zur Mitte des 18. Jahrhundert*, ed. by Robert Eitner, published by the Gesellschaft für Musikforschung, Berlin, 1881, vol. x.

766 *Facsimile edition*. Monteverdi's *Orfeo*, Augsburg, 1927, ed. by Adolf Sandberger, with fine critical notes on previous editions, including that of Malpiero's edition, since the latter contains some small mistakes and omissions. In Malpiero's edition: on p. 76 is omitted the score direction found on p. 47 of the original; it reads: "Qui entrano li Tromb[oni] Corn.[etti] e Regali, e taciono le Viole da bracio, e Organi di legno Clavicem. e si muta la Sena." On p. 87, *Ritornello*, the original soprano clefs of the string instruments are omitted. Again the same omission is made on p. 96. On p. 107 the choral parts in the bass clef are designated by the baritone clef in the original, p. 70; the figured bass part on the same page is written in the baritone clef in the original (omitted in Malpiero's edition).

767 *The violino piccolo alla francese*. Monteverdi mentions this instrument in the score directions only once: p. 41 (27), *Ritornello*. It reads: "Questo ritornello fu sonati di dentro da un Clavicembano [the harpsichord], duoi Chitarroni [the bass lutes, see our No. 244], e duoi *Violini piccioli alla francese*." In the list of instruments the adjective is spelled *piccoli*.

768 *Moser*. Cf. *Zeitschrift für Musikwissenschaft*, April, 1919, pp. 377–380, "Der Violino Piccolo." The earlier hypothesis was that of Julius Rühlmann, *Die Geschichte der Bogeninstrumente*, p. 65; according to Rühlmann, the *violino piccolo* was the pochette (like our No. 267 or 268). This solution is now rejected. Dr. Curt Sachs' standard soprano violin is discussed in Note 771.

769 *Actual tones*. Monteverdi wrote $e_\flat''$ for the highest tone of the *violino piccolo*. On Mr. Moser's hypothesis this would be $e_\flat^3$ actually, or one semitone lower than the highest possible tone in the first position on the first (a'') string of the *violino piccolo*; this would correspond to the b'' on the E-string of the ordinary violin; see Note 780 for fingerings. In both cases the fingering would be the same. The lowest tone of the second violino piccolo in the score of *Orfeo* was c' (c'' in sound). The peculiarity of Monteverdi's writing for the violin family, namely, never to write lower than the open tone of the third string (see p. 301, ii), is an additional proof of the correctness of Mr. Moser's hypothesis, since c' would be played on the fourth or G-string of the standard violin. In no other place in the score, without exception, did Monteverdi use the fourth string on the violin, or on any other instrument of the violin family.

P. 300

770 *The violino ordinario da braccio*. There are only three places in *Orfeo* where the violin is explicitly called for: act ii, p. 43 (28), where the score direction reads "Questo ritornello fu sonato da duoi Violini ordinari da braccio, un Basso de Viola da braccio, un Clavicembano, et duoi Chittaroni"; act iii, pp. 84 (52) and 96 (63). On p. 84 two parts in the soprano clef are marked simply 'violino'; on p. 96 the parts are also designated 'violino.' A reasonable assumption to make is that the terms 'violino ordinario' and 'violino' are equivalent. The sounding compass of the parts in all cases is between *d'* and *b''*; the first violins are taken as low as d' in one instance only, p. 84 (52); otherwise the lowest tone of the first violins is g'.

771 *Orchestras*. Dr. Curt Sachs is responsible for this hypothesis. See his *Handbuch*, 1930, p. 201, the text and note 2. Canon Galpin supports this hypothesis also: cf. his *Textbook of European Musical Instruments*, London, 1937, p. 147. The writer is unable to agree with these esteemed scholars. Exhaustive study of all the string parts in *Orfeo* (explicitly designated and such as, although not designated, would be played by the stringed instruments) as to their sounding compass, position,

rhythm, etc., shows that the violin parts never descended below *d′* and never ascended above *b″*; the usual upper limit for the violins is *a″*, which occurs rather frequently. The fingering charts of the violin and of the viola (see Note 780) show immediately which instrument was actually used, since Monteverdi never wrote in *Orfeo* above the first position; therefore *a″* is out of the question on the viola. Monteverdi is so inflexibly consistent in not using the lowest string on the instruments of the violin family, and in not writing above the first position, that these two criteria can be used with a high degree of safety as a guiding principle in assigning the parts in the score of *Orfeo* to specific instruments. The clefs help to a certain extent, but in their employment Monteverdi was less consistent.

P. 300 772 *The third violins.* The mezzosoprano clef is found in the score of *Orfeo* in the following instrumental pieces: (1) act ii, p. 75 (47), *Sinfonia*, the lowest tone *d′*; (2) act iii, p. 105 (68), *Sinfonia a 7*, p. 128 (82–83), repeated p. 135 (87), the lowest tone *e′*. The bowed string instrument which would be most suitable for these parts is the violin.

773 *The viola da braccio.* In the list of instruments Monteverdi calls for 'Dieci Viole da brazzo' (ten *viole da braccio*). In the score proper he calls for the *viole da braccio* in the following places: (1) act i, p. 14 (10), *Choro*; (2) act ii, p. 48 (32), *Ritornello*, which is repeated several times; (3) act iii, p. 99 (64), Orfeo's aria; p. 103 (67), *Sinfonia*; (4) act iv, p. 125 (80), Orfeo's aria; p. 126 (81), Orfeo's aria; p. 137 (88), *Ritornello*. In all these places there are no direct indications of specific instruments, except the clefs and the internal evidence of the parts, when these are written out individually. Some of them, as the parts in the soprano clef on p. 48 (32), are obviously written for the violin. Other instruments included in this term are discussed in the following notes.

774 *Soprano.* This name for the viola of Monteverdi's time is conjectural and is borrowed from Zacconi. In modern terminology it should be called the 'alto.' The parts are usually written in the alto clef. In one instance, *Sinfonia*, p. 103 (67), which is repeated two more times without changes, pp. 83 (51) and 144 (93), the part which is written in the alto clef with a compass of d′–a′ could be played on the violin. Yet the character of the part is more suitable for the viola; in these instances it would play the soprano part of the ensemble.

775 *Larger.* Praetorius' *Tenor-Alt-Geig* and the Italian *lira da braccio* sizes should be taken as the norm in forming an idea of the sizes of Monteverdi's *soprano viola da braccio*: they were about 47 cm. in body length. See p. 298 of the text for discussion of sizes.

776 *Some cases.* The tenor clef parts in *Orfeo* presumably written for the alto violin are: (1) act i, p. 17 (11), *Ritornello*; (2) act ii, p. 48 (32), *Ritornello*; (3) act iii, p. 83 (51), *Sinfonia*; p. 103 (67), *Sinfonia*; in all cases the lowest tone is *g*.

777 *Tenore.* To the writer's knowledge this is the first time that the tenor violin is suggested as a member of Monteverdi's orchestra. The logic of instrumentation which Monteverdi adhered to with such remarkable consistency forces this conclusion. The reasons for assuming that Monteverdi used the tenor violin are the following. First, the tenor violin existed in his time. Second, the compass of parts in *Orfeo* for instruments of the violin family never exceeded two octaves, and usually was kept within that of a twelfth; thus the extreme sounding compass of the violin parts was from *d′* to *b″*; that of the viola was from *g* to *d″*; that of the violoncello was from G to *d′*, one octave lower than the viola. Assuming that the tenor violin, tuned *F, c, g, d′*, was a member of Monteverdi's orchestra, it is possible to assign to it the parts written in the tenor and the baritone clef within the sounding compass from *c* to *g′*; this is again a twelfth. Third, the lowest F-string would not have been used, in conformance with Monteverdi's practice on other instruments.

There are two more possible assumptions: the parts just mentioned were played either on the viola or on the violoncello. This could be done on the four-stringed viola; but the objection to the use of the viola would be that the fourth string would have to be used, a practice to which Monteverdi obviously had not adhered in the case of the violin and violoncello. The objection to the violoncello would be that the highest tone of the assumed tenor parts would require a shift into the third position, which is out of the question, since in *Orfeo* the string parts for the violin family were written for playing in the first position only.

In other words, in the terms of the standard practice of that time, the assumed tenor parts would be too low for the viola and too high for the violoncello. The fact that they could be played on either instrument now, is no proof that they might have been so played in the 1607 period.

The places in the score of *Orfeo* where, as the writer assumes, Monteverdi used the tenor violin, can be enumerated as follows: A. *The tenor clef.* (1) act i, p. 2 (2), *Ritornello*, which is repeated several times; the compass is from d to e′; p. 11 (8), *Choro*, the compass of the part is given in the original from d to e′ (in Malpiero's edition, for some reason, it is written an octave higher!); p. 31 (18–19), *Ritornello*, from *c* to *d′*; p. 39 (26) *Sinfonia*, from *d* to *g′*, the part being placed rather high; in this particular instance it could not be played on the violoncello of Monteverdi's time, owing to the limitation of fingering to the first position only. (2) Act ii, p. 67 (42), *Sinfonia*, from *d* to *d′*; p. 74 (46), from *d* to *e′*. (3) Act iii, p. 83 (51), p. 103 (67); repeated again in act v, p. 144 (93), *Sinfonia*, in which, it seems, two tenors were used, one within the compass from *e* to *d′*, and another one from c to c′. (4) Act iv, p. 128 (82, 83), *Sinfonia a 7*, again with two tenors: from *c* to *d′* and from *c* to *e′*, p. 137 (88), *Ritornello*, from *d* to *e′*. (5) Act v, p. 150, *Ritornello*, *e–e′*, and, finally, in *Moresca*, p. 153 (100), *d–g′*.

B. *The baritone clef.* (1) Act ii, p. 75 (47), *Sinfonia*, where the instrumentation of the string group would be three violins, two violas, and two tenor violins, each instrument playing a separate part. (2) Act iii, p. 105 (68), *Sinfonia a 7*, repeated on p. 112 (73), with the same instrumentation.

One thing is quite certain. The tenor violins would restore a lost tone color to the string ensemble of Monteverdi's *Orfeo*, if a revival of its performance along the lines indicated should be made.

P. 300 778 *Basso.* Monteverdi, although he called the same instrument by two different names, *basso de viola da braccio* (act ii, p. 43 (28)) and *basso da brazzo* (act iii, p. 96 (63)), had in mind the violoncello of his time. Its size might have been about 80 centimetres, or about 5 cm. longer than the body length of our standard violoncello. See Note 807. Yet the three stringed instruments similar to that on p. 309, fig. 56, and tuned *G, d, a*, are not excluded; Monteverdi's practice of not using the fourth string and the existence of such instruments may indicate that the three-stringed instruments of the violin family were in common use in his time. At least this seems an interesting speculative possibility.

779 *The viola da gamba family.* Mr. Adam Carse in *The History of Orchestration*, New York, 1925, p. 39, states that *Diezi Viole da Brazzo* of Monteverdi may be explained as "Ten arm-viols, i.e., Discant or Tenor Viols, most probably both." This is an unfortunate slip, vitiating most of his subsequent conclusions. The *viole da Brazzo* of Monteverdi are violins (*viole da braccio*) and not viols (*viole da gamba*). This error can be traced to that inadmissible confusion of families discussed in Note 575. Cf. also p. 9 of Mr. Carse's book. The only representatives of the *viola da gamba* family in *Orfeo* were the bass and contrabass viols; it seems that the smaller members of this family dropped out of use in Italy earlier than anywhere else.

P. 301 780 *Two octaves.* The conclusions numbered II, III, and IV will become obvious, if the following fingering tables of the instruments of the violin family of the late sixteenth and the early seventeenth century are studied. The tones set in the heavy frame were used by Monteverdi in *Orfeo*.

THE VIOLINO PICCOLO

Violino piccolo alla francese

String No.	4	3	2	1
Open string	c′	g′	d″	a″
1st finger........	d′	a′	e″	b″
2nd finger.......	e′	b′	f″	c^3
3rd finger	f′	c″	g″	d^3
4th finger	g′	d″	a″	e^3(♭)

THE VIOLIN

Violino ordinario da braccio

String No.	4	3	2	1
Open strings.....	g	d′	a′	e″
1st finger........	a	e′	b′	f″
2nd finger.......	b	f′	c″	g″
3rd finger	c′	g′	d″	a″
4th finger	d′	a′	e″	b″

THE VIOLA

Soprano de Viola da braccio

String No.	4	3	2	1
Open strings.....	c	g	d′	a′
1st finger........	d	a	e′	b′
2nd finger.......	e	b	f′	c″
3rd finger	f	c′	g′	d″
4th finger	g	d′	a′	e″

THE TENOR VIOLIN

Tenore de Viola da braccio

String No.	4	3	2	1
Open strings.....	F	c	g	d′
1st finger........	G	d	a	e′
2nd finger.......	A	e	b	f′
3rd finger	B	f	c′	g′
4th finger	c	g	d′	a′

THE VIOLONCELLO

Basso de Viola da braccio

String No.	4	3	2	1
Open strings.....	C	G	d	a
1st finger........	D	A	e	b
2nd finger.......	E	B	f	c′
3rd finger	F	c	g	d′
4th finger	G	d	a	e′

These fingering tables show very clearly the remarkable uniformity and consistency in practice of playing the principal instruments of the violin family (*viole da braccio*), especially the viola, the tenor, and the bass. These tables suggest strongly that Monteverdi had (*C*), *G*, *d*, *a*, tuning in mind when he wrote the parts for the violoncello and not the tuning one tone lower.

P. 301 781 *About them. De Organographia*, p. 43. If, as the writer maintains, the first instruments of the violin family appeared about 1515–20, the violin was about 100 years old in the time of Praetorius. The size of the violin, as has been shown in Appendix A, was already stabilized at 15 Brunswick inches or 357 mm. (14 English inches).

782 *Violin.* Designations of the violins as three-quarter, half, and one-quarter sized are the nominal trade terms. The actual average sizes are 332 mm., 302 mm., and 297 mm., respectively. Praetorius' instrument is even smaller than the quarter-size since it measures 268 mm. Cf. A. Tolbecque, *L'Art du luthier*, Niort, 1903, p. 204, for the sizes.

783 *Strings.* The *viola pomposa* had five strings. For the body sizes, cf. G. Kinsky, *Musikhistorisches Museum*, ii, pp. 555 f. Also C. S. Terry, *Bach's Orchestra*, p. 137.

P. 303 784 *Quint-bass.* The writer is in agreement with the late Julius Rühlmann in classifying Praetorius' "Bass-Geig de bracio" (table xxi, no. 6) as the large Quint-bass violin. The reasons for this classification were stated in *Geschichte der Bogeninstrumente*, pp. 246 f., and are repeated here, with a slight modification.

Praetorius states in *De Organographia*, p. 48, that the bass of the *Violn de braccio* had four strings: "Deroselben Bass-, Tenor-, und Discantgeig . . . seynd mit 4 Saiten." The tuning of the *Bass-Viol de Braccio* (*ibid.*, p. 26) is that of the four-stringed violoncello (*C*, *G*, *d*, *a*).

The large Quint-bass violin (*Gross Quint-bass*, p. 26) is a five-stringed instrument tuned *FF*, *C*, *G*, *d*, *a*, that is, identically with the *Bass-Viol de Braccio*, except for the additional fifth string, which is tuned a fifth lower. The instrument so tuned would differ but little in size from the violoncello of Praetorius' time (about 80 cm. in body length; see Note 807). An examination of the instrument represented in table xxi, fig. 6, of *Sciagraphia* shows that it has five strings, and its body length measures 85.6 cm.; therefore, it should be classified as a 'large Quint-bass.' Praetorius' nomenclature of individual instruments is not stabilized (see Appendix E) and the name *Bass-Geig de bracio* in table xxi of *Sciagraphia* should not be taken too literally.

785 *Violin.* Cf. C. S. Terry, *Bach's Orchestra*, p. 125.

786 *Museums.* Cf. C. S. Terry, *op. cit.*, p. 137. Also F. W. Galpin, *Textbook*, 1937, p. 147.

787 *Mattheson.* Cf. Julius Schlosser, *Die Sammlung alter Musikinstrumente*, 1920, p. 49.

788 *Below the violin.* If tuned to the violoncello tunings the instrument sounds weak. Tuned an octave lower than the violin, its proper tonal position, the tenor violin sounds fine. The strings of a proper gage should be selected.

789 *Scores.* Cf. C. S. Terry, *Bach's Orchestra*, p. 135. P. 304

790 *Hofmans.* Cf. V. C. Mahillon, *Catalogue descriptif* . . ., i, pp. 327 f.; iii, p. 23; iv, pp. 400, 405, 414; Lütgendorf, *op. cit.*, 1904, p. 294.

791 *Once more.* A critical history of the violin is yet to be written. Commercialism is largely responsible for the distortion of historical perspective and the exaggeration of the relative significance of the violin among musical instruments.

792 *Prototype.* The chapters on the violin in Mr. G. R. Hayes' book *The Viols, and other Bowed Instruments* should be studied for more detailed arguments. Excellent drawings of the old style construction can be found in *Antonio Stradivari*, by W. H. Hill and others (London, 1909); the plate facing p. 193 represents the old and the new bass bars, and the plate facing p. 208 pictures the neck as built by Stradivari and as changed by modern violin-makers. The picture of St. Cecilia by Bernardo Cavallino, plate XIII, also shows the old style neck. P. 306

793 *Tenor.* See text pp. 289 f. and Note 788. P. 307

794 *Thought.* Cf. G. R. Hayes, *The Viols*, 1930, pp. 206 f. Major Hajdecki in his book *Die italienische Lira da Braccio* has not touched the question of the origin of the violoncello. P. 308

795 *Lira da gamba.* This instrument was built somewhat like the bass viol, but the essential differences were a wider body, the number of strings (as many as sixteen on some instruments), and the leaf-shaped head with anterior sagittal pegs and occipital string fastening. Its bridge was very slightly rounded, so the instrument was well adapted for playing chords and polyphonic music. The *lira da gamba* type of music survived, in a modified

form, in that of "the viol used Lyra way." On this point, see G. R. Hayes, *The Viols*, p. 125; also the chapter on the 'Lyra da gamba' (pp. 144–151) of the same book. Fine representations of the instrument can be found in the catalogue of the Vienna Collection (no. 95 by Tieffenbrucker) and the *Musikhistorisches Museum*, ii, pp. 421 and 422. Praetorius and Mersenne both give the figures, description, and tunings of the instrument.

P. 308 796 *Pattern*. On this point there are some interesting ideas in F. Zamminer's *Die Musik und die musikalischen Instrumente*, Giessen, 1855; also see J. Rühlmann, *Die Geschichte der Bogeninstrumente*, pp. 288 f., 298 f.

797 *Mr. Gerald R. Hayes. The Viols*, p. 169, and appendix iii, extracts from Ganassi's *Regola Rubertina*.

798 *Four*. Cf. G. R. Hayes, *op. cit.*, pp. 242 f.

799 *Practice*. Cf. G. R. Hayes, *op. cit.*, p. 246. It is suggested that the instrument referred to by Ganassi as the *viola da braccio senza tasti* was probably the alto violin.

P. 310 800 *Sixteenth century*. For typological details alluded to in the text, cf. G. Kinsky, *Geschichte der Musik in Bildern*, 1929, p. 111, figs. 1, 2, and 3; especially fig. 2, an angel by Ambrogio de Predis painted ca. 1510. Also C. Sachs, *Handbuch*, 1930, p. 190, figs. 62, 63. Through the courtesy of Dr. Frederick M. Watkins of Cornell University and of the Director of the Museo Civico in Modena, Italy, the following data have become available since the text was written.

1. *The four-stringed viol*. The names: the *violetta da gamba*, the *bassetto*, or the *violoncellino*. Made by Cesare Bonoris di Mantova in 1568.

2. *The three-stringed viol*. The instrument is called the *contrabassino*. Originally made in the sixteenth century; restored ca. 1677 by Gherardi in Bologna. Formerly belonged to the family of Lazzari in Capri, a town nine miles north-northwest by rail from Modena. The writer's conclusions in the text are therefore supported by these facts. The sizes of instruments are given in centimetres.

	Violetta da gamba	Contra-bassino
Body, length	85.5	87.5
Width, upper bouts	29.0	33.0
middle bouts	22.0	28.0
lower bouts	36.0	44.0
Ribs	14.0	18.0
Bottom to bridge	35.0	37.0
Vibrating length of strings	78.0	92.5

The backs of both instruments are flat and slanted toward the neck bracket as on viols of the standard type. The lengths of the slanted parts are given as 15 cm. and 21 cm. respectively. Except for the number of strings, these instruments should be classified as members of the *viola da gamba* family. Ganassi wrote his book, *Regola Rubertina*, in 1542.

801 *Viola da gamba*. The outline of body is similar to that of the bass *viola da gamba* by Hans Vohar represented on plate i of Mr. Hayes' book on viols.

802 *Ganassi*. Ganassi implied a consort of instruments with three and four strings. In this connection Monteverdi's consistent practice of writing in the score of *Orfeo* only for three strings becomes significant. The Modena instruments are of great interest in this connection.

803 *Frets*. Also on his reference to the *viola da braccio senza tasti*. Therefore, the technique of playing without frets was practiced in Ganassi's time on the viol when the stopping was done between the seventh and the twelfth (octave) frets. This part is not fretted on some viols. The adherents of the fretless school of viol-playing quite correctly point to this fact as one of the arguments against fretting the viol. They say that if it is possible to play the viol unfretted in a certain part of its compass, why would it not be possible to play it in others or without frets at all? A common-sense observation should prompt an answer. Only four semitones of the whole compass were played on the viol when stopped against the finger-board and only on the highest string. Some viols (Lyra-viol No. 273 of our Collection for instance) had the finger-board completely fretted. Therefore when it was mechanically feasible to provide frets on the disputed part of the finger-board, it was done. In general, this most plausible objection against frets proves, on closer examination, to be not so important as it appears at first.

804 *Too broad*. This inference would be based on the reasoning that the lyra family of instruments consisted of the *lyra da braccio* and the *lyra da gamba*; the violin descended from the *lyra da braccio*; therefore, correspondingly, the violoncello developed from the *lyra da gamba*. The general conclusion would be that the violin family developed from the lyra family and not from the viol family. The middle road, especially with respect to the violoncello, is strongly indicated, not so much musically, but organologically.

805 *Violin*. Both numerical and geometrical analysis show that the violoncello is designed on a somewhat different basis than the violin.

806 *Instruments*. Cf. C. Sachs, *Handbuch*, p. 204. P. 311

807 *Period*. Antonio Stradivari made some violoncellos measuring 80 cm. in body length. Cf. W. Henry Hill et al., *Antonio Stradivari*, London, 1909, p. 312. The 'Tuscan' violoncello measured 31.375 inches, or 79.7 cm. The average standard violoncello size is about 75 cm.

P. 311 808 *Contrabass parts.* Beethoven was the first composer to write the orchestral parts for the violoncello, treating it as an individual instrument. Cf. Cecil Forsyth, *Orchestration*, 1937, p. 433.

809 *J. S. Bach.* Cf. C. S. Terry, *Bach's Orchestra*, pp. 135 ff.

810 *Dr. Curt Sachs. Handbuch*, 1930, p. 205.

811 *Amman.* Cf. G. Kinsky, *Musikhistorisches Museum*, p. 307, the woodcut. Also his *Geschichte der Musik in Bildern*, p. 81, figs. 6, 7.

812 *The viol family.* For the delectation of students of nomenclature the following table is subjoined herewith:

English	*German* (Praetorius)
The Lyra Viol	Viol Bastarda
The Small Bass (Division) Viol	Klein-Bass-Viol de Gamba
The Consort Bass Viol	Gross-Bass-Viol de Gamba
The Contrabass Viol (Violone)	Violn de Gamba Sub-Bass

This table should be compared with Table II, p. 360. Such a sequence of names, as is suggested in this note, would be strictly consistent. The writer had not the courage to add sizes of the German instruments, as he feared this would give credence to Mersenne's tall story about the large-sized viols of long ago. See Note 816 and Note 911 below.

813 *Instrument.* The double-basses average 113 cm.

814 *England.* The 'giant' three-stringer presented by Dragonetti to the Duke of Leinster measured 8 feet 7 inches (English) or 262 cm. Cf. C. Engel, *Descriptive Catalogue of the Musical Instruments*, London, 1874, p. 267. It is assumed that this length includes the rest pin. For another tall story, see *ibid.*, p. 268. Dr. Kinsky gives the length of this instrument as 247 cm. (without the rest pin? Engel's only measure of length is the one given above). Praetorius' instrument was scaled by Dr. Kinsky as 228 cm. Cf. *Musikhistorisches Museum*, ii. p. 570.

815 *Praetorius. De Organographia*, p. 46, under 'NB.'

P. 313 816 *Discant.* The extraordinary character of this combination becomes clear only when the sizes of instruments are taken into consideration.

	Length of Body
The Treble. Kleine Viol de Gamba Bass (xx, 3)	78.5 cm.
The Alto-Tenor. Grosse Contrabass (vi, 4)	114.0 cm.
The Bass. Gar grosse Violn de Gamba Sub-Bass (v, 1)	140.0 cm.

817 *Settled.* Some double-basses which have EE as the lowest tone and some CC are used in modern orchestras. V. C. Mahillon, *Le matériel sonore des orchestres*, p. 16, gives BBB as the lowest tone of the five-stringed double-bass, which is more consistent, since it is a fourth lower than EE.

818 *In fourths.* There is a disagreement on this tuning. C. Engel, *Descriptive Catalogue*, London, 1874, states that it was the English tuning. Kathleen Schlesinger in *Encyclopaedia Britannica*, 11th ed., viii, p. 440, states that three-stringers were so tuned both in England and in Italy. Dr. C. Sachs, *Real-Lexikon*, p. 225 a, and Dr. J. Schlosser, *Sammlung* . . ., p. 70, ascribe it to Italy. Dr. G. Kinsky reverts to England; *Musikhistorisches Museum*, ii, p. 570. Just one of the typical family squabbles among organologists.

819 *Today.* It was not always so. Cf. G. Kinsky, *Musikhistorisches Museum*, ii, p. 571, for variations.

820 *Dr. Richard Strauss.* Hector Berlioz, *Instrumentationslehre*, revised by Richard Strauss, p. 105 a.

821 *Orchestras.* Mostly in Belgium; occasionally in this country.

822 *Instrument.* For CC tuning of the lowest string, see Kathleen Schlesinger, *loc. cit.*, p. 440; BBB was referred to in Note 817. P. 314

823 *Strings.* The alternative is to shift the hand for the fourth tone on the string, which might be inconvenient in a rapid tempo.

824 *Praetorius' tunings. De Organographia*, p. 25, xx, no. 2, under "Gross-Bass Viol de Gamba."

825 *Reconstruction.* F. W. Galpin, *Old English Instruments*, 1932, p. 78. P. 316

826 *Complex.* Cf. Kathleen Schlesinger, *Encyclopaedia Britannica*, 11th ed., vii, p. 513. Dr. C. Sachs, *Handbuch*, 1930, p. 166, has a slightly different derivation. As regards the question of whether or not the crwth was the national instrument of the Welsh people, see Carl Engel, *Researches into the Early History of the Violin Family*, London, 1883, p. 25. Also Kathleen Schlesinger, *loc. cit.*, p. 514. Wewertem's article was printed in *Monatshefte für Musik-Geschichte*, 1881.

827 *Chelys.* Cf. Kathleen Schlesinger, *loc. cit.*, p. 513.

828 *Cithara.* Cf. C. Sachs, *Real-Lexikon*, Berlin, 1913, p. 97 a, where Dr. Sachs refers to 'cousinship' between the instruments; in his *Handbuch*, 1930, pp. 162 ff., there are more fully developed views on the probable origin of the crwth (p. 165).

829 *Bowed-harp.* O. Andersson, *The Bowed-Harp*, chapter on the crwth.

830 *Europe.* O. Andersson, *op. cit.*, p. 256.

831 *Cruit.* O. Andersson, *op. cit.*, p. 244 ff.

832 *Bowed-harp.* Professor Porter's book, *The Crosses and Culture of Ireland*, gives an excellent picture of the

influences active in Irish culture of the pre-Christian and early Christian epoch. Although this book is not directly concerned with musical instruments, it is very illuminating and suggestive to an organologist. Dr. Andersson's problem of the Irish cruit (*The Bowed-Harp*, p. 256) should be considerably simplified, since Professor Porter's book not only substantiates Kiesewetter and Wewertem, but also, it seems, suggests an answer to the problem of its origin. See Note 461.

P. 316 833 *Eleventh century*. F. W. Galpin, *Old English Instruments of Music*, 1932, p. 74. Dr. C. Sachs, *Real-Lexikon*, p. 97 b, estimates it as about the tenth century.

834 *Heron-Allen. De Fidiculis Opuscula*, viii, 1895. It contains both the photo-etching and the cut of the seal. The cut is reproduced in *Encyclopaedia Britannica*, 11th ed., vii, p. 514.

835 *Barrington*. Hon. Daines Barrington, "Some Account of Two Musical Instruments Used in Wales," *Archaeologia*, iii (1775), pp. 30–34. Cited by all writers on the crwth.

836 *Galpin*. Cf. William Bingley, *A Tour round North Wales*, London, 1804, ii, p. 332. Also referred to by many authors. Cf. F. W. Galpin, *op. cit.*, p. 77.

P. 317 837 *Crwth*. G. R. Hayes, *The Viols*, 1930, p. 234.

838 *Aberystwyth*. O. Andersson, *op. cit.*, p. 217, fig. 77.

839 *South Kensington*. Cf. C. Engel, *Descriptive Catalogue*, London, 1874, pp. 294 f., fig. 137. Also A. J. Hipkins, *Musical Instruments, Historic, Rare, and Antique*, Edinburgh, 1888, pp. 47 f., plate xxiv.

840 *Austria*. J. Schlosser, *Die Sammlung alter Musikinstrumente*, 1920, p. 33. The instrument in the Vienna Collection is a copy of one mentioned in the text; the original in the Collection of the Gesellschaft der Musikfreunde is 'of unknown provenance.'

841 *Many years*. Information was derived from the list (typewritten) of instruments made by Canon Galpin in 1911 and now in the Museum files. Cf. also his *Old English Instruments of Music*, 1932, p. 96.

P. 319 842 *Thumb*. The correct playing position is shown on plate xix in the *Old English Instruments of Music* (1932). Figure 35, p. 147, in Carl Engel's *Researches into the Early History of the Violin Family* (1883) is incorrect in many respects, but especially in the position of the bow, which is held under the stopping point.

843 *Rosin*. Cf. Léon Vallas, "Une mémoire sur la trompette marine," *Bulletin Français de la Société Internationale de Musique*, iv (1908), pp. 1176 ff. A curious and important memoir on the *tromba marina* by Jean Baptiste Prin, written in January of 1742, has been reprinted. On p. 1190 is M. Prin's observation that the straight leg of the trembling bridge located directly under the string had to be kept in place by powdered rosin (*la colophaune en poudre*), and the extending leg had to be always clean and polished; otherwise it would not produce the 'trumpety' sound. Glareanus (1488–1563), writing 195 years earlier, gave a comprehensive description of the *tromba marina* which can be found on p. 49 of his *Dodecachordon*, published in Basle in 1547. Praetorius translated Glareanus' description almost verbatim, with a few minor changes. Cf. *De Organographia*, pp. 57 ff.; also G. Kinsky, *Musikhistorisches Museum*, ii, pp. 318, 319.

Glareanus, and after him Praetorius, both state that a piece of ebony or some other hard and polished material was put under the extended leg to increase the trembling effect. In some cases a very small nail was driven into the lower part of that leg to enhance the tremor. Glareanus: ". . . huius protenti pedis extremo calcaneo tenuissimum infigunt clavum ut tremor fortius in solido tinniat . . ." *Dodecachordon*, p. 49.

844 *Drum*. G. Kinsky, *Musikhistorisches Museum*, ii, p. 315.

845 *Tuned to*. C. J. B. Prin, *loc. cit.*, p. 1186, gives D and E also as the tonalities of tuning of the tromba marina. Canon Galpin states that it can be tuned also to BB-flat and as high as F. Cf. his *Old English Instruments of Music*, 1932, p. 98.

846 *Tone*. J. B. Prin, *loc. cit.*, p. 1185, recommends the tuning of the sympathetic strings in unison with the open tone of the bowed string. He states that the sympathetic strings are his invention. In any case these strings are not characteristic of the instrument.

P. 320 847 *Subject*. One of the best books for a general reader is by Philip James, *Early Keyboard Instruments from their Beginnings to the Year 1820*, London, 1930. This book is finely illustrated and has a selected bibliography.

P. 322 848 *Spring*. The Siberian boar's bristle is considered the best. On some modern instruments steel music wire is used for this purpose.

849 *Weight*. To insure certainty of action the jacks are weighted with one or two pieces of lead.

P. 323 850 *Plucking mechanism*. Mr. Arnold Dolmetsch has developed a new plucking mechanism which eliminates this defect of the ordinary jack action. Cf. Robert Donington, *The Work and Ideas of Arnold Dolmetsch*, 1932, p. 9. Also F. W. Galpin, *Textbook of European Musical Instruments*, 1937, p. 112.

851 *Organ*. An impression prevails in some quarters that the harpsichord can be played without special study by any competent pianist. The harpsichord 'touch' is entirely different from that of the pianoforte. Six months, at least, are necessary for an average pianist to master the harpsichord touch. This concerns merely the mechanics of the harpsichord playing. Registration,

on the harpsichord, is an art and depends upon the aesthetic intuition of the player.

P. 328 852 *Order of stops.* On the Shudi harpsichords the stops on the left side were Lute, Octave, Harp. The arrangement of the rest of the stops and pedals was identical with the Kirkman harpsichord.

853 *Full tone.* The Kirkman harpsichord came from England in 1917 in fine condition. In 1937 it was found necessary to restring it and completely overhaul the jack mechanism. The only change of importance is the leading of keys and jacks. The sound-board is in an excellent state of preservation; the tone has a reedy quality, especially in the middle and lower registers, reminding one of the English horn and bassoon.

854 *Disengaged.* The harpsichord nomenclature is somewhat confusing with respect to this term. The word 'stop' is used in the specific sense designating the knob (p. 330, Fig. 67, 23) attached to the lever operating the jack slide; it is similar to the draw-stop of the organ. The entire row of jacks, which is shifted by the jack slide in or out of engagement with the strings, is also called the stop (also the 'register'). The term is used again in the generic sense designating: (1) the stop (knob), (2) the lever, (3) the jack slide, (4) all the jacks, and (5) all the strings which constitute one complete operating unit.

P. 331 855 *Harpsichord.* In addition to the usual reinforcement of the upper partials when two strings of the same tone are tuned in octaves and plucked simultaneously, the phenomenon of sympathetic vibration takes place. This happens, for instance, when one or two stops of the three operated by the lower manual are disengaged. The harpsichord mechanism is so constructed that all three jacks (p. 330, Fig. 67, nos. 7, 8, and 9) are lifted when a given key is pressed down, irrespective of whether some of the stops are engaged or not. When the jacks are lifted, the dampers are taken off the respective strings; the disengaged strings of the same tone are affected and vibrate sympathetically.

Specifically: If the second unison and octave stops (jacks 8 and 9) are engaged and the first unison stop (jack 7) is disengaged, the strings of the first unison stop vibrate sympathetically with those of the second unison and octave stops. The phenomenon is somewhat similar to that on the pianoforte when the damper pedal is lifted, but with this difference: on the harpsichord it is only the strings of the keys which are actually pressed down that vibrate sympathetically. Therefore, this phenomenon is better controlled than the wholesale resonance of the piano.

856 *Play.* This means that all stops, except the lute stop, are engaged. The effect, under proper acoustical conditions, is unbelievably rich and majestic. N.B.: The harpsichord should be played in a small, acoustically perfect hall, or in the intimacy of a home or studio. It is not an instrument for large halls or auditoriums.

857 *Registration.* A fine illustration of a registration of the harpsichord is found in the recently published *Goldberg Variations of J. S. Bach,* edited by Mr. Ralph Kirkpatrick (New York, 1938); see page xxvi of the preface. P. 332

858 *Contrasts.* Each stop has its own dynamic intensity or 'quantum,' if one is permitted to borrow this term from mathematical physics. Therefore, the addition of these intensities is a discontinuous process, however skilfully a good harpsichordist may conceal such accretion. It should be mentioned that some purists object to any attempts to conceal the essential discontinuity of the dynamics of the harpsichord. The 'half-hitch' or a partly shifted pedal permitting a softer playing is an anathema to them.

The tone color of individual stops on the harpsichord also differs. The effect of the lute stop and the harp stop cannot be imitated on the modern pianoforte; only some early pianos of Mozart's time contained a harp stop, very similar to that on the harpsichord.

859 *Photograph.* Mr. Ralph Kirkpatrick very cleverly referred to pianoforte dynamics as "pianistic chiaroscuro dynamics." Cf. his edition of the *Goldberg Variations,* p. ix.

860 *At their disposal.* A good example are the horn parts of some of Beethoven's symphonies. In some instances one feels that he wrote beyond the limits imposed by the technique and resources of the natural horns; yet even Beethoven could not permit his inspiration to burst outside the limits of the possible, and he had to remain satisfied with the means available in his time.

On the subject of the interdependence of means of expression and the inspiration of composers, cf. Philip James, *Early Keyboard Instruments,* pp. 45 f., where references are given to the divergent views of Professor Dent and Mr. Gerald R. Hayes and to Mr. James' own views. This subject deserves a more thorough discussion.

861 *On them.* Some instruments, like our No. 299, have their 'bridges' on the left hand near the hitch pins, but they serve the structural purpose of supporting the strings on a certain level; acoustically such bridges are not necessary, and on many clavichords they are omitted. P. 333

862 *Monochord.* A fine picture of the monochord can be found in table xxxix of Praetorius' *Theatrum Instrumentorum.* P. 334

863 *Century.* Cf. C. Sachs, *Handbuch,* 1930, pp. 142 f.

P. 334 864 *Dr. Otto Andersson.* Cf. his book, *The Bowed-Harp*, pp. 112 f. Referred to before on p. 251.

865 *The oldest known.* There are reasons for thinking that the nail-tangent technique was employed by Greek cithara players.

866 *Origin.* The probable evolutionary sequence of the clavichord would be: (1) the bowed-harp; (2) the organistrum (later reduced to the hurdy-gurdy); (3) the clavichord. In all of these instruments the tangent principle of stopping the strings is the typological connecting link. The hurdy-gurdy keys when struck against the string (the wheel remaining stationary) produce feeble sounds; the application of a balanced keyboard mechanism to operate the tangents, as mentioned by many writers, would be the next logical step.

867 *Berlin Collection.* C. Sachs, *Sammlung alter Musikinstrumente*, Berlin, 1922, pp. 43 f.

P. 335 868 *Study.* Cf. C. Sachs, *Real-Lexikon*, Berlin, 1913, p. 175 a, s.v. 'Hammerklavier'; the bibliography ending 1911; also his *Sammlung Alter Musikinstrumente*, Berlin, 1922. Excellent book by Philip James, *Early Keyboard Instruments*, New York, 1930. The standard book on the history of the pianoforte: Rosamond E. M. Harding, *The Piano-Forte*, Cambridge, England, 1933; this book deserves the highest praise and should serve as a model for writers on musical instruments.

869 *Diatonical scale.* Including, of course, the inevitable B-flat of the short octave.

870 *Upward.* In this note an experiment is tried in designating the tones of the scale in accordance with the system suggested in the American Tentative Standard Acoustical Terminology; see p. 9 for particulars.

P. 337 871 *Heyer Collection.* Georg Kinsky, *Musikhistorisches Museum von Wilhelm Heyer*, i, *Besaitete Tasteninstrumente*, pp. 27 f.; also fig. 1, p. 25.

872 *Sixteenth century.* It has another feature in common with the clavichord of Dominicus Pisaurensis, namely three separate bridges; the first (nearest to the player) carries three double string 'choirs,' the second one has eight choirs, and the third one bears eleven choirs. These bridges cut strings perpendicularly, not at an angle as in the case of curved bridges. According to Dr. Georg Kinsky this is a feature which is found only on the oldest clavichords; cf. *op. cit.*, i, p. 28.

873 *About 1760.* Philip James, *op. cit.*, pp. 51 f.

874 *Pianoforte.* It is not generally realized that some of the early square pianos were built like the clavichord and imitated its feeble tone. The magnificent sounding machines which can drown the fortissimo playing of large symphony orchestras are a development of the late nineteenth century.

P. 338 875 *Stein.* See Metropolitan Museum of Art, Crosby Brown Collection, *Catalogue of Keyboard Instruments*, New York, 1903, p. 138.

876 *Life.* For particulars, see G. Kinsky, *Musikhistorisches Museum*, i, pp. 168 f.

P. 340 877 *Bridge.* For a fine picture of this arrangement see Eugène de Bricqueville, *Notice sur la vielle*, 2. éd. Paris, 1911, the frontispiece. M. Prin's *guidon* is similar in principle and used for the same purpose on the *tromba marina*: cf. Léon Vallas, "Un mémoire sur la trompette marine," *Bulletin Français de la Société Internationale de Musique*, iv, 1908, p. 1189. It seems that M. Prin applied to his *tromba marina* a device which was already in use on the hurdy-gurdy.

878 *Disconnected.* Cf. E. de Bricqueville, *op. cit.*, p. 12.

879 *Potissimum. Op. cit.*, i, p. 303. Odo gave only the rules for locating the tangents. The compass given by him was from C to c, including b-flat; the scale, of course, was that of Pythagoras. Mr. Gerald R. Hayes was disturbed by the word 'fistula': cf. his *The Viols*, p. 228, n. 2. *De Fistulis*, which immediately follows the passage on the organistrum, refers to organ pipes, and has nothing to do with the organistrum.

880 *Normandy.* Carl Engel, *A Descriptive Catalogue of the Musical Instruments in the South Kensington Museum*, p. 113; also Kathleen Schlesinger, *Encyclopaedia Britannica*, 11th ed., xx, p. 268, s.v. 'Organistrum.'

881 *Palace.* G. Kinsky, *Geschichte der Musik in Bildern*, p. 41, 6.

882 *Cathedral.* Carl Engel, *op. cit.*, p. 115.

883 *Simultaneously.* Carl Engel, *op. cit.*, p. 103; the St. Blasius manuscript is dated now as of the twelfth century; also F. W. Galpin, *Old English Instruments of Music*, 1932, p. 108, fig. 19 a.

884 *Strings.* F. W. Galpin, *op. cit.*, p. 108, fig. 19 b.

P. 341 885 *Six.* Carl Engel, *op. cit.*, p. 233, fig. 127.

886 *Five strings. De Organographia*, p. 49, chap. xxiii, 'Lyra.'

887 *Vielle à roue.* E. de Bricqueville, *op. cit.*, pp. 60, 63.

888 *Monochord.* It is possible to regard the 'tangent' stopping technique of the strings on chordophones as a typological criterion; see Note 866. Typological similarity is not necessarily a sign of common origin, but at least it can be suggestive of useful lines of investigation.

889 *Recently.* Cf. E. G. Richardson, *The Acoustics of Orchestral Instruments*, New York, 1929, pp. 30 f., especially p. 33.

P. 342 890 *Real-Lexikon.* Page 16, s.v. 'Aeolsharfe.' On p. 16 of the *Real-Lexikon*, the transliteration in English, 'Eolova arfa,' is correct. On p. 432 it reads 'Zopova arfa.' 'Zopova' is a mistaken reading of 'Eolova,' caused by the somewhat similar shape of the Russian capital letter 'Z' and the 'reverse E' and the small letters 'l' and 'p.'

P. 347 891 *Problem.* Cf. Curt Sachs, in *Archiv für Musikwissenschaft*, i (1918), pp. 3 ff.; also his *Handbuch*, 1930, p. 126.

892 *Bow.* Dr. Andersson's book has been referred to several times before. Its value is not in settling the problem of the bow and its origin, but in bringing to the attention of students many valuable facts about bowed harps and the tangent (or nail) technique of stopping bowed instruments.

893 *Subject.* Cf. Henry Balfour, *The Natural History of the Musical Bow*, Oxford, 1899. *Encyclopédie de la musique*, pt. ii, vol. iii, p. 1744, s.v. 'L'Archet.' E. Heron-Allen, *Violin-Making as it was and is*, chap. vi. Kathleen Schlesinger, *The Precursors of the Violin Family*, ii, chap. iv, pp. 268 ff.; also index, p. 603, s.v. 'Bow.'

P. 348 894 *Thickness.* Cf. F. J. Fétis, *Antoine Stradivari*, Paris, 1856. M. Vuillaume measured Tourte bows and developed a graphic method of determining the decreasing diameters of the stick and linear distances at which these diameters are located.

895 *Details.* Tourte invented the slide (*recouvrement*) which fits over that part of the hair which passes over the lower part of the frog. On old bows this hair was exposed and sometimes bunched up. The slide is fitted in a swallow-tail groove in the frog. In order to hold the hair flat as a ribbon, Tourte affixed a ferrule over the frog and put a wooden wedge between the hair and the beveled portion of the frog, so that the hair is pressed against the ferrule by the wedge and the ferrule itself is prevented from sliding off.

896 *Stick.* Such a notched arrangement is called a *crémaillère*. The principle of the *crémaillère* on bows was known as early as the fifteenth century. Cf. Kathleen Schlesinger, *op. cit.*, ii, p. 283 and fig. 73.

897 *Instruments. Carl Claudius' Samling af Gamle Musikinstrumenter*, Copenhagen, 1931, p 361, no. 642.

P. 355 898 *Absolute size.* A. J. Ellis, "On the History of Musical Pitch," *Journal of the Society of Arts*, 1880, p. 320.

P. 356 899 *Contracted uniformly.* Praetorius' drawings are 13 cm. x 17 cm. For such a comparatively small size errors due to non-uniform contraction of paper would be well within the error of scaling.

P. 357 900 *Statement.* Respectively: (1) the English practice of the seventeenth century and, probably, of the late sixteenth century; (2) the German practice of the last three-quarters of the seventeenth century; (3) the German practice of the late sixteenth and the early seventeenth centuries.

901 *De Organographia.* Some of Praetorius' references to pitch were translated by Dr. A. J. Ellis. It was deemed best to translate here practically the whole of each passage anew.

902 *Chor-Ton.* Praetorius' terminology of pitches was not generally accepted; but the absolute value of the pitch recommended by him, it seems, was adhered to, since the 'classical pitch,' which lasted for nearly two centuries, down to 1820, was very close to his *Chor-Ton*, a′ = 422.8 cycles per second. Cf. A. J. Ellis, *loc. cit.*, p. 320, under (1) MA 424.2. Also Appendix D, p. 378, item 3.

P. 358 903 *Symphonien.* 'Symphonie' in Praetorius refers to an instrument of which no positive knowledge exists. Dr. C. Sachs in the *Real-Lexikon*, p. 367 b (2), suggested that probably a clavichord furnished with 'single choir' strings was meant. Canon Galpin, *Textbook*, p. 108, thinks that it might have been a *clavicymbel* (harpsichord) with gut strings.

904 *Bray.* ". . . sintemal sie in der Tieffe nicht so hart schreien." *De Organographia*, p. 16.

905 *Cammer-Ton. De Organographia*, pp. 14–16. To understand this passage, Appendix D should be studied.

P. 359 906 *Such a pitch.* Later in this quotation Praetorius refers again to these high pitch organs, but does not explain why they were regarded as the 'most convenient.' Dr. Ellis, taking Praetorius' *Chor-Ton* as the basis, figured the pitch of such organs (in just temperament) as 1′ = 565 cycles per second, a figure he put forward with considerable hesitation. Cf. "History of Musical Pitch," *Journal of the Society of Arts*, 1880, p. 332, under MA 567.3. It seems that Praetorius is not very clear in his references to pitches; therefore the pitch of the Halberstadt organ (a′ = 505.8) and that of Arnolt Schlick (a′ = 502.6), both about 1500, should be taken as a norm for the high pitch organs. See Table I, p. 359. "A whole fourth higher or a fifth lower" refers to the same organ, since it gives the same pitch for a′. This is typically an organist's expression. On the piano a given key produces a tone of definite pitch which can be referred to in absolute terms as having so many cycles per second. On the organ a key has relative pitch, since change in registration may raise or lower it an octave or even more. Therefore an organist may refer to a key in general terms. Thus a fourth above A is d; a fifth below is D. Since association of a key with a given octave is meaningless for an organist, unless size of a stop is also specified, he can refer to the organ pitched a fourth higher as 'a fourth higher,' 'a fifth lower,' or 'a fourth higher or a fifth lower.' Therefore there is nothing paradoxical when a high pitch organ, with a′ = 502.6 cycles per second, is referred to as being 'a fifth lower,' as we shall see later. Lack of clear perception of this elementary fact has caused unnecessary confusion.

P. 359 907 *Semitone higher*. Refer to *De Organographia*, pp. 102, 103. 'Present usual tone' is Praetorius' *Chor-Ton* (a′ = 422.8). If he is correct, then the organ 'a fourth higher or a fifth lower' would be pitched to 422.8 x $\frac{4}{3}$ or 563.7 cycles per second; the tonality of such organ would be in E. 563.7 cycles per second is, practically, Mersenne's *Ton de Chambre*.

908 *Conclusions*. Not only does Dr. Ellis' paper remain essentially valid today, but it is the only source on the general history of musical pitch. Unfortunately, this paper is one of the most difficult things to find in libraries. There is an excellent article on musical pitch in the *Encyclopaedia Britannica*, 11th ed., xxi, pp. 660 ff., by Mr. A. J. Hipkins, who collaborated with Dr. Ellis on the history of musical pitch. Less important is the appendix by D. J. Blaikley, in *A Descriptive Catalogue of the Musical Instruments Exhibited at the Royal Military Exhibition, London, 1890*. Published in 1891. The latest statement on the subject is P. A. Scholes, *The Oxford Companion to Music*, p. 731, s.v. 'Pitch.'

P. 360 909 *Two instruments*. Cf. Praetorius, *op. cit.*, p. 25, under *Viole de Gamba*. Also G. Kinsky, *Musikhistorisches Museum von Wilhelm Heyer in Cöln*, ii, p. 437, table; *ibid.*, p. 469, text, and p. 471, fig. 824.

910 *Grösser*. Praetorius, *De Organographia*, p. 47. For translation see p. 277 of this study.

911 *Sixteenth-century viols*. Mersenne tells a story about a bass viol of such large size that a small page was concealed inside and sang the treble; the player played the bass and sang the tenor. This sounds like a good story, if slightly incredible, but it should not be dismissed completely. Praetorius' sizes are considerably larger than those of the English consort viols. Also there is the testimony of Rousseau. Cf. his *Traité de la viole*, p. 19; it is quoted by G. R. Hayes, *Musical Instruments*, ii, pp. 10–11. The writer is inclined to believe Rousseau's testimony, since his description of the design of old viols is supported by the actual instrument in the Museo Civico in Bologna, Italy; photograph in the Crosby Brown Collection in the Metropolitan Museum of Art, New York.

912 *The most convenient*. The real reason why such high pitch organs were considered as convenient can be deduced from the statements made by Arnolt Schlick. It is a transposition of some authentic modes to a different tonal level, so that they could be played in their theoretical tonalities. This practice had nothing to do with transposition of the authentic modes into the plagal ones. It should be remembered that the low pitch organs were built for permitting the Dorian mode to be played with G as the final tone; the rest of the modes were adjusted to this low pitch. Some people preferred theoretical tonalities and played the Dorian mode with D as the final tone; this required the high pitched organ. Since the keyboards of the old organs had F as the lowest tone, there arose certain practical difficulties, much frowned upon by Schlick. See Notes 931 and 933 below.

913 *Standard pitch*. In conversation with the writer, Dr. Curt Sachs mentioned that the set of sixteenth-century recorders found in the Wencelskirche in Naumburg and now in the Berlin Collection are tuned to 440 cycles per second. Here is a curious fact. The arithmetical mean of two pitches of Schlick's time (377 and 502.6) is 440. More precise determination of the implied pitch level of the early sixteenth century gives the average pitch as a′ = 447. See Note 936. Although this is only one instance, it is very significant. As will be shown later, tunings of viols were nominal in the sixteenth century; their actual pitch was determined both by the pitches of the organs and by the tonalities in which the church modes were played. This raises the question of what this actual pitch was. The Wencelskirche recorders seem to indicate an answer.

P. 361 914 *Larger size*. Praetorius' drawings give the sizes of viols of the last quarter of the sixteenth century, as well as of his own time. The writer's impression, derived from a prolonged study of viol sizes, is that both the sizes and the standard pattern of viols were worked out ca. 1575 and have changed very little, in their absolute respect, since that time.

915 *Sizes of viols. Op. cit.*, p. 437.

916 *Drawing of it*. Table xx of Praetorius' *Theatrum Instrumentorum*, for some reason, gives no detailed reference to the viols represented. Viols numbered 1, 2, and 3 are referred to as *Violn de Gamba*. Nevertheless, it is possible to establish what viols are represented there. The body length of viol no. 3 is 78.5 centimetres (Table III); it can be only the *Kleine Bass-Viol*. The body length of *Viol Bastarda* no. 4 is 73.7 centimetres.

Since Praetorius stated that the *Viola bastarda* was somewhat longer than the tenor, the size of the latter is assumed to be about 68.5 cm., or the average size of the bass viols. Hence Praetorius' viol no. 1 is the *Cant* (the treble) and his no. 2 is the *Alt*. The writer is therefore in agreement with Dr. Georg Kinsky's attribution of names to Praetorius' viols. Cf. *Musikhistorisches Museum*, p. 435.

P. 363 917 *Between 35 and 45 cm. Ibid.*, p. 437.

918 *Tenor Viols*. See Table of viol sizes, p. 255 of this study.

919 *Musical usage*. See under No. 273, p. 277.

920 *Dr. Kinsky*. These tunings are too high. See the

next Note 921. The small type passage on p. 435 of the *Musikhistorisches Museum* in which Dr. Kinsky questions the tunings of the treble and alto viols of Praetorius is a misconception. Praetorius assigned the alto tunings (A–a′) to his treble instrument (*Cant*) correctly, since its size is that of the English alto viola.

P. 364 921 *Dr. Georg Kinsky.* Unfortunately, the German nomenclature of recent writers is not consistent. Dr. Kinsky relied entirely on Praetorius both in nomenclature and sizes. This brought him into conflict with the Belgian (English) sizes (see Note 670) and tunings, just mentioned in Note 920. But at least Dr. Kinsky's statements are consistent even when they are wrong. The same thing cannot be said of viol terminology, sizes, and tunings in the excellent catalogue of the Berlin Collection, *Sammlung alter Musikinstrumente*, Berlin, 1922. To facilitate subsequent discussion, pertinent data is tabulated below.

German Viol Nomenclature		Length of Body in cm.	English Viol Nomenclature, 17th century and later
Late 16th and early 17th century (Praetorius)	Later 17th and 18th century		
1. Cantus	Diskant	40	Alto
2.	Kleine Alt	48	Tenor
3. Alt	Alt	57	Lyra-Viol (Viola bastarda)
4. Tenor-Viola	Tenor	68.5	Consort Bass
5. Viola bastarda	Viola bastarda	ca. 75	(?)
6. Kleine Bass	Kleine Bass	78.5	No instrument of this size.

In the Berlin Catalogue one finds viols nos. 165 and 2482 classified as *viola bastarda*. The body lengths of the instruments are 69.5 and 70 centimetres, respectively. This places them in the bass viol class, since they are too large to qualify as lyra-viols in the English series and too small to qualify as the *viola bastarda* of Praetorius. The presence of the rose under the finger-board, which Dr. Curt Sachs regards as the sign of a *viola bastarda* (cf. his article "Die Viola Bastarda" referred to in Note 670, p. 429; also Berlin Catalogue, pp. 117–118; *Handbuch*, 1930, p. 194), is a characteristic of early seventeenth-century instruments. The later practice is not consistent, and the rose is not necessarily the sign of a *viola bastarda*, since it was used on viols of all sizes. Cf. G. R. Hayes, *The Viols*, p. 53. Viols numbered 2481, 168, 2484, 2479, and 2485, measuring (body length) 61, 62, 65, 65, and 66 centimetres respectively, are listed as tenors tuned to G–g′ or even A–a′. Cf. Berlin Catalogue, pp. 117–118 f. According to the best English practice, these viols should be classified as small basses (lyra and division viols) by their sizes. Tunings given for them are too high and the instruments of such a large size (61 centimetres and up) could not possibly be tuned to G–g′, to say nothing of A–a′. The writer made some experiments with the lyra-viol, No. 273 in this study, after it had been repaired and could stand strain. It has a body length of 56.5 cm., yet the most that could be done was to tune this instrument to E–e′, that is, one tone higher than the standard D–d′ tuning of the bass viol; even then the instrument was strained and sounded thin. Tuning it a fourth higher, to G–g′, was simply out of the question. The inconsistency in the Berlin Catalogue nomenclature with respect to these five instruments listed as tenors is this. If they are called tenors because of their size, then they belong to Praetorius' series and should be tuned to D–d′. If they are called tenors because of their tunings, then their sizes are too large, both by the standard English practice and by that of Praetorius, who recommended the English tenor tunings (A–a′) for his *Cantus*, the viol measuring 40.5 cm. in body length. Cf. Praetorius, *De Organographia*, p. 25, and *Theatrum Instrumentorum*, table xx, no. 1, p. 362 of this study, and also Table VII, p. 372 of this study.

922 *End of their existence.* It is difficult even to make assumptions with respect to the early sixteenth-century viols, since no instruments of that period have reached our time. But it seems that about 1575, possibly earlier, both viol and violin bodies were worked out in the forms we know today. With reference to viols the standard pattern is always meant. As to sizes of viols, it is highly probable that Praetorius' viols are of the same size as those of the second half of the sixteenth century. After the reform in viol practices ca. 1600, which was really a change in nomenclature and musical usage, the absolute average sizes remained unchanged. The same instruments were used for lower parts under different names, or, preserving the same name (in Germany), they were tuned lower and later played the same parts as their brethren of the same size, but bearing different names, in various countries.

923 *Organista probatissimus.* The fourth book of *Musice Active Micrologus* by Andreas Ornithoparcus, published in 1517, is dedicated to Schlick in the following words: "Musico consummatissimo ac Palatini Principis organiste probatissime." Cf. Grove's *Dictionary of Music*, iv, pp. 594 f.

Arnolt Schlick's book had a romantic history. The only copy of it was found concealed in the chimney of an old sixteenth-century house when that house was being razed. It was reprinted in *Monatshefte für Musik-Geschichte*, 1869, pp. 78–114.

P. 364 924 *Translation.* Schlick's original sixteenth-century German is so difficult that Herr Ernst Flade published a translation of the *Spiegel der Orgelmacher und Organisten* into modern German (Mainz, 1932). Herr Flade's translation cannot be relied upon completely, since in a few places some important words are omitted and the old designation of tones are translated into modern equivalents without the old equivalents being given. Otherwise, Herr Flade's translation is excellent and indispensable.

This quotation is translated from the original, *loc. cit.*, p. 85 and Herr Flade's text, p. 15.

925 *On the margin.* According to Robert Eitner, the editor of Schlick's reprint, this line measured 4 7-8 Rhenish inches. Multiplied 16 times, this gives the total length of the eight-foot pipe (F) as equal to six and one-half Rhenish feet, or 2040 mm. Cf. Ellis, *loc. cit.*, p. 371, under MA 377.

926 *Praetorius. De Organographia*, p. 14.

927 *That in A.* In this study the pitch of Schlick's organ (a′ = 377) is regarded as belonging to the tonality in A. See Appendix D for particulars.

P. 365 928 *Cornett-tone pitch.* It may seem paradoxical that the organ referred to as being 'a fifth lower' should be really a high pitch organ having a′ = 502.6 cycles per second. Following Praetorius, the pitch of this organ can be also referred to as being 'a fourth higher.' See Note 906 for a complete explanation. The number of cycles, 502.6 (just temperament), is given by Mr. A. J. Hipkins in his article in *Encyclopaedia Britannica*, 11th ed. Dr. Ellis' figure is 504.2 (equal temperament); since the low-pitched organ (a′ = 377) is given by Dr. Ellis in just temperament, Mr. Hipkins adjusted the pitch of the high organ to the same temperament.

929 *Plain Song.* Schlick's book should be read in conjunction with the article published by Herr Raymund Schlecht in the *Monatshefte für Musik-Geschichte*, shortly after Schlick's original text was reprinted there. This excellent and competent article proved of the greatest help to the writer in a correct interpretation of Schlick's text. It is hard to understand why this important contribution has been so long overlooked, since through its use many blunders perpetrated by 'authorities' who used Schlick as their source material could have been avoided. See the Bibliography for the exact reference.

930 *Gamaut.* In the hexachord system the lowest tone was G, designated by the capital Greek letter Gamma. In the first hexachord this tone was called 'ut' (our 'c'). *Gamaut* designated the lowest tone of the hexachordal system.

931 *In gravibus.* Robert Eitner, the editor of *Monatshefte für Musik-Geschichte*, misread the word *gravibus* and used instead the meaningless *grambus*, which he interpreted from the following context as the transposition of the first tone by a fourth. Although Raymund Schlecht explained that this could mean only *gravibus*, and even gave a correct explanation of how this could be misread through the typographical peculiarities of the printing of the sixteenth century (*loc. cit.*, 1870, p. 182), *grambus* sailed forth victoriously into many subsequent works and Eitner's explanation was accepted. Cf. Ellis, *op. cit.*, p. 306; A. J. Hipkins, *Encyclopaedia Britannica*, 11th ed., xxi, p. 661. Mr. Hipkins' explanation given there is misleading. In Schlick's time (it cannot be repeated too often) the keyboards always ended in F (cf. Raymund Schlecht, *loc. cit.*, p. 171). Schlick himself states explicitly that "... ist ein sonder uffmercken und fleiss zü han die werck den organisten brüchlich zü machen, das das clavir des manuals xxiiij. claves naturales, vier fa, vier la, das sein dry octaven, unnd ein tertz perfect." (*Loc. cit.*, p. 88.) That is, the manual of his time had four F's and four A's, three octaves and a major third, or twenty-four natural keys, the compass being from F to a″. The pedal organ had F as the lowest tone, its real pitch depending on the actual length of the F-pipe.

Therefore, Schlick meant by *in gravibus* simply the fact that many church songs ended in low tones. With the keyboards ending in F it was more practicable to play the first tone (Dorian mode) with G as the final tone and utilize the keyboard more completely. See Notes 933 and 934.

932 *The manual.* Arnolt Schlick, *Monatshefte für Musik-Geschichte*, 1869, p. 85. Translated from the original.

933 *Theory.* Theory and practice were not in happy agreement. The lowest note of the authentic modes is D; logically the keyboards of organs should have ended either on D or on AA to accommodate the Dorian and the Hypodorian modes. The hexachord system had G as the lowest tone, so it seems the practice of starting the Dorian mode on G originated long before Schlick's time. For singing songs in this tonality the low pitch organs were necessary to bring the relative pitch to the level of the singers' voices.

934 *Higher octave.* With the lowest D absent, the tones F, G, A, B, and c, were sometimes useless for the organist, so he had to play an octave higher. This difficulty is similar to that of our double bass players. For instance, in the Symphony No. 5 in C-minor of Beetho-

ven the double basses are called upon to play DD and CC. Our standard instruments descending only to EE are not able to produce these tones, and transposition an octave higher has to be resorted to.

P. 365 935 *Independent voices.* Arnolt Schlick, *loc. cit.*, p. 85.

936 *Unison.* For the pitch a′ = 502.6, the tone d′, being a fifth lower, has 335.07 cycles per second; for the pitch a′ = 377, the tone g′, being a major second lower, has 335 cycles per second. This corresponds, approximately, to the tone e′ in our system at 440 cycles per second. A parallel example: the tone e′ is to be played on the clarinet in D in unison with the clarinet in A; the notes would be written as d′ and g′ respectively. 335 cycles per second for e′ correspond to a′ = 447; this might be taken as an average implied pitch of the early sixteenth century.

937 *Convenient range.* The pitches of ancient organs were determined primarily by the vocal range of the human voice. With the keyboards adapted to the hexachordal system of tones, the principal factor in determining the pitch of the organs was the choice of tonalities of the Dorian mode. Sticklers for theoretical tonalities had to have high pitch organs. But, as Schlick proved very conclusively, this practice was not very convenient. So the low pitch organs on which the Dorian mode could be played on G, the Phrygian on A, etc. (cf. the entire second chapter of Schlick's book) were preferred by practical men. Evidently not all organists understood this. So when the Dorian mode was played on G on high pitch organs, singers were forced to 'shout and scream.' Schlick admonished: "des sich dann ein geschickter organist noch gelegenheit der stymmen der person woll zü halten weiss etc." ("A skilful organist will then know how to adapt himself to the compass of voices of singers and so forth.")

Praetorius gives an illuminating comment on some musical practices of his time. "Wiewol auch in *Italia* und andern Catholischen Capellen deutsches Landes jetzt gedachter niedrieger Thon in *tertia inferiore* gar sehr im gebrauch: Sintemahl etliche *Itali* an dem hohen singen, wie nicht unbillich, kein gefallen, vermeynen es habe keine art, könne auch der *Text* nicht recht wol vernommen werden, man krähete, schreie und singe in der Höhe gleich wie die *Grasemägde.*" (*De Organographia*, p. 16.)

P. 366 938 *Transposition. Encyclopaedia Britannica*, 11th ed., xxi, p. 661. See Note 940 for details.

939 *Organ tablatures.* Cf. Gotthold Frotscher, *Geschichte des Orgelspiels und der Orgelkomposition*, Berlin, 1935–36, the facsimile plate facing p. 400.

940 *Pitch.* A. J. Hipkins, *History of the Pianoforte*, London, 1897, p. 87. Italics are ours. The last sentence is a slip of the pen. The highest key of the lower keyboard is given correctly as f^3. This tone is *higher* than c^3. Therefore, the lower keyboard is a fourth higher than the upper. But, since the keys c^3 and f^3 plucked the same string, they were of the same pitch (in terms of cycles per second); nominally they differed 'in pitch,' to use the word 'pitch' with respect to notation. (See Note 941.) The writer disagrees with M. Hipkins' explanation of the reasons for tuning organs a fourth apart. Mr. Hipkins states (*op. cit.*, p. 87): "We learn from Arnolt Schlick that organs were tuned a fourth apart to effect the same purpose in accompanying the Plain Song, a transposition to enable the Plagal modes to lie as conveniently as the Authentic and from this the high and low church pitches arose, at first, as said, a fourth apart, although later only a minor third or a whole tone, the tendency being a compromise." In the footnote Mr. Hipkins in addition to Schlick gives Dr. Ellis as one of his authorities.

In checking the last reference (Dr. Ellis' paper on pitch, p. 306), the writer found that Dr. Ellis mistranslated Schlick. The original text reads: "Ursach das sich der merer theill Chor gesangs endet in grambus (cf. Note 931), als in primo tono." Herr Eitner's note on 'grambus' reads: "Ein unbekannter Ausdruck; zieht man aber das Folgende in Betracht, so kann damit nur die Transposition des tonus primus nach der Quart gemeint sein."

Dr. Ellis evidently has not noticed Herr Schlecht's article (Mr. Hipkins rather, since in note 8, p. 304, Dr. Ellis states that Schlick's book was lent to him by Mr. A. J. Hipkins). At any rate he translated this place as follows: "The reason is that a greater part of church music ends in *grambus* [a word which puzzles Schlick's editor, who says, however, that it can only mean the transposition of the *tonus primus* by a Fourth], than in the first tone." 'Als' does not mean 'than,' but 'as,' 'like,' or 'being.' A correct translation of Schlick's words is given on p. 365 of this study. Arnolt Schlick never implied that organs of his time were tuned a fourth apart for transposition, enabling "the Plagal modes to lie as conveniently as the Authentic." Transposition of the Plagal modes had nothing to do with selection of the organ tunings. What Schlick actually stated was that on the high pitch organs the first tone (the Dorian mode) had to be transposed from G to D; this meant that an authentic mode (the Dorian in this case) was transposed from one system of notation (G) into another (D) without affecting its interval relationships; its final tone on the low pitch organs was, nominally, G; on the high pitch organs it was D. Paradoxically, this transposition had not affected the actual pitch level. If both organs were tuned precisely a fourth apart, i.e., if their pipes were made of the lengths recommended by Schlick, then for the singers the actual pitch level would remain the same. In other words, the organs were treated as transposing instruments with respect to the implied pitch level which was considered as the most convenient for human voices. See Text, p. 366, and Notes 936 and 937.

Mr. Hipkins' suggestion would mean that there should be either two organs tuned a fourth apart, or one organ with keyboards transposing a fourth, in the same church. In his later statement (article on 'Musical Pitch,' *Encyclopaedia Britannica*, 11th ed., xxi, p. 661) he acknowleged that such a practice could not be carried out, since there were no organs with keyboards transposing a fourth. Indeed, there would be no necessity of having any such arrangement, since the whole purpose of the selection of different tonalities of organs (and, therefore, of their pitches) was to accommodate the notation of parts to the proper pitch level of human voices. As Schlick told us, the low pitch organs were more convenient because the keyboard ending in F could accommodate the lowest authentic mode better if its final tone were G. This, in turn, would dictate the tonality (pitch) of the organ, if the average pitch level of voices were selected properly and regarded as a reference point. By suggesting a certain length of pipe for both the low and the high pitch organs and by giving the final tones of the Dorian mode for each, Schlick clearly indicated what he considered as a proper average pitch level for the singers. As already stated, this pitch level was the same (i.e., both organs would sound in unison) if the tonalities of organ parts were properly selected. Our failure to understand sixteenth-century practices arises from the psychological difficulty imposed by the fact that our keyboard instruments are non-transposing. Appendix D on the polydiapasonal scale should be studied in this connection.

P. 366 941 *The low pitch organs.* This can be visualized better if two keyboards were represented by letters in the highest part of their compass, thus:

KEYBOARDS

The Upper:

d' e' f' g' a' b' c'' d'' e'' f'' g'' a'' b'' c^3

The Lower:

g' a' b' c'' d'' e'' f'' g'' a'' b'' c^3 d^3 e^3 f^3

This tabulation shows that the lower keyboard was a fourth higher in notation; but the keys actually plucked the same string and therefore sounded the same tone. The interesting question: To what pitch were the strings on these harpsichords with transposing boards tuned? See Note 913. A harpsichord with transposing keyboards is represented on p. 88 of Mr. Hipkins' *A Description and History of the Pianoforte.*

P. 367 942 *Pitch remain the same.* See *Musical Instruments and their Music*, ii, *Viols*, London, 1930, p. 39. The qualifying part of the sentence is ours and states the fundamental assumptions when viols cannot be tuned a fifth lower. Mr. Hayes assumes throughout his book the existence of one series (English) of sizes of viols. The larger-sized German series, already discussed, were evidently unknown to him; otherwise this important point would certainly have attracted his attention and called for comment.

943 *With organs.* String instruments were played with organs as early as the twelfth century. Cf. *Encyclopaedia Britannica*, 11th ed., xx, p. 268, fig. 6.

P. 368 944 *Alto and Tenor.* Ganassi gives the tuning of these instruments as *G*, *c*, *f*, *a*, *d′*, *g′*. Cf. Johannes Wolf, *Handbuch der Notationskunde*, Leipzig, 1913–19, ii, p. 224. This reduces the interval between the bass and the alto-tenor tunings to a fourth; later the tunings stabilized themselves as given in the text.

Martin Agricola's tunings of viols were given, of course, as follows:

Treble		*f*	*a*	*d′*	*g′*	*c″*
Alto and Tenor		*c*	*f*	*a*	*d′*	*g′*
Bass	G	*c*	*f*	*a*	*d′*	*g′*

Cf. Johannes Wolf, *op. cit.*, ii, p. 221. The intervals between the strings are not in accordance with later practice; the bass tuning differs from the Alto-Tenor tuning only by the addition of the sixth string.

Straightening out the intervals and adding one extra string to each instrument, we get:

Treble	(*c*)		*f*	*b*	*d′*	*g′*	*c″*
Alto and Tenor	(G)		*c*	*f*	*a*	*d′*	*g′*
Bass	(D)	G	*c*	*e*	*a*	*d′*	*g′*

It is curious that such a slight adjustment discloses that Agricola's treble viol was tuned almost the same way as the modern alto viol (cf. Hayes, *op. cit.*, p. 17); to indulge in a little speculation, its size might have been about 40 cm., or the size of Praetorius' *Cant.* Agricola's alto-tenor tunings are the same as those of Ganassi. The bass tuning of Agricola only indicates the trend, since differing but little from those of the alto-tenor, it shows that the bass viol of Agricola's time and locality was either of the same size or only very slightly larger. This conclusion is supported by the relative size of the instruments represented in Agricola's book.

Since the practice of tuning instruments in the sixteenth century, when played individually or in consort of their own kind, was to tune the highest string 'neither too high nor too low' (cf. G. R. Hayes, *op. cit.*, p. 10, n. 3), that is, arbitrarily, it is not illegitimate to transpose the treble and alto-tenor tunings one tone higher:

Treble .... (*d*) *g* *d* *e'* *g'* *d''*
Alto and Tenor ..... (*A*) *d* *g* *b* *e'* *a'*

Comparison of these tunings with corresponding tunings given in the text shows that they are identical. This is the reason for the writer's statement that the 'ordinary' or D-tunings were given, among others, by Agricola.

P. 368 945 *A fifth lower.* "To the eye at least" refers to the fact that with the low and high pitch organs in existence these tunings were nominal and sounded in unison when the high pitch organs were exactly a fourth higher.

946 *Treble.* Cerone's tunings for the treble are: *G*, *c*, *f*, *a*, *d'*, *g'*. In the text the tuning of the treble viols in the G-series of tunings is, of course, a fourth lower than that in the D-series. The low set is referred to as being a fifth lower for simplicity.

947 *Per quartam superiorem.* Since the G-tunings of viols correspond to the tonality of the Dorian mode transposed a fourth higher (*per quartam superiorem*), it is more logical to regard them as being, theoretically, a fourth higher and not a fifth lower with respect to the D-tunings. The actual position of the G-tunings is therefore one octave lower than the theoretical one.

P. 369 948 *Should be.* This deplorable tendency to 'correct' the old writers should be discouraged. In the course of this investigation the writer learned many severe lessons, among others, that the hasty questioning of things which appear absurd or mistaken in the old writings is not always a safe procedure. More often it is the questioner who is wrong.

949 *Contradictory statements.* In addition to the statement made in Note 947, D-tunings are a fourth lower than G-tunings when the latter are put in their proper theoretical position with respect to the former.

950 *Chor-Ton pitch. De Organographia*, p. 16; translated on p. 358 of this study.

951 *Per second.* A. J. Ellis, *loc. cit.*, p. 309.

952 *In unison.* This conclusion is based on the premises that G-tunings were played with the low pitch organs and D-tunings with the high pitch organs. See Note 936.

P. 370 953 *At the moment.* Such a procedure is not purely imaginary. Bernhard Schmid's book of organ tablatures, in which both tonalities of the same church mode, when there were two of them, were printed on the same page, would permit this feat. It seems that old musicians understood this process so well that it never occurred to them that three hundred years later their practices would prove a stumbling block to understanding.

954 *Piece of music.* This is one of the advantages a tablature has over the staff notation. In the latter a violist would have difficulties in reading parts, since, although actually the same pitch, they would be written differently for each organ. This is based on the assumption that music would be written in terms of the keyboard of organs of various pitches.

955 *Books on viols. Op. cit.*, pp. 41 f.

956 *Such difference. Op. cit.*, p. 42. Mr. Hayes refers to the fact that the authors who wrote on viols were, except for Praetorius, writing either of the 'low' or 'high' viol tunings; cf. *ibid.*, pp. 40 f.

957 *Same.* Since the sound of vocal parts was in unison and the difference in notation of parts was only nominal, there would be no necessity of having instruments of two different series of sizes. Not so in the early seventeenth century. Praetorius, as we have seen, gave us hints that not everything was proper either with voices or with viols. This was due to the changes in pitch standards.

958 *Fourth higher.* Cf. G. R. Hayes, *Viols*, p. 242, last two lines of the text and the footnote 4.

P. 371 959 *Organ parts.* The last statement is based mostly on Schlick's explanations. Bernhard Schmid's book of organ tablatures supports Schlick.

960 *Euclidean proof.* G. R. Hayes, *op. cit.*, p. 42.

961 *Imperative.* This was not an easy thing to realize. Praetorius longed for a single standard of pitch and he recommended his *Chor-Ton* as the most suitable. Whenever possible, musicians followed his recommendation; but the old organs, which have a proverbially long life, made a thorough reform impossible. Cf. C. S. Terry, *Bach's Orchestra*, pp. 165 f., for a fine example of difficulties which old musicians had to face.

962 *Inconveniences.* For a complete picture of pitch variations one has to read Dr. Ellis' paper *On the History of Musical Pitch.* It should be reprinted.

963 *Preferred.* Most writers give D-tunings. They were eventually adopted as the standard tunings of viols when the pitch was settled and the sizes of viols properly adjusted.

964 *Harmonii.* See p. 368 of this study. Also *De Organographia*, p. 44.

P. 372 965 *De Organographia.* G-tunings are given there on p. 25; D-tunings are mentioned in the famous passage quoted here on p. 368.

966 *Much better.* This conservatism of the German musicians was a good thing. The old nomenclature of

viols, which they preserved to our day, when properly related to the sizes of viols in the seventeenth century, is one of the most incontrovertible objective evidences that the viol sizes were larger in Praetorius' time.

P. 372

967 *Consort.* Cf. G. R. Hayes, *Viols*, p. 40.

968 *Were regarded.* See Notes 947 and 949. The change itself was so simple and obvious that among contemporary English authorities no one, it seems, made any comments. The earliest indirect reference is that of Praetorius; cf. *De Organographia*, p. 44; also p. 368 of this study.

P. 373

969 *Equivalent.* On bowed instruments there are three functionally interdependent elements: their size, their tunings, and the standard of musical pitch. The last-named is an independent variable and its change must necessarily affect both sizes and tunings. As already stated several times, at the turn of the century (1600), in addition to the early sixteenth-century practices of tuning organs to a low and a high pitch, there was a tendency to find a compromise pitch. Since this pitch varied considerably from both the low and high ecclesiastical pitches, it became imperative that some adjustment should be made with respect to the viol. The English kept the tunings constant (D-tunings according to Praetorius), but adjusted the sizes of their consort viols; Rousseau referred to this change as a 'reduction' of sizes. It should be understood that the absolute sizes of the viols remained the same, but the whole series were 'promoted' to the lower tonal positions. The Germans kept the sizes of viols constant, but lowered the tunings. As Table VII, p. 372, shows, the processes are equivalent. The names of viols being a matter of convenience, they were adjusted by the English and retained by the Germans. This explains the difference between the English and German nomenclatures.

970 *Proof.* It is unsafe to disregard Praetorious' viol sizes. For a balanced picture, the whole problem of sizes, not only in Germany but also in England, should be considered. Dr. Kinsky's unfortunate extension of Praetorius' sizes into a period when they no longer applied is excusable, since he was an enthusiastic pioneer in scaling the sizes of Praetorius' instruments (his work was published in 1912); he had not the benefit of Mr. G. R. Hayes' authoritative statement (1930) on the English practice. It appears that Mr. Hayes must have missed, for some reason, Dr. Kinsky's valuable work; there is not a single reference in his book on viols to the second volume of the *Musikhistorisches Museum.* Otherwise, the glaring discrepancies in the sizes of the German (Praetorius–Kinsky) and the English viols would have become so obvious that the problem could not be disregarded. Praetorius' reference to the D-tunings of the English can be taken as an indication that the latter had already adjusted their sizes.

971 *En France. Op. cit.*, p. 22. Translation: ". . . those who make viols reduced them to a convenient size for holding them between the legs, whence they came to be called leg viols. . . . It is true that the English reduced their viols to a convenient size before the French (did), as it is easy to judge by the ancient viols of England, which we hold in particular esteem in France."

P. 374

972 *Ratios.* See p. 274 of this study, the passage beginning "And to be exact in that . . .," etc. 'As short again' with reference to the treble viol means 'twice as small' or 'half the size.'

P. 375

973 *Dynamic symmetry.* Cf. Jay Hambidge, (1) *Dynamic Symmetry*, 1920; (2) *Dynamic Symmetry in Composition as Used by the Artists*, Cambridge, Mass., 1923; (3) *Practical Applications of Dynamic Symmetry*, New Haven, 1932. L. D. Caskey, *Geometry of Greek Vases*, Boston, 1929, contains a fine introduction, restating in simple language some basic principles of dynamic symmetry.

974 *Exact.* The closer to this ratio, 1.236 of the 'U' (the curve 'C' of the graph) the outline of the viol comes, the more harmoniously proportioned it appears. *Viola da gamba* no. 805 of the former Heyer Collection (cf. *Musikhistorisches Museum* . . ., ii, p. 447, for picture, p. 454 for description) has this ratio almost exact. In this case U = 24.25 cm.; L = 30 cm. 24.25 x 1.236 = 29.97 cm. The correct English nomenclature of this instrument would be the tenor. The division viol No. 274 of this Collection has the size L = 37.08 cm. by calculation and 37 cm. as measured; the bass viol No. 275, L = 40.17 cm. calculated, and 40 cm. as measured.

P. 376

975 *Graph.* Mace's rule for locating the bridge on the *viola da gamba* is discussed on p. 262 of this study.

P. 377

976 *Pitches.* Dr. A. J. Ellis listed about 320 various pitch standards which were used from ca. 1361, the year the famous Halberstadt organ was built, until 1880.

977 *Instruments in C.* In 1880, N. A. Rimsky-Korsakoff, when he began to compose the opera *Snow Maiden* in his village summer home, had at his disposal a piano, old, broken, and tuned a whole tone too low. He used to call it the 'piano in B-flat.' Cf. *My Musical Life*, New York, 1923, p. 197.

978 *Condition.* Cf. Praetorius, *De Organographia*, p. 14, where he refers to the troubles experienced in his time.

979 *Difficulties.* The European-built clarinets tuned to 435 cycles per second cannot be put exactly in tune with the clarinets built to 440 cycles. The shorter barrels bring the 435-clarinet in tune in some part of its register, but the rest of the scale is out of tune in various degrees.

P. 377 980 *Systems.* The actual tones selected were from *f′*-sharp to *c″* inclusive; only the number of cycles per second of these tones were used as the basis of the poly-diapasonal scale; otherwise there is no connection between the equal tempered and the suggested poly-diapasonal scales.

P. 378 981 *Consulted.* Cf. C. M. von Hornbostel, "Eine Tafel zur logarithmischen Darstellung von Zahlenverhältnissen," *Zeitschrift für Physik*, vi, pp. 29–34 (1921). This table permits the quick conversion of a number of cycles per second into cents and vice versa.

982 *Musical pitch.* Cf. A. J. Ellis, "On the History of Musical Pitch," *Journal of the Society of Arts*, March 5, 1880, p. 316. 370 cycles per second is an arbitrary number selected by Dr. Ellis because no historical pitch had this low number. The lowest pitch cited by Dr. Ellis is the mean tone a′ of 373.1 cycles per second given by an organ pipe of four 'pieds du roi' (an obsolete French measure, 'royal feet').

983 *This pitch.* Very necessary conditions for the viola da gamba: (1) the bass bar should be correctly proportioned (rather small), and not strengthened, as is done with some instruments adapted for modern fretless playing at our present standard pitch; (2) the strings should be thin and correctly selected for the low pitch.

984 *Standard.* According to the procedure adhered to by the American Standards Association, the 'American Tentative Standard' is the next to the last step in many intermediate steps before a proposal sponsored by certain responsible and recognized organizations becomes an 'American Standard.' A tentative standard can still be changed; after it is approved as a standard, changes are very difficult.

BIBLIOGRAPHY

BIBLIOGRAPHY

A COMPLETE bibliography of musical instruments would be enormous. The following list includes only books and articles referred to in the text and notes or consulted in the preparation of this study. Inclusion does not imply that the work is authoritative, but only that it contains particular features of interest. Several important works are not mentioned because they were not accessible. The items marked with an asterisk are considered especially valuable for the study of musical instruments, either from an historical or from an organological point of view.

*Adlung, Jacob. *Musica mechanica organoedi. Das ist: Gründlicher Unterricht von der Struktur, Gebrauch, und Erhaltung, &c. der Orgeln, Clavicymbel, Clavichordien und anderer Instrumente* . . . Johann Lorenz Albrecht, ed. 2 vols. Berlin, 1768.

*Agricola, Martin. *Musica Instrumentalis Deudsch* . . . Wittemberg, 1528 und 1545. Reprint, Leipzig, 1896.

Allen, *see* Heron-Allen.

*Altenburg, Johann Ernst. *Versuch einer Anleitung zur heroisch-musikalischen Trompeter- und Pauker-Kunst.* Halle, 1795. Reprint, Leipzig, 1911.

Altenburg, Wilhelm. *Die Klarinette.* Heilbronn, 1904.

—— "Zur Entwicklungsgeschichte des Klarinettenbaues." *Zeitschrift für Instrumentenbau*, xxv, pp. 390 f. (1905).

—— "Eine Wiedereinführung des Bassethorns." *Ibid.*, xxviii, pp. 555 a f.

Altmann, Wilhelm, and Borissowsky, Wadim. *Literaturverzeichnis für Bratsche und Viola d'amore.* Wolfenbüttel, 1937.

Ambrosius, Theseus. *Introductio in Chaldaicam Linguam . . . et Descriptio ac Simulachrum Phagoti Afranij* . . . Pavia, 1539. *See also* Valdrighi, and Cecil Forsyth, *Orchestration*, London, 1914, p. 487.

**American Tentative Standard Acoustical Terminology.* The Standard No. Z24.1–1936. Sponsored by the Acoustical Society of America. Approved and published by the American Standards Association. New York, 1936.

*Andersson, Otto. *The Bowed-Harp: A Study in the History of Early Musical Instruments.* From the original Swedish edition revised by the author. Kathleen Schlesinger, ed. London, 1930.

Ann Arbor. The Stearns Collection. *See* Stanley, Albert.

Apian-Bennewitz, Paul Otto. *Die Geige, der Geigenbau und die Bogenverfertigung.* Weimar, 1892.

Arban, Joseph. *Arban's . . . Method for the Trumpet or Cornet.* New York, [?].

Arbeau, Thoinot. *See* Tabourot.

*Armstrong, Robert Bruce. *Musical Instruments.* Part i: *The Irish and the Highland Harps.* Edinburgh, 1904. Part ii: *English and Irish Instruments.* 1908.

*Audsley, G. A. *The Art of Organ-Building.* New York, 1905. 2 vols.

*—— *The Organ of the Twentieth Century* . . . New York, 1919.

*Aznar y García, Francisco. *Indumentaria española* . . . Madrid, 1880. Contains colored facsimiles of the miniatures of the musicians in the *Cantigas de Santa Maria.*

Bach, Vincent. *The Art of Trumpet Playing.* Garden City, 1920. Privately published.

Bacher, Joseph. *Die Viola da Gamba.* Kassel, 1932.

Bach-Jahrbuch. Leipzig, 1904 and later years.

Bach Trumpets. "Die Höhen Bach-Trompeten." *Zeitschrift für Instrumentenbau*, xxx, pp. 194 f. *See* Blandford, Sachs.

Balfour, Henry. *The Natural History of the Musical Bow*. Oxford, 1899.

—— *The Old British "Pibcorn" or "Hornpipe," and its Affinities*. London, 1890.
Reprint from *Journal of the Anthropological Institute*, xx, pp. 142–154.

*Barnes, William H. *The Contemporary American Organ, its Evolution, Design, and Construction*. New York, 1937.

Bartholinus, Casparus. . . . *De Tibiis Veterum et earum Antiquo Usu Libri Tres*. Rome, 1677. Second ed., Amsterdam, 1679.

*Barton, Edwin Henry. "Sound." See *Dictionary of Applied Physics*.

*—— *A Text-Book on Sound*. London, 1926. First published in 1908.

Bechler, Leo, and Rahm, Bernhardt. *Die Oboe und die ihr verwandten Instrumente* . . . Leipzig, 1914.

*Bedos de Celles, François. *L'Art du facteur d'orgues*. Paris, 1776–78. 2 vols. Reprint, Kassel, 1934– .

*Berlioz, Hector. *Grand traité d'instrumentation et d'orchestration modernes*. Nouvelle éd. Paris, [188–]. First ed., Paris, 1844.

—— *A Treatise upon Modern Instrumentation and Orchestration* . . . Mary Cowden Clarke, tr. First ed., London, 1856, and several subsequent ones.

—— *Instrumentationslehre, von Hector Berlioz*. Revised and supplemented by Richard Strauss. Leipzig, 1905.

*Bermudo, Juan. *Declaracion de instrumentos musicales*. Ossuna, 1555.

*Besseler, Heinrich. *Die Musik des Mittelalters und der Renaissance*. Wildpark-Potsdam, 1931–34. 10 parts.

Bianchini, Francesco. *De Tribus Generibus Instrumentorum Musicae Veterum Organicae Dissertatio*. Rome, 1742.

Blaikley, David James. *Acoustics in Relation to Wind Instruments*. London, 1890.

—— "The single and double reed instruments." *English Music, 1604 to 1904*, pp. 333–354.

—— Miscellaneous papers on wind instruments. Cf. Dayton C. Miller, *Catalogue of Books and Literary Material Relating to the Flute*, Cleveland, 1935, p. 19.

*Blandford, Walter F. H. "Bach's Trumpets." *The Monthly Musical Record*, July, 1931.

*—— "The 'Bach' Trumpet." *Ibid.*, lxv, March–April, May, June, 1935.
This is the most competent contribution on a much misrepresented subject.

*—— "Bach's Horn Parts." *The Musical Times*, Aug., 1936.

Bobillier, Marie. *Dictionnaire pratique et historique de la musique*, par Michel Brenet (pseud.). Paris, 1926.

—— *La musique militaire*, par Michel Brenet. Paris, 1917.

Boehm, Theobald. *Die Flöte und das Flötenspiel in akustischer, technischer, und artistischer Beziehung*. Munich, 1871. For a translation, *see* Miller, D. C.

Bonanni, Filipo. *See* Buonanni.

Borland, John E. "The Brass Instruments." *English Music, 1604 to 1904*, pp. 445–477.

Boston, Museum of Fine Arts. "The Leslie Lindsey Mason Collection of Musical Instruments." *The Museum of Fine Arts Bulletin*, no. 91, Boston, 1917. Reprints are available.

Boston Symphony Orchestra. *Catalogue of the Casadessus Collection of Old Musical Instruments*. Boston, 1926.

Bottée de Toulmon, Auguste. *Dissertation sur les instruments de musique employés au moyen-âge*. Paris, 1844.

Bouasse, Henri. *Verges et plaques. Cloches et carillons*. Paris, 1927.

*—— *Tuyaux et résonateurs. Introduction à l'étude des instruments à vent*. M. Fouché, collab. Paris, 1929.

*—— *Instruments à vent*. Vol. i. *Anches métallique et membraneuses. Tuyaux à anche et à bouche. Orgue. Instruments à embouchure de cor*. Paris, 1929. Vol. ii. *Instruments à piston, à anche, à embouchure de flûte*. M. Fouché, collab. Paris, 1930.

—— *Cordes et membranes. Instruments de musique à cordes et à membranes.* Paris, 1926.

Professor Bouasse's writings are stimulating and refreshing. He does not rely entirely on the quantitative (objective) approach. His old-time common-sense qualitative analysis leads sometimes to surprising results. He believes that a well-developed ear is still the best acoustical apparatus for certain investigations. How old-fashioned and how true!

Brancour, René. *Histoire des instruments de musique . . .* Pref. by Ch. M. Widor. Paris, 1921.

Brenet, Michel, pseud. *See* Bobillier, Marie.

Bricqueville, Eugène de. *Un coin de la curiosité. Les anciens instruments de musique.* Paris, [1894].

—— *Les musettes.* Paris, 1894.

—— *Notice sur la vielle.* 2. éd. Paris, 1911.

—— *Les vents d'instruments de musique au XVIIIe siècle.* Paris, 1908.

—— *La Viole d'amour.* Paris, 1908.

*Buhle, Edward. *Die musikalischen Instrumente in den Miniaturen des frühen Mittelalters.* i. *Die Blasinstrumente.* Leipzig, 1903.

*—— *Verzeichnis der Sammlung alter Musikinstrumente im Bachhause zu Eisenach.* Curt Sachs, ed. Leipzig, 1919.

Buonanni, Filippo. *Gabineto armonico pieno d'istromenti sonori indicati . . .* Rome, 1722.

Caccini, Giulio. *La nouve musiche.* Florence, 1601. Reprint, Francesco Vatielli, ed. Rome, 1934.

Cantigas de Santa Maria.

A great collection of tunes made by Alfonso X ('El Sabio'), king of Castile and León (1252–1284). *See* Aznar y García. *Grove's Dictionary of Music,* 1927 edition, has colored reproductions of pictures of musicians.

Carse, Adam. *The History of Orchestration.* London and New York, 1925.

*—— *Musical Wind Instruments. A history of the Wind Instruments used in European Orchestras and Wind-Bands from the Later Middle Ages to the Present Time.* London, 1939.

The best book on the wind instruments extant.

Caskey, Lacey D. *Geometry of Greek Vases.* Boston, 1922.

Century Dictionary, The. New York, 1914 and other years.

Cerone, Domenico Pietro. *Regole necessarie per il canto fermo.* Naples, 1609.

*Cerreto, Scipione. *Della prattica musica vocale et strumentale . . .* Naples, 1601.

Cervený, V. F., & Söhne. *Preisliste der . . . Musik-Instrumente.* Königgrätz in Böhmen, 1910.

Chouquet, Gustave. *Le Musée du Conservatoire National de Musique. Catalogue descriptif et raisonné.* With three supplements by Léon Pillaut. 1875 and 1884, 1894, 1899, 1903.

Clappé, Arthur A. *The Wind-Band and its Instruments.* New York, 1911.

—— *The Principles of Wind-Band Transcription.* New York, 1921.

*Claudius Collection. *Carl Claudius' Samling af Gamle Musikinstrumenter.* Copenhagen, 1931.

Fine illustrations.

*Coerne, Louis Adolphe. *The Evolution of Modern Orchestration.* New York, 1908.

Coussemaker, Edmond de. *Mémoire sur Hucbald . . . et sur les instruments de musique.* Paris, 1841.

—— *Scriptorum de musica medii aevi novam seriem a Gerbertina alteram collegit nuncque primum edidit . . .* Paris, 1864–76. 4 vols. Facsimile reproduction, Milan, 1931.

—— "Essai sur les instruments de musique au moyen âge." *Annales archéologiques,* iii, pp. 76–88, 147–165 (1845).

*Coutagne, Henry. *Gaspard Duiffoproucart et les luthiers lyonnais du XVIe siècle.* Paris, 1893.

Disproved fairy tales about this early maker. *See* Niederheitmann.

Daubeny, Ulric. *Orchestral Wind Instruments, Ancient and Modern.* London, 1920.

A fine book, but the statements about the Flügelhorn are not correct. Thus, on p. 77: "... the Flügel horn, a true treble to the French horn ..."; on p. 127: "Horn family: flugelhorn, French horn, and Wagner tubas, tenor and tenor bass." These statements are misconceptions; the Flügelhorn is a bugle and not a horn.

Davis, R. N. The *Imperial Method for the Slide Trombone.* Philadelphia, 1898. Cincinnati, 1901.

*Davison, Archibald Thompson. *Music Education in America, What is Wrong with it? What shall we do about it?* New York, 1926.

Day, Charles Russell. *See* Royal Military Exhibition.

*Densmore, Frances. *Handbook of the Collection of Musical Instruments in the United States National Museum.* Bulletin 136. Washington, 1927.

Dick, Friedrich. *Bezeichnungen für Saiten- und Schlaginstrumente in der altfranzösischen Literatur ...* Giessen, 1932.

Dictionary of Applied Physics. Sir Richard Glazebrook, ed. London, 1923. 5 vols. Vol. iv, pp. 688–733, "Sound," by E. H. Barton.

*Diderot, Denis, and Alembert, Jean Lerond d', eds. *Encyclopédie.* Paris, Neuchâtel, 1751–65. 17 vols. *Recueil de planches,* Paris, 1762–72. 11 vols. *Supplément,* Amsterdam, 1776–77. 4 vols. *Suite du Recueil de planches,* Paris, 1777. *Table,* Paris, 1780. 2 vols.

*Djevad Bey, Ahmed. *État militaire Ottoman depuis la fondation de l'Empire jusqu'à nos jours.* Tom. i, livre 1. *Le corps des janissaires depuis sa création jusqu'à sa suppression.* G. Macrides, tr. Constantinople and Paris, 1882.

*Dolmetsch, Arnold. *The Interpretation of the Music of the XVIIth and XVIIIth Centuries.* London, 1915.

—— *Dolmetsch and his Instruments. Evolution of the Dolmetsch Instruments.* Haslemere, Surrey, 1929.

*—— "The Lute." *The Connoisseur,* viii, pp. 213–217 (April, 1904); ix, pp. 23–28 (May, 1904).

*—— "The Viols." *The Connoisseur,* x, pp. 134–138 (Nov., 1904); xiii, pp. 112–116 (Oct., 1905). "The Lute" and "The Viols" are little known popular contributions, finely illustrated.

*Donington, Robert. *The Work and Ideas of Arnold Dolmetsch. The Renaissance of Early Music.* Haslemere, Surrey, 1932.

Doursther, Horace. *Dictionnaire universel des poids et mesures anciens et modernes.* Brussels, 1840.

Dräger, Hans Heinz. *Die Entwicklung des Streichbogens und seine Anwendung in Europa bis zum Violenbogen des 16. Jahrhunderts.* Berlin, also Kassel, 1937.

Drechsel, F. A. *Zur Akustik der Blasinstrumente.* Leipzig, 1927.

Drevnosti Rossiĭskago Gosudarstva. S. G. Stroganov and F. G. Solntsev, editors. St. Petersburg, 1849–53. 6 vols. and Atlas, 6 vols.

A magnificently illustrated edition of the antiquities of the Russian state.

Drinker, Henry S., Jr. *The Chamber Music of Johannes Brahms.* Philadelphia, 1932.

Dufourcq, Norbert. *Esquisse d'une histoire de l'orgue en France du XIIIe au XVIIIe siècle.* Paris, 1935.

Eichborn, Hermann. *Die Trompete in alter und neuer Zeit.* Leipzig, 1881.

—— *Das alte Clarinblasen auf Trompeten.* Leipzig, 1894.

—— *Die Dämpfung beim Horn.* Leipzig, 1897.

Einstein, Alfred. *Zur deutschen Literatur für Viola da Gamba im 16. und 17. Jahrhundert.* Leipzig, 1905.

*Ellerhorst, Winfred. *Handbuch der Orgelkunde.* Einsiedeln, Switzerland, 1936.

*Ellis, Alexander J. *The History of Musical Pitch.* London, 1880. Reprinted with corrections and appendix from the *Journal of the Society of Arts,* 1880.

Of the utmost importance for the organologist.

Encyclopaedia of Islām, The. A Dictionary of the Geography, Ethnography, and Biography of the Muhammadan Peoples. Leiden, 1908–36. 4 vols. *Supplement.* 1934–38. 5 parts.
The articles on musical instruments are by Dr. H. G. Farmer. They should not be overlooked.

**Encyclopédie de la musique et Dictionnaire de Conservatoire.* Paris, 1913–31. 11 vols. Especially important is pt. ii, vol. iii, *Technique instrumentale*, 1927.

Engel, Carl. *A Descriptive Catalogue of the Musical Instruments in the South Kensington Museum.* London, 1870. Second ed., 1874.

—— *Researches into the Early History of the Violin Family.* London, 1883. Revised by A. J. Hipkins.

**English Music, 1604 to 1904.* Second ed. London and New York, 1911. *See* Blaikley, Borland, Finn, Galpin, Southgate.

Euting, Ernst. *Zur Geschichte der Blasinstrumente im 16. und 17. Jahrhundert.* Berlin, 1899.

*Evliyā Çelebi. *Turkish Instruments of Music in the Seventeenth Century* . . . H. G. Farmer, tr. and ed. Glasgow, 1937.

Famintsyn, A. S. *Gusli.* St. Petersburg, 1890.

—— *Domra.* St. Petersburg, 1891.

Farmer, Henry George. *Byzantine Musical Instruments in the Ninth Century.* London, 1925.

—— *Memoirs of the Royal Artillery Band . . . An Account of the Rise of Military Music in England.* London and New York, 1904.

—— *Military Music and its Story. The Rise and Development of Military Music.* Introduction by Albert Williams. London, 1912.

—— *An Old Moorish Lute Tutor* . . . H. G. Farmer, ed. and tr. Glasgow, 1933.

*—— *The Organ of the Ancients, from Eastern Sources (Hebrew, Syriac, and Arabic).* With a foreword by the Rev. Canon F. W. Galpin. London, 1931.

*—— *Studies in Oriental Musical Instruments.* London, 1931.

*—— *Turkish Instruments. See* Evliyā Çelebi.

*—— *The Encyclopaedia of Islām.* Articles on musical instruments.

Fétis, F. J. *Antoine Stradivari, Luthier célèbre connu sous le nom de Stradivarius.* Paris, 1856.

*—— *Histoire générale de la musique* . . . Paris, 1869–76. 5 vols.

*Findeisen, N. F. *Schilderungen aus der Geschichte der Musik in Russland von der ältesten Zeit bis zum Ende des XVIII. Jahrhunderts.* Moscow, 1928–29. 2 vols.
In Russian. Only the title and picture names are translated into German. The most important history of music in Russia, written by the outstanding Russian musicologist; it should be translated into English.

Finn, John. "The Recorder, Flute, Fife, and Piccolo." *English Music, 1604 to 1904.*

Fissore, Robert, *Traité de lutherie ancienne* . . . par R. Dupuich [pseud.] 1. éd. Paris, 1894. Later eds., 1899 and n.d.

Fitzgibbon, Henry Macaulay. *The Story of the Flute.* London, 1914.

Flade, Ernst. *Der Orgelbauer Gottfried Silbermann.* Leipzig, 1926.

—— *See* Schlick.

Fletcher, Giles. *Of the Russe Common Wealth.* Edw. A. Bond, ed. London, Hakluyt Society, 1856.
The edition of 1591 is very rare.

Fleury, Édouard. *Les instruments de musique sur les monuments du moyen-âge du Département de l'Aisne* . . . Laon, 1882.

Flood, William Henry Grattan. *A History of Irish Music.* Dublin, 1905. Third ed., 1913.

—— *Early Tudor Composers . . . (1485–1555).* London, 1925.

★—— *The Story of the Bagpipe.* London and New York, 1911.

—— *The Story of the Harp.* London and New York, 1905.

—— A reply to Canon Galpin's article on the origin of the clarsech, in *The Musical Times* (London), March, 1912.

★Forsyth, Cecil. *Orchestration.* London, 1914.

Fraser, Alexander Duncan. *Some Reminiscences and the Bagpipe.* Edinburgh, 1907.

Frederick, H. A. "American Tentative Standard Acoustical Terminology." *Journal of the Acoustical Society of America,* ix, pp. 60–71 (July, 1937).

★Frotscher, Gotthold. *Geschichte des Orgelspiels und der Orgelkomposition.* Berlin, 1935–36. 2 vols.

★Gafori or Gaffurio, Franchino. *Practica musice . . .* 1496. First ed. of Gafori's main work.

★—— *Theorica musice . . .* Milan, 1492. Revised ed.; the first was printed at Naples in 1480. A facsimile reprint, Rome, 1934.

★—— *. . . De Harmonia Musicorum Instrumentorum Opus.* Milan, 1518.

Galilei, Vincenzo. *Dialogo . . . della musica antica, et della moderna.* Florence, 1581. Second ed., 1602.

★Galpin, Francis William. *The Music of the Sumerians . . . the Babylonians and Assyrians.* Cambridge, 1937.

★—— *Old English Instruments of Music, their History and Character.* Third ed., revised. London, 1932.
The first edition was published in 1910. Many instruments of this Collection are illustrated in this book.

—— "The Origin of the Clarsech or Irish Harp." *The Musical Times,* Feb., 1912. *See* Flood.

★—— "The Sackbut, its Evolution and History." Musical Association, *Proceedings,* xxxiii, 1906–07. (Nov., 1906).

—— *A Textbook of European Musical Instruments.* London, 1937.

—— "Viola Pomposa." *Music and Letters,* London, xii, pp. 354–364 (1931).

★—— "The Water Organ of the Ancients and the Organ of to-day." *English Music, 1604 to 1904.*

★—— "The Whistles and Reed Instruments of the American Indians of the Northwest Coast." Musical Association, *Proceedings,* 1902–03.

★Ganassi, Silvestro, dal Fontego. *. . . Fontegara . . .* Venice, 1535. Modern reprint in *Collezione di Trattati e Musiche Antiche Edite in Fac-Simile,* Milan, 1934.

★—— *Regola Rubertina.* Vol. i: *Regola che insegna a sonare de Viola d'arco tastada.* Venice, 1542. Vol. ii: *Lettione seconda pur della prattica di sonare il Violone d'arco da tasti.* 1543. Modern reprint, Max Schneider, ed., Leipzig, 1924.

Garnault, Paul. *Instruments d'Amour.* Nice, 1927.

★—— *Le Temperament, son histoire, son application aux violes de gambe et guitares.* Paris, 1924.

—— *La Trompette Marine.* Nice, 1926.

★—— "Les Violes." *Encyclopédie de la musique,* part ii, vol. iii, pp. 1753–93.

Gaspari, Gaetano. *Catalogo della Biblioteca del Liceo Musicale di Bologna.* Bologna, 1890–1905. 4 vols.

★Gehot, Joseph. *Complete Instruction for Every Musical Instrument . . . to which is added the Scale or Gamut for Thirty-Five Different Instruments.* London, printed for G. Goulding [178–?].
Important as an early work of an American writer. A copy in the Boston Public Library.

Geiger, Leroy F. *Violin Making made Clear and Concise.* L. M. Cole, ed. Chicago, 1935. Reprinted from *Popular Homecraft Magazine.*
One of the best instruction books on violin-making for amateurs.

★Gerbert, Martin, ed. *Scriptores Ecclesiastici de Musica Sacra potissimum.* St. Blasien, 1784. 3 vols. Facsimile reprint, Milan, 1931. *See* Coussemaker.

★Gerle, Hans. *Musica Teusch auf die Instrument die Grossen uund* [!] *kleynen Geigen auch Lautten . . .* Nürnberg, 1532; second ed., 1546.

*Gevaert, François Auguste. *Nouveau traité d'instrumentation.* Paris, 1885. English translation: *A New Treatise on Instrumentation,* by E. F. E. Suddard, London [1906?].

*Glareanus, Henricus. *Δωδεκάχορδον.* Basel, 1547.

Goehlinger, Franz August. *Geschichte des Klavichords.* Basel, 1910.

*Goodrich, Wallace. *The Organ in France* . . . Boston, 1917.

*Gregory, Julia. *Catalogue of Early Books on Music* (before 1800). Library of Congress, Division of Music. O. G. Sonneck, ed. Washington, 1913.

*Greilsamer, Lucien. "La facture des instruments à archet." *Encyclopédie de la musique,* pt. ii, vol. iii, pp. 1708–52.

*Grillet, Laurent. . . . *Les ancêtres du violon et du violoncelle, les luthiers et les fabricants d'archets.* Paris, 1901 and 1905. 2 vols.

Grove, Sir George, ed. *Grove's Dictionary of Music and Musicians.* 3d ed. H. C. Colles, ed. New York, 1927–28. 5 vols.

Guer, Jean Antoine. *Moeurs et usages des Turks* . . . Paris, 1747. 2 vols.

Guthrie, Matthew. *Dissertations sur les antiquités de Russie. Contenant . . . les instrumens de musique* . . . St. Petersburg, 1795.

*Hajdecki, Alexander. *Die italienische Lira da Braccio. Eine kunst-historische Studie zur Geschichte der Violine.* Mostar (Herzogovina), 1892.

The first writer to suggest the importance of the Italian *lira da braccio* as an ancestor of the violin.

*Halbig, Hermann. "Die Geschichte der Klappe an Flöten und Rohrblattinstrumenten bis zum Beginn des 18. Jahrhunderts." *Archiv für Musikwissenschaft,* vi, pp. 1–53 (May, 1924).

Hambidge, Jay. *Dynamic Symmetry.* New Haven, 1920.

Hammerich, Angul. *Les lurs de l'âge de bronze, au Musée national de Copenhague.* E. Beauvois, tr. Copenhagen, 1894.

Harap, Louis. "On the Nature of Musicology." *The Musical Quarterly,* xxiii, pp. 18–25 (Jan., 1937).

*Harding, Rosamond E. M. *The Piano-Forte; its History traced to the Great Exhibition of 1851.* Cambridge, 1933.

A standard work; extensive bibliography.

Hart, George. *The Violin: its Famous Makers and their Imitators.* London, 1875. Later eds., 1884, 1887, 1909. French translation by Alphonse Roger, Paris, 1886.

*Hayes, Gerald R. *Musical Instruments and their Music, 1500–1750.* Vol. i: *The Treatment of Instrumental Music.* London, 1928. Vol. ii: *The Viols, and other Bowed Instruments.* London, 1930.

One of the most fundamental and important works of the Dolmetsch school. It is not possible to exaggerate its value. It should be in the hands of every student of old instruments. Although it is eminently readable, its true worth comes out only after prolonged study.

Heckel, Wilhelm. *Der Fagott. Kurzgefasste Abhandlung über seine historische Entwicklung, seinen Bau und seine Spielweise.* Biebrich a. Rhein, 1899. Enlarged ed. by W. H. Heckel, Leipzig, 1931.

*Heinitz, Wilhelm. *Instrumentenkunde.* Potsdam, 1929.

Helmholtz, Hermann. *Die Lehre von den Tonempfindungen* . . . Brunswick, 1863. Second ed., 1865. Third ed., 1870. English translation by Alexander J. Ellis, *On the Sensations of Tone as a Physiological Basis for the Theory of Music,* London, 1875. Third ed. of the translation, 1895; 4th ed., 1912.

Now obsolescent, but important historically.

*Henry Arnaut de Zwolle. *Les traités d'Henry-Arnaut de Zwolle et des divers anonymes.* (MS B. N. Latin 7295.) G. Le Cerf, ed., E. R. Labande, collab. Paris, 1932.

Very important for the study of fifteenth-century musical instruments.

Heron-Allen, Edward. *Violin-Making, as it was and is; . . . A Historical, Theoretical, and Practical Treatise on the Science and Art of Violin-Making* . . . London, 1884. Later eds., 1885, 1889.

—— *De Fidiculis Bibliographia: being an Attempt towards a Bibliography of the Violin and all other Instruments played with a Bow.* London, 1890–94. 2 vols.

—— *De Fidiculis Opuscula.* London, 1882–95. 8 parts.

*Herrad of Landsberg, abbess of Hohenburg, d. 1195. *Hortus Deliciarum.* A. Straub, ed. Plates: Paris, 1879–99. Text: Strassburg, 1901.

*Hermann, Erich. *Über die Klangfarbe einiger Orchesterinstrumente und ihre Analyse.* Stuttgart, 1908.

Heuss, Alfred. *Die Instrumental-Stücke des "Orfeo" und die venetianischen Opern-Sinfonien.* Leipzig, 1903.

Heyer Collection of Musical Instruments. *See* Kinsky.

Hill, William E., and Sons. *The Salabue Stradivari . .* [*"Le Messie"*]. London, 1891.

—— *The "Tuscan." A Short Account of a Violin by Stradivari made for Cosimo de Medici . . . dated 1690.*

*Hill, William Henry and others. *Antonio Stradivari, his Life and Work.* London, 1902. Second ed., smaller format, 1909.

*—— *The Violin-Makers of the Guarneri Family (1626–1762).* London, 1931.

Hipkins, Alfred James. Articles in *Grove's Dictionary of Music,* 1927: 'Clavichord,' 'Harpsichord,' 'Jack,' 'Mute,' 'Pianoforte.'

*—— *A Description and History of the Pianoforte and of the Older Keyboard Stringed Instruments.* London, 1896.

Excellent; the glossary of technical terms.

—— *Dorian and Phrygian Reconsidered from a Non-Harmonic Point of View.* London, 1902.

Greek Music is a new edition of this work, with additions, printed for private circulation by his daughter, Edith J. Hipkins, in 1932.

*—— *Musical Instruments, Historic, Rare, and Unique.* Edinburgh, 1888. Cheaper edition, 1921.

*Holyoke, Samuel. *The Instrumental Assistant; Volume ii . . . with Instructions for the French Horn and Bassoon.* Exeter, New Hampshire, 1807.

*Hornbostel, Erich M. von, und Sachs, Curt. "Systematik der Musikinstrumente. Ein Versuch." *Zeitschrift für Ethnologie,* 1914, pp. 553–590.

Hornbostel, E. M. von. "Eine Tafel zur logarithmischen Darstellung von Zahlenverhältnissen." *Zeitschrift für Physik,* vi, pp. 29–34 (1921).

*Howard, Albert Andrew. "The Αὐλός or Tibia." *Harvard Studies in Classical Philology,* iv, pp. 1–60 (1893).

—— "The Mouthpiece of the Αὐλός." *Ibid.,* x, pp. 19–22 (1899).

The first article gives the sizes of the *auloi,* but the scale is not determined correctly. *Cf.* Kathleen Schlesinger, *The Greek Aulos,* p. 44, note, and pp. 75 f.

Huggins, Lady Margaret. *Gio: Paolo Maggini, his Life and Work.* London, 1892.

*Hunt, Edgar H., and Donington, Robert. *A Practical Method for the Recorder.* London, 1935. 2 vols.

Iaremich, Stepan Petrovich. *M. A. Vrubel, Life and Works.* Moscow, 1911. (In *Russian Artists,* Igor Grabar, ed., a series of illustrated monographs.) In Russian.

Jacquot, Albert. *La musique en Lorraine.* Paris, 1882. Third ed., 1886.

—— *La lutherie lorraine et française . . .* Preface by J. Massenet. Paris, 1912.

Jahn, Fritz. "Die Nürnberger Trompeten und Posaunenmacher im 16. Jahrhundert." *Archiv für Musikwissenschaft,* April, 1926.

*James, Philip. *Early Keyboard Instruments from their Beginnings to the Year 1820.* London, 1930.

Kalkbrenner, August. *Wilhelm Wieprecht, Direktor der sämtlichen Musikchöre des Garde-Corps, sein Leben und Werken.* Berlin, 1882.

Kappey, J. A. *Military Music. A History of Wind-Instrumental Bands.* London and New York, 1894.

Karamzin, N. M. *Histoire de l'empire de Russie.* St.-Thomas and Jauffret, trs. Paris, 1819–26. 11 vols.

Kastner, Georges. *Les Danses des Morts . . .* Paris, 1852.

—— *La harpe d'Éole et la musique cosmique.* Paris, 1856.

*—— *Manuel général de musique militaire . . .* Paris, 1848.

—— *Méthode . . . des Timbales . . . précédée d'une notice historique . . .* Paris, [?].

Kelley, Edgar Stillman. *Musical Instruments.* Boston, 1925.

Kieffer, Jean D., and Bianchi, Thomas X. de. *Dictionnaire turc-français.* Paris, 1835–37. 2 vols.

Kiesewetter, Rafael Georg. *History of the Modern Music of Western Europe, from the First Century to the Present Day . . .* R. Müller, tr. London, 1848.
The German original was published in 1834.

*Kinkeldey, Otto. *Orgel und Klavier in der Musik des 16. Jahrhunderts.* Leipzig, 1910.

Kinsky, Georg. "Doppelrohrblatt-Instrumente mit Windkapsel." *Archiv für Musikwissenschaft,* June, 1925.

*——, ed. *Geschichte der Musik in Bildern.* Leipzig, 1929. English translation, *A History of Music in Pictures,* London, 1930 and 1937.
Indispensable iconography of musical instruments.

*—— *Kleiner Katalog der Sammlung alter Musikinstrumente.* Cöln, 1913.
Contains the list and a few pictures of the wind instruments of the former Wilhelm Heyer Collection, now in the Grassi Museum in Leipzig; has to serve as a substitute for the intended third volume of the large catalogue.

*—— "Kurze Oktaven auf besaiteten Tasteninstrumenten. Ein Beitrag zur Geschichte des Klaviers." *Zeitschrift für Musikwissenschaft,* November, 1919.
The best study on the short octaves.

*—— *Musikhistorisches Museum von Wilhelm Heyer in Cöln. Katalog.* Vol. i: *Besaitete Tasteninstrumente. Orgeln und orgelartige Instrumente. Friktionsinstrumente.* Cöln, 1910. Vol. ii: *Zupf- und Streichinstrumente.* Cöln, 1912.

Kirby, Percival Robson. *The Kettle-Drums. A book for Composers, Conductors, and Kettle-Drummers.* London, 1930.

Kircher, Athanasius. *Musurgia Universalis, sive Ars Magna Consoni et Dissoni . . .* Rome, 1650. 2 vols.

—— *Phonurgia Nova, sive Conjugium Mechanico-Physicum Artis et Naturae Paranympha Phonosophia Concinnatum . . .* Campidonae, 1673.

Kleefeld, Wilhelm. "Das Orchester der Hamburger Oper 1678–1738." Internationale Musik-Gesellschaft, *Sammelbände,* i, pp. 219–290 (Leipzig, 1900).

Kling, Henri. *Modern Orchestration and Instrumentation.* Gustav Saenger, tr. New York, 1902 and 1905.

*Körte, Oswald. *Laute und Lautenmusik bis zur Mitte des 16. Jahrhunderts.* Leipzig, 1901.

*Kool, Jaap. *Das Saxophon.* Leipzig, 1931.

*Landowska, Wanda. *Music of the Past.* Tr. from the French by William A. Bradley. New York, 1924.

Langwill, Lyndesay G. "Some Notes on the Bassoon. With Particular Reference to its Fundamental Scale." *Musical Progress and Mail,* August, 1933.

—— "The Alto-Fagotto — misnamed Tenoroon — the Caledonica, and their Inventor." *Musical Progress and Mail,* April, 1934.

*—— "The Curtal (1550–1750). A Chapter in the Evolution of the Bassoon." *The Musical Times,* lxxviii, pp. 305–309 (April, 1937).

—— "A 17th-Century Wood-Wind Curiosity." (A description of the Gross-Doppel-Quint-Pommer.) *The Musical Times,* lxxix, pp. 573–574 (Aug., 1938).

Laurencie, Lionel de la. "Le Luth." *Encyclopédie de la musique,* pt. ii, vol. iii, pp. 1972–83.

Le Blanc, Hubert. *Défense de la basse de viole contre les entreprises du violon et les prétentions du violoncel.* Amsterdam, 1740.

Leichtentritt, Hugo. *Music, History, and Ideas.* Cambridge, Harvard Univ. Press, 1938.

*—— "Was lehren uns die Bilderwerke des 14–17. Jahrhunderts über die Instrumentalmusik ihrer Zeit?" Internationale Musik-Gesellschaft, *Sammelbände*, vii, pp. 315–364 (Apr.–June, 1906).

Leman, Anatoliĭ Ivanovich. *Letters about the Violin and Violoncello.* (The 'Red booklet.') St. Petersburg, 1900.

*—— *A Book about the Violin. No. 1.* Second ed. Moscow, 1903.

*—— *Acoustics of the Violin.* Moscow, 1903.

—— *No. 2. Concerning the Violin, 1889–1906.* St. Petersburg, 1906.

—— *No. 3. Concerning the Violin, Violoncello.* St. Petersburg, 1908.

*—— *A Book about the Violin. No. 4.* St. Petersburg, 1908.

—— *The Russian Violin.* St. Petersburg, 1909.

—— *Violinists and Violins; Violoncellists and Violoncelli.* St. Petersburg, 1910.

—— *New Data on the Russian Violin.* St. Petersburg, 1911.

—— *Meditations on the Violin.* St. Petersburg, 1912.

—— *The Seventh Symphony.* (*A Book about the Violin, No. 7.*) St. Petersburg, 1912.

—— *Goldene Tafel.* St. Petersburg, 1910. In German.

All these works (all in Russian, except the last title) are available in the Harvard College Library.

A. I. Leman is a Russian violin-maker, a man of artistic talent, refined taste in music, and solid scientific training. His instruments can be compared in tonal qualities, elegance of outline, beauty of varnish, and workmanship only with the best of Stradivari. His outstanding contribution is the *Acoustics of the Violin,* in which he formulated the 'law of consonances' and the 'law of maximum vibrational response.'

Library of Congress, Division of Music. *See* Gregory.

*Lütgendorff, Willibald Leo, Freiherr von. *Die Geigen- und Lautenmacher vom Mittelalter bis zur Gegenwart.* Frankfurt a. Main, 1913. 2 vols.

Luscinius, Ottomarus. *Musurgia seu Praxis Musicae.* Strassburg, 1536.

*Mace, Thomas. *Musick's Monument; or, A Remembrancer of the Best Practical Musick* . . . London, 1676.

Maggs Bros. *Music. Early Books, Manuscripts, Portraits, and Autographs (1473–1928).* Catalogue No. 512. London, 1928.

*Mahillon, Victor Charles. *Catalogue descriptif & analytique du Musée Instrumental du Conservatoire Royal de Musique de Bruxelles.* 2e éd. Ghent, 1893–1922. 5 vols.

—— *Éléments d'acoustique musicale & instrumentale.* Brussels, 1874.

—— *Instruments à vent.* i. *Le Trombone, son histoire, sa théorie, sa construction.* ii. *Le Cor.* iii. *La Trompette.* Brussels, 1906–07.

*—— *Le matériel sonore des orchestres de symphonie, d'harmonie et de fanfares, ou Vade Mecum du compositeur* . . . Brussels, 1897.

*—— *Experimental Studies on the Resonance of Conical, Trunco-Conical, and Cylindrical Air Columns.* F. A. Mahan, tr. London, 1901.

Mahrenholz, Christhard. *Die Berechnung der Orgelpfeifenmensuren vom Mittelalter bis zur Mitte des 19. Jahrhunderts.* Kassel, 1938.

Mairy, Adrienne. "Le Luth." *Encyclopédie de la musique,* pt. ii, vol. iii, pp. 1983–90.

**Manessesche Liederhandschrift, Die.* Faksimile-Ausgabe. Introductions by Rudolf Sillib, Friedrich Panzer, Arthur Haseloff. Leipzig, 1924–27.

Several plates have representations of musicians and musical instruments.

Manson, William L. *The Highland Bagpipe.* Paisley and London, 1901.

★Marsigli, Conte Luigi Fernando. *Stato militare dell'Imperio Ottomano.* The Hague, 1732. In Italian and French.

Mason, Daniel Gregory. *The Orchestral Instruments and what they do.* New York, 1909.

★Mattheson, Johann. *Das neu-eröffnete Orchestre.* Hamburg, 1713.

Mehta, N. C. *Studies in Indian Painting.* Bombay, 1926.

Meibomius, Marcus, ed. *Antiquae Musicae Auctores Septem.* Amsterdam, 1652. 2 vols.

★Menke, Werner. *History of the Trumpet of Bach and Handel.* Gerald Abraham, tr. London, 1934.

Mersenne, Marin. *Les preludes de l'harmonie universelle . . .* Paris, 1634.

★—— *Harmonie universelle . . . où il est traité de la nature des . . . toutes sortes d'instrumens harmoniques.* Paris, 1636–37. 2 vols.

★—— *Harmonicorum Libri XII.* Paris, 1648. 2 vols. Vol. 2 is entitled *F. Marini Mersenni Harmonicorum Instrumentorum Liber Primus . . . Quartus.*

★Metropolitan Museum of Art, New York. *Catalogue of the Crosby Brown Collection of Musical Instruments of All Nations.* Hand-Book no. 13, i, *Europe.* New York, 1902, 1904. *See* Morris.

Meyer, Kathi, ed. *Katalog der internationalen Ausstellung Musik im Leben der Völker.* Frankfurt am Main, 1927.

Meyers Lexikon. Seventh ed., Leipzig, 1924–33.

★Miller, Dayton C. *Catalogue of Books and Literary Material Relating to the Flute and other Musical Instruments.* With annotations. Privately printed. Cleveland, 1935.

An excellent foundation for a more general bibliography. This work is necessarily limited to the specific interest of its esteemed author, who made the most outstanding collection of flutes.

★—— *The Flute and Flute-Playing in Acoustical, Technical, and Artistic Aspects,* by Theobald Boehm . . . tr. and annotated by D. C. Miller. Cleveland, 1908.

★—— *The Science of Musical Sounds.* New York, 1916. Second ed., 1922.

Miškovský, Josef. *Václav František Červený.* V. Českém Brodě, 1896.

A short biography of a remarkable maker of brass wind instruments, whom Dr. Schafhäutl called the "Érard of brass instrument making."

★Monteverdi, Claudio. *Orfeo.* Facsimile, edited by Adolf Sandberger, of the edition of 1609. Augsburg, 1927.

★—— *Tutti le Opere di Claudio Monteverdi.* G. Francesco Malpiero, ed. Asolo, 1926–32. 14 vols.

Moreck, Kurt. *Die Musik in der Malerei.* Munich, 1924.

★Morris, Frances. *Catalogue of the Crosby Brown Collection of Musical Instruments.* Vol. ii. *Oceanica and America.* New York, 1914. Pp. 267–268: *Bibliography of the Musical Bow.*

Morrow, Walter. "The Trumpet as an Orchestral Instrument." Musical Association, *Proceedings,* xxi, pp. 133–147 (June 11, 1895).

Moser, Andreas. "Der Violino Piccolo." *Zeitschrift für Musikwissenschaft,* April, 1919.

Moule, A. C. "List of Musical and other Sound Producing Instrument of the Chinese." *Journal of the North China Branch of the Royal Asiatic Society,* 1908.

★Mozart, Leopold. *Versuch einer gründlichen Violinschule.* Augsburg, 1756. Reprinted, Vienna, 1922.

Music Loan Exhibition. *An Illustrated Catalogue of the Music Loan Exhibition held . . . by the Worshipful Company of Musicians at Fishmongers' Hall, June and July, 1904.* London, 1909.

Naumann, Hans. *Die Minnesinger in Bildern der Manessischen Handschrift.* Insel-Bücherei No. 450. Leipzig, [?]. See *Manessesche Liederhandschrift.*

Nef, Karl. *Geschichte unserer Musikinstrumente.* Leipzig, 1926.

★—— *An Outline of the History of Music.* Carl F. Pfatteicher, tr. New York, 1935.

Neukomm, Edmond. *Histoire de la musique militaire.* Paris, 1889.

*Neusidler, Melchior. *Teutsch Lautenbuch* . . . Strassburg, 1574.

Nicholson, Charles. *A School for the Flute.* New York, [1836]. 2 vols.

Niederheitmann, Friedrich. *Cremona. Eine Charakteristik der italienischen Geigenbauer und ihrer Instrumente.* Leipzig, 1877. 7th ed., 1928.

This book belongs to that romantic period when the history of the violin was not studied but, literally, 'made.' Niederheitmann, along with many other 'experts,' believed that the famous Parisian violin-maker, J. B. Vuillaume, discovered six violins allegedly made by Gaspard Duiffoproucart between 1510 and 1517. It was later proven that the 'father of the violin' was born in 1514, and that these fascinating instruments, so conscientiously described by Niederheitmann, were made by Vuillaume. *See* Coutagne.

*Nikitin, Afanasiĭ. . . . *Die Fahrt des Athanasius Nikitin über die drei Meere; Reise eines russischen Kaufmannes nach Ostindien, 1466–1472.* Karl H. Meyer, ed. and tr. Leipzig, [1920].

Norlind, Tobias. *Systematik der Saiteninstrumente; i. Geschichte der Zither.* Stockholm, 1937.

Novoselsky, A. *Sketches on the History of Russian Folk Instruments.* Moscow, 1931.

O'Curry, Eugene. *On the Manners and Customs of the Ancient Irish.* London, 1873. 3 vols.

Odo, abbot of Cluny, d. 942. *Quomodo organistrum construatur. See* Gerbert.

O'Neill, Francis. *Irish Folk Music.* Chicago, 1910.

—— *Irish Minstrels and Musicians.* Chicago, 1913.

Chapters on bagpipes, pipers, etc.

*Ornithoparchus, Andreas. *Musice Active Micrologus* . . . Leipzig, 1517. English translation by John Dowland, London, 1609.

*Panum, Hortense. *Middelalderens Strengeinstrumenter og deres Forløbere.* 3 vols. Copenhagen, 1915–31.

*Parès, Gabriel. *Traité d'instrumentation et d'orchestration à l'usage des musiques militaires d'harmonie et de fanfare.* Paris, 1898. 2 vols.

*Pierre, Constant. *La facture instrumentale à l'Exposition Universelle de 1889.* Paris, 1890.

Piersig, Fritz. *Die Einführung des Hornes in die Kunstmusik* . . . Halle, 1927.

Pincherle, Marc. *Feuillets d'histoire du violon.* Paris, 1927.

*—— "La Harpe." *Encyclopédie de la musique*, pt. ii, vol. iii, pp. 1892–1927.

Excellent bibliography.

Pitch, Musical. France. Ministère d'état. *Rapport et arrêtés pour l'établissement en France d'un diapason musical uniform.* Paris, 1859.

Playford, Henry. *Harmonia Sacra* . . .. *with a Thorough-Bass for the Theorbo-Lute, Bass-Viol, or Organ.* London, 1714. 2 vols.

*Playford, John. *A Breefe Introduction to the Skill or Musick, for Song & Violl.* London, 1654. First ed. Other editions are subtitled:

1658 — . . . *Viol de Gambo, and also on the Treble-Violin.*
1660 — . . . *Viol, and also for the Treble-Violin.*
1666 — . . . *Bass-Viol, and also for the Treble-Violin.*
1694 — . . . *corrected and amended by Mr. Henry Purcell.* 12th edition.
1697 — . . . *for the Treble, Tenor, and Bass-Viols; and also for the Treble Violin.*

—— *Musick's Delight on the Cithren* . . . London, 1666.

*—— *Musick's Recreation on the Viol, Lyra-Way* . . . London, 1661.

Originally published in 1652 as *Musick's recreation on the Lyra Viol.* On this work, which I have had no opportunity to examine, see Gerald R. Hayes, *Musical Instruments and their Music. ii. The Viols* . . ., p. 128, note.

Polnoe Sobranie Russkikh Letopiseĭ. Published by the Russian Archaeographical Commission. 1841–1921. 24 vols.

★Porter, Arthur Kingsley. *The Crosses and Culture of Ireland*. New Haven, 1931.
An important work, throwing new light on the early culture of Ireland and the Celtic Church.

Pougin, Arthur. . . . *Le violon, les violonistes et la musique du XVIe au XVIIIe siècle*. Paris, 1924.

★Praetorius, Michael. *Syntagma Musicum*.
This great work was published at Wittemberg and Wolfenbüttel in four parts: (1) the first volume, in Latin, in 1615; (2) the second volume, *De Organographia*, in 1619; it is in German despite its Latin title; (3) the third volume, also in German, in 1618; (4) the illustrated supplement to the second volume, *Theatrum Instrumentorum seu Sciagraphia*, in 1620.

★Pratt, Waldo Selden. *The History of Music*. New York, 1907.

★Prunières, Henry. *Monteverdi, his Life and Work*. Marie D. Mackie, tr. London, 1926.

Pulver, Jeffrey. *A Biographical Dictionary of Old English Music*. London, 1927.

★—— *A Dictionary of Old English Music and Musical Instruments*. London, 1923.

★Quantz, Johann Joachim. *Versuch einer Anweisung die Flöte traversiere zu spielen*. Berlin, 1752; Breslau, 1780; Breslau, 1789.
This work should be translated into English without cuts. It discusses problems of musical aesthetics and proper performance of music on various orchestral instruments. Many remarks and suggestions are valid today.

Ramos de Pareja, Bartolomeo. *De Musica Tractatus, sive Musica Practica* . . . Bononiae, 1482.

—— Reprint, *Musica Practica*, Johannes Wolf, ed., Leipzig, 1901.

Redfield, John. *Music: A Science and an Art*. New York, 1928 and later years.
Stimulating. Some of its ideas should be received with caution.

Rendall, F. G. "The Saxophone before Sax." *The Musical Times*, lxxiii, pp. 1077–79 (Dec., 1932).

★Riaño, Juan F. *Critical and Bibliographical Notes on Early Spanish Music*. London, 1887.

Ricaut, Sir Paul. *The Present State of the Ottoman Empire*. London, 1668. Also in French and Italian translations.

Richardson, Edward Gick. *The Acoustics of Orchestral Instruments and of the Organ*. London, 1929.

Riemann, Hugo. *Catechism of Musical Instruments*. Translated from the German. London, 1890.

★—— *Hugo Riemanns Musiklexikon*. Twelfth ed., by Josef Müller-Blattau, Mainz, 1939– . Issued in parts. First ed., 1882. Eleventh ed., by Albert Einstein, Berlin, 1929.

★Rimsky-Korsakov, Nikolaĭ Andreevich. *Letopis' moei muzykal'noi zhizni*. Andrei Nikolaevich Rimsky-Korsakov, ed. Fifth Russian ed. Moscow, 1935.

★—— *My Musical Life*. Judah A. Joffe, tr., Carl Van Vechten, ed. New York, 1923.

★—— *Osnovy Orkestrovki*. Maximilian Steinberg, ed. St. Petersburg, 1913.

★—— *Principles of Orchestration*. Edward Agate, tr. Berlin, etc., 1922. 2 vols.

Ritter, August G. *Zur Geschichte des Orgelspiels, vornehmlich des deutschen, im 14. bis zum Anfange des 18. Jahrhunderts*. Leipzig, 1884. 2 vols.

Ritter, Hermann. *Die Viola alta* . . . Leipzig, 1876. Third ed., 1885.

★Rockstro, Richard S. *A Treatise on the Construction, the History, and the Practice of the Flute* . . . London, 1890. Revised ed., 1928.

Röhn, Franz. "Geigenköpfe." *Atlantis*, vi, pp. 692–699 (Nov., 1934).
Excellent photographs of viol heads.

★Rokseth, Yvonne. *La musique d'orgue au XVe siècle et au début du XVIe*. Paris, 1930.

Rose, George. "The Evolution of the Pianoforte." *The Connoisseur*, xiii, pp. 182–195 (Nov., 1905).
Fine illustrations, including a picture of A. J. Hipkins, F.S.A., at the harpsichord.

*Rousseau, Jean. *Traité de la viole.* Paris, 1687.

*Rousseau, Jean Jacques. *Dictionnaire de Musique.* Paris, 1767. Second ed. 1781–82, 3 vols.

*Royal Military Exhibition, London, 1890. *A Descriptive Catalogue of the Musical Instruments Exhibited at the Royal Military Exhibition, London, 1890.* Compiled by Capt. Charles R. Day. London, 1891.
Contains descriptions of several instruments now in the Museum Collection.

Rühlmann, Julius. "Das Waldhorn." *Neue Zeitschrift für Musik*, lxvi, pp. 293–295, 301–303, 309–311, 317–320, 325–327 (Aug.–Sept., 1870).

*—— *Die Geschichte der Bogeninstrumente.* Text and atlas. Richard Rühlmann, ed. Braunschweig, 1882.

*Rupp, Émile. *Die Entwicklungsgeschichte der Orgelbaukunst.* Einsiedeln, 1929.

Rushworth & Dreaper. *Collection of Antique Musical Instruments and Historical Manuscripts.* Liverpool, 1932.

Ruth-Sommer, Hermann. *Alte Musikinstrumente: Ein Leitfaden für Sammler.* Second ed. Berlin, 1920.

*Sachs, Curt. *Handbuch der Musikinstrumentenkunde.* Leipzig, 1920. Second ed., 1930.

—— *Das Klavier.* Berlin, 1923.

—— *Die modernen Musikinstrumente.* Berlin, 1923.

—— *Musik und Oper am kurbrandenburgischen Hof.* Berlin, 1910.

*—— *Real-Lexikon der Musikinstrumente, zugleich ein Polyglossar für das gesamte Instrumentengebiet.* Berlin, 1913.
Absolutely indispensable for an organologist.

*—— *Sammlung alter Musikinstrumente bei der staatlichen Hochschule für Musik zu Berlin.* Beschreibender Katalog. Berlin, 1922.

*—— "La signification, la tâche et la technique museographique des collections d'instruments de musique." *Mouseion*, viii, nos. iii–iv, pp. 153–184 (1934).

—— "Die Streichbogenfrage." *Archiv für Musikwissenschaft*, i, pp. 3 f. (Oct., 1918).

—— "Eine unkritische Kritik des Klarinblasens." *Archiv für Musikwissenschaft*, ii, pp. 335 f. (July, 1920).

—— *Vergleichende Musikwissenschaft in ihren Grundzügen.* Leipzig, 1930.

—— "Die Viola Bastarda." *Zeitschrift der internationalen Musikgesellschaft*, xv, pp. 123–125 (1914).

Salinas, Francisco de. *De Musica Libri Septem . . .* Salamanca, 1577.

Sambamoorthy, P. *Catalogue of the Musical Instruments Exhibited in the Government Museum, Madras.* Madras, 1931.

Sandys, William, and Forster, Simon A. *The History of the Violin and other Instruments Played with the Bow . . .* London, 1864.

*Sauerlandt, Max. *Die Musik in fünf Jahrhunderten der europäischen Malerei, etwa 1450 bis etwa 1850.* Königstein and Leipzig, 1922.

Savvaitov, Pavel I. *Description of Ancient Russian Furniture, Dresses, Arms, and Armor.* St. Petersburg, 1896.

Schaeffner, André. "Le Clavecin." *Encyclopédie de la musique*, pt. ii, vol. iii, pp. 2036–60.

*—— *Origine des instruments de musique.* Paris, 1936.

—— "Wanda Landowska." *La Revue Musicale*, 1927, No. 8.

*Schafhäutl, Karl Emil von. "Die Musikinstrumente." *Bericht der Beurteilungscommission bei der allgemeine deutschen Industrie Ausstellung in München, 1854.* Section iv, pp. 169–170. Munich, 1855.

*Schlecht, Raymund. "Ein Beitrag zur Musikgeschichte aus den Anfange des 16. Jahrhunderts, nach dem 'Spiegel der Orgelmacher und Organisten von Arnolt Schlick,' 1511." *Monatshefte für Musik-Geschichte*, ii, pp. 165–176, 181–188, 197–207 (1870).
An important study of Schlick's work.

★Schlesinger, Kathleen. *The Greek Aulos: A Study of its Mechanism and of its Relation to the Modal System of Ancient Greek Music* . . . Intr. by J. F. Mountford. London, 1939. An epoch-making book.

★—— *Encyclopaedia Britannica.* Eleventh edition. Articles on musical instruments.
For some inconceivable reason these scholarly contributions were not included in the 'humanized' fourteenth edition of the *Encyclopaedia Britannica.* The omission considerably reduced its value to the students of musical instruments. At least, these articles should be reprinted separately.

★—— *The Instruments of the Modern Orchestra & Early Records of the Precursors of the Violin Family.* London, 1910. 2 vols.
Volume ii contains an excellent bibliography.

★Schlick, Arnolt. *Spiegel der Orgelmacher und Organisten.* Heidelberg, 1511.
The original text reprinted in *Monatshefte für Musik-Geschichte,* i (1869), pp. 77–114.

—— *Spiegel* . . . Neudruck in moderner Sprache, übertragen und herausgegeben von Ernst Flade. Mainz, 1932.

★—— . . . *Tabulaturen etlicher Lobgesang und Lidlein uff die Orgeln und Lauten, etc.* Modern reprint. Klecken, 1924.

★Schlosser, Julius, Ritter von. *Die Sammlung alter Musikinstrumente. Kunsthistorisches Museum in Wien.* Vienna, 1920.
The catalogue of a collection of ancient musical instruments which, though small, is yet one of the most important. Such instruments as the tartoelds and sourdines are unique.

—— *Unsere Musikinstrumente: Eine Einführung in ihre Geschichte.* Vienna, 1922.

★Schneider, Wilhelm. *Historisch-technische Beschreibung der musicalischen Instrumente* . . . Leipzig, 1834.

Scholes, Percy Alfred. *The Columbia History of Music through Ear and Eye.* Period i: *To the Opening of the Seventeenth Century.* London, 1930. Period ii: *From the Beginning of Opera and Oratorio to the Death of Bach and Handel.* London, 1931.

★—— *The Oxford Companion to Music.* London and New York, 1938. Second ed., 1939.

—— *A List of Books about Music in the English Language, Prepared as an Appendix to the Oxford Companion to Music.* London and New York, 1940.

Schubart, Christian F. D. *Ideen zu einer Ästhetik der Tonkunst.* Ludwig Schubart, ed. Vienna, 1806.

Schubert, Franz Ludwig. *Katechismus der Musik-Instrumente.* Leipzig, 1862.

★—— *Die Blechinstrumente der Musik.* Leipzig, 1866.

Shapiro, Meyer. "The Romanesque Sculpture of Moissac." *The Art Bulletin,* vol. xiii, nos. 3 and 4.

Sibire, Antoine. *La chélonomie, ou Le parfait luthier.* Paris, 1806. New ed., Brussels, 1885.

★Simpson, Christopher. *Chelys, Minuritionum Artificio exornata: . . . The Division Viol, or, The Art of Playing ex tempore upon a Ground.* London, 1667.

Skinner, William. *The Belle Skinner Collection of Old Musical Instruments, Holyoke, Massachusetts.* Fanny Reed Hammond and Nils J. Ericsson, compilers. Holyoke, Mass., 1933.

★Slonimsky, Nicolas. *Music since 1900.* New York, 1937.

Smith, Edmund W. *The Moghul Architecture of Fathpur-Sikri.* Volume iii. Allahabad, 1897.

Smith, Vincent A. *Akbar the Great Mogul.* Oxford, 1917.

Solntsev, F. G. *Kievskiĭ Sofiĭskiĭ Sobor.* St. Petersburg, 1871–87. From the series *Drevnosti Rossiĭskago Gosudarstva.*

Southgate, Thomas Lea. "The Evolution of the Pianoforte."

—— "The Regal and its Successors." Both articles are in *English Music, 1604 to 1904.*

Soyer, A.-M. "Les instruments à vent" (*Encyclopédie de la musique,* part ii, vol. iii, pp. 1401–82.)

★Speer, Daniel. *Grund-richtiger, kurz, leicht und nöthiger Unterricht der musicalischen Kunst.* Ulm, 1687.

Speth, Ewald. "Die Schwingungsvorgange in der Geige." *Zeitschrift für Instrumentenbau,* 1929, no. 3, pp. 78 f.

*Stanford, Sir Charles Villiers, and Forsyth, Cecil. *A History of Music.* New York, 1916. New edition, 1928.

Stanley, Albert A. *Catalogue of the Stearns Collection of Musical Instruments.* Ann Arbor, Michigan, 1918. Second ed., 1921.

Stebbing, L. Susan. *A Modern Introduction to Logic.* London, 1930.

Steinberg, Lester Simon. *The Treatment of the Natural Horns and Trumpets in the Symphonies of the Mannheim School, Haydn, Mozart, and Beethoven.* Harvard University Honors Thesis, 1937. (Typewritten.)

Stokes, Margaret. *The High Crosses of Castledermot and Durrow.* Dublin, 1898.

The Strad: A Monthly Journal for Professionals and Amateurs of All String Instruments Played with the Bow. London, 1890– .

*Straub, Alexandre, ed. *See* Herrad of Landsberg.

*Straeten, Edmond vander. *La musique aux Pays-Bas avant le XIXe siècle.* Brussels, 1867–88. 8 vols.

*Straeten, Edmund van der. *The History of the Violin; its Ancestors and Collateral Instruments, from Earliest Times to the Present Day.* London and Toronto, 1933. 2 vols.

*—— *The History of the Violoncello, the Viol da Gamba, their Precursors* . . . London, 1915.

*—— "Revival of the viols." *The Strad,* London.

A long and informative series of articles, beginning with vol. xix, May, 1908, p. 358, and ending in vol. xxiii, June, 1912. One of the best contributions on the history of the viol family.

—— "The literature of the viols." *The Strad,* xlii, pp. 212 f. (Aug., 1931.)

—— *The Romance of the Fiddle* . . . London, 1911.

Tabourot, Jehan. *Orchesography* . . . Translated from the original edition published at Langres, 1588. Cyril W. Beaumont, tr., pref. by Philip Heseltine. London, 1925.

Tans'ur, William. *A New Musical Grammar: or, The Harmonical Spectator* . . . London, 1746. 3d ed., 1756.

—— *The Elements of Musick Display'd.* London, 1772.

*Terry, Charles Sanford. *Bach's Orchestra.* London, 1932.

Tolbecque, Auguste. *Souvenirs d'un musicien en province.* Niort, 1896.

*—— . . . *L'Art du luthier.* Niort, 1903.

Tomás de Santa María. *Libro llamado Arte de tañer fantasia, assi para tecla como para vihuela, y todo instrumēto, en que se pudiere tañer a tres y a quarto vozes, y a mas* . . . Valladolid, 1565.

Travers, Émile. *Les instruments de musique au XIVe siécle d'après Guillaume de Machaut.* Paris, 1882.

Treder, Dorothea. *Die Musikinstrumente in den höfischen Epen der Blütezeit.* Greifswald, 1933.

**Utrecht Psalter.* Autotype facsimile; published by the Palaeographical Society. London, 1875.

Vadding, M., and Merseburger, Max. *Das Violoncello und seine Literatur.* Leipzig, 1920.

Valdrighi, Luigi Francesco. *Nomocheliurgographia antica e moderna* . . . Modena, 1884. *Il Phagotus di Afranio (del Albonesi).* Musurgiana series, no. 4. Modena, 1881.

*Vallas, Léon. "Une mémoire sur la trompette marine." *Bulletin Français de la Société Internationale de Musique,* 1908, pp. 1176 f.

Venn, Lyn. "The 'Chest of Viols' and its Music." *The Strad,* 1920, pp. 195 f., 213 f.

*Vidal, François. *Lou Tambourin. Istòri de l'estrumen prouvençau seguido de la metodo dóu galubet e dóu tambourin* . . . Aix, 1864.

*Vidal, Louis Antoine. *Les instruments à archet* . . . Paris, 1876. 3 vols.

Viollet-le-Duc. *Dictionnaire raisonné du mobilier français de l'epoque carlovingienne à la renaissance.* Paris, 1858–75. 6 vols. "Instruments de musique," vol. ii, part 4, pp. 243–327.

*Virdung, Sebastian. *Musica getutscht und auszgezogen durch Sebastianum Virdung Priesters von Amberg . . .* Basel, 1511. Facsimile ed. (200 copies), Robert Eitner, ed., Berlin, 1882; facsimile ed., Leo Schrade, ed., Kassel, 1931.

Viskovatov, Alexander V. *Historical Description of Uniforms and Armaments of Russian Troops.* St. Petersburg, 1841–61. 29 vols.
In Russian; magnificent lithographs.

Wasielewski, Wilhelm Joseph von. *Geschichte der Instrumentalmusik im XVI. Jahrhundert.* Berlin, 1878.

—— *Die Violine im XVII. Jahrhundert und die Anfänge der Instrumentalcomposition.* Bonn, 1874.

—— *Die Violine und ihre Meister.* 5th ed. Waldemar von Wasielewski, ed. Leipzig, 1910.

—— *The Violoncello and its History.* Isobella S. E. Stigand, tr. London, 1894.

Welch, Christopher. *History of the Boehm Flute.* London, 1885. Third ed., 1896.

*—— *Six Lectures on the Recorder and other Flutes.* London, 1911.

Welcker von Gontershausen, Heinrich. *Neu eröffnetes Magazin musikalischer Tonwerkzeuge . . .* Frankfurt a/M., 1855.

—— *Der Clavierbau in seiner Theorie, Technik, und Geschichte . . .* Frankfurt a/M., 1864. 4th ed. 1870.

*Wellesz, Egon. *Die neue Instrumentation.* Berlin, 1928–29. 2 vols.

White, Georgia Atwood. *A History of the Harp.*
An unpublished MS to which the writer has had access.

Widor, Charles Marie. *The Technique of the Modern Orchestra.* Edward Suddard, tr. London, 1906.
The sequel to Berlioz's *Instrumentation and Orchestration.*

Wieprecht, Wilhelm Friedrich. *Die Militair-Musik . . .* Berlin, 1885.

Willemin, Nicolas Xavier. Choix de . . . instruments de musique . . . Paris, 1839. 2 vols. (*Monuments français inédits.*)
Fine colored plates of musical instruments.

Wit, Paul de. *Katalog des musikhistorischen Museums von Paul de Wit, Leipzig.* Leipzig, 1903.

—— *Perlen aus der Instrumenten-Sammlung von Paul de Wit in Leipzig.* Leipzig, 1892.

*Wolf, Johannes. *Geschichte der Mensural-Notation von 1250–1460.* Leipzig, 1904. 3 vols.

*—— *Handbuch der Notationskunde.* Leipzig, 1913–19. 2 vols.

Yousoupov, Nikolaĭ Borisovich. *Luthomonographie, historique et raisonnée. Essai sur l'histoire du violon et sur les ouvrages des anciens luthiers célèbres . . .* Munich, 1856.

*Zacconi, Lodovico. *Prattica di musica . . . divisa in quattro libri.* Venice, 1596.

*Zamminer, Friedrich. *Die Musik und die musikalischen Instrumente in ihrer Beziehung zu den Gezetzen der Akustik.* Giessen, 1855.

*Zarlino, Gioseffo. *De tutte l'opere del R. M. Gioseffo Zarlino . . .* Venice, 1588–89. 4 vols.

Zeitschrift für Instrumentenbau. Leipzig, 1880– .
A trade magazine containing articles and data on musical instruments not to be found elsewhere.

INDICES

INDEX NOMINUM

INDEX RERUM

ADDENDA AND CORRIGENDA

Page 8, Table II. *For* 844.359 *read* 884.359.
Correction communicated through the courtesy of Mr. J. W. McNair, ASA, Secretary of the Sectional Committee on Acoustical Standards. The Tentative Standard Acoustical Terminology Z24.1–1936 contains this misprint.

Page 22, Fig. 2. Reproduced from Djevad Bey, *État militaire Ottoman*, etc., a part of *Planche* 5.

Page 23, Fig. 3. Reproduced from Marsigli, *Stato militare dell'Imperio Ottomano*, vol. ii, Table xxxiii, a part of the cortege on the left hand side of the plate.

Page 84, line 5. *For* kind if pipes *read* kind of pipes.

Page 117, line 20. *Insert* described *between* is *and* in.

Page 163, line 4. *For* 187. *read* 187 and 410, Note 382.

Page 182. Alternative name of the instrument No. 195 is the "valve horn."

Page 184, last line. *For* Anzatz *read* Ansatz.

Page 186, line 38. *For* Anzatz *read* Ansatz.

Page 204. The instrument No. 316 should be placed after No. 223. The instrument No. 316 belongs to Division II: Section B: Free Reeds.

Page 231, line 14. *For* Newslider *read* Newsidler.

Page 231, line 22. *For* Hoffman *read* Hoffmann.

Page 231, line 27. *For* Hoffman *read* Hoffmann.

Page 231, line 28. *For* Hoffman *read* Hoffmann.

Page 258, Fig. 49. The title should read "The Fiedel Type of Viol Body."

Page 273, list of names. *For* Martin Hoffman *read* Martin Hoffmann.

Page 273, list of names. *For* Johann Christian Hoffman *read* Johann Christian Hoffmann.

Page 273, list of names. *For* Stadlman *read* Stadlmann.

Page 359, Table I. *For* Arnold *read* Arnolt.

Page 389, Note 93. *For* 'fictitious' *read* 'factitious.'

Page 390, Note 107. *Th. Solnzev* is the same person as *Solntsev, F. G.*, on p. 467.

Page 426, Note 600. *Add*: Julius Ruhlmann, *Geschichte der Bogeninstrumente*, Atlas, Plate xi, Fig. 4, represents the same instrument with *seven* strings.

Page 442, Note 906. *For* I′ = 565 cycles *read* a′ = 565 cycles.

PLATES

PLATE I

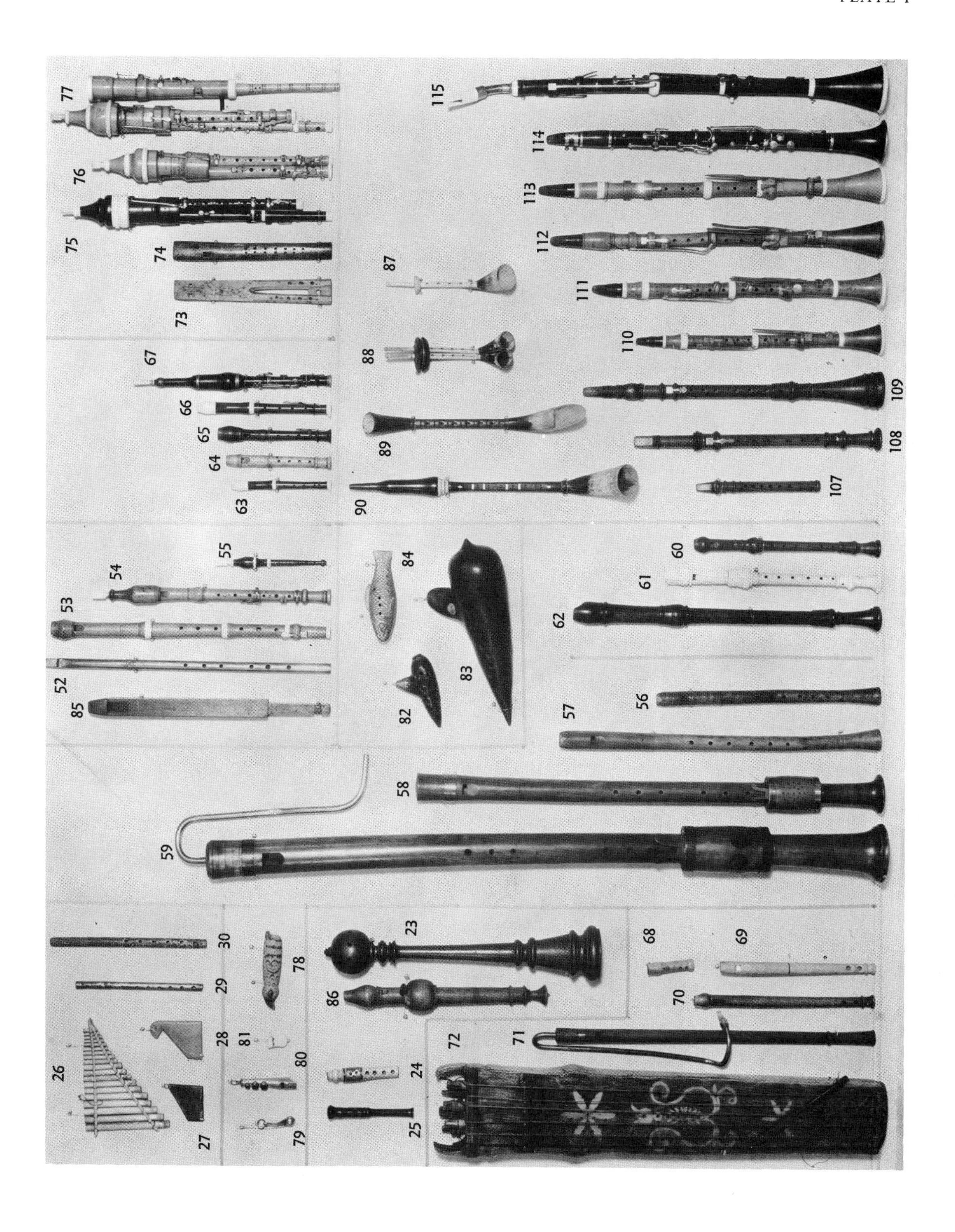

77
76
75
74
73
115
114
113
112
111
110
109
108
107
87
88
89
90
67
66
65
64
63
55
54
53
52
85
84
83
82
60
61
62
56
57
58
59
30
29
28
26
27
81
80
79
78
23
86
24
25
68
69
70
71
72

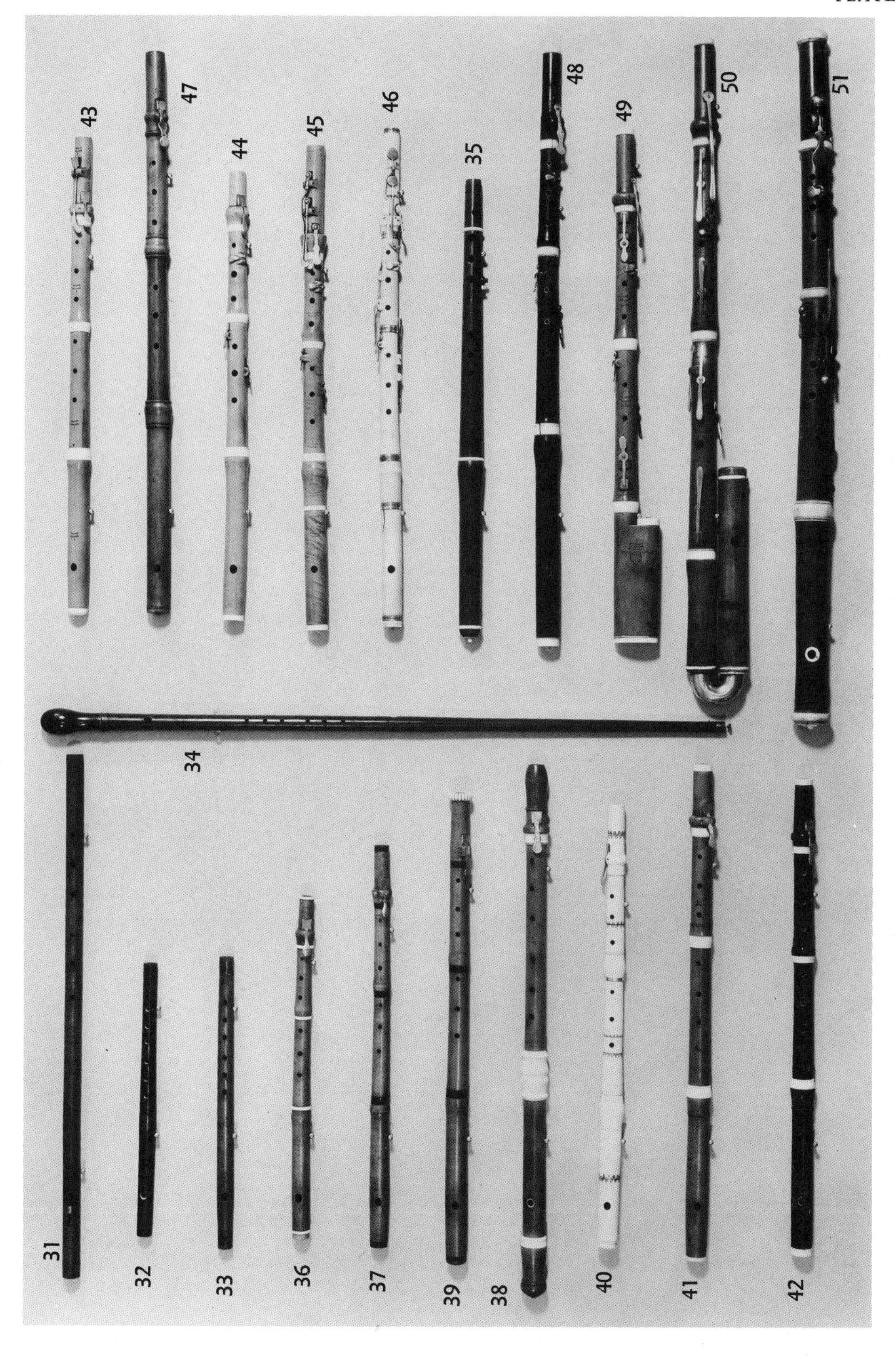
43
47
44
45
46
35
48
49
50
51
34
31
32
33
36
37
39
38
40
41
42

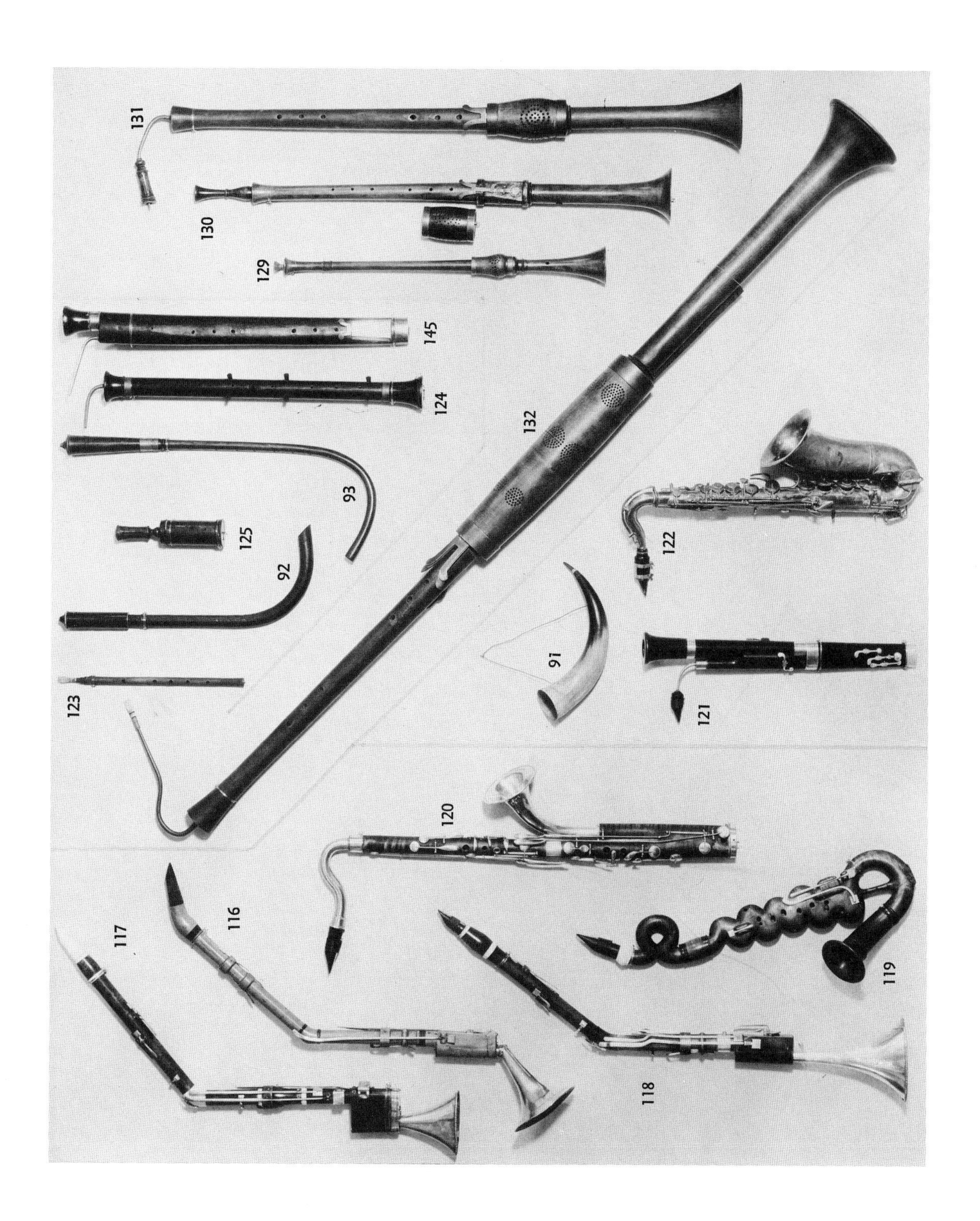
131
130
129
145
124
132
93
125
92
123
91
122
121
120
116
117
119
118

PLATE IV

161
162
160
163
165
164
151
150
148
149
104
147
146
144
143
141
142
140
96
139
137
95
136
94
127
134
135
128
138
133

PLATE V

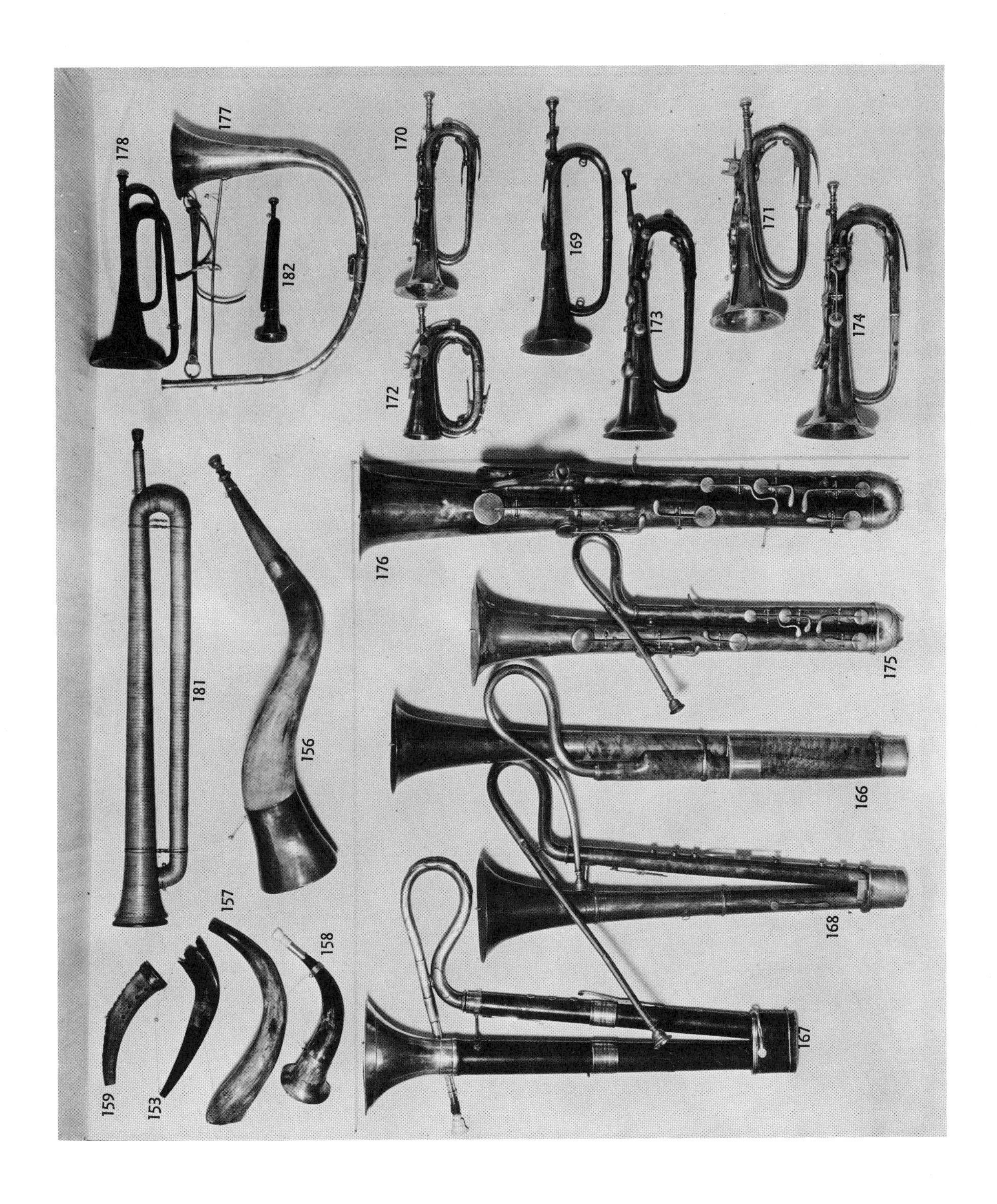
178
177
182
170
169
172
173
171
174
176
175
181
156
166
168
157
158
167
159
153

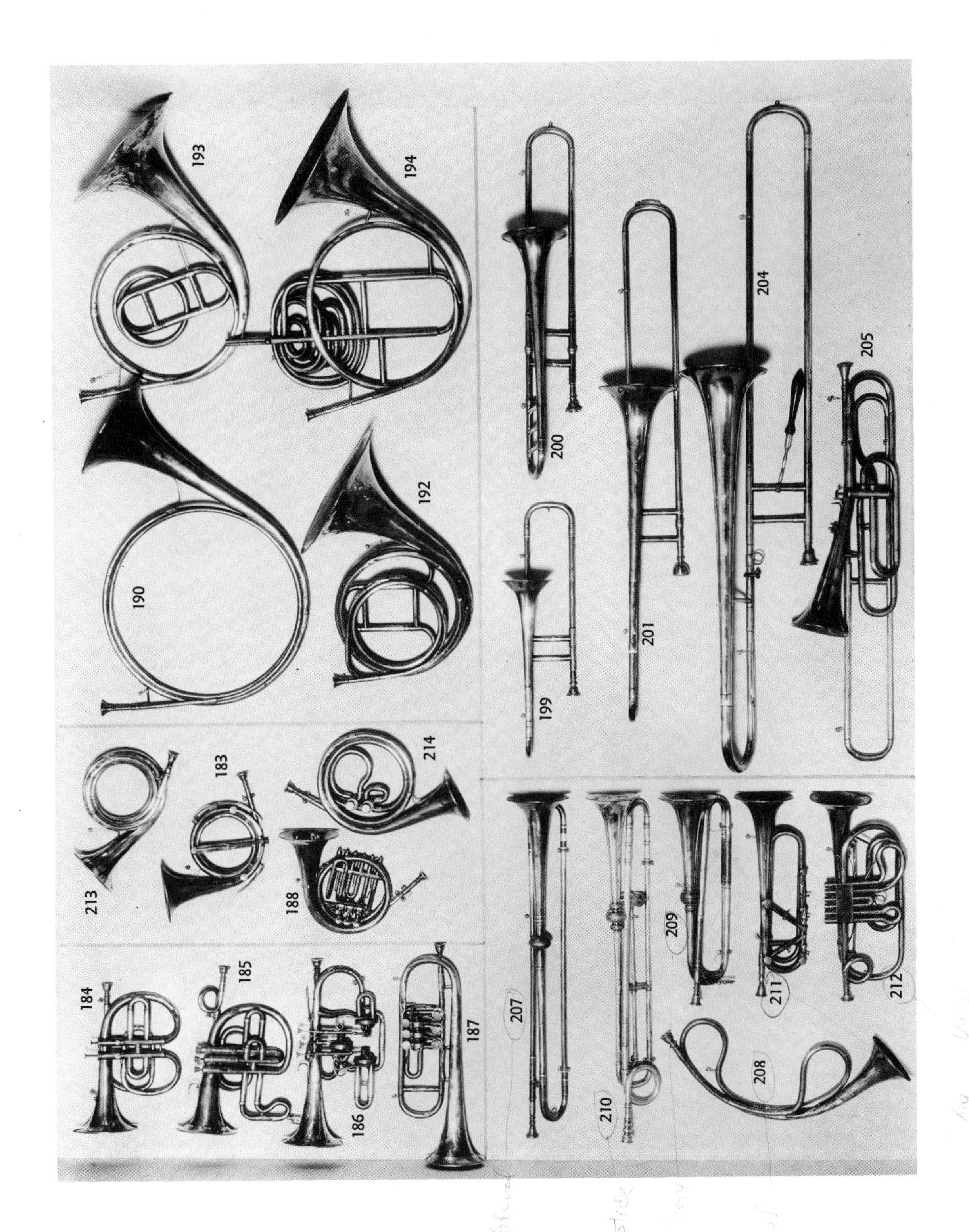
193
194
190
192
200
199
201
204
205
213
183
214
188
184
185
186
187
207
210
209
211
212
208

PLATE VII

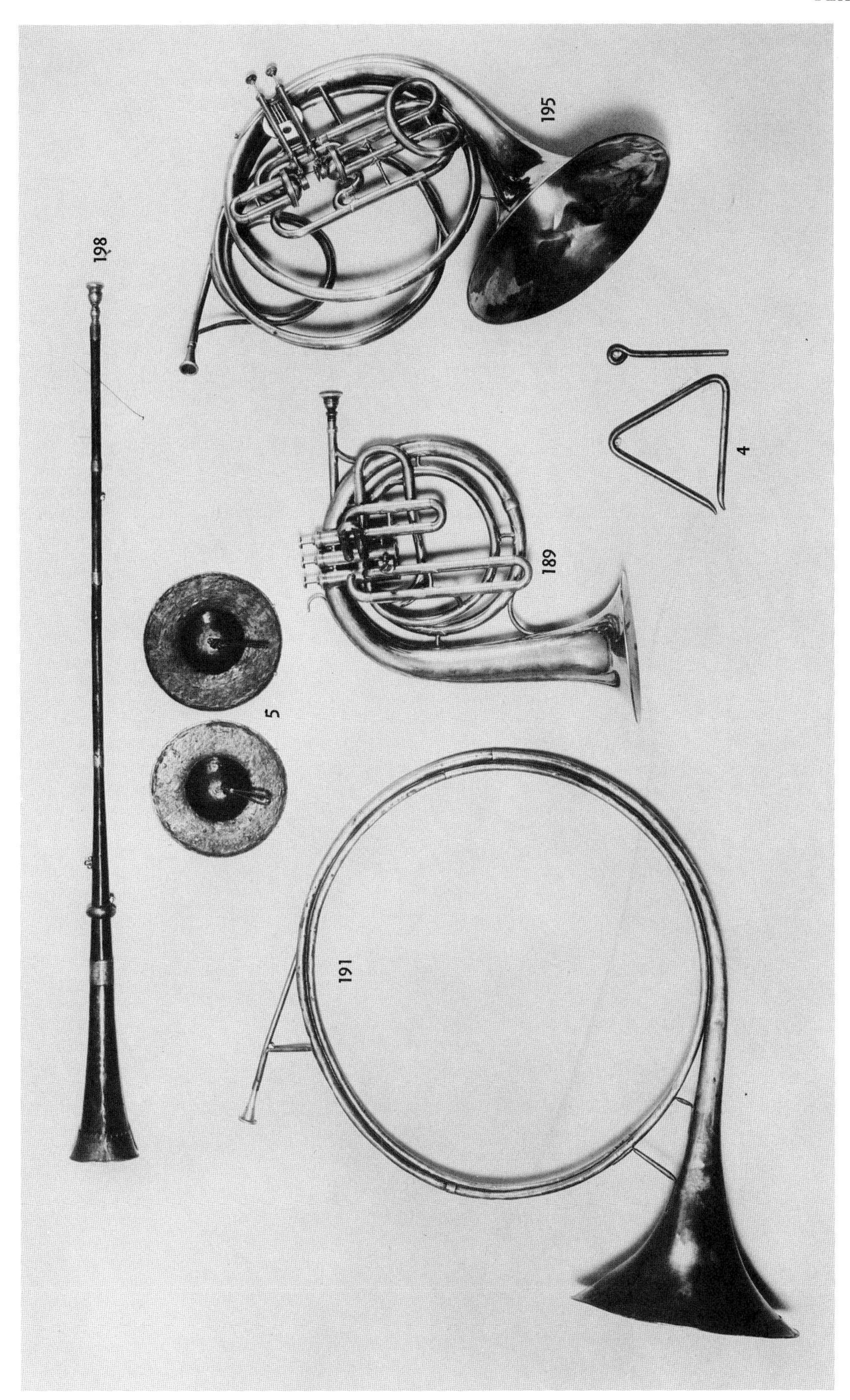

PLATE VIII

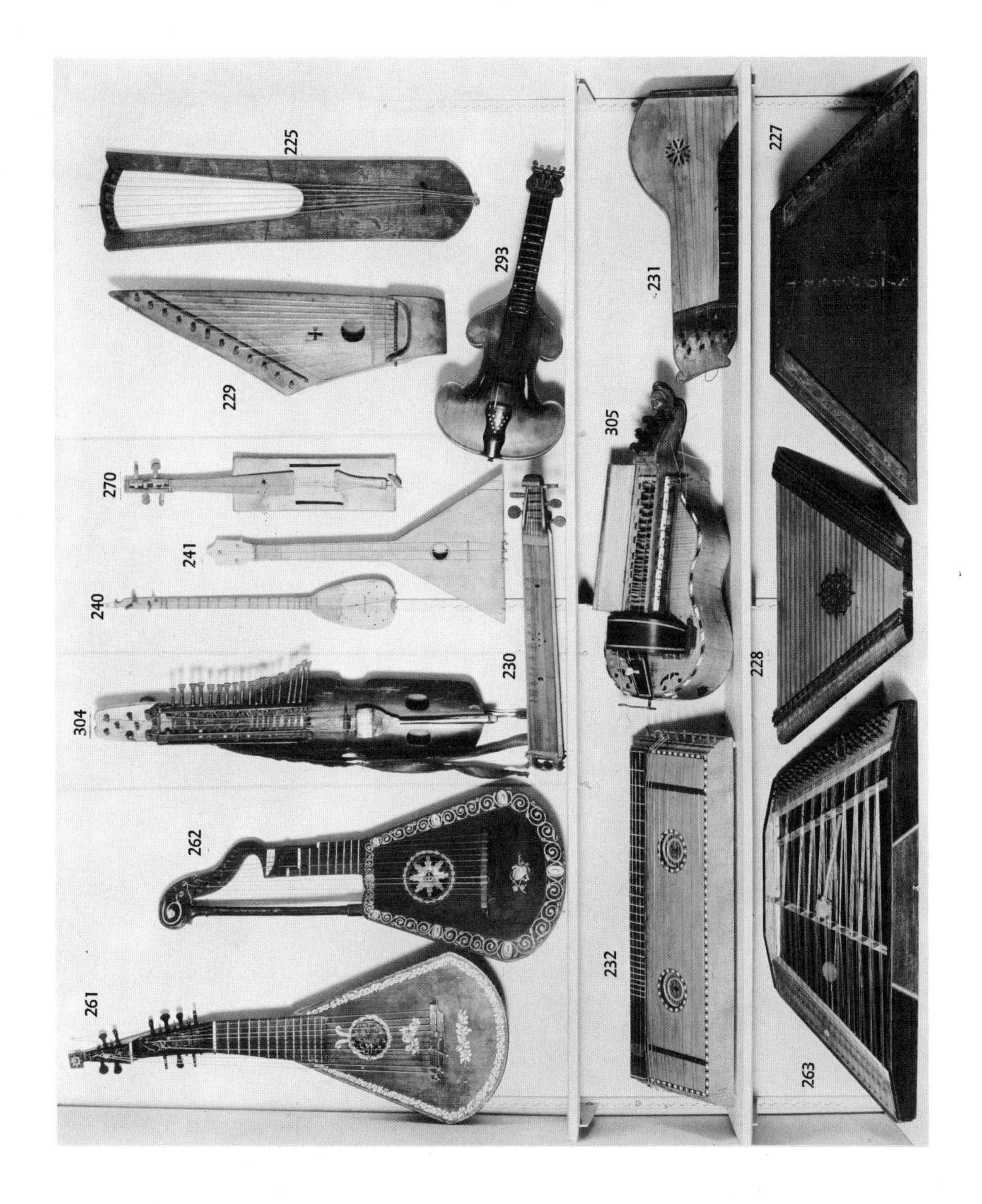

PLATE IX

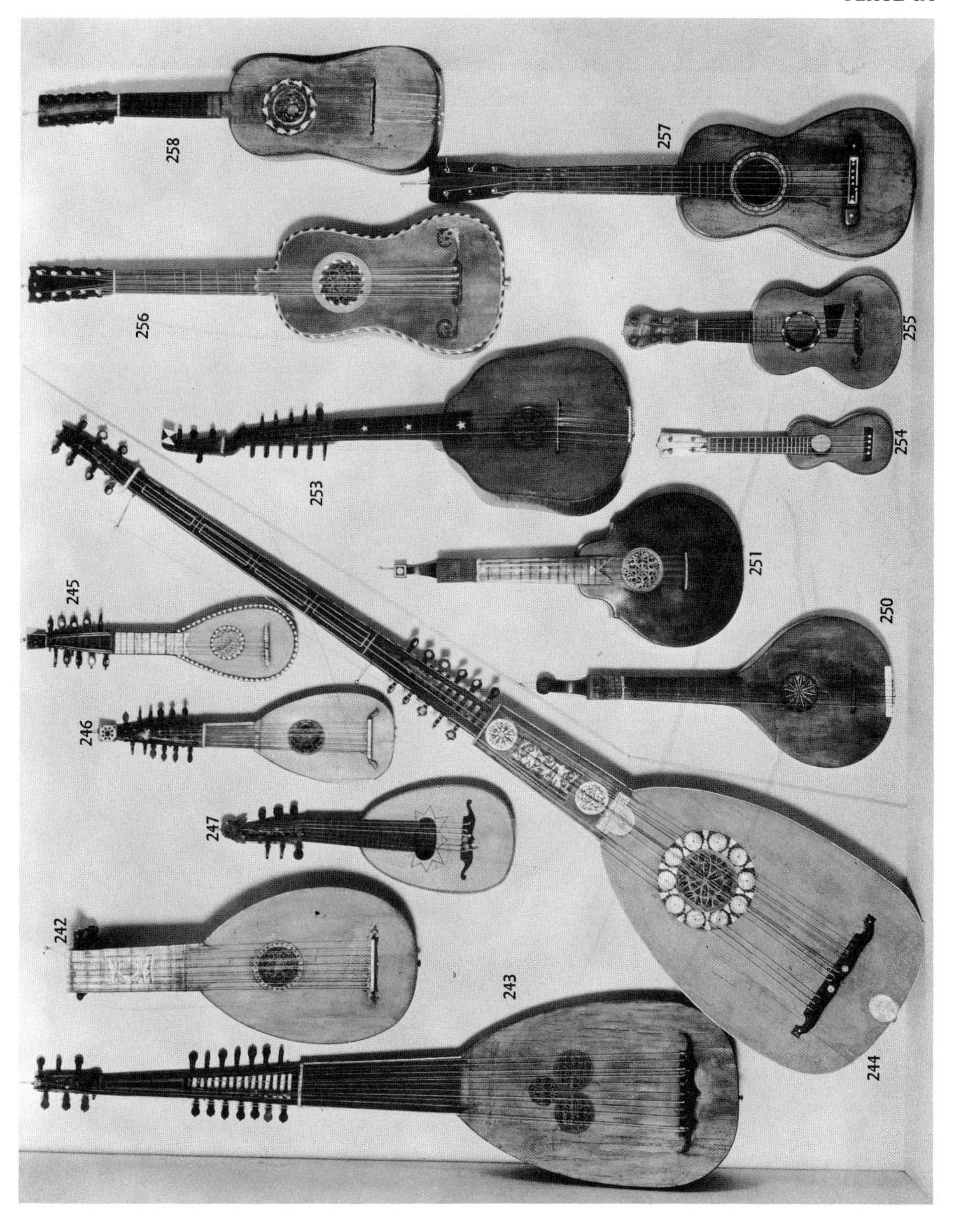

265
266
291
290
269
267
268

PLATE XI

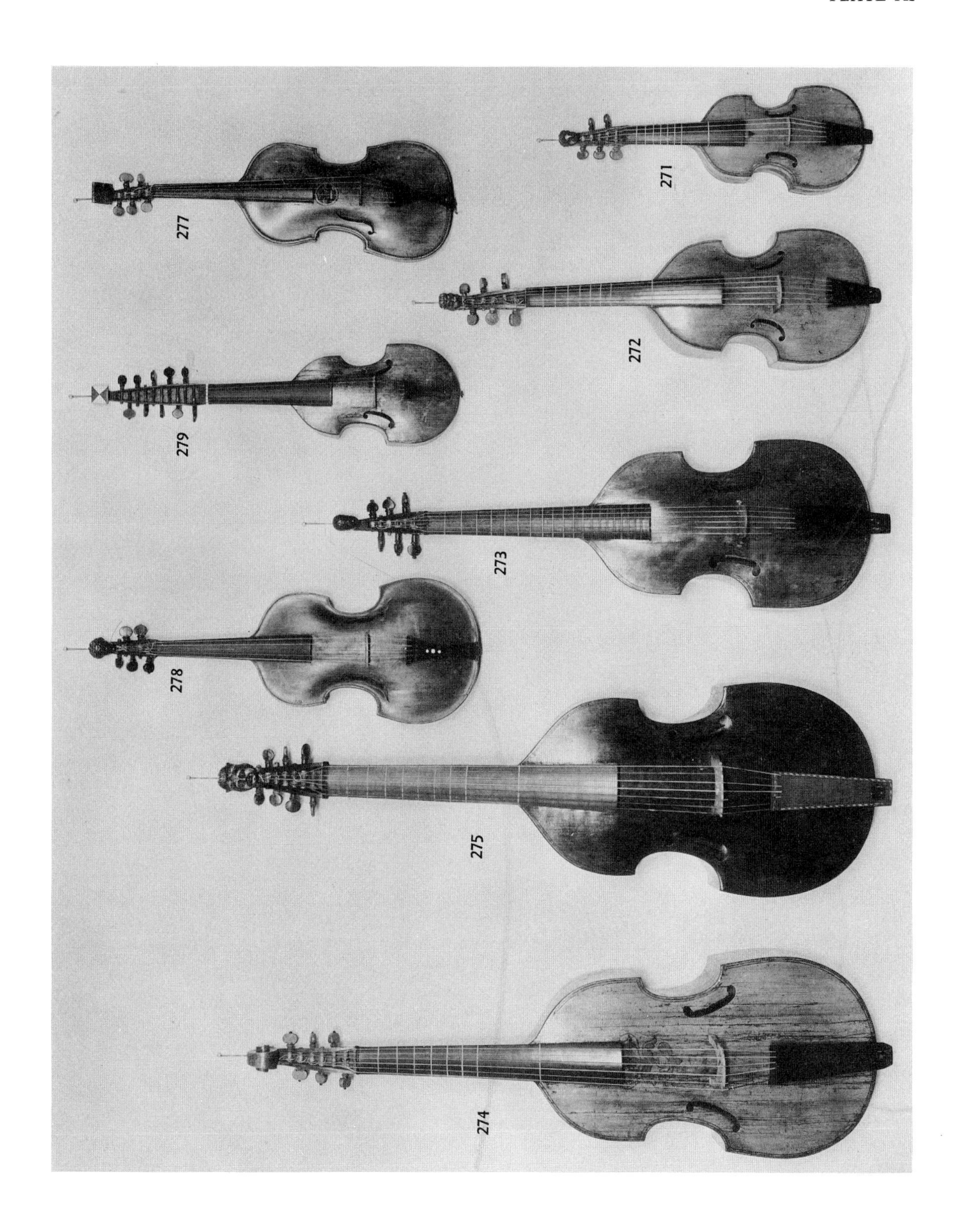

282
281
283

ST. CECILIA

By Bernardo Cavallino (1622–56). Neapolitan School

Museum of Fine Arts, Boston

286
284
280
289
276
287

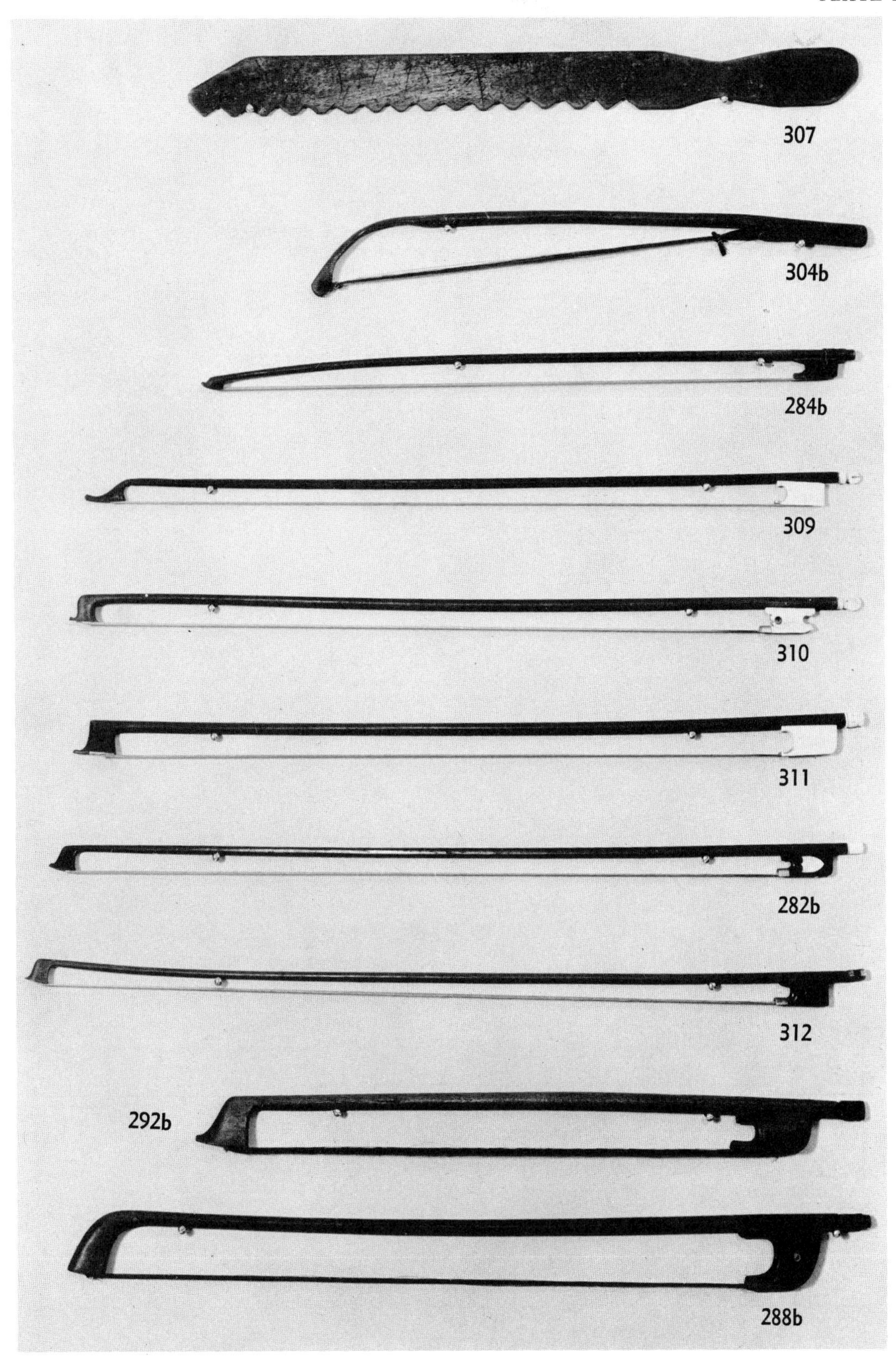
307
304b
284b
309
310
311
282b
312
292b
288b

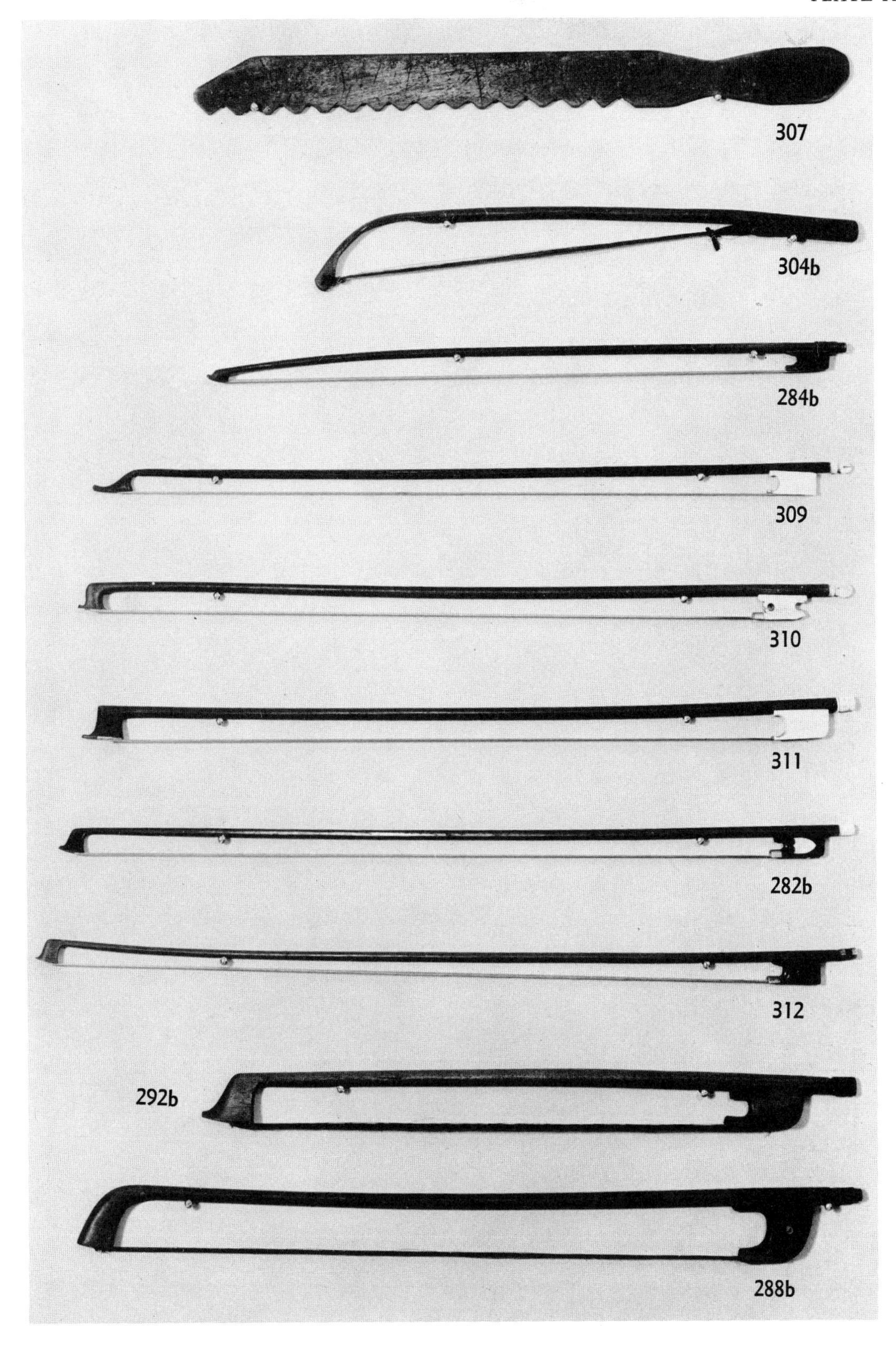
307
304b
284b
309
310
311
282b
312
292b
288b

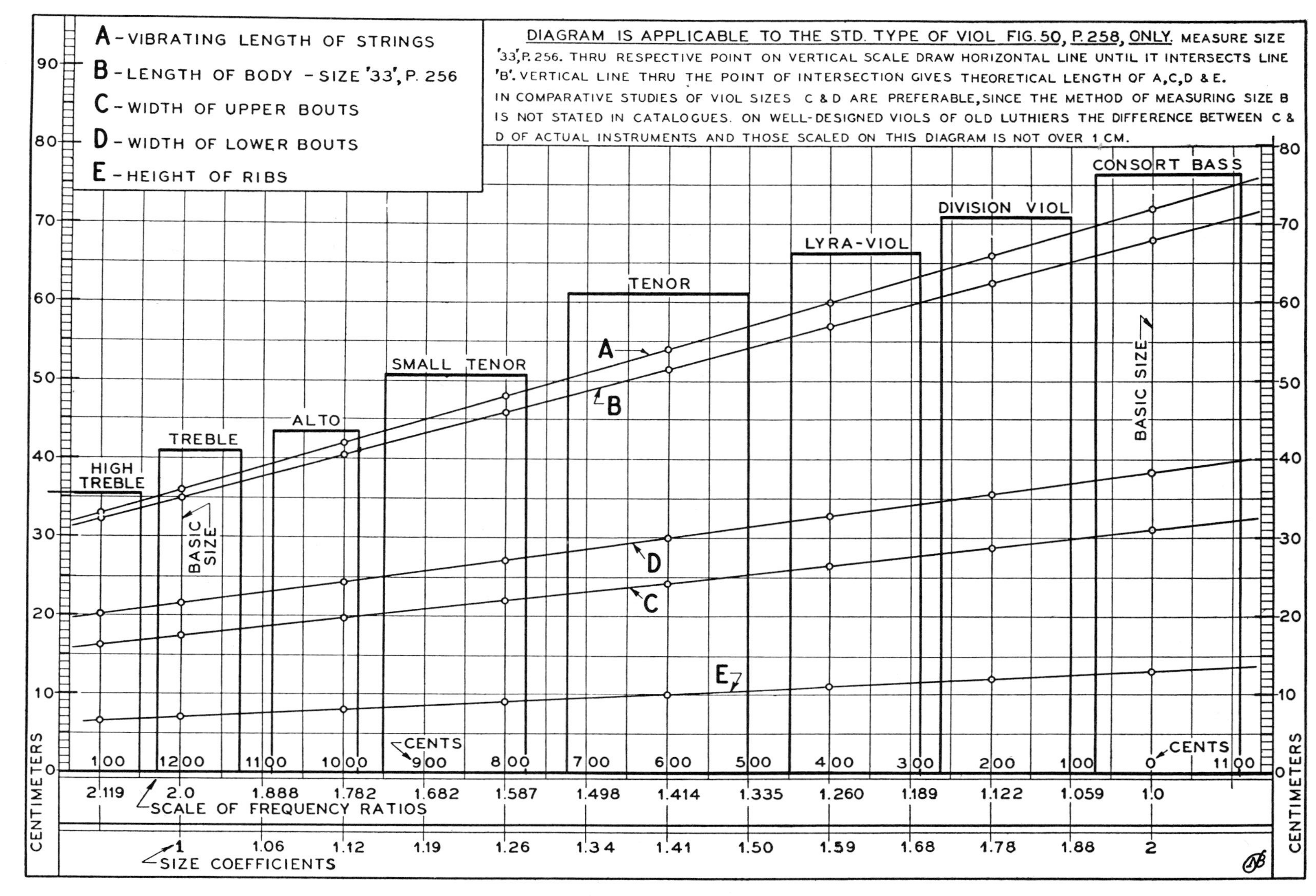

BASIC PROPORTIONS OF VIOLS - ENGLISH SERIES